Southeast Asia and the ASEAN Economic Community

Roderick Macdonald
Editor

Southeast Asia and the ASEAN Economic Community

palgrave
macmillan

Editor
Roderick Macdonald
Université du Québec à Montréal
Montréal, QC, Canada

ISBN 978-3-030-19721-6 ISBN 978-3-030-19722-3 (eBook)
https://doi.org/10.1007/978-3-030-19722-3

This Palgrave Macmillan imprint is published by the registered company Springer Nature Switzerland AG
The registered company address is: Gewerbestrasse 11, 6330 Cham, Switzerland

Preface

This book is an introduction to the ASEAN Economic Community and the economies of Southeast Asia. It is aimed at businesses looking to expand into the region and at academics interested in international business and in economics of the region. It is a first step that may bring the reader to pursue deeper and more specific research. It will also interest the layperson wishing to expand his or her knowledge of this part of the world.

My first decision as editor of this book was to seek out local prestigious authors rather than international experts established in English-speaking countries. The intention was to provide greater local flavor and insight, greater familiarity with local events as covered by local media, and access to information in the first language of the researcher. There was a trade-off in this decision: in some countries, researchers must sanitize their remarks under direct or indirect pressure from government and/or colleagues.

Nor was it always possible to get an author from the country covered.

The authors of the chapter on Myanmar are currently in Austria and in the United States of America. However, Thomas Bernhardt worked for several years as researcher and policy analyst at the Myanmar Centre for Economic and Social Development (CESD) in Yangon, while Aung Hein was a research coordinator at the Centre for Economic and Social Development (CESD), a think tank at the forefront of reforms in Myanmar.

In the cases of Indonesia and Singapore, health and other issues of the researchers required that I actively and extensively intervene in the research for and composition of the chapters. Hopefully these chapters have not lost their local flavor.

Sophal Ear became a refugee from Cambodia at an early age but has maintained contact with his old homeland while developing his career in international relations. He recruited Sigfrido Burgos, with whom he had collaborated on *The Hungry Dragon*, a book about China's resource quest.

The chapter on the influence of China in the region was a singular case. Chinese writers did not respond to invitations to collaborate. When I asked a wise (and retired) Singaporean expert what was happening, he observed that they would be uncomfortable participating in a Western publication because they feared they would be collaborating in a publication hostile to China, with dire effects for their career. Luckily, I was able to obtain the help of Stephen Marks, a long-established authority on Southeast Asia who spent years working in Indonesia and with current interests in China's influence in the region. He in turn enlisted the help of Cheryl Yau, a student from Singapore.

Finally, in the case of the description of the ASEAN Economic Community itself, I was able to obtain the contribution of David Martin Jones, an expert on political thought and conflict very familiar with Southeast Asia, and he brought Sarah Choong Ee Mei into the project. Originally from Malaysia, Sarah currently consults for the International Organization for Migration (IOM) in Geneva.

There is no list of abbreviations or glossary in this book. We have expanded acronyms on first use as well as offered explanations of the more esoteric concepts. Virtually all readers will have access to sources on the Internet to supplement this.

All of us have kept a moderate tone when describing these countries and their institutions. Perhaps here I can permit a little emotion. Southeast Asia is a wonderful part of the world. Thailand is known as the Land of Smiles, but smiles are to be found all across Southeast Asia. Of course, there are difficulties and tensions, but people are cheerful and happy. There are far fewer gray hairs in Southeast Asia than in OECD countries: most countries have young populations that provide an atmosphere of enthusiasm and exuberance. Over nine years visiting this part of the world, I experienced only one unfortunate incident: having my pocket picked one Saturday afternoon on a busy street in Kuala Lumpur. I was tired and not very alert, but the experience granted me one more hilarious story to tell my friends and family. And I can say now that I have many friends and indeed family in Southeast Asia.

I would like to thank the researchers and authors for their remarkable work in contributing to this volume, as well as for their comments on my own contributions. Jesus P. Estanislao, former Finance Secretary of the Philippines and co-founder of the Center for Research and Communications, is the first person who explained to me the structure and history of ASEAN. I remain indebted to him. George Ekins, who worked as reference librarian in the parliament of Canada before his retirement, was merciless in pointing out flaws in my chapters. The flaws that do remain are the fruits of my obstinacy. Doctoral students at Universitas Gunadarma in Depok, Indonesia, and undergraduate students at the International School of Business (ISB) at the University of Economics, Ho Chi Minh City (Trường Đại học Kinh tế Thành phố Hồ Chí Minh), have my gratitude for bearing with my exploration of many of the institutional indicators (ease of doing business, economic freedom, competitiveness, etc.) that pervade this book. Luong Quang of the International Civil Aviation Organization and Nguyễn Thị Hải Hằng of Học Viện Hàng Không Việt Nam (VAA, the Aviation University of Vietnam) introduced me to the region ten years ago, and Hai Hang in particular did much to cushion the culture shock transitioning from Singapore to Cambodia. I am grateful to them both.

Manila, Philippines Roderick Macdonald
March 19, 2019

Contents

Notes on Contributors

Thomas Bernhardt is an advisor for Sustainable Development and Finance in the Department for International Financial Institutions of the Austrian Federal Ministry of Finance. Previously, Thomas worked as an economist for the United Nations Industrial Development Organization (UNIDO) and as a researcher and policy analyst at the Myanmar Centre for Economic and Social Development (CESD) in Yangon. He has published widely on economic development issues with a focus on industry, trade, global value chains, finance, and labor markets.

Sigfrido Burgos is a freelance writer and independent researcher on international affairs. He authored *The Hungry Dragon: How China's Resource Quest Is Reshaping the World* with Sophal Ear.

Sarah Choong Ee Mei is a consultant for the International Organization for Migration (IOM), the UN's migration agency based in Geneva, Switzerland.

Evelyn S. Devadason is a professor at the Faculty of Economics and Administration, University of Malaya. Her research focuses on international trade and regional integration. Her research work has seen print in international journals such as *World Development, Journal of International Development, Pacific Review, Journal of Contemporary Asia, and Journal of Contemporary China*, among others. She has also been engaged in a number of international research projects, including the International Confederation of Free Trade Unions - Asian and Pacific Regional Organisation (ICFTU-APRO), Asian Development Bank Institute (ADBI), Asian Development Bank (ADB), World Bank, ERIA Economic

Research Institute for ASEAN and East Asia - UNCTAD United Nations Conference on Trade and Development (ERIA-UNCTAD), Food Industry Asia (FIA), and a partnership between The Danish Ministry of Foreign Affairs, the United Nations Economic Programme and the Technical University of Denmark (UNEP-DTU), for research and consultation on energy, climate and sustainable development.

Sophal Ear is Associate Professor of Diplomacy and World Affairs at Occidental College and author of *Aid Dependence in Cambodia: How Foreign Assistance Undermines Democracy* as well as *The Hungry Dragon: How China's Resource Quest Is Reshaping the World.*

Aung Hein is a Master in Public Affairs candidate at the Woodrow Wilson School of Public and International Affairs at Princeton University and was a research coordinator at the Centre for Economic and Social Development (CESD), Myanmar. Before this, he was a faculty member at the pre-collegiate program, teaching classes in international political economy and existential philosophy. He was a Coro fellow in public affairs in St. Louis, Missouri, in 2010–2011.

David Martin Jones is visiting professor in the War Studies Department, King's College, University of London.

Roderick Macdonald is Professor of Management and Technology at the *École des sciences de la gestion, Université du Québec à Montréal*, Canada. He has authored books and articles on business strategy in new industries, fundamental economic notions used in business, and moral analysis. His previous books with Palgrave Macmillan are *Genesis of the Financial Crisis* and *Eurocritical: A Crisis of the Euro Currency.*

George Manzano has worked in government, academe, and international institutions. As a member commissioner of the Philippine Tariff Commission, he contributed to the process of trade policy formulation. He has given several trade policy courses including the regional trade policy course of the World Trade Organization (WTO). He likewise served as an economic affairs officer in the United Nations Economic and Social Commission for Asia and the Pacific (ESCAP). His research interests include international economics, free trade areas, and service trade.

Stephen V. Marks is Elden Smith Professor of Economics and Coordinator of the International Relations Program at Pomona College and has extensive experience in trade, competition, and tax policy consulting and research in Indonesia and Laos. He has published widely on trade policy issues and in 2010 was named a Presidential Friend of Indonesia.

Siti Fatimahwati Pehin Dato Musa has been Lecturer of Economics in Universiti Brunei Darussalam School of Business and Economics since 2008. She has a PhD in agricultural economics and rural development from Newcastle University, United Kingdom, 2016. Her research interest revolves around development economics, agricultural economics, specifically issues of food security and youth in agriculture, and issues of youth unemployment.

Ma. Anne Teresa Rivera is currently an economist for a global building materials company where she tracks and analyzes key issues in Asia and Europe. Her main interest is marrying economic knowledge and operational insights to guide business strategy. She is passionate about development and culture and loves how storytelling fosters constant engagement with the world.

Vilém Semerák is a senior lecturer at the Institute of Economic Studies of Charles University and a researcher at the Economics Institute of the Czech Academy of Sciences. He teaches economics of transition, international trade, and occasional guest courses for Dijon Campus of Sciences Po Paris. His most recent activities focus on economic reforms in Myanmar and China.

Hotniar Siringoringo is professor in the Faculty of Economics and the Director of Institute for Research of Gunadarma University, Jakarta, Indonesia. She has published peer-reviewed articles and books on statistics, research methodology, system simulation, and operations research. She is a member of the National Assessment and Accreditation Council of Higher Education in Indonesia and research proposal reviewer on national competition, and she sits on the editorial board of various journals and has established university-to-university collaborations between Gunadarma University and various universities across Europe, Asia, and America.

Piti Srisangnam is a professor at Chulalongkorn University and was deputy director for Academic Affairs of the Centre for European Studies from 2010 to 2012 and deputy director for Academic Affairs of the ASEAN Studies Center in 2012, both at Chulalongkorn University, before he became director of the Center in 2013. Apart from producing academic articles and books, he also hosts three radio programs related to current issues in ASEAN and manages "Sachinomi Sushi," a Japanese restaurant!

Seck Tan is assistant professor at the Singapore Institute of Technology and adjunct assistant professor at Lee Kuan Yew School of Public Policy, National University of Singapore; he is the author of 15 academic articles and book chapters as well as 20 conferences.

Buavanh Vilavong is the deputy director general of the Department of Industry and Handicraft under the Laotian Ministry of Industry and Commerce. He previously worked in Foreign Trade Policy Department and the Department of Import and Export and formed part of a team negotiating entry to the World Trade Organization (WTO). He has operational experience in the areas of trade negotiations as well as coordinating internal reforms and technical assistance to support the WTO accession process of Laos.

Bernardo Villegas was a member of the Constitutional Commission that drafted the Philippine Constitution under the government of President Corazon Aquino. He has been an advisor of the recent Philippine Presidents. He is a professor and senior vice president at the University of Asia and the Pacific (UA&P), visiting professor at IESE, co-founder and chairman of the Center for Research and Communication, and a member of the Board of Trustees of the Makati Business Club.

Quan Hoang Vuong is the founder and director of the Centre for Interdisciplinary Social Research and senior researcher at Phenikaa University. He is also a member of the editorial board of *Scientific Data* and an associate editor of *Palgrave Communications*. His works cover monetary policies, entrepreneurship, innovation and creativity, and more recently public health and culture, with an extensive focus on Vietnam.

Thu Trang Vuong is a third-year bachelor student of the European Campus of Dijon, Sciences Po Paris. She has worked on topics related to entrepreneurship and public health with the aim of providing insights for policymaking. Her main disciplines of interest for future research include comparative politics and political sociology.

Cheryl Jia Min Yau is a senior in international relations and economics at Pomona College and is from Singapore.

List of Figures

List of Images

List of Tables

CHAPTER 1

Southeast Asia and the AEC, an Introduction

Roderick Macdonald

Occupying two million square miles to the South of China and to the East of India, the total population of Southeast Asia is a little less than 9% of the world's population and produces a very little over 3.5% of world GDP. Productivity (excluding outliers Singapore, Malaysia and Brunei Darussalam) is about half the world average. Infrastructure is poor in most countries. With the exceptions of Singapore and Brunei Darussalam, the urban centres have badly congested traffic. Southeast Asia is composed of 11 countries (listed in Table 1.1), so the region is also one of the most complicated zones to market or operate a production network. It presents a diversity of political regimes, legal systems, three major religions (four if you count the four million Hindus of Bali; five if you include the influence of Confucianism in Vietnam), five scripts, eight to ten major languages, depending how you count them, and economies varying from one of the wealthiest in the world (Singapore) to one with a GDP per capita less than 10% of the world average (Cambodia). Half of these countries are mainland countries, half of them are composed of islands. The diversity becomes even greater upon closer examination. For example, there are over 300 ethnicities in Indonesia alone and over 20 languages having more than a million speakers.

R. Macdonald (✉)
Université du Québec à Montréal, Montréal, QC, Canada
e-mail: macdonald.roderick@uqam.ca

R. Macdonald (ed.), *Southeast Asia and the ASEAN Economic Community*, https://doi.org/10.1007/978-3-030-19722-3_1

Table 1.1 Rainy seasons across Southeast Asia

Country	*Rainy seasons*
Brunei Darussalam	September to January and May to July
Myanmar	June to October
Cambodia	May to November
East Timor	December to April
Indonesia	Jakarta: October to March Bali: December to February
Laos	May to October
Malaysia	October to December (to February in Borneo)
Philippines	June to October
Singapore	Strictly speaking, November to December. However, there could be heavy rain at any time
Thailand	May to October for most of Thailand
Vietnam	Late May to November

Source: Compiled by author from experience and various weather and climate sites on the Internet

At first glance, Southeast Asia is not worth the trouble.

However, according to one survey (EY ASEAN 2017), a growing percentage of companies around the world are looking to increase investment or trade with the region: 87% of US companies, 86% of Australian companies, 85% of European Union (EU) companies and 55% of Japanese companies (who already have a strong presence).

The Association of South East Asian Nations (ASEAN) and in particular the ASEAN Economic Community (AEC) have been working towards a simplification of this diverse market. Further, there are four principal reasons why this region is important to business: growth, stability, location and a tipping point:

1. The economies of this region are growing quickly—an average of over 5% a year.[1]
2. They have maintained this growth rate stably for decades (PwC 2018, p. 11).
3. They are located next to the two growth centres that are China and India and are aligned along the sea route between China and India, the Middle East, Africa and Europe. About 30% of world maritime trade passes through the South China Sea (ChinaPower 2017).
4. Finally, the rise of the middle class in these countries is timed perfectly to contribute to the further growth of their economies (Brueckners et al. 2018, p. 49). The growth of the middle class

suggests growth of discretionary income leading to increased demand for consumer goods and to an improved education base for acquiring economically relevant skills to stimulate the supply side.

To reinforce these reasons: ASEAN economies collectively are larger than that of India. They will surpass Japan in ten years. The total population of 630 million people includes 60% below the age of 30. There was a 50% increase in the size of the labour force between 1995 and 2015 (Cfr PwC 2018, p. 15, Fig. 1.5), bringing it to just over 300 million, and nearly 60 million people more are projected to enter the region's workforce by 2030. The consumption-oriented middle-income class is one-third of the population today and will be two-thirds of the population by 2030.

The existence of the AEC makes all these data more compelling, because it has the fundamental mandate of integrating this region for the mobility of goods, capital and labour.

This book is an introduction to the ASEAN Economic Community. An understanding of the participating countries and their economies is prerequisite to understanding the AEC. An understanding of the AEC organization itself is also necessary—it is not a copy of the European Economic Community. Appreciating the integration of the ASEAN economies with the global economy is also necessary, particularly with their major trading and investment partners, the European Union, China, Japan and the US.

This introductory chapter describes the geography, history and economies of the region and gives a preview of the other chapters in this book.

Geography of the Region

Indonesia straddles the equator to the South. It stretches almost from Myanmar (Burma[2]) on the west all the way to the province of Irian Jaya on the island of New Guinea, which is next to Australia. Myanmar thrusts into China in the north. Myanmar is also the most westerly of these nations, bordering on Bangladesh and India, while to the east the Philippines lies 1200 kilometres to the south of Taiwan. Timor Leste (East Timor) is 2500 miles to the south of the Philippines, almost 1000 kilometres south of the equator. The region is a great square about 2500 kilometres to a side, half of which is water. To be more precise, it is a trapezoid with the western corners skewed to the north and separated by 4500 kilometres. There are two archipelagos: Indonesia (18,000 islands) and the Philippines (over 7000 islands).

Singapore is also an island at the tip of a peninsula occupied by Malaysia. Brunei Darussalam is located on the island of Borneo, which also includes territories of Malaysia and Indonesia. East Timor also shares an island with Indonesia. There are thus six maritime countries in Southeast Asia. East Timor is not part of the ASEAN organization nor the AEC as of 2019.

The five mainland countries of Southeast Asia, from West to East, are Myanmar, Thailand, Cambodia, Lao People's Democratic Republic (PDR) and Vietnam. The most striking geological feature of the mainland is the presence of the Southeast Asian Massif, dividing the region into multiple areas of highlands and lowlands. Communication with the highlands is more difficult than across the lowlands. Agriculture in the highland has tended to be "swiddening" or shifting cultivation—typically the slash and burn of forest land to cultivate it temporarily before abandoning it to move on to a new plot. The lowlands are characterized by rice paddies with permanent irrigation schemes. The highland-lowland division also applies in the larger maritime countries. The highland regions tend to be characterized by a diversity of small, more or less isolated, ethnic groups, while the lowlands have produced the more populous groups that gave rise to nationalities, although not always coinciding with the country borders established by European colonial history from 1511 (Portuguese Malacca) to 1984 (British Brunei).

In general, all parts of Southeast Asia are tropical with two seasons, wet and dry, brought by the monsoon winds. There are two monsoons—northeast and southwest. The impact of each monsoon varies depending on latitude and proximity to the coast and to mountains. Thus, the months and distinctness of the seasons vary. Table 1.1 provides a rough guide to the seasons in various cities. To this should be added the temperature variations in the northern part of Southeast Asia, particularly in the highlands.

Typhoons are another weather phenomenon that impacts part of Southeast Asia seasonally: although they may develop at any time of year, most occur between May and October. The Philippines, Vietnam, Cambodia, Thailand and Laos are most affected by typhoons. These bring heavy rain, high winds, storm surges and lead to landslides. Lands closest to the equator such as Singapore and Indonesia experience few or no typhoons. Indeed, there is little variation in their equatorial climate year round, with slight difference between wet and dry seasons.

History of the Region

Early Identity and Influences

The current country borders in Southeast Asia have much to do with the resolution of the Second World War and also with centuries of European colonization. It would be a mistake, however, to reduce these nations to European creations. Vietnam, for example, has a history stretching back several thousand years. The official historical text of the Lê Dynasty (1428–1788 A.D.), the Đại Việt Sử ký toàn thư, points to Lộc Tục, Kinh Dương Vương, the first king of the Vietnamese people in 2879 B.C. Of course, there is some aura of myth around this. Keith Taylor (1983) associates the "first birth" of Vietnam with the Dong Son culture that lasted from 1000 B.C. to the first century after Christ. The history of Myanmar (today called Myanmar) traces back to the Pyu city-states of the second century before Christ. Although the Khmer ethnic group probably migrated from what today is Southeastern China no later than 2000 B.C., current scholarship suggests dating the beginnings of Khmer culture (and thus arguably the origins of Cambodia) by the fourth century of our era (Murphy 2016, p. 368). Murphy also proposes the emergence of the Dvāravatī polity and culture in central Thailand. Ethnic Malays descend from the Deutero-Malays (deriving from the Cham in what are now southern Cambodia and southern Vietnam) who arrived around 300 B.C. The earliest major civilization for both Malaysia and Indonesia was the thalassocratic Srivijaya Empire (700–1100 of our era). The Laguna Copperplate Inscription, the oldest known Philippine document, is from 900 A.D.

The dominant societies in the region tended to be lowlands, often coastal, with centres that radiated influence diminishing with distance and geographic obstacles, rather than possessing the clear and distinct boundaries that are associated with nation states. "Mandala" (Wolters 1982), "Negara" (Geertz 1981) and "galactic polity" (Tambiah 1977) are so many similar concepts proposed to convey this sense of a powerful centre radiating influence. There have been a myriad of minor centres and a small number of major centres that have waxed and waned in Southeast Asia over the centuries, such as those mentioned above regarding the origins of different cultures, and more recently, the Champa in southern and central Vietnam from 192 to 1832, the Pagan (within today's Myanmar in the eleventh to thirteenth centuries), Lan Na (within today's Thailand in the late thirteenth to sixteenth centuries), the

Sultanate of Malacca (the century before the Portuguese arrived and, through various vicissitudes, on until 1920) and so on.

These polities, and to some extent the more isolated ethnic minorities in the highlands, underwent three major influences before the arrival of European colonizers: those of India, China and Arabia. From 200 B.C. until 1500, traders from the Pallava kingdom in the Indian continent brought goods and Brahman scholars so that their culture reached all classes including the elite: notably Sanskrit, Hinduism and Buddhism. Chinese influence was strongest in Vietnam, especially from 111 B.C. to 938 A.D., although Chinese traders arrived in the Philippines by 982. The most notable influences were Confucianism (without adopting its patriarchal bent) and Mahayana Buddhism (Theravada Buddhism began to replace Mahayana Buddhism in the rest of Southeast Asia starting in the eleventh century). The conversation about Middle East influence upon Southeast Asia has tended to centre on a discussion of the impact of Islam. Sunni Islam is of course the most populous religion in the region. The spice trade brought merchants from Oman and Yemen in the ninth century through to the fifteenth century when Europeans began to take over the trade.

Although these influences were real and lasting, they did not replace the cultures present in Southeast Asia.

The Europeans and Japan

Several Italian city-states acted as middlemen between the Middle Eastern spice traders and Europe. The expansion of the Ottoman Empire led to Venice alone controlling the trade with the Middle Eastern and Indian merchants who sourced in the "spice islands." The rest of Europe sought to circumvent this control. Vasco da Gama rounded the Cape of Good Hope in 1498, opening a direct route for Europeans. The Portuguese controlled this route until the Dutch took over in the seventeenth century, followed by the British in the eighteenth century.

Although European colonization lasted four centuries, it had little influence upon Southeast Asian culture, with the exception of the Christianization of most of the Philippines, accentuating the mixed ethnicity of the Malay Peninsula and expanding the culinary repertoire of urban Vietnamese cuisine.

In 1511, the Portuguese general Alfonso de Albuquerque conquered the Sultanate of Malacca, beginning Portugal's colonial presence in the region. Portugal held Malacca until 1641 and also held East Timor from

1702 to 1975. Although the Portuguese were the European pioneers, their main impact upon the region was to disorganize the trade along the Malacca Strait and to contribute some vocabulary to Indonesian and Malaysian (more or less the same language).

Spain (in the Philippines), the Netherlands, Great Britain and France had a greater impact, particularly in drawing the general national boundaries of Myanmar, Malaysia with Singapore, Indonesia, Laos, Cambodia and Vietnam.

Spain had made an attempt to reach the "spice islands" before Portugal but arrived in America instead. Charles I of Spain later appointed Ferdinand Magellan to organize an expedition that rounded the Americas via the Magellan Strait (just north of Tierra del Fuego) and crossed the Pacific Ocean, reaching the Philippines and then the spice islands (roughly today's Indonesia) in 1521. Spain maintained the Philippines as a colony from 1521 to 1898, when the Spanish–American War brought the Philippines under the rule of the US. Anti-colonialist sentiments and rebellions had begun in the 1870s and continued until suppressed by the US. The US Bureau of Insular Affairs administered the Philippines until 1935.

The Dutch (in Indonesia), the British (in Myanmar, Malaysia and Singapore) and the French (in Cambodia, Laos and Vietnam) all established colonies in Southeast Asia with extensive territories and fought to define their boundaries.[3] Only Thailand remained uncolonized. The colonial regimes lasted until interrupted by Japanese occupation during the Second World War.

Propaganda from Japan in the decades preceding the Second World War proposed a pan-Asian rejection of colonialism and white domination. While the military occupation of Southeast Asia by Japan hardly gave the impression of a liberation by a stronger brother, it is possible that this propaganda awakened a sense of nationalism[4] among the literate and indirectly reinforced the borders drawn by the European colonists. Japanese again promoted the rejection of European colonization in the weeks before its surrender.

Philippines: Before the war, the Philippines Commonwealth had self-government with the limitation that legislation required approval by the president of the US. After occupying the Philippines, Japan declared the [second] "Republic of the Philippines" on October 14, 1943, with José P. Laurel as President. The Commonwealth government continued in exile, however. Further, there was active resistance in the Philippines, with over 250,000 guerrilla fighters by the end of the war. On October 20, 1944, the allied forces landed in Leyte and Laurel dissolved the (Japan-sponsored second Philippine) Republic on August 17, 1945. Japan surrendered the Philippines on September 2, 1945. The Treaty of Manila recognized the independence of the Republic of the Philippines as on July 4, 1946, and the end of American sovereignty over the Philippine Islands.

Vietnam: During the Second World War, Japan governed French Indochina through the intermediary of the Vichy regime. Towards the end, on March 9, 1945, the Japanese ousted the French administration from all zones except Cochinchine (the southern third of Vietnam) and sought declarations of independence from the three nations of Cambodia, Laos and Vietnam. On March 11, the Emperor Bảo Đại declared the independence of Annam (central Vietnam) and Tonkin (North Vietnam) as constituting the empire of Vietnam. The Viet Minh (the communist forces led by Ho Chi Minh among others) seized Hanoi on August 26, 1945. Bao Dai abdicated on August 25. When Japan formally surrendered to the allies on September 2, 1945, Ho Chi Minh proclaimed the independent Democratic Republic of Vietnam. He declared that all "Vietnamese people are determined to mobilise all their physical and mental strength, to sacrifice their lives and property in order to safeguard their independence and liberty."[5] Three French soldiers were killed when forces landed at Haiphong to reassert France's authority, and France shelled the city in retaliation. The Viet Minh replied with an attack against the French in Hanoi. These actions began the First Indochina War that lasted from December 19, 1946, until July 20, 1954.

The Second Indochina War, known as the Vietnam War in the US and as the American War in Vietnam, lasted from November 1, 1955, to April 30, 1975, and was fought on the soil of Cambodia, Laos and Vietnam.

The 1954 Geneva Accord dissolved the colony of French Indochina, established Laos, Cambodia and Vietnam, which was "temporarily" divided at the 17th parallel pending reunification elections. The Viet Minh held the north, and the State of Vietnam, associated with the French Union, became limited to the south under Emperor Bảo Đại as Head of State. He appointed Ngô Đình Diệm as his prime minister and moved to Paris. Diem orchestrated the State of Vietnam referendum of 1955 and changed the regime to the Republic of Vietnam on October 26, 1955. There followed eight years of tension between North and South as well as Buddhist agitation against the Diem regime. A coup put an end to his government and his life. Instability followed, with multiple military governments into the early 1970s. Meanwhile, the Second Indochina War escalated and then came to a close with the withdrawal of American forces and the fall of Saigon on April 30, 1975. The North and South of Vietnam were reunified into the Socialist Republic of Vietnam on July 2, 1976.

Laos: The Viet Minh supported the Pathet Lao in their resistance against colonial France. France gradually relinquished control until Laos became a constitutional monarchy on October 22, 1953. There followed two decades of intrigue and civil war with the outside influences of Vietnam, Russia, France and the US until the Pathet Lao took control and proclaimed the (communist) Lao People's Democratic Republic on December 2, 1975.

Cambodia: It was a protectorate of France from 1867 to 1953 including the years under the Vichy regime. After the war, Cambodia's first democratic election saw the Democratic Party came to power in 1946 with 50 of the National Assembly's 67 seats. In June 1952, King Norodom Sihanouk dismissed the government and seized power. In January 1953, he dissolved the National Assembly and promulgated martial law. He then went to France to seek independence. Making little headway, he began a public relations campaign in the US, Canada and Japan, before returning to Cambodia in May.

Although King Sihanouk had not received a warm reception in France, the reality was that post-war France was hardly able to maintain control over its colonies. Already at war in Vietnam, the French government entered into independence negotiations with Cambodia in August 1953, with complete independence as a constitutional monarchy coming on November 9, 1953. There followed 17 years of machinations, both within the country and in playing both sides in the US-Vietnam War, until a coup displaced Sihanouk. Next came five years of civil war, the victory of the communist Khmer Rouge in 1975, three years of its brutal regime and then the invasion and occupation by Vietnam from 1978 to 1992. Norodom Sihanouk was once again King of Cambodia in 1993. Co-Prime Minister Hun Sen took control with a coup d'état in 1997 and remained in power as of 2019.

Thailand: On June 24, 1932, the Khana Ratsadon (People's Party), a group of military officers and civilians, overthrew King Prajadhipok and replaced the absolute monarchy with a constitutional monarchy. On

March 15, 1933, a civilian leader of the Party, Dr Pridi Phanomyong, submitted a draft economic plan that outlined needed reforms to raise the standard of living of the poor by redistributing land and guaranteeing private property. Three months of factional infighting followed, with Pridi fleeing into exile and culminating in a military coup on June 20, 1933. Pridi Phanomyong eventually returned to Siam on September 29, 1933. During the Second World War, he became regent of Thailand (1944–1946) and prime minister of Thailand in 1946. Phibunsongkhram (Phibun) was one of the military leaders of Khana Ratsadon. While Pridi had tended to socialism and was anti-Japanese, Phibun admired fascism and was pro-Japanese. He centralized power by appointing close military officials to government posts, encouraged a patriotism that bordered on nationalism and cultivated a cult-like following of his person. He changed the name of the country from Siam to Thailand. The French-Thai War (October 1940 to May 1941) ended with the presence of Japan in neighbouring Indochina via the French Vichy regime. Japan reached Malaysia via Thailand with a December 8 invasion initially against the will of Phibun, but within a couple of weeks, he signed a military alliance with Japan after witnessing that country's success in Malaysia. His enthusiasm waned, however, as the economic difficulties of war and the perceived arrogance of the Japanese led to disaffection of the Thai people. Meanwhile, the Regent Pridi carried out a resistance against Phibun and Japan. At the end of the war, Pridi declared Phibun's 1942 declaration of war unconstitutional and thus void. The US interceded to prevent any punitive measures against Thailand. Thailand has seen 20 constitutions since 1932 (Thavevong 2017), all based on a constitutional monarchy.

Myanmar: Aung San (father of Aung San Suu Kyi, current State Counsellor of Myanmar) was born into a Burmese family active in the resistance against the British colonizers. Politically involved from his university days (1933), he had to flee the country in 1940, returning in February 1941 with Japanese support. Japan declared Myanmar an independent nation on August 1, 1943, and named Aung San War Minister. He became disillusioned with the Japanese, realizing they did not permit true independence. On March 27, 1945, he led a Myanmar National Army revolt against occupation. After the war, he became president of the Anti-Fascist People's Freedom League, an amalgamation of various resistance groups. The British governor named him premier of the British-Myanmar Crown Colony, responsible for defence and external affairs. On January 27, 1947, he signed an agreement with British Prime Minister Clement Attlee foreseeing Myanmar's independence. He was assassinated on July 19, 1947.

U Nu (which means Mr Nu) was foreign minister under the Japanese and replaced Aung San after his assassination. It was he who signed the Nu-Attlee Treaty of October 1, 1947, by which Myanmar became independent. The forms of government since then have been as follows: Union of Myanmar (1948–1974), Socialist Republic of the Union of Myanmar (1974–1988), Union of Myanmar (1988–2011) and Republic of the Union of Myanmar (2011–current). There was a military coup in 1962. Over a period of 26 years, a socialist military regime intended to improve the lot of peasants, but the specific actions included the reduction of foreign trade, the nationalization of much of the economy and diversion of investment away from industry into agriculture. The resulting crash of the economy led to an uprising that was suppressed after a military coup brought the installation of a military government which named itself the State Law and Order Restoration Council (SLORC) on September 18, 1988. The military government changed the name of the country from Burma to Myanmar in 1989. It was at this time that the city of Rangoon became Yangon. The government organized elections in 1990. Aung San Suu Kyi's National League for Democracy won 80% of the seats although she had been placed under house arrest previous to the election. The junta rejected the results and continued to govern.

The military government proposed a new constitution on May 10, 2008, giving the military an automatic 110 seats in the 440-seat House of Representatives. The Union Solidarity and Development Party won 259 of the 330 remaining seats. Western observers had reservations about the electoral process (e.g. Martin 2010) while China and Russia endorsed it. A series of political reforms from 2011 to 2015 included the release of Aung San Suu Kyi. An April 1, 2012, by-election for 45 seats saw her National League for Democracy won 41 seats. That party won a majority of seats in both houses in the "Assembly of the Union" in the 2015 general election. In spite of this, the 2008 constitution limits what the Assembly can do, so that the military remains the true power in Myanmar (Selth 2018).

Malaysia: Japan quickly occupied the Malay Peninsula, Singapore and Borneo including Brunei. They roused Malay nationalism and dealt harshly with ethnic Chinese. Unsurprisingly, the resistance Malayan People's Anti-Japanese Army was predominantly ethnic Chinese. It was linked to the Malayan Communist Party, also predominantly ethnic

Chinese. This led to ethnic Malays fearing the Malay Communist Party after the Japanese left and the British returned.

Previous to the Second World War, British influence in what is now Malaysia had been distributed over three kinds of territories: federated Malay States, five unfederated Malay States and the crown colony (under direct British rule) of the Straits Settlements (Dindings, Labuan, Malacca, Penang and Singapore). After the war, the federated Malay States, the unfederated Malay States, Penang and Malacca were transformed into the Malayan Union with a British governor. The regime was unpopular with ethnic Malays and on February 1, 1948, the Federation of Malaya replaced the Malayan Union.[6]

At this point in time, the Federation was about 50% ethnic Malay, 40% ethnic Chinese and 5% ethnic Indian (Tamil).[7] Although the Federation in theory provided equal citizenship opportunity for the Chinese, some felt betrayed by the British, and the Malayan Communist Party agitated for immediate independence with equality for all races. Its recourse to violence combined with British concessions led to a split with more moderate Chinese, and the "Malayan Emergency" dwindled in importance by 1954, although Chin Peng (a hero of the resistance against Japan) maintained armed opposition until 1989.

A general election was held in 1955, and Tunku Abdul Rahma became the Chief Minister and led the Federation to independence (within the Commonwealth of Nations) on August 31, 1957. From 1961, he worked with Lee Kuan Yew of Singapore and with the British towards the merger of Singapore, North Borneo (now Sabah), Sarawak and Brunei with the Federation. This led to the creation of Malaysia on September 16, 1963. Originally, it was to include 15 states, but Brunei declined the invitation. Sukarno[8] in Indonesia rejected the plan, as did the Philippines that claimed North Borneo. Today there are 13 states, of which 11 are on Peninsular Malaysia and 2 on Borneo.

Singapore[9]: It had been in shambles after the War: a major port on a major trading route, its harbour had been badly damaged and of course world trade had been interrupted. Lawlessness and food shortage were problems and utilities were dysfunctional. The Straits Settlements, a colony ruled by Britain, included Penang, Malacca and Singapore, Labuan, Christmas Island and the Cocos-Keeling Island. Singapore and the Cocos-Keeling and Christmas islands became a separate crown colony on April 1, 1946. The Cocos were transferred to Australia on November 23, 1955, and Christmas Island on October 1, 1958.

A new constitution allowing elections came into effect on March 1, 1948. The first elections, held three weeks later, were restricted to the 20,000 British subjects, and only six seats were available for popular vote. In 1955, a majority of seats were up for more extensive popular vote, and the April election resulted in a coalition government. Communists groups began agitating through strikes, student protests and riots. The British Parliament transformed the colony of Singapore into a state in August 1958 with all seats in the Legislative Assembly to be decided by popular vote the following year. Lee Kuan Yew led the People's Action Party to win 43 of the 51 seats. He would remain in power as prime minister until November 1990, and the party remains in power to this day. In 1961, Dr Goh Keng Swee (Minister of Finance) began to implement a four-year development programme to industrialize Singapore.

As mentioned above, Singapore became part of the new Malaysia on September 16, 1963. The next two years saw strife within Singapore (as part of Malaysia) both as a result of ethnic and political tensions and as a result of Indonesia's *Konfrontasi* with at least 42 terrorist-style bombings in Singapore over three years. Further, Singapore had a high portion (76%) of ethnic Chinese, exacerbating ethnic tensions within Malaysia. The Parliament of Malaysia expelled Singapore on August 9, 1965. Singapore's government transformed the new nation into a republic, naming the ethnic Malay Yusof bin Ishak President of the Republic. Independence was proclaimed on Radio Singapore at 10:00 in the morning. Lee Kuan Yew remained as Prime Minister (the Legislative Assembly now became the Parliament).

Indonesia: Soekarno (also spelled Sukarno) studied engineering and received his degree in 1926. With Dr Tjipto Mangunkusumo, he founded the *Perserikatan Nasional Indonesia* in 1927. In 1928, the party's name was changed to *Partij Nasional Indonesia* and adopted the red and white flag of today's Indonesia, as well as the current national anthem *Indonesia Raya*. The colonial government arrested Soekarno and others in 1929. Freed in 1931, he was arrested again in 1933 and exiled to the South of Sumatra.

Both the Dutch commander in the Dutch East Indies (today's Indonesia) and the Dutch governor general surrendered to the Japanese on March 9, 1942. Received as liberators by much of the population, the Japanese fomented a nationalist sentiment. They facilitated speaking tours by Soekarno and Mohammed Hatta, another Indonesian nationalist in 1944.

On March 1, 1945, Japan's Army launched the *Badan Penyelidik Usaha Persiapan Kemerdekaan*, a committee with the mandate of preparing Indonesian independence (as part of Greater Asia). Eight Japanese were in the 59-member committee, as were Soekarno and Hatta. On June 1, Soekarno enunciated the *Pancasila* for this committee. The *Pancasila* is the five-point foundational theory of the Indonesian State, and remains in use today, although the formulation has been modified. Japan surrendered on August 15, and Soekarno proclaimed Indonesia's independence on August 17. Four years of conflict with the Dutch followed, until the transfer of sovereignty on December 27, 1949.

Although established as a democracy, Indonesia was governed by two strongmen for four decades until the Asian Financial Crisis in 1997. The political history of Indonesia thus covers three periods: the old order of Soekarno (1949–1967), the new order of Suharto (from 1967 to the Asian Financial Crisis of 1997) and the current reform era which has consisted in five presidencies up to 2018: three of short duration immediately following Suharto, the stabilizing ten-year administration of Susilo Bambang Yudhoyono (2004–2014) and that of Joko Widodo (2014 onwards).

Negara Brunei Darussalam[10]**:** Britain established a residency (an office administering the relations between Britain and a colony) in Brunei in 1906. Japan entered Brunei on December 16, 1941, and occupied the country by December 22. They kept most of the native administration in their posts. Their forces surrendered at Labuan on September 10, 1945. British Military Administration then oversaw the country until July 6, 1946. Omar Ali Saifuddin III became Sultan in 1950 and continued to be advised by the British Resident. The Brunei People's Party was founded in 1956 with the goal of independence from the UK and democratization of government. Incorporation into Indonesia was seen as a second choice, the third choice being amalgamation with Sarawak and the British North Borneo to form the North Borneo Federation. In 1959, a new constitution made Brunei a self-governing state with Islam as the state religion. Britain retained responsibility for defence and foreign affairs. When the 1962 election returned all ten electable seats to Brunei People's Party, the sultan annulled the election and ruled by decree. The Brunei Revolt in 1962 was unsuccessful except that it may have influenced the sultan's 1963 decision not to join the Federation of Malaysia. A new constitution agreement was signed on September 23, 1959, and another agreement with amendments was signed on November 23, 1971. Finally, at midnight on January 1, 1984, Sultan Hassanal Bolkiah read the Proclamation of Independence.

In summary, European powers had great influence on the boundaries of the countries of Southeast Asia. Nascent resentment of colonialism was cultivated by Japan before and during the Second World War. European ideologies such as communism and liberalism were used to further nationalist ambitions in Southeast Asia. Political manoeuvring within each country did much to determine the regime of each.

ASEAN: From Individual Countries to a Region

Various individual nations came into being in Southeast Asia in the aftermath of the Second World War. All of these nations were desperately poor. It seemed that some sort of collaboration or sharing of experiences might be useful, and the war was followed by two decades of discussion, with a plurality of opinions and postures in each of the countries of the region and also within outside powers interested in the region. This discussion led to a series of organizations and treaties.

The United Nations came into being on October 24, 1945; it set up the Economic Commission for Europe on March 20, 1947. The Philippines, India and China pressed for a similar commission for Asia. This eventually led to the Economic Commission for Asia and the Far East (ECAFE) on March 28, 1947.[11] This commission had the objective of economic cooperation between members, both donor nations and beneficiaries. The USSR and China were both members, as were the UK and the US. Neither Japan nor Korea were included.[12]

Australia, Canada, Ceylon, Great Britain, India, New Zealand and Pakistan attended the 1950 Commonwealth Conference on Foreign Affairs that led to the Colombo Plan for Cooperative Economic Development in South and Southeast Asia. Ceylon was the only country arguably from the region at the time, the only Commonwealth nation in the general area. Laos (1951), South Vietnam (1951–1975), Myanmar (1952), Indonesia (1953), Philippines (1954), Thailand (1954), Malaysia (1957) and Singapore (1966) followed in joining the plan. Vietnam (reunited) also joined in 2004, as did Brunei Darussalam (2008). Underlying this initiative was a belief that development was a scientific problem to be resolved by applying Western financial aid to duplicate the accomplishments of the West. For many of the Western parties, financial aid could help stop the spread of communism, except that it would "be swallowed up and lost in ineffective administration" (Alister McIntosh quoted in Oakman 2010, p. 41). The plan financed infrastructure and also skill development for the operation of the infrastructure. It brought together several nations of Southeast Asia but as part of a larger group and was not a Southeast Asian initiative.

Yoshida Shigeru (Japan's prime minister from 1946 to 1947 and from 1948 to 1954) wrote in 1954 that "Japan's own existence [...] depends on the economic development of, and the maintenance of stability in, the Southeast Asian countries" (Pressello 2018). Japan explored the idea of a fund to Asian aid development in the mid-1950s and early 1960s. The US did not welcome the notion. In January 1963, the Thai Paul Sithi-Amnuai proposed an Asian bank at the Economic and Social Commission for Asia and the Pacific (ESCAP) conference on intraregional trade. The commission, with both Russia and China as members, was receptive to the concept. This eventually led to the founding of the Asian Development Bank on December 19, 1966, in Manila, with Takeshi Watanabe as its first president. Although it would pay an important role in development and was headquartered in the Philippines, the bank had a mandate beyond Southeast Asia. Japan provided much of its financing.

The Truman Doctrine foresaw agreements between countries to forestall the spread of communism. The Manila Pact of 1954 was one such agreement that created the SEATO alliance: Southeast Asia Treaty Organization. The Philippines and Thailand were the only two Southeast Asian nations in the organization. Pakistan, the two Oceanic nations of Australia and New Zealand, France, the UK and the US were the other parties. The headquarters were in Australia, but the first secretary general was the Thai Pote Sarasin. SEATO proved ineffectual, although it did set up some educational facilities in Thailand and was not wound up until 1977.

The Cold War context also led to various treaties and organizations in the Asia Pacific with a more or less explicit mandate of stopping the spread of communism.

The road to ASEAN began in 1958 and 1959, when Tunku Abdul Rahman, Chief Minister of the Federation of Malaya, visited Ceylon (now Sri Lanka) and the Philippines to explore the idea of some sort of Southeast Asian collaborative forum. He also sent feelers to Indonesia. In a Kuala Lumpur press conference on February 8, 1958, he urged Southeast Asian countries to make an effort "to build up their own unity and understanding. If they did not do this, they would have to look outside the area for protection and the full meaning of independence would be lost" (quoted in Tarling 2006, p. 96). Malaysia, Indonesia and the Philippines combined would go a long way towards a collaboration of the Malay race across the Malay Peninsula and the "Malay archipelago" (roughly, the islands between the Southeast Asia mainland and Australia). However, Indonesia had already set up the *Konferensi Asia-Afrika* and, within Southeast Asia, preferred to concentrate on bilateral agreements—perhaps because Soekarno hoped to dominate such agreements as the largest country in the region.

The approach had to evolve to remain viable as other countries (such as Myanmar and Cambodia) were approached. The project was given first one name (Southeast Asia Friendship and Economic Treaty) and then another (Association of South East Asian States). Finally, the foreign ministers of Malaya, the Philippines and Thailand met in Bangkok and established the Association of Southeast Asia (ASA) on July 21, 1961.[13] Tensions between the Philippines and Malaysia over North Borneo shortened the life of ASA. Differences in Cold War rhetoric (coming from the Philippines and Thailand but avoided in the case of Malaysia) also repulsed the interest of potential participants such as Myanmar and Laos. Indonesia and Singapore eventually rallied to the efforts of Malaysia, the Philippines and Thailand and, on August 8, 1967, the five nations established "an Association for Regional Cooperation among the countries of South-East Asia to be known as the Association of South-East Asian Nations (ASEAN)." Table 1.2 lists member nations with the dates they joined ASEAN.

Table 1.2 Accessions to ASEAN

Republic of Indonesia	August 8, 1967
Malaysia	August 8, 1967
Republic of the Philippines	August 8, 1967
Republic of Singapore	August 8, 1967
Kingdom of Thailand	August 8, 1967
Brunei Darussalam	January 7, 1984
Socialist Republic of Vietnam	July 28, 1995
Lao People's Democratic Republic	July 23, 1997
Republic of the Union of Myanmar	July 23, 1997
Kingdom of Cambodia	April 30, 1999

Source: ASEAN University Network at http://www.aunsec.org/historyofasean.php. Accessed April 15, 2019

Originally ASEAN had primarily a security vocation and thus of solidarity against outside threat rather than meddling in internal domestic issues. As such, a basic principle is that of non-interference in domestic affairs: "this principle is the major content in most important documents of ASEAN such as The Zone of Peace, Freedom and Neutrality Declaration (ZOPFAN) sealed in year 1971 and Treaty of Amity and Cooperation of Southeast Asia in year 1976" (Keling et al. 2011). The Philippines and Thailand have since argued for a greater authority to accelerate adoption of ASEAN guidelines, but the principle remains in place.

In 1991, ASEAN's economic ministers meeting led to the creation of AFTA, the ASEAN Free Trade Area. Seven years later, the ministers confirmed the framework for AIA, the ASEAN Investment Area, with the objective of developing ASEAN as a desirable investment area over the coming decade.

The Asian Financial Crisis saw the heads of state of the participating nations meet in Kuala Lumpur on December 15, 1997, and produce Vision 2020, a document in which they announced their resolve to "advance economic integration and cooperation by undertaking the following general strategies: fully implement the ASEAN Free Trade Area and accelerate liberalization of trade in services, realise the ASEAN Investment Area by 2010 and free flow of investments by 2020." The ASEAN Trade in Goods Agreement was signed on February 26, 2009. On November 20, 2007, the heads of state signed the declaration of the ASEAN Economic Community Blueprint with a strategic schedule for that community. The ASEAN Agreement on Customs was signed on March 29, 2012. The AEC came into effect on December 31, 2015.

The Economies of ASEAN and AEC in 2018

Together, Southeast Asian economies constitute the most rapidly growing economic region in the world, thanks to diversification into more complex manufacturing, according to Ricardo Hausmann (quoted in McKenney 2018). Since the middle-income class with its disposable income will be two-thirds of the projected population of nearly five billion by 2030, there is great promise of continued growth. This section provides an overview of the economies of the members of the AEC, covering their size, capital, trade, productivity and demand. It ends with an examination of the digital economy of the region.

Table 1.3 Overview of size and wealth of Southeast Asian economies

Country name	*Population in millions 2017*	*GDP (million current US$) 2017*	*GDP per capita (current US$) 2017*
Indonesia	264.0	1,015,539.02	3846.86
Philippines	104.9	313,595.21	2988.95
Vietnam	95.5	223,864.00	2343.12
Thailand	69.0	455,220.92	6593.82
Myanmar	53.4	69,322.12	1298.88
Malaysia	31.6	314,500.28	9944.90
Cambodia	16.0	22,158.21	1384.42
Lao PDR	6.9	16,853.08	2457.38
Singapore	5.6	323,907.23	57,714.30
Brunei Darussalam	0.4	12,128.09	28,290.59
Totals and average	647.4	2,767,088.16	4274

Source: Author's calculations for totals and average GDP per capita; data taken from the World Bank national accounts data and OECD National Accounts

Size: ASEAN's projected 2018 GDP of US$3 trillion is greater than that of India and about 30% the GDP projected for China. Table 1.3 provides a breakdown of GDP by country as well as GDP per capita, which varies 50-fold in nominal GDP from the richest (Singapore) to the poorest (Cambodia). There is also a considerable variation in size from Indonesia, with over one-third of the total ASEAN population, to Brunei, with less than half a million. The region as a whole has long outperformed both advanced economies and the world average in terms of growth, with the exception of the 1997 financial crisis (Fig. 1.1). The growth rate varies across the region. The Philippines grew at 6.6% in 2017; Brunei Darussalam (sensitive to the price of oil) did not grow at all (see Table 1.4). If we exclude the small population countries of Singapore and Brunei Darussalam, ASEAN seem set to grow only a little slower than India, with the sole exception of Thailand (see Table 1.5). Singapore, an advanced economy, will probably grow at 2.5%–3.0% a year. Although Brunei Darussalam is attempting to diversify, its GDP varies with the price of oil.

Capital, debt and savings: However, if the ASEAN region is slightly outpaced by China and India, it presents a far more conservative government debt profile in Fig. 1.2. The region has also been conservative regarding foreign reserves since the 1997 financial crisis as shown in Table 1.6. Even Lao PDR has more than the Euro area's half percent.

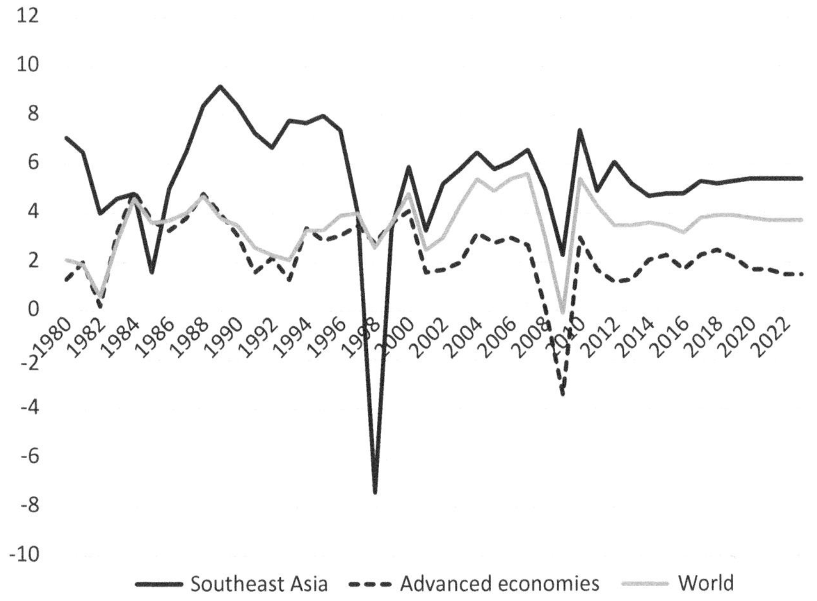

Fig. 1.1 Real GDP growth measured by annual percent change in GDP. Data source: IMF datamapper

Table 1.4 Real GDP growth in ASEAN in percent

Region		*2016*	*2017*	*Projection 2018–2022*
ASEAN		4.8	5.1	5.2
Fastest growth	Philippines	6.9	6.6	6.4
Slowest growth	Brunei Darussalam	−2.5	0	0.5
	Singapore	2.0	3.2	2.3
	Thailand	3.2	3.8	3.6

Data source: IMF datamapper

Gross fixed capital formation[14] varies from Cambodia's 23% of GDP in 2016 (slightly below the world average) to nearly 35% of GDP for Myanmar, Indonesia and Brunei Darussalam—see Table 1.7. These figures are comparable with that of India (28.5%) but fall short of China (42% in 2017). Foreign direct investment (FDI) inflows (investment funds coming into the country as opposed to FDI outflows) have

Table 1.5 Projected real growth for ASEAN, China and India

	2019	*2020*	*2021*	*2022*	*2023*
India	7.8	7.9	8.1	8.1	8.2
Cambodia	6.8	6.5	6.3	6	6
Lao PDR	7	7	6.9	6.8	6.8
Philippines	6.8	6.9	6.9	7	7
China, People's Republic of	6.4	6.3	6	5.7	5.5
Vietnam	6.5	6.5	6.5	6.5	6.5
Myanmar	7	7.2	7.3	7.4	7.5
Indonesia	5.5	5.6	5.6	5.6	5.6
Thailand	3.8	3.6	3.6	3.5	3.5

Data source: IMF. World economic outlook for April 2018. https://www.imf.org/external/datamapper/NGDP_RPCH@WEO/BRN/KHM/CHN/IDN/LAO/MMR/PHL/SGP/THA/VNM. Accessed September 30, 2018

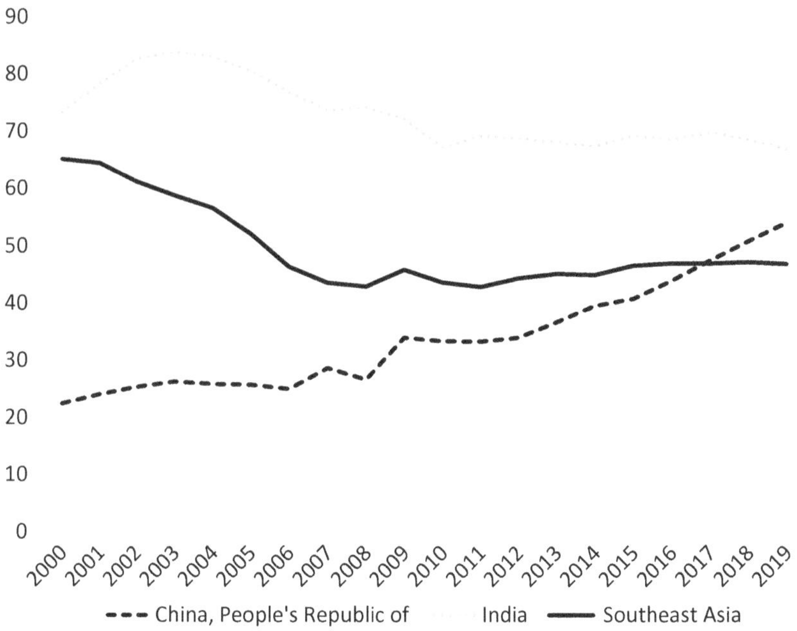

Fig. 1.2 General government gross debt (percent of GDP) of ASEAN, China and India. Data source: IMF

Table 1.6 Foreign reserves as percent of external debt in 2016

Cambodia	86.5
Indonesia	36.8
Lao PDR	6.2
Malaysia	47.2
Myanmar	75.7
Philippines	104.3
Thailand	141.4
Vietnam	42.0
Brunei Darussalam	n.a.
Singapore	n.a.

Source: World Bank, International Debt Statistics

Table 1.7 Gross fixed capital formation as a percentage of GDP from largest to smallest percentage in 2015

	2008	*2009*	*2010*	*2011*	*2012*	*2013*	*2014*	*2015*	*2016*	*2017*
Brunei Darussalam	13.7	17.5	23.5	25.9	32.8	39.5	27.3	35.0	34.4	34.6
Myanmar	15.7	19.0	22.9	29.2	29.9	31.4	35.2	34.7	n.a.	n.a.
Indonesia	27.7	31.1	31.0	31.3	32.7	32.0	32.5	32.8	32.6	32.2
Lao PDR	31.7	33.9	27.5	28.1	32.5	30.6	29.8	31.6	29.0	29.0
Singapore	28.3	29.3	26.1	25.5	26.7	27.9	28.4	27.8	26.6	24.8
Malaysia	20.6	22.0	22.4	22.2	25.4	26.5	26.0	26.1	25.8	25.3
Vietnam	31.8	33.9	32.6	26.8	24.2	23.6	23.8	24.7	23.7	23.1
Thailand	26.4	23.1	24.0	25.8	27.0	25.4	24.6	24.5	24.0	n.a.
Philippines	19.7	19.0	20.5	18.7	19.6	20.6	20.7	22.0	24.6	25.2
Cambodia	17.3	20.1	16.2	16.0	17.4	18.9	21.0	21.4	21.7	21.9

Data source: World Bank national accounts data and OECD National Accounts data files

hovered around US$130 billion over the past few years, with the European Union dominating as shown in Fig. 1.3.[15] The major sources of FDI are the EU, Japan and China, in that order. However, China's activity is more recent and increasing. Of the three major sources, China directs a greater portion to real estate than either Europe or Japan, as shown in Fig. 1.4.

Gross domestic savings rates, measured as a percentage of GDP, vary across three distinct groups, as Table 1.8 indicates: high savers such as Singapore, medium savers such as Indonesia and low savers such as Cambodia. Savings seem to be a function of the amount of discretionary income, with poorer countries less able to save. About 35 million people in the region earn less than the international poverty line cut-off of US$1.90

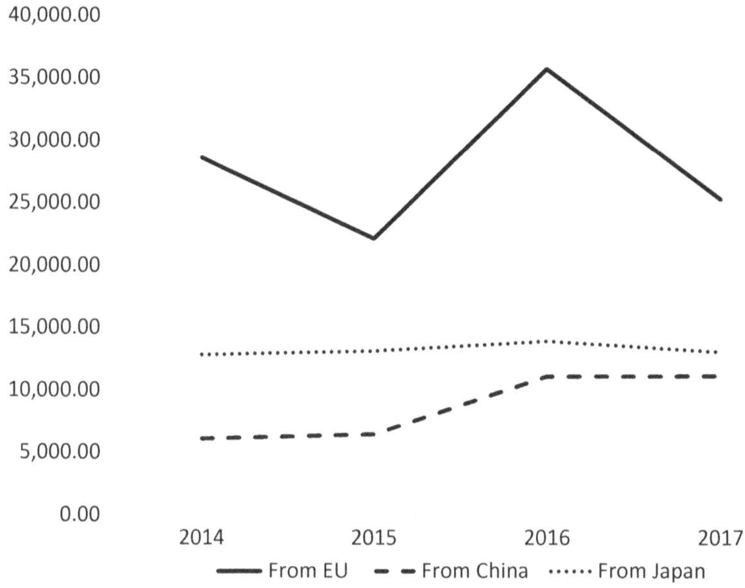

Fig. 1.3 Flows of inward foreign direct investment (FDI) to ASEAN. Data source: ASEANStats DataPortal

a day; of these, 90% live in Indonesia and the Philippines. Of course, these two countries account for more than half the population of the region.

Trade: Intra-ASEAN trade (between ASEAN members) and extra-ASEAN trade (with the rest of the world) accounted for 24% and 76% of total trade, respectively, in 2015. Total extra-ASEAN trade (imports plus exports) is equivalent to two-thirds of GDP (compared to the 56% world average in 2016 and 84.3% in 2016 and 87.1% in 2017 for the Euro area), with China accounting for almost as much as the next two largest trading partners, the EU and Japan (see Table 1.9). While total imports and exports are more or less balanced, trade with China is clearly skewed to imports. Figure 1.5 shows the evolution of trade balances from 2010 to 2017. The portions of intra- and extra-ASEAN trade raise the question of the degree to which the AEC really constitutes an economic block. Chapter 13 on the ASEAN Economic Community and the concluding Chap. 14 will raise this question again. However, the purpose of the AEC is not to isolate ASEAN from the rest of the world but on the contrary to make member nations more competitive in world trade.

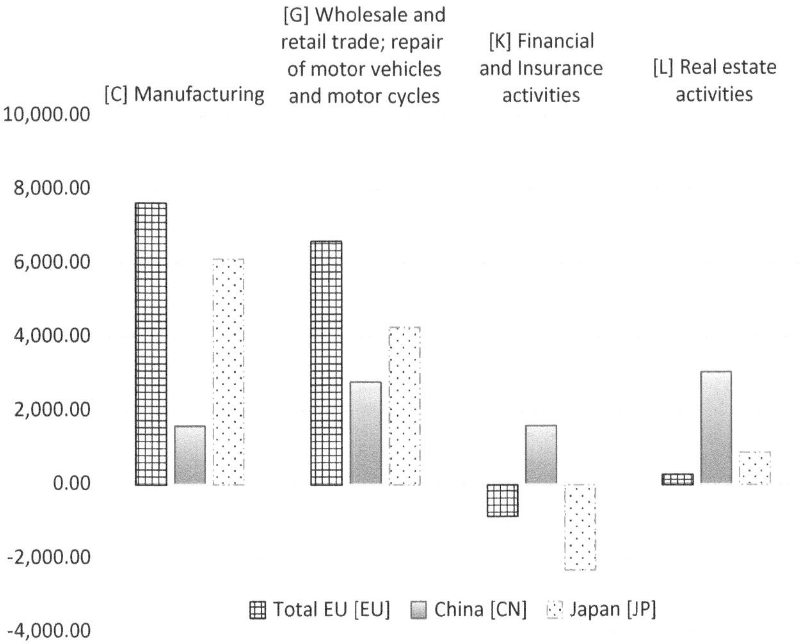

Fig. 1.4 FDI to ASEAN by source to selected sectors for 2017. Data source: ASEANStats DataPortal

Table 1.8 Gross domestic savings rates as percentage of GDP, 2016

Singapore	53.3
Brunei Darussalam	52.6
Thailand	33.0
Indonesia	32.7
Malaysia	32.6
Myanmar	30.0
Vietnam	24.9
Lao PDR	20.3
Cambodia	18.7
Philippines	15.3

Data source: World Bank national accounts data, and OECD National Accounts data files

Table 1.9 ASEAN international 2017 merchandise trade in US$ billion

Partner	*Total*	*Export*	*Import*	*Balance*	*Balance/Total in percent*
Extra-ASEAN	1984.37	1011.32	973.05	38.28	1.9
China	441.57	187.03	254.55	−67.52	−15.3
European Union	261.27	157.84	103.43	54.41	2.1
Japan	219.00	105.54	113.47	−7.93	−3.6

Data source: ASEANStats data portal

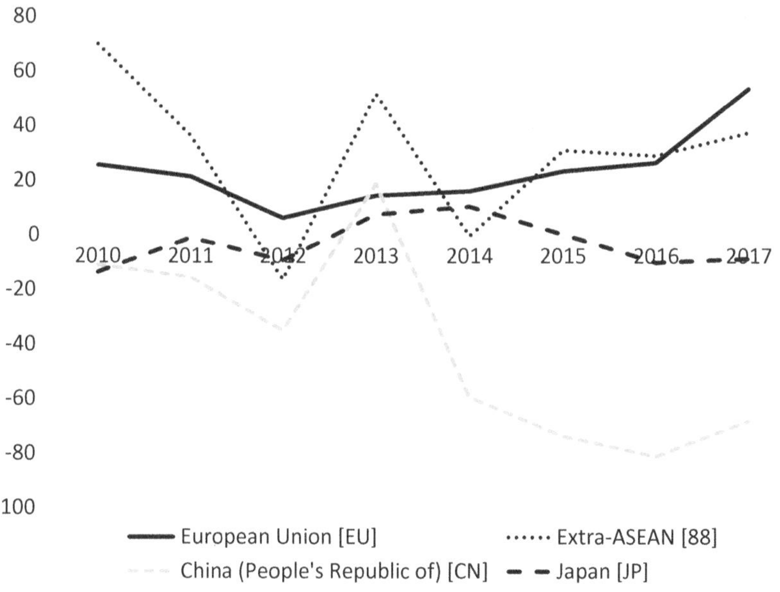

Fig. 1.5 Trade balance by Year and Partner. Data source: ASEANStats data portal

Productivity: Table 1.10 provides figures for the portion of the population employed. For reference, the EU average is around 65%. Productivity varies widely, as measured by GDP per person employed. The figure for Brunei Darussalam is more than 25 times that of Cambodia, as Table 1.11 shows. More importantly, after eliminating the petroleum-based economy of Brunei Darussalam and the advanced economy of Singapore, only

Table 1.10 Employment to population ratio (%) for the population 15 years and older

Country	*%*	*Year*
Brunei Darussalam	56.9	2017
Cambodia	82.6	2015
Indonesia	64.2	2017
Lao PDR	77.7	2010
Malaysia	65.6	2017
Philippines	57.6	2017
Singapore	65.3	2016
Vietnam	74.7	2017
Myanmar	60.3	2017
Thailand	67.8	2016

Data source: International Labour Organization, ILOSTAT database. Data retrieved in September 2018

Table 1.11 GDP in US$ per person employed (Constant 2011 PPP $)

Brunei Darussalam	$167,876.44
Singapore	$141,424.58
Malaysia	$55,527.59
Thailand	$28,303.40
Indonesia	$23,787.86
Philippines	$18,617.96
Myanmar	$11,757.91
Lao PDR	$10,973.18
Vietnam	$10,232.48
Cambodia	$6176.77

Data source: International Labour Organization, ILOSTAT database. Data retrieved in November 2017

Malaysia returns a figure above the world average (constant 2011 PPP US$35,430 in 2017; nominal figures not available). This is problematic at first glance. Labour may be cheaper in much of the ASEAN region, but why invest here if labour is less productive? (See Table 1.12 for monthly wages and monthly GDP per person employed.) This logic is somewhat misleading however, because that same labour can be made more productive when an investor provides better tools and machinery. It is also partly accurate, because labour needs better education and training in order to work with better tools and machinery. See Table 1.13 for education levels in the ASEAN region. Table 1.14 gives scores and rankings on the Global Human Capital Index that combines scores for formal education with an apprecia-

Table 1.12 Monthly wages in 2014 for some ASEAN countries, China and India

Country	*Currency*	*2014 monthly wage*	*Source*	*Monthly wage in 2014 US$*	*Monthly GDP per capita in 2014 US$*	*Monthly GDP per person employed (constant 2011 PPP $)*
Cambodia	KHR	642,000	National Institute of Statistics	155	91.15	451.97
Indonesia	IDR	1,952,589	Statistics Indonesia of the Republic of Indonesia	131	290.97	1801.12
Malaysia	MYR	2775	Department of Statistics of Malaysia	670	931.98	4346.85
Philippines	PHP	9582	National Statistical Office of the Philippines	177	236.91	1340.57
Singapore	SGD	4727	Statistics Singapore	3449	4746.42	12,040.45
Thailand	THB	13,244	National Statistical Office of Thailand	411	496.15	2157.33
Viet Nam	VND	4,473,000	General Statistics Office of Vietnam	192	167.67	740.16
China	CNY	4697	National Bureau of Statistics China	684	640.29	1896.95
India	INR	9194 (data for 2013)	Government of India Ministry of Statistics and Programme Implementation	126	131.33	1217.83

Data source: Wages from ILO 2016, p. 102. The primary sources used by ILO are listed in the fourth column. Wages in US$ calculated using 2014 exchange rates from Exchange-Rates.org. Monthly GDP per capita in US$ calculated from annual figures provided by World Bank national accounts data and OECD National Accounts data files

The similar figures for monthly wage and monthly GDP per capita for Singapore are coincidental (or rather a result of the exchange rate)

tion of the quality of that education and the development of skills on the job, among other considerations. Further, that labour needs a better infrastructure (roads, rail, bridges and ports) to be more productive. One indicator of infrastructure is the ratio of paved road to total road length. In

Table 1.13 Secondary education completion rates for ASEAN

Country name	*% Lower secondary completion rate*	*Year of data*	*(%) population 25+ with completed upper secondary education*	*Year of data*
Singapore	n.a	n.a.	70.9	2015
Brunei Darussalam	101.3	2016	n.a.	
Philippines	83.2	2015	58.5	2013
Malaysia	84.5	2016	50.9	2010
Thailand	78.7	2015	32.7	2016
Indonesia	95.1	2016	28.9	2011
Vietnam	87.6	2016	25.7	2009
Lao PDR	66.8	2016	n.a.	
Myanmar	54.3	2017	n.a.	
Cambodia	47.4	2016	6.3	2009

Data source: UNESCO Institute for Statistics
Lower secondary completion rate as percent of the relevant age group; percent of the population over 25 having at least completed upper secondary education. Sorted by percent with upper secondary completed, with the exception of Brunei Darussalam

Table 1.14 Score and rankings (out of 130 countries) for AEC members in the global human capital index 2017

Country	*Score*	*Ranking*
Singapore	73.3	11
Malaysia	68.3	33
Thailand	66.2	40
Philippines	64.4	50
Brunei Darussalam	62.82	58
Vietnam	62.19	64
Indonesia	62.19	65
Lao PDR	58.36	84
Myanmar	57.67	89
Cambodia	57.28	92

Data source: World Economic Forum 2017, pp. 8–9
Scores "can be roughly interpreted as a percentage reflecting the degree of effective human capital utilization in a given country relative to the ideal outcome" (World Economic Forum 2017, p. 6)

decreasing ratios, Singapore, Brunei Darussalam, Philippines, Thailand and Malaysia are all above 75%. Indonesia and Vietnam are above 50%. Myanmar is around 40%. Laos and Cambodia are both below 10% (ASEANstats). In comparison, the figure was 54% for China and 50% for India in 2008. Table 1.15 provides scores and rankings for the infrastructure.

Table 1.15 Infrastructure ranking and score on the World Economic Forum global competitiveness index 2017–2018

Country	*Rank*	*Score*
Singapore	2	6.5
Malaysia	22	5.5
Thailand	43	4.7
Indonesia	52	4.5
Brunei Darussalam	60	4.3
Vietnam	79	3.9
Philippines	97	3.4
Lao PDR	102	3.3
Cambodia	106	3.1
Myanmar	n.a.	n.a.

Data Source: World Economic Forum 2018
Higher scores (maximum of 7) are better and give priority in ranking

Another factor affecting productivity is the structure of the economy understood as the proportion of workers employed in each of agriculture, industry and services. In a highly productive economy, a small portion of the population is able to supply sufficient foodstuffs for all.[16] Southeast Asia is a case in point, and the remarkably large number of farm workers are the least productive (and poorest) workers in the economies of the region. There have been some productivity improvements in agriculture and fisheries—another low value-added industry—across Southeast Asia, but farm sizes have been *decreasing* in Indonesia, the Philippines and Thailand. The importance of agriculture and fisheries decreased between 1998 and 2012 and presumably continues to decrease today, both in terms of employment and in terms of portion of the GDP (OECD/FAO 2017, p. 62). Table 1.16 lists AEC member nations from least to highest proportion of agricultural workers. Brunei Darussalam is able to use the revenue from petroleum to import most food. Cambodia is strikingly out of sequence (in terms of GDP per capita), suggesting that its industry is very simple. Garments, footwear and other light manufacturing are the main industrial activities there.

Demand: As observed in the opening paragraphs of this introduction, the region most likely will experience a rapid growth in the size of the middle class with consequent increase in demand. This has not yet happened, although Malaysia has seen a 50% increase in household[17] final consumption expenditure per capita over 2008–2017—an indication of increasing demand (see Fig. 1.6).

Table 1.16 Portions of total employment in agriculture, industry and services

Country	*% employed in agriculture*	*% employed in industry*	*% employed in services*	*GDP per person employed constant 2011 PPP US*
Singapore	0.1	16.3	83.6	141,424.58
Brunei Darussalam	0.5	17.7	81.8	167,876.43
Malaysia	11	27.4	61.5	55,527.60
Philippines	26	17.7	56.3	18,617.96
Cambodia	26.7	27	46.3	6176.77
Indonesia	31.2	21.7	47.1	23,787.86
Thailand	32.8	22.6	44.6	28,303.40
Vietnam	40.9	25.1	34.1	10,232.48
Myanmar	49.9	16.6	33.5	11,757.10
Lao PDR	61.3	9.7	29	10,973.18

Data source: International Labour Organization, ILOSTAT database

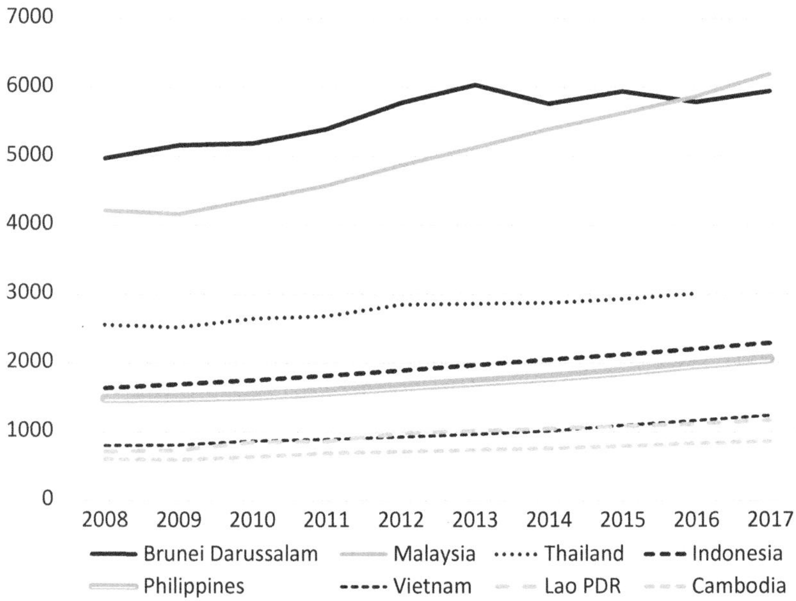

Fig. 1.6 Households' final consumption expenditure per capita, including the expenditures of non-profit institutions serving households. Note: Singapore excepted as an outlier with three times the expenditure of Malaysia. Myanmar excepted due to lack of data, although the figure was slightly lower than that of Cambodia in 2010. Data source: World Bank national accounts data and OECD National Accounts data files

Elements of the digital economy: Southeast Asia is the fastest growing Internet region in the world (Anandan et al. 2016). One measure of the Southeast Asian e-commerce market is "shipped orders of new merchandise sold by business to consumers." The figure for 2015 was US$5.5B; the figure for 2017 was US$10.9B in gross merchandize value including VAT—it doubled in two years (Google Temasek 2017). The projection for 2025 is US$88.1 billion (Ibidem).

Out of 19 regions worldwide, Southeast Asia as a region ranks third highest for mobile connections, Internet users (in millions), number of monthly mobile-active accounts on the top social network in each country (with a 51% penetration rate), number of mobile connections and the number of mobile broadband connections. In general, the number one spot goes to Eastern Asia (China, Japan, Korea and Taiwan) and the number two spot to Western Asia (Bangladesh, Bhutan, India, the Maldives, Nepal, Pakistan and Sri Lanka)[18] (Kemp 2018). This is explained by a reasonably high penetration rate and large populations. In the case of Southeast Asia, individual users have multiple phones and tablets, leading to a world highest 1.5 connections per capita: on average, each person has 1.5 connections to the internet.

Regarding online transactions, in a survey of 40 countries including 6 from Southeast Asia, only 3 of these were in the top 36 (!) countries for percentage of the population who bought something online. However, the profile changes when we focus on transactions from a mobile device. In a survey of 34 countries, 5 of the 6 AEC members surveyed were in the top 10 countries for the portion of Internet users who access via a mobile only. Thus it is not surprising that 3 of top 10 countries for online purchases from a mobile device and 6 of the top 22 were in the AEC region. The region also accounted for three of top ten countries for percentage of the total population that accesses banking services via a mobile device (Kemp 2018).

English is dominant on the Internet with 50% of web content and the language of 50% of Facebook users. Still, 4 of the top 12 languages used on Facebook are from AEC countries. The reason is that four of the top eight countries by percentage share of total global Facebook monthly active users are AEC members. Of the top ten countries with the largest growth in number of mobile social media users from 2016 to 2017, three were AEC members (Kemp 2018). There is room for more web content in languages of Southeast Asia.

All of this suggests that Southeast Asia is a zone to watch for innovations in connectedness. It means that retailers should think in terms of mobile transactions and suggests that manufacturers and wholesalers must be networked to be competitive.

The Structure of This Book

AEC member nations present a rich and diverse economic zone, and this book can only provide an initiation, orienting further and more specific research, be it applied or academic. Rather than attempting to be complete, this book compromises to constitute a starting point. Part I covers the large AEC economies moving geographically in a general counterclockwise direction starting with the Philippines and moving through Vietnam, Thailand, Malaysia, Singapore and Indonesia. Chapter 2, besides describing the Philippines, also provides the reader with further background on ASEAN and the AEC, as well as the notion of economic freedom which is invoked in many of the subsequent chapters. Part II treats the smaller economies: Brunei Darussalam, Cambodia, Laos and Myanmar. Part III deals with two general issues: the presence and influence of China upon the region and the AEC organization as well as its history and that of ASEAN. A conclusion will summarize and build on the main points covered in Parts I, II and III.

Notes

1. IMF 2018, World Economic Outlook, Table 1, provides an average for ASEAN 5—the largest and slowest growing economies with the exception of the Philippines. OECD 2018, Economic Outlook for Southeast Asia, China and India, p. 20 provides figures for ASEAN countries. The ASEAN secretariat itself gives a slightly more conservative figure of 4.8% for 2017. Cfr. Investing in ASEAN-2017, p. 6.
2. The military regime changed the name of Burma to Myanmar, and the latter is used in this book.
3. Trade had motivated their arrival, but this led to occupation of territory. The growing demand for spice was inelastic relative to the Portuguese supply in the sixteenth century. The Dutch and the English joined in the trade in the late sixteenth century but also were only somewhat sporadic in supplying the European market, leading to price swings. The problem was the scale of the undertaking. Individual expeditions were capitalized on a one-time basis. England was the first to create a permanent company sending

multiple expeditions to Southeast Asia. Some 200 merchants and nobles invested some £70,000 in a venture which on December 31, 1600, obtained a charter from the Queen of England granting a 15-year monopoly on all English trade between the Cape of Good Hope and the Straits of Magellan. This would become the British East India Company and lasted until the nineteenth century. The Dutch followed suit in 1602 with the formation of the publicly traded Dutch East India Company (*Vereenigde Oostindische Compagnie*; VOC). King Louis XIV chartered the *Compagnie française pour le commerce des Indes orientales* in 1664.

4. Some nationalism was already extent in most of the colonies/territories previous to the Second World War. Religion played some role. It was one factor among many in the Moslem areas like present-day Brunei, Indonesia and Malaysia but not dominant. Theravada Buddhism, on the other hand, was a stronger source of nationalism in Cambodia, Myanmar and Thailand (see Keyes 2016).
5. The full declaration is available at many web sites in English and in Nguyễn 2002, p. 71.
6. For a graphic summary of the evolution of the Malaysian peninsula and British Borneo from the eighteenth century until 1984, see https://upload.wikimedia.org/wikipedia/commons/3/3d/Malaysia_tree_diagram.svg.
7. Estimates vary. See, for example, Jensen 1967, p. 6, using religion as a proxy for ethnicity, and Panikkar 1943, p. 98.
8. He had adopted the 1920s concept of Indonesia Raya—a Greater Indonesia including the Malay Peninsula and all of Borneo. Indonesian opposition led to the 1963–1966 *Konfrontasi*—a low-level, undeclared war along what is today's border between Malaysian and Indonesian Borneo. The idea was that the division between Malaysia and Indonesia was an after-effect of colonization by two different European countries that separated the Malays into two different nations.
9. The Singapore government provides web pages with a reasonably detailed timeline of Singapore at http://eresources.nlb.gov.sg/history. See also http://countrystudies.us/singapore/.
10. This the full official name of the country. Negara means (more or less) "state." Darussalam means "abode of peace." The word Brunei has the same historical derivation as "Borneo."
11. Cfr. United Nations, Economic and Social Commission for Asia and the Pacific (ESCAP) (2014). Asia and the Pacific: A Story of Transformation and Resurgence.
12. There were jurisdictional and sovereignty issues that impeded the early participation by Japan and Korea. Korea was divided at the 38th parallel between the USSR-run North and the US-run South. As for Japan, the Supreme Command of Allied Powers (SCAP) administered the country and was responsible for external affairs. Japanese advisers accompanied SCAP repre-

sentatives to ECAFE at its inception before Japan became an associate member in 1952 and full member in 1954 (Mie 2008). ECAFE was renamed the Economic and Social Commission for Asia and the Pacific (ESCAP) in 1974.

13. For a somewhat more detailed relation of events from the Second World War to the founding of the ASA, see Shimada 2010, pp. 31–55. For events over the short history of ASA, see Pollard 1970 and Tarling 2007.
14. GDP can be measured on the use side as well as the production side. On the use side, it is used for investment, consumption, net exports and government spending on goods and services. Gross capital formation is the measure of investment and "consists of outlays on additions to the fixed assets of the economy plus net changes in the level of inventories. Fixed assets include land improvements (fences, ditches, drains, and so on); plant, machinery, and equipment purchases; and the construction of roads, railways, and the like, including schools, offices, hospitals, private residential dwellings, and commercial and industrial buildings. Inventories are stocks of goods held by firms to meet temporary or unexpected fluctuations in production or sales, and work in progress. According to the 1993 SNA, net acquisitions of valuables are also considered capital formation. Data are in constant 2010 U.S. dollars" (World Bank national accounts data). Non-economist readers can find the definition of other technical terms on the Internet, such as at http://documents.worldbank.org/curated/en/541831468326979631/pdf/322800PUB00PUB0d0bank0glossary01996.pdf.
15. This works out to about 5% of GDP. However, this does not compare directly with capital formation as the World Bank points out: "FDI can be used to finance fixed capital formation, however it can also be used to cover a deficit in the company or paying off a loan. Thus, you cannot say FDI is always included in gross fixed capital formation." https://datahelpdesk.worldbank.org/knowledgebase/articles/195312-is-foreign-direct-investment-fdi-included-in-gro. Accessed September 24, 2018.
16. Imports and exports do affect this indicator. Singapore imports most of its food. It can afford to do so. In theory, a highly productive agricultural economy (most workers being agricultural workers) could export most of its food. In practice, agriculture does not add as much value as industry and many services.
17. The data also include expenditures by non-profit institutions serving households (NPISH) that are not mainly financed and controlled by government and which provide goods or services to households for free or negligible symbolic amounts. These include political parties, churches, and so on, and their expenditures are far less than those of households.
18. In addition, Afghanistan is an eighth member state of the South Asian Association for Regional Cooperation. The author did not ascertain if Afghanistan is included in this statistic, as it would not have affected rankings.

References

Anandan, Rajan, Rohit Sipahimalani, Alap Bharadwaj, Jaideep Jhangiani, Danny Kim, and Soumi Ramesh. 2016. *e-conomy SEA: Unlocking the $200B Digital Opportunity.* https://www.thinkwithgoogle.com/intl/en-apac/trends-and-insights/e-conomy-sea-unlocking-200b-digital-opportunity/. Accessed October 1, 2018.

Brueckners, Markus, Era Dabla-Norris, Mark Gradstein, and Daniel Lederman. 2018. The Rise of the Middle Class and Economic Growth in ASEAN. *Journal of Asian Economics* 56 (2018): 48–58.

ChinaPower. 2017. *How Much Trade Transits the South China Sea?* https://chinapower.csis.org/much-trade-transits-south-china-sea/. Accessed February 8, 2019.

EY ASEAN. 2017. *Rediscover ASEAN. A Growth Story of Ten Countries.* EY ASEAN (related to Ernst & Young Global Limited). https://www.ey.com/Publication/vwLUAssets/EY-rediscover-asean-a-growth-story-of-10-countries/$FILE/EY-rediscover-asean-a-growth-story-of-10-countries.pdf. Accessed March 23, 2019.

Geertz, Clifford. 1981. *Negara: The Theatre State in Nineteenth-Century Bali.* Princeton: Princeton University Press.

Google Temasek. 2017. *e-Conomy SEA Spotlight 2017.* Jointly published by Google (Mountain View) and Temasek (Singapore).

ILO. 2016. *Global Wage Report 2016/17.* Geneva: International Labour Organization.

IMF. 2018, July. *World Economic Outlook Update.* https://www.imf.org/en/Publications/WEO/Issues/2018/07/02/world-economic-outlook-update-july-2018. Accessed September 24, 2018.

Iokibe, Makoto, Caroline Rose, Junko Tomaru, and John Weste, eds. 2008. *Japanese Diplomacy in the 1950s: From Isolation to Integration.* Milton Park: Routledge.

Jensen, Clara Sayre. 1967. *Religion and Politics in South and Southeast Asia.* Ph.D. Thesis, University of Illinois.

Keling, Mohamad Faisol, Hishamudin Md. Som, and Mohamad Nasir Saludin. 2011. The Development of ASEAN from Historical Approach. *Asian Social Science* 7 (7).

Kemp, Simon. 2018. *Digital in 2018.* Vancouver: Hootsuite. https://hootsuite.com/pages/digital-in-2018. Accessed September 22, 2018.

Keyes, Charles. 2016. Theravada Buddhism and Buddhist Nationalism: Sri Lanka, Myanmar, Cambodia, and Thailand. *The Review of Faith & International Affairs* 14 (4): 41–52.

Martin, Michael F. 2010. *Myanmar's 2010 Elections: Implications of the New Constitution and Election Laws.* Washington: Congressional Research Service.

McKenney, Chuck. 2018. *Southeast Asia Surging in CID's New Global Growth Projections*. http://atlas.cid.harvard.edu/rankings/growth-projections/. Accessed October 8, 2018.

Mie, Oba. 2008. *Japan's Entry into ECAFE*. Chapter 5 in Iokibe et al. 2008.

Murphy, Stephen A. 2016. The Case for Proto-Dvāravatī: A Review of the Art Historical and Archaeological Evidence. *Journal of Southeast Asian Studies* 47 (3): 366–392.

Nguyễn, Thế Anh. 2002. The Formulation of the National Discourse in 1940–45 Vietnam. *Journal of International and Area Studies* 9 (1): 57–75.

Oakman, Daniel. 2010. *Facing Asia: A History of the Colombo Plan*. Acton (Australia) ANU Press. Online version prepared from the 2006 printed edition by Pandanus Books (Canberra).

OECD/FAO. 2017. *OECD-FAO Agricultural Outlook 2017–2026*. Paris: OECD Publishing.

Panikkar, K.M. 1943. *The Future of South-East Asia*. London: George Allen & Unwin Ltd.

Pollard, Vincent K. 1970. ASA and ASEAN, 1961–1967: Southeast Asian Regionalism. *Asian Survey* 10 (3, March): 244–255.

Pressello, Andrea. 2018. *Japan and the Shaping of Post-Vietnam War Southeast Asia Japanese Diplomacy and the Cambodian Conflict, 1978–1993*. Milton Park: Routledge.

PwC Growth Markets Centre. 2018. *The Future of ASEAN – Time to Act*. https://www.pwc.com/gx/en/growth-markets-centre/publications/assets/pwc-gmc-the-future-of-asean-time-to-act.pdf. Accessed September 19, 2018.

Selth, Andrew. 2018. All Going According to Plan?: The Armed Forces and Government in Myanmar. *Contemporary Southeast Asia: A Journal of International and Strategic Affairs* 40 (1): 1–26.

Shimada, Kazuhisa. 2010. *"Working Together" for Peace and Prosperity of Southeast Asia, 1945–1968: The Birth of the ASEAN Way*. Ph.D. Thesis, University of Adelaide. https://digital.library.adelaide.edu.au/dspace/bitstream/2440/63422/8/02whole.pdf Accessed September 19, 2018.

Tambiah, Stanley J. 1977. The Galactic Polity: The Structure of Traditional Kingdoms in Southeast Asia. *Annals of the New York Academy of Sciences* 293 (1): 69–97.

Tarling, Oleh Nicholas. 2006. *Regionalism in Southeast Asia: To Foster the Political Will*. Milton Park: Routledge.

Tarling, Nicholas. 2007. From SEAFET and ASA: Precursors of ASEAN. *IJAPS* 3 (1): 1–14.

Taylor, Keith Weller. 1983. *The Birth of Vietnam*. Berkeley: University of California Press.

Thavevong, Kittipong. 2017, May 24. With 20 Constitutions, Thailand Joins a Select League. *The Nation*. http://www.nationmultimedia.com/detail/big_read/30316132. Accessed September 19, 2018.

Wolters, O.W. 1982. *History, Culture, and Region in Southeast Asian Perspectives*. Institute of Southeast Asian Studies.

World Economic Forum. 2017. *The Global Human Capital Report 2017*.

———. 2018. *The Global Competitiveness Report 2017–2018*.

PART I

Six Large Economies

CHAPTER 2

The Philippines

George Manzano, Ma. Anne Teresa Rivera, and Bernardo Villegas

Introduction

Today, the Philippines is in the limelight as one of the economic bright spots in Southeast Asia. Turning around from stagnant economic growth from the 1980s to the early 2000s, the country has outperformed most of its regional neighbours in the last decade. Several factors have also inspired a renewed confidence for its future: its robust domestic demand, its demographic sweet spot, and the growing reform momentum seen to translate to further improvements in the country's competitiveness. In 2017, the Philippines was brought to the forefront of regional and global economic discussions, after taking helm of the Association of Southeast Asian Nations (ASEAN) Chairmanship and hosting the 50th anniversary of the ASEAN.

This chapter provides an overview of the Philippines. The first section briefly describes the country's unique features as shaped by its economic

G. Manzano (✉) • B. Villegas
University of Asia and the Pacific, Pasig, Philippines
e-mail: george.manzano@uap.asia; bernardo.villegas@uap.asia

M. A. T. Rivera
CEMEX, Madrid, Spain
e-mail: teresa.rivera@uap.asia

R. Macdonald (ed.), *Southeast Asia and the ASEAN Economic Community*, https://doi.org/10.1007/978-3-030-19722-3_2

and political history. The second section outlines the country's more recent economic performance, its growth drivers, as well as the challenges and opportunities that lie ahead. The third section discusses the Philippines' progress in terms of economic freedom to contextualize internal institutional dynamics in relation to the country's growth. The fourth section provides some background on the ASEAN Economic Community, its objectives, the Philippines' participation in the ASEAN framework's development, and the outlook for the Philippines in relation to its neighbours. The fifth section provides a summary of the growth prospects for the country and key areas for government investment. The chapter concludes with the challenges that must be addressed to supplement the Philippines' recent economic performance and how with all these, the Philippines fits into or stands out in the ASEAN Economic Community.

History in Brief

The Philippines underwent occupation by Spain, the United States, and Japan in the nineteenth and twentieth centuries and up to now, influences from these nations are evident in the local culture, languages, arts, government structure, and even education (Wa-Mbaleka et al. 2014). English is widely used. The Philippines' Constitution and form of government were also largely patterned from the United States.

The Philippines finally gained independence in 1946. To support nationalism and as part of efforts to minimize foreign participation in the economy, the succession of governments from the 1950s to the 1960s focused on import substitution that saw the rise of exclusivist economic nationalism (Sicat 2015). Under Ferdinand Marcos' leadership which started in 1965, the Philippines became a founding member of the Association of Southeast Asian Nations in 1967. After almost eight years of rule as president, Marcos declared martial law, leading to authoritarian rule for almost a decade. During this time, the country undertook massive foreign-currency loans from transnational banks (Hays 2015). Dissatisfaction with the government especially with the perceived widespread corruption, excessive government borrowing, a slowdown in economic growth, and perceived abuses led to Marcos' overthrow and the restoration of democracy in 1987. Under the leadership of President Corazon Aquino, the Philippines revised the Constitution in 1987 and restored political institutions to their pre-martial law framework (Sicat 2015). The succeeding governments contended with economic and political challenges rooted in the preceding three decades: among these were wide government and trade deficits, government debt amounting to more than 60% of the gross domestic product (GDP), cronyism, and massive income inequality. Adding to this was the six-year limit to the presidential term which made it politically difficult to implement long-term reforms.

In the mid-2000s, the Philippines started to show signs of strength, mainly due to robust domestic demand fuelled by the steady inflow of cash remittances and the growth of the Information Technology-Business Process Outsourcing (IT-BPO) sector. By the late 2000s, the Philippines was lauded as being among the most resilient economies in Asia, even growing positively during the 2008–2009 global financial crisis. In the early 2010s, the Philippines received its first-ever investment grade credit rating, pointing to a renewed optimism in the Philippines (Hays 2015). Up to this point, analysts have pointed out that while the Philippine economy expanded steadily, growth was not broad-based and thus did not substantially reduce income inequality. In this regard, the administration of President Rodrigo Duterte launched its socioeconomic agenda in 2016, focusing on sustaining the country's growth while aiming to redistribute wealth through an expansionary fiscal policy and massive human capital investments.[1]

National Characteristics

The Philippines is culturally similar to some Latin American countries such as Peru, Argentina, and Mexico due to shared colonial histories and the resulting Western influence and the assimilation of Western cultural traits and habits. For example, the Philippines is predominantly Catholic (about 80%), like most Latin American countries. It is in fact one of the only two predominantly Catholic countries in Asia, the other being East Timor. Catholic-inspired festivities are celebrated in the Philippines up to this day, and Hispanic influence is evident in Philippine cuisine. Many Filipino surnames also derive from Spanish surnames. The Philippines also became one of the few electoral democracies in Southeast Asia, influenced by liberal-humanistic thought from Europe and the American government.

The Philippines is an archipelago of more than 7100 islands. Its population of more than 100 million is spread across about 2000 inhabited islands. The islands are clustered into three major regions: Luzon (northern), Visayas (central), and Mindanao (southwestern). The clusters vary in terms of culture, language, and practices with religion being a main distinction. That is, the population in the northern and central islands is predominantly Christian, while those in the southwestern parts mostly identity as Muslim (Cultural Atlas n.d.). Owing to this archipelagic nature, the society is diverse and described by village and regional identities. Each region has its own subculture characterized by sets of cultural practices, beliefs, cuisines, and traditions. The various regional languages—with eight major languages and about 170 other spoken dialects—are a proof of the internal differentiation (Cultural Atlas n.d.).

From the "Sick Man of Asia" to Its "Rising Tiger"

After the Second World War, economic growth in the Philippines lagged behind that of its Asian neighbours, earning it such titles as "the Sick Man of Asia" and "the Latin American Asian." From the 1950s to the 1980s, economic performance in the Philippines was inhibited by lower foreign direct investment (FDI) inflows compared to its neighbours due to political constraints and perceptions of corruption, judicial inefficiency, difficulties in doing business, and political instability (Kind 2000). In addition, the county's trade policy, focused on import substitution, made the Philippines unattractive to investors looking to expand production in Asia (Kind 2000).

However, in the mid-2000s, positive developments in the Philippines marked an economic turnaround for the country. From an average GDP growth of 1.7% between 1980 and 1990 to 2.3% in 1990–1999, GDP growth doubled to about 4.2% between 2000 and 2009 (Coleman et al. 2014). Over the 2009–2013 period, the Philippines further accelerated with a GDP growth rate of 6.3%, higher than the 6.0% average for Southeast Asia. More notably, the Philippines' strength became evident as its growth coincided with the slowdown in its neighbours' pace of growth, including China, Indonesia, and Thailand. In fact, the Philippines was dubbed as Asia's "Next Tiger" owing to its strong economic performance characterized by a surge in its manufacturing and service sector output, rising domestic wages, and robust remittance flows driving domestic demand and government reforms leading to improvements in the business climate (Coleman et al. 2014). A description of the Philippines' more recent economic performance is provided in the next section.

Overview: The Philippine Economy

The Philippines is now touted as one of the most dynamic economies in Southeast Asia. In 2016, it registered the highest gross domestic product (GDP) growth in the region at 6.9%. In the following year, Philippines grew by 6.7%, which was the second highest in the region. Moreover, the

Philippines grew by an average of 6.6% from 2013 to 2017, surpassing the growth rates of Malaysia (5.2%) and Indonesia (5.1%), the perennial pace-setters among the bigger ASEAN members (see Fig. 2.1).

During the same period, inflation in the Philippines remained stable, averaging 2.7%, proximate to the regional average of 2.8%. This indicates that the relatively rapid growth was not accompanied by the spectre of inflation, implying that there is further scope for continued growth in the years ahead (see Fig. 2.2).

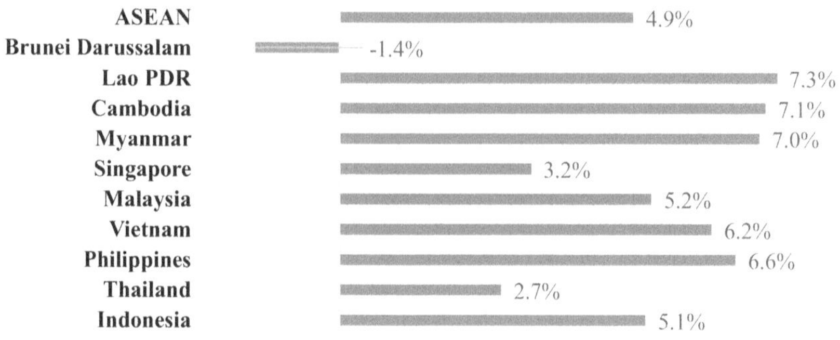

Fig. 2.1 ASEAN average GDP growth (2013–2017). Data source: World Bank Data Bank. Accessed on 5 June 2018, from http://databank.worldbank.org/data/source/world-development-indicators

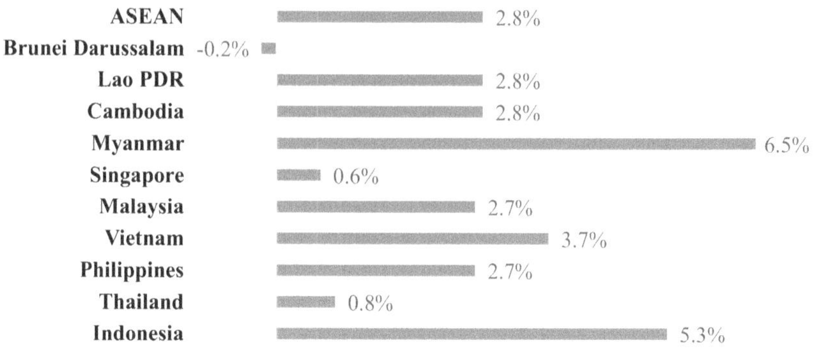

Fig. 2.2 ASEAN average inflation (2013–2017). Data source: World Bank Data Bank. Accessed on 5 June 2018, from http://databank.worldbank.org/data/source/world-development-indicators

Sectoral Development

As of 2017, the country's service sector comprised 57% of the total domestic output and industry 34%, while agriculture accounted for the remaining 9%. From 2013 to 2017, agriculture registered a compounded average growth of 0.9%, clearly outpaced by the industry sector which grew by 5.8% and services which expanded by 5.4% in the same period. However, in terms of labour, as of 2017, agriculture accounted for 25% of total employment and industry represented 18%, while services registered 57%. This clearly shows the underperformance of the agricultural sector compared to the rest of the economy. In fact, the latest available indicators in Table 2.1 show that, unsurprisingly, the farmers and fishermen have remained the poorest in the country. Two of five rural persons (small farmers, subsistence fisherfolk, and landless farm workers) live in poverty compared to one out of eight urban persons.

In fact, the Philippines lags way behind some of its ASEAN neighbours in agricultural productivity and exports. One possible explanation for this lack of performance of the Philippines in agricultural exports is that previous governments have tended to focus on trying to achieve rice self-sufficiency, thus leaving fewer resources for product diversification (Villegas 2016b). Improving the productivity of the agricultural sector is undoubtedly one of the ways of achieving inclusive growth. Among the country's poorest are agricultural workers and the causes of rural poverty are well known: low investment leading to low productivity, lack of non-farm or off-farm jobs, inadequate physical and knowledge infrastructure, and poor governance.

Table 2.1 Poverty incidence for basic sectors, 2006–2015

	2006	*2009*	*2012*	*2015*
Philippines	26.6	26.3	25.2	21.6
Farmers	38.5	38.0	38.3	34.3
Fishermen	41.2	41.3	39.2	34.0
Children	35.2	35.3	35.2	31.4
Self-employed and unpaid family workers	30.6	29.9	29.0	25.0
Women	25.9	25.7	25.6	22.5
Youth	21.1	21.6	22.3	19.4
Migrant and formal sector workers	16.0	16.8	16.6	13.4
Senior citizens	16.9	16.1	16.2	13.2
Individuals in urban areas	12.6	12.6	13.0	11.5

Data source: Philippine Statistics Authority. Accessed on 5 June 2018, from http://psa.gov.ph/poverty-press-releases/data

Drivers of Growth

As previously stated, the Philippine economy is considered one of the most dynamic in the region. In 2017, Philippines grew by 6.7%, marking the country's sixth consecutive year of above 6.0% growth (see Fig. 2.3).

The robust economic expansion in recent years has been fuelled mainly by domestic demand factors such as consumption. Such spending, in turn, is fuelled by steady income from foreign sources such as remittances by overseas Filipino workers (OFWs) and the Information Technology-Business Process Outsourcing (IT-BPO) sector (Fig. 2.4), considered the major contributors to employment generation and income rise in the past decade.

Today, about 10 million Filipinos are working abroad, while about 1.3 million are employed in the BPO sector. In 2017, overseas cash remittances hit a record high in 2017 at US$28.1 billion (~10% of GDP) while IT-BPO receipts were estimated to have reached ~US$25 billion (~9% of GDP).

In addition, there has been an uptick in the construction and real estate sectors as the Philippines entered a construction boom, driven by private investments, outpacing other sectors of the economy (see Fig. 2.5).

Adding to these developments is an improvement in the country's labour outcome. Table 2.2 shows that unemployment rate stood at 5.7% as of 2017, much lower than the average of 6.7% in the preceding six years. Underemployment also showed an improvement from 18.8% in 2010 to 16.1% in 2017, indicating an improvement in the quality of jobs. The labour participation rate declined in 2017 compared to the previous

Fig. 2.3 Philippine annual GDP growth. Data source: World Bank Data Bank. Accessed on 5 June 2018, from http://databank.worldbank.org/data/source/world-development-indicators

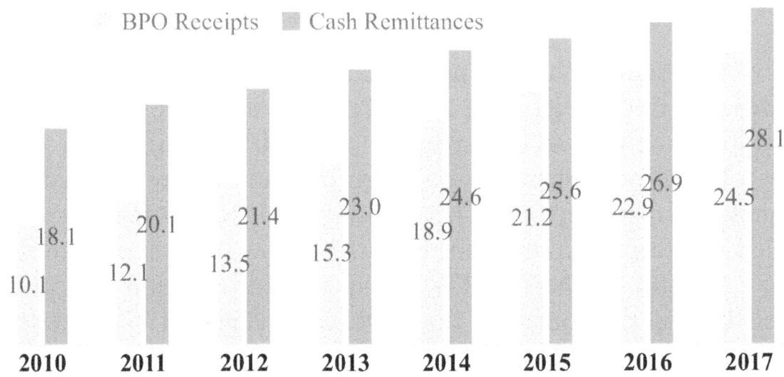

Fig. 2.4 Information Technology-Business Process Outsourcing (IT-BPO) revenues and cash remittances from overseas (2010–2017, US$ billion). Data source: Central Bank of the Philippines. Accessed on 5 June 2018, from http://www.bsp.gov.ph/statistics/statpage01.asp. Note: 2015–2017 IT-BPO revenues estimated by author, no official data available

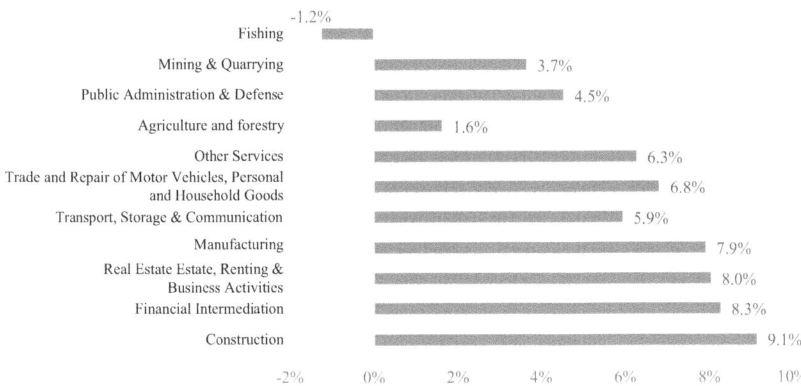

Fig. 2.5 Five-year compounded annual growth of gross value added by economic subsector (2013–2017). Data source: Philippine Statistics Authority. Accessed on 5 June 2018, from https://psa.gov.ph/nap-press-release/data-series

years but this is mainly attributed to the change in the basic educational system.

In 2016, the Philippine government implemented the Kinder-to-Grade 12 (K12) education policy in the country. This scheme mandated kindergarten and increased the duration of basic education from 10 years to

Table 2.2 Philippine labour statistics

	2010	*2011*	*2012*	*2013*	*2014*	*2015*	*2016*	*2017*
Labour force (million persons)	38.6	39.9	40.5	41.2	42.5	43.0	43.8	44.6
Labour participation rate	61.4%	62.2%	61.7%	61.4%	62.2%	63.7%	61.5%	61.2%
Unemployment rate	7.4%	7.0%	7.0%	7.1%	6.6%	6.3%	5.5%	5.7%
Underemployment	18.8%	19.3%	20.0%	19.3%	18.4%	18.5%	18.3%	16.1%

Data source: Philippine Statistics Authority. Accessed on 5 June 2018, from http://psa.gov.ph/statistics/survey/labor-and-employment/labor-force-survey

12 years by adding 2 more years of schooling at the high school level. The shift was done to be at par with its ASEAN counterparts and to meet global standards in basic education. The government also overhauled the curriculum to incorporate more technical-vocational subjects designed to provide graduates practical skills by the time they graduate from high school, allowing them the option of working instead of seeking tertiary education. This was envisioned to tackle unemployment among the youth.

Investments as part of the GDP have likewise blossomed in the recent past. From an average of 20.0% of GDP for the period 2010 to 2015, gross capital formation rose to the range of 24.3–25.0% of GDP in 2016 and 2017 (see Fig. 2.6).

This trend was mirrored by bank credit growth which posted a compounded average growth rate of 10.5% from 2010 to 2015 and posted an annual growth of 15.9% and 17.2% in 2016 and 2017, respectively.[2] As of end-2017, the sectors that secured the most loans from the banking system were real estate activities (18.2%), wholesale and retail trade (13.0%), manufacturing (11.5%), and utilities (10.0%). Because investment spending has a long-term nature, the investment performance over the recent past indicates that investors have a bullish outlook on the Philippine economy.

This conjecture is supported by a clear improvement in consumer and in domestic and foreign investor sentiment. Business confidence has remained broadly steady in the last seven years, with the Business Confidence Index (BCI) averaging 44%, indicating the net amount of surveyed firms which are optimistic about the Philippine economy, as shown

Fig. 2.6 Investment, % of GDP. Data source: World Bank Data Bank. Accessed on 5 June 2018 from http://databank.worldbank.org/data/source/world-development-indicators

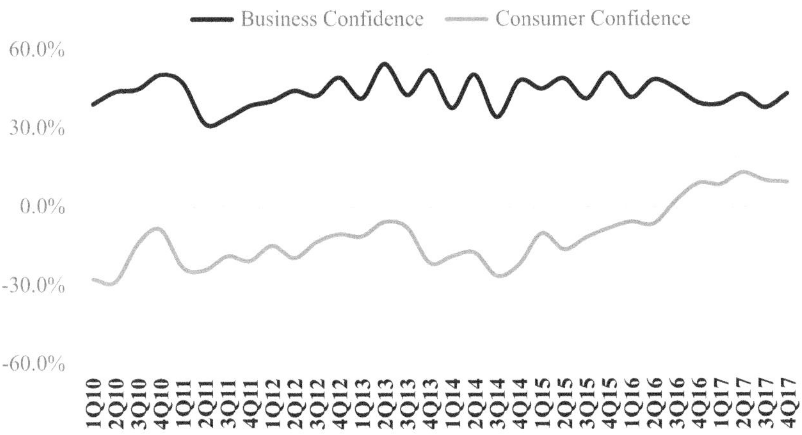

Fig. 2.7 Business and consumer confidence indices, % (2010–2017). Data source: Central Bank of the Philippines. Accessed on 5 June 2018 from http://www.bsp.gov.ph/statistics/surveys.asp

in Fig. 2.7.[3] At the same time, consumer confidence posted a continuous improvement in the last five years and finally reached positive territory in the third quarter of 2017 (also see Fig. 2.7).[4] This indicates that Filipino consumers have generally become more bullish about their spending, employment, and wage outlook.

Fig. 2.8 Foreign direct investments, US$ billion. Data source: Central Bank of the Philippines. Accessed on 5 June 2018 from http://www.bsp.gov.ph/statistics/efs_ext2.asp#FCDU

In parallel, foreign investors' interest in the Philippines showed an improvement in recent years. Foreign direct investments (FDIs) in the country posted a compounded annual growth rate of 37.7% from 2010 to 2017, although coming from a very low base. In 2017, FDI reached a record high of US$10.4 billion, 21.4% higher than the previous year (see Fig. 2.8). This represented about 3.7% of the country's GDP. Most of the investments were placed in the manufacturing sector, construction, and real estate.

Despite this, the Philippines has a long way to catch up with some of its regional neighbours in terms of attracting FDI. As shown in Table 2.3, there has only been a marginal increase in the share of FDI as a share of GDP from 2010 to 2016, and the Philippines continues to lag behind neighbours such as Singapore, Vietnam, and Malaysia.

The historically low FDI into the Philippines has been attributed to the Constitutional restrictions against foreign investments which have persisted in the last three decades. Currently, total foreign ownership is disallowed for such industries as mass media, public utilities, construction, mining, educational institutions, as well as in land ownership. Economists have argued that these provisions are restrictive, protectionist, and anti-competitive and have thus hampered inclusive growth and economic development.

Fiscal policy has largely been expansionary. National government spending grew by 12.9% in 2016 (an election year) and the streak was sustained in 2017 when it grew by 11.4% (see Table 2.4).

Table 2.3 FDI as % of GDP

	2010	*2011*	*2012*	*2013*	*2014*	*2015*	*2016*
Indonesia	2%	2%	2%	3%	3%	2%	0%
Thailand	4%	1%	3%	4%	1%	2%	1%
Philippines	1%	1%	1%	1%	2%	2%	3%
Vietnam	7%	5%	5%	5%	5%	6%	6%
Malaysia	4%	5%	3%	3%	3%	3%	5%
Singapore	23%	18%	19%	21%	23%	24%	25%
Myanmar	2%	4%	2%	4%	3%	7%	5%
Cambodia	12%	11%	13%	12%	10%	9%	11%
Lao PDR	4%	3%	3%	4%	7%	10%	6%
Brunei Darussalam	4%	4%	5%	4%	3%	1%	-1%

Source: World Bank Data Bank. Accessed on 5 June 2018 from http://databank.worldbank.org/data/source/world-development-indicators

Table 2.4 National government spending (Trillion PHP)

	2010	*2011*	*2012*	*2013*	*2014*	*2015*	*2016*	*2017*
National government spending	1.7	1.7	2	2.2	2.3	2.5	2.8	3.1
Year-on-year growth	7.1%	0.9%	14.8%	7.8%	6.2%	9.4%	12.9%	11.4%
% of GDP	19.6%	17.9%	18.9%	18.7%	18.1%	18.8%	19.5%	20.2%

Source: World Bank Data Bank. Accessed on 5 June 2018 from http://databank.worldbank.org/data/source/world-development-indicators

In particular, the current administration has given special attention to increase infrastructure spending, as part of an overall economic agenda to create jobs, raise the country's investment status, and improve competitiveness. After years of underspending, in 2016 and 2017, the government posted significant improvement in its disbursement achievement rate as clearly seen in Fig. 2.9.

Despite the accommodating fiscal policy employed, the fiscal balances remain manageable. Government net debt has actually decreased from 68% of GDP in 2003 to 49.7% in 2010 and finally only 37.8% in 2017 (see Table 2.5). Public deficit settled at 2.4% and 2.2% of GDP in 2016 and 2017, respectively, which are broadly in line with the target band of about 3.0% (also in Table 2.5).

On the external front, the Philippines has experienced a current account deficit of less than 1% of GDP in 2016 and 2017. Trade balance of goods

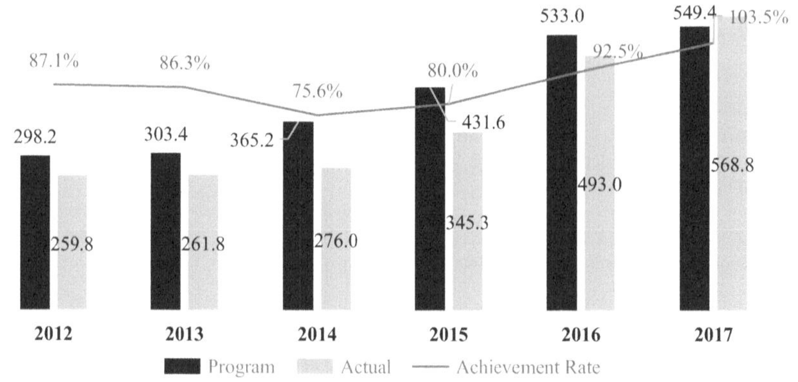

Fig. 2.9 Infrastructure and capital outlay disbursement (billion PHP). Data source: Department of Budget and Management—Philippines. Accessed on 5 June 2018 from https://dbm.gov.ph/index.php/dbcc-matters/reports/ng-disbursement-performance. Note: Historical achievement rates are author's calculations

Table 2.5 Fiscal position, 2010–2017

	2010	*2011*	*2012*	*2013*	*2014*	*2015*	*2016*	*2017*
Government debt (% of GDP)	49.7	47.5	47.9	45.7	42.1	41.5	39.0	38.9
Public deficit (% of GDP)	3.5%	2.0%	2.3%	1.4%	0.6%	0.9%	2.4%	2.2%

Data source: World Bank Data Bank. Accessed on 5 June 2018 from http://databank.worldbank.org/data/source/world-development-indicators

and services has been negative over several years. Imports continued to outstrip exports in 2017, reaching US$92.7 billion (up by 10.2% year on year) versus the total exports of US$62.9 (up by 9.5% year on year) as shown in Table 2.6. However, it must be noted that capital goods accounted for much of the imports in the last two years, indicating growing investments in fixed assets which are likely to increase productive capacity and support economic growth in the coming years. In addition, the government's infrastructure plan up to 2022 will imply stronger import demand, thereby potentially causing the current account deficit to widen and the peso to weaken further.

As discussed earlier, the Philippines has a trade deficit in merchandise goods trade, although it enjoys a surplus in services trade. The Philippines,

Table 2.6 International trade position, 2010–2017

	2010	*2011*	*2012*	*2013*	*2014*	*2015*	*2016*	*2017*
Exports (% of GDP)	35%	32%	31%	28%	29%	28%	28.0%	0.3
Imports (% of GDP)	37%	36%	34%	32%	33%	34%	37%	40.5%
Current account deficit (% of GDP)	3.6%	2.5%	2.8%	4.2%	3.8%	2.5%	−0.4%	−0.8%

Data source: World Bank Data Bank. Accessed on 5 June 2018 from http://databank.worldbank.org/data/source/world-development-indicators

an active member of the World Trade Organization (WTO), has just completed its Trade Policy Review in March 2018. It is a founding member of the Asia Pacific Economic Cooperation (APEC) and hosted the APEC summits in 1997 and 2015. Engaging in free trade agreements (FTAs) is an integral component of Philippine trade policy. To date, the Philippines has signed eight FTAs, mostly ones which involve ASEAN and its dialogue partners. Japan is the only partner for which the Philippines has a bilateral FTA, although there is a lot of interest in pursuing FTAs with the European Union and the United States. The latest FTA that has been successfully negotiated by the Philippines is with the European Free Trade Association (EFTA) comprising Norway, Switzerland, Iceland, and Liechtenstein.

On monetary policy, the Philippine Central Bank has mainly managed to keep the inflation rate at bay—its primary mandate—in the past decade. This is remarkable given the course of fast growth since 2010. The inflation rate settled at 1.8% in 2016 and 3.2% in 2017, well within the government's 2.0–4.0% comfort range. The increase in public spending as well as the expansion of investments such as construction did not stoke price spirals. In addition, subdued global oil prices and timely imports of rice kept food prices in check. The IMF attributes the low inflation to stable commodity prices and well-anchored inflation expectations.[5] The manageable inflation expectations, in turn, can be attributed to a rather strong monetary position.

However, in 2018, the first tranche of the government's tax reform package was implemented. It involved raising levies on fuel, coal, sugared drinks, and cigarettes. Rising global commodity prices also added to price pressures and ushered in a continued acceleration in inflation, which posted several three-year and five-year highs in the first four months. The uptick in inflation prompted the Central Bank to raise its policy interest rates for the first time in nearly four years in May 2018. Still, the Central Bank maintained that while inflation may breach the government's 2.0–4.0% target range in

2018 and 2019, the uptrend is expected to be temporary and caused by supply-side factors. The Central Bank asserted that inflation was not caused by demand pull, which would have been symptomatic of overheating.[6]

Economic Freedom

The Index of Economic Freedom is an indicator of the degree to which a country's policies and institutions support economic freedom, that is, the ability of members of a society to direct their own labour and property—to work, produce, consume, and invest, in the way they please.[7] Launched in 1995 by the Heritage Foundation and the Wall Street Journal, the Index was designed to provide an objective measure for countries' political and institutional set-up in relation to economic growth. It is widely believed that these non-economic factors influence how efficiently the factors of production are utilized and therefore have a profound effect on economic growth and development (Hussain and Haque 2016, p. 2).

Economic freedom is distinct from political freedom or the capacity to participate in the political process on equal conditions and from civil freedom which is characterized by protection of personal rights such as access to fair trials, freedom of assembly, freedom of religion, and free of speech (Berggren 2003, p. 194).

The Index is based on four broad categories or "pillars" of economic freedom. These are four key aspects in the economic environment over which a government exercises considerable influence. The pillars are further broken down to 12 quantitative and qualitative factors. The first is "Rule of Law," which measures the extent to which a country's legal environment and institutions facilitate economic activity. "Rule of Law" is meted by the existence and protection of property rights, intellectual property rights, and judicial effectiveness. The second is "government size" which is assessed through the levels of government integrity, tax burden, government spending, and fiscal health. The third pillar is "regulatory efficiency" which reflects the regulatory processes that influence market activity. Factors considered under this pillar are those that indicate levels of business freedom, labour freedom, and monetary freedom such as ease of doing business, minimum wages, labour laws, price controls, and inflation. Finally, the last pillar is "open markets" which is assessed through the absence of constraints to trade, investment capital flow, and the efficiency and independence of financial institutions.[8]

Table 2.7 Index of Economic Freedom: Philippines, Asia Pacific Average, and Global Average (2014–2018)

	2014	*2015*	*2016*	*2017*	*2018*
Economic freedom index—Philippines	60.1	62.2	63.1	65.5	65
Category	Moderately Free	Moderately Free	Moderately Free	Moderately Free	Moderately Free
Regional (Asia Pacific) average	58.5	58.8	59	60.4	61.0
Regional ranking (out of 43)	16	13	14	14	13.0
Global average	60.3	60.4	60.7	60.9	61.1
Global ranking (out of 186)	89	76	70	58	61.0

Data source: Heritage Foundation. Index of Economic Freedom. Accessed on 10 June 2018 from https://www.heritage.org/index

A positive association between economic growth and regulatory and institutional factors as measured by the Index of Economic Freedom has previously been established, lending credence to the importance of this measure in the study of a country's development (Hussain and Haque 2016, p. 10).

Based on the Heritage Foundation's annual reports on the Global Index of Economic Freedom (where a score of 0 signifies "no economic freedom" and 100 indicates "total economic freedom"), the Philippines has improved substantially in the last five years, from a score of 60.1 in 2014 to 65.0 in 2018. Table 2.7 shows that Philippines has consistently outperformed the average for the Asia Pacific region and, since 2015, has also fared better than the global average. Consequently, the Philippines improved its regional ranking from the 16th to the 13th for the period and more notably climbed up the global ranking from 89th in 2014 to 61st in 2018.

The improvement for the period 2014–2016 was largely attributed to institutional and legislative reforms implemented by the administration of President Benigno Aquino Jr (2010–2016) to combat corruption, raise regulatory efficiency, improve fiscal management, enhance regional competitiveness, and liberalize the banking sector (Kim and Singham 2016, p. 351).

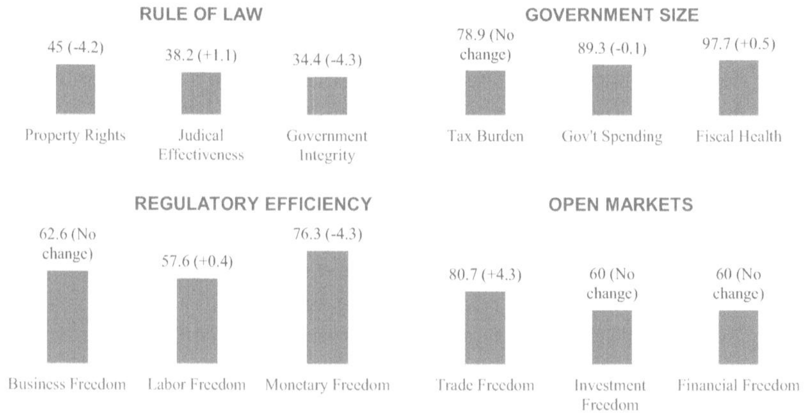

Fig. 2.10 2018 Index of Economic Freedom: Philippines. Data source: Heritage Foundation. 2018 Index of Economic Freedom. Accessed on 10 June 2018 from https://www.heritage.org/international-economies/commentary/2018-index-economic-freedom

In 2017, the Philippines jumped 12 spots higher in the global ranking, with its Index improving from 63.1 to 65.5 on the back of solid economic growth and improvements in fiscal policy, government spending, and monetary stability (Miller and Kim 2017, *Index of Economic Freedom 2017*, p. 168).

However, in 2018, the country's economic freedom score declined by 0.5 and consequently lowered its rank from the 58th to the 61st freest economy in the world (Miller et al. 2018, p. 336). Figure 2.10 describes the year-on-year change in the Philippines' score on the four pillars of economic freedom.

The 2018 Index of Economic Freedom reports that the decline in the Philippines' score is based on the following changes in the different pillars of economic freedom:

- Rule of Law *declined* due to lower scores for property rights and government integrity. While property rights are protected by law, enforcement remained weak. Judicial effectiveness was perceived as low because of inefficiency, delays, and vulnerability to political influence. On one hand, President Rodrigo Duterte consolidated power by marginalizing his opponents and received massive criticism for his brutal crackdown on illegal drugs which also reflected his authoritarian tendencies. On the other hand, the "war on illegal drugs" has been a cornerstone of the Duterte administration's agenda on peace and order. President Duterte, in the aftermath of his election victory, cited that the illegal drug trade has become pandemic. However, there is mixed reception on how the means carried out to address the drug issue.

- Government size *improved* marginally due to the perceived improvement in fiscal health. This is as public debt, budget surpluses, and government spending remained at healthy levels.
- Regulatory efficiency *declined* due to the drop in monetary freedom as the government maintained some price controls on pharmaceuticals, food, and household fuel items while labour and business regulatory conditions remained unchanged.
- Open markets *improved* as the average applied tariff rate dropped to 2.1% from 4.3% in 2017. Meanwhile, policies affecting investment freedom and financial freedom remained stable.

Admittedly, as shown in Table 2.8, the Philippines has to catch up with some of its ASEAN neighbours.

In any case, the Philippines' robust growth has been matched by consistent improvement in the level of its economic freedom over recent years. This bodes well for a broader-based development.

Table 2.8 2018 Index of Economic Freedom—ASEAN

	Index	*ASEAN ranking*	*Global ranking*
Singapore	88.8	1	2
Malaysia	74.5	2	22
Thailand	67.1	3	53
Philippines	65.0	4	61
Indonesia	64.2	5	69
Brunei	64.2	6	70
Cambodia	58.7	7	101
Laos	53.6	8	138
Vietnam	53.1	9	141

Data source: Heritage Foundation. 2018 Index of Economic Freedom. Accessed on 10 June 2018 from https://www.heritage.org/international-economies/commentary/2018-index-economic-freedom

The Philippines in the AEC

Origins of ASEAN

The Association for South East Asian Nations (ASEAN) marked its 50th anniversary in 2017. Founded in 1967 by the governments of Indonesia, Malaysia, Singapore, Thailand, and the Philippines, the ASEAN was formed to address emerging political and security problems in the region. While these five founding countries were quite politically and economically diverse, they had a common interest in crafting a defined security arrangement to counteract the rise of communist insurgency in the region (Drysdale 2017). Thus, economic considerations were not in the forefront during the institution of the ASEAN. As the political tensions subsided, the ASEAN shifted attention to address economic issues. The leaders realized that integrating the economies in the region more deeply would be a good strategy to position the region in the light of the growth in world trade. Hence, the ASEAN Free Trade Agreement (AFTA) was crafted in 1993. Broadly, the AFTA was designed to encourage regional trade by elimination of tariffs and non-tariff barriers and to attract more foreign investments into the region.

Thus, the AFTA has guided the regional cooperation efforts of ASEAN which are geared to increase the region's competitive advantage as a production base, promoting regional integration while remaining open to the world markets. Over time, membership grew to a total of ten members, with the latest accession of Cambodia in 1999.

The ASEAN later fortified its economic agenda by establishing the ASEAN Economic Community (AEC) which serves as a blueprint for a deeper form of economic integration that addresses not only trade liberalization but also development issues. The AEC was deliberately more comprehensive than the earlier attempts towards integration, such as the AFTA, in that it includes services, investments, trade facilitation, and trading arrangements with major economic blocks among others. Furthermore, the institutional architecture of the AEC is more formal than the earlier ASEAN set-up.

The great interest in the AEC is underpinned by the notion of ASEAN's "coming of age," as an increasingly important institution, not only in Asia, but on the global stage. There are good reasons for this optimism and these have to do with the extent of the market that ASEAN offers as well as the advantages of ASEAN as a production hub.

Extent of the Market

Over the recent past, economic growth in the ASEAN has been faster than other emerging regions. Improving competitiveness in trade, increasingly affluent domestic markets, and good economic management buoyed this spectacular performance. The ASEAN has also demonstrated resilience to global crises, as it learnt its lesson from the ASEAN financial crisis of 1997.

The ASEAN leaders have long recognized that much can be gained from integrating the ten individual markets into one big ASEAN market. First, a huge market will allow producers to raise their production capacities and take advantage of scale economies. A large market can also accommodate more firms, thus facilitating start-ups, which eventually leads to greater product diversification. Second, the process of integrating markets entails trade liberalization, allowing international trade to flourish and in turn enhance competition on the ground. Either way, the ASEAN consumer welfare is better served. Third, a large market is more attractive to foreign direct investments (FDIs) than smaller ones. Taken as a whole, an integrated ASEAN market is well positioned to compete against established destinations such as China and India for much-needed FDI infusion.

Indeed, growth projections for the ASEAN region have been quite optimistic (see Table 2.9). For example, the forecast average economic growth rate of 5.3% for the ASEAN-5[9] over the period 2018–2020 is higher than the corresponding forecasts for the world economy and the broad group of emerging markets and developing economies (International Monetary Fund 2018). However, China and India are expected to grow even faster over the same period. The robust projections for the medium-term growth prospects of the ASEAN region bode well for the region's attractiveness in attracting FDI.

Within the ASEAN, the overall performance of the Philippine economy has been commendable. IMF forecasts place the Philippines and Indonesia among the fastest-growing economies in the region, among the more established ASEAN-5 members (see Table 2.10). Of course, owing to their low bases, Myanmar, Lao PDR and Vietnam are projected to grow even faster than the ASEAN-5 subgrouping. Vietnam particularly has shown growth at a rapid clip, fuelled by foreign investments. It is interesting to note that the perennial growth leaders of the ASEAN—Singapore, Malaysia, and Thailand—are not expected to grow as fast as their historical records attest. Some observers conjecture that the forces of low population growth rates and ageing may have hampered the long-run economic growth potentials of these countries (Bonoan and Martin 2016, pp. 11–16).

Table 2.9 Gross domestic product projections in constant prices (percent change)

	Projections							
	2015	*2016*	*2017*	*2018*	*2019*	*2020*	*2021*	*2022*
World	3.4	3.2	3.6	3.7	3.7	3.7	3.8	3.8
Advanced economies	2.2	1.7	2.2	2.0	1.8	1.7	1.7	1.7
Euro area	2.0	1.8	2.1	1.9	1.7	1.6	1.5	1.5
Major advanced economies (G7)	2.0	1.8	2.1	1.9	1.7	1.6	1.5	1.5
Other advanced economies (excludes the United States, Euro area countries, and Japan)	2.0	2.3	2.7	2.6	2.6	2.5	2.5	2.2
European Union	2.3	2.0	2.3	2.1	1.8	1.8	1.7	1.7
Emerging market and developing economies	4.3	4.4	4.7	4.9	5.0	5.0	5.1	5.0
Emerging and developing Asia	6.8	6.4	6.5	6.5	6.6	6.5	6.4	6.3
Emerging and developing Europe	4.7	3.2	5.2	4	3.8	3.2	3.2	3.2
China	6.9	6.7	6.8	6.6	6.4	6.2	6.0	5.8
India	8.0	7.1	6.7	7.4	7.8	7.9	8.1	8.2
Japan	1.1	0.9	1.8	1.2	0.9	0.2	0.7	0.6
ASEAN-5	4.9	4.9	5.3	5.3	5.3	5.3	5.3	5.3
Latin America and the Caribbean	0.1	-0.7	1.3	1.9	2.6	2.6	2.7	2.7

Data source: IMF World Economic Outlook, October 2017, WEO Update, January 2018 and WEO database. Accessed on 24 March 2018 from https://www.imf.org/external/pubs/ft/weo/2018/01/weodata/index.aspx

Table 2.10 ASEAN GDP projections in constant prices (percent change)

ASEAN	*Projections*							
	2015	*2016*	*2017*	*2018*	*2019*	*2020*	*2021*	*2022*
Brunei Darussalam	−0.4	−2.5	−1.3	0.6	8.7	8.9	11.2	5.3
Cambodia	7.2	7.0	6.9	6.8	6.8	6.5	6.3	6.0
Indonesia	4.9	5.0	5.2	5.3	5.5	5.5	5.5	5.5
Lao PDR	7.3	7.0	6.9	6.9	7.1	7.1	7.0	7.0
Malaysia	5.0	4.2	5.4	4.8	4.8	4.9	4.9	4.9
Myanmar	7.0	6.1	7.2	7.6	7.5	7.5	7.5	7.5
Philippines	6.1	6.9	6.6	6.7	6.8	6.8	6.8	6.8
Singapore	1.9	2.0	2.5	2.6	2.6	2.6	2.6	2.6
Thailand	2.9	3.2	3.7	3.5	3.4	3.1	3.0	3.0
Vietnam	6.7	6.2	6.3	6.3	6.2	6.2	6.2	6.2

Data source: IMF World Economic Outlook, October 2017, WEO Update, January 2018 and WEO database. Accessed on 24 March 2018 from https://www.imf.org/external/pubs/ft/weo/2018/01/weodata/index.aspx

The ASEAN, with more than 600 million people, offers a robust consumer market. Indonesia boasts the largest domestic market which amounts to about 261 million. The Philippines comes second with more than 100 million, followed by Vietnam and Myanmar with close to 90 and 51 million, respectively. Meanwhile Singapore and Brunei are among the members with the smallest population bases but with the highest per capita incomes.

Actually, one of the anchors of the attractiveness of the Philippines to foreign investments is the size of its labour force. A Hong Kong Shanghai Banking Corporation (HSBC) study on the future biggest economies in Asia states that the Philippines has one of the most promising prospects in Asia as it sets itself to be the world's sixteenth largest economy in 2050 (Ward 2012). The Philippines is currently enjoying the demographic dividend, a considerable advantage over some ASEAN members which are facing the dim prospects of a greying population (Guarin and Martin 2016). Table 2.11 shows ASEAN members' projected populations and the corresponding GDP growth rate predicted until 2050.

Coming from different economic backgrounds and stages of growth, there is understandably great disparity in incomes in the region. That the average Singaporean is more than forty times richer than the average Myanmar citizen is something that has to be addressed by ASEAN. Yet it must be noted that the region is seeing the per capita income of its members

Table 2.11 Population projections, 2050

ASEAN	*Population in 2050*	*2015[a]–2050 average growth rate*
Brunei	0.5 million	0.7%
Cambodia	23 million	1.1%
Indonesia	321 million	0.7%
Lao PDR	11 million	1.2%
Malaysia	42 million	0.9%
Myanmar	59 million	0.2%
Philippines	157 million	1.3%
Singapore	7 million	0.5%
Thailand	62 million	−0.3%
Vietnam	100 million	0.3%

Data source: The World Bank. 2015. Health Nutrition and Population Statistics: Population estimates and projections. Last updated: 1 July 2015

[a]2015 population is a forecasted figure, not actual. Taken from Emmanuel P. Bonoan and Kristine Joy Martin, 2016. Transforming into one ASEAN Market. In Moving Across Borders: The Philippines and the ASEAN Economic Community: 2016 Investment Guide by KPMG in the Philippines. KPMG and University of Asia and the Pacific, Manila, Table 4, p. 13

Table 2.12 Projection of ASEAN GDP per capita in current US$, 2015–2020

ASEAN	*2015*	*2016*	*2017*	*2018*	*2019*	*2020*
Brunei Darussalam	31,047.07	26,935.12	29,711.86	33,233.46	33,623	34,281.84
Cambodia	1167.72	1277.70	1389.63	1498.82	1614.14	1732.72
Indonesia	3369.36	3604.28	3875.77	4051.65	4290.87	4585.36
Lao P.D.R.	2212.40	2416.86	2542.45	2705.90	2918.09	3146.04
Malaysia	9505.32	9374.12	9812.80	11,237.42	12,240.57	13,180.30
Myanmar	1147.34	1210.46	1263.89	1338.49	1414.09	1555.29
Philippines	2882.77	2953.367	2976.31	3095.12	3247.06	3509.74
Singapore	54,939.86	55,241.28	57,713.34	61,766.82	64,413.39	66,893.16
Thailand	5830.84	5970.43	6590.64	6992.23	7510.00	7940.75
Vietnam	2087.53	2171.83	2353.69	2545.91	2774.40	3014.53

Data source: IMF World Economic Outlook Database (April 2018). Accessed on 2 May 2018 from http://www.imf.org/external/datamapper/NGDPDPC@WEO/WEOWORLD/APQ/KHM/IDN/LAO/MYS/MMR/PHL/SGP/THA/VNM

increase at a positive clip as can be gleaned from the per capita income projection in Table 2.12. The improvements in the purchasing power of the consumers in the region make the area not only a growing consumer market but a dynamic one at that. The expanding proportion of the middle class among the households is expected to usher in changes in spending patterns. Studies show that the spending on durable goods such as cars and furniture increases rapidly as incomes rise, indicating very elastic demand (Meyer 2013).

ASEAN as a Competitive Production Hub

The ASEAN Economic Community (AEC) is the master plan designed to propel the region both as a lucrative marketplace to sell products and services and as a competitive production hub for local and international investors.

Crucial to developing the AEC is to attract a flow of foreign direct investments to increase productive capacity and employment, facilitate technology transfer, and augment sources of foreign exchange.

To this end, the ASEAN has initiated projects such as the ASEAN Comprehensive Investment Agreement (ACIA) to attract foreign capital through greater investment liberalization, investment protection, promotion, and facilitation.

To enhance the attractiveness of the AEC to inward FDI, particularly among firms engaged in global production chains, the AEC called for

Table 2.13 Foreign direct investments inward flows in ASEAN (in US$ billion)

	2007	*2009*	*2012*	*2013*	*2014*	*2015*	***2016** (preliminary)*
ASEAN	8.4	8.8	25.5	18.2	21.6	21.6	24.7
Rest of the world	70.5	34.6	94.0	101.8	111.5	99.0	73.4
Total	78.9	43.4	117.5	120.1	133.1	120.5	98.0

Data source: ASEAN Statistical Yearbook 2016/17. ASEAN Secretariat. Accessed on 6 June 2018 from http://passthrough.fw-notify.net/download/145091/http://www.aseanstats.org/wp-content/uploads/2018/01/ASYB_2017-rev.pdf

initiatives to create a more competitive environment in the region. Apart from trade liberalization programmes such as elimination of tariffs, policymakers engaged in cooperative efforts to improve connectivity and facilitation. In addition, mutual recognition agreements (MRAs) for mobility of professionals are pursued to promote greater trade in services in the region. As flows of factor inputs increase, a more competitive environment for production is fostered.

For the past few years, foreign direct investments into the ASEAN have considerably risen, indicating the relative success of policy efforts to enhance the ASEAN as a production platform.

Table 2.13 reports the flows of inward FDI to the ASEAN from 2007 to 2016. The flow of FDI to the ASEAN grew alongside the state of world economy. To illustrate, FDI weakened during the global financial crisis of 2007–2009. However, strong domestic markets, favourable production conditions in the ASEAN, and active investor promotion helped to continue attracting FDIs into the region.

Among individual countries, the United States and Japan are the biggest investors in the ASEAN, both accounting for ~12% of the total (see Fig. 2.11). The rise of China as an economic powerhouse in Asia can be gleaned from an uptick in its investment performance in ASEAN. From US$2 billion in 2007, China's investment has surged to US$9.8 billion by 2016, representing a 285% growth rate.

Considering the regional blocs, the EU is the most important investor into the AEC with its share of total FDI increasing from 16% in 2013 to 33% in 2016.

Most notably, intra-ASEAN FDI has grown rapidly from US$8.4 billion in 2007 to US$18 billion by 2013, and further to about US$25 billion by 2016, representing 25% of total investments into the region (see Fig. 2.12).

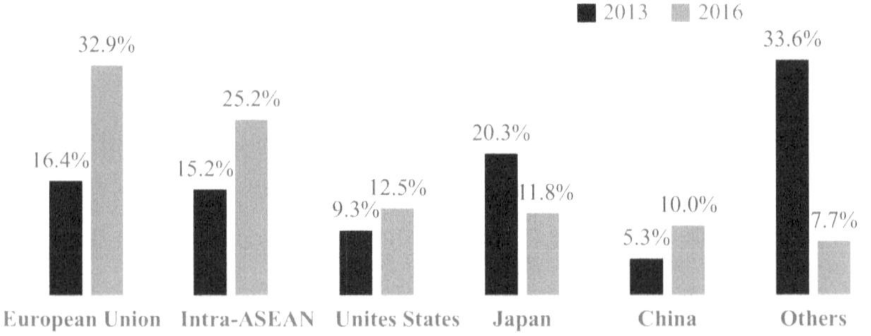

Fig. 2.11 Sources of foreign direct investments to the ASEAN (% of total). Data source: ASEAN Secretariat—ASEAN FDI Database as of 31 October 2017. Accessed on 8 June 2018 from https://data.aseanstats.org/fdi_by_country.php. Note: 2016 data are preliminary

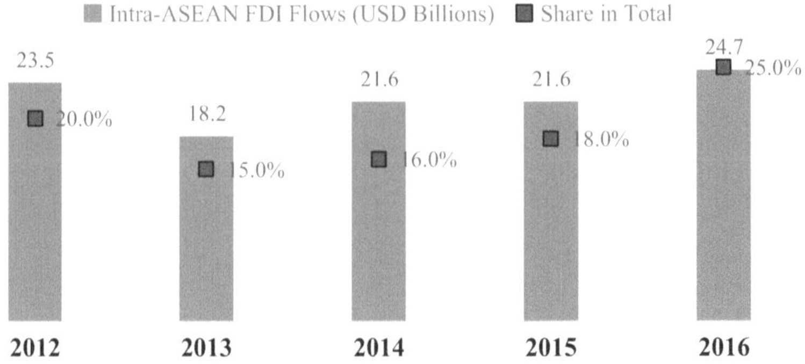

Fig. 2.12 Intra-ASEAN investment flows (in US$ billion). Data source: ASEAN Secretariat—ASEAN FDI Database as of 31 October 2017. Accessed on 8 June 2018 from https://data.aseanstats.org/fdi_by_country.php. Note: 2016 data are preliminary

Table 2.14 shows that Singapore and Malaysia were the most active investors among ASEAN members, accounting for 61% and 21% of the total intra-regional FDI in 2016. The Philippines has not been actively investing as much in the region. In fact, its outward FDI to other ASEAN countries even declined from US$893 million in 2012 to US$158 million in 2016, representing about 1% of the total.

As for receiving FDI, Table 2.15 shows that there is still a very wide disparity among the members. Singapore continues to dominate as host

Table 2.14 Intra-regional foreign direct investments inward flows in ASEAN (in US$ million)

	2011	*2012*	*2013*	*2014*	*2015*	*2016*
Singapore	12,716.8	9814.7	13,267.9	15,241.2	14,695.1	15,053.5
Malaysia	3999.4	3906.6	1176.3	1385.8	3503.2	5248.5
Thailand	(2209.7)	1228.3	968.5	3554.8	1242.9	2534.5
Indonesia	1856.1	6168.7	2333.3	1254.7	726.4	1086.8
Vietnam	288.3	427.6	338.8	332.7	409.5	283.4
Brunei	155.6	848.9	268.4	(620.0)	55.9	195.1
Philippines	(555.9)	893.0	(387.0)	406.5	824.1	157.9
Myanmar	118.5	98.8	95.7	97.7	31.0	51.8
Lao	0.4	0.1	1.1	1.9	2.2	23.7
Cambodia	33.1	2.4	(1.6)	20.5	47.1	(5.4)

Data source: ASEAN Secretariat—ASEAN FDI Database as of 31 October 2017. Accessed on 8 June 2018 from https://data.aseanstats.org/fdi_by_country.php.

Note: 2016 data are preliminary

Table 2.15 FDI inflows to the ASEAN by receiving country (in US$ billion)

	2012	*2013*	*2014*	*2015*	*2016*
Singapore	60.9	55.8	77.5	62.4	53.9
Vietnam	8.4	8.9	9.2	11.8	12.6
Malaysia	9.4	12.1	10.9	10.2	11.3
Philippines	2.8	3.9	5.8	5.6	7.9
Indonesia	19.1	18.4	21.8	16.6	3.5
Myanmar	1.4	2.6	0.9	2.8	3.0
Thailand	12.9	15.9	3.7	8.0	2.6
Cambodia	1.6	1.3	1.7	1.7	2.3
Lao PDR	0.3	0.4	0.9	1.1	1.1
Brunei	0.9	0.7	0.6	0.2	−0.2

Data source: ASEAN Secretariat—ASEAN FDI. Accessed on 1 June 2018 from http://asean.org/?static_post=foreign-direct-investment-statistics

Note: Database as of 31 October 2017

country by accounting 55% of all FDI flowing into the ASEAN in 2016. Other top investment recipients are Vietnam and Malaysia which received 13% and 12% of total ASEAN FDI in 2016, respectively.

In fact, Vietnam is one of the fastest-growing investment destinations in the region. From only US$6.7 billion in 2007, Vietnam's FDI has expanded to US$12.6 billion in 2016. Although lower than its counterparts and under the regional average of US$9.8 billion, the Philippines is slowly catching up. FDI receipts for the country had a compounded annual growth rate of 30.0% from 2012 to 2016, reaching US$2.9 billion in 2016, which represents 8.1% of the regional total.

As shown in Table 2.16, the bulk of the FDIs in the ASEAN over the period 2014 to 2016 went to the manufacturing and the finance sectors. On average, the service sectors account for the bulk of the FDIs, surpassing agriculture, mining, and utilities. The same sectoral distribution of the foreign investments at the intra-ASEAN level is observed. Again, the sectors of manufacturing and financial services received the most FDI in

Table 2.16 Flows of inward direct investment to ASEAN by economic sectors (in US$ million)

Economic sector	*2012*	*2013*	*2015*	*2016*
Agriculture, forestry, and fishing	1746.86	2330.21	5389.53	2680.08
Mining and quarrying	6461.77	8103.63	6241.40	4223.95
Manufacturing	−8881.53	39,921.25	29,179.76	7943.27
Electricity, gas, steam, and air conditioning supply	192.19	1193.77	2015.60	2942.44
Water supply, sewerage, waste management, and remediation	247.69	597.91	−39.96	366.20
Construction	−7.16	702.91	1112.42	1843.57
Wholesale and retail trade; repair of motor vehicles and motorcycles	24,314.19	14,965.70	7562.10	18,862.85
Transportation and storage	3344.09	2783.01	3644.53	4578.37
Accommodation and food service	148.74	21.25	476.03	632.42
Information and communication	2407.64	1827.02	2038.90	2060.77
Financial and insurance	57,008.91	23,485.76	36,318.14	33,635.33
Real estate	11,546.89	9323.34	8935.31	8598.91
Professional, scientific and technical	5506.39	421.06	247.02	561.86
Administrative and support service	244.86	62.17	245.75	329.13
Public administration and defines; compulsory social security	0.00	0.00	0.00	18.44
Education	2.26	65.77	1.55	64.28
Human health and social work	293.36	131.15	138.38	−131.31
Arts, entertainment, and recreation	119.14	221.20	−14.34	724.50
Other services	11,091.04	10,242.29	13,057.56	2160.29
Unspecified	1462.98	3197.01	3961.84	5947.14
Total activities	117,544.71	120,050.92	120,511.50	98,042.49

Data source: ASEAN Secretariat—ASEAN FDI Database as of 31 October 2017. Accessed on 8 June 2018 from https://data.aseanstats.org/fdi_by_country.php

Note: 2016 data are preliminary

2016 with US$9 billion and US$3.5 billion investments, respectively. It is interesting to note that the agricultural sector also attracted substantial intra-ASEAN FDI.

Cost of Doing Business as a Key Determinant of Participating in AEC as a Production Hub

Among the AEC's desired characteristics are enhanced connectivity and a competitive and innovative business environment among the member countries. The AEC, in competition with other regions in the world, is positioning itself as a conducive host to global production networks (GPNs) and regional value chains (RVCs). RVCs arise when a company breaks up its production process into different parts and allocate these parts to the most cost-efficient countries (Wood 2014). By doing so, companies enjoy lower costs arising from the benefits of specialization and economies of scale at the parts and components level. It is thus important for countries to be plugged into the RVCs. The different endowments of countries—labour cost, natural resources, as well as the quality of institutions and regulations—play a part in the choice of location of the RVCs.

As the AEC positions itself to be a conducive region for GPNs or RVCs to flourish, it has to implement reforms through regional cooperation. Efforts aimed at deepening integration through reducing trade barriers, improving connectivity, and lowering transaction costs are all carried out with the aim of fostering the RVCs. Countries that are more likely to gain from RVCs are those that exhibit superior cost of doing business attributes.

How Does the Philippines Compete in Terms of the Costs of Doing Business?

The World Bank's Doing Business format provides a framework in ranking relative competitiveness of countries in terms of business facilitation by providing objective measures of business regulations. The quantitative measures of regulations include starting a business, dealing with construction permits, getting electricity, registering property, getting credit, paying taxes, enforcing contracts, and resolving insolvency and labour market regulation, among others.

Table 2.17 presents the Doing Business indicator rank and the business snapshots of each ASEAN country. According to the table, in general, Malaysia is the most promising ASEAN country to locate one's business. It has the highest rank among the region (12 out of 185 countries). Still,

Table 2.17 ASEAN business snapshots

Country	*Doing Business Indicator (2018)*	*Index 2017*
Cambodia	135 due to improvements of starting a business and dealing with construction permits	131
Indonesia	72 due to improvements of getting electricity and credit, registering property, and protecting minority investors	91
Lao PDR	141 due to improvements in getting electricity	139
Malaysia	24 due to improvements in getting credit and paying taxes indicators	23
Philippines	113 due to improvement in the paying taxes indicator	99
Singapore	2 due to improvement in trading across borders	2
Thailand	26 due to improvements in getting credit, starting a business, getting electricity, protecting minority investors, paying taxes and enforcing contracts	46
Vietnam	68 due to improvements in paying taxes, getting electricity, and getting credit	82

Data source: The World Bank: Doing Business. 2018. In Moving Across Borders: The Philippines and the ASEAN Economic Community: 2016 Investment Guide by KPMG in the Philippines

it needs to enhance the workforce education and business and tax processes as suggested by the Enterprise Survey in 2009 to further attract investment (Ishido and Fukunaga 2012). Thailand also has a high Doing Business score. According to the criteria, the constraint in this country, however, is the stringent policy in foreign equity ownership restrictions.

The index for Doing Business of the Philippines in 2018 slipped from the 2017 rankings registering a rank of 113 out of 190 countries. Still, the distance to frontier (DTF) measure registered a slight improvement in 2018, indicating that the Philippines is moving closer to best practices. Among the most notable improvements were the introduction of an online system of tax filing and the efforts to reduce the time to get an electricity connection. In 2017, the business reforms in the Philippines clustered around dealing with construction permits and paying taxes.[10] However, the Philippines only ranked the seventh among the ten ASEAN members in the Ease of Doing Business in general.

One of the most important developments in this area is the passage of the "Ease of Doing Business and Efficient Government Service Delivery Act of 2018" on 31 May 2018. The law is meant to strengthen the drive to cut red tape and unnecessary delays arising from excessively bureaucratic systems. Overall, the law seeks to lessen transaction costs by putting in place a framework that facilitates the applications for licenses, permits, certification, and so on.

Human Resources: The Ultimate Resource

By and large, labour determines the productive capacity and greatly influences the economic performance of a country. A large and high-quality workforce emits a positive signal to investors. It is notable that in terms of working population, net exporters of labour in the ASEAN are also the countries with the largest workforce and the youngest median age (Antonio and Manzano 2016). Measured in number of workers, the Philippines has the third largest workforce in the ASEAN as of 2017, next only to Indonesia, which also has the biggest population, and Vietnam.

The Philippines possesses a youthful population. Contrasted against some of the rapidly ageing countries in the region, this characteristic opens a lot of possibilities. This has implications for the ability to absorb investments, which further increases the productive capacity of the nation. The human resources of the Philippines can be tapped in many sectors. Some of these factory workers can be directed to the rapidly expanding manufacturing enterprises that are relocating to the Philippines from Northeast Asia, service workers for the business process outsourcing (BPO) and tourism sectors, and highly skilled engineers and scientists who will be employed in the knowledge industries such as in information technology and software, biotechnology, and material sciences—the three areas that will define the technological breakthroughs in the twenty-first century (Villegas 2013a).

The Philippines as a Dynamic Part of the ASEAN Production Hub: Way Forward

It is said that the AEC is the driver of transformation of ASEAN member states (Maria et al. 2017). Indeed, the AEC puts in place a blueprint for strategic and orderly integration in the region. It crafts a policy and action agenda for the members to collaborate in an effort to transform the region into a very attractive place to invest and do business. Breaking down barriers to trade, linking the different countries by policy-induced connectivity initiatives, and putting into place trade-facilitating practices are all meant to bring down transaction costs in the region. To transform the ASEAN into a meaningful production hub requires a collaborative effort among the members. To illustrate, providing seamless connectivity among the members requires harmonized regulations and other institutional arrangements such as airline routes or even agreements on customs procedures.

Despite the grand ambitions, the AEC remains just a plan. It does not have force of law to compel the ASEAN members to carry out the provisions. To be operative, the AEC provisions have to be implemented at the domestic level by way of national laws. The Philippines is fully committed to the ASEAN process. The Department of Trade and Industry (DTI), the lead agency in matters of ASEAN, has unveiled its strategic thrusts in the 3Cs: compliance to meet AEC obligations consistent with national goals, collaboration among government agencies and all interested parties, and communication to all stakeholders to elicit participation and competitiveness (Llanto, *Philippines*, 2017, p. 193).

The Philippines has structural advantages in human resources. Furthermore, the Philippine economy can depend on sizeable remittance inflows over the next years. The Philippine economy has been on the rise supported by strong economic fundamentals. Improvements in fiscal space, tame inflation, adequate level of gross international reserves, and upgrades in credit standing are some of the positive outcomes from institutional reforms and getting the policy mix right.

In terms of development in governance, the Philippines has made strides in advancing the AEC vision, particularly in the competition area. Just recently, in 2016, the Philippine Competition Commission (PCC) was established. It is an independent quasi-judicial body which will enforce a national competition policy. It is hoped that this development will help create a business environment that enhances the confidence of investors in the Philippine market. In addition, the National Competitiveness Council, a body composed of key government agencies and private representatives, oversees efforts to reduce the cost of doing business through regulatory reform and improvements in governance (Llanto, *Philippines*, 2017, p. 189).

Challenges in AEC for the Philippines

Though the Philippines has made progress in complying with its commitments in the AEC Blueprint, there remain some obstacles. Observers point out that the Philippines is lagging behind its commitments in the service sector. To illustrate, as measured by the Services Trade Restrictiveness Index (STRI),[11] the commitment of the Philippines in the

ASEAN Agreement on Services (AFAS) Seventh Package was only 0.33, compared to the ASEAN average of 0.36 as cited by Llanto (2017). Another challenge for the Philippines is to address the constitutional restrictions on foreign ownership in public utility investments which is a key sector in infrastructure to build up. Other related roadblocks to investments include prohibition on land ownership and restrictions on the practice of professions. Addressing the economic provisions of the Constitution is a promising avenue for the Philippines for it to fully benefit from the AEC.

Prospects

Undoubtedly, the outlook for the Philippines is bright, and this can be attributed to at least five main prospective growth drivers: demographic dividend, robust labour and service exports, the manufacturing industry's resurgence, the construction boom, and the tourism sector.

Demographic Dividend

Most ASEAN countries enjoy the advantage of a young demographic and an expanding middle class, making the region an attractive investment destination (Villegas 2013b). An overriding advantage of the Philippines lies in its demographic dynamics. It is at the stage where the demographic dividend is beginning to manifest. The share of the working-age population is becoming to be dominant relative to the share of the non-working-age population.

The Philippines is one of the biggest (along with Indonesia and Vietnam) markets in the region. With a population of about 103–105 million as of 2018, and with a median age of 24–25 as of 2018,[12] the Philippines is enjoying a demographic dividend that is expected to last until 2050 (Mapa 2015). This makes the country attractive to investors offering all types of consumer goods and services who want to capture a large domestic market, particularly of a growing middle class. In the context of the rapidly ageing Southeast Asian neighbours, particularly Thailand and Singapore, the Philippines offers abundant and cost-competitive human resources vital for the production sector.

Labour and Services Exports

Two of the pillars of the robust economic growth of the country since the early 2000s are the steady increase in overseas Filipino workers and the rapid rise of the Business Process Outsourcing (BPO) sector, which are both sources of foreign exchange driving consumption, investment, and middle-class growth.

About ten million Filipinos are abroad,[13] sending an average of US$25 billion a year.[14] Remittances from abroad are expected to continue to be a major source of income for the country, for several reasons:

First, according to the Central Bank, the sources of remittances have become more diversified. As shown in Fig. 2.13, the distribution of remittance source countries has changed in the last seven years. From being concentrated in the Americas (53%) and Europe (17%) in 2010, the 2017 distribution was more diverse, with notably larger shares from the Middle East (28% from only 16% in 2010) and Asia (19% from 13%). The diversification of income sources reduces the risk of a shock (or at least the impact of shock) to the remittance inflows to the Philippines and in case of economic crises in the source countries.

Second, according to the World Bank, the expected recovery in major economies including Europe and the United States in the next two years would help raise remittances (Arteta and Stocker 2018).

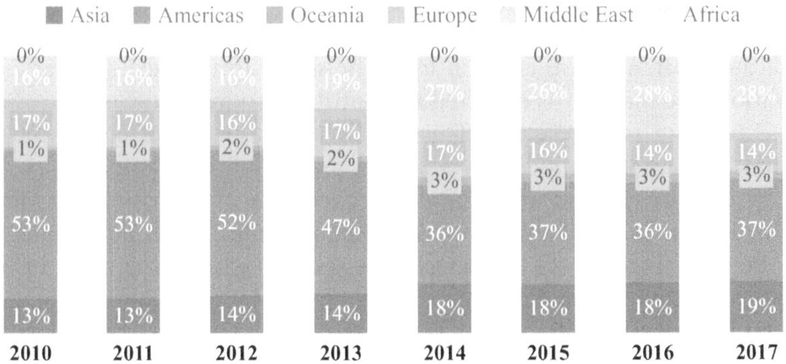

Fig. 2.13 Distribution of cash remittances from overseas Filipinos by source (%). Data source: Central Bank of the Philippines. Cash remittances by countries and by sources. Accessed on 8 June 2018 from http://www.bsp.gov.ph/statistics/keystat/ofw2.htm

Third, the ageing population of several advanced economies such as Japan and China, and their interest in English-speaking workers which the Philippines has in abundance, could raise the demand for OFWs in the coming years.[15]

The Information Technology-Business Process Outsourcing (IT-BPO) Sector is also expected to continue to thrive, driven by cost competitiveness, Filipino workers' service-oriented culture, and the growing market demand in the Asia Pacific region. The Filipino's proficiency in English, as well as the level of education, particularly at the tertiary level, are among the major factors that bring foreign and local firms to invest in IT-BPO operations in the country.

In fact, the Information Technology and Business Processing Association of the Philippines (IBPAP) has projected that the industry will grow by an annual rate of 9.2% from 2017 until end of the Duterte Administration in 2022 (Frost and Sullivan 2018). The sector is seen to earn close to US$40 billion by 2022, accounting for 15.5% of the global market (from 12.6% in 2016). Further, by 2022, the total employed in the sector is estimated to be 1.8 million (Frost and Sullivan 2018). IBPAP believes that as the global business process outsourcing grows globally, there is real opportunity for growth in specializing in mid- and high-skilled tasks that require strong analytical skills and a strong grasp of logical reasoning. In this case, IBPAP's projection indicates that some 73% of the workforce will be engaged in medium and high-level skilled jobs in 2022 from just 53% in 2016, while low-skilled workers will account for only 27% by 2022 (from about 50% in 2016) (Villegas 2017a). These projections indicate substantial job creation from the sector in the next six years. In addition, the industry is expected to contribute to more inclusive growth by expanding to new cities. This implies the dispersal of employment, capital investments, and business development to more regions.

In addition, critical and major improvements in the country's infrastructure—as planned by the current administration—will be supportive of the growth of the IT-BPO sector by providing access to more urban centres outside of the country's capital, as well by reducing the costs of doing business.

Related to the IT-BPO sector growth is the Philippines' ability to attract more investments from multinational companies seeking to create efficiencies by relocating to the Philippines (Villegas 2017b). The Philippines has particularly sought to attract foreign investors by providing incentives for building regional operating headquarters (ROHQs). In particular, the government granted fiscal and non-fiscal incentives for multinational corporations (MNCs) relocating their ROHQs in the Philippines, in competition with other choice regional hubs such as Hong Kong and Singapore. As of 2016, there were 158 ROHQs in the Philippines with a combined US$2 billion in employee wages and benefits, employing over 50,000 workers. These ROHQs benefit from the development of the service industry. ROHQ workers perform various high-level services that require above-average skills and provide above-average wages and salaries to professionals. In addition, ROHQs have significant multiplier effects on other sectors of the economy because they engage local service firms for their operational support and project needs, creating thousands of additional jobs for highly skilled workers (Villegas 2017b).

The current government is implementing a series of tax reforms to boost workers' incomes, raise revenues for the government to support its infrastructure and social programmes, and to rationalize fiscal policies. There have been suggestions to remove the fiscal and non-fiscal incentives provided to ROHQs. In this regard, it must be noted that the incentives are a major factor in motivating ROHQs to stay in the country, at a time that other countries—Vietnam and Thailand—are emerging as competitors (Villegas 2017b). It must be remembered that fiscal incentives have been critical in attracting and maintaining talents in ROHQs, reducing the attrition rate of highly desired candidates lost to jobs overseas because of the regional/global flexibilities and business competencies they have developed. It must be stressed that these ROHQs, being in the premier and highly skilled segment of the service industry, cannot afford the high rate of attrition typical of outsourcing firms. Thus, the continuous operations of ROHQs locally could help attract top local talents and be a training ground for upgrading their skills and moving into higher-value services.

Resurgence in Manufacturing

As a consequence of being "the Sick Man of Asia" in the last century, the Philippine manufacturing sector has consistently underperformed. The combination of overvalued exchange rates and rigid labour laws has channelled resources towards capital intensive manufacturing technology which deviated from the comparative advantage of the Philippines at that time. However, as stated in an earlier part of this discussion, manufacturing growth in the last decade outpaced total GDP growth. The key sectors for manufacturing are furniture and fixtures, chemical and chemical products, publishing and printing, basic metal industries and machinery and equipment (except electrical and transport equipment)—demand for which are expected to grow alongside the economy.

Quite recently, bright prospects for manufacturing growth for the country, geared towards the increasingly buoyant export markets in the region, have emerged. In particular, the rapid rise in labour costs amidst growing demand in countries such as Japan, South Korea, and Taiwan is shifting the focus of investments towards Southeast Asia (Villegas 2017c). Admittedly, the Philippines has to contend with its neighbours that offer better investment climates for manufacturing. For example, Vietnam in the past three years has outperformed the Philippines in the expansion of its manufacturing industry in the light of its more investor-friendly policies. A number of Southeast Asian countries have embarked on industry strategies that leverage on emerging technologies. Thailand, for instance, is gearing itself to attract FDIs for development of high technology, the so-called new-age industries (Villegas 2017c). Similarly, Malaysia is also aiming to move into even higher value-added sectors. Given the competition, the Philippines must make steps to change its policies to attract more foreign investments, upgrade its infrastructure to reduce business costs and raise competitiveness, and continuously train workers to support the industry's growth.

Construction Boom

To enhance the country's competitiveness, raise productivity, and to achieve a 7.0–8.0% annual GDP growth between 2016 and 2022, the current administration launched a ten-point socioeconomic agenda, locally dubbed as "Dutertenomics." Central to the plan is an ambitious infrastructure programme aimed at increasing public infrastructure investment, commonly referred to as "Build, Build, Build."[16] The grand plan was introduced in 2017 as part of the Philippine Development Plan 2017–2022. In particular, the government aims to implement at least PHP 8 trillion worth of infrastructure projects including public-private partnerships (PPPs) and foreign investments between 2017 and 2022, to bring the country's infrastructure into its "golden age." The government aims to implement massive infrastructure projects until 2022 including international airports, major expressways, inter-island bridges, industrial parks, and public transportation systems. The Philippines is also seeking aid from other countries for both financing and technological know-how in infrastructure. In fact, the government has secured significant pledges from foreign investors, mostly from Japan and China. Examples include the first subway to be built in the country, the Mega Manila Subway, to be funded by Japan, and the Mindanao Railway, to be funded by China. The government's public infrastructure programme aims to raise infrastructure spending to at least 7.0% of the GDP by the end of Duterte's term in 2022. This is expected to boost domestic growth, expand capital formation, and boost business and consumer confidence (World Bank 2017). There is thus a distinct move to channel developmental resources to areas outside the capital, such as Mindanao. Given the preference of President Duterte to shift the form of government towards federalism, the shift should even be more pronounced in the future.

Tourism

One of the key industries that can benefit from the current government stance on improving infrastructure is the tourism industry. Currently, Philippine tourism pales in comparison to its ASEAN neighbours like Thailand, Malaysia, and Singapore which enjoy tourist arrivals of three to six times that of the Philippines (see Fig. 2.14).

The state of the country's infrastructure is a major hindrance to attracting tourists. Besides the lack of infrastructure, there are other structural factors that do not favour Philippine tourism. For one, all ASEAN countries, except the Philippines, have land borders with one or more ASEAN countries, and three of them share land borders with China (Villegas 2017d). The existence of land borders naturally facilitates tourism, all

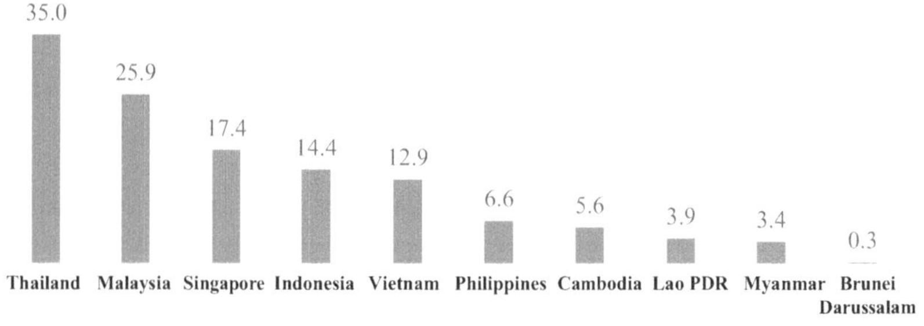

Fig. 2.14 Tourist arrivals in 2017—ASEAN (million persons). Data source: UOB Bank. ASEAN Snapshot: Special Coverage in Tourism. Accessed on 8 June 2018 from https://www.uobgroup.com/web-resources/uobgroup/pdf/research/mir-20180502.pdf

other things being equal. The Philippines is located well to the east of the population centre (central axis of the population) of ASEAN that runs more or less north between Singapore and Malaysia. Indeed, a significant portion of the other ASEAN countries' international arrivals is mostly by land. In contrast, being archipelagic, the Philippines received the bulk of its tourists in 2017 by air travel, of which 63.5% arrived through the country's main airport, the Ninoy Aquino International Airport in Manila.[17] Moreover, the transportation infrastructure cost per head of the population of the other ASEAN countries is significantly lower than that of the Philippines (Villegas 2017d). Thus, the Philippines is the most expensive ASEAN country to reach from other ASEAN markets.

Given the geographical constraints, it is quite clear that a significant increase in interconnectivity through more efficient air and sea travel to the Philippines can enable the Philippine tourism industry to catch up with foreign tourist arrivals enjoyed by its ASEAN neighbours (Villegas 2017d). In addition to better infrastructure, there should also be the development of a regional network of urban and non-urban destinations offering good quality accommodations at all levels, including bed and breakfast facilities, especially in the more rural destinations (Villegas 2017d).

The Duterte Administration is keen on addressing the obstacles to the development of the tourism industry. Among the first infrastructure projects that were approved by the investment committee of the Duterte Administration were the international airports in key tourism sites such as Bohol, Bacolod, Iloilo, Cagayan de Oro, and Davao (Villegas 2017d). Originally planned as projects under the private-public partnership (PPP) programme, these were later subsumed under the so-called hybrid model in which the government will finance and implement the construction, using ODA funding if necessary, and then assign the operations and maintenance to the private sector. The Philippines has a huge number of attractions that can attract domestic and foreign tourists. The National Tourism Development Plan (NTDP) 2016 to 2022 of the Department of Tourism projects 12 million foreign tourists. There is general consensus that the tourism and hotel sectors are powerful catalysts for inclusive and regional growth in the country.

Challenges

Despite the many successes that the Philippines has achieved in the past decade, it continues to face perennial problems that will be crucial in shaping the outcomes for the country's future generations. One of them is the

Table 2.18 Poverty incidence and GDP growth—Philippines (2006–2015)

	2006	*2009*	*2012*	*2015*
Poverty incidence	26.6%	26.3%	25.2%	21.3%
GDP growth	5.6% (average: 2004–2006)	4.0% (average: 2007–2009)	6.0% (average: 2010–2012)	6.3% (average: 2013–2015)

Data source: Philippine Statistics Authority. Social Statistics. Accessed on 12 June 2018 from http://psa.gov.ph/poverty-press-releases

country's slow progress towards poverty reduction. Despite a GDP growth averaging 5.4% between 2006 and 2015, at the latest count (2015), 21.3% of the country's population still live below the poverty line (see Table 2.18).

According to the Asian Development Bank (2009), economic growth in the 2000s did not translate into poverty reduction. The same report says that poverty levels vary greatly by regions, indicating the necessity of regionally targeted programmes (Asian Development Bank 2009). Further, poor Filipino households are susceptible to key shocks and sources of vulnerability on their incomes and expenditures including labour and employment shocks (job losses and lower wages), price shocks, demographic, health-related shocks (illness or death of a household member), and natural disasters (Albert et al. 2015). Without social safety nets addressing these, the poverty gap will remain.

It is generally known that poverty levels are linked with educational attainment. Inequalities in education attainment especially among household heads have been the root of vulnerable employment. While basic education is free in the country, the opportunity costs for poor families to send children to school are rather high, as children may be expected to work and contribute to household income and livelihood (Albert et al. 2015). Thus, reducing the gap in educational outcomes among families—especially the young working-age population—could have a great impact on poverty reduction.

Part of why the efforts have been insufficient is because the local government capacity to implement poverty reduction programmes is weak, as governance and institutional constraints remain in the programme responses (Asian Development Bank 2009). For instance, governance is constrained by corruption and the political culture of patronage. It has been observed that some local politicians make use of the patronage system to stay in power and could shift the use of resources that are intended for poverty reduction to other purposes. In certain local cases, the combination of weak institutions given competing interests, weak leadership, and inequitable distribution of income, wealth, and political power has also undermined the proper implementation of reforms. Particularly, the lack of job security and tenure in regulatory and bureaucratic offices and political interference have led to institutional underperformance, flawed policies and failure to deliver development outcomes (Llanto and Gonzalez, *Policy Reforms and Institutional Weaknesses: Closing the Gap*, 2007).

Crucial to reducing poverty and improving outcomes in the Philippines are improving access to education and creating more jobs, raising foreign direct investments, increasing service and manufacturing sector contribution to output, improving government effectiveness, and elevating agricultural productivity (Villegas 2016a).

Improving access to education will help level the opportunities for workers. Aside from this, improving the quality of education and the matching between the labour pool's skills and the job market needs are important in helping more people out of poverty. Higher FDI inflows will generally facilitate the adoption of more advanced technology and know-how, raising overall productivity. If implemented in the agriculture sector where most of the poor are employed, FDI could highly impact poverty reduction. Meanwhile, greater FDI flows into the agricultural sector will raise its contributions to national output in the same manner that growth among labour-intensive industries could raise the income of a considerable number of workers, helping them out of poverty (Villegas 2016a). Finally, better governance could also facilitate poverty reduction as projects in the agricultural sector could be carried out in a timelier fashion.

Another challenge that the country faces is job creation. Today, while labour migration is a pillar to economic growth, the reality is a number of these Filipinos choose to work abroad due to lack of job opportunities locally. In the long run, this could impact domestic growth. In fact, despite the abundant supply of workers in the labour market, research reveals labour shortages in select industries. In 2017, the government reported occupational shortages in a number of sectors including human health and social work activities, construction, and waste management and remediation activities (Philippine Statistics Authority 2018). The government also noted insufficiency of applicants in a number of professions including physiotherapists, nursing professionals, economists, dentists, pharmacists, social work and counselling professionals, vocational education teachers, and midwifery professionals (Philippine Statistics Authority 2018)

Generally, inefficiencies in public management also result in bottlenecks limiting productivity in the country. These inefficiencies are evident, for example, in the bureaucratic red tape and the persistent traffic problems in the country. Policy and regulatory processes in the Philippines such as securing government permits and licenses are complicated and tedious, raising the cost of doing business in the country. The passage of legislation fostering ease of doing business is the right policy move to address the issue of high transaction cost. Another indication of inefficiency is the persistent traffic in the capital, Metro Manila, caused by insufficient transport infrastructure and poor traffic management. In fact, Japan International Cooperation Agency (JICA) estimated that in 2012, the daily productivity loss due to traffic in the capital, Metro Manila, was PHP 2.4 billion, while their preliminary estimate for 2017 was at PHP 3.5 billion (JICA and NEDA 2014).[18]

Another major challenge is revising the Constitution to liberalize local markets and enable further growth. The current version of the Constitution was drafted and revised in 1987, after the dictatorship of Ferdinand Marcos. The framers of the Constitutions wanted to place safeguards to ensure that another authoritarian ruler would not lead again. The composition of the Constitutional Commission of 1986 was quite varied in terms of representatives coming from different political persuasions, united only in their opposition to the Marcos regime, a veritable "rainbow coalition." However, the relatively protectionist provisions they put in place have led to institutional problems affecting further economic growth.

Currently, the Constitution limits foreign ownership in several sectors, particularly in public utilities. Because of such ownership constraints and their effects on corporate control, foreign investments have not been very forthcoming in the last three decades. Unlike its neighbours with their more liberal investment regimes, the Philippines ranked quite poorly in the ability to attract foreign direct investments in the past decades.

This "Filipino First" approach has actually spawned a good number of oligopolistic industries which have kept prices of domestic goods or services unreasonably high (Villegas 2017e). It is necessary to liberalize the industries to attract more foreign investments and induce competition for the benefit of consumers and the industries. Because ownership of companies in key sectors such as utilities and construction is limited to local investors, there is a great chance of regulatory capture by vested interest groups that thrive under inward-looking policies enshrined in the Constitution (Villegas 2017e). Such observation found echo in the allegation that the protectionist provisions in the Constitution have encouraged monopolies and oligopolies in the strategic sectors of the economy: communications, transportation, ports, and so on deemed "public utilities" with undesirable consequences on the cost and quality of services (Chikiamco 2017).

Governance, in general, is a great challenge. Defects in governance could result in adverse selection problems involving foreign investors. To illustrate, it is possible that a defective investment regime could allow only those foreign investors with high levels of risk tolerance but who may not be the most efficient ones. This leads to rent-seeking behaviour, reinforcing the elite capture and further constraining competition that could otherwise facilitate greater efficiency and increased consumer welfare (Villegas 2017e).

Economic provisions need to be amended for the needed flexibility to enable the Philippines to properly compete, adapt, and prosper in a changing and dynamic global economy. To carry this out, a number of imperatives should be in order. First, government efforts should be directed to ensure free competition and dismantle monopolies and disempower oligarchs at the same time. Second, the government should promote market efficiency by reducing barriers to entry by foreign investors primarily in vital industries such as utilities. The greater competition will benefit local consumers and export-oriented industries. Third, the Philippines must enhance international competitiveness by meeting trade agreement obligations and increasing foreign investments (Villegas 2017e).

Final Remarks

Currently, the Philippine economy is strategically well-positioned in the region, in a "sweet spot," as outlined in the second section of the chapter. Growth, anchored on a resurgence in manufacturing and a construction boom, is robust. A steady inflow of workers' remittances, close to US$30 billion coming from millions of overseas Filipino workers (OFWs), and the more than US$25 billion earnings from the Information Technology-Business Process Outsourcing sector continue to stimulate consumption spending. Even the erstwhile constraint, infrastructure deficiencies, that have long hobbled Philippine aspirations towards an investment-led growth, is being addressed by President Duterte's Build-Build-Build infrastructure programme. Reforms of the tax system directed at making it less regressive are in place. There are, however, concerns that the tax reform programme, which called for higher excise taxes for fuel, sweetened beverages and other items, has induced inflationary pressures. Likewise, the immediate needs of the poor are being addressed through an expanded Conditional Cash Transfer (CCT) started by President Benigno Aquino III, which is an instrument to keep children, especially in the rural areas, longer in the school system.

The third section has underscored the performance of the Philippines in the area of economic freedom. Though there was an improvement over the period 2014–2017, there was a dip in the Economic Freedom index in 2018. The fourth section discussed Philippine's performance set against the backdrop of the AEC. The Philippine economy has been performing well relative to the region and strides have been experienced in the Ease of Doing Business indicators. Still, there are challenges for the country in attracting foreign direct investments both from within ASEAN and from outside of ASEAN.

The fifth section has raised the prospects of the Philippine economy. The demographic dividend, further developments in the exports of services, particularly the Information Technology-Business Process Outsourcing (IT-BPO) sector, and tourism are some of the factors that bode well for the continuing expansion of the economy. The final section discussed the main challenges of the country—making progress in poverty reduction and improving the investment climate further.

The Philippines has kept an active profile in ASEAN matters. As Chair of the 50th Anniversary of ASEAN, the Philippines has championed the cause of the Micro Small and Medium Establishments. Further, leveraging on its demographic profile, the Philippine economy is well positioned to take advantage of the ASEAN integration initiatives both as a consumer market and as a production hub. It has the population base to attract not only home-market-oriented investments but also export-oriented ones. All told, there is high expectation to see the Philippines attain a high growth trajectory in the near future.

Notes

1. See the National Economic Development Authority's Philippine Development Plan 2017–2022 for more information at http://www.neda.gov.ph/2017/07/26/philippine-development-plan-2017-2022/.
2. IMF. November 2017. Philippines: 2017 Article IV Consultation-Press Release; Staff Report, IMF Country Report No. 17/334.

3. The Business Confidence Index (BCI) drawn from the Business Expectations Survey by the Central Bank of the Philippines. It is a leading indicator of business activity in the economy and companies' operations. The BCI is computed as the percentage of firms that answered in the affirmative less the percentage of firms that answered in the negative with respect to their views on a given indicator. For example, a BCI of 0% indicates the number of respondents with an optimistic outlook is equal to the number of respondents with a pessimistic outlook.
4. The Consumer Confidence Index (CCI) is drawn from the quarterly Consumer Expectations Survey conducted by the Central Bank of the Philippines. It is an advance indicator of consumer sentiments for the current and the next quarters and the year ahead and their expectations on selected economic indicators such as inflation, unemployment rate, and borrowing rate. The CCI is computed as the percentage of households that answered in the affirmative less the percentage of households that answered in the negative with respect to their views on indicators such as overall condition of the economy, household finances, and household income.
5. IMF. November 2017. Philippines: 2017 Article IV Consultation-Press Release; Staff Report, IMF Country Report No. 17/334, p. 2.
6. Chipongian, Lee. BSP working on controlling a spiralling inflation. Manila Bulletin. 4 May 2018. https://business.mb.com.ph/2018/05/04/bsp-working-on-controlling-a-spiralling-inflation/. Accessed 11 June 2018.
7. 2018 Index of Economic Freedom. https://www.heritage.org/index/about. Accessed 4 June 2018.
8. Ibid.
9. ASEAN-5 refers to the ASEAN founding members—Indonesia, Malaysia, the Philippines, Thailand, and Singapore.
10. The World Bank: Doing Business. 2018. In Moving Across Borders: The Philippines and the ASEAN Economic Community: 2016 Investment Guide by KPMG in the Philippines. KPMG and University of Asia and the Pacific. Manila, pp. 48–64. http://www.doingbusiness.org/reforms/overview/economy/philippines. Accessed 24 March 2018.
11. The Services Trade Restrictiveness Index (STRI) is a metric launched by the Organization for Economic Development (OECD) in 2014 to catalogue barriers to service trade and allow policymakers to assess reform options. Read more at http://www.oecd.org/tad/services-trade/services-trade-restrictiveness-index.htm.
12. Authors' estimates based on data from the Philippine Statistics Authority.
13. There is a difference between the estimate of the stock of overseas Filipinos and estimates coming from surveys in the Philippines. Estimates vary widely. A survey was conducted by the Philippine Statistics Authority as

reported in "2017 Survey on Overseas Filipinos." Accessed from https://psa.gov.ph/content/total-number-ofws-estimated-23-million-results-2017-survey-overseas-filipinos. Accessed on 10 June 2018. Estimates from the Commission on Overseas Filipinos put the 2013 figure closer to 10.2 million, from http://www.cfo.gov.ph/downloads/statistics/stock-estimates.html. Accessed on 18 June 2018.

14. Average total cash remittances from Filipinos overseas, taken from the Central Bank of the Philippines. http://www.bsp.gov.ph/statistics/key-stat/ofw2.htm. Accessed on 10 June 2018.
15. See S. Medenilla's article discussing the hiring of more Filipinos in Japan at https://news.mb.com.ph/2017/09/10/japan-poised-to-hire-100000-ofws-to-address-worsening-labor-shortage/ and Barbara Dacanay's article discussing hiring of workers in China at: https://gulfnews.com/news/asia/philippines/china-s-deal-to-hire-300-000-filipinos-finalised-1.2205241.
16. Based on the Philippine Development Plan 2017–2022. Read the chapter on "Accelerating Infrastructure Development" for further details: http://pdp.neda.gov.ph/wp-content/uploads/2017/01/19-04-07-2017.pdf.
17. For instance, in 2017, 69.2% of tourists to Malaysia arrived by land. Tourists mostly came from countries with which Malaysia shares land borders, namely Singapore (47.7%), Indonesia (10.4%), Thailand (7.1%), and Brunei (6.4%). In 2016, 74.2% of tourist arrived in Laos via land travel, with the majority coming from connected countries namely Thailand (47.0%) and Vietnam (24.0%). In contrast, the Philippines received 97.1% of its tourists in 2017 by air travel, of which 63.5% arrived through the country's main airport, the Ninoy Aquino International Airport in Manila (statistics were derived from the official government database of Malaysia, Lao PDR, and the Philippines).
18. JICA's preliminary estimate for the daily traffic cost as of 2017 was at PHP 3.5 billion. Read more at: http://cnnphilippines.com/transportation/2018/02/23/JICA-P3.5-billion-traffic.html.

References

Albert, Jose Ramon, Jesus Dumagan, and Arturo Martinez Jr. 2015. *Inequalities in Income, Labor, and Education: The Challenge*. Discussion Paper Series. Manila: Philippine Institute for Development Studies. https://dirp4.pids.gov.ph/webportal/CDN/PUBLICATIONS/pidsdps1501.pdf. Accessed July 7, 2018.

Antonio, Henry, and George Manzano. 2016. Reaping the Fruits of Labor Mobility in the AEC. In *2016 Investment by KPMG in the Philippines*, 18–28. Manila: KPMG and University of Asia and the Pacific.

Arteta, Carlos, and Marc Stocker. 2018. Turning of the Tide? In *World Economic Prospects 2018*, ed. World Bank, 1–58. Washington, DC: World Bank Group. https://openknowledge.worldbank.org/bitstream/handle/10986/.../9781464812576.pdf

Asian Development Bank. 2009. *Poverty in the Philippines: Causes, Constraints, and Opportunities.* Mandaluyong: Asian Development Bank.

Berggren, Niclas. 2003. The Benefits of Economic Freedom: A Survey. *The Independent Review*. VIII (2): 194–199. http://www.independent.org/pdf/tir/tir_08_2_2_berggren.pdf. Accessed June 8, 2018.

Bonoan, Emmanuel, and Kristine Joy Martin. 2016. Transforming into One ASEAN Market. In *Moving Across Borders: The Philippines and the ASEAN Economic Community 2016 Investment Guide by KPMG in the Philippines*, 11–17. Manila: KPMG and University of Asia and the Pacific.

Chikiamco, Calixto. 2017. *Dismantling the Post-EDSA Order*. September 11. http://www.fef.org.ph/calixto-chikiamco/dismantling-the-post-edsa-order/. Accessed June 28, 2019.

Coleman, Gary, Ira Kalish, Dan Konigsburg, and Gregorio Navarro. 2014. *Competitiveness – Catching the Next Wave – The Philippines.* UK: Deloitte.

Cultural Atlas. n.d. *Filipino Culture – Core Concepts.* https://culturalatlas.sbs.com.au/filipino-culture/filipino-culture-core-concepts. Accessed June 10, 2018.

Drysdale, Peter. 2017. ASEAN: The Experiment in Open Regionalism that Succeed. In *The ASEAN Economic Community Into 2025 and Beyond*, ed. Rebecca Sta. Maria, Shurijo Urata, and Ponciano Intal Jr., 64–86. Economic Research Institute for ASEAN and East Asia (ERIA).

Frost and Sullivan. 2018. *The Philippine IT-BPM Sector Roadmap 2022.* Industry Roadmap, Manila: IT-BPAP. http://www.boi.gov.ph/files/Roadmaps/TID/Executive%20Summary%20Accelerate%20PH%20Future-Ready%20Roadmap%202022_with%20corrections.pdf. Accessed June 10, 2018.

Guarin, Michael, and Kristin Joy Martin. 2016. Establising as a Production Base. In *2016 Investment Guide by KPMG in the Philippines.* Manila: KPMG and University of Asia and the Pacific.

Hays, Jeffrey. 2015. *Economic History of the Philippines.* June. http://factsanddetails.com/southeast-asia/Philippines/sub5_6g/entry-3916.html. Accessed June 16, 2018.

Hussain, Mohammed, and Mahfuzul Haque. 2016. Impact of Economic Freedom on the Growth Rate: A Panel Data Analysis. *Economies*, 1–15. https://doi.org/10.3390/economies4020005. Accessed June 6, 2018.

International Monetary Fund. 2018. *World Economic Outlook.* Washington, DC: International Monetary Fund. https://www.imf.org/en/Publications/WEO/Issues/2018/01/11/world-economic-outlook-update-january-2018. Accessed March 24, 2018.

Ishido, H., and I. Fukunaga. 2012. *Liberalization of Trade in Services: Towards a Harmonized ASEAN ++ FTA*. Working Paper No. 2012-12, Economic Research Institute for ASEAN and East Asia. http://www.eria.org/ERIA-PB-2012-02.pdf. Accessed May 5, 2018.

JICA and NEDA. 2014. *Roadmap for Transport Infrastructure Development for Metro Manila and Its Surrounding Areas*. Study, Manila: Japan International Cooperation Agency (JICA) and National Economic Development Authority (NEDA). http://www.neda.gov.ph/wp-content/uploads/2015/03/FR-SUMMARY.-12149597.pdf. Accessed July 7, 2018.

Kim, Terry, and Shanker Singham. 2016. *2016 Index of Economic Freedom*. Washington, DC: The Heritage Foundation. https://www.heritage.org/index/pdf/2016/countries/philippines.pdf. Accessed June 6, 2017.

Kind, Hans Jarle. 2000. *The Philippines – The Sick Man of Asia? Economic Development in the Philippines After 1948*. Working Paper. Bergen: Foundation for Research in Economics and Business Administration. https://brage.bibsys.no/xmlui/bitstream/handle/11250/166586/A24_00.pdf. Accessed June 10, 2018.

Llanto, Gilbert. 2017. Philippines. In *ASEAN and Member States: Transformation and Integration*, ed. Ponciano Intal Jr. and Lurong Chen, 188–193. ASEAN and Member States: Transformation and Integration.

Llanto, Gilbert, and Albert Gonzalez. 2007. *Policy Reforms and Institutional Weaknesses: Closing the Gap*. Discussion Paper Series. Manila: Philippine Institute for Development Studies. http://www.eaber.org/sites/default/files/documents/PIDS_Llanto_07_2.pdf. Accessed July 20, 2018.

Mapa, Dennis. 2015. *Demographic Sweet Spot and Dividend in the Philippines: The Window of Opportunity Is Closing Fast*. Study, Manila: University of the Philippines. http://philippines.unfpa.org/sites/default/files/pub-pdf/DemographicSweetSpoandDividendinthePhilippines_FINAL_DRAFT_Ver4_OCT2015-withcover_0.pdf. Accessed June 10, 2018.

Maria, Rebecca Sta, Shujiro Urata, and Ponciano Intal, Jr. 2017. The ASEAN Community into 2025 and Beyond. In *The Sean Economic Community into 2025 and Beyond*, 61. Economic Research Institute for ASEAN and East Asia (ERIA).

Meyer, Jorg. 2013. *Towards More Balanced Growth Strategies in Developing Countries: Issues Related to Market Sie, Trade Balances, and Purchasing Power*. Discussion Paper, United Nations Conference on Trade and Development. unctad.org/en/PublicationsLibrary/osgdp20134_en.pdf. Accessed April 30, 2018.

Miller, Terry, and Anthony Kim. 2017. *2017 Index of Economic Freedom*. Washington, DC: The Heritage Foundation. https://www.heritage.org/index/pdf/2017/book/index_2017.pdf. Accessed June 6, 2018.

Miller, Terry, Anthony Kim, and James Roberts. 2018. *2018 Index of Economic Freedom*. Washington, DC: The Heritage Foundation. https://www.heritage.org/index/pdf/2018/book/index_2018.pdf. Accessed June 6, 2018.

Philippine Statistics Authority. 2018. *Occupational Shortages and Surpluses: 2015–2016*. Manila: Philippine Statistics Authority.

Sicat, Gerardo. 2015. *Philippine Economic History Since the 1930s in Perspective*. June 17. http://www.fef.org.ph/gerardo-sicat/philippine-economic-history-since-the-1930s-in-perspective/. Accessed June 1, 2018.

van der Kroef, Justus M. 1958. The Role of Islam in Indonesian Nationalism and Politics. *The Western Political Quarterly* 11 (1): 33.

Villegas, Bernardo. 2013a. Preparing Knowledge Workers for ASEAN. *Business and Society Section*. Manila: Manila Bulletin, August 26.

———. 2013b. Yahoo News. *ASEAN Connectivity – Manila Bulletin*, May 10. https://ph.news.yahoo.com/asean-connectivity-181720037.html. Accessed June 10, 2018.

———. 2016a. Catching Up with the ASEAN Agriculture Part II. *Manila Bulletin*, August 26. http://2016.mb.com.ph/2016/08/21/catching-up-in-asean-agriculture-part-ii/. Accessed June 12, 2018.

———. 2016b. Catching up in ASEAN Agriculture (Part I). *Manila Bulletin*, August 14. http://2016.mb.com.ph/2016/08/14/catching-up-in-asean-agriculture-part-i/. Accessed June 8, 2018.

———. 2017a. *Amending Economic Provisions of Constitution (Part I)*. April 9. https://business.mb.com.ph/2017/04/09/amending-economic-provisions-of-constitution-part-i/. Accessed June 12, 2018.

———. 2017b. Attracting Regional Headquarters of MNCs. *Manila Bulletin*, April. https://news.mb.com.ph/2017/04/27/attracting-regional-headquarters-of-mncs/. Accessed June 10, 2018.

———. 2017c. *Bright Prospects for Hotel Industry*. August 28. https://business.mb.com.ph/2017/09/03/bright-prospects-for-hotel-industry-part-2/. Accessed June 8, 2018.

———. 2017d. Not Too Late for Manufacturing (Part II). *Manila Bulletin*, August 20. https://business.mb.com.ph/2017/08/20/not-too-late-for-manufacturing-part-ii/. Accessed June 10, 2018.

———. 2017e. *The Largest Foreign Exchange Earner*. February 12. https://business.mb.com.ph/2017/02/12/the-largest-foreign-exchange-earner/. Accessed June 8, 2018.

von der Mehden, Fred R. 2014. Saudi Religious Influence in Indonesia. Middle East Institute. https://www.mei.edu/publications/saudi-religious-influence-indonesia. Accessed 25 June 2019.

Wa-Mbaleka, Safary, Claudia Blath, Janice Lloren, and Wenwan Duan. 2014. A Brief Ethnography on Philippine English. *International Forum*: 38–55. http://www.academia.edu/11536889/A_Brief_Ethnography_on_Philippine_English. Accessed June 10, 2018.

Ward, Karen. 2012. *The World in 2050: From the Top 30 to the Top 100*. HSBC Global Research.

Wood, Justin. 2014. *Redrawing the ASEAN Map: How Companies Are Crafting New Strategies in Southeast Asia*. The Economist Intelligence Unit. https://www.eiuperspectives.economist.com/sites/default/files/RedrawingASEAN.pdf. Accessed May 24, 2018.

World Bank. 2017. *Philippines Economic Update April 2017*. May 4. http://www.worldbank.org/en/news/feature/2017/05/04/philippines-economic-update-april-2017. Accessed June 8, 2018.

World Travel and Tourism Council. 2017. *Travel & Tourism Economic Impact 2017 Indonesia*. London: WTTC.

CHAPTER 3

The Vietnamese Economy at the Crossroads

Thu Trang Vuong, Vilém Semerák, and Quan Hoang Vuong

Introduction

Vietnam is a typical transition economy in its later stages: a rather weak currency, an economy flooded with foreign investment, and 'equitization' as a daily buzzword. Ever since the *Đổi Mới* reforms of 1986, the country has been changing drastically. In roughly 25 years, Vietnam has sextupled its GDP from over USD 36 billion in 1993 to more than USD 220 billion in 2017. Poverty reduction has succeeded with only 5.8% of the population remaining under the poverty line (Vuong and Pham 2009) as opposed

T. T. Vuong (✉)
European Campus of Dijon, Sciences Po, Paris, France
e-mail: thutrang.vuong@sciencespo.fr

V. Semerák
Institute of Economic Studies of Charles University, Prague, Czech Republic

Economics Institute of the Czech Academy of Sciences, Prague, Czech Republic

Q. H. Vuong
Phenikaa University, Hanoi, Vietnam

Université Libre de Bruxelles, Brussels, Belgium
e-mail: qvuong@ulb.ac.be; hoang.vuongquan@phenikaa-uni.edu

R. Macdonald (ed.), *Southeast Asia and the ASEAN Economic Community*, https://doi.org/10.1007/978-3-030-19722-3_3

to close to 60% in 1993. The political economy has transformed from a closed and centrally planned one to one of the most open economies in the world (World Bank 2017b). One must not, however, overlook the fact that Vietnam has a relatively low GDP per capita (USD 2545.9 as of 2018) compared to other ASEAN (Association of Southeast Asian Nations) countries such as Thailand (USD 6992.3) or Singapore (USD 61,766.8) (IMF 2018).

While the transition of Vietnam could be clearly filed under East Asian models whose eminent representative is the Chinese economy, the country still differs greatly from China. Not only is the Vietnamese economy much smaller than that of China, Vietnam has also absorbed more Western influence after decades of being a French protectorate followed by 20 years with American intervention in its southern part. The Vietnamese economy has turned out to be an equally curious mix of capitalism and socialism in its economic culture (Vuong and Pham 2009). As the market mechanism worked its way into the core of the economy of Vietnam, the government that supposedly insisted on a planned economy turned towards advocating for innovation and, most intriguingly, entrepreneurial spirit, which is quintessential to the capitalist economy itself (Vuong et al. 2016). Today, an ambivalent image of Vietnam prevails: a third-world authoritarian country as painted in human rights reports alongside the image of a country showing fast Human Development Index improvements, a rising Asian tiger with a large, attractive market, which faces various socio-economic conundrums from urbanization to public transport.

This chapter explores the transition economy of Vietnam, one of the few remaining countries under communist rule to this day, and the role of the particular variant of entrepreneurship of Vietnam in the process of transition (Vuong 2014).

Vietnam Today

Historical Background

Vietnam is a small country with a long history. Traces of human inhabitation in prehistoric Vietnam dated back to the Palaeolithic era. The first primitive government of Văn Lang was formed in Northern Vietnam at around 700 A.D. (Chapuis 1995). The country was colonized early on by China for about a thousand years, during which the Chinese led fierce policies of oppressive taxing, mainly on metal to curb weaponry production and further lower the possibility of revolts. Assimilation of aboriginal

Viet tribes through forced marriages with Chinese was also widespread. This period left a mark on Vietnamese culture and set the base for profound East Asian—principally Chinese—influence that would be reinforced over and over throughout the next periods of Vietnamese history. For this reason, despite being in the Southeast Asian geopolitical region, Vietnam is much closer to the East Asian sphere of influence in customs, culture, and religion (Joyaux 1970). This is highly relevant to any analysis of Vietnamese socio-cultural, economic, and political organization, which bears striking resemblances to that of the Chinese model from the feudal era to today's philosophy of politics and polity.

The year 938 A.D. officially marked Vietnamese independence from Chinese colonial rulers. As Vietnamese feudality evolved, it could be noticed that one of the most important consequences of Chinese influence on Vietnam was religion. In all five continental Southeast Asian countries, Buddhism is the most widely practiced religion. However, while the populations of Thailand, Myanmar, Cambodia, and Laos practised variants of Theravada Buddhism, it was Mahayana Buddhism that had been introduced from China into Vietnam (Thual 2002). Principles of Mahayana Buddhism, rituals, religious structures (pagoda), and holidays were mixed with indigenous faiths, such as the worship of local gods or of ancestors, and integrated into traditional customs. In the same manner, Confucianism was also imported into Vietnam and became an integral part of the Vietnamese mentality and way of life (Vuong and Vuong 2018). Among the three major religions of Vietnam (Confucianism, Buddhism, and Taoism), Confucianism dominates social culture (Vuong et al. 2018) and served as the basis for morality and social behaviour, the educational system, the mechanism of selection of imperial officials, and the power dynamics in most social and political relations, the most important one being the divine entitlement of the king to absolute obedience from his subjects. Economically speaking, the effect of Confucian principles results in a sort of mistrust towards merchants and commercial activities (Vuong and Tran 2009) that is more prevalent where centres of feudal power had been in the past, namely, Northern and Central Vietnam.

Before the nineteenth century, the geopolitics of Vietnam was very much linked to China. Feudal Vietnam not only belonged directly to the Chinese sphere of influence but imported the primary pillars of its social structure—namely, the Confucian religion and philosophy and the method of selection of imperial officials—from China as well (Vuong 2011). This created a certain sense of subordination, even of reverence at times, especially in the ruling power that had often resorted to asking for help from Chinese forces to suppress popular revolts at the risk of China taking the opportunity to manipulate and dominate Vietnam (Joyaux 1970). In fact, the feudal era in Vietnam was marked with resistance against Chinese invasions, which made China the most constant threat to Vietnamese sovereignty and almost the 'ultimate enemy' of the Vietnamese people in the Vietnamese mentality. This hostility clashed with the aforementioned sense of subordination, often taking shape as conflicts between the pro-China-governing powers and the patriots, with popular anti-China sentiments in the populace (Tran 1920).

Vietnam first came into contact with the West through the arrival of Catholic priests in the sixteenth century. It was in attempts of evangelization that one of these missionaries developed a system of Latin transcription of the Vietnamese language. As European powers began their second global conquest in the nineteenth century, Vietnam officially became a French protectorate from 1884 (Brocheux and Hémery 2001; Tran 1920). Under the French administration, the use of Latin characters for writing rose into prominence and later became the official written language of Vietnam (*Quốc ngữ*). This set Vietnam apart both from other continental Southeast Asian countries and from East Asian countries and gave Vietnamese people an edge in both the study of the English language and computer programming languages later on.

As the Second World War broke out, the people of Vietnam found themselves under three forces of oppression: the French administration, the puppet feudal government, and the Japanese occupiers. The exploitation of the people pushed unrest in the mass in addition to the already-budding resistance among intellectual and climaxed with the famine of 1945 (Gunn 2011) that incited spontaneous countrywide revolts against occupying Japanese forces. It was at this conjuncture that Vietnamese patriots—pre-eminently Hồ Chí Minh, who had taken great inspiration from the French Communist Party and the Russian Bolsheviks during his time abroad—latched onto communism as the solution, the road to liberation. After overthrowing Japanese occupiers, a provisory, communist-oriented government was established with Hồ Chí Minh as the President. The Vietnamese people considered themselves to have regained their own country and declared independence in 1945.

The French, on the other hand, insisted on their sovereignty over Vietnam and returned to reclaim their protectorate after the end of the World War (Valette 1993). This in turn led to the First Indochina War, a resistance war led by the communist Việt Minh on the Vietnamese side. The Geneva Accords of 1954 split the country in half at the 17th latitude (Randle 1970) and a pro-American, anti-communist government, the Republic of Vietnam, was installed in the South. The People's Democratic Republic of Vietnam in the North, governed by the Communist Party, led a war against the South; Vietnam became a physical front of the Cold War, with the North supported by the Soviet Union (USSR) and the People's Republic of China (PRC) and the South by the US and to a lesser extent the British. With the victory of the North, Vietnam officially became a communist country and remains such to this day. It was arguably the wars themselves rather than the victory that solidified the power of the Communist Party in the country as well as the place of communist rhetoric in the Vietnamese mentality. Communists were seen as *the* emancipators of the nation from colonial forces and fascist occupiers. The communists themselves were conscious of their historical role and succeeded in making use of their position to impose the Marxist-Leninist ideology on the country.

Economically, this translated to a socialist economy modelled after the central planning methods of the USSR and the PRC (Vuong 2014). This set Vietnam apart from former Eastern bloc countries, upon which communism had been forcefully imposed by an external force. In Vietnam, the imposition was done by a force that was first regarded as emancipatory (much like how the Bolshevik was seen by farmers after the Russian Revolution of 1917) and that had, through war, convinced generations that the Communist Party and their way of governing was the only way to fend off external threats. Evidently, the biggest difference in results is that Vietnam remains a single-party, communist country to this day. This leads us to consider the second aspect that set Vietnam apart from European former communist countries: in Eastern Europe, the transition was initiated after lifting the Iron Curtain and the fall of communist rule. In the case of Vietnam, despite the political regime, the economy is no longer one of central planning but a market economy in transition, open to foreign trade, and only named *socialist-oriented market economy* for ideological reasons.

Economic Overview

The Vietnamese economy appears to be growing healthily. Its GDP, which amounts to over VND 5000 trillion (approximately USD 219.4 billion) in 2017, has been on a generally upward trend with some fluctuations

(GSO 2017). According to the country's General Statistics Office, 2017 was a year of spectacular growth with a GDP increase of 6.81% over the year. Compared to GDP growth in other countries in the region, Vietnam ranked in the upper middle, after Cambodia, Philippines, and Lao PDR (ADB 2017). For 2018, the government even anticipated a better economic expansion rate, estimated at 7.1%.

With a population of nearly 96 million, and a per capita GDP estimated at USD 2550 by the end of 2018, Vietnam offers a sizeable market that promises to keep getting more attractive, not only for its purchasing power but also by its labour force. In fact, Vietnam was one of the countries with the highest speed of productivity improvement in the ASEAN region. In 2017, its labour productivity amounted to over USD 4000 *per capita*, and the average yearly increase in productivity was 4.7% during the period of 2011–2017. However, this is mitigated by the fact that Vietnamese productivity in level remained relatively lower, compared to many ASEAN countries, and the gap has kept widening (GSO 2017).

Economic growth has led to improvements in infrastructure and living standards. Over 99% of the population has access to electricity (2014) as opposed to 73% in 1990, higher than world average as well as neighbouring countries such as Lao PDR (78.1%), Cambodia (56.1%), or Indonesia (97%) (World Bank 2017b).

On the other hand, it should be noted that Vietnam is not an exception to the global trend of inequality in BRICS and emerging economies. The poorest 20% population received only 7.1% of national income; Vietnam's GINI index had been steadily rising, from 0.420 in 2002 to 0.436 in 2015 (GSO 2017). Malnutrition remained a problem that affected nearly one out of four children under five years of age.

The shift in composition of sector contribution into GDP was also a matter of consideration. True to the *Industrialization—Modernization* slogan that remained a stark principle in Vietnamese economic policies, industry and service together made up over 75% of the country's total GDP in 2016. Both sectors have been expanding in volume, growing about 5–8% every year since 2005. Their share in total GDP has been growing as well, although this has seemingly slowed down in the recent years, with yearly increases under 0.5 percentage point in the last decade (GSO 2018). The current composition of sector contribution into total GDP almost seemed to have frozen in place (Fig. 3.1). This puts into question the claims that the Vietnamese economy is still transitioning from purely agricultural to being more industry and service oriented. These sectors might have been

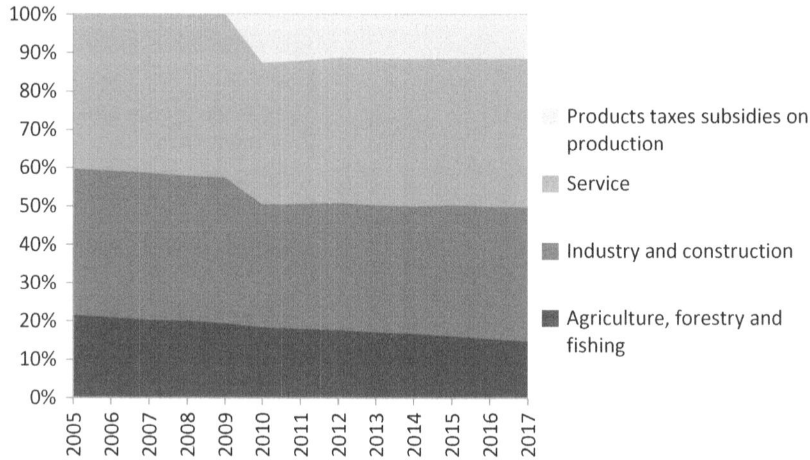

Fig. 3.1 GDP at constant 2010 prices by economic sector: 2005–2017 (%). Data source: GSO 2018

prioritized in economic policy-making and were developing as a result of that, but recent progress seems rather slow compared to the robust transformation envisioned by government officials (Fig. 3.2).

It should be noted that FDI has been concentrated mainly in manufacturing and real estate activities (GSO 2018; see Appendix, Figs. 3.15 and 3.16 for details). The manufacturing sector in Vietnam, as seen above, mainly consists of the textile/garment industry and the electronics parts industry, which relies heavily on imports of primary materials and generates modest added value. Real estate on the other hand generated little to no added value. In other words, out of the two main target sectors of FDI, one was export based and still low in added value, while the other did not generate added value at all.

In the private sector, over 126,000 new businesses were registered with a total capital of nearly VND 1300 trillion (approximately USD 58 billion) in 2017. In trade, one can observe a general trend to a trade deficit in Vietnam; additionally, the total volume of imports usually tops exports by around USD 1–7 billion, although this gap could be up to USD 18 billion (GSO). In addition, given the weight of heavy and mining industries as well as the significance of tourism to the Vietnamese economy, environmental protection understandably held a permanent place in government agenda and plans; however, only 2.5% of marine

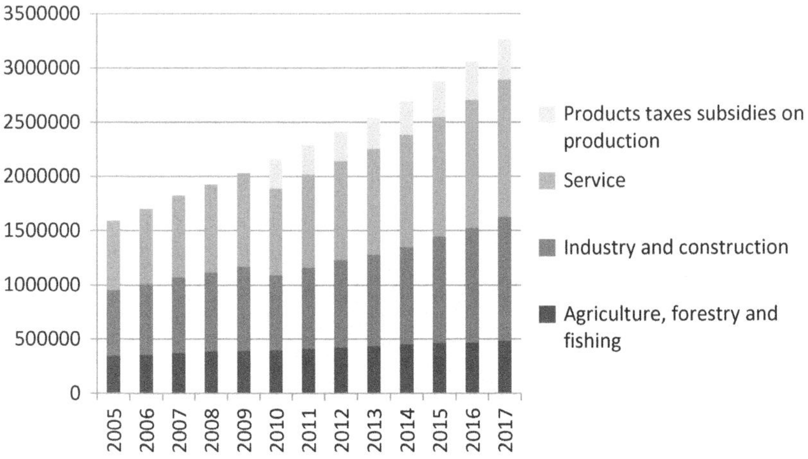

Fig. 3.2 GDP at constant 2010 prices by economic sector: 2005–2017 (VND billion). Data source: GSO 2018

and terrestrial areas was nationally protected, very low compared to most other countries in the region (over 20% in Cambodia, 12.5% in Thailand, and 6% in Indonesia).

On the other hand, a considerable number of sectors are partly, if not entirely, under state control, namely, energy (including fuel, petrol, and electricity), transportation infrastructure (airlines, railways, etc.), and banking. The state controls 100% of authorized capital of Electricity of Vietnam (EVN) and Petrovietnam (PVN), the two largest corporations in the energy industry by total assets (VND 770 trillion and VND 692 trillion, respectively, as of 2016). In transportation, 86% of authorized capital of Vietnam Airlines was state owned (see Appendix, Table 3.4); Vietnam Railways, on the other hand, was 100% owned by the state (Decree 11/2018/NĐ-CP). In the banking sector, aside from the two state-owned banks (Vietnam Bank for Social Policies and Vietnam Development Bank), the state also owned over 50% shares in many of the largest domestic commercial banks, including Vietinbank (64% state owned), BIDV (95% state owned), Agribank (100% state owned), Vietcombank (77% state owned), and so on (according to reports from the State Bank of Vietnam). Out of those, BIDV and Vietinbank were the largest banks of Vietnam by total assets, with BIDV totalling over VND 1202 trillion in assets as of December 2017 and Vietinbank VND 1095 trillion as of December 2017 (Vietinbank 2018).

Many of these state-owned enterprises have been undergoing the process of equitization under governmental directives. State-owned enterprises were tiered by percentage of capital owned by the state; equitization methods varied from issuing stocks to redirecting capital to State Capital Investment Corporation (SCIC), a capital management firm currently controlling a large amount of state capital in equitized enterprises (Decision 58/2016/QĐ-TTg). Decree 09/NQ-CP issued in 2018 stipulated the elaboration of a governmental committee for control of state capital in equitized enterprises, including SCIC (see Appendix, Table 3.4, for the full list of enterprises under the committee's control), to strengthen state control on all enterprises partly or entirely owned by the state. Some regarded this committee as being similar to SCIC to the point of redundancy (Pham 2019), while others insisted on its higher extent of control (Thành Đạt 2018). It should be noted that there seemed to be a contradiction in the political discourse regarding state-owned enterprises and equitization: on one hand, there was a concrete plan for reducing state capital in equitizing enterprises (Decision 1232/QĐ-TTg); on the other, with the creation of the aforementioned committee, it seemed that the state was also attempting to tighten its grip on the same equitizing/equitized enterprises.

Political Regime and Culture

The Government of Vietnam

Political regimes and politics have a profound influence on the national economy (DeRouen 1995, Farber et al. 2006). In socialist countries, the implementation of central planning mechanisms was imposed on the economy for ideological reasons, at least initially; government influence is then even more important. Vietnam has a socialist regime, so it is to be expected that the political system has a strong presence in, and a profound impact on, the transition process.

Currently, having a grip on political power is the Communist Party of Vietnam—commonly referred to as *the* Party, as it is the only political party that exists and legitimately resides in Vietnam. The Party was formerly the Labour Party of Vietnam, a direct descendant of the Communist Party of Indochina (Vietnam inherited the core of this party, being the main protagonist in the struggle for independence in Indochina during the First Indochina War).

Political discourse and official statistics both suggest that economic growth had been observed since the August Revolution of 1945 and especially towards the end of the First Indochina War (1945–1954), with a hiatus over 1988–1989. Cereal and other harvests amounted to 2.95 million tonnes, up 13.7% compared to 1946 (Nguyễn 2005). Industrial production in the years 1950–1954 was reportedly successful in both mining and metallurgy (20,000 tonnes of coke coal, 0.8 tonnes of antimony in 1946–1950, 19.5 tonnes of tin, 43.0 tonnes of lead in 1952–1953) and manufacturing (169.3 metres of cloth, 31,700 tonnes of paper). After the peace of Geneva in 1954, the North was governed by the Communist Party. During the Second Indochina War waged against the pro-America regime of South Vietnam, the economy of the Democratic Republic of Vietnam operated under socialist principles. By 1965, 88.8% farmer households took part in cooperatives. Agricultural product volume increased 4.1% per year on average (1961–1965). Industry wise, over 1.132 state-owned industrial factories had been constructed. The five-year plan of 1961–1965, implemented in the North only, was reported as a success. From 1965 to 1975, despite being in the midst of warfare, agricultural production did not fall, with 5,468,800 tonnes of harvest recorded in 1974. Total industrial and artisan production in the same year was reported as exceeding plans by 4%. The public sector produced 88.4% of total GDP (Government Portal 2006).

After the fall of Saigon and the unification of Vietnam in 1975, the Fourth National Congress of Vietnam took place and issued a number of important decisions, which include (a) the central planning mechanisms already in place in the North were to be imposed upon the South and (b) the first nationwide five-year plan (1976–1980) of unified Vietnam was to be carried out (Vuong et al. 2011). Under the command economy, commonly referred to as *Bao cấp* (literal translation: *complete subsidies*) in Vietnam, the national economy manifested the characteristics of a typical socialist economy: rigid central planning, lack of foreign trade activities and shortage of goods, social category-based rations managed through the use of stamps for most commodities and corruption on many levels, and so on (Đặng 2008). In times of peace, the shortcomings of central planning started to be revealed. The economy was stagnating: in the 1975–1985 period, the GDP only increased 4.6% and income 3.7% a year on average, while the population was growing at an annual pace of 2.3% on average (Government Portal 2006). Faced with constant shortages and harsh living conditions, managers at local cooperatives and factories began to look for ways to generate more earnings. Mechanisms typical of the free market began to emerge underground, namely clandestine contracts in rural factories, the formation of provincial *imex* (import-export) companies, smuggling of second-hand foreign goods from sailors, and so on. According to documentation by Đặng (2008), cooperative managers sought out other cooperatives and made secret deals, producing extra output that they called *second plan* (the implication being that the production quota from the centrally devised five-year plans was the *first plan*); others even produced for the free ('black') market, calling it a *third plan*. These activities became an *everybody knows, nobody tells* phenomenon and multiplied across the country. They were so widespread that eventually the Central acknowledged the shortfalls of central planning and started allowing the economy more freedom, thereby installing *de facto* market mechanisms even before the 1986 reforms—*Đổi Mới*—took place (Vuong et al. 2011). Vuong et al. (2011) also argued that precursors of entrepreneurial attributes, namely, the ability to create and transmute value, were already present even under central planning and were determinant factors in the success of the reforms.

The fact that Vietnam had never had the definite political rupture experienced in most Eastern bloc countries resulted in a transition that could be characterized as quite rogue in nature. As unlawful trading with natural market mechanisms became widespread, the government finally implemented top-down policies in *Đổi Mới*, starting in late 1986 promulgated at the Sixth National Congress of the Communist Party of Vietnam (CPV). Though there was a shift to a more market-oriented economy, the CPV still needed to perpetuate the initial Marxist-Leninist ideologies to maintain their authority and to stay in power. For this reason, they were reticent in the face of transition policies and reforms, not only out of concerns over economic destabilization but also because they could not outright declare a transition without contradicting the ideology that they had imposed on the country for decades. One of the most telling examples of this was that the government had baptized the Vietnamese economy a 'socialist-oriented market economy'. It should be noted that the notion of *transition* is never mentioned in Vietnamese media or political agendas without *the economy*, making phrases such as 'transition economy' or 'economic transition' a single word, *de facto*. (In Vietnamese, 'transition' has a very close meaning to 'evolution', a political taboo.) Instead, to this day, the government promotes slogans such as 'modernization and industrialization in order to advance to socialism' (so much so that the terms had been hollowed of the meaning).

In short, Vietnam lacked political drive for transition; the 1986 reforms took place for practical reasons. The government was not only very gradualist in its approach to economic reforms but also had to be careful in the presentation of their measures so as not to admit the failure of central planning. For this reason, the residual of central planning era behaviours—namely rent-seeking behaviours and disregard for standardized procedures along with preference for unofficial shortcuts—remains a prominent, accepted part of the Vietnamese economy, especially in the public sector.

The Economic Culture of Vietnam: Confucian and Communist Legacies

Not only was the political regime unfavourable for real transition, but also there are cultural elements that hinder the development of a free-market economy. The most important aspect of Vietnamese culture in regard to this hindrance is the Confucian system of values. In fact, Confucianism has long been considered to be the pillar of the Vietnamese society (Vuong et al. 2018), as its philosophy and teachings served as a source of legitimacy for the imperial court as well as a base for many social institutions and mechanisms, including the selection of imperial officials. One could even make the remark that Confucianism is as fundamental to Vietnam (and China, to an extent) as Christianity has been to Europe. For this reason, it is not a surprise that Confucian principles can have profound economic implications.

Vuong and Tran (2009) had pointed out basic principles of the Confucian system of values: worship of designated superiors, conformity to the hierarchy, and mistrust towards merchants. If the Protestant faith was the source of the capitalist *ethos* which encouraged profit-seeking, Confucian traditions portrayed the business class as dishonest and potentially dangerous people. There was no prestige in successfully accumulating wealth, especially not through trading, as the Confucian social hierarchy placed merchants at the lowest of the four classes in society (scholars/intellectuals, farmers, workers, merchants). For this reason, being merchants were often seen as a last resort taken out of necessity, and if given the chance to ascend in society, merchants themselves would gladly take up a different occupation. These pejorative connotations associated with the status of merchants were a part of the Vietnamese Confucian mindset and resounded well with the Marxist-Leninist criticism of capitalism. During the entire socialism construction era, these elements had been encouraged by the communist government with capitalism-bashing propaganda and muted any development of true entrepreneurship spirit.

Additionally, Confucianism maintained five types of unequal relationships, based not only on social status but also on familial hierarchy and gender (Vuong and Tran 2009), as a pillar of its teachings, which also served to reinforce the legitimacy of the authority of feudal rulers. Indeed, unequal relationships were necessary for superiors to impose obedience on those they wanted to put under subordination. This Confucian element has been absorbed into Vietnamese culture and induces a mentality that is not only tolerant but also, at times, in favour of state paternalism. In fact, state intervention, such as price regulation for certain commodities (especially those concerning children, such as powdered milk for infants or grade-school supplies), is rarely contested. In the face of unfortunate events in which the bearers of the damage were groups traditionally regarded as more vulnerable and disadvantaged, such as farmers or customers, an intervention is even demanded as an effective—albeit short-term, one may argue—tool for economic stability and security. This is often fuelled by media coverage with an emphasis on the humane aspect of the problem, to further call for intervention. The brief crises of price drops due to excess production followed by government-initiated rescue campaigns in 2017 (Bảo Phương 2017; Công Quang 2017), in which the government not only encouraged people to buy off the excess commodities but resorted to buying them itself with taxpayer money, as well as numerous scandals of breach of food hygiene safety standards that often led customers to ask for more protection, illustrate the case.

It should be noted that this Confucian legacy resonated with the attempt at total control over all economic activities by the communist regime during the central planning era. One need only consider the fact that, to this day, the government of Vietnam still devises five-year plans despite the fact that central planning has been recognized as not feasible and replaced with market mechanisms. This is not merely a ceremonial act, either; in fact, the planning approach with arbitrary quota is still often taken in economic policy-making. For example, in 2006, the government published a five-year plan for private small and medium enterprise (SME) sector development with very specific quantified goals such as to increase the number of private SMEs to 320,000 and maintain a yearly rate of 22% increase in the number of SMEs (Decision No. 236/2006/QD-TTg). There is a certain central planning culture embedded in Vietnamese economic decision-making, reminiscent of the command economy era before *Đổi Mới*, and it is not contested by the state paternalism mentality that is the legacy of traditional Confucian values.

In light of this, the cultural element added inertia to an economy that was already held back by its authoritarian regime. A market economy cannot function properly without a business class consisting of producers who seek to maximize their profits. Yet, this class was not only politically bashed during the pre-*Đổi Mới* period but has also been shunned in the Vietnamese mentality. Entrepreneurs were few and far between, inexperienced from being under central planning and discouraged by culture from doing business. This lack of a strong business class made the market economy of Vietnam function in a rather forced manner, at least in the beginning.

Global Integration and Transformation of Economic Behaviour

Trade Liberalization and Consumer Behaviour

Prior to the reforms of 1986, Vietnam had been relatively autarkic: trade was highly restricted and limited only to countries of the socialist bloc; additionally, the US had also placed an embargo on Vietnam at the fall of Saigon in 1975. The command economy showed its shortfalls one after the other, as the state budget saw deficits while foreign aid from communist countries declined, especially in the last two years of the 1970s; targets in the first five-year plan set by the Fourth Congress were not at all met (Vuong et al. 2011). The economy stagnated, and shortages were a common nationwide occurrence. Most of the population did not have many personal belongings—the simplest commodities such as clothes or kitchen utensils were scarce and strictly rationed—or money in cash—as goods were exchanged for stamps. For this reason, the average Vietnamese consumer under central planning was very keen on saving up and reserving in anticipation of a future shortage. They also made use of relationships and connections—a legacy of the Confucian mentality (Vuong and Tran 2009)—where possible, forming a sort of so-called *shadow economy* and, later on, black markets, that would bruise the efficiency of the already poorly performing economy.

After price liberalization and a series of socio-economic reforms as mentioned above, the country started to open up to economic integration (Vuong et al. 2011). Over the course of several decades, Vietnam has signed over a hundred bilateral agreements, the major ones being the agreement with European Union (EU) in 1992 and with the US in 2000, and joined regional associations as well, such as ASEAN in 1995. Bilateral deals seemed to increase trade flows dramatically, promoting Vietnamese exports especially (Vuong 2014). In 2007, Vietnam gained accession to the WTO after a long process of negotiations that started in 1995 and over 20 bilateral trade agreements concluded with member states. This could be considered a milestone of trade liberalization in Vietnam, as the agreements with WTO included deeper institutional reforms and fewer regulations in terms of foreign trade. The years following the accession witnessed a boost in Vietnam's economic performance (Vo and Nguyen 2009). Increase of welfare was expected (Nguyen and Tran 2006) and did happen, however, with an unequal distribution that led to more disparity between higher and lower income, as well as between urban and rural households (Pham et al. 2008; Fosse and Raimondos-Møller 2012; Le 2014).

Most previous studies suggest that middle- to high-income households, especially in the city, experienced a more significant improvement of welfare. From the consumer's point of view, this may be explained by the fact that economic integration had increased both variation and quantity of products, enabling the customer to not only choose the type of product but also to obtain the number of products to their liking. This was a very different situation from the highly regulated distribution mechanism under the command economy, where one might not be able to obtain certain commodities even if one had cash. Further, the buying capacity of the Vietnamese consumer had grown along with the effects of the reforms. Non-state small and medium enterprises (SMEs) not only increased in number but also maintained high efficiency (Le and Harvie 2010), creating jobs and raising household income. In addition, Vietnamese labour had more freedom to work abroad, which increased remittance flows; these international remittances were in turn often beneficial to the improvement of household spending capacity (Pfau and Giang 2009).

Consumer behaviour morphed along with these transformations. Cultural sensitivity and ethnocentrism still played a role in determining the role of imported product consumption (Nguyen et al. 2008), and Vietnamese customers retained their shopping habits at traditional markets (Maruyama and Le 2007). However, there was a shift to hedonistic consumerism in the Vietnamese population, especially among the younger generations, which was in stark contrast with the previous behaviour in the shortage economy under central planning. There was also a shift in the share of income to more luxurious goods. Middle- to high-income Vietnamese consumers began to engage in status consumption: to spend on goods that would benefit their social image and status (Drury 2011; Nguyen and Tambyah 2011). Luxury consumption similar to that of China started to be observed in the Vietnamese economy, which was also linked with status and face-saving (Le Monkhouse et al. 2012).

While this appeared to be quite a positive sign of the Vietnamese population creating value and accumulating wealth, one should be careful not to take the lavish spending at face value. On the one hand, status and luxury consumption only occurred within a certain group of the population, while the rest, especially in rural areas, still faced various degrees of economic difficulty, even down to poverty (Figuié and Moustier 2009). On the other hand, a great portion of consumers with hedonistic behaviour belonged to the middle-income category. Some of them lacked the buying capacity to engage in such status spending, but face-saving turned out to be enough of a motivation for them to borrow to spend. This led to the problem of personal debts, which has not been addressed enough in the literature on Vietnamese consumer behaviour.

The Rise of the Internet and Its Economic Implications

The Internet changed the world, from the everyday life of each individual to the behaviour of political regimes and economic markets. Kalathil and Boas (2003) studied authoritarian regimes across the globe to show that information technologies have the potential to promote at least some degree of democratization in Vietnam (Nguyen and Vuong 2016). In addition, the Internet serves as a platform for business and the digital marketplace is expected to strengthen the invisible hand—that is, to improve the efficiency of market mechanisms (Brownrigg 1991; Bakos 1998) and encourage foreign trade at the level of firms (Nguyen and Barrett 2006).

Fifteen years after *Đổi Mới*, in 2000, Vietnam connected with the World Wide Web. At the time, Internet users understandably only made up a minuscule 0.3% of the Vietnamese population. The diffusion of the Internet started off rather slowly due to cost and infrastructure (Lam et al. 2004). Boymal et al. (2007) suggested that the reason for the low rates of Internet subscriptions in Vietnam at the time was due to the Central's innovation policy being more ideologically and politically driven rather than inspired by realistic socio-economic needs. Yet, by 2013, Vietnam already ranked among 20 countries with the most Internet users in the world (Ngo and Gim 2014). In 2016, Internet users made up 46.5% of the Vietnamese population (World Bank 2017a). In the end, the spread of the Internet applications into the daily life of Vietnamese people was impressively rapid, resulting in the birth and growth of the online marketplace among Vietnamese economic agents.

In fact, the Internet has largely modified the Vietnamese consumer behaviour. Numerous studies have shown that many businesses, especially goods and services providers, have taken up the online channel to expand their clientele (Ngo and Gim 2014; Nguyen et al. 2007; Ho and Chen 2014). Despite hesitation linked to the risks of indirect transactions, customers have proved to be quite willing to adopt online shopping, especially when they could form a bond of trust with providers through their experience of customer service and their perception of goods' quality. Customers have also developed methods specific to online shopping, such as group buying, a practice in which many customers gather together to place one common order so as to lower shipping fees (Ho and Chen 2014) and which is the most common when the goods were to be shipped from overseas (the business, in this case, usually provided this service as an intermediate agent). This showed that e-commerce was such an integral part of the Vietnamese economy that customers had formed specific behaviours around these types of economic activities.

Despite this, little attention has been given to the marketplace platforms of e-commerce in Vietnam. In fact, while the Internet-based commerce is often studied as a trading platform in itself, online is not as homogenous and takes place on different types of storefronts that vary in the manner in which online businesses operate in relation to shifting trends in customers' behaviours. These types of small business storefronts range from self-maintained e-commerce portals, in which the seller sets up an independent domain name and coordinate production and delivery on their own, to marketplace platforms along the line of Amazon and eBay where individuals can sell without having to coordinate shipping services. In the middle of this emerged a hybrid type of business storefront that was highly popular in Vietnam: the Facebook online store.

Indeed, in the last 10 years or so, social media sites have risen in popularity in Vietnam, Facebook being the most prominent. Although the primary use of the site was socialization, along the way, Facebook developed more and more features such as the ability for just about anyone to set up their own online shop and sell goods without the need of a physical showroom. Although Southeast Asia-based online marketplaces such as Lazada, Shopee, or even the exclusively Vietnamese EnBac were relatively popular among online shoppers, Facebook remains one of the leading platforms for small online businesses in Vietnam. This choice might have been made out of convenience or mimetic behaviour. Additionally, there could be a number of underlying rational reasons for economic agents to choose a platform that was primarily a social media to conduct business: networking opportunities, more individualized customer interactions, more freedom and control in concrete business operations (e.g. in shipping goods).

These Facebook-based businesses were often small-scale retail service providers; retailed commodities included but were not limited to foodstuff (raw ingredients, delicate gourmet, etc.), household equipment (kitchen apparels, furniture, etc.), clothing and accessories (from off-brands to high-end luxury items), and electronic gadgets. They were very reminiscent of the traditional wet markets or 'street economy' of Vietnam, as there was little focus on branding but much more on customer relations. The multiplication of small online businesses seemed to be a good sign that free-market mechanisms were becoming natural in the Vietnamese economy. However, one should rather assess these signs with care, as they were likely a response to the demands of consumers that were becoming more and more consumerist despite profound lifestyle differences between income groups in society.

The Economic Leaders of Transitional Vietnam

The Vietnamese Superclass

The superclass is not homogeneous, but its members exist across the globe and are fairly similar in at least one respect: the amount of wealth they possess, which naturally leads to the influence they can exert on governments (Rothkopf 2008). They are the oligarchs of Russia, the cronies of the Middle East, the plutocrats of America—basically the wealthiest people on planet earth. Although this economic elite is often contested and condemned, sometimes for very good reasons, it is undeniable that they are an important part of the economy. Whether or not their existence is intrinsic to free-market economies is up for debate, but at face value, every country has a so-called superclass. Vietnam is not an exception.

What is, then, the nature of this Vietnamese superclass? In the first section, it was shown how political-historical and cultural-religious elements hindered the formation of a strong class of business owners. In fact, when the economy first opened up to the world and started transitioning, the political elite was the only class that had the power to accumulate wealth. And in an increasingly capitalistic emerging economy, it was the wealthy who in turn have power. This seemingly closed circle consolidated the economic power of an interest group that initially sprung from political power. One could say that power dynamics in Vietnam was deeply marked by one-on-one, case-by-case relationships rather than relations between social groups. When privatization took place, it was often those who had previously been in power or had had close relations with those in power, who were selected for high positions in these enterprises—which was not unlike the *nomenklatura* method of personnel selection[1] for privatized companies in China. In this method of keeping control over large companies even after privatization, one could see how the Confucian legacy carried on: this manner of personnel appointment and promotion was very reminiscent of the recommendation-based mechanisms of officer selection in feudal times.

However, these people alone do not constitute the entirety of the Vietnamese economic elite today. As Vuong et al. (2011) has pointed out, precursors of entrepreneurial elements were already present in the society before reforms. As such, these elements continued to develop in the free market into particular cases of successful business actors who rose in economic power. Being few and far between, they did not constitute a class of business owners but existed more as outliers. Despite this, these few successful entrepreneurs still existed; they earned their place among the economic elite, alongside those who drew economic power from political power, purely through market mechanisms. They are the people we call the *plutocrats* of Vietnam—the self-made portion of the Vietnamese superclass. Although they did not originally derive wealth from political power, their accumulated wealth held economic weight and earned them political influence.

Individuals that constituted the Vietnamese superclass were often well known in the Vietnamese public, as many among them were heads of popular brands of commodities. Surprisingly, these ultra-wealthy individuals could be quite well liked, popularized by the media as successful business owners and women and looked up to as pioneers in modernizing the economy and making the country prosperous. For instance, Phạm Nhật

Vượng, Chairman of the Vingroup Corporation,[2] which was involved in a multitude of domains such as real estate, retail, healthcare, educations, and so on, was known as the wealthiest person in Vietnam by virtue of his USD 2.4 billion personal wealth. His wife and Vice Chairwoman, Phạm Thu Hương, also ranked among the top ten wealthiest persons in Vietnam. Remarkable figures in the Vietnamese superclass could be more or less well known to the public by their names, but their companies were often recognized by most Vietnamese, such as Trịnh Văn Quyết, Chairman of FLC Group JSC, primarily involved in financial investment and real estate; Mai Kiều Liên, Chairman and CEO of Vinamilk, the largest dairy company of Vietnam; Đoàn Nguyên Đức, Chairman of Hoàng Anh Gia Lai JSC and one of the most influential business owners in Southeast Asia as ranked by Wall Street Journal; and so on.

Some among this superclass are well known not only for their company brand but also for their diversification into more social-related sectors, namely healthcare and education. Phạm Nhật Vượng's Vingroup, with its private hospital Vinmec (established in 2012), and private school, Vinschool (established in 2013), was not the only example. Trương Gia Bình, co-founder, Chairman, and CEO of FPT, the largest information technology service provider of Vietnam, had also founded VINASA (Vietnam Software Association) and FPT University. A more controversial figure would be Thái Hương, Chairwoman of TH True Milk, a younger but quickly growing player in the dairy industry of Vietnam, who had opened TH School in 2016. Others hosted charitable public campaigns: Đặng Lê Nguyên Vũ, founder of Trung Nguyên Coffee, dubbed *Coffee King of Vietnam* and often evoked as a *zero-to-hero* role model, had initiated numerous events and public programmes with the aim of promoting entrepreneurship among the youth.

It was clear that the Vietnamese superclass has eminent social and political influence; the question that remains is how they utilize it. One would assume some sort of conflict to come into play between the entrepreneurs and the old money. The politically powerful rich could be adamant to defend the current political *status quo* as guarantors of their wealth. The plutocrats could either go against the political ruling class in favour of more economic freedom and more opportunity for doing business or seek political power and collude with the political-economic elite to secure their own business and prevent new competition. In reality, the relation between the purely economic plutocrats and the rich who gained from political status is ambiguous. There is a conversion between the two categories of superclass: the plutocrats are neither showing particular interest in acquiring a place in the political system nor actively making use of their economic weight to influence current rulers. They simply accepted the political *status quo* as they have themselves integrated into it. On the other hand, the politically powerful rich have been immersed in the open market economy for decades and have seen entrepreneurs rise to become part of the economic elite. This experience transformed them into orienting more towards business rather than politics but without severing the umbilical cord between themselves and the ruling power (as, in some cases, the important stockholders or managers of large privatized enterprises were literal children of high government officials). The Vietnamese superclass, rather than fracturing, entered a compromise in which both plutocrats and political wealthy shifted towards one another, creating a small group that had a strong presence both in the economy and in politics.

To put it simply, the lack of a socially defined business class consisting of the middle class or upper-middle class employers and the solidification of the two seemingly opposed groups of the political elite make it very likely that despite being small in number, the superclass will lead the economy onwards.

Aspirations for Prosperity: The Start-Up Fever

Entrepreneurship is a crucial aspect of the economy and even more so in the case of emerging economies. Post-socialist countries often struggled with strengthening the private sector after years of state monopoly; post-reforms Vietnam was not an exception, at least in the beginning. Nowadays, the casual observer would say that the market economy performs very well in Vietnam. As robust as the private sector is in Vietnam, it is also dominated by foreign actors. For example, commodities imported from Japan or Thailand are considered to be of relatively lower cost and higher quality. Domestic brands often need nationwide campaigns with national pride undertones and emotional appeal towards customers, with arguments such as one should support compatriots by buying *Made in Vietnam* products. This is in line with our previous assessments about the absence of a collective business identity in Vietnam.

Nevertheless, the said absence does not necessarily translate to the non-existence of Vietnamese entrepreneur communities. Quite the contrary: entrepreneurial endeavours have been surging in recent years. The image of successful business owners in their 30s, smiling in smart casual and earning six figures with just an app and a small core team composed of a handful of close-knit equally young colleagues, seduces Vietnamese millennials more than the plutocrats—who are often of the previous generation and active in primary or secondary sectors such as agriculture, real estate, food and commodity production, and so on. Perhaps it was the closeness that had struck a chord with Vietnamese youth: the plutocrats are, after all, of a different generation and appear to live in a different world by virtue of their wealth alone; on the other hand, millennial entrepreneurs give off a more *self-made man* vibe, triggering a sense of self-consciousness in the youth.

As such, success stories of young business owners in the West, those of the brains behind Facebook, Uber, and so on, were eventually followed by tales of new, successful Vietnamese entrepreneurs as well. Aside from the occasional outliers, they were usually middle class, ranging from the mid-20s to the late 30s in age, most often equipped with a university degree that might or might not be related to their entrepreneurial endeavours. There was a distinct focus on information technology, more specifically the use of the Internet, which could be explained by the low-fixed cost and accessible nature of web-app development, but perhaps also by the fact that their most recent inspirations were success stories of Internet-based services. The fruits of their attempts at the time of media coverage could be a functioning company with tax records or only at the stage of a successfully gathered pot of investment funds.

The idea of start-ups attracted not only fresh graduates and hopeful investors but also policy-makers. The government had, in fact, made numerous initiatives to promote entrepreneurship in Vietnam. The publicly funded National Entrepreneurship Program had taken place every year since 2003, but public attention skyrocketed in 2014 as VCCI (Vietnam Chamber of Commerce and Industry) took over and gave the programme, renamed Start-up Festival, a makeover. In 2017, the reality show 'Start-up Nation' (*Quốc gia Khởi nghiệp*) started being broadcasted on national television channel VTV1, which effectively turned entrepreneurship into an element of mainstream pop culture. Socio-cultural programmes aside, the government had promulgated legally binding directives, such as Prime Minister Decision 1665/QĐ-TTg (dated October 30, 2017), which provided a set of guidelines with the purpose of encouraging entrepreneurial spirit among students. However, the targets set by the decision were not only unrealistically ambitious but also rather groundless in terms of scientific basis—for example, one of the directives stipulated that every institution of higher education must have at least two student-initiated start-up projects.

The heightened wave of enterprising attempts could well be qualified as a start-up *fever*. It did not stem from entrepreneurial spirit, but rather an act of mimicking and following the trend. Many people set up businesses less in response to demands of innovation and more based on their own aspiration to what they perceive would be the life of an entrepreneur, based on the image largely constructed by recent media coverage. It was not a coincidence that the Vietnamese start-up fever did not begin with the rise to prominence of the likes of Facebook or Uber themselves, rather lined up with the Chinese start-up wave chronologically; mimetic behaviour did not stop at national borders. For this reason, the Vietnamese entrepreneurial community has witnessed catastrophic failures. One such example was the debt scandal of *The KAfe*, a popular chain of café-restaurant serving fusion cuisine in Hanoi. Founded by young businesswoman Đào Chi Anh in 2013, the start-up received much praise before it even started going into business, solely for the fact that the founder had succeeded in raising over VND 5.5 billion of capital from Cassia Investment Funds (Hồng Minh 2016). In 2016, *The KAfe* made headlines for long overdue debts of over VND 4 billion to food suppliers (A.N 2015) and started closing down stores across Hanoi. The tale of *The KAfe* ended with CEO Đào Chi Anh resigning and the Vietnamese start-up being acquired in 2017 by a company from Hong Kong (Minh Sơn 2017). This is only one out of many start-ups of the same fate, many of those not coming as far as *The KAfe* had before closing down.

More than a few Vietnamese young entrepreneurs aspired to make quick money, to have the status of founder and CEO, or simply to have a job without job-hunting, rather than aspiring to do business because they saw the demand and were willing to put efforts into innovation if need be. In this regard, they lacked true entrepreneurial spirit. This explains why a majority of businesses set up in Vietnam's start-up fever could not withstand rigorous market competition. And if even start-ups founded by people who truly wanted to do business suffered from the lack of real demand, then start-up projects forced into existence in higher education establishments as stipulated by Decision 1665/QĐ-TTg would very likely be doomed for failure from their conception.

Whether this was detrimental to the economy as a whole is a different question. It is true that start-up failures were costly, but at the same time, the start-up fever has excited both public opinion and market dynamics. Vuong et al. (2016) point out that entrepreneurial efforts, whether successful or fruitless, boosted creativity as perceived by the entrepreneurs themselves. The experience of failure itself could be educational, and perhaps the intensity of the start-up fever would reinforce and develop entrepreneurial characteristics on both an individual and a collective level. Whether or not the positive effects countered the cost of mass business failures is a question to be subjected to further empirical investigation and theorization.

Vietnamese Foreign Trade

Trade Overview

After *Đổi Mới*, numerous efforts of trade integration and the 1994 embargo lift of the Clinton administration, trade has been expanding vigorously, along with which the trade deficit also has grown. The gap between imports and exports has recently been reduced and exports have even been recorded to slightly top imports in 2012, as well as in preliminary reports for 2016. Even so, there is an undeniable trend to a trade deficit in Vietnam, which is traditionally regarded as being linked to a high volume of imports in machinery and intermediate goods contributing to industrial development (Fig. 3.3).

According to the Department of Vietnam Customs (2018), in April 2018, the main exports of Vietnam included primarily electrical machinery, components and parts; textile, garment, and footwear; agriculture, forestry, and fishery primary products; and iron and steel. Main imports also included electric machinery and accessories, followed by other industrial primary and intermediate goods such as metals, plastics, and chemicals. This aligns with the general trend in the past two decades of trade shifting from primary materials to intermediate and manufactured goods (see Appendix, Figs. 3.17–3.18, and Tables 3.5, 3.6, 3.7, and 3.8). It can be inferred that Vietnam's main export industries consisted of textile/garment and electronics, which both rely heavily on imports of raw materials and parts (Tran and Nørlund 2014). These are notably labour-intensive industries with modest added value despite their growing export volumes.

Given that industrialization is still considered an ongoing process in the transition economy of Vietnam, trade policies should accommodate these

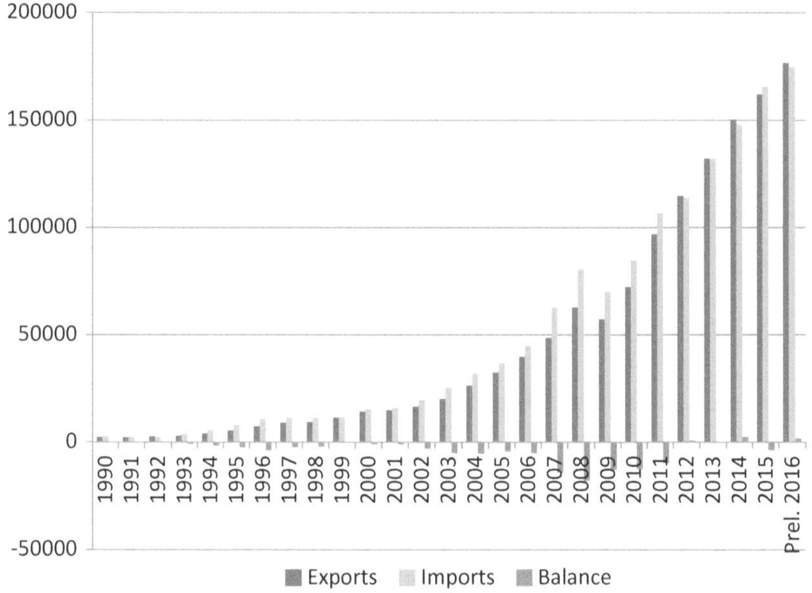

Fig. 3.3 Export, import, and trade balance (export minus import): 1990–2016 (USD million). Data source: GSO 2018

specific attributes of Vietnamese trade in a way that would favour industrial development. However, in matters of both trade and development of export-oriented industries, Vietnamese decision-making lacks overarching principles as a direction for strategies and plans to follow (Ohno 2009). Privatization of state-owned enterprises—termed *equitization* for ideological reasons in Vietnam—was done largely under the pressure of foreign donors, investors, trade partners, and international organizations (Tran and Nørlund 2014). The government has not defined its role in developing export industries, so while there are prioritized industries, protected industries cannot be pinpointed as easily.

Within the ASEAN Region

To give an overview of the weight of the Vietnamese economy in the region, Table 3.1 presents ASEAN countries with several key indicators (data as of May 2018).

Table 3.1 Key indicators on ASEAN countries: 2017

	GDP (USD bln)	*Population (mln)*	*Area (sq. km)*	*Exports (USD bln)*	*Imports (USD bln)*	*Fixed investment (% of GDP)*
Brunei	11.4	0.4	5770	5.6	4.3	36.1
Cambodia	20	15.9	181,040	12.3	13.1	22
Indonesia	3250	26.3	1,811,569	168.9	150.1	32
Laos	15.8	7.1	236,800	5.5	6.7	36
Malaysia	296.6	31.6	330,800	200.7	180.8	26.3
Myanmar	63.2	53.4	676,590	11	17.7	37.9
Philippines	304.9	103.3	300,000	85.3	112.6	25.2
Singapore	297	5.6	719	511.2	434.3	23.5
Thailand	407	68.9	513,120	280.5	220.5	24.2
Vietnam	205.3	94.7	330,967	192.2	186.9	24.8

Data source: CIA World Factbook

Joining ASEAN was a milestone in the economic integration process for Vietnam. However, the weight of ASEAN countries in trade is not as significant as one would have thought. In fact, exports and imports to ASEAN played a relatively unimpressive part in the past. The ASEAN region accounted for a very low share of trade volume for Vietnam, only accounting for 11.2% of imports and 14.3% of exports in 2016, especially when compared to other countries, notably Myanmar and Thailand (Figs. 3.4 and 3.5).

Trading with ASEAN slowed down in favour of accelerating trade with other countries and regions in the world, namely the US, EU and China. In particular, exports to the US and imports from China dramatically increased (Figs. 3.6 and 3.7).

It is safe to say that despite the very positive government reports on regional economic integration, in reality, ASEAN does not hold a lot of weight in the economy of Vietnam, not even in Vietnamese foreign trade. Vietnam's greatest trading partner remains China, and Vietnamese aspirations are mostly turned westward. The general mentality is to aim for European and American standards, as the ultimate destination for exports. Imports of consumer goods from European countries, the US, and Japan are regarded by most Vietnamese as being of the highest quality; on the other hand, goods from ASEAN countries do not benefit from such kinds of 'default' positive attitudes.

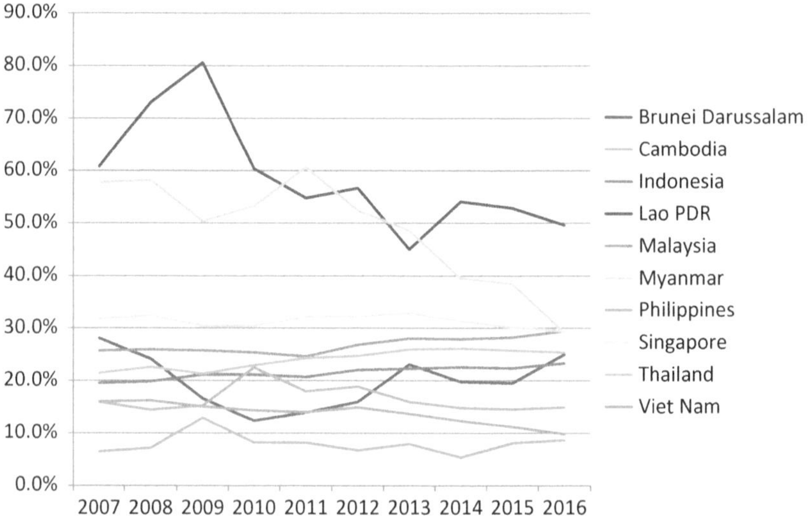

Fig. 3.4 The share of volume of exports of goods to ASEAN by countries from 2007 to 2016. Data source: ADB Database 2018, accessed March 30, 2018

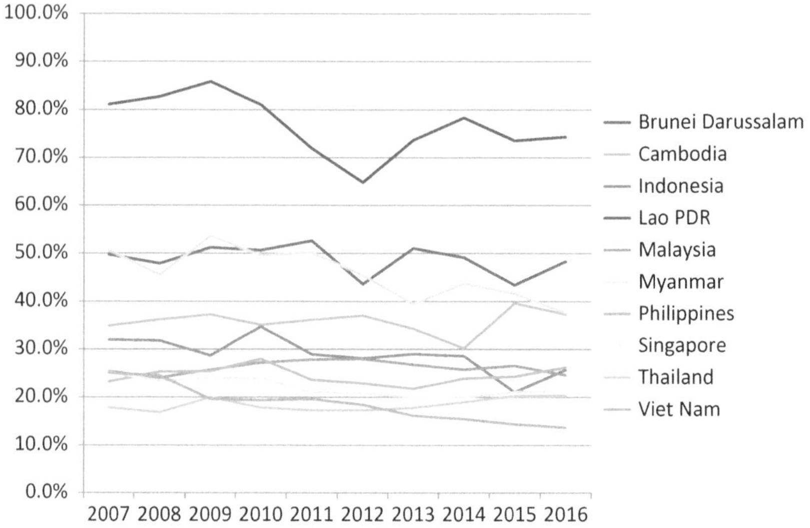

Fig. 3.5 The share of volume of imports of goods from ASEAN by countries from 2007 to 2016. Data source: ADB Database 2018, accessed March 30, 2018

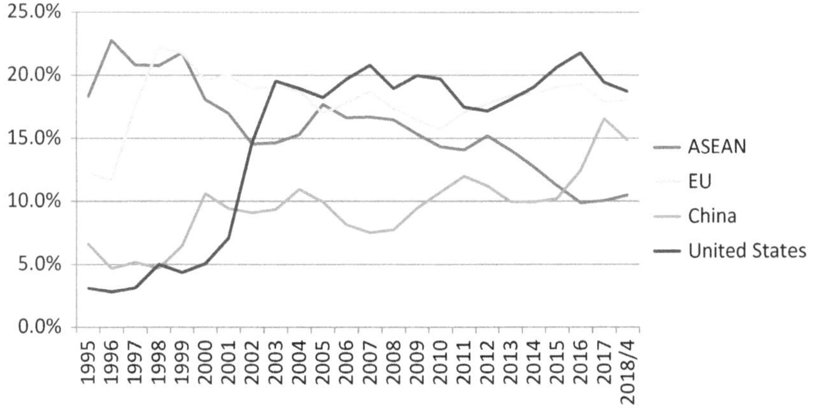

Fig. 3.6 Shares of the total volume of export of goods from Vietnam by countries and regions (USD billion): 1995–April 2018. Data source: GSO 2018; General Department of Vietnam Customs 2018

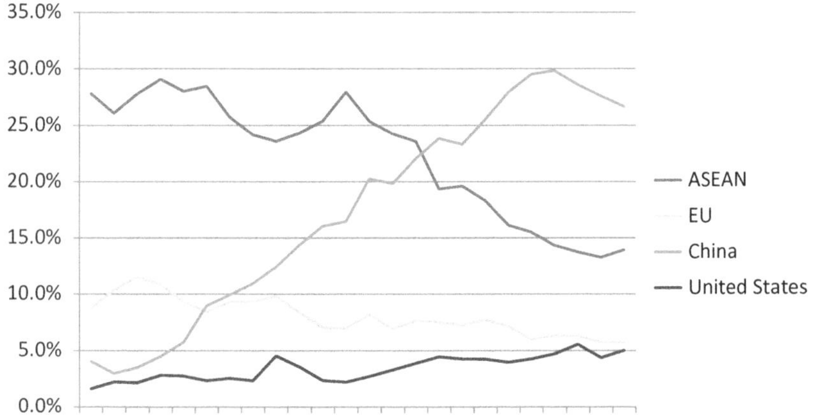

Fig. 3.7 Shares of the total volume of import of goods into Vietnam by countries and regions (USD billion): 1995–April 2018. Data source: GSO 2018; General Department of Vietnam Customs 2018

Legislation at the ASEAN level was not especially ample, and unlike the European Union, ASEAN was much looser in terms of enforcing their directive on member countries, as one of the founding principles of the association was non-interference and action-taking at the national level rather than directed by a core region-wide bureaucracy, which does not exist in ASEAN (Lian and Robinson 2002). Historically, the only legally binding document at the supranational level was the ASEAN treaty itself, whose economic implications were not as significant as political clauses. When it comes to foreign affairs, policy coordination at the regional level, albeit carried out with increasingly sophisticated measures, was very limited. In strategic decision-making with powerful economies such as China or the US, ASEAN was not a coherent block: member countries, when weighing regional versus national interest, often favoured the latter. For this reason, entering the Vietnamese market would not be complicated in terms of legality.

Staying in the Vietnamese market is a different matter. According to the Enterprise Survey, corruption indicators of Vietnam are relatively high compared to other ASEAN countries, which coincided with low scores on economic freedom as assessed by both the Fraser Institute (6.30 in 2016, third quartile) and the Heritage Foundation (53.1 in 2018, ranked 141 in the world). Given how trade volume increases every year as Vietnam aligns itself with numerous international bodies (such as ASEAN) and has concluded trade agreements with various countries, the most recent being Trans-Pacific Partnership (TPP), limited economic freedom did not seem to hinder economic growth in general. However, the high cost of corruption could be taxing on smaller businesses in the market, which directly contrasts with the Vietnamese government's attempts on boosting SMEs and the private sector in general.

China Trade and FDI

Vietnam belongs to the East Asian sphere of influence, as mentioned above. Relations with China arguably have a more significant weight in Vietnamese decision-making regarding economic matters as much as any other. In fact, China has been a top exporter for nearly a decade (see Fig. 3.4) with a 28.6% share of imports into Vietnam and figures among Vietnam's biggest markets with 12.4% of Vietnamese exported goods heading to China in 2016 (GSO 2018).

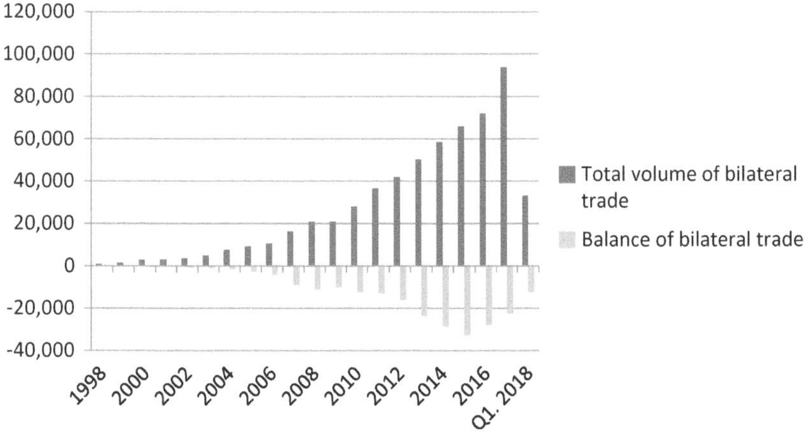

Fig. 3.8 Bilateral trade between Vietnam and China: 1998–Q4.2018 (million USD). Data source: GSO 1998–2017; General Department of Customs (Q1. 2018)

Trade between Vietnam and China grew significantly in the past two decades, especially from 2010. It could be observed that the more Vietnam trades with China, the higher the trade deficit on the side of Vietnam. In fact, 1999 and 2000 were the only two years in which Vietnam had a slight trade surplus of USD 73 million and USD 135 million, respectively, which made up about 5% of the total bilateral trade volume. From 2007 to 2015, the deficit was always hovering around 50% of total volume and on an increasing trend, with the exception of 2011 (when the trade deficit was at 36% total volume) and 2012 (deficit at 39% total). Given how China has become Vietnam's top import partner, Chinese imports seemed to be the main source of the trade deficit in Vietnam. However, from 2016, the trade deficit has shown signs of decrease despite total bilateral trade still rapidly increasing. In fact, the ratio of trade deficit to total volume has fallen from 50% in 2015 to 24% in 2017, the lowest since 2005 (Fig. 3.8).

China also contributed significantly to the tourism industry of Vietnam. Tourism has always been one of the most important tertiary industries of Vietnam: in 2017, the tourism industry earned a total of VND 510.9 trillion (approximately USD 22.4 billion), making up 10% of GDP. For this reason, the fact that Chinese visitors accounted for over four million arrivals to Vietnam in 2017—nearly double the number of arrivals from South Korea and five times that from Japan—added considerable weight to China in its presence in the Vietnamese economy (see Table 3.2).

Table 3.2 Top 12 countries of origins of visitors by the number of arrivals to Vietnam in 2017

Country	*Arrivals*
China	4,008,253
South Korea	2,415,245
Japan	798,119
Taiwan	616,232
United States	614,117
Russia	574,164
Malaysia	480,456
Australia	370,438
Thailand	301,587
United Kingdom	283,537
Singapore	277,658
France	255,369

Data source: Vietnam National Administration of Tourism 2018

FDI from China into Vietnam was quite low but generally increasing in the share of total FDI into Vietnam. This rising trend was, however, not consistent, dropping to just over 2% in 2014, only to later shoot from 3.09% in 2015 to 10.8% in 2016 (see Table 3.3). The boost in the share of Chinese investment in total FDI carried on into 2017. This is mainly explained by the formalization of Chinese investments in Vietnam, many of which were previously done through unofficial channels.

China FDI into Vietnam has been small in scale and concentrated in labour-intensive industries, mining, and forestry. The majority of Chinese investors and business owners do not regard the Vietnamese market as significant. With the exception of business owners from the southern provinces of China, the business class in China consider Vietnam to be backward and of weak purchasing power. For this reason, it became common practice to supply the Vietnamese market with low-quality, poorly manufactured commodities, and in the case of food and beverage, some of which might even have expired. As a consequence, most Vietnamese consumers were unaware of high-quality, high-tech products from China and generally held the vision that Chinese goods were cheap and of low quality. Trust was also rather limited in trade relations and bilateral investment. The recent sharp increase in Chinese share of FDI in Vietnam suggested a possible change in the attitude of both sides.

A specificity of Vietnam-China economic relations lies in Chinese communities in Vietnam. The great majority of Chinese-owned businesses operate on a family business model and was usually in close cooperation with the Chinese community in Vietnam. Many of these businesses are

Table 3.3 FDI inflow from China into Vietnam: 2007–2017

FDI from China in Vietnam											
Year	*2007*	*2008*	*2009*	*2010*	*2011*	*2012*	*2013*	*2014*	*2015*	*2016*	*2017*
FDI from China (million USD)	397	522	728	987	1291	2368.6	2882.6	427.3	744.1	1950.7	4694.1
FDI from China/total FDI (%)	0.99	1.05	1.27	1.51	1.77	3.33	3.67	2.11	3.09	10.8	14.2

Data source: Foreign Investment Agency 2018

also currently undergoing a generational shift. The first generation was weathered entrepreneurs who had sustained their business through historical changes—from the market economy under the Republic of Vietnam in the south, to Hanoi's victory and implementation of socialist central planning, to the *Đổi Mới* reforms of 1986 and economic transition. The current generation, gradually taking over family businesses, grew up when Vietnam had already been unified and benefited from standardized, professional training in business administration.

These communities and businesses constitute a significant part of the Vietnamese economy. Chinese business owners dominate quite a few brands of consumer goods and distribution networks, namely Thiên Long (stationery), Thành Thành Công (sugar), Biti's (footwear), Mỹ Hảo (detergents), Duy Tân (plastics), and so on. Most of these Chinese-Vietnamese business owners are integrated into society and considered themselves Vietnamese. This being said, a certain distance not only remains between them and the Vietnamese society but also arise between them and Chinese relatives outside of Vietnam. For this reason, political tensions between Vietnam and China could perversely affect their productivity and, consequently, the economy. For instance, in 2014, the illegal infiltration of the Chinese HD981 oil drilling platform into Vietnamese maritime territory (Tuoitrenews 2014) and the surrounding controversy sparked anti-China sentiments in the Vietnamese population (Thế Kha 2014; Mặc Lâm 2014). This led to numerous demonstrations across the nation, some of which resorted to brute force, such as the violent protests in Bình Dương (VNExpress Reporters 2014). These events induced confusion and fear among business owners of Chinese origins. Their usual reaction, when faced with this kind of socio-political instability, was to preserve assets by reducing firm production to minimal levels.

Economic relations between Vietnam and China are largely tied to politics. Given how significant China is to the Vietnamese economy, recent tensions could be a source of concern. However, it is unlikely that either side—China or Vietnam—would risk breaking the current relatively stable relations (Nguyen et al. 2018).

Trade with Other Partners

Aside from China and ASEAN, notable trade partners include the EU and US as shown in Figs. 3.5 and 3.6, but also Japan, South Korea, and Oceania (Fig. 3.9).

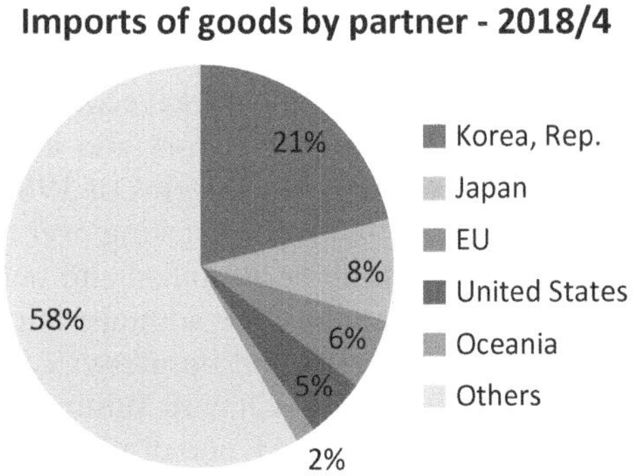

Fig. 3.9 Exports and imports of goods by partner: April 2018 (Year to Date). Data source: GSO 2018; Department of Vietnamese Customs 2018

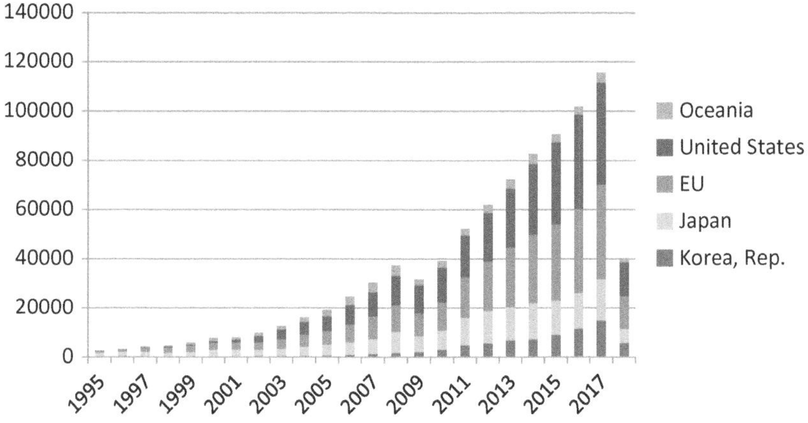

Fig. 3.10 Exports of goods to large partners: 1995–April 2018. Data source: GSO 2018; Department of Vietnamese Customs 2018

The US and EU make up nearly 40% of Vietnam's export volumes and, as such, constitute Vietnam's largest export markets. In terms of imports, South Korea is the second biggest partner after China, followed by Japan. It can also be observed that the more the trade volume has expanded, the larger the share of these respective export and import partners grew (Figs. 3.10 and 3.11). South Korea and Japan are not only large import partners but also considerable contributors to the Vietnamese tourism industry, as seen in Table 3.2 in the previous subsection.

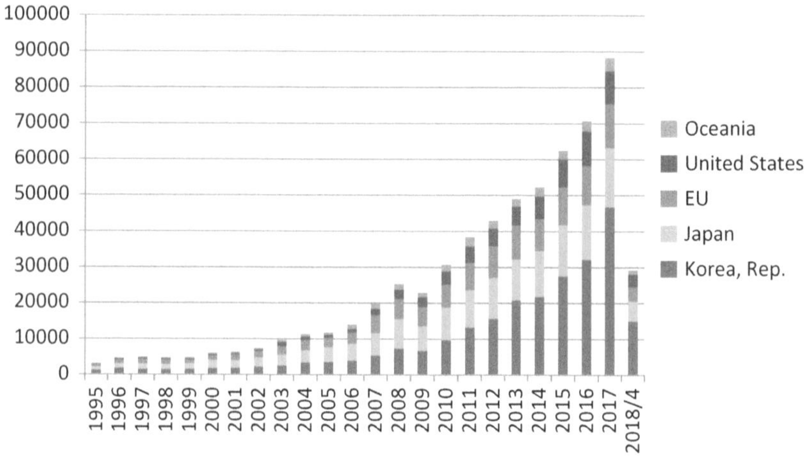

Fig. 3.11 Imports of goods from large partners: 1995–April 2018. Data source: GSO 2018; Department of Vietnamese Customs 2018

In terms of FDI, South Korea and Japan have consistently topped the chart as most significant investors into Vietnam. As of May 2018, South Korea has invested in 6883 projects with an accumulated fund of over USD 59.5 billion, making it the leading investor in Vietnam, followed by Japan with 3755 projects worth USD 50.6 billion in total (Foreign Investment Agency, hereafter FIA 2018). Manufacturing is the most attractive sector (56.8% of total accumulated FDI in 1992–2014) to Korean FDI, within which the electronics industry is the most important sub-sector (25.6% of total accumulated FDI in the same period). Most of this concentration of FDI in the Vietnamese electronics industry was accounted for by massive facilities factories set up by Samsung Electronics (Oh and Mah 2017). While South Korea is still the long-standing leading investor, Japan has taken the number one spot in terms of FDI in 2017 with over USD 9.1 billion invested in Vietnam in total (FIA 2018), mainly in real estate activities, more specifically housing projects (Tomiyama 2017). It should be noted that Japan and Vietnam are also both members of the Trans-Pacific Partnership, which is expected to boost trade and investment relations between the two countries. In fact, Vietnamese officials have echoed these expectations as well as made promises of favourable conditions for Japanese investments (VietNamNews 2018). As to whether Japan would take over South Korea's place as leading investor in Vietnam, the matter is still ambiguous as statistics of the first five months of 2018 showed that South Korea was once again top investor after placing after Japan in 2017 (FIA 2018).

Whither the Vietnamese Market Economy?

Macroeconomic Stability Under Political Influence

Macroeconomic stability has always been a main priority for the Vietnamese government. Three main problems are to be tackled: inflation, the repayment of public debts, and a high commercial lending rate.

The first issue to be addressed is inflation. Vietnam underwent a period of high inflation after the end of the war, particularly from 1985 to 1988. Prior to *Đổi Mới* in 1986, there had been numerous attempts at reforming the stagnating economy under central planning. One such attempt was the *General Adjustment of Price-Wage-Currency* reform package, which was introduced in 1985 and resulted in enormous inflation rates that persisted throughout the 1980s, reportedly hitting 587% at its peak (Đặng 2008; Vuong and Pham 2009). Nguyen (1999) has pointed out that the reason for acute inflation during the 1985–1988 period was supply rigidity, especially in agricultural staples, due to the inefficient public sector under the classical socialist model (Fig. 3.12).

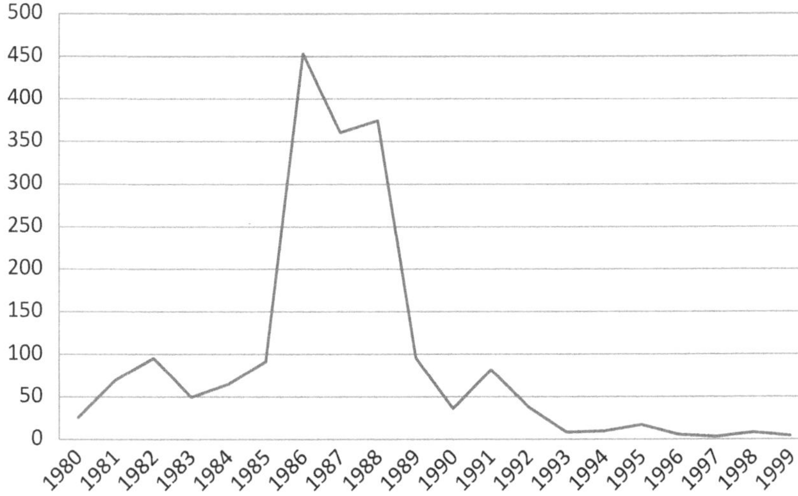

Fig. 3.12 The inflation rate, the annual per cent change of CPI, 1980–1999. Source: World Economic Outlook Database 2018 (IMF)

Inflation slowed down in the 1990s and despite being brushed by the 1997 Asian financial crisis, Vietnam re-emerged in 2000–2003 with negative-to-modest inflation rates. Prices were sensitive to the world market, as inflation could be seen to jump to two-digit rates during periods of world crises, namely the 2007–2008 world financial crisis (23.1% in 2008) and the 2012 Eurozone crisis (18.7% in 2011, 9.1% in 2012). From 2013 onwards, there has been a downward trend, but after inflation fell to under 1% in 2015, the rates abruptly picked up in 2016 (2.7%) and continued to rise above 3% in 2017 (Fig. 3.7). This has been considered a success, as the target set by the government for 2017 was to keep inflations under 4% (the same goal applied to 2018 per Government Resolution 01/NQ-CP by Prime Minister Nguyen Xuan Phuc on January 2, 2018). This being said, reports from IMF and Asian Development Bank (ADB) all forecasted a rate of approximately 4% in the years to come. Since the beginning of 2018, monthly inflation rates have been fluctuating around 2.6–3.1% year-over-year, according to data provided by the General Statistics Office of Vietnam (GSO) on CPI progression (GSO 2018) (Fig. 3.13).

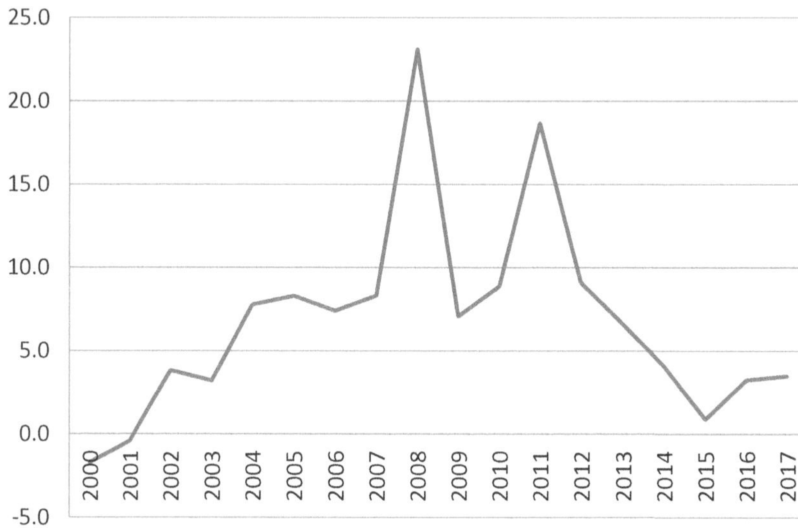

Fig. 3.13 The inflation rate, the annual per cent change of CPI: 2000–2017. Data source: World Bank; Asian Development Bank

Vietnam's 4% inflation was high compared to emerging economies in the region, such as Lao PDR or Cambodia. Indeed, the Vietnamese government recognizes inflation as a chronic problem, especially with inflation inertia being the main determinant of high inflation rates (Nguyen et al. 2012). The extant literature does not agree on how this problem should be resolved. While Goujon (2006) and Nguyen et al. (2012) suggest that restrictive monetary policy and fixed exchange rates would help lower the rates of inflation, Pham and Riedel (2012) argue that the financial sector should be liberalized to ensure macroeconomic stability. Vietnamese decision-makers have always leaned more towards restrictions and fixed exchange rates, especially since 2008. One might expect shifts in policies as the new government led by Prime Minister Nguyen Xuan Phuc was put in place after the XIVth CPV Congress in 2016.

Another emerging issue is the repayment of public debts, attributed to low-investment efficiency represented by higher ICOR (see Fig. 3.10) and increasing trends in public borrowing. According to *the 2017 Government Report on Social Economic Development*, central government debts in Vietnam added up to an equivalent of 62.6% of GDP. While the debt-to-GDP ratio had dropped a few percentage points compared to 2016, debt value had increased by VND 270 trillion (USD 11.8 billion) to over VND 3100 trillion (USD 140 billion). It is noteworthy that due to disparities in accounting in Vietnam and international accounting standards, public debts in Vietnam might have been higher than what official figures suggested (Le 2016). Per capita debt was approximately USD 1000/person, which, despite being quite average in the region and modest compared to countries such as Thailand, Malaysia, and Singapore, received much media attention and public criticism. External debt was also significant, 45.2% of GDP; the share of external debt was being reduced in government debt structure, conforming to government strategy on public debt restructuring following the prime minister's decision numbered 958/QD-TTg (Fig. 3.14).

Le (2016) attributed this level of public debt to several main causes, namely: demand for public spending exceeding economic growth; government borrowing in order to offset chronic public deficit; and inefficient investment, shown in Vietnam's high incremental capital-output ratio. Most official reports propose long-term, general measures such as

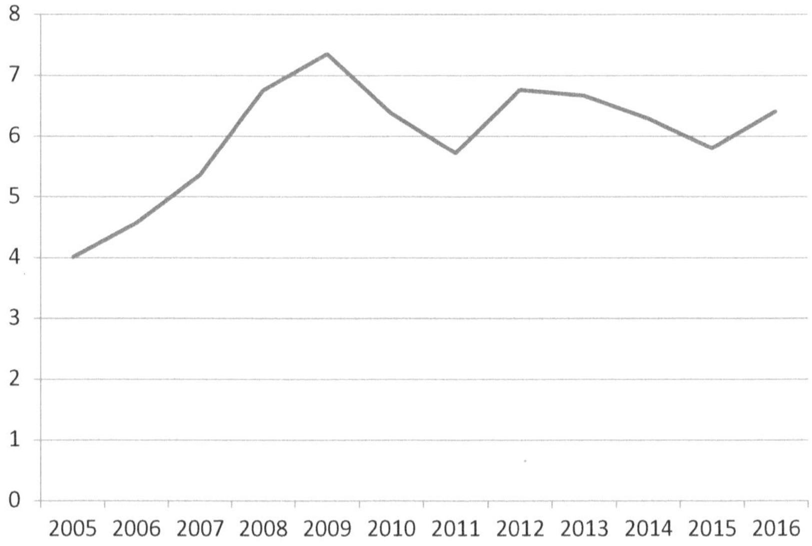

Fig. 3.14 Incremental capital-output ratio (ICOR; constant 2010 prices) during 2005–2016. Data source: GSO 2017

improving budget revenues, reducing public expenditure, improving efficiency in investment, and so on. However, the imperative need of repaying existing public debts calls for short-term actions to be taken: making use of the bond market and building a market for debt trading.

In the private sector, high commercial lending rates add to the issue of inflation and recur as a threat to the system. Bad debt was also a key issue: according to the 2017 General Financial Market Overview released by the National Financial Supervision Commission, the rate of non-performing bank loans over gross loans was 9.5% in 2017, which was three times higher than the 3% goal set by the government, but an improvement from the rate of 11.6% in 2016. Debt-ridden commercial banks are inefficient, especially as a component of the transmission mechanism. Resources have been concentrated in the restructuring of debt and of malfunctioning banks; however, bad debts were an excuse, and it was mainly the abuse of bank powers, cross-holding, and overbankedness that has been addressed.

Sustainability Assessment

In the recent decades, sustainable economic development, linked to improving basic material living standards from 'grassroots' levels (Barbier 1987), has become the keyword in institutional reports across developed as well as emerging economies. As an economy in transition, Vietnam also saw arise the question of sustainability and use of resources. In this section, we shall discuss matters related to uses of natural and social resources.

A common saying in Vietnam holds that, 'Forests of gold, seas of silver' (*Rừng vàng, biển bạc*). This is a reference to the ample natural resources with which the country is endowed: fertile lands and tropical climate in favour of agricultural development and rich biodiversity; diverse geological composition favouring the mining industry; natural gas exploitation and oil rigs in the sea; and so on, to name a few. The mere richness of natural resources reduces the incentive to shift the structure of export products from primary to more secondary and tertiary. While very lucrative, these industrial activities were not only taxing on the environment but also induced a certain dependency on resources and in the mentality of decision-makers. As such, issues regarding natural resources in Vietnam have noteworthy specificities: political rulers, and sometimes even public opinion, are less concerned with impacts on the environment itself and are rather more focussed on immediate economic consequences. One such example was the Formosa incident, the most prominent environmental disaster in Vietnam in 2016.

Formosa, formally Formosa Plastics Group, was a Taiwanese conglomerate with two investment projects in Vietnam. The 2016 incident concerned Formosa Hà Tĩnh Steel Corporation, situated in the Vũng Áng Economic Zone. In April 2016, mass deaths of both farmed fish and wild fish were detected. Dead fish continued to wash up the shores in tons for weeks, and seafood consumption had reportedly caused food poisoning among people in the region. The incident was devastating for the concerned Central Vietnam provinces, as it led to not only an enormous loss in output for farmers but also instilled anxiety among the population and was thus detrimental not only to the fisheries industry but also to tourism in the region. Subsequent events revealed that the cause was indeed severe water poisoning due to waste water containing illegally high concentrations of cyanide, phenol, and iron hydroxide being dumped in the sea by Formosa factories (Minh Hà and Đông Sơn 2016). This information was made public in late June, two months after the first instance of the incident.

Prior to this revelation, in the midst of national panic, action by the government had been largely criticized as reticent and lacking in transparency. Public opinion had indeed shifted the focus of the controversy from environmental destruction to government transparency. Even after the formal apology and a compensation of USD 500 million by Formosa, activists remained adamant (Nguyen and Vuong 2016), but only on the issue of transparency rather than the environment. Conversely, over a year later, as the heat of the controversy has died down, misuse of allocated compensation funds by provinces directly damaged by the incident (Hải Sâm 2018) has received virtually no attention from activists.

Issues regarding social resources involve politics in an even more profound manner. Most of the focus has been on capital investment, the general mentality perceiving financial capital as topmost desirable in boosting economic growth. This translates into a political rhetoric rather in favour of subsidiaries and external investment, despite FDI net inflow already at USD 12.6 billion (6.1% of GDP) as of 2016—quite high compared to countries in the region such as Thailand (0.8% of GDP), Malaysia (4.6% of GDP), or Myanmar (5.2% of GDP) (World Bank 2018). Since 2013, Vuong has coined the term *resource intoxication* to characterize the phenomenon of the economy becoming economically worse off despite increasing endowments of physical and capital resources (Nguyễn 2013) and the corporate sector being kept in the downward spiral of low efficiency-poor performance (Vuong and Napier 2014). Indeed, sustainable economic growth in the long run concerned political and institutional structure (Woolcock 1998) and social cohesion (Ritzen and Woolcock 2000), as well as higher productivity and higher labour quality, linked to education which has been shown to be a determinant of growth (Chen and Feng 2000). Rather than focusing on any of these determinants, however, the government largely concerned itself with acquiring foreign investment and, recently, with aligning the development of the country with the Fourth Industrial Revolution.

Conclusion

More than 30 years after the official launch of *Đổi Mới* that allowed economic freedom and market mechanisms to start flourishing, the socialist-oriented market economy of Vietnam has apparently entered its final stages of transition. The Vietnamese Communist Party retains the monopoly of political power and institutional reforms have been insignificant; for this reason, the government remains powerful in terms of policy-making, facing no political opponent. In addition, the legacy of a deeply Confucian society that had been abruptly forced into modernity through colonization means a certain tolerance, even fondness, for state paternalism in the Vietnamese population.

However, despite the lack of political rupture and gradualism of reforms, the Vietnamese economy has transformed completely. Central planning was completely abolished in favour of a market economy—albeit with minor price regulations for certain goods—resolving shortages and economic stagnation in general. Foreign trade opened up to the world with bilateral agreements and regional economic integrations, boosting production and exports.

Faced with these changes, the Vietnamese people have been quick to pick up consumerist behaviours, which may signify increased spending capacity for certain groups of society, but should also serve as a warning, given the economic vulnerability of a large portion of the population. Policy-makers and consumers alike should not forget that it is difficult to determine whether transition had truly ended or how a fully transitioned economy should look like—especially considering the national specificities of Vietnam. The economic growth Vietnam has experienced for the past few decades has led to the formation of the Vietnamese plutocrats—strong economic actors that are starting to gain influence over political actors as well as inspiring entrepreneurship among younger generations. While the establishment of a socially defined class of business owners remains far in the future, it is clear that Vietnam's economic growth will henceforth be led not by the political power but the economic elite—the *superclass*.

The Vietnamese economy has been characterized by high inflation, high public debt, inefficient public spending, and trade deficits. As a small and open economy, Vietnam is sensitive to prices in the world market, which adds to the problem of inflation, and the large volume of imports means a certain dependence on foreign supply. Vietnam depends little on ASEAN—intra-ASEAN trade was, in fact, quite modest compared to other member countries—and has had much more significant trade volumes with China and the US.

Appendix

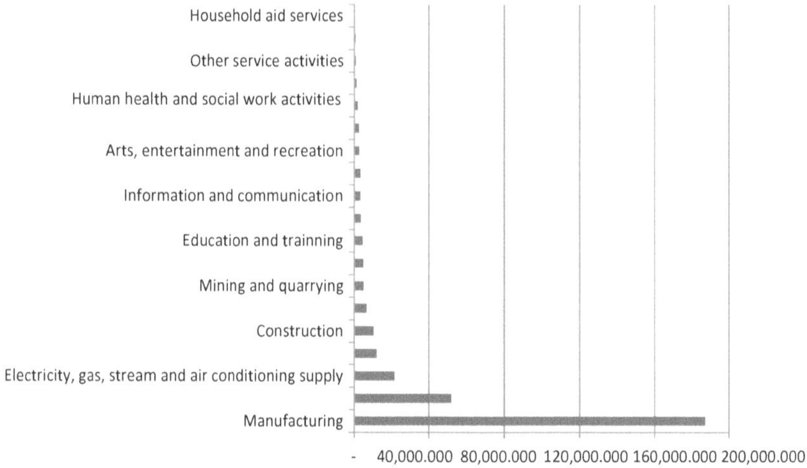

Fig. 3.15 Total accumulated FDI by economic activity as of May 2018 (USD Million). Source: Foreign Investment Agency Vietnam 2018

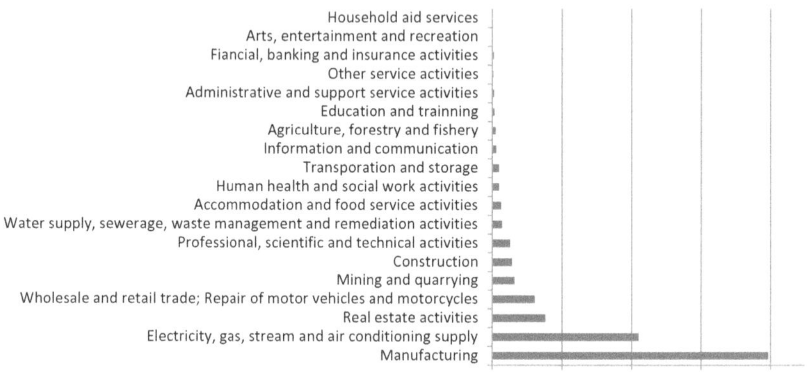

Fig. 3.16 FDI by economic activity: 2017 (USD Million). Source: Foreign Investment Agency Vietnam 2018

Table 3.4 State-owned enterprises under committee control

Corporation	*State ownership*	*Sector*	*Ministry in control*
SCIC	100%	Finance	Ministry of Finance
EVN	100%	Energy/Electricity	Ministry of Industry and Trade
Petrolimex	76%	Energy/Fuel	Ministry of Industry and Trade
PetroVietnam	100%	Energy/Petrol	Ministry of Industry and Trade
Vinachem	100%	Chemicals	Ministry of Industry and Trade
Vinacomin	100%	Energy/Coal	Ministry of Industry and Trade
Vinataba	100%	Tabacco	Ministry of Industry and Trade
ACV	95%	Transportation/Airport	Ministry of Transport
VEC	100%	Transportation/ Infrastructure	Ministry of Transport
Vietnam Airlines	86%	Transportation/Airlines	Ministry of Transport
Vietnam Railways	100%	Transportation/ Railways	Ministry of Transport
Vinalines	100%	Transportation/Marine	Ministry of Transport
Vinacafe	100%	Agriculture	Ministry of Agriculture and Rural Development
Vinafor	51%	Agriculture	Ministry of Agriculture and Rural Development
Vinafood I	100%	Food	Ministry of Agriculture and Rural Development
Vinafood II	51%	Food	Ministry of Agriculture and Rural Development
VRG	75%	Agriculture	Ministry of Agriculture and Rural Development
Mobifone	100%	Technology & Communication	Ministry of Information and Communications
VNPT	100%	Technology & Communication	Ministry of Information and Communications

Source: Article 9 – Chap. 2 – Decree 131/2018/NĐ-CP (http://cmsc.gov.vn/documents/20181/34931/Ngh%E1%BB%8B+%C4%91%E1%BB%8Bnh+131_08102018160309.pdf); Commission for the Management of State Capital at Enterprises—Official Webpage (http://cmsc.gov.vn); Government Portal—List of State-owned Enterprises (http://vanban.chinhphu.vn/portal/page/portal/chinhphu/DoanhNghiep); Government Portal—Equitization and Modernization of State-owned Enterprises (http://doimoidoanhnghiep.chinhphu.vn/thong-tin-doanh-nghiep.html)

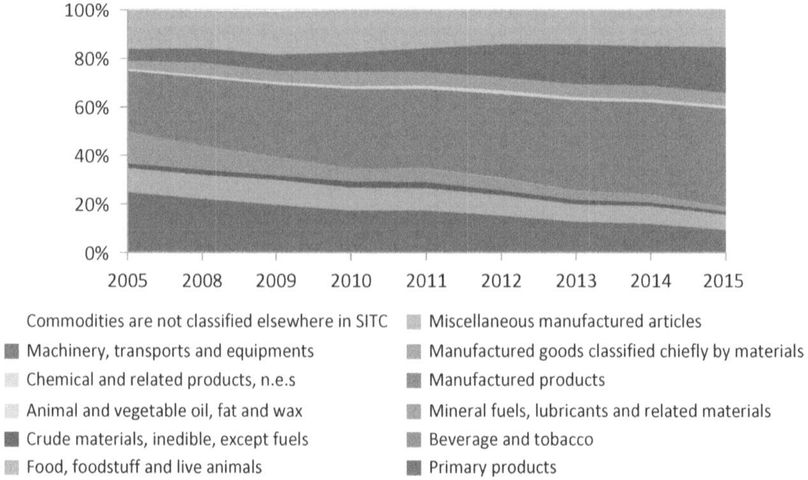

Fig. 3.17 Structure of exports by standard international trade classifications: 2005–2015. Source: GSO 2018

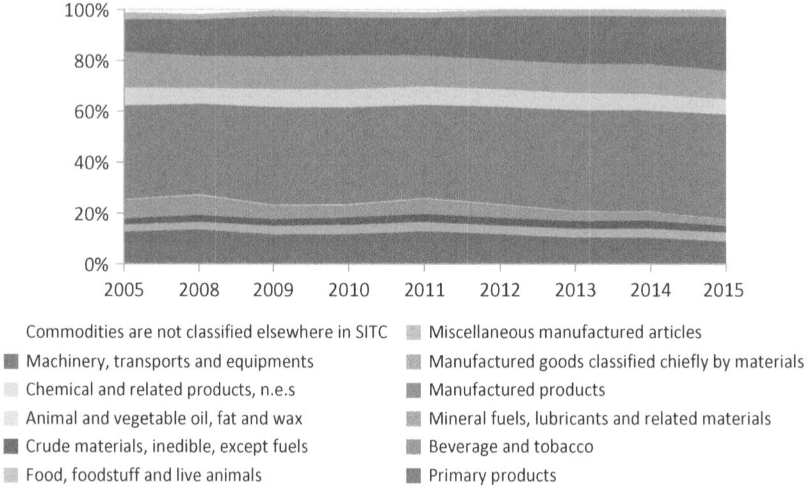

Fig. 3.18 Structure of imports by standard international trade classifications: 2005–2015. Source: GSO 2018

Table 3.5 Structure of exports by commodity groups: 1995–2005 (%)

Heavy industrial products and minerals	25.3	28.7	28	27.9	31.3	37.2	34.9	31.8	32.2	36.4	36.1
Minerals											
Light industrial and handicraft goods	28.4	29	36.7	36.6	36.7	33.9	35.7	40.6	42.7	41	41
Agricultural products	32	29.8	24.3	24.3	22.1	17.7	16.1	14.3	13.3	12.8	13.7
Forest products	2.8	2.9	2.5	2	1.5	1.1	1.2	1.2	1	0.7	0.8
Aquatic products	11.4	9.6	8.5	9.2	8.4	10.1	12.1	12.1	10.8	9.1	8.4
Non-monetary gold											0

Source: GSO 2018

Table 3.6 Structure of exports by commodity groups: 2006–2016 (%)

	2006	*2007*	*2008*	*2009*	*2010*	*2011*	*2012*	*2013*	*2014*	*2015*	*Prel. 2016*
Heavy industrial products and minerals	36.2	34.4	37	30.9	31	35.8	42.1	45	44	45.4	45.3
Minerals					11.5	12	10.7	8.2	7	3.8	
Light industrial and handicraft goods	41.2	42.6	39.8	44.8	46.1	41.6	37.8	37.8	39.4	40	
Agricultural products	13.4	14.5	14.7	14.6	14.7	14.9	13.5	10.6	10.1	9.1	10.3
Forest products	0.8	0.8	0.7	0.8	1.1	1.3	1.2	1.4	1.3	1.4	
Aquatic products	8.4	7.7	7.2	7.5	7	6.3	5.3	5.1	5.2	4.1	4
Non-monetary gold	0	0	0.6	1.4	0.1	0.1	0.1	0.1	0	0	

Source: GSO 2018

Table 3.7 Structure of imports by commodity groups: 1995–2005

	1995	*1996*	*1997*	*1998*	*1999*	*2000*	*2001*	*2002*	*2003*	*2004*	*2005*
Machinery, instrument, accessory	25.7	27.6	30.3	30.6	29.9	30.6	30.5	29.8	31.6	28.8	25.3
Fuels, raw material	59.1	60	59.6	61	61.7	63.2	61.6	62.3	60.6	64.5	64.4
Consumer goods	15.2	12.4	10.1	8.5	8.4	6.2	7.9	7.9	7.8	6.7	8.2
Food						0		0	0	0	0
Foodstuffs	3.5	2.9	2.1	2.4	2.5	1.9	3	2.5	2.4	2.4	3
Pharmaceutical and medicinal products	0.9	1.9	3.1	2.8	2.3	2.2	2	1.8	1.6	1.4	1.4
Others	10.8	7.6	5	3.2	3.6	2.1	3	3.6	3.8	2.9	3.7
Non-monetary gold											2.2

Source: GSO 2018

Table 3.8 Structure of imports by commodity groups: 2006–2016

	2006	*2007*	*2008*	*2009*	*2010*	*2011*	*2012*	*2013*	*2014*	*2015*	*Prel. 2016*
Machinery, instrument, accessory	24.6	28.6	28	31.6	29.6	29.6	35.1	38.2	38.1	43.2	41.4
Fuels, raw material	63.4	61.9	60.8	58.6	59.4	59	55.8	52.6	53	47.9	49.7
Consumer goods	7.8	7.4	7.8	9.3	9.9	9.5	9	9.1	8.8	8.8	8.9
Food	0	0	0	0.1	0	0	0	0	0	0	
Foodstuffs	2.8	2.5	2.8	3	3.3	3.5	3.3	3.5	3.7	3.8	
Pharmaceutical and medicinal products	1.3	1.2	1.1	1.7	1.6	1.5	1.6	1.5	1.4	1.4	1.5
Others	3.7	3.7	3.9	4.5	5	4.5	4.1	4.1	3.7	3.6	
Non-monetary gold	4.2	2.1	3.4	0.5	1.1	1.9	0.1	0.1	0.1	0.1	

Source: GSO 2018

Notes

1. The *nomenklatura* system consists of lists of positions over which party committees exercise the power of appointment, with lists of reserve cadres for positions as well as processes for making the appropriate personnel changes.
2. He and his wife co-founded the predecessor of Vingroup in Ukraine.

References

A.N. 2015. Bị tố chây ì không thanh toán nợ, CEO The Kafe Đào Chi Anh nói: "Không phải cứ tự nhiên bị ép trả tiền là trả". *CafeBiz*, June 29. http://cafebiz.vn/bi-to-chay-i-khong-thanh-toan-no-ceo-the-kafe-dao-chi-anh-noi-khong-phai-cu-tu-nhien-bi-ep-tra-tien-la-tra-20160629004857114.chn. Accessed June 3, 2018.

ADB. 2017. Asian Development Outlook 2017 Update. In *Asian Development Outlook*. Asian Development Bank.

Bakos, Yannis. 1998. The Emerging Role of Electronic Marketplaces on the Internet. *Communications of the ACM* 41 (8): 35–42. https://doi.org/10.1145/280324.280330.

Bảo Phương. 2017. 'Đại khủng hoảng' thịt lợn và cuộc giải cứu chưa từng có. *VietNamNet*, August 31. http://vietnamnet.vn/vn/kinh-doanh/thi-truong/dai-khung-hoang-thit-lon-va-cuoc-giai-cuu-chua-tung-co-395973.html. Accessed June 3, 2018.

Barbier, Edward B. 1987. The Concept of Sustainable Economic Development. *Environmental Conservation* 14 (02): 101. https://doi.org/10.1017/s0376892900011449.

Boymal, Jonathan, Bill Martin, and Dieu Lam. 2007. The Political Economy of Internet Innovation Policy in Vietnam. *Technology in Society* 29 (4): 407–421. https://doi.org/10.1016/j.techsoc.2007.08.003.

Brocheux, Pierre, and Daniel Hémery. 2001. *Indochine, la colonisation ambiguë*. La Découverte.

Brownrigg, Edwin B. 1991. The Internet as an External Economy: The Emergence of the Invisible Hand. *Library Administration & Management* 5 (2): 95–97.

Chapuis, Oscar. 1995. *A History of Vietnam: From Hong Bang to Tu Duc*. Cambridge University Press.

Chen, Baizhu, and Yi Feng. 2000. Determinants of Economic Growth in China: Private Enterprise, Education, and Openness. *China Economic Review* 11 (1): 1–15. https://doi.org/10.1016/s1043-951x(99)00014-0.

Công Quang. 2017. Người Sài Gòn "giải cứu" dưa hấu cho nông dân Quảng Ngãi. *Dân Trí*, April 7. http://dantri.com.vn/kinh-doanh/nguoi-sai-gon-giai-cuu-dua-hau-cho-nong-dan-quang-ngai-20170407150107735.htm.

Đặng, Phong. 2008. *Tư duy kinh tế Việt Nam: chặng đường gian nan và ngoạn mục, 1975–1989*. Hanoi, Vietnam: Nhà xuất bản Tri thức.
Department of Vietnam Customs. 2018. *Preliminary Assessment of Vietnam International Merchandise Trade Performance in the First 4 months of 2018*. Department of Vietnam Customs.
DeRouen, Karl R. 1995. The Indirect Link: Politics, the Economy, and the Use of Force. *Journal of Conflict Resolution* 39 (4): 671–695. https://doi.org/10.1177/0022002795039004004.
Drury, Rebecca. 2011. Hungry for Success: Urban Consumer Demand for Wild Animal Products in Vietnam. *Conservation and Society* 9 (3): 10. https://doi.org/10.4103/0972-4923.86995.
Farber, André, Van Nam Nguyen, and Quan Hoang Vuong. 2006. *Policy Impacts on Vietnam Stock Markets: A Case of Anomalies and Disequilibria 2000–2006*. Working Papers CEB, Bruxelles.
FIA. 2018. *Foreign Investment Monthly Reports*. Foreign Investment Agency.
Figuié, Muriel, and Paule Moustier. 2009. Market Appeal in an Emerging Economy: Supermarkets and Poor Consumers in Vietnam. *Food Policy* 34 (2): 210–217. https://doi.org/10.1016/j.foodpol.2008.10.012.
Fosse, Henrik Barslund, and Pascalis Raimondos-Møller. 2012. Reducing Tariffs According to WTO Accession Rules: The Case of Vietnam. *Review of Development Economics* 16 (2): 331–341. https://doi.org/10.1111/j.1467-9361.2012.00665.x.
Goujon, Michaël. 2006. Fighting Inflation in a Dollarized Economy: The Case of Vietnam. *Journal of Comparative Economics* 34 (3): 564–581. https://doi.org/10.1016/j.jce.2006.06.001.
Government Portal. 2006. *Một vài nét về kinh tế-xã hội Việt Nam*. http://www.chinhphu.vn/portal/page/portal/chinhphu/NuocCHXHCNVietNam/ThongTinTongHop/kinhtexahoi. Accessed June 3, 2018.
GSO. 2017. *Press Release: 2017 Socioeconomic Report*. General Statistics Office.
———. 2018. *Consumer Price Index*. General Statistics Office.
Gunn, Geoffrey C. 2011. The Great Vietnamese Famine of 1944–45 Revisited. 東南アジア研究年報 52: 81–105.
Hải Sâm. 2018. Trích hơn 100 triệu tiền đền bù sự cố Formosa đi du lịch. *VietNamNet*, April 8. http://vietnamnet.vn/vn/thoi-su/chong-tham-nhung/trich-hon-100-trieu-tien-den-bu-su-co-formosa-di-du-lich-440513.html.
Ho, Thi Huong Lan, and Yizeng Chen. 2014. Vietnamese Consumers' Intention to Use Online Shopping: The Role of Trust. *International Journal of Business and Management* 9 (5). https://doi.org/10.5539/ijbm.v9n5p145.
Hồng Minh. 2016. Đào Chi Anh đã làm gì trong 3 năm điều hành The KAfe? *CafeBiz*, October 28. http://cafebiz.vn/dao-chi-anh-da-lam-gi-trong-3-nam-dieu-hanh-the-kafe-20161027180137624.chn. Accessed June 3, 2018.
IMF. 2018. World Economic Outlook, April 2018: Cyclical Upswing, Structural Change. In *World Economic Outlook*. International Monetary Fund.

Joyaux, François. 1970. Les relations sino-vietnamiennes: perspectives politiques et économiques. *Tiers-Monde* 11 (42): 291–300. https://doi.org/10.3406/tiers.1970.1704.

Kalathil, Shanthi, and Taylor Boas. 2003. Open Networks, Closed Regimes: The Impact of the Internet on Authoritarian Rule (Table of Contents). *First Monday* 8 (1). https://doi.org/10.5210/fm.v8i1.1024.

Lam, Dieu, Jonathan Boymal, and Bill Martin. 2004. Internet Diffusion in Vietnam. *Technology in Society* 26 (1): 39–50. https://doi.org/10.1016/j.techsoc.2003.10.004.

Le, Minh Son. 2014. Trade Openness and Household Welfare Within a Country: A Microeconomic Analysis of Vietnamese Households. *Journal of Asian Economics* 33: 56–70. https://doi.org/10.1016/j.asieco.2014.05.005.

Le, Thi Khuong. 2016. Bàn về nợ công Việt Nam hiện nay. *Tạp chí Ngân hàng*, December 2.

Le, Viet, and Charles Harvie. 2010. *Firm Performance in Vietnam: Evidence from Manufacturing Small and Medium Enterprises*. Economics Working Papers.

Le Monkhouse, Lien, Bradley R. Barnes, and Ute Stephan. 2012. The Influence of Face and Group Orientation on the Perception of Luxury Goods. *International Marketing Review* 29 (6): 647–672. https://doi.org/10.1108/02651331211277982.

Lian, Koh Kheng, and Nicholas A. Robinson. 2002. Regional Environmental Governance: Examining the Association of Southeast Asian Nations (ASEAN) Model. In *Global Environmental Governance: Options and Opportunities*, ed. Daniel C. Esty and Maria H. Ivanova, 101–121. Connecticut, US: Yale School of Forestry & Environmental Studies.

Mặc Lâm. 2014. Khắp nước biểu tình choống Trung Quốc. *RFA*, May 10. https://www.rfa.org/vietnamese/in_depth/anti-cn-protest-whole-country-ml-05102014224400.html.

Maruyama, Masayoshi, and Viet Trung Le. 2007. Supermarkets in Vietnam: Opportunities and Obstacles. *Asian Economic Journal* 21 (1): 19–46. https://doi.org/10.1111/j.1467-8381.2007.00245.x.

Minh Hà, and Đông Sơn. 2016. Công bố nguyên nhân sự cố môi trướng làm hải sản chết bất thướng tại 4 tỉnh ven biểu miền Trung. *Quân đội nhân dân*, June 30. http://www.qdnd.vn/xa-hoi/cong-bo-nguyen-nhan-su-co-moi-truong-lam-hai-san-chet-bat-thuong-tai-4-tinh-ven-bien-mien-trung-482056.

Minh Sơn. 2017. Startup KAfe Group trở thành công ty con của doanh nghiệp Hong Kong. *VNExpress*, April 2. https://startup.vnexpress.net/tin-tuc/hanh-trinh-khoi-nghiep/startup-kafe-group-tro-thanh-cong-ty-con-cua-doanh-nghiep-hong-kong-3564395.html.

Ngo, Tan Vu Khanh, and Gwangyong Gim. 2014. Factors Affecting the Online Shopping Behavior: An Empirical Investigation in Vietnam. *International Journal of Engineering Research and Applications* 4 (2): 388–392.

Nguyen, Tri Hung. 1999. *The Inflation of Vietnam in Transition*. CAS Discussion Paper.

Nguyễn, Bá Khoáng. 2005. 60 năm phát triển kinh tế – xã hội từ nước Việt Nam dân chủ cộng hoà đến nước Cộng hoà xã hội chủ nghĩa Việt Nam. *General Statistics Office*, August 23. http://www.gso.gov.vn/default.aspx?tabid=382&idmid=2&ItemID=2998. Accessed June 3, 2018.

Nguyễn, Trinh. 2013. Tiến sĩ Vương Quân Hoàng: Chống "ngộ độc" nguồn lực. *Thanh Niên*, January 15. https://thanhnien.vn/van-hoa/tien-si-vuong-quan-hoang-chong-ngo-doc-nguon-luc-42437.html.

Nguyen, Tho D., and Nigel J. Barrett. 2006. The Knowledge-Creating Role of the Internet in International Business: Evidence from Vietnam. *Journal of International Marketing* 14 (2): 116–147. https://doi.org/10.1509/jimk.14.2.116.

Nguyen, Thi Tuyet Mai, and Siok Kuan Tambyah. 2011. Antecedents and Consequences of Status Consumption Among Urban Vietnamese Consumers. *Organizations & Markets in Emerging Economies* 2 (1): 24.

Nguyen, Chan, and Kim Dung Tran. 2006. The Impact of Trade Liberalization on Household Welfare in Vietnam. *SSRN Electronic Journal*. https://doi.org/10.2139/ssrn.888534.

Nguyen, Pham Muoi, and Quan Hoang Vuong. 2016. In Vietnam, Digital Is Democratizing. *CIMA*.

Nguyen, Trang T.M., Tho D. Nguyen, and Nigel J. Barrett. 2007. Hedonic Shopping Motivations, Supermarket Attributes, and Shopper Loyalty in Transitional Markets. *Asia Pacific Journal of Marketing and Logistics* 19 (3): 227–239. https://doi.org/10.1108/13555850710772914.

Nguyen, Tho D., Trang T.M. Nguyen, and Nigel J. Barrett. 2008. Consumer Ethnocentrism, Cultural Sensitivity, and Intention to Purchase Local Products—Evidence from Vietnam. *Journal of Consumer Behaviour* 7 (1): 88–100. https://doi.org/10.1002/cb.238.

Nguyen, Huu Minh, Tony Cavoli, and John K. Wilson. 2012. The Determinants of Inflation in Vietnam, 2001–09. *ASEAN Economic Bulletin* 29 (1): 1. https://doi.org/10.1355/ae29-1a.

Nguyen, Hong Kong, Quan Hoang Vuong, Tung Ho, and Thu-Trang Vuong. 2018. The 'Same Bed, Different Dreams' of Vietnam and China: How (Mis) Trust Could Make or Break It. *SSRN Electronic Journal*. https://doi.org/10.2139/ssrn.3185278.

Oh, Ji Hyun, and Jai S. Mah. 2017. The Patterns of Korea's Foreign Direct Investment in Vietnam. *Open Journal of Business and Management* 05 (02): 253–271. https://doi.org/10.4236/ojbm.2017.52023.

Ohno, Kenichi. 2009. Avoiding the Middle-Income Trap: Renovating Industrial Policy Formulation in Vietnam. *Asean Economic Bulletin* 26 (1): 25–43. https://doi.org/10.1355/ae26-1c.

Pfau, Wade Donald, and Long Thanh Giang. 2009. Determinants and Impacts of International Remittances on Household Welfare in Vietnam. *International Social Science Journal* 60 (197–198): 431–443. https://doi.org/10.1111/j.1468-2451.2010.01733.x.

Pham, Hung Hiep. 2019. *Giải pháp mạnh xử lý cuộc khủng hoảng*. RPE Discussion Papers.

Pham, Thi Thu Tra, and James Riedel. 2012. On the Conduct of Monetary Policy in Vietnam. *Asian-Pacific Economic Literature* 26 (1): 34–45. https://doi.org/10.1111/j.1467-8411.2012.01335.x.

Pham, Thi Ngoc Linh, Michael P. Burton, and David Vanzetti. 2008. *The Welfare of Small Livestock Producers in Vietnam Under Trade Liberalisation – Integration of Trade and Household Models*. 2008 Conference (52nd), February 5–8, Canberra, Australia.

Randle, Robert F. 1970. *Geneva 1954. The Settlement of the Indochinese War*. Princeton University Press.

Ritzen, Jozef, and Michael Woolcock. 2000. *Social Cohesion, Institutions, and Growth: Implications for Countries in Transition*. Annual Bank Conference on Development Economics (Europe), Paris, June 26–28, 2000.

Rothkopf, David. 2008. *Superclass: The Global Power Elite and the World They Are Making*. New York: Farrar, Straus and Giroux.

Thành Đạt. 2018. State Capital Committee: A Copy of SCIC? *VOA*, February 6. https://www.voatiengviet.com/a/scic-uy-ban-von-nha-nuoc/4270943.html. Accessed June 3, 2018.

Thế Kha. 2014. Cử tri cả nước bất bình về giàn khoan Hải Dương 981. *Người Lao Động*, May 20. https://nld.com.vn/thoi-su-trong-nuoc/cu-tri-ca-nuoc-bat-binh-ve-gian-khoan-hai-duong-981-20140520115317109.htm. Accessed June 3, 2018.

Thual, François. 2002. *Géopolitique du bouddhisme*. Paris: Éditions des Syrtes.

Tomiyama, Atsushi. 2017. Japan returns as top investor in Vietnam. *Nikkei Asian Review*, December 28. https://asia.nikkei.com/Economy/Japan-returns-as-top-investor-in-Vietnam.

Tran, Trong Kim. 1920. *Việt Nam Sử Lược*. Hanoi: NXB Văn Học.

Tran, Angie Ngoc, and Irene Nørlund. 2014. Globalization, Industrialization, and Labor Markets in Vietnam. *Journal of the Asia Pacific Economy* 20 (1): 143–163. https://doi.org/10.1080/13547860.2014.974343.

Tuoitrenews. 2014. Chinese Vessels Try to Scare Vietnam's Ships Further Away from Illegal Rig. *Tuoi Tre News*, June 9. https://tuoitrenews.vn/society/20194/chinese-vessels-try-to-scare-vietnams-ships-further-away-from-illegal-rig. Accessed June 3, 2018.

Valette, Jacques. 1993. *Indochine, 1940–1945: Français contre Japonais*. Paris: SEDES.

Vietinbank. 2018. *Financial Statement*. http://investor.vietinbank.vn/FinancialStatements.aspx. Accessed June 3, 2018.

VietNamNews. 2018. Việt Nam Rolls Out Carpet for Japanese Investment. *VietNamNews*, May 21. http://vietnamnews.vn/economy/449009/viet-nam-rolls-out-carpet-for-japanese-investment-president.html#IYOk1q4kDwV1CxfB.97. Accessed June 3, 2018.

VNExpress Reporters. 2014. Hơn 400 người đập phá trong cuộc biểu tình bị bắt. *VNExpress*.

Vo, Tri Thanh, and Anh Duong Nguyen. 2009. Vietnam After Two Years of WTO Accession: What Lessons Can Be Learnt? *Asean Economic Bulletin* 26 (1): 115–135. https://doi.org/10.1355/ae26-1h.

Vuong, Quan Hoang. 2011. Vietnam's Economic History: The Feudalism System. *Stratfor World View*. Accessed June 21, 2011.

———. 2014. Vietnam's Political Economy in Transition (1986–2016). *Stratfor World View*. Accessed May 27, 2014.

Vuong, Quan Hoang, and Nancy K. Napier. 2014. Resource Curse or Destructive Creation in Transition. *Management Research Review* 37 (7): 642–657. https://doi.org/10.1108/mrr-12-2012-0265.

Vuong, Quan Hoang, and Minh Chinh Pham. 2009. *Kinh tế Việt Nam: Thăng trầm và Đột phá*. Hanoi: NXB Chính trị quốc gia.

Vuong, Quan-Hoang, and Tri Dung Tran. 2009. The Cultural Dimensions of the Vietnamese Private Entrepreneurship. *SSRN Electronic Journal*. https://doi.org/10.2139/ssrn.1442384.

Vuong, Thu Trang, and Quan Hoang Vuong. 2018. *L'Indochine française du XIXe–XXe siècle – politique et religions*. Working Papers CEB, Bruxelles.

Vuong, Quan Hoang, Van Nhue Dam, Daniel van Houtte, and Tri Dung Tran. 2011. The Entrepreneurial Facets as Precursor to Vietnam's Economic Renovation in 1986. *The IUP Journal of Entrepreneurship Development* 8 (4): 42.

Vuong, Quan Hoang, Quang Hoi Vu, and Thu Trang Vuong. 2016. Relationship Between Past Experience, Social Network Participation and Innovative Capacity: Vietnamese Entrepreneurship in Transition. *International Journal of Transitions and Innovation Systems* 5 (3/4): 299. https://doi.org/10.1504/ijtis.2016.083587.

Vuong, Quan-Hoang, Quang-Khiem Bui, Viet-Phuong La, Thu-Trang Vuong, Viet-Ha T. Nguyen, Manh-Toan Ho, Hong-Kong T. Nguyen, and Manh-Tung Ho. 2018. Cultural Additivity: Behavioural Insights from the Interaction of Confucianism, Buddhism and Taoism in Folktales. *Palgrave Communications* 4 (1). https://doi.org/10.1057/s41599-018-0189-2.

Woolcock, Michael. 1998. Social Capital and Economic Development: Toward a Theoretical Synthesis and Policy Framework. *Theory and Society* 27 (2): 151–208. https://doi.org/10.1023/a:1006884930135.

World Bank. 2017a. *Country Partnership Framework for the Socialist Republic of Vietnam for the Period FY18–FY22*. World Bank.

———. 2017b. *Vietnam – Country Partnership Framework for the Period FY18–FY22*. Washington, DC: World Bank Group.

———. 2018. *Enterprise Surveys*. World Bank.

CHAPTER 4

Thailand at the Frontier of Upper Middle Income

Piti Srisangnam

Introduction

Thailand, officially the Kingdom of Thailand, and formerly known as Siam, is a nation state located on the Indochina and Malay Peninsula in the Southeast Asian Region, bordering its neighbours of Lao PDR and Cambodia in the east, the Gulf of Thailand and Malaysia to the south, Myanmar and the Andaman Sea to the west (resulting in Thailand's maritime borders being adjacent to the islands of the Andaman Sea and the Nicobar Islands of India), and the countries of Myanmar and Lao PDR to the north with the Mekong River acting as a natural border in certain parts of the geography.

Following a long-drawn political divide which began in 2005, the National Council for Peace and Order (NCPO) has intervened, obtaining administrative powers in the process in a coup d'état on May 22, 2014, and annulled the Constitution of Thailand of 2007. Later on, in 2017, a new Constitution of Thailand (2017) was announced, making it the 20th

P. Srisangnam (✉)
ASEAN Studies Center and Faculty of Economics,
Chulalongkorn University, Bangkok, Thailand
e-mail: piti.s@chula.ac.th

R. Macdonald (ed.), *Southeast Asia and the ASEAN Economic Community*, https://doi.org/10.1007/978-3-030-19722-3_4

Constitution of Thailand. The Constitution states that Thailand is and shall be a Constitutional Monarchy, governed by parliamentary democracy, also known as Democracy with the King as the Head of State. His Majesty King Maha Vajiralongkorn Bodindradebayavarangkun (born on July 28, 1952), the only son of King Bhumibol Adulyadej and Queen Sirikit, is the King of Thailand since 2016. The Thai government retroactively declared his reign to have begun on October 13, 2016, upon his father His Majesty King Bhumibol's passing. As the tenth monarch of the Chakri Dynasty, he is also styled as Rama X.

Thailand defines its three governing powers, according to the Secretariat of the Senate (2017), as follows:

1. The Legislative Power, consisting of the National Legislative Assembly (NLA) with members not exceeding 220 in total, who act as interim members for the parliament, the senate, and the house of representatives, with no rigidly defined terms. According to the 2017 Constitution of the Kingdom of Thailand, after the general election in March 2019, the Royal Thai Parliament will be bicameral, consisting of a 250-member nominated Senate and a 500-member House of Representatives, of whom 350 are elected from single-member constituencies and 150 members from party lists.
2. The Administrative Power, with the Prime Minister, appointed by the King in accordance with the resolution of the National Legislative Assembly, and ministers not exceeding 35 in total, appointed by the King in accordance with the Prime Minister's recommendations. The cabinet exercises administrative powers, with the Prime Minister presiding over the administration and being the head of the government. The cabinet has no definitive term.
3. The Judicial Power, consisting of the court system, comprising the Court of Justice, the Constitutional Court, and the Administrative Court as the organizations exercising this power. These organizations are headed by the President of the Supreme Court, the President of the Constitutional Court, and the President of the Supreme Administrative Court, respectively.
4. As for the local administrative authorities, these are categorized into the local administration and the Council of Local Government Organizations, with public servants/officials from both the administrative and judicial branches coming from direct elections of the people.

According to the Office of the Royal Society, Thailand's regions are categorized into the Northern, Northeastern (Isaan), Central, Eastern, Western, and Southern regions (Office of the Royal Society 2017), whereas the administrative jurisdictions are categorized into the following:

1. The central administrations, comprising ministries, bureaus, and departments
2. The regional bureaucracy, comprising 76 provinces, 878 districts (amphoes), and 7255 sub-districts (tambons)
3. The local bureaucracy, consisting of the provincial administration organizations, municipalities, sub-district administration organizations, the Bangkok Metropolitan Administration, and the Pattaya City Administration

Thailand is the world's 50th largest country, covering 513,115 square kilometres, and is also the world's 20th most populous country, with an estimated 68,863,514 citizens in 2016 (UNESA 2017) and an official population census of 2010 of 64,785,909 citizens (The National Statistics Office 2011).

In economic terms, the Thai economy is the world's 20th largest economy in terms of GDP at PPP and the 26th largest by measure of nominal GDP (IMF 2017; World Bank 2017a). The International Monetary Fund (IMF) has estimated that in 2018, Thailand's GDP will be 466.623 million USD, with GDP per capita at 6744 USD/person/year (GDP (PPP) = $1.296 trillion, GDP (PPP) per capita = $18,734). According to the World Bank (2017b), Thailand holds the status of a newly industrialized country, as well as being a major exporter since the 1990s, and its economy is focused on manufacturing, agriculture, and tourism as leading sectors (Image 4.1 and Fig. 4.1).

Economic Policy and Historical Background

After the end of WWII, the economy of Thailand was in a downturn until 1950, at which time the Phibunsongkhram government accepted economic and military aid from the US during the Cold War period. This was meant as both a means to maintain Field Marshal Phibunsongkhram's own position and a means to restore economic livelihood, as well as to ensure Thailand's security in a turbulent regional situation during the Cold War. As such, the economic policies of Thailand in the post-WWII and the

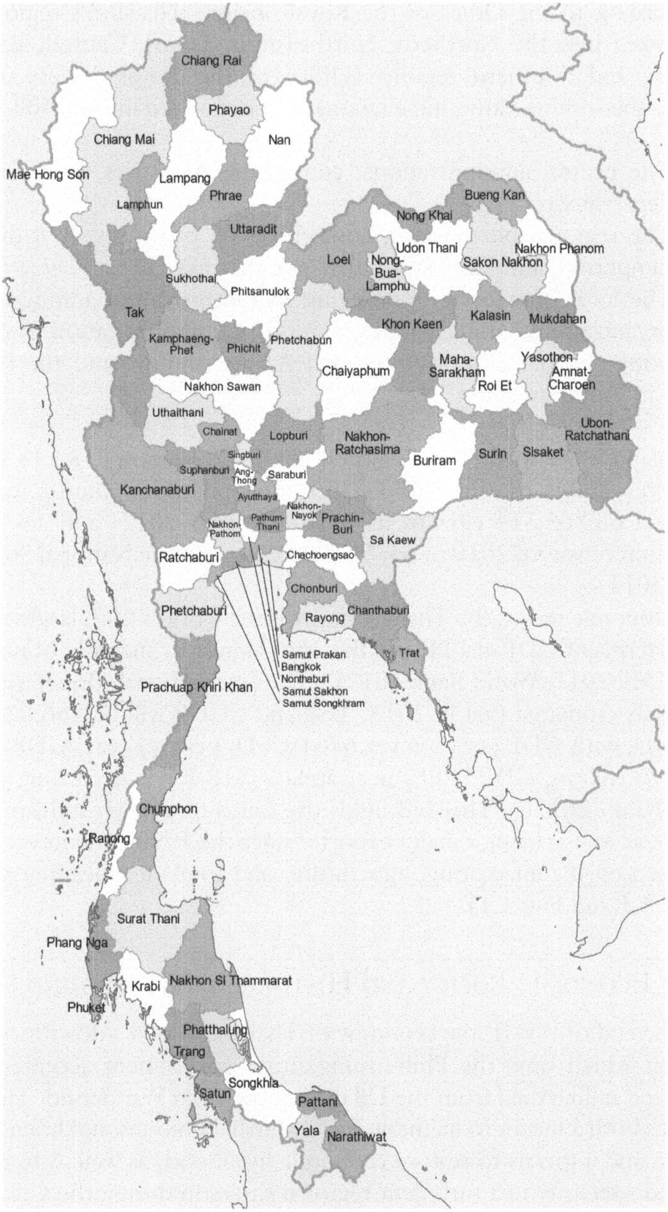

Image 4.1 Map of Thailand. Source: Original by NordNordWest Modifications by Paul_012 https://en.wikipedia.org/wiki/File:Thailand_provinces_en.svg

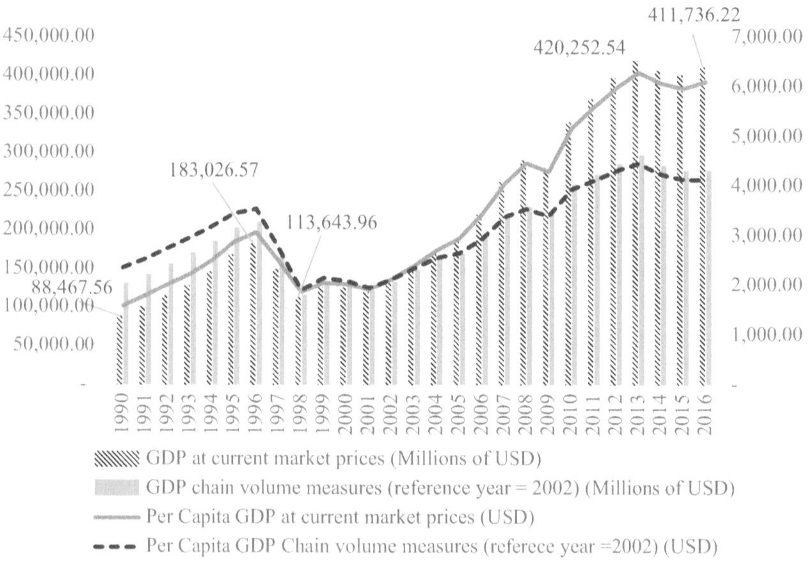

Fig. 4.1 Gross domestic product of Thailand. Right-hand-side axis: Per capita GDP. Left-hand-side axis: GDP in USD million. Data source: World Bank

Cold War periods were geared towards economic nationalism, and the Phibunsongkhram administration had established many state-owned enterprises to operate the various functions of the economy, in favour of national security. This prompted a number of scholars to define the economic policies of these periods as "bureaucratic capitalism" (Nilnopkoon 2012; Satitniramai 2012). Distinct phenomena during 1955–1959 were the financial assistance granted by the US for national security purposes, the establishment of numerous state enterprises, and protectionist trade policies. One of the major positive changes with continued benefits was the attempt to update Thailand's exchange rate regime from a multiple exchange rate system to a fixed unified exchange rate system, which would result in Thailand's improved efficiency in international trade and investment during the mid-1980s.

In addition to this improvement of the exchange rate regime, Thailand's foreign policies interfaced well with the policies of both the US and China for most of the period 1960s–1970s, which was another positive factor for Thailand. When it received the World Bank's expert assistance which led to the establishment of economic organizations, such as the Bureau of Budget, the Office of the National Economic and Social Development Board (NESDB), the Board of Investment (BOI), and the Bank of Thailand (BOT), as well as the formation of the faculties of Economics in Chulalongkorn University and Thammasat University, this marked a significant leap forward for Thailand in terms of human capital in economics, considered a vital element in economic development. During the 1960s–1970s, Thai economic policies shifted from economic nationalism to market-oriented import-substituting industrialization (ISI). These factors have resulted in a rapid expansion of the Thai economy at that time, reaching as high as 7 percent per year throughout the entire period (Nixon 1967).

Thailand faced another economic downturn during the 1970s–1980s, caused by the oil crisis combined with shifting policies of the US in terms of economic and military funding assistance, as well as the Vietnamese army's occupation of Cambodia, which meant that Thailand at the time was located right next to three important communist countries (Lao PDR, Cambodia, and Vietnam), while its western borders were adjacent to Burma (the former name of Myanmar at the time) which had announced itself to be a socialist country under military regime. These circumstances within the region led to the First ASEAN Summit in Indonesia in 1976, which came after the establishment of the Association of Southeast Asian Nations (ASEAN) in 1967, in which five ASEAN member countries (Thailand, Malaysia, Singapore, Indonesia, and the Philippines) needed to strengthen their partnerships and cooperation in response to the turbulent regional situations at the time.

The 1980s saw a new need for Thailand to reform and enhance its economic system. The Thai baht was depreciated three times in succession between 1981 and 1984, in order to stimulate a new force of growth—exports. During the period, export-oriented industrialization became the major policy agenda for the Thai economy, and the exchange rate regime was re-defined again in 1984, with the introduction of the multiple-currency basket peg system, which remained Thailand's monetary policy goal up to July 2, 1997, when the fixed exchange rate regime finally succumbed to the wake of the 1997 Asian Financial Crisis.

The shift towards a currency basket that was heavily weighted towards the US dollar (as high as 80 percent) had resulted in a rapid depreciation of Thai baht when the USD was weakened from the 1985 Plaza Accord. Combined with the infrastructural development projects that have been pursued by the previous governments since the 1960s and the rising domestic purchasing power during the 1980s, the interval between the latter half of the decade up to the mid-1990s appeared to be a golden period for the Thai economy. During this time, capital flows were abundant, and domestic consumption, exports, and investments rapidly flourished, especially with the large influx of foreign direct investment (FDI) from various countries that entered Thailand, along with new technology capitals that augmented Thai production capabilities, especially from Japan. During the 1990s, Thai GDP had enjoyed a rapid growth rate of 9.5 percent per year on average, according to the IMF World Economic Outlook Database calculations, peaking at 13.3 percent in 1988. Thailand's export figures soared during the same period, with growth reaching an average of 14.8 percent per year and peaking at 26.1 percent in 1988 (IMF 2012).

After this period of rapid expansion, however, and despite continued momentum in the growth of exports, especially after the realization of the ASEAN Free Trade Area (AFTA) in 1992/1993, and the multilateral decline in tariff rates from the WTO initiatives during 1994–1995, the competitiveness of the Thai economy began to decline with large trade and current account deficits outgrowing even the high export expansions and economic progress. When it became clear that the Thai economy could not compete in wage rates with other emerging economies of the time, especially China, the inflows of foreign capital which had been abundant before began to decline. The government at the time responded to the situation by liberalizing capital flows through a system known as the Bangkok International Banking Facility (BIBF) in 1993. While this allowed the inflow of capitals to continue, the nature and composition of the capital changed from direct investments to loans, and what followed was the widespread usage of such loans for speculative investment projects that led to an economic bubble. This occurred at the same time when the Thai exchange rate regime was using a fixed rate target through currency baskets, leading to rampant speculations that the government would eventually need to devalue its currency relative to other foreign currencies. Ultimately, monetary policy errors coupled with speculative attacks on the Thai currency led to the most devastating economic crisis of Thai history—the 1997 Asian Financial Crisis. At that time, Thailand had a total of private and public debt of 109,276 million USD, while the national foreign exchange reserve was only at 38,700 million USD (calculated by the author from Bank of Thailand 2018).

Given these factors, rapid speculative attacks from hedge funds were the last straw for the Thai economy, and when the Bank of Thailand at that time made the mistake of dedicating its foreign exchange reserve towards the defence of the fixed exchange rate regime, it resulted in the depletion of the Thai foreign reserves, quickly reduced by as much as 24,000 million USD. Eventually, on July 2, 1997, the Thai foreign reserve amounted to only 2850 million USD, which was clearly inadequate to maintain the fixed exchange rate system any longer. Thailand was abruptly compelled to shift to a managed floating exchange rate system, which saw the drastic and severe depreciation of the baht from 25THB/USD to as low as 56THB/USD. As many debt obligations were denominated in foreign currencies, this sudden change had rendered debtors utterly unable to repay their obligations in time, and the production sector froze since it could not import additional inputs from abroad for its activities at such an exchange rate. What immediately followed was the fall of 56 Thai financial institutions, and the stock exchange index of Thailand had plummeted from its peak at 1753.73 points in 1997 to a meagre 207.31 points in 1998. The unemployment rate rose from 1.5 percent in 1996 to 4.4 percent in 1998. The gross national product diminished from 3.115 trillion USD in 1996 to 2.749 trillion USD in 1998 (a negative economic growth of 10.5 percent for the year). Thailand would need almost a decade to rise to the GDP levels of 1996 again (IMF 2012). This required Thailand to receive financial and academic assistance from the IMF, totalling 17.2 million USD (IMF 2000).

The disastrous effects of the 1997 crisis prompted the Thai economy to reconsider and reform its economic policies and exercise much caution in its monetary policy. Transactions by the financial institutions in the system, although more liberalized than before, were also subject to very strict scrutiny and regulations, at par with international best practice standards, and even exceeded them in certain areas. Fiscal policies were directed towards strengthening social safety nets and welfare systems to cope with the aftermaths of the crisis. Thailand also shifted its international trade and investment strategies to become more of a leader in pushing for economic, trade, and investment integration within the regional and sub-regional levels, as in the role of Thailand in determining the ASEAN 2020 Vision announced in the ASEAN Summit of 1997, hosted in Malaysia to mark the 30th anniversary of ASEAN.

In the domestic economy, the government led by Thaksin Shinawatra, a former telecommunications tycoon who turned to politics, forming the

Thai Rak Thai Party, began its endeavour to stimulate the economy in 2001, through a series of populist policies, which were dubbed with the nickname of "Thaksinomics". During its time, the Thai Rak Thai Party's administration employed various populist policies both to promote growth and to garner support for the government. Examples of Thaksin's populist policies, or "Thaksinomics", included a four-year debt moratorium for farmers to gain their trust and the subsidies for petrol and fuels for vehicles for reducing the impacts of soaring global oil prices since January 2004. His administration also ordered state-owned banks to grant more loans with low interest rates to farmers, small enterprises, and villages. The state-owned electricity company, Electricity Generating Authority of Thailand (EGAT), was also ordered to give partial subsidies on electricity prices. One of his highly popular policies was "the 30 Baht Universal Healthcare Program", under which, state hospitals offered universal healthcare coverage at an affordable rate of 30 baht or approximately 0.75 USD per visit. This helped many people especially those with lower income who were previously unable to access healthcare services, but the implementation of the system also raised criticisms from physicians in practice. He stimulated the development of Small and Medium-Sized Enterprises (SMEs) in the rural areas with the "One Tambon, One Product program" or "OTOP" (one sub-district, one product) to promote their growth (Wehrfritz 2008).

On the other hand, Thaksin was a fervent proponent of privatization of state-owned enterprises and continuously pushed for the state-owned EGAT (Electricity Generating Authority of Thailand) electricity company to be privatized. However, the privatization did not happen since the social movement fought against this policy so hard. Thailand's state-owned power company, EGAT, looks set to halt the construction of new domestic power plants and suspend its investment plans abroad after a Thai court ruled that its privatization plans were illegal. In response to a petition it received in November 2005, the court nullified two government decrees that gave consent for EGAT to pursue with plans to sell 25 percent of its assets to private investors. The petition was filed by 11 civic groups that feared partial privatization would result in price hikes and would ultimately be detrimental to national assets. The court ruled that the government had broken several regulations by commencing with plans to privatize the company, including allowing a member of the privatization committee with potential conflicting interests. Before the ruling was given, EGAT's chief executive had warned that if privatization was stopped, the company would be forced to withdraw foreign investment and cut back with infrastructure improvements (Power Engineering 2006).

Thaksin's administration also launched the "Mega Projects" that involved over 50 billion USD investments in public infrastructures, such as public transit, road systems, the construction of a large-scale international airport, Suvarnabhumi Airport, and the established cartels or consortiums for raising export prices, in the rubber industry, for example (Wehrfritz 2008).

Despite high rates of growth that flourished at an average of 5.1 percent between 2001 and 2006 during the Thaksin Shinawatra's administration, where Thailand saw a rise in its International Institute for Management Development (IMD) Global Competitiveness Scoreboard ranking from the 31st place in the global community in 2002 to the 25th place in 2005, the period was also plagued by widespread corruption and conflicts of interests problems from politicians, together with accusations of misusing state policies to benefit friends and relatives, and Thailand's inequality situation and gaps had also significantly worsened. These unsolved problems eventually led to a military coup in 2006. An Army General, Sonthi Boonyaratglin, organized a coup with a group of soldiers, calling themselves the Council for Democratic Reform under the Constitutional Monarchy (CDRCM), on September 19, 2006. Thaksin was away in New York to give a speech at the UN General Assembly at that time, and this coup ended his administration, leading to his self-imposed exile which continues to this day. Later in 2008, the Supreme Court's Criminal Division for Holders of Political Positions sentenced that Thaksin was guilty of misusing the office and administrative power while he was the prime minister, by using them to allow his wife to buy public land at auctions with loopholes. The court sentenced him in his absence to serve two years in prison. Currently, six cases about him remain in court, where most of them are focused on charges of misuses of authority to grant abnormal benefits to friends, relatives, and family, which caused damages to the country's administrative system.

The period which followed between 2006 and 2011 was characterized by the severe lack of political stability in Thai society and the economy, and economic policies became very inconsistent between different administrations after the coup. During that period, Thailand had as many as five prime ministers, namely, General Surayud Chulanont (2006–2008), Samak Sundaravej (2008), Somchai Wongsawat (2008), Abhisit Vejjajiva (2008–2011), and Yingluck Shinawatra (2011–2014).

Under General Surayud Chulanont, the Thai economy faced a sharp decline in economic growth rate, with the rates decreasing from 6.1 percent in 2006 to 4.8 percent in 2007, due to political instability and the worldwide effects of the Subprime Economic Crisis. The outbreak of the Subprime Crisis resulted in severe economic problems for both the US and the EU, both of which have been Thailand's major export destinations, leading to a rapid decline in Thai exports at the time. The succeeding administrations of Samak Sundaravej and Somchai Wongsawat also faced numerous problems as they were Thaksin's political nominees in practice while he was abroad as a refugee from charges and allegations of corruption. The Samak and Somchai administration did not last long in office, and the economic growth rate of Thailand in 2008 fell to 2.8 percent and continued to fall until a negative growth rate of −2.3 percent was reached for the first time since the 1997–1998 Asian Financial Crisis.

Abhisit Vejjajiva became the next prime minister of Thailand in late 2008, in a period of turbulent global economy and tensions in domestic politics. Nevertheless, Thailand was able to enjoy a growth rate of 10 percent by the year 2010. Along with this high growth rate, the Thai stock market index and the baht finally rebounded, reaching peak levels for the first time since the dreaded Asian Financial Crisis in 1997. Abhisit's administration promoted the "People's Agenda" that focuses on improving the living conditions of poor and working-class citizens.

The political and economic situations in Thailand began to look grim again when Ms Yingluck Shinawatra succeeded to office. She had explicitly presented herself as the political representative of her brother Thaksin Shinawatra, who has been living in self-imposed exile after his conviction and court charges. Her Pheu Thai Party—which was the reformed Thai Rak Thai Party—secured its victory through a policy guaranteeing the procurement price of paddy rice at the defined rate of 15,000 THB per ton (roughly 450 USD), 4000 THB above the previous rate set by the Democrat Party before. This specified rate was very attractive to rice farmers, as it is at almost 50 percent above the rice price in the global market. Since almost 40 percent of labour force in Thailand works in the agricultural sector, and rice is the dominant subsector in agriculture, Yingluck secured victory after Abhisit's administration ended, and she was sworn into office on August 10, 2011, after a period of political turmoil (Biswas et al. 2015).

The core concept of the policy was in three steps and these were rather straightforward but had implementation problems. The government would purchase rice from farmers at inflated prices and then stockpile it to drive up the price of rice in the global market by reducing supplies. The plan was to sell the rice again when prices are high and recover the price loss incurred earlier from the global market. But the true hazard of this policy was that it undermined the rice production structure of Thailand in the long term, since it effectively eliminates the need for rice farmers to select and develop breeds of rice that give good quality products. In effect, farmers around the country abandoned their higher quality rice breeds that needed a longer time to produce and raced to plant low-grade breeds that could be harvested as early as possible and were cheap in costs, so that they could receive procurement payments from the state and earn the margins.

As a result, the government was left with very low-grade supplies of rice that could not be properly sold in the global market. As time passed, these unsold supplies of rice which amounted to more than 17.5 million tonnes had started to decay, and the rice export capabilities of Thailand suffered. The value of Thai rice exports had decreased by 35 percent in 2011/2012, and 39 percent in 2012/2013, but the government had made a loss of more than 20 billion USD in buying the pledged supply of rice (Biswas et al. 2015). Political problems started to appear again and political unrest eventually led to another military coup by General Prayuth Chan-ocha, with the name of the National Council for Peace and Order (NCPO), seizing administrative power in May 22, 2014.

Prayuth's administration, after the 2014 coup, launched its "Thailand 4.0" economic initiative in 2016. According to Apornrath (2017), the Thailand 4.0 initiative is a "*master plan to free Thailand from the middle-income trap, making it a high-income nation in five years*".

The Prayuth government mentions the different stages of development that came before the 4.0 era. Thailand 1.0 was the pre-modern Thai agrarian economy which was dominant decades ago. After light industries and manufacturing emerged in Thailand, its economy moved on to Thailand 2.0 that relied on textiles, food processing, and other light industries, not requiring much capital. Currently, Thailand is in its Thailand 3.0 state where it focuses on heavy industries and energy, which, according to Apornrath (2017), contribute as much as 70 percent of Thailand's GDP. The current government's vision of Thailand 4.0 is as a high-technology and innovation-based economy to increase value-added in products and services, and this initiative is described by three elements: (1) to elevate Thailand to a high-income developed country; (2) to make Thai society a more inclusive society; and (3) to give importance to sustainable development and sustainable growth (Languepin 2016).

In the hopes of linking Thailand with other emerging economies in Mainland ASEAN (Cambodia, Lao PDR, Myanmar, and Vietnam), a number of economic corridors and dedicated special economic zones (SEZs) were established and are currently designated as a major part of Thailand's ongoing economic strategy. The Eastern Economic Corridor (EEC) Development Plan under the Thailand 4.0 Initiative is aiming to revitalize and enhance the Eastern Seaboard Development Program, an important strategic economic infrastructure which has strengthened Thailand's industrial production capacities for over 30 years, securing its competitive advantage. To implement this policy, the EEC Policy Committee, chaired by the prime minister of Thailand, has been established in hopes of promoting innovation in industries and advanced technologies that may transform Thailand's investment and production in the areas in the east and promote significant economic progress, focusing initially on three main provinces—Chachoengsao, Chonburi, and Rayong.

In order to realize such ambitious goals, the government must also provide multiple supporting measures to promote rapid economic growth within the EEC, which has a large coverage of over 13,000 square kilometres. These announced measures are expected to consist of development of key infrastructures, transportation and logistics systems, public utilities, investment promotion and facilitative measures, and human resources. The One-stop Service Center is expected to be established to fulfil these roles (EECO 2017).

Natural Resources, Strengths, and Comparative Advantages

Thailand's land area covers 513,120 square kilometres and includes a variety of geographic patterns. The northern regions of Thailand are the Thai highlands made up of multiple mountain ranges, with the highest peak being the Doi Inthanon Peak, located 2565 metres above sea level. These mountain ranges act as the foundations of Thailand's four key rivers, the Ping, Wang, Yom, and Nan rivers, which form the important freshwater system in Thailand's northern provinces. This combination of mountains and rivers has endowed the northern provinces with valuable minerals, forests, and fertile hilly plains for agriculture and livestock. This region of Thailand, along with the northern parts of Laos and Myanmar and the adjacent southern part of China, was historically known collectively as

"Lanna" and "Lanxang", which means the place for plentiful rice paddies and livestock, respectively.

The Northeastern Region or Isaan is characterized by its plateau geography, known as the Khorat Plateau, which slopes down eastward and separates from the Khmer Plains in Cambodia. The Isaan region is vitalized by three key rivers, which are the Mekong, Chee, and Mun Rivers, giving birth to a wide area of plateaus that can be used for rice plantations. The best breeds of Thailand's rice are from this region, especially the Hom Mali Rice or the famous Thai Fragrant Long-Grain Rice. The region's nature also makes it suitable for raising livestock and various types of farming, including salt and potash production as well.

Central Thailand is largely a congregation of river basins centred around Thailand's most important river, the Chao Phraya River, which comes from the combination of the four great rivers of the north, the Ping, Wang, Yom, and Nan Rivers. The Chao Phraya River acts as both the lifeline for agriculture and transportation, functioning as a key route of logistics since ancient times. Nevertheless, Thailand's river-based transportation system has largely gone into dormancy, especially since the 1960s when the country experienced a boom in its road infrastructure and traffic. The Chao Phraya River proceeds on to the Gulf of Thailand (covering more than 320,000 square kilometres of area), which is considered to be one of the most fertile and biologically diverse ecosystems in the world. The abundance of marine resources in the area comes from the sediments from the various rivers flowing into the gulf, namely, the Chao Phraya River, Meklong River, Bang Pakong River, and the Tapi River. As a result, many cities, old and new, have sprouted at the river mouths over the course of the Thai history, such as the Bangkok metropolis, Samut Prakarn, Samut Sakorn, Samut Songkhram, Chon Buri, Chachoengsao, and Rayong. These cities are also the locations of important commercial ports (Bangkok Port, Laem Chabang Seaport, Map Ta Phut Seaport, and Sattahip Seaport) and are located near important sources of food from agriculture, fisheries, and processed foods. Given the importance of these cities, many industrial zones and manufacturing factories have flocked around them as well. In addition to these strong points, there are also reserves of natural gas in the Gulf of Thailand, which provides some security to Thailand's energy security.

The southern regions of Thailand are located on an isthmus which connects to the Malay Peninsula. The Tanintharyi Mountain Range, spanning across a length of more than 1700 kilometres, forms the spine of this region, separating the Gulf of Thailand which leads to the Pacific Ocean, from the Andaman Sea in the Indian Ocean. The Andaman Sea is very important to the fishery industries and also provides Thailand with valuable natural gases and other minerals which generate much income and downstream industries for the country. Breathtaking isles, beaches, and coral reefs have also populated the surrounding areas with tourist destinations that attract substantial income to the country each year. Tourism is the most important source of income in Thailand's service sector. The tourism industry started to play a significant role in the Thai Economy in 1987, when the government and the private sector cooperated to launch a grand "Welcome to Thailand" Campaign for the first time, resulting in rapid tourism growth ever since.

Thailand's geographical landscape permits the development of an agricultural industry and processed agricultural products industry, especially large-scale food industries, attracting a significant portion of Thai labour force. At first, the food manufacturing industry of Thailand relied much on foreign investment and technology, but Thai entrepreneurs have been learning and investing heavily in their own R&D for many years, resulting in their ability to operate on a large scale with high comparative advantage in agricultural and food industries.

The Thai service subsectors, especially in tourism, hotels, and food, are derived from Thailand's geographical advantages and diversity, ranging from the mountainous North to the oceanic isles and beautiful seas in the southern parts, coupled with Thailand's unique culture and heritage. Thai cuisines, combined with Thai people's hospitality, contributes to Thailand being a highly popular destination for tourists from around the world.

Thailand's manufacturing sector enjoyed high competitive advantage in textiles, electric appliances, and electronics in the past. More recently, Thailand excels in computer parts and integrated circuits. But it should also be mentioned that regardless of the export and manufacturing values remaining at high levels, the comparative advantage of Thailand has been steadily decreasing, as Thailand relies much on its young labour force, and attracted investors through relatively low-wage rates in the past. Most of the production operations were done as Original Equipment Manufacturers, or contracted manufacturing, without any substantial establishment of Thailand's own brands or technology. As Thailand now becomes an ageing society, the previously abundant supply of labour has dwindled, and Thailand is left without its own technology or brands in this industry as well, which means that it will soon lose much of its competitive advantage in the sector (Fig. 4.2).

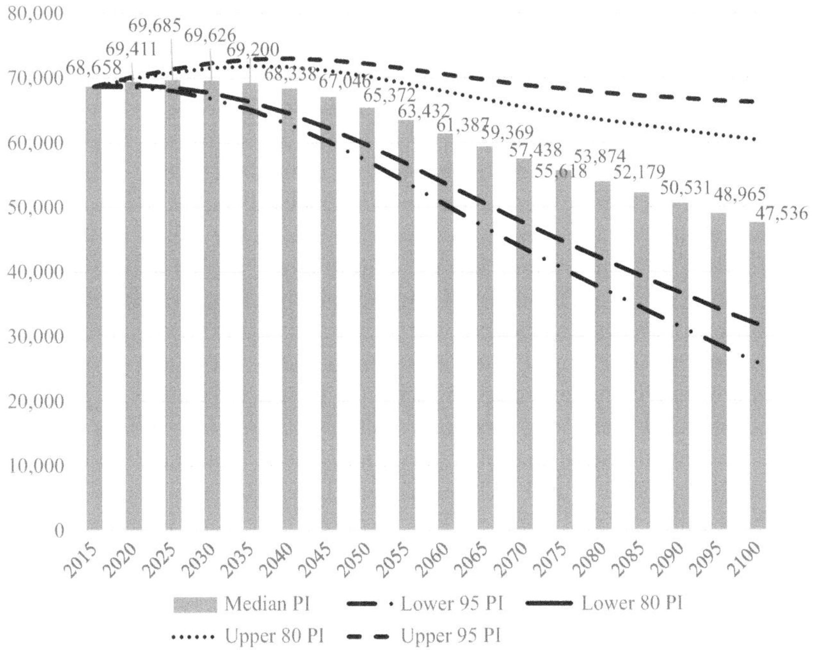

Fig. 4.2 Thailand population statistics (2010, 2020, 2030, 2040). Source: Compiled by author from United Nations, Department of Economic and Social Affairs, Population Division (2017). Probabilistic Population Projections Based on the World Population Prospects: The 2017 Revision. Population Division, DESA. http://esa.un.org/unpd/wpp/andPopulation Development Plan in the 11th National Economics and Social Development Plan, Office of the National Economics and Social Development Board, Thailand. Data source: United Nations/DESA Population Division. Available at https://population.un.org/wpp/Download/Probabilistic/Population/

Unskilled Labour and Migrant Workers

According to the 2010 population census, Thailand has a total of 64,785,909 citizens (National Statistical Office of Thailand 2012), and the most recent 2017 estimate has been 68,414,135 (UNESA 2017). Life expectancy at birth for Thais is currently at 74.9 years, and the median age of the population is currently at 37.7 years, which is higher than the Southeast Asian regional average, being at the second highest place in the region after Singapore (40 years) and a place above Brunei (30.6 years) (Statista 2018).

When we consider the population pyramid, it becomes evident that Thailand is an ageing society, with a total dependency ratio at 40 percent in 2015 (youth dependency ratio = 25.2 percent and elderly dependency ratio = 14.8 percent). Thailand's children aged between 0 and 14 years are at 6,503,133 persons, or 16.93 percent of the total population, whereas senior citizens of over 65 years old are at 7,238,248 persons, which is 10.58 percent of the entire population in 2017 (CIA Factbook 2018). It should be noted that while the total population of Thailand has been growing at a highly reduced rate, reaching as low as 0.4 percent per year (2017 data), the proportion of senior citizens has been rising at an alarmingly high rate as people aged 60 and over are increasing at approximately five percent each year, while population aged 80 and over increases by over six percent per year. It is estimated that the year 2019 will be the first year that Thailand will have more seniors (aged 60 and over) than children (aged below 15 years) (Institute for Population and Social Research, Mahidol University 2017).

In the near future, the number of senior citizens will continue to surge and Thailand will become a full-fledged aged society perhaps as soon as 2021, when the share of population aged 60 and over exceeds 20 percent of the total population. This is because the population cohort born during 1963–1983, the generation which experienced high birth rates of over million persons per year, will soon become senior citizens (right now, this group of the population is aged between 35 and 55 years). If no significant changes or measures are made to tackle this pattern, Thailand will most likely enter the super-aged society stage in 2031, when population over 60 years old reaches 28 percent of total Thai population (Institute for Population and Social Research, Mahidol University 2017). Towards the end of the 2030s, this major population cohort will be aged 55–75 years, and about a third of the population will be older than 60 years.

As a result, Thailand will face a very important challenge in human capital: the shortage of labour resulting from this demographic structure. The World Bank has forecasted that the decrease of the Thai labour force in this manner will surely deteriorate its economic performance and growth (World Bank 2016). One of the attempts to deal with this challenge has been to allow inward movement of labour from Thailand's neighbour countries in the ASEAN region, through the Memorandum of

Understanding (MOU) on Cooperation in the Employment of Workers between Thailand, Lao PDR, Cambodia, and Myanmar.

This MOU started in the 1990s, when Thailand's labour migrant status shifted from being a net-sending country to a net-receiving country in terms of migrant workers. Rapid economic development and multiple other factors caused this change and led to the large inflow of unskilled workers from its neighbours in the region. The major sources for these workers are Myanmar, Cambodia, and, to a lesser extent, Laos.

This phenomenon was not only due to economic development by itself, but also to the fact that Thais prefer higher paying jobs with better working conditions and social status. Manual and physical labour tasks almost always come with low levels of payment and are associated with negative social status, often combined with physical exhaustion and sometimes dangerous or unsanitary work conditions. As such, many Thai workers have moved away from these jobs and the gaps needed to be filled by unskilled migrants from other countries. For a long time, however, workers from Thailand's neighbours, especially from Myanmar, Lao PDR, and Cambodia, employed to do these jobs have tended to be illegal immigrants who are unaccounted for. In the attempt to compromise regulatory frameworks with the reality of the informal economy in Thailand, various governments have launched numerous measures, such as relieving penalties for illegal immigrants, allowing for temporary employment and facilitation of registrations. But, as the demographical structure of Thailand and the following unskilled labour shortage problem is a long-term structural issue, the demand for unskilled workers will always remain strong and cannot be remedied simply with temporary measures.

Given Thailand's export intensiveness and fierce cost-based competition between many similar developing countries manufacturing similar products, it relies much on low-wage labour. It becomes inevitable that migrant workers with low-wage costs are vital in maintaining Thailand's export competitiveness in such a manner. This means that the temporary measures, such as registration processes, will be inadequate in the long term, and in reality, the number of illegal migrant workers has not decreased. In fact, the number has grown larger every year despite efforts to discourage them. Also, migrant workers have been frequently re-registering as well. All of this suggests that the many employed measures are not effective solutions to the long-term structural problem of unskilled labour shortage that has become a defining trait of the Thai economy.

As such, in 1999, the Bangkok Declaration on Irregular Migration was introduced and this was supported by 19 countries in the Asia-Pacific region, where the key element of this declaration has been to promote mutual cooperation in addressing labour migration issues, and this was also the starting point for other three important bilateral Memoranda of Understandings (MOUs), which were made between Thailand and Cambodia, Laos, and Myanmar, respectively (Vasuprasat 2010).

A comprehensive amnesty programme for workers who have migrated illegally was launched in 2004, where registration windows were opened and allowed existing workers to receive temporary worker ID cards. It is worth mentioning that the majority of migrant workers in Thailand has long been from Myanmar. Still, the measure was not adequate, and these registration windows needed to be opened again in 2009 and 2011. Another attempt in addressing the problem was the 2008 amendment of the Alien Employment Act, which facilitated the legal employment of foreign workers and contributed to the implementation of the MOU and NV procedures on the issue of migrant workers.

Thailand is currently in a crucial tipping point in its economic history, as it is currently an upper-level middle-income country, emphasizing on its industrial and manufacturing sectors in an attempt to escape the middle-income trap phenomenon. This means that it requires inexpensive low-skilled labour to maintain its competitive edge in the labour-intensive industries, which is a gap that needs to be filled by migrant workers from its neighbours. One reason for this is that Thai unskilled labourers are deemed to be more costly, yet less productive and more prone to laziness and malingering in their performance. Coupled with the ageing population in Thai demographics, the issue will become even more pronounced in the long term. As such, Thailand will need a solid framework for long-term strategies and policies on migrant labour which will take into account the interests of various stakeholder groups. This remains absent and lacking at the moment. Substantial research and forecasts on the labour situation in the new labour landscape governed by the MOU are required, as well as into the effects on Thai society and the economy.

International and social pressures on labour standards and best practices have resulted in positive developments in the migrant labour situation as the government has been more attentive towards the issues of migrant labour rights, human trafficking problems, and the protection of human rights and combating labour exploitation and abuses. Globally, consumers in developed countries, such as the US, Europe, and Australia, have become much more sophisticated in matters of human rights and whether their goods are produced ethically. Similarly, the international public sectors are also concerned with labour welfare issues, such as the Trafficking in Persons Report (TIP) in the US. In this light, multiple measures have been introduced and implemented to ensure greater degree of welfare protection for migrant labours, including the revision of ministerial regulations for workers who are employed in the domestic household work sector and the fisheries sector, which are the two most common sectors that have been employing migrant workers from Thailand's neighbouring countries. Other measures include a stronger labour inspection system, formal registration for workers in the fisheries sector, and there has been stronger collaborative efforts between NGOs and the government authorities in promoting labour welfare and safety as well.

The current military government gave its attention to the various aspects of the labour movement issue in Thailand since 2014 when it came to power, and the attitude of the government, combined with public expectations and speculations, poses significant effects on migrant labour situations, both positively and adversely. For example, several actions and statements of the government caused panic among workers, resulting in a massive outflow of Cambodian workers and a consequent sudden labour shortage for several sectors dependent on low-wage labour from the neighbouring country, such as the agricultural and certain industrial subsectors. Following this event, the Thai economy has become more aware of the importance and contribution of migrant labours in the Thai production economy.

During the same month that the Cambodian workers' brief exodus occurred, the US TIP Report, mentioned earlier, had downgraded Thailand to the lowest level of "Tier 3", on alleged grounds of severe and worsening trafficking situations in Thailand. In response to this sudden downgrading, the National Council for Peace and Order (NCPO), acting as the country's administration, organized two bodies: the committee and the sub-committee on Solving Problems of Migrant Workers to handle the issue and improve the migrant labour outlook. The NCPO administration also established one-stop service centres for registration of migrant workers throughout various provinces, hoping to formalize the previously informal migrant labour sector and mitigate the human trafficking and illegal immigrant problems. Following these measures, immense numbers of migrant workers, exceeding 1.6 million irregulars, registered during the period between June 26 and November 29 of that year. This marked an important point in formalizing the migrant labour force—while not the entirety of the migrant workers in Thailand, they counted as a significant portion of the group. The government then attempted to facilitate the registration processes and ease up the application of work permits and extensions, as well as to establish common standards throughout the country, by reducing costs, red tapes, and obstacles, including the tackling of corrupt practices which have been denounced by the government.

Competitiveness and Ease of Doing Business

During 2017–2018, The Global Competitiveness Report (GCR) made by the World Economic Forum (WEF) has ranked Thailand at the 32nd place within a total of 137 countries examined, an advance of two ranks since the previous report. Among the nine ASEAN countries ranked, Thailand is ranked 3rd, following Singapore (3rd globally) and Malaysia (23rd globally), and is close to Indonesia which is ranked 36th. Other countries in ASEAN were Brunei (46th), Vietnam (55th), Cambodia (94th), and Laos (98th). The key items that can make much difference for Thailand in the near future include solid improvements in infrastructure, macroeconomic environment, market efficiency, health and education development, financial market development, and technological readiness.

Thailand has been ranked 41st in terms of basic requirements (scoring at 5.1 points), 35th for efficiency enhancers (4.6 points), and 47th for innovation and sophistication factors (3.9 points). It can then be observed that among the three main components, innovation and sophistication factors for businesses is currently the weakest item for Thailand. Business sophistication is an appreciation of both firm strategy and operations, as well as the network of businesses (cluster development, quality of suppliers, control of international distribution, etc.). This index remains the same as in the previous report of 2016–2017, where Thailand was also ranked 47th in this category.

For the 12 subcategories of indicators that the GCR uses in ranking countries' competitiveness, the observations for Thailand can be concluded as follows (STI 2018; Schwab and Sala-i-Martin 2018):

a. Basic requirements: In 2017–2018, Thailand enjoys a higher rank from 44th in the previous report to its current place at 41st. Looking at the components, the institutional factors are ranked 78th (from 84th), infrastructural quality at 43rd (from 49th), and macroeconomic environment exhibits notable improvement from 13th place to the current 9th ranking. Yet, health and primary education remains low, and fell from 86th to 90th place.

b. Efficiency enhancers: During the past year, Thailand enjoyed a slightly increasing rank from 37th to 35th. The subfactor components indicate that many of these have improved, such as higher education and training (62nd to 57th), goods market efficiency (37th to 33rd), labour market efficiency (71st to 65th), and technological readiness (71st to 65th). The only worsened component was the financial market development, which went down slightly from 39th to 40th. The market size indicator remains at 18th, same as last year.
c. Innovation and sophistication factors: Overall, Thailand is placed 47th, which is the same ranking as last year. But when taking a look at the components, two subfactors have improved, which are business potential (42nd from 43rd) and innovation (50th from 54th).
d. Technological readiness factor: Thailand scores 4.5 out of 7 for this item, placing Thailand in the 61st ranking. This is a slight improvement from 4.3 points to 63rd place in the last year's ranking. Most of the subfactors related to the private sector are ranked in the middle zones. The availability of latest technologies enjoyed much higher ranking from 70th to 56th, firm-level technology absorption 42nd from 43rd, and FDI and technology transfer 40th from 42nd. Most of the rankings related to Information and Communication Technology (ICT) and Internet remain at lower levels compared to other countries, such as the Internet users as percentage of the population which stands at 47.5 percent and ranking 86th, whereas Iceland, the top country, has 98.2 percent of Internet usage. Fixed broadband Internet subscriptions per 100 population for Thailand is at 10.7 per 100 persons and ranking 86th, while Switzerland ranking at the top has 46.3 per 100 persons. During the past year, the statistics for Internet bandwidth in kb/s/user has significantly worsened from 53rd place to the 75th; still, mobile broadband subscriptions per 100 people has notably improved from 34th ranking to 24th, with 94.7 persons per 100 population of subscription.
e. Innovation statistics: During 2017–2018, Thailand has moved up to the 50th place (3.5 points out of 7), from the previous 54th place in the 2016–2017 evaluation (3.4 points). The innovation indexes can be further classified into the following categories. Capacity for inno-

vation for Thailand is at 4.1 points, ranking 69th, from 70th in the previous year, where the top performer is Switzerland which has 6.2 points. The quality of scientific research institutions remains the same as last year at 4.0 points and is ranked 56th, while Luxembourg is the highest-ranking country with 6.6 points. Company spending on R&D is 3.6 points and moved up to 43rd ranking from last year's 46th, with Luxembourg being the top country in this area as well (6.1 points). University-industry collaboration in R&D for Thailand is at 3.9 points, being ranked 39th (from 41st), and, again, Luxembourg is the top performer with 5.8 points. Government procurement of advanced technology products is at 3.4 points, moving up to 56th ranking from last year's 65, with Qatar being the top-ranked country at 5.6 points. The availability of scientists and engineers is at 4.1 points, compared to Finland in the first place at 6.0, where Thailand is now ranked 56th (from last year's 57th). And finally, PCT patent applications per 1 million population is at 66th ranking (from 70th in the last evaluation), which counts for 1.5 patents per 1 million Thai people. While the patent application statistics of Thailand has improved, it is still extremely low when compared to the world's top performer, Japan, whose patent application is at 334.9 per 1 million population.

The "2018 Doing Business Report" by the World Bank Group places Thailand in the 26th ranking, out of a total of 190 economies examined. This report focuses on the ease of doing businesses for SMEs in various countries, and Thailand has seen significant improvement from the previous year's ranking of 48th place. The methodology used for handling the data was applied for both years. According to Office of the OPDC (2018), the following reasons contributed to the improvement in Thailand's rankings (Figs. 4.3, 4.4, 4.5, 4.6, 4.7, and 4.8).

a. Starting a business: Certain outdated rules have been abolished, such as the requirement for a company's seal, and the previously required approval of companies' work rules and regulations that were formerly needed from the Department of Labour Protection and Welfare.
b. Getting electricity: Access to electricity in Thailand has been made easier as a geographic information system was implemented. This

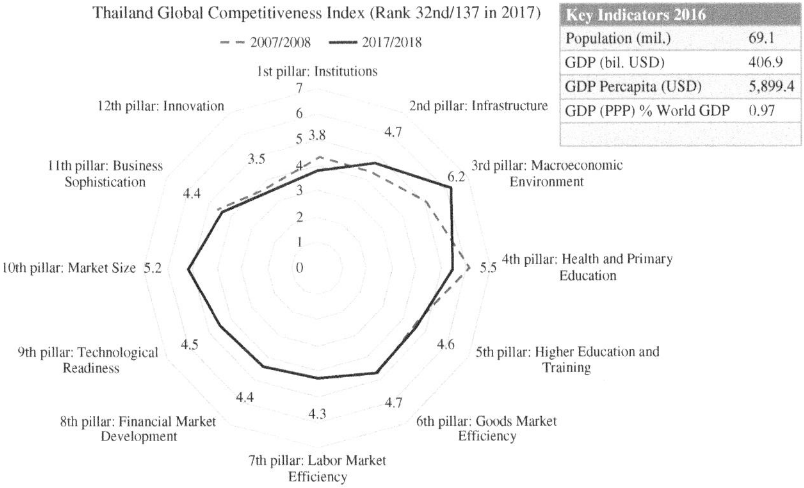

Fig. 4.3 Thailand Global Competitiveness Index (2017). Data source: World Economic Forum Data (http://reports.weforum.org/global-competitiveness-index-2017-2018/countryeconomy-profiles/#economy=THA)

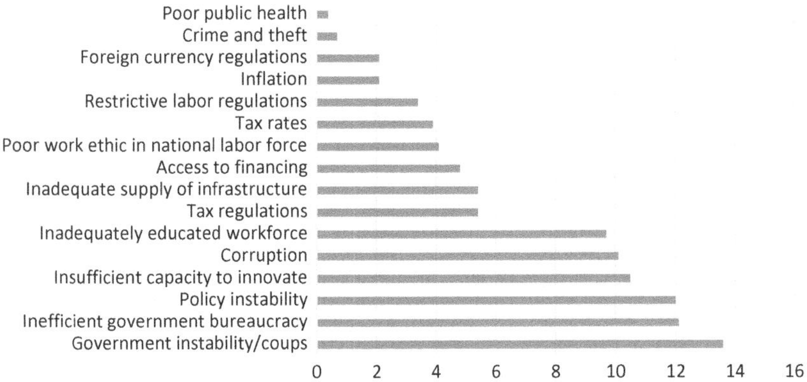

Fig. 4.4 Most problematic factors for doing business in Thailand (2017/2018). Data source: World Economic Forum Data (http://reports.weforum.org/global-competitiveness-index-2017-2018/countryeconomy-profiles/#economy=THA)

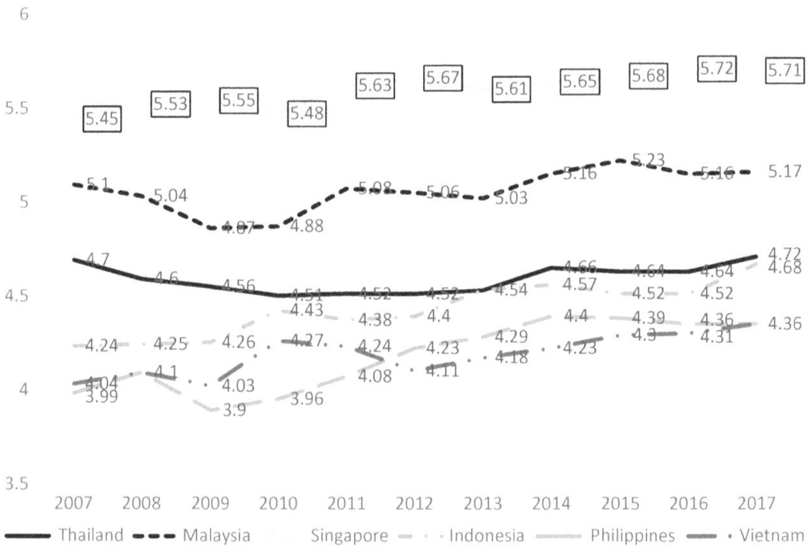

Fig. 4.5 Thailand Global Competitiveness Index 2007–2017. Source: Adapted by author from World Economic Forum Data

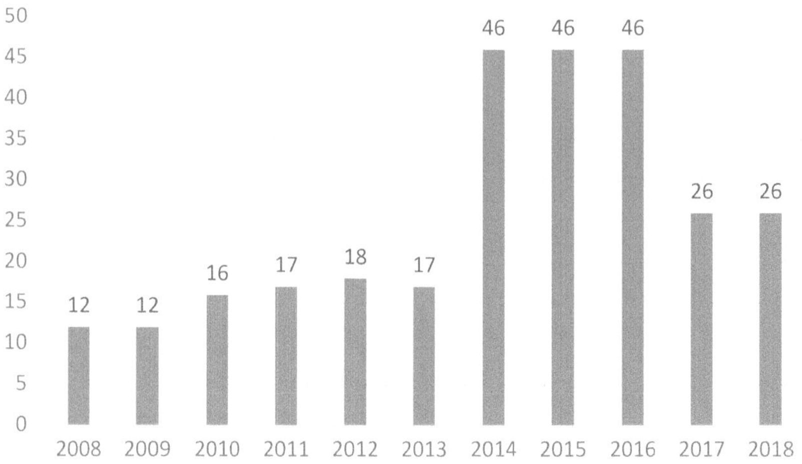

Fig. 4.6 Ease of doing business: Thailand (rank global). Source: Adapted by author from the World Bank

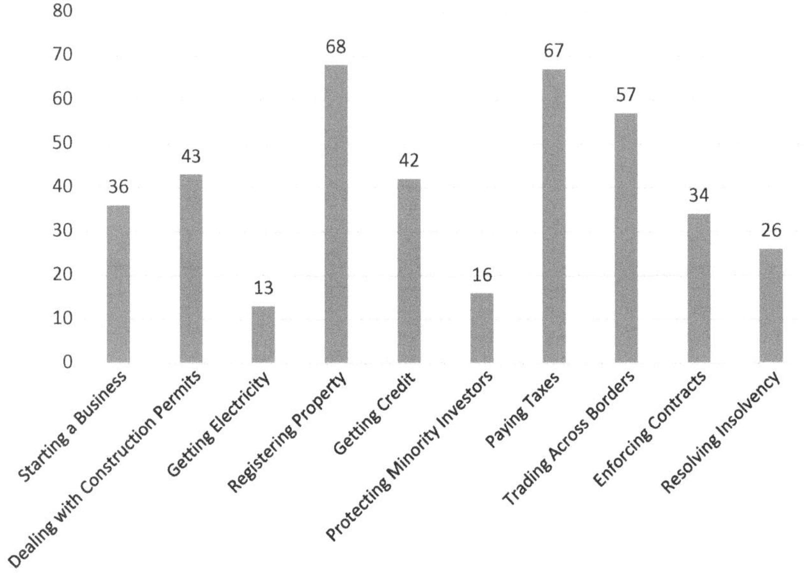

Fig. 4.7 Ranking on doing business topics: Thailand (2017). Source: Adapted by author from the World Bank (http://www.doingbusiness.org/content/dam/doingBusiness/country/t/thailand/THA.pdf)

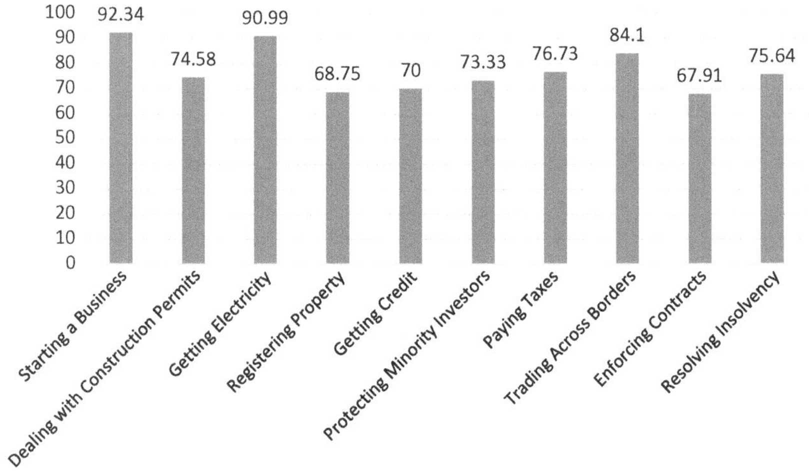

Fig. 4.8 Distance to Frontier (DTF) on doing business topics: Thailand. Source: Adapted by author from the World Bank (http://www.doingbusiness.org/content/dam/doingBusiness/country/t/thailand/THA.pdf)

promoted access since it eliminated the need for external site inspections.

c. Registering property: The geographic information has also been useful in improving the reliability of administering land plots through the system, as the maps for most of Bangkok have been scanned.
d. Getting credit: The collateral system has been updated to incorporate a wider range of assets and allows a general description of possible collaterals. Also, the security interest can be automatically attached to the original asset's proceeds. Out-of-court enforcement of collaterals was also allowed, along with the establishment of clear grounds for relief from a stay for secured creditors during reorganization procedures.
e. Protecting minority investors: Legal actions can be made against directors when prejudicial-related party transactions are made, which is a measure to enhance protection of minority investors. This means that shareholder rights are promoted, and they are able to enjoy greater levels of ownership and have a role in major corporate decisions.
f. Paying taxes: Difficulties and costs of paying taxes have been reduced through the use of automatic risk-based systems, used for selecting companies to be audited, and the reduction of the property transfer tax rates.
g. Enforcing contracts: Another ease of doing businesses comes from the electronic system for paying court fees. This has positive effects on reducing the costs of enforcing contracts. Contract enforcement is also augmented by more automated and efficient processes that reduce time costs as well.
h. Resolving insolvency: The voting procedures for reorganization plans were updated, thereby increasing the ease of resolving insolvencies.

Economic Needs and Weaknesses

I. Resource Scarcities (Ageing Society and Severe Degradation of Natural Resources)

The issue of human resource scarcity caused by the ageing society demographics was addressed above. Here, we will focus on the resource-scarcity problem that is the result of deteriorated natural resources and environment in Thailand.

The many previous decades of Thai economic history were marked with imbalanced development which did not give adequate considerations to environmental quality and natural resource management, resulting in severe degradations of the Thai environment and vast depletion of natural resources (UNEP n.d.).

The 12th National Economic and Social Development Plan (2017–2021), Thailand's main development framework, has aimed to respond to these problems by incorporating the goals of "stability, prosperity, and sustainability" into its development details. The balanced development of Sufficiency Economy philosophy proposed by King Rama IX, which places weight on social well-being and natural resource quality, along with steady economic progress, is part of the developmental agenda (NESDB 2017). As environmental concerns become more important in the present world, the UN Sustainable Development Goals 2030 was also endorsed by the policy authorities, and "green growth" towards sustainable development and environmentally friendly progress has been set as a key approach.

The Thai National Assembly has also introduced its 20-year National Strategy (2017–2036) to address the environmental agenda, along with several other key developmental issues. Various ministries have adopted this strategy, and the Ministry of Natural Resources and Environment aims to enhance its key policy guidelines towards more sustainable environmental development paths (NESDB 2018), including the National Environmental Quality Management Plan (2017–2021), which emphasizes four key natural resources-related agendas. These four key agendas are environmental quality management, protection and rehabilitation of natural resources, increased efficiency of natural resource usage, and international cooperation on climate change (ONEP 2017).

II. Inability to Escape the Middle-Income Trap

During the 1990s, Thailand was categorized as a lower middle-income country by the World Bank. Two decades later, on July 1, 2011, it was reclassified as an upper middle-income country. While this may seem good news, a troubling fact is that Thailand has remained in the "middle-income group" for almost three decades, with debatable hopes for the future. Jitsuchon (2012) listed the reasons for this persistent situation as the labour shortage and the resource shortages already noted above, the absence of education to upgrade low-skilled workers, the absence of skills needed for the job market in general education, insufficient R&D spending, low taxation levels leaving the government without funds for infrastructure and welfare expenditures, monopolistic power of state-owned enterprises and lack of competition in vital sectors, especially high-value service industries, and most manufacturers sticking to simple manufacturing. He added that political reality has made macroeconomic stability more problematic.

All of these issues, according to Jitsuchon, are the result of institutional weakness: no one has made the tough decisions necessary to coax business towards the development of the economy.

III. Serious Income Distribution Problems

In 2016, Thailand was ranked the third most unequal country in the world, outdone only by Russia and India (Fernquest 2016), and from the latest data from Forbes and Credit Suisse, that estimated the total asset value of Thailand at 434 billion USD, it is reported that the richest 1 percent of the adult population in Thailand (equal to 521,850 persons) own as much as 56.2 percent of the entire country's property value. When we look at the 10 percent of the richest adult population, they own 78.7 percent of all national assets, or more than 341.55 billion USD, compared to the remaining 90 percent or 47 million adult Thais who collectively own only 21.3 percent of the country's wealth or merely 92.4 billion USD (Credit Suisse 2017).

A noteworthy fact is that 21.84 percent of the country's entire wealth is owned by only five families of successful business owners—the Chearavanont family, owner of the Charoen Phokapant Group (CP), with around 30 billion USD worth assets, the Chirathivat of the Central Group, with around 21.2 billion USD worth assets, the Yoovidhya Family of the Red Bull Group, 21 billion USD worth assets, the Sirivadhanabhakdi Family, 17.4 billion USD worth assets, and the Srivaddhanaprabha of the King Power Group, 5.2 billion USD worth assets (Forbes Thailand 2018). While this represents the success of Thai large-business conglomerates, it also means that more than 47 million Thai people combined together still have much less assets worth than the five wealthiest families in the country.

On a wider level, the extreme economic and political inequality in Thailand comes mostly from two reasons which are the structural power of wealth and capital and state policies. Many studies have shown a rural-urban divide which has been a long-standing gap. In the past when the governments and state promoted the industrialization of the Thai economy, the working class grew, but when high capital-intensive industries emerged more and more, the industrial sector had difficulties in absorbing all the migrants from rural regions who sought employment in urban and industrial areas. The mismatch between industry demand for labour skills and what the migrant rural workers could offer led to the creation of a very large informal economy. In this way, the welfare systems of the state which were already limited could have no way to cover all of these people. This was partially the cause of inequality since state assistance and welfare was aimed at the formal sector, which had relatively small number of participants. In the dimension of education, state investments tend to be focused in urban areas, thereby stagnating opportunities for educational advancements. People from rural areas and farming families were, for a long time, unable to access the higher education system. Back in the 1960s, farmers and labour workers comprised as much as 85 percent of total Thai population, but the university students from the farming and labourer families were only 15.5 percent of all, and it declined further to 8.8 percent in the mid-1980s. As the income gaps between educated and uneducated or lower educated groups of people were wide, it means that the poorer people were excluded the opportunities of moving up their financial status as they were unable to attain higher education and were forced to remain in the low-paying unskilled labour sectors. Also, on the big picture, education budgets have been only small fractions of total government expenditure for many years, which is another weakness in the education system of Thailand.

The taxation structures in the past were also discriminative in practice against the lower income groups, regressive taxes on rice siphoned wealth from smaller-scale farmers to rich businessmen in the cities, and the high rates of manufacturing protections were detrimental to the agricultural sector altogether. For many years since the 1990s, many types of taxes and policies have been regressive and pro-rich, a trend which continued well into 2012 and recent years. While progressive tax rates are pro-poor, Thailand's actual regressive tax structures ended up being pro-rich at the expense of the poor, and the effects were amplified by the low-wage/high-profit policies from businesses which the many governments have failed to address, resulting in the transfer of wealth from the poor to the rich capital owners (Hewison 2015).

Thailand's uneven structural power of capital is also the result of Thai people's inability to adapt to structural changes in the past, especially the transition periods between 1970s and 1980s, when the Industry 2.0, where labour workers worked together with machines in the conveyor assembly lines, was replaced by Industry 3.0 which depended much on computers and automated systems. These capital inputs were replacing manual labour of semi-skilled workers, who have been the majority of Thai workforce. They were faced with two choices as a result: (1) advance themselves into high-skilled workers and professionals or (2) accept underemployment below their true skills and receive lower wages than they were to get. Of course, the second choice was much less difficult, since the educational and occupational skills of Thai workers were never continuously augmented, and many found themselves unable to move up these skill or education attainment ladders at all. As a result, a large portion of the Thai workforce has long been underemployed. Only a lucky few were able to successfully develop themselves into high-skilled workers and professionals. This went on continuously for more than four decades and resulted in very wide gaps between the rich who receives economic opportunities and the poor, leading to accumulation of wealth for only a small group of people, and the rest of the population stuck in chronic poverty. These are the causes of Thailand's severe economic and social inequality.

Economic Freedom

From a study conducted by the Heritage Foundation, Thailand is ranked 53rd worldwide in the Index of Economic Freedom in 2018, with a score of 67.1 (up by 0.9 points from 2017). Thailand has seen continued improvements since after the year 2015 when the score dropped due to the military coup of 2014. In 2014, Thailand was ranked 72nd (this means that the Index of Economic Freedom for Thailand has increased by 3.8 points between 2014 and 2018). The subcategory with the highest improvement has been the indexes for trade freedom, both in terms of business freedom and in terms of investment freedom, compared to several other index rankings that remain decreased after the military coup, which are the indexes for rule of law, government integrity, and property rights. When compared to other ASEAN countries, Thailand ranks the third highest in economic freedom after Singapore (88.8 points) and

Malaysia (74.5 points) and is on similar levels with the Philippines (65 points) and Indonesia (64.2 points). Within the Asia-Pacific Region, Thailand currently ranks 12th (Heritage Foundation 2018).

An important obstacle to Thailand's trade liberalization is the presence of many non-tariff measures (NTMs), which still remain in large numbers and are highly complicated. The Economic Research Institute for ASEAN and East Asia (ERIA) report in 2014–2015 had identified as many as 1630 NTMs of Thailand and marks the highest number of NTM measures in the ASEAN Community, at twice the amount of the Philippines' 854 NTMs in the second place. The report has also observed that Thailand has NTMs covering all imported items. The numbers for both the simple average and weighted average methods of calculation for NTM import coverage ratios stand at 100 percent, which is no different from other ASEAN countries, which are Cambodia, Lao PDR, the Philippines, Singapore, and Vietnam (Ing et al. 2016). The most frequently employed types of NTMs in Thailand are the sanitary and phytosanitary (SPS) measures[1] and the technical barriers to trade (TBT), covering 48.3 percent and 34.9 percent of NTM usages, respectively. Also, the price control measures, considered as F-type NTMs, take up around 1.3 percent of NTMs. In terms of organization, Thai NTMs are most frequently employed by the Ministry of Public Health, Ministry of Agriculture and Cooperatives, Ministry of Industry, and Ministry of Commerce, respectively. NTMs are most frequently used on food stuffs, vegetable products, and animal products (Intaravitak 2016).

Aside from trade factors, Thailand's investment climate receives negative effects from its internal political instability, and political interferences threaten to intervene with the judicial systems, while corruption remains a problem that undermines government integrity indexes. Sadly, the corruption problem is encountered at all levels in the society. Independent judiciary handles contractual rights enforcement and property rights, but the legal process in such matters often operates slowly, and Thailand still suffers from rampant problems of counterfeiting and piracies, which are detrimental to the country's intellectual property (IP) outlook and utilization. The bribery problem in Thailand is another issue to be worried about. Businesses view bribery of officials as an unsavoury but normal element in doing business activities, and the problem is made more severe with low levels of salaries for public servants, thereby encouraging them to accept bribes (the Heritage Foundation 2018).

Compliance with AEC Institutions

Thailand has been one of the major contributing members in laying the foundations of the ASEAN Community's policies, starting from the very beginning when the Association of Southeast Asian Nations (ASEAN) was established on August 8, 1967, in Thailand. At that time, Thailand was mediating disputes between Indonesia, the Philippines, and Malaysia on certain matters, and in the process of reconciliation, the four countries realized that regional cooperation would be essential or the stability and future prosperity of the region would be compromised.

The key person who originated this historic moment, Thanat Khoman, Foreign Minister of Thailand, described the detail of his crucial role in the advent of ASEAN as follows: "*At the banquet marking the reconciliation between the three disputants, I broached the idea of forming another organization for regional cooperation with Adam Malik* [foreign affairs minister of Indonesia]. *Malik agreed without hesitation but asked for time to talk with his government and also to normalize relations with Malaysia now that the confrontation was over. Meanwhile, the Thai Foreign Office prepared a draft charter of the new institution. Within a few months, everything was ready. I therefore invited the two former members of the Association for Southeast Asia (ASA), Malaysia and the Philippines, and Indonesia, a key member, to a meeting in Bangkok. In addition, Singapore sent S. Rajaratnam, then Foreign Minister, to see me about joining the new set-up. Although the new organization was planned to comprise only the ASA members plus Indonesia, Singapore's request was favorably considered.*" Moreover, Thanat Khoman summarized the events at the end of the inaugural session of the Association of Southeast Asian Nations on the day of its establishment, August 8, 1967, as "*What we have decided today is only a small beginning of what we hope will be a long and continuous sequence of accomplishments of which we ourselves, those who will join us later and the generations to come, can be proud. Let it be for Southeast Asia, a potentially rich region, rich in history, in spiritual as well as material resources and indeed for the whole ancient continent of Asia, the light of happiness and well-being that will shine over the uncounted millions of our struggling peoples*". His descriptions elaborated the details of how the ASEAN Community came to be (Flores and Abad 1997).

Later, in 1992, amidst the turbulent changes in the global power and order after the fall of the Soviet Union, Communism, and the Berlin Wall, and the persistent lags in the global multilateral trade negotiations in the

Uruguay Round of the WTO, the Thai Prime Minister at the time, Anad Panyarachun, joined with the Prime Ministers Goh Chok Tong, of Singapore, and Dr Mahathir bin Mohamad, of Malaysia, in realizing the ASEAN Free Trade Agreement, signed in Singapore on January 28, 1992.

The primary objectives of AFTA have been to increase the competitiveness of ASEAN as the global market's production base, to be achieved by lowering barriers within the region, both tariffs and NTMs, and to attract foreign direct investment capital flows into ASEAN economies. The Common Effective Preferential Tariff Scheme is the primary mechanism towards these stated goals. The schedules were outlined in 1992, as phases, to gradually improve the regional competitiveness in producing goods to satisfy global market demand.

Thailand's major contribution occurred again in 1997, during the outbreak of the worst economic crisis in the history of Thailand, Southeast and East Asia, when Surin Pitsuwan, then Minister of Foreign Affairs of Thailand, who later became the ASEAN Secretary General, proposed the framework of ASEAN Vision 2020, which sees ASEAN as a community of harmony for Southeast Asian nations, marked with peace, stability, and prosperity, outward looking, and shares strong bonds with each other in partnership, to care for the people of the region.

This ASEAN Vision 2020 eventually led to the Bali Concord II in 2003, laying the foundations for the ASEAN Community, which consists of three pillars: The ASEAN Political-Securities Community (APSC), ASEAN Socio-Cultural Community (ASCC), and the ASEAN Economics Community (AEC).

When the core structures and the blueprints of these three pillars became solid, Thailand as the chair of the ASEAN Summit in 2009 (led by Prime Minister Abhisit Vejjajiva and assisted by Former Ambassador Pradab Phibunsongkhram) was also the proponent of the Master Plan on ASEAN Connectivity (MPAC), to connect the procedures of the three main pillars together to promote a strong and harmonious ASEAN Community. In all historic events that formed the ASEAN Community of today, Thailand has contributed fully to the progress of the community and performed its roles consistently.

Also, from Thailand's perspectives, the ASEAN Community is also vital to its national strategies, since much of Thailand's natural resource supply has been depleted following its long period of opening up to the global market, since the 1960s. Its ageing society and current demographic structures are also resulting in the scarcity of labour and workers. At the same time, many Thai workers have now, after many years, amassed adequate wealth and are readier than ever to invest overseas. The modern global economy, with significant declines in the economies of Thailand's former key trade partners, namely, the US and EU, now forces Thailand to switch and depend highly on its neighbours within the region, in terms of the emerging markets for Thai exports. Thailand's neighbour countries are also desirable investment destinations for Thai investors, since they still have fertile natural resources and abundant young labour force. Moreover, Thailand's ASEAN partners offer a variety of investment benefits, such as GSP (Generalized System of Preferences) and EBA (everything-but-arms), and are characterized by steadily growing markets, as the purchasing powers of the consumers are rising as their economies develop (Sermcheep 2017).

Other benefits of investments in AEC emerging economies are not limited only to the AEC benefits, but also by other regional trade agreements, namely, ASEAN-China Free Trade Agreement (ACFTA), ASEAN-Japan Closer Economic Partnership Agreement (AJCEP), ASEAN-Korea Free Trade Agreement (ASEAN-ROK FTA), ASEAN-Australia-New Zealand Free Trade Agreement (AANZFTA), and ASEAN-India Free Trade Agreement (AIFTA). These FTAs lead to more opportunities to invest in our ASEAN dialogue partners as most of ASEAN+1 FTAs also include investment agreements. In addition to these channels, the Regional Comprehensive Economic Partnership (RCEP, ASEAN+6) Agreement with China, Japan, Korea, Australia, New Zealand, and India is also under way and will be an important element in the future of the region. These are important considerations for Thailand in advancing its economic progress in the future.

As a result, during the 3–4 years prior to the official establishment of the ASEAN Community in 2015, the government of Thailand has allocated considerable amount of money in promoting the awareness of the Thai public about the importance of ASEAN, especially with regard to the ASEAN Economic Community or AEC, with the result that Thailand has one of the highest degrees of awareness about the AEC. Awareness does not necessarily mean deep and complete understanding of the AEC structures and principles, a fact that can be observed from the statistics of applications for trade agreement benefits, which remain much lower than expected.

Apart from these facts, the domestic process of regulatory reforms and internal enforcements of rules and laws related to trade, investment, and liberalization within the AEC has also been lacking and incomplete. Protectionist concepts of thinking remain dominant among some policy regulators and businessmen, resulting in the emphasis on protecting domestic goods rather than liberalizing trade for mutual regional benefits, and the use of multiple non-tariff measures (NTMs) in Thailand's international and regional trade, which was already addressed in the Economic Freedom section on how Thailand, as a member of ASEAN, has as many as 1630 NTMs in force today, which is the highest amount in ASEAN.

There is also another issue that limits the usage of trade benefits in the case of Thailand, which is the incomplete progress of trade facilitations (TFs).[2] It should be noted that FTA benefits, while they ought to be expected, do not come automatically, since firms need to apply for the certificates of origin (COOs) in order to gain these trade benefits. Yet, the average utilization of FTA benefits was merely 47 percent in 2012 for all FTAs, which points out the presence of some obstacles. The findings of Suksri et al. (2015) suggest that there are three main reasons explaining the low rate of FTA utilization of Thai firms: (1) the small trade volumes of many firms limit their profitability of applying for FTA benefits, given their scale, (2) other schemes provide better benefits than FTAs to some firms, and (3) Thai firms of all sizes, as to be expected, still lack adequate information on FTAs and how to make the most from them.

Conclusion on Thailand and the AEC

Thailand is located in the best geographic location, being the centre of mainland ASEAN among emerging economies such as Cambodia, Lao PDR, Myanmar, and Vietnam. At the same time, it is a link between Mainland ASEAN and Maritime ASEAN member states such as Malaysia, Singapore, Indonesia, Philippines, and Brunei. At the global level, Southeast Asia, which is located at the heart of Indo-Pacific Region, can be considered as one of the most crucial strategic locations in the modern world, in the dimensions of both geo-politics and geo-economics. Linking two of the most economically active oceans of the world—Indian Ocean and Pacific Ocean—it boasts the highest levels of trade and investment and is associated with a multitude of traditional and non-traditional national and regional securities issues. Beside the strength of the location, Thailand also has a large market with high purchasing power which comes from a population of over 68 million classified as upper middle-income economy.

Further, the current government has made great strides in reforming the country through the 20-year National Strategic Plan (2016–2026), an effort of reform in every dimension and every level. However, the weaknesses of the country should be analysed in order to make more appropriate decisions regarding trade and investment in Thailand, such as the ageing society and the development of human resources in both quantitative and qualitative dimensions in order to catch up with the Fourth Industrial Revolution. Thailand must find a way to escape the middle-income trap and diminish the inequality between the rich and the poor.

Thailand has been one of the major contributing members in laying the foundations of the ASEAN Community's policies, starting from the very beginning to the establishment of the ASEAN Economic Community (AEC) in 2015. AEC is a major milestone in the regional economic integration agenda in ASEAN, offering opportunities in the form of a huge market of almost USD 3 trillion and over 650 million people. In 2017, AEC was collectively the third largest economy in Asia and the seventh largest in the world. ASEAN already integrated into global value chains with the six dialogue partners, namely, China, Japan, South Korea, India, Australia, and New Zealand. Soon, this group of ASEAN+6 will conclude the Regional Comprehensive Economic Partnership Agreement (RCEP). RCEP is the world's largest economic bloc, covering nearly half of the global economy; in 2017, prospective RCEP member states accounted for a population of 3.4 billion people with a total gross domestic product (GDP, PPP) of 49.5 trillion USD, approximately 39 percent of the world's GDP. All of this represents opportunity, but Thailand needs to exploit it with more aggressive industrial policy. It must do so in a world more complex—a multiplex world (Amitav Acharya 2018)—than that in which Britain, US, Japan, Korean, and Taiwan achieved development.

Notes

1. Sanitary and phytosanitary (SPS) measures are measures to protect humans, animals, and plants from diseases, pests, or contaminants.
2. A trade facilitation is a simplification and harmonization of international trade procedures.

References

Acharya, A. 2018. *The End of American World Order*. Wiley. ISBN 9781509517084.

Apornrath Phoonphongphiphat. 2017. Thailand 4.0: Are We Ready? *Bangkok Post*, January 2. https://www.bangkokpost.com/archive/thailand-4-0-are-we-ready-/1173133. Accessed February 12, 2018.

Bank of Thailand. 2018. *Thailand Key Economic Indicators* (available in Thai). https://www.bot.or.th/Thai/Statistics/Indicators/Pages/default.aspx. Accessed February 8, 2018.

BBC. 2017. *Yingluck Trial: Ex-PM 'flees Thailand' Ahead of Verdict*. http://www.bbc.com/news/world-asia-41046993. Accessed February 12, 2018.

Biswas, A., Kastner, M., and Tortajada, C. 2015. The Rice and Fall of Yingluck Shinawatra: The Former Thai Prime Minister Faces a Potential Jail Term Over a Bungled Rice Scheme. *The Diplomat*, May 21. https://thediplomat.com/2015/05/the-rice-and-fall-of-yingluck-shinawatra/. Accessed February 12, 2018.

CIA Fact Book. 2018. The World Fact Book: Thailand. https://www.cia.gov/library/publications/the-world-factbook/geos/th.html.

Credit Suisse. 2017. *Global Wealth Report 2017: Where Are We Ten Years After the Crisis*. https://www.credit-suisse.com/corporate/en/articles/news-and-expertise/global-wealth-report-2017-201711.html. Accessed May 8, 2018.

EECO. 2017. *"About EEC" Eastern Economic Corridor Office (EECO)*. http://www.eeco.or.th/en/background. Accessed February 12, 2018.

Fernquest, Jon. 2016. *Thailand Third Most Unequal Country in World*. Bangkok Post, November 29. https://www.bangkokpost.com/learning/advanced/1147468/thailand-third-most-unequal-country-in-world. Accessed May 8, 2018.

Flores, J.M., and Abad, J. 1997. "ASEAN at 30" a Publication of the Association of Southeast Asian Nations in Commemoration of its 30th Anniversary on 8 August 1997. http://asean.org/asean/about-asean/history/. Accessed May 23, 2018.

Forbes Thailand. 2018. *Thailand's 50 Richest*. http://forbesthailand.com/pr-detail.php?did=2420. Accessed May 8, 2018.

Heritage Foundation. 2018. *2018 Index of Economic Freedom: Thailand*. https://www.heritage.org/index/pdf/2018/countries/thailand.pdf. Accessed May 23, 2018.

Hewison, K. 2015. Inequality and Politics in Thailand. *Kyoto Review of Southeast Asia*, Issue 17, March. Center for Southeast Asian Studies, Kyoto University. https://kyotoreview.org/issue-17/inequality-and-politics-in-thailand-2/. Accessed May 8, 2018.

IMF. 2000. *Recovery from the Asian Crisis and the Role of the IMF*. International Monetary Fund. http://www.imf.org/external/np/exr/ib/2000/062300.htm#box 1. Accessed February 8, 2018.

———. 2012. *Thailand*. World Economic Outlook Database, April. International Monetary Fund. http://www.imf.org/external/pubs/ft/weo/2012/01/weodata/weorept.aspx?pr.x=51&pr.y=10&sy=1980&ey=1984&scsm=1&ssd=1&sort=country&ds=.&br=1&c=578&s=NGDP_R%2CNGDP_RPCH%2CNGDPD&grp=0&a=. Accessed February 7, 2018.

———. 2017. *World Economic Outlook Database*. International Monetary Fund, October 24. https://www.imf.org/external/pubs/ft/weo/2017/02/weodata/index.aspx. Accessed February 7, 2018.

———. 2018. *Thailand*. International Monetary Fund. http://www.imf.org/external/pubs/ft/weo/2017/02/weodata/weorept.aspx?pr.x=52&pr.y=7&sy=2016&ey=2018&scsm=1&ssd=1&sort=country&ds=.&br=1&c=578&s=NGDPD%2CPPPGDP%2CNGDPDPC%2CPPPPC&grp=0&a=. Accessed February 7, 2018.

Ing, L.Y., Cordoba, S., and Cadot, O. 2016. *Non-Tariff Measures in ASEAN*. Economic Research Institute for ASEAN and East Asia and United Nations Conference on Trade and Development. ERIA Research Project FY2015 No.01. http://www.eria.org/RPR-FY2015-01.pdf. Accessed May 23, 2018.

Intaravitak, C. 2016. Non-Tariff Measures in Thailand. In *Non-Tariff Measures in ASEAN*, ed. L.Y. Ing, S. Cordoba, and O. Cadot. Economic Research Institute for ASEAN and East Asia and United Nations Conference on Trade and Development. ERIA Research Project FY2015 No.01. http://www.eria.org/RPR-FY2015-01.pdf. Accessed May 23, 2018.

Jitsuchon, S. 2012. *Thailand in a Middle-income Trap*. TDRI Quarterly Review, Thailand Development Research Institute, June, pp. 13–20. https://tdri.or.th/wp-content/uploads/2012/12/t5j2012-somchai.pdf. Accessed May 11, 2018.

Languepin. 2016. Thailand 4.0, What Do You Need to Know? *Thailand Business News*, September 15. https://www.thailand-business-news.com/economics/54286-thailand-4-0-need-know.html. Accessed February 12, 2018.

National Statistics Office. 2011. *100th Anniversary of Population Censuses in Thailand: Population and Housing Census 2010: 11th Census of Thailand*. http://popcensus.nso.go.th/doc/8-thailand%20census.doc. Accessed February 7, 2018.

———. 2012. *100th Anniversary of Population Censuses in Thailand: Population and Housing Census 2010: 11th Census of Thailand*. http://popcensus.nso.go.th/doc/8-thailand%20census.doc. Accessed May 7, 2018.

NESDB. 2017. *The 12th National Economics and Social Development Plan (2017–2021)*. Office of the National Economics and Social Development Board. http://www.nesdb.go.th/ewt_dl_link.php?nid=6422. Accessed May 7, 2018.

———. 2018. *Thailand's 20-Year National Strategy (2017–2036) (Draft as of May 2018)*. Office of the National Economics and Social Development Board. http://www.nesdb.go.th/download/document/SAC/NS_DraftplanMay2018.pdf. Accessed May 11, 2018.

Nilnopkoon, Somsak. 2012. *The Thai Economic Problems After the Second World War and the Government Strategies in Dealing with Them*. Silpakorn University.

Nixon. 1967. *Foreign Affairs*, Vol. 46 (1), October, pp. 113–125. Reprinted by permission of Foreign Affairs, 2002. Copyright 1967 by the Council on Foreign Relations, Inc. https://history.state.gov/historicaldocuments/frus1969-76v01/d3. Accessed February 7, 2018.

Niyomsilp, P. n.d. ASEAN Vision 2020. King Prajadhipok's Institute. Available in Thai at http://wiki.kpi.ac.th/index.php?title=%E0%B8%A7%E0%B8%B4%E0%

B8%AA%E0%B8%B1%E0%B8%A2%E0%B8%97%E0%B8%B1%E0%B8%A8%E0%B8%99%E0%B9%8C%E0%B8%AD%E0%B8%B2%E0%B9%80%E0%B8%8B%E0%B8%B5%E0%B8%A2%E0%B8%99_2020.

ONEP. 2017. *Thailand Environmental Quality Management Plan 2017–2021*. Office of Natural Resources and Environmental Policy and Planning (ONEP) prepared by Patcharasorn Karatna. Presented to National Policy Dialogue on the Urban Nexus in Thailand Conference, 2 March 2017, United Nations Conference Centre (UNCC), Bangkok, Thailand. http://www.unescap.org/sites/default/files/ONEP%20_%20NEQMP.pdf. Accessed May 11, 2018.

OPDC. 2018. *Doing Business 2018 Thailand Ranks 26th Out of 190 Countries in DB 2018*. Office of the Public Sector Development Commission (OPDC). http://www.oppb.coj.go.th/doc/data/oppb/oppb_1519637828.pdf. Accessed May 11, 2018.

Power Engineering. 2006. *EGAT Privatization Prevented by Court*. https://www.power-eng.com/articles/2006/03/egat-privatization-prevented-by-court.html. Accessed October 9, 2018.

Satitniramai, A. 2012. Politics of Thailand Economic Developments (1955–1963). Available in Thai at https://tdri.or.th/2015/03/20150309/. Accessed Feb 8, 2018.

Schwab, Klaus, and Xavier Sala-i-Martin, eds. 2018. *The Global Competitiveness Report 2017–2018*. Geneva: World Economic Forum.

Sermcheep. 2017. The Rise of Outward Foreign Direct Investment from ASEAN. In Cassey Lee, and Sineenat Sermcheep, editors "Foreign Direct Investment in ASEAN". ISEAS – Yusof Ishak Institute. Pp. 6-25.

Statista. 2018. *Median Age of the Population in South East Asian Countries in 2015*. https://www.statista.com/statistics/590942/median-age-of-the-population-in-south-east-asia/. Accessed May 7, 2018.

STI. 2018. "บทวิเคราะห์การจัดอันดับความสามารถในการแข่งขันของประเทศไทย ประจำปี 2017–2018 โดย World Economic Forum: WEF". สำนักงานคณะกรรมการนโยบายวิทยาศาสตร์ เทคโนโลยีและนวัตกรรมแห่งชาติ. National Science Technology and Innovation Policy Office (STI). http://www.sti.or.th/news-detail.php?news_type=2&news_id=250. Accessed May 11, 2018.

Suksri, P., S. Sermcheep, and P. Srisangnam. 2015. Survey on the Use of Free Trade Agreements in Thailand. In *The Use of FTAs in ASEAN: Survey-based Analysis*, ed. L.Y. Ing and S. Urata, 243–270. ERIA Research Project Report 2013–5. Jakarta: ERIA.

UNEP. n.d. *Thailand Case Study*. Stockholm Convention, United Nation Environmental Programme. http://chm.pops.int/Portals/0/download.aspx?d=UNEP-POPS-NIP-Thailand-1.English.pdf. Accessed May 11, 2018.

UNESA. 2017. *World Population Prospects: The 2017 Revision*. ESA.UN.org (custom data acquired via website), United Nations Department of Economic and Social Affairs, Population Division. https://esa.un.org/unpd/wpp/DataQuery/. Accessed May 7, 2018.

Wehrfritz, G. 2008. The Economics of Thailand's Thaksin Is Catching On. *Newsweek*, August 22. http://www.newsweek.com/economics-thailands-thaksin-catching-88109. Accessed February 8, 2018.

World Bank. 2016. *Thailand Economic Monitor – June 2016: Aging Society and Economy*. http://www.worldbank.org/en/country/thailand/publication/thailand-economic-monitor-june-2016-aging-society-and-economy. Accessed May 7, 2018.

———. 2017a. *GDP (Current US$)*. World Development Indicators, World Bank. https://data.worldbank.org/data-catalog/world-development-indicators. Accessed February 7, 2018.

———. 2017b. *Thailand and the World Bank*. World Bank on Thailand Country Overview. http://www.worldbank.org/en/country/thailand/overview. Accessed February 7, 2018.

———. 2018. *Doing Business 2018: Reforming to Create Jobs. Economic Profile: Thailand*. A World Bank Group Flagship Report. http://www.doingbusiness.org/~/media/WBG/DoingBusiness/Documents/Profiles/Country/THA.pdf. Accessed May 11, 2018.

Vasuprasat, P. 2010. Agenda for Labour Migration Policy in Thailand: Towards Long-Term Competitiveness; ILO/Japan Project on Managing Cross-Border Movement of Labour in Southeast Asia; ILO Regional Office for Asia and the Pacific. Bangkok: ILO, xiii, 50, xviii, 58 p.

ธนาคารแห่งประเทศไทย. (2561). "เครื่องชี้ภาวะเศรษฐกิจที่สำคัญ". คำนวณจากฐานข้อมูลโดยผู้เขียน. https://www.bot.or.th/Thai/Statistics/Indicators/Pages/default.aspx. Accessed February 8, 2018.

พัชร์ นิยมศิลป. (n.d.). "วิสัยทัศน์อาเซียน 2020" ฐานข้อมูลการเมืองการปกครอง. สถาบันพระปกเกล้า. http://wiki.kpi.ac.th/index.php?title=%E0%B8%A7%E0%B8%B4%E0%B8%AA%E0%B8%B1%E0%B8%A2%E0%B8%97%E0%B8%B1%E0%B8%A8%E0%B8%99%E0%B9%8C%E0%B8%AD%E0%B8%B2%E0%B9%80%E0%B8%8B%E0%B8%B5%E0%B8%A2%E0%B8%99_2020. Accessed February 8, 2018.

ราชบัณฑิตยสถาน. (2545). อักขรานุกรมภูมิศาสตร์ไทย ฉบับราชบัณฑิตยสถาน เล่ม 1. ราชบัณฑิตยสถาน. หน้า 4.

ศูนย์ข้อมูลกลางกระทรวงมหาดไทยและจังหวัด (2561). ข้อมูลสถิติที่สำคัญของจังหวัด และ ดัชนีชี้วัดจังหวัดบูรณาการ (สำหรับประชาชนทั่วไป). http://www.moi.go.th/MOIWEB/MOILogin?user_id=guest&user_password=guest&flag=1. Accessed February 7, 2018.

อภิชาต สถิตนิรามัย. 2012. การเมืองของการพัฒนาเศรษฐกิจยุคแรก 2498-2506. https://tdri.or.th/2015/03/20150309/. Accessed February 8, 2018.

สถาบันวิจัยประชากรและสังคม. 2017. สถานการณ์ผู้สูงอายุไทย พ.ศ. 2559. มูลนิธิสถาบันวิจัยและพัฒนาผู้สูงอายุไทย (มส.ผส.) สถาบันวิจัยประชากรและสังคม มหาวิทยาลัยมหิดล. http://www.dop.go.th/download/knowledge/th1512367202-108_0.pdf. Accessed May 7, 2018.

สำนักเลขาธิการวุฒิสภา. 2017. รัฐธรรมนูญแห่งราชอาณาจักรไทย พุทธศักราช 2560. http://click.senate.go.th/wp-content/uploads/2017/06/%E0%B8%A3%E0%B8%B1%E0%B8%90%E0%B8%98%E0%B8%A3%E0%B8%A3%E0%B8%A1%E0%B8%99%E0%B8%B9%E0%B8%8D-2560.pdf. Accessed February 7, 2018.

สำนักงานราชบัณฑิตยสภา (2560). ชื่อจังหวัด อำเภอ ตำบล เขต และแขวง Changwat, Khet and Amphoe Directory. http://www.royin.go.th/wp-content/uploads/2015/03/%E0%B8%8A%E0%B8%B7%E0%B9%88%E0%B8%AD%E0%B8%88%E0%B8%B1%E0%B8%87%E0%B8%AB%E0%B8%A7%E0%B8%B1%E0%B8%94-%E0%B8%AD%E0%B8%B3%E0%B9%80%E0%B8%A0%E0%B8%AD-%E0%B8%95%E0%B8%B3%E0%B8%9A%E0%B8%A5-%E0%B9%80%E0%B8%82%E0%B8%95-%E0%B9%81%E0%B8%A5%E0%B8%B0%E0%B9%81%E0%B8%82%E0%B8%A7%E0%B8%87-22%E0%B8%81%E0%B8%9E60.pdf. Accessed February 7, 2018.

CHAPTER 5

Malaysia: Trade, Foreign Direct Investment and Regional Integration

Evelyn S. Devadason

Introduction

Malaysia, though small, is the 3rd largest economy in Southeast Asia and the 38th largest in the world. Malaysia was recently ranked 25th out of 137 countries in terms of national competitiveness (WEF 2017a), 65th out of 159 countries in the Economic Freedom of the World Index (Gwartney et al. 2017) and 22nd freest economy out of 180 countries in the Heritage Index of Economic Freedom (Miller et al. 2018). It continues to be ranked among the world's top 25 exporting nations, 24th largest exporter and 26th largest importer (MITI 2017; WTO 2017). Outward-looking policies, trade and foreign direct investment (FDI) have made Malaysia one of the most prominent exporters in the

The research leading to these results has received funding from the European Union H2020 Framework Programme CP-2016-under grant agreement no. 770562 (IF002AB-2018).

E. S. Devadason (✉)
Faculty of Economics and Administration, University of Malaya, Kuala Lumpur, Malaysia
e-mail: evelyns@um.edu.my

R. Macdonald (ed.), *Southeast Asia and the ASEAN Economic Community*, https://doi.org/10.1007/978-3-030-19722-3_5

world and subsequently helped the economy make the transition from low to upper middle-income status. While the economy is grappling to graduate into the ranks of an advanced economy, further challenges are emerging.

As a highly open and trade-dependent economy, the country has become very vulnerable to global market sentiment. The recent slowdown in external demand, the trade exposure to China and uncertainties over the trade policies of the United States (US), lower commodity prices and larger capital and intermediate imports have begun to deteriorate external balances. This trend runs contrary to the long history of trade and strong surpluses recorded in the current account. Recent data indicate that the current account surplus had declined from 3.8 per cent of gross domestic product (GDP) in the fourth quarter of 2016 to 1.6 per cent of GDP in the first quarter of 2017 (World Bank 2017). Though the economy still grew at 4.2 per cent in 2016 (World Bank 2017), the resilience and global positioning of the economy is being called into question. Similarly, questions arise about the relevance and effectiveness of industrial policy of the yesteryears for transforming the economy under the present interconnected and complex environment.

This chapter therefore examines how Malaysia has responded to global challenges through product and market diversification, investment promotion and trade strategies. To set the background of the study, this chapter begins with a historical overview of the Malaysian economy since Independence. It then profiles the changes in the trade structure and direction of trade, namely, the FDI-trade nexus that generated supply chain linkages, and reviews the industrial policy drive since the 1990s.[1] Then follows an in-depth examination of Malaysia's regional links through the trade and investment patterns with the Association of Southeast Asian Nations (ASEAN). The discussion on Malaysia's regional connection is complemented with a review of its global position based on several performance-based rankings. Finally, this chapter concludes, sanguinely, with suggestions for a reframing of the industrial policy with a focus on the firm. It also identifies some thorny issues that need to be addressed by the state.

Historical and Developmental Snapshots

To provide a context for the study, this section highlights the key features of the Malaysian economy, focusing briefly on its political history since Independence and structural and economic transformation since the 1970s.

Malaysia is a federal constitutional elective monarchy in Southeast Asia, consisting of 13 states (*Negeri*) and 3 federal territories. Having gained Independence from the British Empire on 31 August 1957, the then Federation of Malaya became Malaysia on 16 September 1963, after its unification with North Borneo, Sarawak and Singapore. Due to political and economic differences between the ruling parties of Malaysia and Singapore, the latter separated from Malaysia to become an independent and sovereign state on 9 August 1965. From the legacy of the British colonial rule, the government system in Malaysia is modelled after the Westminster parliamentary system. The head of state is the king (*Yang di-Pertuan Agong*), while the prime minister is the head of government. Malaysia is currently (since 9 May 2018, the 14th general election) governed by the *Pakatan Harapan* alliance, which succeeded the long-standing *Barisan Nasional* (National Front) coalition ruling party since Independence.

At Independence, the country was saddled with the challenge of a plural society, inherited from the colonial past. The Malays (55 per cent of the population) were engaged in the relatively poor and low-productive agrarian sector, while the Chinese (35 per cent of the population) dominated modern sector activities. The focus of the government for a decade since Independence therefore was on preserving communal harmony and political stability, while developing the economy. Economic policymaking was geared towards redressing ethnic and regional economic imbalances through rural development schemes and the provision of social and physical infrastructure. Though the economic expansion from 1957 to 1969 was somewhat respectable, it failed to address the disparity of economic power among ethnic communities. Following this, ethnic tensions rose and bloody race riots erupted on 13 May 1969. This remained a dark blot in the history of Malaysia.

That May 1969 incident was also significant in that it heralded a culture of passivity, as the citizens were thereafter refrained from questioning the regime in place and debating on sensitive issues such as citizenship, national language, sovereignty of the rulers and the special position of the Malays, issues that were considered to undermine racial harmony and national unity. Fast forward to present day, Malaysia has come to be regarded as a politically stable country. Unfortunately, the pace of democratization has not kept pace with its economic expansion, and therefore, the Economist Intelligence Unit reported that Malaysians live in a situation of "flawed democracy." It scored Malaysia as 6.54 (on a scale from 1 to 10) in the

2017 Democracy Index, with a ranking of 59 out of 167 countries (Free and Independent News, 31 January 2018). The country was considered "largely unfree" in the Media Freedom Index, a result of the security laws that prosecute civil dissent. Against this backdrop of the ethnicity interactions with the politics of Malaysia, the following discussion shifts to the economic transformation of the country that truly began since the 1970s.

Soon after Independence, in 1960, Malaysia recorded a population of just 8.2 million and GDP per capita of USD 1048.6. Since then, the Malaysian economy has grown rapidly, such that by 2016, the population and GDP per capita had reached 31.2 million and USD 11,031.8, respectively. Figure 5.1 shows that negative GDP growth rates over the period of review occurred only during the 1985 economic recession, 1998 Asian financial crisis and the 2008 global financial crisis. Notwithstanding the three episodes of economic downturns, Malaysia still recorded a healthy 6.3 per cent average annual GDP growth from the 1960 to 2016 period. Structural transformation was the outcome of economic growth. Before 1964, Malaysia was largely an agrarian economy, whose mainstays were rubber and tin. The dependence on primary commodities that were subject to price volatility and unstable export demand was a core developmental issue then. Therefore, the state initiated a long-term economic diversification strategy in terms of moving away from agriculture to industry, apart from diversifying the agriculture sector with new crops such as

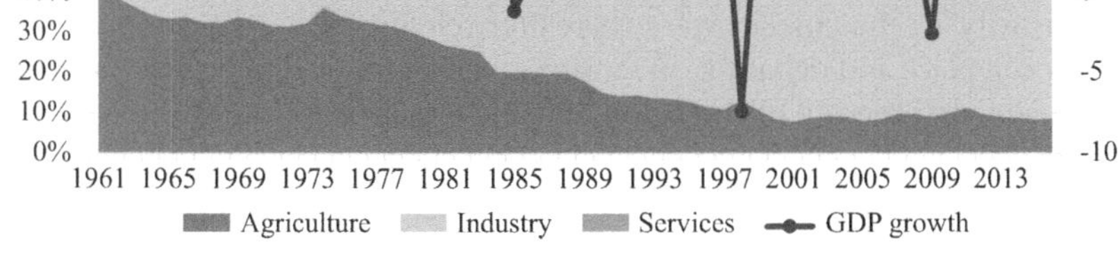

Fig. 5.1 Malaysia: GDP growth (per cent) and sectoral value added (per cent of GDP), 1961–2016. Source: World Development Indicators: http://databank.worldbank.org/data/reports.aspx?source=world-development-indicators

palm oil. The contribution of the agriculture sector declined somewhat drastically from 40.6 per cent in 1960 to 20.3 per cent in 1985, and it currently only accounts for 8.7 per cent of GDP. By the mid-1980s, the agriculture-to-industry transition was regarded as completed. Alternatively, the value-added contribution of the industrial sector to GDP increased over time, even surpassing that of the services value added, especially, for the periods 1972–1983 and 1997–2006. However, the services sector share of GDP has remained the largest since 2007 and reached 53 per cent in 2016. As such, the services sector has emerged as the largest employer (61.5 per cent of total employment), followed by the industry and agriculture sectors at 27.4 per cent and 11.1 per cent of total employment, respectively.

Resulting from the early diversification process, the 1970s ushered a new era of economic growth, marked by a shift from the previous import substitution strategy since the late 1950s to an export-oriented industrialization drive. This policy shift coincided with the New Economic Policy (NEP),[2] which resulted in greater state intervention through increased public investments and the rise of state-owned enterprises (SOEs). A major feature of the export orientation strategy was to attract FDI in the manufacturing sector through tax concessions and other incentives. The 1970s phase saw the rise of resource-based and labour-intensive manufactured exports (textiles, garments, electrical and electronics or E&E) and imports of capital-intensive goods, reflecting the comparative advantage of economy in the former. To ensure a more balanced industrial growth, a second round of import substitution strategy was again deployed in the 1980s (1980–1985) to develop heavy industries such as the locally manufactured car, steel and cement industries. These industries were accorded high rates of effective protection. However, the protected industries failed to compete internationally, and the government re-emphasized a second round of export-oriented strategy in the mid-1980s. Worth noting here is that outward orientation was promoted alongside the import substitution strategy.

Efforts to accelerate the pace of industrialization further increased under the premiership of Mahathir Mohamad (the fourth Prime Minister of Malaysia) from 1981 until 2003, especially with his 1983 privatization programme "Look East Policy"[3] and vision for Malaysia to attain a developed status by 2020 (known as "Vision 2020"). The paradigm shifts to the newly rising Asia under the "Look East Policy" saw increased investment inflows from East Asia, particularly from Japan. The leading investors in the

1980s were Singapore, Japan, the United States (US), the United Kingdom (UK) and West Germany. Hence, industrialization became the developmental priority for decades thereafter.

The industrial development experience throughout the 1980s and 1990s generated a large demand for labour, resulting in the tightening of the domestic labour market. This is shown by the dramatic drop in the unemployment rate from its peak of 7.4 per cent in 1986 to 3.1 per cent in 1995 (Fig. 5.2). To overcome the problem of labour shortages, foreign workers were employed from neighbouring countries, namely Indonesia, Thailand, the Philippines and Bangladesh. In the case of manufacturing, the share of foreign workers in total employment grew from a mere 1.6 per cent in 1985 to 30.2 per cent in 2014 (based on unpublished returns from the Department of Statistics, Malaysia). This is not just specific to manufacturing: the agriculture, services and construction sectors have also become heavily dependent on foreign workers. With 2.1 million foreign workers, Malaysia has now emerged as having the fourth largest number of migrants and the seventh highest ratio of migrants to total population in East Asia-Pacific (World Bank 2015).

Fig. 5.2 Malaysia: Labour force, total employment and unemployment rate, 1982–2017. Note: The left axis refers to labour force ('000) and total employed ('000), while the right axis refers to unemployment rate (per cent). Source: Department of Statistics, Malaysia: https://www.dosm.gov.my/v1/index.php?r=column/ctimeseries&menu_id=NHJlaGc2Rlg4ZXlGTjh1SU1kaWY5UT09

The push for industrialization, starting from the 1970s and largely driven by capital and labour inflows, shaped the economy in several ways. First, the ownership of large plantations shifted from foreigners to locals, including the state and federal governments. Overall, foreign ownership fell substantially from 63.4 per cent in 1970 to 25.1 per cent in 1990 (Drabble 2000). Despite this shift in wealth ownership, foreign capital was still accorded a central role in the development of the economy. The government relaxed the limits on foreign equity ownership in the manufacturing and services sectors. The deregulation of the FDI equity guidelines resulted in foreign capital largely taking the form of wholly foreign controlled entities from joint venture investments with Malaysian companies. Joint venture investments represented 60 per cent of FDI in 1980 (Beaumont 1990). By 1995, it had declined to 40 per cent of FDI (OECD 1999). In 1995, 36 per cent of FDI was in projects that were wholly foreign controlled vis-a-vis wholly Malaysian-owned ventures at 23 per cent. Though joint ventures still remained dominant, there was a clear shift from wholly-owned Malaysian ventures to wholly-owned foreign ventures between the 1980s and 1990s, as the latter only constituted 2 per cent of FDI in 1984 (OECD 1999). Most of the wholly foreign-owned companies were engaged in export-oriented activities.

Second, the FDI-export-oriented strategy also led to an increase in trade intensity from the import side. An enterprise survey showed that 45 per cent of the manufacturing firms in Malaysia use inputs or supplies of foreign origin. Comparatively, the reliance of firms on foreign inputs is high in Malaysia, as only 17 per cent of the manufacturing firms in East Asia and the Pacific utilize imported inputs/supplies (World Bank 2014).

Third, manufacturing jobs generated through the inflow of capital led to rising Malay and female participations in this sector. This is because during that phase of growth, the leadership under the *Barisan Nasional* coalition was committed to narrow wealth distribution between the Malays and Chinese through race-based affirmative action policies prescribed in the NEP. The National Development Policy (NDP) that succeeded the NEP in 1990 and was supposed to focus on development continued implicitly with race-based policies. Hence, *Bumiputera* entrepreneurship flourished, and the ownership of the Malays in the country's wealth increased from 2 per cent before the NEP in 1970 to approximately 19 per cent in 2015 (The Star, 24 June 2015). The 1983 privatization drive, which initially seemed to run contrary to the goal of restructuring equity under the NEP, in fact accelerated the transfer of

Bumiputera share ownership from trust agencies to private individuals. Though the NEP ended in 1990, ethnic considerations continued to dominate politics henceforth. Interestingly, the "back-to-the-future" Prime Minister Mahathir Mohamad (2018–), who backed affirmation action during his previous premiership (1981–2003), is once again advocating for policies to help the ethnic Malays under the new *Pakatan Harapan* government (Naidu 2018).

In terms of labour force participation, the manufacturing labour force had also been feminized, with the proportion of female employment increasing from 29 per cent in 1970 to 41 per cent in 1980 (Jomo and Edwards 1993). The expansion of female employment was not only attributed to female-dominated jobs in the textiles, clothing and electronics industries, but also to employers' preferences for female workers who are considered suitable for routine tasks and are willing to accept low wages and inferior working conditions. This invariably resulted in labour market dualism, which was also tied to the segmented manufacturing sector, comprising resource-based exports, import-substituting industries and export-oriented industries. Despite the progress made in terms of female labour participation since the 1980s, their overall participation in the labour market still remained low at 54.7 per cent in 2017 relative to the male labour force participation at 80.1 per cent (DOS online database). The 2017 Global Gender Gap reports that Malaysia only closed 67 per cent of its overall gender gap and ranked 104 out of a total of 144 countries (WEF 2017b). Likewise, Malaysia ranked only 65th in the Gender Disparity Index, signalling legal barriers imposed on women that impede their abilities in formal economic activity (Gwartney et al. 2017).

Fourth, the inflow of labour altered the demographic structure of the population. Previously, Indians were the third largest community in the country, after the dominant racial group of Malays and *Bumiputera*, who made up approximately 69 per cent of the population, followed by the Chinese at 23 per cent. At present, the immigration population of about 19 per cent has displaced the Indian ethnic group to become the third largest community in Malaysia (The Straits Times, 17 September 2016). Retrospectively, Malaysia's multi-ethnic population bears testament to its long history of immigration, which dates to the period under the British colonial rule. During that time, foreign nationals from China and India came to work in the mining and rubber plantations, respectively. Their settlement in Malaysia (Malaya then) defined the ethnic fabric of the country that we see today. The present-day large inflows of migrant workers (including undocumented workers) have also reinforced the dualism in the labour market. The mismanagement of the large inflows of migrant workers has, in turn, led these to be highly vulnerable to human trafficking. It is therefore of no surprise that Malaysia had slipped to the Tier-2 Watch List (refers to countries that do not fully meet the minimum standards of the Trafficking Victims Protection Act and some additional criteria) in the 2018 Trafficking-In Persons Report (Zolkepli 2018).

From the historical record of Malaysia, its successes, challenges and insights can be gleaned from several factors, namely, its openness to capital and labour inflows, followed by the extensive restructuring in its primary and secondary sectors and its management of inter-ethnic stability through affirmative action. Being open and diversifying the economy are strategies that continue to remain in the developmental process of the economy. The next section is therefore dedicated to the discussion on the changing dynamics in the country's openness strategy since the 1990s.

Changing Trade Posture and Investment Dynamics

Trade represents the life-blood of the Malaysian economy, and this is reflected by its total trade-to-GDP ratio of 132.5 per cent in 2016 (or on average 147.2 per cent of GDP for the 1990–2016 period) (calculated from World Development Indicators online). The emphasis on the second round of export-oriented industrialization in fact dates to the mid-1980s, with increased participation of FDI.[4] By the 1990s, the government had introduced a plethora of investment incentives for private investors, followed by tariff reductions. Following from that time, the basic tenet of the national development strategy has been an open trade and investment regime (Athukorala 2005).

Malaysia has recorded consistent surpluses in her trade balances over the 1990–2016 period (Fig. 5.3), though the growth of trade surpluses has somewhat slowed down since the 2008–2009 global financial crisis. The annual average growth of trade surpluses declined by 4.7 per cent between 2008 and 2016, relative to an increase of 8.5 per cent on average for the overall 1990–2016 period. The manufacturing sector, more specifically, is important in that it is the largest component of exports, with a contribution of 82.2 per cent of total exports of the country in 2016 (WTO 2017). Within manufacturing, E&E remained the dominant export earning industry since the 1990s. In 2017, the E&E industry commanded 44.1 per cent of total exports of manufactured goods. The main exports

Fig. 5.3 Malaysia: Exports, imports and trade balances of goods and services, 1990–2016 (USD million). Note: In constant 2010 US dollars. Source: World Development Indicators: http://databank.worldbank.org/data/reports.aspx?source=world-development-indicators

of the E&E industry included semiconductors, automatic data processing machines and telecommunication equipment (MOF 2018).

Since 2000, the manufacturing sector has witnessed some structural changes in terms of market and product concentration. Export destinations have diversified from traditional markets such as the European Union (EU), US and Japan to East Asia (ASEAN, China, Hong Kong, Republic of Korea and Taiwan). As for product concentration, though the E&E sector continues to account for a significant proportion of Malaysia's exports, the shares of non-E&E and commodities' (such as petroleum, chemicals and machinery) exports have begun to rise. This is reflected in the decline in the export concentration index in Fig. 5.4. Noteworthy is that the downward trend in the export concentration index is tracked closely by the import concentration index. The latter has dropped below the former since 2008. Generally, exports and imports of Malaysia are more homogeneously distributed over a series of products. This is because there is a strong relationship in Malaysia between exports and imports in that the goods produced for exports have strong import content. This is explained by the significance of the intermediate goods trade. In 2017, intermediate goods alone accounted for 58.4 per cent of total gross imports to Malaysia (MOF 2018). Also, the same countries serve as destinations for export and sources of import.

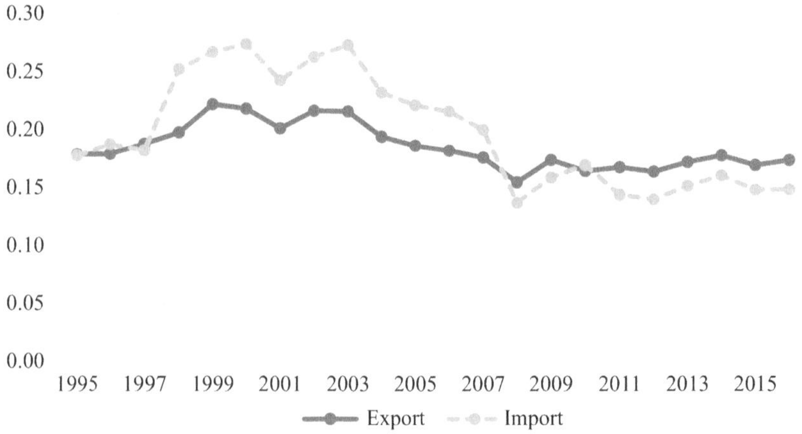

Fig. 5.4 Malaysia: Product concentration of exports and imports, 1995–2016. Notes: (1) Product concentration is measured based on the Herfindahl-Hirschman Index as follows:

$$H_j = \frac{\sqrt{\sum_{i=1}^{n}\left(\frac{x_{ij}}{X_j}\right)^2} - \sqrt{1/n}}{1-\sqrt{1/n}}$$

where

H_j = country or country group index
x_{ij} = value of export for country j and product i

$$X_j = \sum_{i=1}^{n} x_{ij}$$

and
n = number of products (SITC Revision 3 at three-digit group level)

(2) An index value closer to 1 indicates a country's exports or imports are highly concentrated on a few products. On the contrary, values closer to 0 reflect exports or imports being more homogeneously distributed among a series of products. (3) The data is not available for 1990–1994
Source: UNCTADSTAT: http://unctadstat.unctad.org/wds/ReportFolders/reportFolders.aspx

The shifts in trade patterns towards intermediate goods following the internationalization of production significantly altered the process of industrialization in Malaysia. Over the years, the manufacturing sector shifted to the lower end of the value chain. This was reflected in the low domestic value added (DVA) content of exports (Rasiah 2011). The gradual downgrading of the manufacturing sector was attributed to the low level of technology development and human capital availability (Tham 2015; Rasiah 2017). The problem was compounded with the FDI-oriented industrialization process that was largely focused on export expansion and employment growth,[5] resulting in minimal technology acquisition through capital flows. As shown in Fig. 5.5, the DVA of manufactured exports to the world only recorded a marginal increase from 39.5 per cent to 47.6 per cent between 2000 and 2011, and it remained much

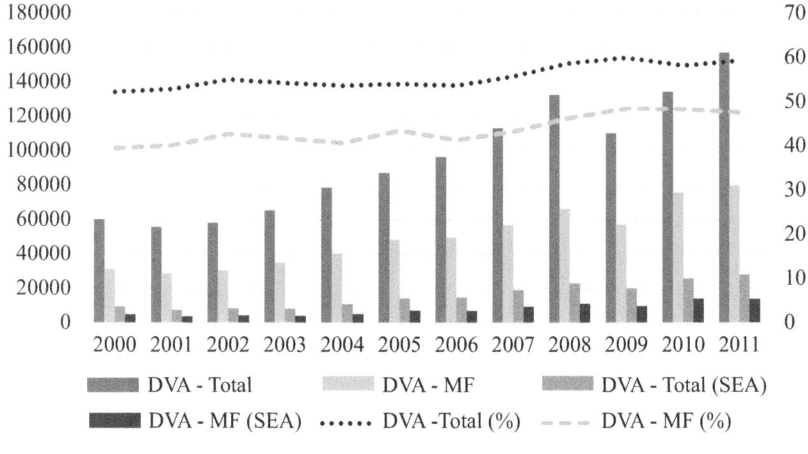

Fig. 5.5 Malaysia: Domestic Value-Added (DVA) exports, 2000–2011. Notes: (1) Total—total trade; MF—manufactures only; SEA—Southeast Asia. (2) The left axis refers to DVA content of exports (USD million), for total trade/manufactures in Malaysia to the world/Southeast Asia. It represents the exported value added that has been generated anywhere in the domestic economy (i.e. not just by the exporting industry). (2) The right axis refers to DVA share of gross exports (per cent), for total trade/manufactures in Malaysia. It is a "DVA intensity measure" and reflects how much value added, generated anywhere in the domestic economy, is embodied per unit of total gross exports. (3) Latest data available is 2011. The data is also not available for 1990–1999. Source: OECD.Stat: https://stats.oecd.org/index.aspx?queryid=75537

lower than that for total exports to the world. Domestic value added in exports below 75 per cent is considered to be a low share and is typical of economies that provide low-cost manufacturing. The DVA share of E&E exports recorded even much lower levels than that for total manufacturing. Further scrutiny of the E&E industry in Malaysia indicates a loss in market due to reduced competitiveness of the sub-sector of information technology (IT) and consumer electronics and electronic components by 4.06 per cent and 1.06 per cent between 2012 and 2016, respectively (sourced from ITC online). The low DVA and negative competitiveness effect indicates that the country is certainly not getting the commensurate production-linked gains of exports. This has inadvertently caused a fall in the significance of the manufacturing sector for the Malaysian economy since 2000. In 2017, the manufacturing sector only contributed 23 per cent to GDP. Malaysia is therefore considered to be facing "negative" or "premature" deindustrialization[6] (Chandran and Devadason 2017; Tan 2014).

On a global level, Malaysia has also moved away from being an investment destination for low-cost labour manufacturing activities. This is reflected in a decline in inward FDI (IFDI) from 5.9 per cent of GDP in 1990 to 3.3 per cent of GDP in 2016 (Fig. 5.6). The magnitude of IFDI

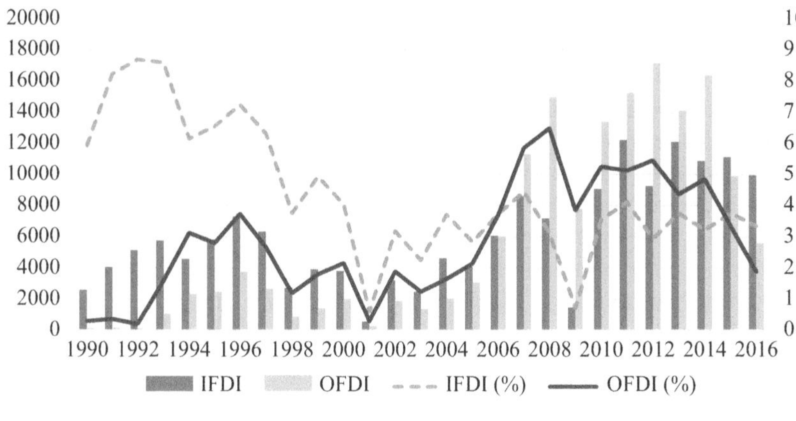

Fig. 5.6 Malaysia: Foreign Direct Investment (FDI) flows, 1990–2016. Notes: (1) IFDI—inward FDI; OFDI—outward FDI. (2) The left axis refers to FDI flows in USD million at current prices. (3) The right axis refers to FDI flow as a percentage of GDP. Source: UNCTADSTAT: http://unctadstat.unctad.org/wds/ReportFolders/reportFolders.aspx

dipped during the 1997–1998 crisis period, and the contraction continued until 2001. Malaysia failed to regain its pre-crisis IFDI level as it is currently challenged by lower cost competitors from emerging economies such as China and Vietnam (Athukorala and Wagle 2011; Sermcheep 2017). For example, Vietnam is moving up the E&E value chain and creating increasing competition for Malaysia in lower value-added segments of the industry. Interestingly, for the 2007–2014 period, outward FDI (OFDI) from Malaysia consistently surpassed IFDI. OFDI by Malaysia is mainly in services relative to manufacturing, and for manufacturing, it is largely listed in industries such as fabricated metal products, machinery and equipment, palm oil, wood and wood-based products, including furniture (Tham et al. 2015).

The regression of the manufacturing sector and the waning attractiveness of Malaysia to multinational enterprises (MNEs) have given credence to the argument that the Malaysian economy is caught in a "middle-income trap.[7]" Consequently, there is now a strategic push in Malaysia to seek out new growth areas and move towards higher value-added and knowledge-based industries. These policy shifts are outlined in the next section.

Shifting Focus of Industrial Policy

Industrial policy has indeed played an important role in transforming the Malaysian economy from one dependent on the primary sector to one driven by the manufacturing sector. Importantly, the industrial policy for decades had been centred on export growth. The government is now promoting technology-based industrialization, by adopting a targeted approach in attracting quality investments in high-technology, capital-intensive and knowledge-intensive industries; high value-added industries; and research and development (R&D) activities as well as in new growth areas (WTO 2017). Table 5.1 gives a chronological review of the key industrial plans and policies since the 1990s.

Malaysia devised Five-Year Malaysia Plans and Industrial Master Plans to direct the development of country. The ongoing plans for the country are the 11th Malaysia Plan (11MP, 2016–2020) (Government of Malaysia 2016) and the Third Industrial Master Plan (IMP3, 2006–2020). The goals that underlie the 11MP include increasing Malaysia's export potential and trade balance, and promoting investment, among others. These goals are to be achieved through trade liberalization, trade facilitation and

Table 5.1 Malaysia: Selected plans, programmes and initiatives

Year	*Long-term plans*
IMP1, 1986–1995	Emphasis on broad-based manufacturing
IMP2, 1996–2005	Cluster-based approach to move up the value-added chain
IMP3, 2006–2020	Focus on higher value-added and knowledge-based economy
9MP, 2006–2010	Centred on improving overall economic competitiveness, developing its manufacturing sector and deepening its human capital base
10MP, 2011–2015	Focus on 12 national key economic areas (NKEAs) with a shift from manufacturing services
11MP, 2016–2020	Focus on rapidly delivering high-impact outcomes to both the capital economy and people economy at an affordable cost
	Specific plans/programmes/initiatives
MSC, 1996	Fiscal incentives for local and foreign companies that develop or utilize multimedia technologies to produce or enhance their products and services and for process development
Small and Medium Enterprises (SME) Development Plan, 2000	To increase the capacity and capabilities of SMEs
K-Economy Master Plan, 2003	Focus on knowledge, creativity and innovation
Economic Transformation Programme (ETP), 2010	Targeting NKEAs, identified on the bases of their potentials to contribute to output growth and their multiplier effects
Malaysia Productivity Blueprint (MPB), 2017	Target initiatives to open up potential productivity at national, sectoral and industrial levels
Digital Free Trade Zone (DFTZ), 2017	To facilitate small and medium enterprises (SMEs) to capitalize on the convergence of exponential growth of the internet economy and cross-border e-commerce activities
	Recent measures/regulations
Apr 09	Liberalization of 27 services sub-sectors, with no equity condition imposed
May 15	New tax incentives for economic corridors such as 100 per cent income tax exemption up to 15 years for newly established companies or existing entities that expand operations into less developed areas

(*continued*)

Table 5.1 (continued)

Year	*Long-term plans*
Oct 17	Additional investment incentives such as accelerated capital allowance of 200 per cent on the first RM10 million qualifying capital expenditure incurred in the year of assessments 2018–2020 for manufacturing and manufacturing-related services sectors and capital allowance for the purchase of information and communication technology (ICT) equipment and computer software packages with effect from year of assessment 2017 and expenditure incurred on the development of customized software

Source: Author's own compilation from the literature.

Notes: IMP—Industrial Master Plan; MP—Malaysia Plan

regulatory reform initiatives. The strategic thrusts underscored in the IMP3 were aimed at broadening the industrial policy, by including services and introducing horizontal policies (small and medium enterprise development, human resource development, technology and logistics). The thrusts related to trade and investment, more specifically, seek to enhance Malaysia's position as a major trading partner by integrating domestic companies into the regional and global production networks and generating investments in targeted growth areas.

The long-term plans and programmes mentioned above and detailed in Table 5.1 indicate distinct shifts in the economic strategy of the country. The stark differences in the strategies reveal one shortcoming: there was no continuity in the plans, especially between the First and Second Industrial Master Plans (Chandran and Devadason 2017; Tham 2015). Moving from a broad-based (industry) strategy to a cluster-based approach to industrialization, the subsequent and current emphasis is on information and communication technology (ICT) as a new source of growth. This was clearly manifested through the launch of the Multimedia Super Corridor (MSC) in 1996. The MSC status companies enjoy fiscal and non-fiscal incentives that include exemption from income tax, investment tax allowance (ITA), duty-free importation of multimedia equipment, employment of foreign knowledge workers without restriction and freedom to source capital globally. By the end of 2015, there were 3881 MSC status companies, where foreign-owned companies anchored 79 per cent of total export sales in that year (The Sun Daily, 17 March 2017). Similarly, foreign companies also dominated special economic zones[8] such as the free industrial zones (FIZs)[9] and the industrial estates (IEs), with 88 per cent and 59 per cent of total investment capital in both zones, respectively (ASEAN Secretariat 2017). To uphold its investment liberalization to attract FDI, in 2009, Malaysia further eased up on foreign equity restrictions in key services sectors to attract FDI (even eliminating the 30 per cent *Bumiputera* share in a number of services industries). Following which, Malaysia has emerged as the third largest recipient of FDI in ASEAN.

With a continued focus on cluster development, a new regional model that transcends the boundaries of various Malaysian states (Hutchinson 2016; Athukorala and Narayanan 2018) was introduced under the Ninth Malaysia Plan (9MP, 2006–2010) (Government of Malaysia 2006). This transborder strategy resulted in the creation of five regional economic corridors[10] located in strategic investment regions that act as platforms in promoting free trade and business incentives. The corridors are the Iskandar Malaysia in Southern Johor (IRDA), the East Coast Economic Region (ECER), the Northern Corridor Economic Region (NCER), the Sabah Development Corridor (SDC) and the Sarawak Corridor of Renewable Energy (SCORE). This strategy, which is unique to Malaysia among ASEAN economies, has indeed attracted much investor interest. For example, the total cumulative investment in IRDA by the end of 2017 reached RM221 billion, exceeding its target of RM141 billion (Sharidan 2017).

The new thinking of agglomeration economies (developing economic specialities in specific geographic locations) through the cluster development strategy of corridors was extended in the Tenth Malaysia Plan (10MP, 2011–2015) (Government of Malaysia 2011), when the corridors were matched with national key economic areas (NKEAs). Specifically, IRDA is to focus on creative industries, the ECER is to develop the petrochemical sector, the NCER is to specialize in the automotive and aeronautics sectors, the SDC is to focus on tourism and palm oil processing and the SCORE is to leverage its cheap hydropower to produce aluminium, steel and glass. Intervention through industrial policy that shifted towards cluster-based development, apparently, has been re-cast from a regional perspective through these corridors, to propel economic growth through trade and investment.

In terms of specific policy instruments, fiscal and investment incentives have been widely utilized as tools of industrial policy in Malaysia. Trade and investment barriers, historically, have reduced to levels that are considered to be relatively low, with exceptions for the automotive, alcoholic beverages and agricultural sectors. Notwithstanding that, the current investment instruments in Malaysia are no longer sufficient to attract FDI

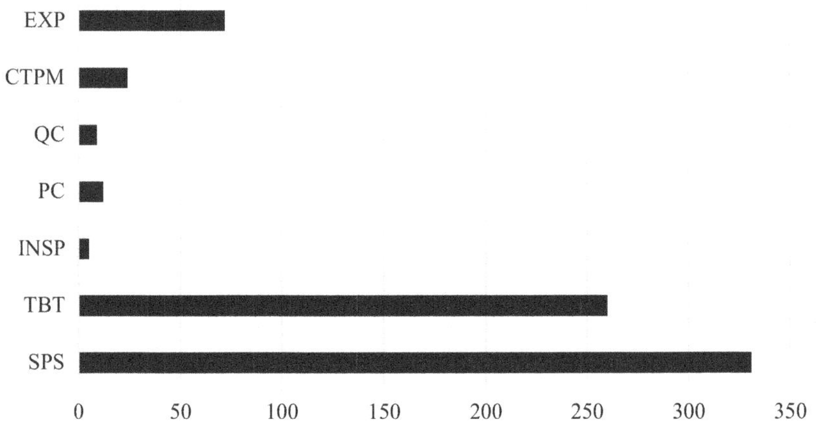

Fig. 5.7 Malaysia: Number of non-tariff measures, 2016. Notes: SPS—sanitary and phytosanitary; TBT—technical barriers to trade; INSP—pre-shipment inspection; PC—price control; QC—quantity control; CTPM—contingent protective measures; EXP—export-related measures. Source: ERIA-UNCTAD online: http://asean.i-tip.org/Default.aspx

as regional competitors have begun to offer similar incentive packages, and investors are now seeking greater transparency in the regulatory environment. In this context, while tariffs have been reduced substantially through trade liberalization, non-tariff measures (NTMs)[11] seem to be assuming greater importance. Figure 5.7 shows that technical measures, namely sanitary and phytosanitary (SPS) and technical barriers to trade (TBTs),[12] constitute the largest number (591 measures or 82.9 per cent) of NTMs in Malaysia. Obviously, NTMs are becoming popular policy instruments to regulate trade in Malaysia. There are however some outstanding issues with respect to NTMs, mainly that some NTMs may in fact be disguised non-tariff barriers (NTBs). A study by the Economic Research Institute for ASEAN and East Asia (ERIA) confirmed that Malaysia (after Indonesia) had the highest incidence of NTBs in ASEAN (Tangkitvanich and Rattanakhamfu 2018). Consequently, in the World Bank's Global Doing Business 2018 Report, Malaysia's ranking dropped one notch to 24th place overall among the 190 economies covered in the survey. The 2017 Malaysia Productivity Blueprint (MPB) has therefore identified one out of its six initiatives to be the removal of NTBs that impede business growth.

Policy interventions (through the various plans, programmes and regulations) and policy instruments, discussed above, are considered necessary to address market failures and regulate trade and investment. Unfortunately, some of the policy interventions have not produced the desired outcomes. For example, approximately 90 per cent of the 3000 MSC-status companies are still trapped at the start-up level even after two decades of their existence (The Star, 20 January 2016). Likewise, there are some unsuccessful economic zones (e.g. Port Klang free zone, Tanjung Kling free trade zone and Pulau Jerejak industrial estate; see ASEAN Secretariat 2017) that have struggled to attract investors, while there has been uneven progress in the development of the five economic corridors.[13] As for policy instruments, the current macro-industrial policy is not framed to handle the internationalization of production and the building of micro intra- and inter-firm relationships. The rise of NTMs and the advent of regional production networks (which will be elaborated further in the next section) are anchored in a different set of realities that require new forms of industrial policy, which target firms and go beyond trade liberalization. For example, efforts to remove NTBs and procedural obstacles can be addressed at the national level, but NTMs need to be streamlined or harmonized at the regional level to facilitate trade along the supply chain.

Growing Regional Connections

ASEAN is integral to Malaysia's development strategy, as it is both of geopolitical significance and of economic relevance to Malaysia. It has held a special place in the country's trade policy (Nambiar 2017). ASEAN represents approximately one-fourth of Malaysia's trade, having increased marginally from 24.3 per cent in 1990 to 26.6 per cent in 2016 (Fig. 5.8). Though total trade between Malaysia and ASEAN has somewhat reached a plateau, the engagement between Malaysia and ASEAN members (and among other ASEAN members) has become more balanced with time. In 1990, Singapore was the largest ASEAN trading partner of Malaysia, commanding 77.7 per cent of total Malaysian trade with ASEAN, followed by Thailand at a distant second (12.2 per cent). In 2016, Singapore (still the largest ASEAN partner), Thailand, Indonesia and Vietnam emerged as the core ASEAN trading partners of Malaysia, representing 46.4 per cent, 21.5 per cent, 14.2 per cent and 10.6 per cent of total trade with the region, respectively (calculated from ARIC online). Rooted in their shared history and geographical proximity, Singapore naturally remains the larg-

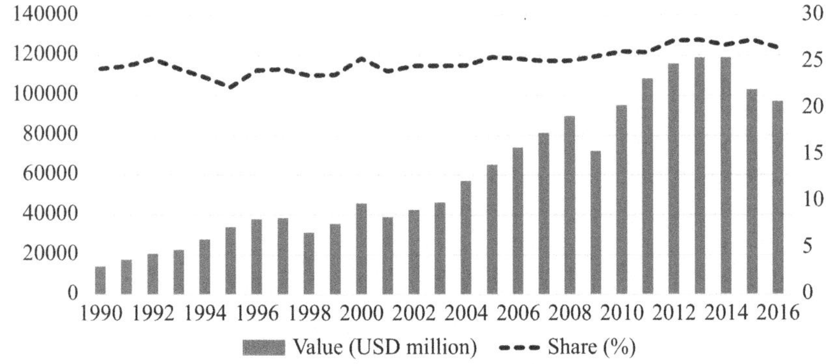

Fig. 5.8 Malaysia: Trade with ASEAN, 1990–2016. Notes: (1) The left axis refers to total trade with ASEAN (in USD million). (3) The right axis refers to share of total trade with ASEAN in global trade (in per cent). Source: ARIC: https://aric.adb.org/integrationindicators

est ASEAN trading partner and (and investor) for Malaysia. Malaysia supplies a number of intermediate and finished products in E&E, machinery, crude oil and optical and scientific equipment to Singapore.

From the investment perspective, ASEAN is also becoming an important investment source and destination for Malaysia. Approximately 20.7 and 25.1 per cent of Malaysia's total inward and outward investments were ASEAN bound for the 2010–2016 period (Fig. 5.9). For that period, OFDI to ASEAN recorded a healthy growth rate of 25.4 per cent on average, relative to that to the world which declined by 9.7 per cent. The saturation of the domestic market, the support of the government through tax exemption, tax incentives and special funds and institutional support through investment guarantee agreements (IGAs)[14] have driven outward investments (Tham et al. 2015; Sermcheep 2017). These recent developments in two-way investment flows are also indications of Malaysia becoming increasingly integrated with the region.

ASEAN took further priority as a strategic partner for Malaysia when the latter assumed the position of host and chair of ASEAN in 2015 and was tasked with the responsibility of inaugurating the ASEAN Economic Community (AEC). The AEC, semi-completed, was fully rolled out in November 2015 under Malaysia's chairmanship. Though Malaysia no longer helms the chairmanship of ASEAN, Malaysia continues to assume an active role in driving regional economic integration under the second

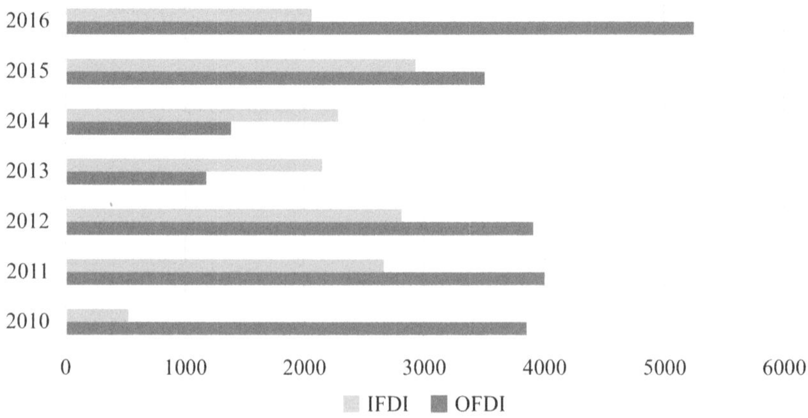

Fig. 5.9 Malaysia: Inward and outward investments with ASEAN (in USD million), 2010–2016. Notes: (1) IFDI—inward foreign direct investment; OFDI—outward foreign direct investments. (2) The data is not available prior to 2010. Source: ASEANstats: https://data.aseanstats.org/

phase of the AEC Blueprint, namely, to resolve the long-standing issues of NTBs. Prior to the AEC, Malaysia had signed six regional free trade agreements (FTAs) through ASEAN[15] (Table 5.2). (It is worth mentioning here that Malaysia has also concluded several bilateral FTAs, which are relatively easier than regional FTAs given that they represent fewer players and narrower differences of interests). The FTA partners in Table 5.2 absorbed 62.4 per cent of Malaysia's total exports in 2016 (MITI 2017). Besides formal government-to-government engagements through FTAs, Malaysia is also engaged in sub-regional cooperation with specific ASEAN members, such as the Indonesia-Malaysia-Thailand Growth Triangle (IMT-GT) and the Brunei Darussalam–Indonesia–Malaysia–Philippines East ASEAN Growth Area (BIMP-EAGA), to foster deeper integration. In the case of the IMT-GT, Malaysia played an instrumental role by shouldering the operational budget for the establishment of the Centre for IMT (CIMT) in the country and according it an international organizational status.

Growing trading and investment activities with ASEAN are also propelled by more intra- and inter-company linkages and outsourcing activities within the region. Malaysia is indeed an active player in the regional production networks,[16] and the density of the networks is particularly

Table 5.2 Malaysia: Free trade agreements, by status[a]

Agreement	*Status*	*Year*
ASEAN Free Trade Area (AFTA)	Signed and in effect	1993
ASEAN-People's Republic of China Comprehensive Economic Cooperation Agreement (ACFTA)	Signed and in effect	2005
ASEAN-[Republic of] Korea Comprehensive Economic Cooperation Agreement	Signed and in effect	2007
ASEAN-Japan Comprehensive Economic Partnership	Signed and in effect	2008
ASEAN-Australia and New Zealand Free Trade Agreement	Signed and in effect	2010
ASEAN-India Comprehensive Economic Cooperation Agreement	Signed and in effect	2010
ASEAN-Hong Kong, China Free Trade Agreement	Signed but not yet in effect	2017
ASEAN-Pakistan Free Trade Agreement	Proposed/under consultation and study	2009
ASEAN-EU Free Trade Agreement	Proposed/under consultation and study	2015
ASEAN-Eurasian Economic Union Free Trade Agreement	Proposed/under consultation and study	2016
ASEAN-Canada Free Trade Agreement	Proposed/under consultation and study	2017
Japan-Malaysia Economic Partnership Agreement	Signed and in effect	2006
Malaysia-Pakistan Closer Economic Partnership Agreement	Signed and in effect	2008
Malaysia-New Zealand Free Trade Agreement	Signed and in effect	2010
Malaysia-India Comprehensive Economic Cooperation Agreement	Signed and in effect	2011
Malaysia-Chile Free Trade Agreement	Signed and in effect	2012
Malaysia-Australia Free Trade Agreement	Signed and in effect	2013
Malaysia-Turkey Free Trade Agreement	Signed and in effect	2015
Malaysia-Gulf Cooperation Council Free Trade Agreement	(FA) signed	2011
United States-Malaysia Free Trade Agreement	Negotiations launched	2006
Malaysia-[Republic of] Korea Free Trade Agreement	Proposed/under consultation and study	2011
Malaysia-Syria Free Trade Agreement	Proposed/under consultation and study	2011
Malaysia-Iran FTA	Proposed/under consultation and study	2017
Malaysia-EU Free Trade Agreement	Negotiations launched	2010
Malaysia-European Free Trade Association Free Trade Agreement	Negotiations launched	2012

(*continued*)

Table 5.2 (continued)

Agreement	*Status*	*Year*
Preferential Tariff Arrangement-Group of Eight Developing Countries	Signed and in effect	2011
Trade Preferential System of the Organization of the Islamic Conference	Signed but not yet in effect	2014
Comprehensive and Progressive Agreement for Trans-Pacific Partnership (CPTPP)	Signed but not yet in effect	2018
East Asia Free Trade Area (ASEAN+3)	Proposed/under consultation and study	2004
Comprehensive Economic Partnership for East Asia (CEPEA/ASEAN+6)	Proposed/under consultation and study	2005
Free Trade Area of the Asia-Pacific	Proposed/under consultation and study	2014
Regional Comprehensive Economic Partnership (RCEP)	Negotiations launched	2013
Trans-Pacific Partnership (TPP)	Discontinued	2018

Source: ARIC online, https://aric.adb.org/fta-country

[a]A free trade agreement (FTA) can either be proposed, under negotiation, signed but not yet in effect or signed and in effect.

notable in the E&E industry. The established position of Malaysia in the regional production networks can be attributed to three key factors: the developed E&E clusters spurred by economic zones resulting in the dominance of the E&E in Malaysia's own trade structure; the established supply chains built with Japan in 1985 and subsequently the US in 1995; and building of ties with China, which is at the current centre of the production network[17] and also the largest trading partner of Malaysia since 2009. However, Malaysia is still engaged in lower DVA export content of manufactures destined to ASEAN relative to that for total manufactured exports to the world (see Fig. 5.3). An important challenge that ensues is how Malaysia can best utilize the regional production networks to increase its DVA, which in turn is constrained by innovation and the "catch-up" process with the more advanced regional economies.

Global Track Record

To complement the preceding discussion on Malaysia's regional strength and connections, this section provides an overview of Malaysia's global standing. It reviews the global performance of the economy based on its rankings and scores across dimensions of competitiveness, economic freedom and ease of doing business for the private sector.

Ranked at 25th out of 137 countries in the 2017–2018 Global Competitiveness Report, Malaysia is considered "most competitive" within the 24 upper-middle income countries. That said, Malaysia has slipped in its global competitiveness as it ranked higher at 18th position out of 140 countries in 2015–2016. The sub-indices of competitiveness indicate that Malaysia scored relatively low in terms of technological readiness (ranked 46th position) and higher education and training (ranked 45th position). The low ratings for technological readiness corroborate the discussion in the preceding sections that highlight the low technology transfer through FDI and the low technology absorption at the firm level, which then explains the low DVA content of its exports. In terms of education and training, Malaysia has made great strides in the education enrolment rates, but the quality of the tertiary education has not kept pace with the country's economic development. The low quality of education, in general, is evidenced by the poor performance of Malaysian students in the Programme for International Student Assessment (PISA). Though Malaysian students recorded some improvement based on the 2015 PISA relative to the 2010 assessment, their scores are still below the global average standard and below that for most East Asian economies.

The state of the global competitiveness of Malaysia can be related to its economic freedom. According to the recent 2018 Heritage Foundation Freedom Index, Malaysia was reported as the 22nd freest economy out of 180 countries, while it ranked 6th among 43 countries in the Asia-Pacific region (Miller et al. 2018). The economic freedom score for Malaysia at 74.5, albeit not economically "free" (still below a score of 80), was much higher than the global average of 61.1. (Note: the scores range from 0 to 100). The overall score change since 1995 was 2.6, and for the period 1995–2018, the economic freedom scores for Malaysia hit lowest levels during the crises periods of 1997 and 2008 (Fig. 5.10). In fact, over the period of review, Malaysia was considered "moderately fee" (recording scores between 60 and 70) until 2014. In 2018, the highest score across the various components of freedom was recorded for trade freedom and the lowest for government integrity. Similarly, the Fraser Institute 2017 Economic Freedom rating classified Malaysia in the second quartile of "mostly open" economies (Gwartney et al. 2017). Ranked 65th (out of 159 countries) in Economic Freedom, Malaysia was again scored poorly in

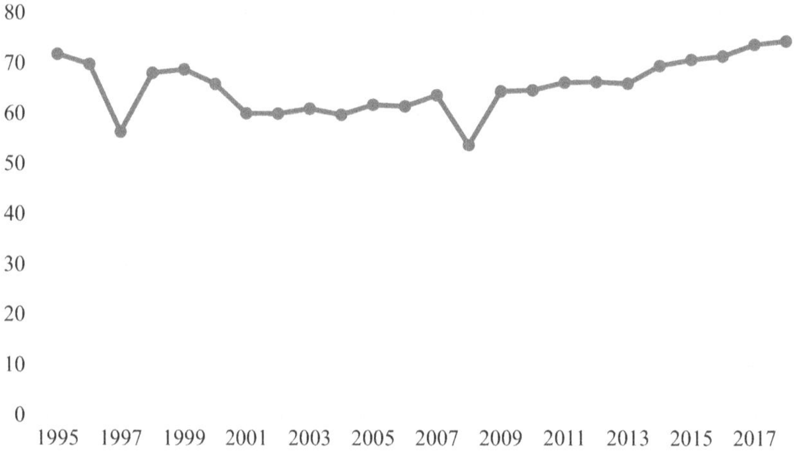

Fig. 5.10 Malaysia: Index of economic freedom scores, 1985–2018. Notes: (1) The economic freedom scores range from 0 to 100. (2) Scores of 80 or more—free; scores of between 70 and 80—mostly free; scores of 60 to 70—moderately free; scores of 50 to 60—mostly unfree; scores of below 50—repressed. Source: Miller, T., Kim, A.B., Roberts, J.M., Tyrrell, P. and Whiting, T.K. (2018). *2018 Index of Economic Freedom*, The Heritage Foundation: Washington, DC: https://www.heritage.org/index/pdf/2018/book/index_2018.pdf

terms of its legal system and property rights (5.8) and size of government (6.0) relative to its overall ratings of 7.2. (Note: the ratings are based on a scale from 0 to 10). Within both components, judicial independence and government enterprises and investments were rated the lowest. Judicial independence, specifically, was said to have been compromised on several accounts, namely, in 1988, during the judicial crisis when the then lord president of the Supreme Court was removed from office and five other Supreme Court judges were suspended, the sacking of the deputy prime minister on corruption and sodomy charges in 1998 and the acquittal of the previous prime minister of a multi-billion dollar money laundering scandal involving Malaysia's state fund 1Malaysia Development Berhad (1MDB) in 2015. Acknowledging the possibility of collusion and the absence of a legal system that is independent of politics, the present ruling party is committed to restore the separation of powers between the executive, legislature (Parliament) and judiciary. Ultimately, upholding the rule of law and controlling corruption[18] are critical elements of the business environment as it affects all economic interactions.

Apart from judicial enterprises, the low economic freedom ratings for the component of SOEs (also referred to as government-linked companies or GLCs and government-linked investment companies or GLICs) reflect their pervasive role in the Malaysian economy. In fact, Malaysia ranks fifth in the world in terms of countries with the highest SOE presence among their largest firms (Menon 2017). The GLCs, which are largely engaged in industrial and infrastructure projects, are perceived to be less efficient than private firms though they have been accorded preferential treatment in terms of access to government contracts and favourable regulations. Despite the divestment programme initiated in 2004, the GLCs and GLICs[19] continue to expand their activities into new areas and crowd out private investment in specific segments.

The nexus between the judiciary and politics and the state and business poses a challenge for good governance in Malaysia. The state-business interactions have generated crony capitalism, and according to the newly constructed 2016 index by *The Economist*, Malaysia was ranked 2nd among 22 countries in terms of the percentage of billionaire's wealth coming from cronyism. Corroborating this finding is the drop in the 2017 corruption perception index of the Transparency International from 51 points in 2008 to 47 points in 2017 (on a scale of 0 to 100, where 0 is highly corrupt and 100 is very clean) (Fig. 5.11). Malaysia recorded an all-time low of 62 out of 180 countries in 2017, over the period of review in Fig. 5.11. It was estimated that Malaysia lost approximately RM46.9 billion (USD 11.6 billion) in 2017 due to corruption within the public sector (Kana 2018).

Apart from the shortcomings in terms of the rule of law and government integrity, Malaysia has also somewhat declined in its performance in business rankings. According to the World Bank (2018), Malaysia ranked 24th globally in the ease of doing business rankings and 4th in Asia. Figure 5.11 shows that after attaining a high rank of sixth position globally in 2013, Malaysia has been sliding down the rankings for the ease of doing business. Though Malaysia has made 23 reforms in improving business regulations over the past 15 years (Jagdev 2017), much remains to be done in the area of starting a business, where its ranking is the lowest at 111th position. For example, to obtain a construction permit, companies need to complete about 37 procedures, which involves an average of

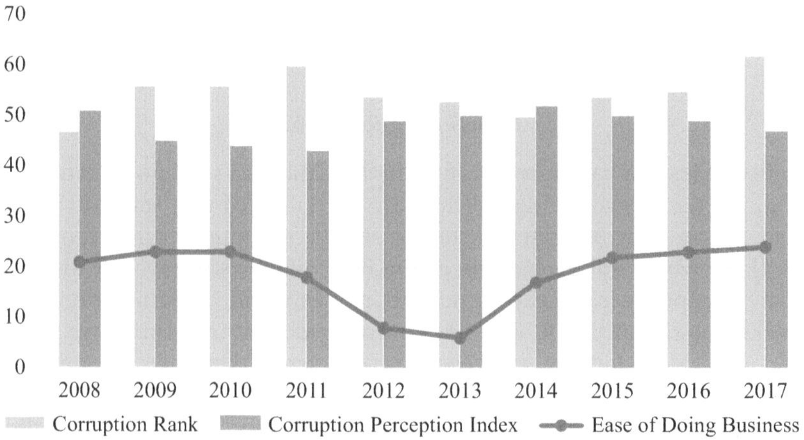

Fig. 5.11 Malaysia: Ranking and scores for ease of doing business and corruption, 1995–2017. Notes: (1) A high rank (1–20) indicates simpler and more-friendly business regulations. (2) The rank is based on how corrupt the public sector is perceived to be. The perceived level of public sector corruption is on a scale of 0 (highly corrupt) to 100 (very clean). Sources: Compiled by the author from Trading Economics data: https://tradingeconomics.com/malaysia/corruption-rank; https://tradingeconomics.com/malaysia/corruption-index; https://tradingeconomics.com/malaysia/ease-of-doing-business

140 days. Unlike the poor rating for starting a business, Malaysia has made it into the top 10 of 190 countries for electricity reliability. Comparatively, it takes a shorter time of 31 days to get connected to the electrical grid in Malaysia relative to 78 days across high-income countries. Likewise, trading across borders is considered cheap in Malaysia as it takes only about ten days to export and eight days to import. The distance to the frontier for trading across borders is rather high at 82.8.[20]

From a global standpoint, Malaysia has indeed come a long way to have reached the ranks of a "mostly free" and "mostly open" economy by having a pro-trade and pro-business culture. That said, several constraints prevail that affect the outcomes. Malaysia still lags behind other dynamic emerging economies in the region in technology and human capital, two important efficiency enhancers in the face of increasing global competition and technological advancement. Malaysia also falls short in good governance practices, which is important for maintaining a conducive business environment and further attracting capital inflows.

Concluding Remarks

Industrialization has indeed been central to Malaysia's accumulation process, wherein restructuring policies have been marked with state intervention. Accordingly, Malaysia pursued an active trade intensive policy, reliant on IFDI, which still remains integral to its economic strategy. The diversification in product and export markets, the expansion of production networks, the rise in OFDI and the growing trade and investment ties with the ASEAN region are some positive outcomes that have emerged in response to domestic and global challenges through the 1990s and 2000s. These changes in trade and investment patterns coincided with the market-oriented industrial policies of both decades, which in turn focused on regulating links to the regional and global economy through trade and FDI. Towards this end, the Malaysian government enforced a range of industrial policy instruments that include fiscal incentives, FDI promotion incentives, special zones and NTMs and regional integration strategies through FTAs, IGAs and sub-regional cooperation.

Though the export-oriented FDI growth model has successfully transformed Malaysia into an industrialized, "mostly free" and "mostly open" economy, the country is now trapped in low value-added activities within the manufacturing sector. Unfortunately, the industrial policies that drove successes in manufacturing were not able to withstand domestic constraints linked to absorptive capacity and technology, counterintuitive policies associated with domestic class formations[21] and the dual investment regime. Industrial strategies and policies, therefore, have to be continually revised to push the structural transformation of the manufacturing sector.[22] For this purpose, market distortions need to be identified and political captive addressed before executing the design and implementation of any new policies. The proliferation of production networks with the ASEAN region and beyond, which have blurred boundaries, increased vulnerability and altered the process of industrialization, injects further complexity to the industrial policy choice. In fact, the internationalization of production puts emphasis on the firm and renders a case for a change in industrial policy. In particular, some consideration should be given for Malaysian industrial policy to target specific firm-level characteristics instead of the current intense focus on industry-wide targeting (all firms within the industry/ sector). Investment incentives are needed to increase the linkage leverage between domestic (supplier) firms and MNEs (lead firms) that control global production and technology development. Ultimately, successful industrialization for Malaysia will hinge on (firm-level) innovation to deliver productivity gains and move up the value chain. This in turn depends on efficiency enhancers such as technology and human capital and a business environment that encourages entrepreneurial activity.

More importantly, the scaled heights of bad governing practices and corruption are overarching challenges to the observed low-technology and human capital base. As the country eases itself into this new phase of political development under the *Pakatan Harapan* alliance, reforms are under way. There are already winds of change with aggressive moves to improve institutional quality and remove rent-seeking activities. In pushing for domestic reforms, it is important that the new government does not neglect its commitments to the regional and global fora. Namely, the government should push for the completion of the Regional Comprehensive Economic Partnership (RCEP) and ratify the Comprehensive and Progressive Trans-Pacific Partnership (CPTPP) Agreement, as these are also agreements that will set Malaysia on the right course of governance and transparency (see also Rebecca 2018). On a final note, it is yet to be determined if a new Malaysia can emerge from these reforms and if those changes can support the economic policies and shift the process of industrialization to the next level.

Notes

1. The earlier phases of the industrial policies in Malaysia, namely the export-oriented industrialization drive in the early 1970s, a second round of import-substituting industrialization in the early 1980s and a second round of export push in the late 1980s, have been well documented in the literature. Therefore, this chapter is confined to the shift towards market-oriented policies since the 1990s.
2. The NEP (1971–1990) was a social re-engineering and affirmative action programme.
3. The 'Look East Policy'—to emulate Japan, South Korea and Taiwan—was the brainchild of Mahathir during his premiership (1981–2001) and is now reignited under his 2018 premiership.

4. Multinational enterprises (MNEs) account for over 80 per cent of manufacturing exports (65 per cent of total exports) (Athukorala and Wagle 2011).
5. Approximately 40 per cent of jobs in Malaysia are created in export-related activities (MITI 2017).
6. Negative deindustrialization refers to the shift into services without having gone through a proper experience of industrialization. In short, it represents unsuccessful manufacturing.
7. The "middle-income trap" is the situation in which rapidly growing economies stagnate at middle-income levels and fail to graduate into the ranks of high-income countries.
8. There are 22 FIZs, 18 free commercial zones (FCZs) and more than 500 IEs in Malaysia as of December 2016 (see ASEAN Secretariat 2017).
9. Malaysia has been a frontrunner in the region in advancing FIZs since the 1970s, whereby incentives such as pioneer status, labour utilization relief, investment tax credits, accelerated depreciation allowances and export refinancing facilities are granted to foreign-owned companies that are operating in FIZs (Zainal and Bhattasali 2008).
10. Economic corridors are large economic areas involving a number of contiguous states or provinces. Their development draws on the sectoral and geographical strengths of the constituent areas to support economic clusters and benefit from economies of scale (ASEAN Secretariat 2017).
11. NTMs are defined as policy measures other than ordinary customs tariffs that can potentially have an economic effect on international trade in goods, changing quantities traded or prices or both.
12. SPS refers to measures to protect human, animal and plant life, while technical measures are imposed to fulfil policy objectives such as national security requirements; prevention of deceptive practices; protection of human safety; protection of the environment; quality matters; and the protection of human, animal or plant life or health (other than for SPS reasons).
13. The NCER, which includes the state of Penang and the successful Penang FIZ, is at a relatively advanced stage in implementation (Athukorala and Narayanan 2018) relative to the other economic corridors.
14. The IGA between Malaysia and ASEAN came into force on 29 February 1989. For a list of Malaysia's signed and in force IGAs, see http://www.miti.gov.my/index.php/pages/view/771.
15. ASEAN is a pioneer in regional FTAs in East Asia by establishing its internal FTA (ASEAN FTA or AFTA) and ASEAN+1 FTAs (with China, Korea, Japan, Australia-New Zealand and India; see Table 5.2).
16. The supply (and not the demand) part of the networks is regionally concentrated, as the ASEAN trade is largely dependent on extra-regional demand.

17. The centre of the regional production network shifted from the US and Japan to China in mid-2000s.
18. The long-standing ruling party of the United Malays National Organization (UMNO) since Independence in 1957 until its recent defeat in May 2018 has led to cronyism and a degree of corruption in the bureaucracy.
19. At the time of writing, the current ruling party known as *Pakatan Harapan* (the opposition) that defeated the long-standing *Barisan Nasional* coalition in 2018 is in the process of removing all political appointees at GLCs and GLICs.
20. The distance to the frontier is on a scale of 0–100, where 0 represents the lowest performance and 100 represents the frontier.
21. See Tan (2014) for a detailed account of the adverse effects of Malaysian industrialization from national accumulation strategies, driven by internal factors related to changes in domestic class formations and reinforced by broader changes in global accumulation processes. These policies are, however, beyond the scope of this chapter.
22. The manufacturing sector should not be neglected on grounds that the economy is undergoing a process of deindustrialization, as misconstrued by those who advocate for emphasis on services-led growth at the expanse of manufacturing.

References

ASEAN Secretariat. 2017. *ASEAN Investment Report 2017: Foreign Direct Investment and Economic Zones in ASEAN*. Jakarta: ASEAN Secretariat.

Athukorala, Prema-Chandra. 2005. Trade Policy in Malaysia: Liberalization Process, Structure of Protection, and Reform Agenda. *ASEAN Economic Bulletin* 22 (1): 19–34.

Athukorala, Prema-Chandra, and Suresh Narayanan. 2018. Economic Corridors and Regional Development: The Malaysian Experience. *World Development* 106: 1–14.

Athukorala, Prema-Chandra, and Swarnim Wagle. 2011. Foreign Direct Investment in Southeast Asia: Is Malaysia Falling Behind. *ASEAN Economic Bulletin* 28 (2): 115–133.

Beaumont, P.G. 1990. The Role of Foreign Investment in Malaysia. *Jurnal Ekonomi Malaysia* 21 & 22: 65–77.

Chandran, V.G.R., and Evelyn S. Devadason. 2017. Energizing the Manufacturing Sector: Can Malaysia Move Forward. *Journal of Southeast Asian Economies* 34 (3): 523–551.

Drabble, John H. 2000. *An Economic History of Malaysia: The Transition to Modern Economic Growth*. Basingstoke and New York: Macmillan and St. Martin's Press.

Free and Independent News. 2018. Malaysians in Live in a 'Flawed Democracy'. January 31. http://www.freemalaysiatoday.com/category/nation/2018/01/31/report-malaysians-live-in-a-flawed-democracy/. Accessed June 24, 2018.

Government of Malaysia. 2006. *Ninth Malaysia Plan 2006–2010*. Kuala Lumpur: Government Press.

———. 2011. *Tenth Malaysia Plan 2011–2015*. Kuala Lumpur: Government Press.

———. 2016. *Eleventh Malaysia Plan 2016–2020*. Kuala Lumpur: Government Press.

Gwartney, James, Robert Lawson, and Joshua Hall. 2017. *Economic Freedom of the World – 2017 Annual Report*. Canada: Fraser Institute.

Hutchinson, Frank. 2016. *Evolving Paradigms in Regional Development in Malaysia*. ISEAS Economics Working Paper No. 2016–05. Singapore: ISEAS-Yusof Ishak Institute.

Jagdev, Singh Sidhu. 2017. Vital to Improve the Ease of Doing Business. *The Star*, November 4. https://www.thestar.com.my/business/business-news/2017/11/04/vital-to-improve-the-ease-of-doing-business/. Accessed June 30, 2018.

Jomo, Kwame Sundaram, and Chris Edwards. 1993. Malaysian Industrialisation in Historical Perspective. In *Industrialising Malaysia: Policy, Performance, Prospects*, ed. K.S. Jomo, 14–39. London: Routledge.

Kana, Ganeshwaran. 2018. The Burden to the Country. *The Star*, June 30. https://www.thestar.com.my/business/business-news/2018/06/30/the-burden-to-the-country/. Accessed June 30, 2018.

Menon, Jayant. 2017. *Government-linked Companies: Impacts on the Malaysian Economy*. Policy IDEAS No. 45. Kuala Lumpur: Institute for Democracy and Economic Affairs (IDEAS).

Miller, Terry, Anthony B. Kim, James M. Roberts, Patrick Tyrrell, and Tori K. Whiting. 2018. *2018 Index of Economic Freedom*. Washington, DC: The Heritage Foundation.

Ministry of Finance (MOF). 2018. *Malaysia: 2018 Economic Report*. Kuala Lumpur: Government Press.

Ministry of International Trade and Industry (MITI). 2017. *MITI Report 2016*. Kuala Lumpur: MITI.

Naidu, Sumisha. 2018. Affirmative Action Still Needed to Bridge Gap and Avoid Conflict Between Malays, Chinese: Mahathir. *Channel News Asia*, June 25. https://www.channelnewsasia.com/news/asia/affirmative-action-malays-mahathir-malaysia-10468360. Accessed June 30, 2018.

Nambiar, Shankaran. 2017. Malaysia. In *ASEAN and Member States: Transformation and Integration*, ed. Ponciano Intal Jr. and Lurong Chen, 164–179. Jakarta: Economic Research Institute for ASEAN and East Asia.

Organisation for Economic Co-operation and Development (OECD). 1999. Malaysia. In *Foreign Direct Investment and Recovery in Southeast Asia*, 99–153. Paris: OECD.

Rasiah, Rajah. 2011. Is Malaysia Facing Negative Deindustrialization? *Pacific Affairs* 84 (4): 715–736.

Rasiah, Rasiah. 2017. The Industrial Policy Experience of the Electronics Industry in Malaysia. In *The Practice of Industrial Policy Government—Business Coordination in Africa and East Asia*, ed. John Page and Finn Tarp, 123–144. Oxford: Oxford University Press.

Rebecca, Fatima Sta Maria. 2018. *Malaysia's Trade Policy: Time for Review, Issue No. 34*. Singapore: ISEAS-Yusof Ishak Institute.

Sermcheep, Sineenat. 2017. The Rise of Outward Foreign Direct Investment from ASEAN. In *Outward Foreign Direct Investment in ASEAN*, ed. Cassey Lee and Sineenat Sermcheep, 5–29. Singapore: ISEAS-Yusof Ishak Institute.

Sharidan, M. Ali. 2017. How the Economic Corridors Are Faring. *Business News*, May 13. https://www.thestar.com.my/business/business-news/2017/05/13/how-the-economic-corridors-are-faring/. Accessed February 12, 2018.

Tan, Jeff. 2014. Running Out of Steam? Manufacturing in Malaysia. *Cambridge Journal of Economics* 38: 153–180.

Tangkitvanich, Somkiat, and Saowaruj Rattanakhamfu. 2018. The ASEAN Economic Community and the East Asian Agenda. In *Asian Economic Integration in an Era of Global Uncertainty*, ed. Shiro Armstrong and Tom Westland, 185–218. Canberra: ANU Press.

Tham, Siew Yean. 2015. Diversification and Industrial Policies in Malaysia. In *Development and Modern Industrial Policy in Practice: Issues and Country Experiences*, ed. Jesus Felipe, 320–345. Cheltenham: Edward Elgar.

Tham, S.Y., Y.N. Teo, and Andrew Jia Yi Kam. 2015. Outward Foreign Direct Investment from Malaysia. *Journal of Southeast Asian Economies* 32 (3): 358–374.

The Economist. 2016. Comparing Crony Capitalism Around the World: The Economist's Crony-capitalism Index. May 5. https://www.economist.com/graphic-detail/2016/05/05/comparing-crony-capitalism-around-the-world. Accessed June 29, 2018.

The Star. 2015. Dr. M: Affirmative Action Under NEP Has Finally Paid Off. June 24. https://www.thestar.com.my/news/nation/2015/06/24/dr-m-affirmative-action-under-nep-has-finally-paid-off/. Accessed June 24, 2018.

———. 2016. MDeC: 90% of MSC-status Firms Still at Start-up Level. January 20. https://www.thestar.com.my/business/business-news/2016/01/20/90pc-of-msc-status-firms-still-at-start-up-level/. Accessed March 20, 2018.

The Straits Times. 2016. The Dilemma of Having Foreign Workers in Malaysia. September 17. https://www.straitstimes.com/opinion/the-dilemma-of-having-foreign-workers-in-malaysia. Accessed June 24, 2018.

The Sun Daily. 2017. New Investments in MSC Malaysia Companies Down. March 17. http://www.thesundaily.my/news/2197156. Accessed February 12, 2018.

World Bank. 2014. *Enterprise Surveys – Malaysia 2015 Country Profile*. Washington, DC: World Bank.

———. 2015. *Malaysia Economic Monitor – Immigrant Labour*. Washington, DC: World Bank.

———. 2017. *Malaysia Economic Monitor: Data for Development*. Kuala Lumpur: World Bank.

———. 2018. *Doing Business 2018: Reforming to Create Jobs*. Washington, DC: World Bank.

World Economic Forum (WEF). 2017a. *The Global Competitiveness Report 2017–2018*. Geneva: World Economic Forum.

———. 2017b. *The Global Gender Gap Report 2017*. Geneva: World Economic Forum.

World Trade Organization (WTO). 2017. Trade Policy Review – Report by Malaysia, WT/TPR/G/366, December 20. https://www.wto.org/english/tratop_e/tpr_e/s366_e.pdf. Accessed March 20, 2018.

Zainal, Aznam Yusof, and Deepak Bhattasali. 2008. *Economic Growth and Development in Malaysia: Policy Making and Leadership*. Working Paper No. 27. Washington, DC: World Bank.

Zolkepli, Farik. 2018. Muhyiddin: Malaysia Has Slipped in 2018 Human Trafficking Rating. *The Star*, June 30. https://www.thestar.com.my/news/nation/2018/06/30/muhyiddin-malaysia-has-slipped-in-2018-human-trafficking-rating/. Accessed June 30, 2018.

Online Databases

ASEANstats: https://data.aseanstats.org/.

Asia Regional Integration Center (ARIC): https://aric.adb.org/integrationindicators.

Department of Statistics (DOS), Malaysia: https://www.dosm.gov.my/v1/index.php?r=column/ctimeseries&menu_id=NHJlaGc2Rlg4ZXlGTjh1SU1kaWY5UT09.

ERIA-UNCTAD: http://asean.i-tip.org/Default.aspx.

International Trade Centre (ITC): https://tradecompetitivenessmap.intracen.org/TPIC.aspx.

OECD.Stat: https://stats.oecd.org/index.aspx?queryid=75537.

Trading Economics: https://tradingeconomics.com/indicators.

UNCTADSTAT: http://unctadstat.unctad.org/wds/ReportFolders/reportFolders.aspx.

World Development Indicators (WDI): http://databank.worldbank.org/data/reports.aspx?source=world-development-indicators.

CHAPTER 6

Singapore: Working Towards Prosperity

Roderick Macdonald and Seck Tan

Overview of the Economy

Singapore is a wealthy country, and its economy has solid foundations. Weak points are its size (population 5.6 million) and its ageing demographic. There is also some concern because the growth rate has plateaued for the past five years at under 4%.

The years before and after the global crisis that began in 2007 illustrate the resilience of the economy of Singapore: GDP per capita increased 4.65% in 2007, the lowest in the five years preceding the crisis. It then shrunk 0.6% during the global recession that followed the crisis before rebounding in 2010 with a 15.2% annual growth rate. This is typical. Singapore's economy is closely linked to the global economy but has rapidly returned to steady growth after each crisis. Encouraged by the government, businesses use slowdowns to upgrade the skills of employees and redirect investment, leading to higher productivity post crisis. GDP per

R. Macdonald (✉)
Université du Québec à Montréal, Montréal, QC, Canada
e-mail: macdonald.roderick@uqam.ca

S. Tan
Singapore Institute of Technology, Singapore, Singapore
e-mail: Seck.Tan@Singaporetech.edu.sg

R. Macdonald (ed.), *Southeast Asia and the ASEAN Economic Community*, https://doi.org/10.1007/978-3-030-19722-3_6

capita in 2017 was (in constant 2010 US$) 55,236 (comparable to 59,532 for the USA). Although Singapore is a small country, it provides a reasonable range of mid-to-high-end manufacture and services.

The government has been aggressive in directing domestic and foreign funds towards growth. Growth is financed in part by foreign direct investment, which has varied between 15 and 20% of GDP with the exception of two crisis points (see Fig. 6.1). Government debt, at 112.3% of GDP, appears moderately high at first glance, two to three times higher than that of neighbouring countries. However, this debt finances government assets, with a positive return after debt servicing (Ministry of Finance 2016). Further, most of the debt is domestic, with external debt equal to about 20% of gross national income (GNI), including private debt as well as public and publicly guaranteed debt. Taxes are low. The corporate tax rate is 17% (and only 8.5% tax rate on the first S$300,000 of taxable

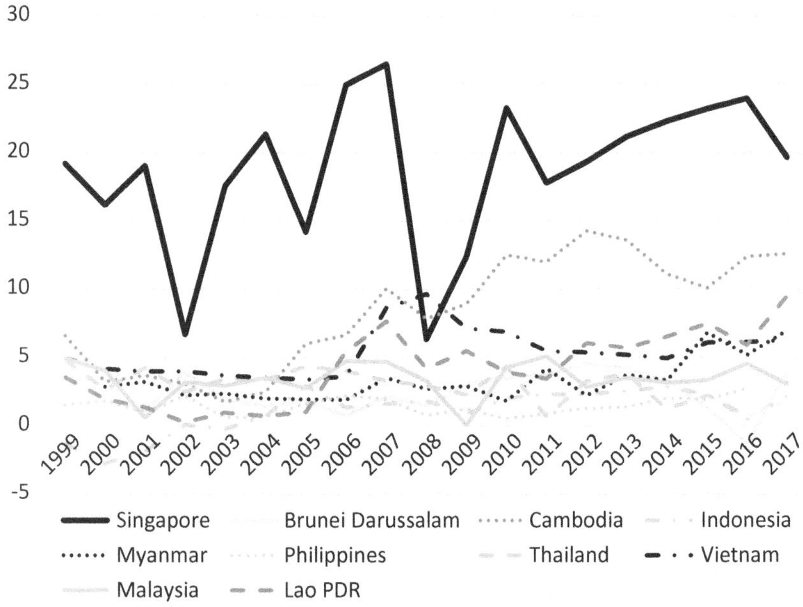

Fig. 6.1 Net inflows of foreign direct investment as a percent of GDP. Data source: International Monetary Fund, International Financial Statistics and Balance of Payments databases, World Bank, International Debt Statistics and World Bank

income), freeing more private funds for investment and upgrading skills. The income tax scheme is progressive and rates minimal. For example, residents pay only S$7950 on the first S$120,000 of income; there is a 22% tax rate over S$320,000. General sales tax will be raised to 9% between 2021 and 2025. Lower taxes leave firms more funds to reinvest and individuals with more disposable income to consume or save. The government has access to a portion of the investment returns from the sovereign wealth funds—Temasek and GIC (formerly Government of Singapore Investment Corporation) as well as from the Monetary Authority of Singapore, contributing more funds than any tax to Singapore's budget (Stolarchuk 2019). These funds are invested in businesses and are managed for returns (as opposed to job creation, self-sufficiency in some industry or other social goals), but also in collaboration with growth-oriented economic policy. Pensions (and also home purchases) are financed by an obligatory saving scheme, the Central Provident Fund, that the government can use in two ways to influence the economy: through the investment of these savings and by varying the contribution rates. Singapore also enjoys a higher than average percentage of high net-worth individuals, with a mean wealth per capita of S$380,000 in 2015. As a thriving offshore financial services centre (important for facilitating transactions of multinational corporations), it also benefits from increased funds deposited, even if it operates as a conduit rather than a sink offshore financial centre.[1] All of this increases the funds available as credit or for investment directed by public policy.

Singapore is a success story, particularly in contrast with other members of the ASEAN Economic Community. Singapore consistently places among the top world rankings in competitiveness, economic freedom, control of corruption and ease of doing business. The efficiency of its bureaucracy and the fairness of enforcement of contracts might suggest an enlightened and well-governed Western country. However, Singapore presents a special case that needs to be understood, and this understanding is best conveyed by a founding myth.

The Founding Myth

The State of Singapore Act was passed in Britain on August 1, 1958. The People's Action Party won the elections of May 30, 1959, the 1958 act was adopted as the Constitution of Singapore on June 3, 1959, and Lee Kuan Yew installed as Prime Minister on June 5, 1959.

Legally a sovereign nation, Singapore faced two sources of threats to its identity, as does any nation: internal and external.

Within, the ideas of communism were widespread in part of the community and political agitation was rampant, feeding on disparities in material success, ethnic divisions, the example of Communist China and the propaganda and other efforts of Russia and China during the Cold War period. The perception of vulnerability and uncertainty was very strong.

The threat from outside of Singapore was a basic strategic reality. The island of Singapore was 581.5 square kilometres of land sandwiched between Malaysia (a kilometre across the Johor Strait) and Indonesia (150 kilometres across sea to Batam), the fourth largest country in the world. Even when relatively undeveloped, Singapore had virtually no wilderness or natural resources. It was militarily undefended. There was no possibility of self-sufficiency. Further, Singapore could not aspire to produce any world-class enterprise due to lack of scale in terms of resources, variety of local talent and domestic market.

The evident solution was to become part of Malaya. Lee Kuan Yew and Tunku Abdul Rahma of the Federation of Malaya worked towards the creation of Malaysia (from Malay-SI-a) on September 16, 1963. Purportedly, Tuku had reservations because of the impact of Singapore upon the proportions of the ethnic mix in the new country, bringing the ethnic Chinese population closer in size to that of ethnic Malays. He led the parliament of Malaysia to expel Singapore on August 9, 1965. The evident solution had failed.

The *Konfrontasi* campaign by Soekarno of Indonesia added to the tension, with over 40 terrorist bombings since 1962. Soekarno nurtured the idea of a pan-Malay nation including the Malay peninsula, current Indonesia, and all of Borneo. He thus opposed the formation of the Federation of Malaysia.

Then the British navy rapidly retired from Singapore during 1968–1971, with a residual presence until 1976. This both exposed the young nation militarily and eliminated the 20% of its economic activity that had consisted of servicing that navy. Trade had been 300% of GDP, and now dropped to 200%, a bad sign for an economy reliant on trade.

This is the founding myth of Singapore, based on hard facts: it is a very vulnerable nation, and its people have to work hard together to assure survival. This "work hard together" would be assured by three principles: meritocracy, an openness to anyone wishing to join them, and a strong government that runs the island like a business corporation. This last principle distinguishes Singapore from its neighbours, where government process tends to be manipulated by "elite" business or military interests. The second principle has a twist: if you do not join them, you are a threat to the unity of the nation. There is great freedom to contribute to the prosperity of Singapore, but one must work in concert with the plans of the government. Although Singapore is technically a representative democracy, there is no real contest for power (Freedom House 2018; or media freedom cfr Reporters Without Borders 2019).

Singapore is perceived as a free-market laissez-faire, hard core capitalist state, in part because of a history of strong state intervention to assure the efficiency of business transactions.[2] However, there also has been a strong state presence through ownership of businesses. Government-linked enterprises represent about 37% of stock market capitalization.[3] Credit to government and government-linked enterprises (the term used in Malaysia and Singapore to denote business wholly or partially owned by government) has been increasing, even relative to GDP, as Fig. 6.2 shows. The

Fig. 6.2 Credit to government and state-owned enterprises to GDP (%). Data source: International Financial Statistics (IFS), International Monetary Fund (IMF) via the Global Financial Development of the World Bank

country has a widely praised programme to help citizens purchase their own homes, and as a consequence, the state has built housing for 80% of the population. Although state-owned enterprise elsewhere is often inefficient and can be a locus of corruption in other countries, Singapore government-linked enterprises perform well.

The third principle, meritocracy, is an aspiration of Singapore's government and it has by and large succeeded. One of the challenges in establishing a meritocracy is that natural talent and early upbringing are important factors in the capacity of new citizens. Although educational streaming is based above all on merit in Singapore, family home conditions affect academic performance and poverty still tends to beget poverty. Efforts to deal with this in the 1980s went so far as to provide various incentives to encourage less successful Singaporeans to have smaller families and for successful men to marry more highly educated women. This episode is long in the past but does illustrate the degree to which government has focussed upon the pursuit of security, founded upon material success.

A History of Growth

Today Singapore has a population of about six million. Reclaimed land has added 140 square kilometres to the territory. In five decades of economic development, Singapore has evolved from a modest trading post to an alluring world-class metropolitan city. Singapore's current developed nation status is an enormous contrast to its early days of independence when strikes and riots were routine.

Figure 6.3 reveals strong growth since 1961, with the exception of six inflection points: 1964, 1975, 1985, 1998, 2001 and 2008. The slowed growth in 1964 corresponds to the lone full calendar year in which Singapore was part of Malaysia and which was marked by severe race riots and the *Konfrontasi* campaign of Indonesia that disrupted Singapore's trade. All other inflection points derive from worldwide trade disruptions: the 1974 world trade recession following the oil shocks of 1971 and 1973, a recession in the USA spreading worldwide in the 1980s, the 1997–1998 Asian financial crisis, the telecommunications shock of 2001 followed by a slowdown caused by 9/11 and the global financial and economic crisis of 2007–2011. With trade representing 2.5–4 times GDP since its independence, Singapore necessarily is affected by trade shocks. However, in each case, the downturn was modest with only slight and brief incursions into negative growth, and the economy rebounded quickly. For much of its history, growth of GDP

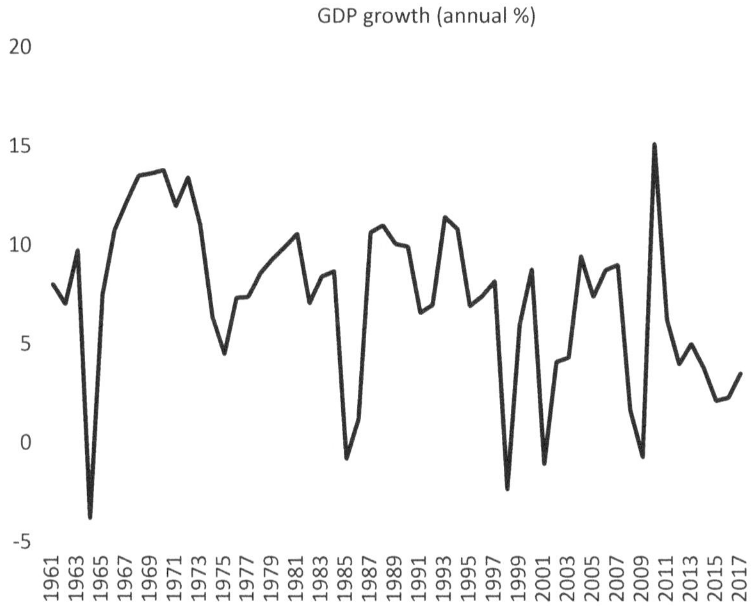

Fig. 6.3 Annual GDP growth rate 1961–2017. Data source: World Bank

has been closer to 10% than to 5%. This persistence is not the result of spontaneous free-market growth, nor is it the result of a consistently applied economic policy. On the contrary, policy was modified several times. Singapore has varied its economic policies over the decades in order to lead its workforce up the productivity and value ladder. In addition, Singapore has continued to refine its bureaucracy to increase the efficiency of procedures necessary for business. It is "business-friendly."

The Twentieth Century: From Policy to Results

Singapore had been heavily reliant on the hinterland of Malaysia for resources in the 1950s and early 1960s. In anticipation of a common Malayan market, an import-substitution strategy (ISS) was adopted. A strategy of this nature would have had to be based on a policy of self-sufficiency. Being self-sufficient offers multiple benefits that include immunity to exchange rate volatility, specialization in specific types of goods and services, ensuring quality and excellence and creativity and innovation.

However, there were limitations to ISS's success for Singapore. ISS is dependent on a large population and consumers with adequate disposable income. Singapore in the 1950s–1960s did not have a sufficiently large population to sustain ISS consumption. Still, although there were potential deficiencies (Baer and Samuelson 1977) of ISS and inadequacies (Bruton 1998), ISS remained the preferred option.

In the event, ISS had to be abandoned as an option when separation from Malaysia in 1965 set Singapore off on an export-oriented trajectory. The export-led strategy was heavily championed by a UN Team led by Dr. Winsemius and Mr. Tang I-Fang. This team did not believe in a common Malayan market due to the mismatch in market size and the differing dominant ethnic groups in both countries (Malay in Malaysia, Chinese in Singapore). Being the first UN Industrialization Survey Team to call on Singapore, their goal was to create the highest number of jobs in the shortest time possible. Dr. Winsemius and his team drafted a ten-year plan to transform Singapore from an *entrepôt* to a manufacturing and industrialized centre. Further, ISS was halted at the insistence of International Monetary Fund (IMF) and the World Bank (WB) on global market-driven liberalization. These were strong pressures for change from the policies first pursued while Singapore was still a state of Malaysia.

The government of Singapore began to pursue exports as the basis of economic development and thus national security. Huff (1994) observed that one of the characteristics of Singapore's economy is that it is a planned economy. However, the detail rather than the fact of planning is what is most striking. There is no mystical or magical thinking, only an understanding of the challenges ahead and a pragmatic choice of actions in order to meet them. This began soon after self-government and continued for the rest of the twentieth century. Examination of the State of Singapore development plan 1961–1964, as well as two early budget speeches, illustrates this.

The Ministry of Finance published the State of Singapore development plan 1961–1964 with the main objective of increasing employment opportunities. This was to be achieved primarily by attracting private capital through the promise of higher profits. These were to be made possible by the provision of low-cost power and water and good logistics. To this end, Singapore budgeted expenditures for the provision of electricity, water and gas (S$147 million), the creation of industrial estates in Kaliang and Jurong (S$85 million) and the provision of S$100 million in capital to the Economic Development Board for government participation in industrial enterprises. S$117 million was foreseen for the development of transport and communications. S$350 million would go to social development,[4] of which nearly half was for housing and nearly one-third for education (Ministry of Finance 1961).

In his December 13, 1965, budget speech, the Minister of Finance Lim Kim San[5] reiterated the importance of creating manufacturing jobs to assure the development of Singapore. This would be done by a limited number of businesses capable of manufacturing competitive products. The idea was to sell 200–300 products to developed economies without disrupting them. On December 5 of the next year, he observed that "In order to achieve rapid technological advancement and to develop to the full potential quality of our workers, it will be necessary to organize a mass program of training within industries for specialized skills." He then described a pilot programme in progress for specific trades and announced the erection of a "Metal Industry Development Center and Prototype Production and Training Center for machine building, electronics, precision instruments, printing and plastic will be set up. Specialized production teams including workers will be sent overseas for on-the-job training. Such schemes will be directed towards the creation of specific factories. By building up a large reservoir of techniques and skilled workers, and by gearing training to the industrial promotion program, we can quickly enter into a more sophisticated stage of industrial development." The minister further observed that the higher skilled workers would only contribute to the economy if they had jobs, and to this end, it was necessary to continue attracting multinationals to manufacture in Singapore, to encourage the expansion of manufacturers in Singapore and to keep targeted firms in fast-evolving industries current. He then announced a series of fiscal incentives for these purposes (Lim 1966).

Perhaps even more important than the pragmatic, detailed realism of these and subsequent policies was a strong linkage between policy and actual implementation, enabled by the cohesion between political actors and the civil service. Kumar and Siddique (2010) observed that "In Singapore, the dominance of one-party rule and the continuity of such political power have meant that policy consistency is matched by personalities dedicated to fulfilling the overall strategic design. … The level of loyalty towards the political system and the corresponding trust from the political hierarchy were important catalysts to creating the Singapore model. …individuals can be found in other agencies and ministries, exercising a strong personality cult that is in consonance with the demands of the political system." Staff competence and initiative in decision-making style throughout the organization (Low 2016) were also part of the formula.

Increasing labour costs, labour shortages, the rise of protectionism among developed countries for labour-intensive industries and the rise of nations whose competing economies featured lower labour costs all brought Singapore to implement a new stage in economic policy in the late 1970s, upgrading labour skills still further and encouraging businesses towards more advanced processes and outputs as well as increased R&D.

The result of this was a long run of ever-increasing GDP and ever-increasing exports—so much so that the trade balance became consistently positive and so large that it became a significant fraction of GDP, passing 10% in the early 1990s and varying around 20% in the twenty-first century.[6]

Singapore's economic development has been described as a movement from exclusively trade to low-skilled, simple manufacturing (1960s), then to intermediate, higher skilled manufacturing (1970s and 1980s), on to high technology (1990s) and then on to business, financial and health services (twenty-first century).[7] There would be a lot of truth in this as the leaders of Singapore made an effort to increase domestic technical knowledge, support capacity and business sophistication. At the same time, history was a little more complicated. The rise of business services underlines this. The Global Financial Centres Index (2018) rates Singapore as number 4 in the world, and the Boston Consulting Group Wealth Report 2018 ranks Singapore third in the world for offshore finance. The rise of this financial service began in 1968 when Singapore licensed Bank of America to handle transactions for non-residents, leading to the "Asian dollar" or "Asian Eurodollar" market. Hodjera (1978) remarked that, from that time onward, "the long-run strategy of the authorities has been to stimulate the development in Singapore of a large financial sector, based on very highly skilled services to be provided to the whole south and east Asian region." The relative importance of GDP from manufacturing increased until about 1973 and remained more or less stable until about the end of 1984 (Fig. 6.4). Thereafter services returned to contributing over two-thirds of GDP.

In fact, two things happened in 1984: services rose in importance, and overall economic performance fell. Manufacturing decreased in absolute terms as well as relative to GDP. GDP from services did increase in absolute terms, but total GDP still decreased in 1985. A recession had begun in Singapore and lasted through the year. Although the downturn after

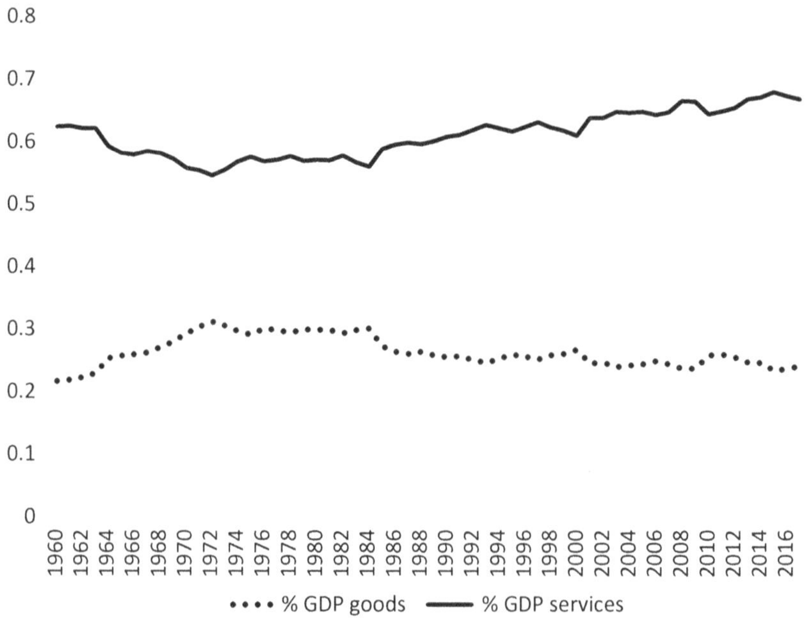

Fig. 6.4 Goods and services components of GDP. Data source: SingStat

the Asian financial crisis was more brutal, the 1985 recession was far more traumatic for Singapore. Once again, however, the government carried out a cold analytical diagnosis, listed the internal and external factors, and then moved to address those factors it controlled. Among its many actions was one that would reduce costs and also reduce saving. The Central Provident Fund had been established in 1955, before Singapore became an independent nation, as the pension plan of the country. This was a contribution-based scheme, with contributions by both employees and employers and fixed rates for both. In early 1986, the contribution of employers was reduced provisionally (for a two-year period) from 25% to 10% of wages. As a result, wages costs decreased by 12%, bringing firms back to 1982 levels of competitiveness (for more details on this pivotal period, see Grice and Drakakis-Smith 1985; Chan 1986; Lee 1987; Rigg 1988; for a comparison with other economic downturns, see Woo 2018).

Nonetheless, manufacturing was becoming more sophisticated, at least from 1980 onwards, as indicated by Fig. 6.5. Many authors dub the period

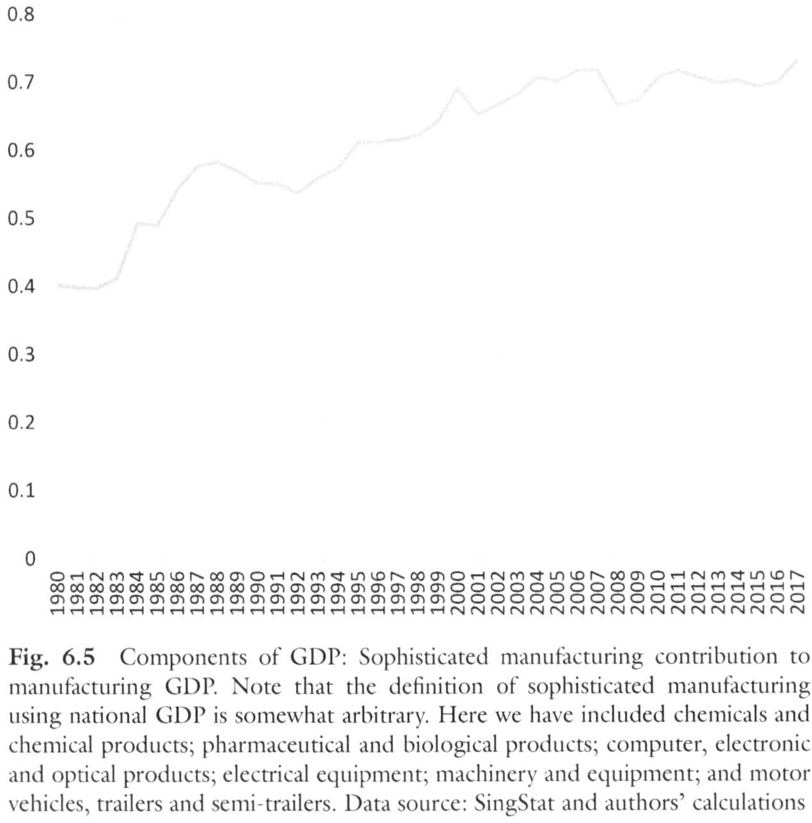

Fig. 6.5 Components of GDP: Sophisticated manufacturing contribution to manufacturing GDP. Note that the definition of sophisticated manufacturing using national GDP is somewhat arbitrary. Here we have included chemicals and chemical products; pharmaceutical and biological products; computer, electronic and optical products; electrical equipment; machinery and equipment; and motor vehicles, trailers and semi-trailers. Data source: SingStat and authors' calculations

1979–1984 the second industrial revolution of Singapore. The Economic Development Board gave importance to the pharmaceutical, biotechnology, medical technology, electronics and engineering industries with investments in the 1990s. More sophisticated services were also growing in importance, as indicated by Fig. 6.6. Categorizing some industries as more sophisticated than others is somewhat arbitrary—for example, both chemicals and electrical machinery included simple as well as sophisticated processes. In addition, much of the growing sophistication occurred within industries, resulting in greater productivity, rather than through changes in the mix of industries (see Ministry of Trade and Industry 2008 pages 12–14 for an analysis of productivity growth). Figure 6.7 shows that the value added per worker for industry increased more rapidly in

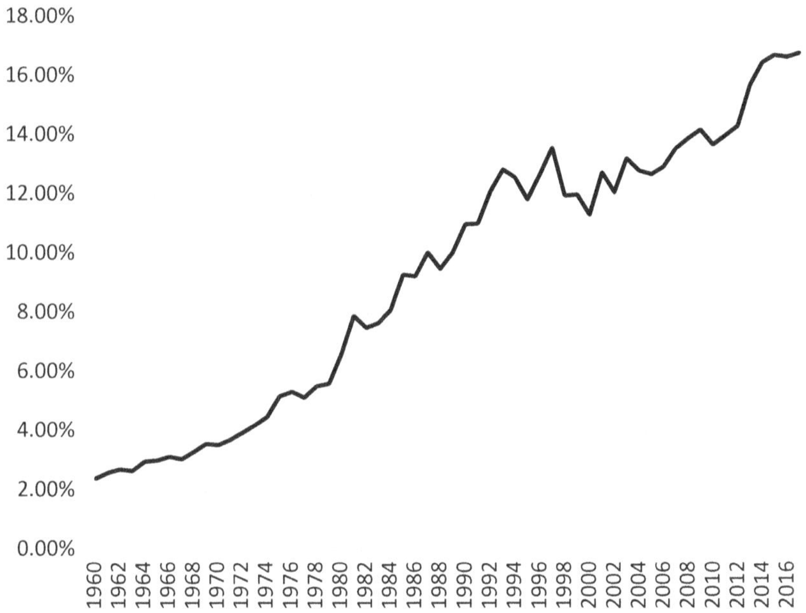

Fig. 6.6 Contribution of information, communication, business and financial services and insurance to GDP in percent. Data source: Singapore Department of Statistics and authors' calculations

Singapore than in Germany, Japan and Switzerland, the highest ranked on the Economic Complexity Index. Unfortunately, the Economic Complexity Index itself does not provide insight to this evolution (this is explained in the appendix).

Human Capital (Resource) Development

The core idea of the early stages of Singapore's development was the provision of opportunities for employment. During the early stages of Singapore's development (1960–1980), job creation, FDI and learning from developed economies were critical in switching from low-wage, import-substitution strategy (ISS) to high-wage, export-oriented industrialization. This would require adopting best practices from the Japanese (who were then regional leaders) and the Westerners (USA and United Kingdom). However, these best practices were adapted to suit Singapore's

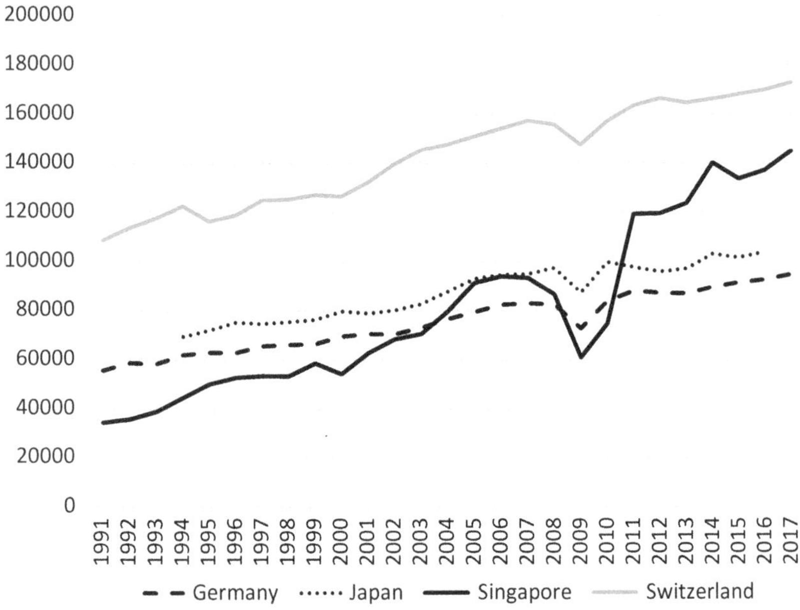

Fig. 6.7 Value added per worker. Data source: Derived by the World Bank using World Bank national accounts data, OECD National Accounts data files, and employment data from International Labour Organization, ILOSTAT database. Data are in constant 2010 US$ and are for industry including construction

requirements (see UNDP Global Centre for Public Service Excellence 2015 for further elaboration).

In the ideal scenario, foreign investors equipped the local labour force with skill sets and relevant expertise. A transferability of applicable skill sets to local labour force gives an advantage with respect to workers in other countries, offering an attractive opportunity to foreign investors. Both ideals provided the foundation for Singapore's human capital development in meeting investor demand and fulfilling market conditions.

Previous education is necessary before these skills can be learnt. Education in Singapore begins when a child is five with two years of pre-primary, six years of primary, four years of secondary and two years of pre-college. This is the roadmap of Singapore education; however, there are also options such as technical and polytechnic courses. In any case, the majority of the labour force would have undergone more than a decade of formal education prior to contributing to the economy. English and a choice of mother tongue (Mandarin, Malay and Tamil) were offered, as linguistics capability was essential in Singapore's role as an international trading player (cfr. Goh and Gopinathan 2006 and Maynes 2011). This would not have been possible without the wise allocation of UN funding for education investment, industrial development and urban planning. These pillars laid the groundwork for selected Singapore scholars to go on the UN Development Programme (UNDP) (UNDP Global Centre for Public Service Excellence 2015) with the expectation that they contribute to nation building upon their return.

An economic restructuring during its early years resulted in Singapore experiencing labour shortages from 1973 to 1984. From that experience, human capital development took priority for the local authorities (Tan 2015) in the form of education, industrial training towards skill-intensive jobs and schemes to improve working conditions and enhance productivity.

From the late 1980s and beyond, there was a subsequent shift to the new markets of China and India and this called for a revised strategy. The new strategy was to utilize the expertise acquired from the developed economies in serving opportunities in China and India (emerging economies). This was critical as Singapore shifted to a knowledge-based economy.

Without a skilled and industrious labour force, the path of Singapore's trajectory may have taken a different route, with economic achievements taking a longer time to come to fruition. The city-state continues to attract global talent. This increases the need for the local labour force to reskill and upgrade in order to compete with a genuine edge.

The Twenty-First Century: New Horizons

At the turn of the millennium, Singapore continued to be an important trade and transportation hub, provided regional headquarters for multinational corporations, boasted competitive manufacturing in relatively advanced industries and had added financial and other sophisticated services. The nation had weathered the Asian financial crisis well. Gross capital formation as a percentage of GDP dropped from the high 30s to the high 20%. Figure 6.8 reveals that investment actually continued to grow in absolute terms, with the only hiccoughs being the years following the Asian financial crisis and the recession following the global financial crisis. Once again, it was the impact of the huge positive trade balance upon the demand side algebra of GDP (see again endnote 6) that made the rate of investment appear to diminish.

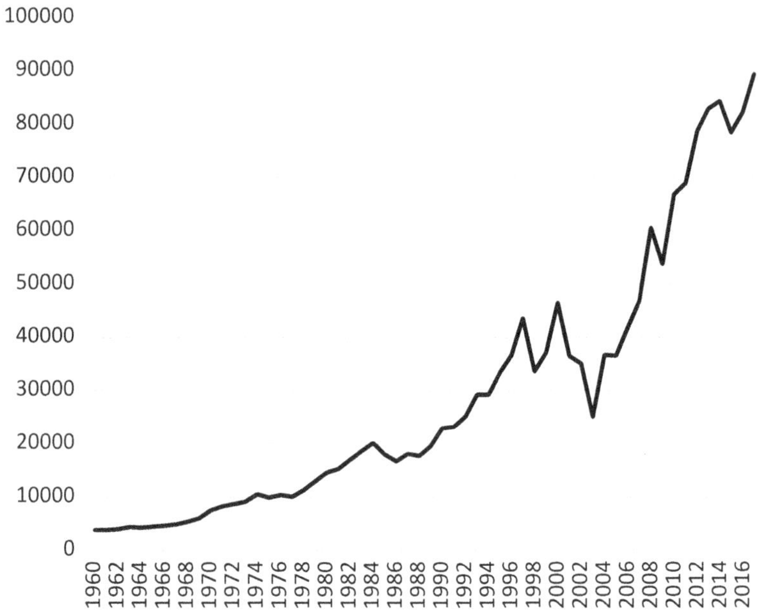

Fig. 6.8 Gross capital formation (Constant 2010 US$). Data source: World Bank national accounts data, and OECD National Accounts data files

There was nonetheless a limit upon growth through increasing sophistication. While a large and growing portion of Singapore's workforce has become capable of increasingly sophisticated production in manufacturing and services, there is a limit to the breadth of diverse technical know-how within a population of six million. Further, the workforce of Singapore will begin to shrink in 2020 and is ageing. A painful observation for Singapore is that GDP growth closely follows the growth of the foreign workforce (Tan 2018). Arguably, though, this might be a coincidence. GDP growing slightly less than the total workforce would give this same result since most of the workforce growth is foreign. In any case, there is also a limit to the scope of manufacturing operations within the domestic boundaries of Singapore. This could lead to diminishing returns on investment, even as Singapore's capacity for investment continued to increase.

GDP continued to increase nonetheless. New markets, or at least the rapid growth of previously small markets, and new development of an established export industry—tourism—contributed to the growth of

GDP. In spite of these, however, exports began to falter in 2011 even as GDP continued to grow. More of the value added created in Singapore manufacturing and services was being consumed in the country, and the current account (exports less imports of goods and services) grew rapidly. Still Singapore sought to stimulate growth, looking to the immediate region and beyond. The following pages cover these points in greater detail.

A New Growth Market

The first few decades of the new century were helped by the rise of a previously small market: China and with mainland China, Hong Kong. Tables 6.1 and 6.2 show how new destinations became important in the first decades of the century. In particular, Fig. 6.9 illustrates how exports to China and Hong Kong have increased, while those to the other principle destination, the USA, have varied considerably but with a flat trend. Between them, Hong Kong and mainland China accounted for a quarter of Singapore's exports in trade and services in 2018, in about equal measure. Further, Singapore has a positive trade balance with both, in contrast to the notable exception of trade with the USA.

Tourism is an exported service, so efforts to increase tourism can lead to increased added value in exports. Although tourism was expanding in the Asia Pacific region, receipts from tourism were flat in Singapore over the last five years of the twentieth century, at around US$6 billion. The aftermath of the Asian financial crisis, the interruption of travel after the destruction of the World Trade towers in New York on September 11, 2001, and the SARS epidemic in early 2003 all contributed to maintain flat receipts until tourists eventually hurried to catch up. Arrivals and receipts rebounded thereafter, but the government made a somewhat controversial decision in 2005 to further stimulate tourism. On April 18, 2005, Prime Minister Lee Hsien Loong presented a proposal to develop integrated resorts (Lee 2005). This was controversial because the resorts would include casinos (as well as other amusement, convention, dining, retail and hotel facilities), in this way seeming to contradict the squeaky clean reputation of Singapore. To mitigate this, he also announced measures to reduce any corrupting impact upon Singaporean mores. In 2006, the Las Vegas Sands Corporation of the USA and the Genting Group of Malaysia were selected to build two resorts, and the Marina Bay Sands (US$5.7 billion) and Resorts World Sentosa (US$4.8 billion) opened their doors in 2010 (Singapore Infopedia 2011 and Meinhardt (Singapore)

Table 6.1 Principle destination of exports in 2000

Export Partner	*Exports (US$ billion)*	%
World	138	100%
Malaysia	25	18%
USA	24	17%
China and Hong Kong	16	12%
Japan	10	8%
Thailand	6	4%
Korea, Rep.	5	4%
Germany	4	3%
Netherlands	4	3%

Source: Authors' calculations on data from WITS, World Bank

Table 6.2 Principle destination of exports in 2018

Export Partner	*Exports (US$ billion)*	%
World	373	100%
China + Hong Kong	100	27%
Malaysia	40	11%
Indonesia	28	7%
USA	24	6%
Japan	17	5%
Korea, Rep.	17	4%
Thailand	15	4%
Vietnam	12	3%

Source: Authors' calculations on data from WITS, World Bank

n.d.). Currently casino revenues are declining, but integrated resorts have boosted tourism. In 2015, the prime minister stated that that the two IRs have contributed between 1.5 and 2% of GDP (Lim 2015), about US$5 billion every year. This and other measures led to a doubling of tourism's contribution to GDP from 2003 to 2017 as Fig. 6.10 shows.

Although both tourism and the new markets of mainland China and Hong Kong did bolster exports and GDP, and while the trade balance of Singapore has been growing, the volume of exports has faltered since 2011. GDP, in contrast, continued to grow albeit more slowly. Though neither self-sufficient nor seeking to be self-sufficient, Singapore was generating and consuming more added value within its own borders, as trade shrank from 380% of GDP in 2011 to 310% in 2016. Services have been

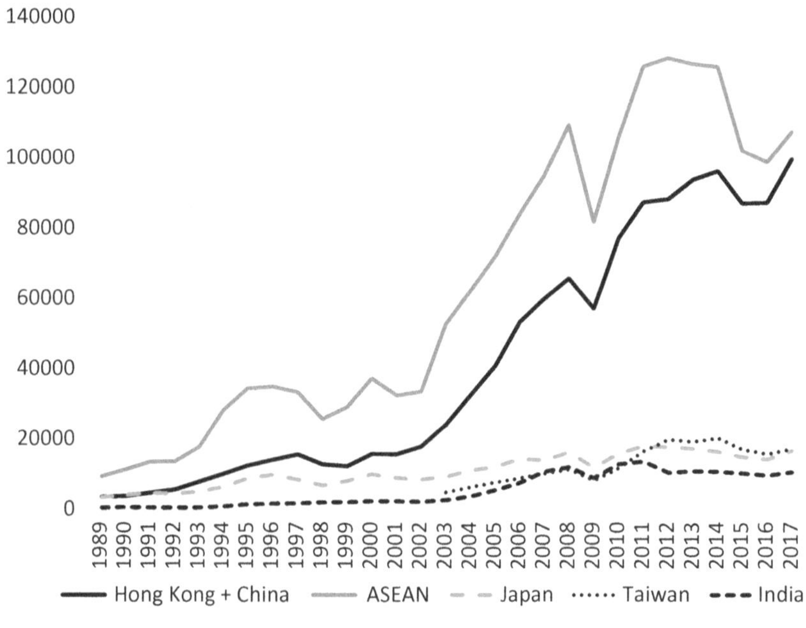

Fig. 6.9 Evolution of exports to principle Asian destinations. Taiwan is not listed in the WITS database. Data sources: WITS, National Statistics of the Republic of Taiwan and author's calculations

the greatest contributor to GDP growth in recent years, and in particular, financial and insurance services (see Fig. 6.6).

Singapore's exports had grown vertiginously in the twentieth century; however, exports to neighbouring countries were rather disappointing. Neighbouring economies had not kept pace with Singapore and were unable to absorb Singapore's exports. Singapore would have fared even better had other ASEAN neighbours grown as rich with consequent purchasing power. Whether intentionally or not, Singapore has twice tried to address this problem, first by trade (mostly in the twentieth century) and second by investment (mostly in the twenty-first century).

An Attempt to Develop Regional Trade

Prompted by a lack of endowments and sluggish advancement in ASEAN integration, Singapore searched for more free trade agreements (FTAs)

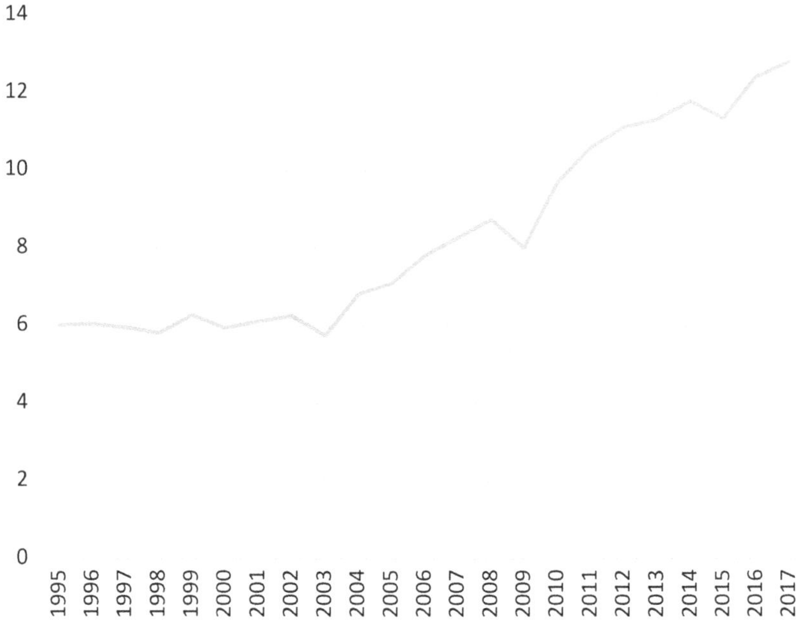

Fig. 6.10 Direct contribution of tourism to GDP (Units are US$ billion). Data source: World Travel and Tourism Council

with other global trading partners. Unfortunately, this was viewed as undermining the ASEAN spirit by allowing a "back door" (Daquila and Le 2003) entry for its global partners into the ASEAN markets. That is, other global trading partners would sign an FTA with Singapore and be granted access into the ASEAN markets by virtue of bilateral arrangements. Singapore ensured that its relationships with ASEAN members would not be undermined by a "back door" entry. In a bid to appease its ASEAN neighbours, the city-state took the initiative by fostering closer economic and trading ties with its immediate neighbours and leading regional economies, namely, Malaysia and Indonesia.

Indonesia, Malaysia and Singapore formed the SIJORI Growth Triangle known as the Subregional Economic Zone (SREZ). This growth triangle was first proposed in December 1989 (Ahmad 1992) for the city-state to address the "back door" perception. Singapore engaged with the allegation by including the Riau Islands in its FTA negotiation with the USA (Daquila and Le 2003). When the growth triangle was finally inked in

December 1994 (Sparke et al. 2004), Indonesia would have its goods accessible to the USA and in return, USA would gain entry to Indonesia's Information Technology sector (Daquila and Le 2003). Singapore would transfer labour-intensive industries to Johor (Malaysia) and Riau Islands (Indonesia). And as Johor and Riau continued to enjoy tariff discounts from developed nations, Singapore would shift its firms within the triangle to enjoy these privileges, in addition to access to land and water (Peng 2002) (Image 6.1).

SIJORI offered benefits for the three ASEAN economies.

1. Indonesia's Riau Islands of Batam and Bintan: Batam would set up eight industrial estates at the Batamindo Industrial Park to house AT&T, CIBA Vision, Epson, Philips, Seagate, Sanyo, Siemens and Thomson, and Bintan island was expected to benefit

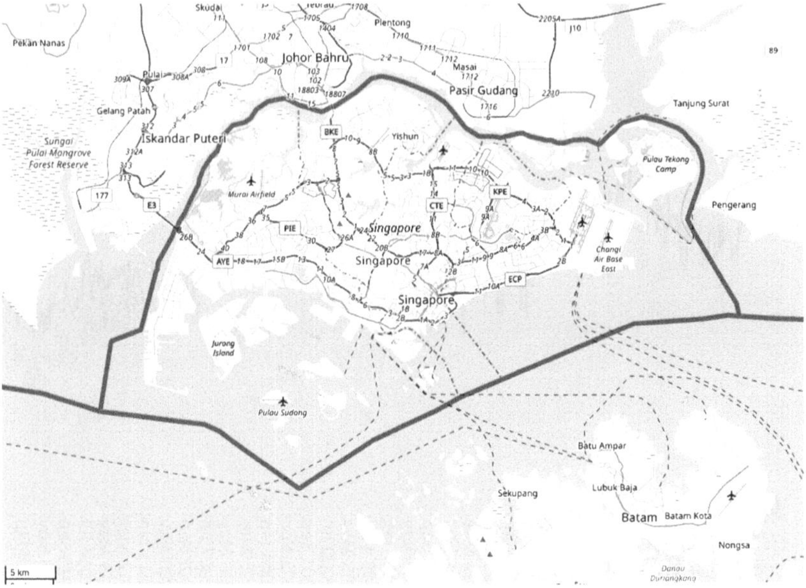

Image 6.1 Malaysia and Indonesia territory in the vicinity of Singapore. The Malaysian city of Johor Bahru is indicated, as is Batam, the largest city in the Indonesian province of Riau Islands. Adjusted to greyscale by authors from a source © OpenStreetMap contributors. See openstreetmap.org

from the capital overflows via industrial parks and high-end tourist facilities (Chang 2001; Grundy-Warr et al. 1999)
2. Malaysia's Johor: Benefited from cross-border industrial relocation and tourism development projects (Guinness 1992; Parsonage 1992)
3. Singapore: Led and provided financial developments and services in Johor, Batam and Bintan (Guinness 1992)

It was hoped that a regional planning initiative as a "growth triangle" between Singapore—Riau (Indonesia)—Johor (Malaysia) could be beneficial to all three economies if combined with political stability and low production costs (Perry 1992).

The SIJORI Growth Triangle was announced in 1989 and extended to additional regions of Indonesia and Malaysia in 1994. Unfortunately, as Fig. 6.11 illustrates, the trade share with Indonesia and Malaysia did not increase, although absolute dollar value did.

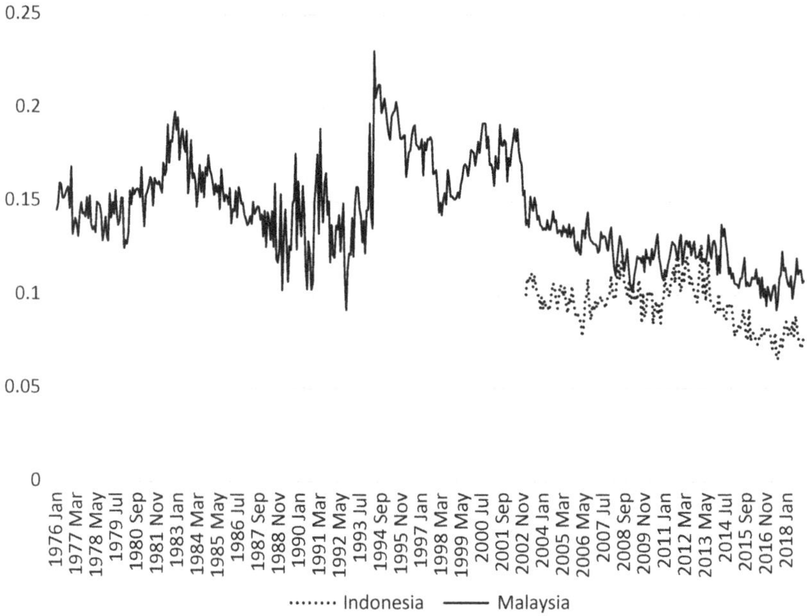

Fig. 6.11 Importance of Indonesia and Malaysia as export destinations. No data are available for Indonesia prior to 1993. Data source: SingStat

It was important for participating governments to pursue complementary human resource development strategies rather than compete (Debrah et al. 2000) to enjoy the growth triangle's benefits. This was not to be the case. As the partnership developed, competition between the economies overshadowed cooperation. Singapore benefited from its earlier investment in labour skill formation. Because it took advantage of its comparative edge in human capital development, foreign firms did not need to devote many resources to staff training and development. This did not resonate well with Indonesia and Malaysia as their local labour did not benefit from such a programme. Further, numerous state-initiated training programmes under the Skills Development Fund of Singapore (Debrah et al. 2000) did not help the cause.

The triangle was meant to vastly improve cross-border cooperation, but cooperation between the economies was poorly defined and failed to take off (Grundy-Warr et al. 1999). A possible explanation for a less than ideal pace of development was that some issues (such as taxes and duties) in Johor (Malaysia) and the Riau Islands (Indonesia) could only be addressed at the federal level and not at the local level. This resulted in differing levels of autonomy and delays in decision-making (Grundy-Warr et al. 1999).

Although various contextual elements limited integration and cooperation across the three economies (Sparke et al. 2004; Siddiqui 2010), the best explanation of why SIJORI failed was offered by Peng (2002). Although the implementation of any SREZs will be demanding, it helps if it falls under the same jurisdiction, for example, the Chinese economy. Consequently, the growth triangle led to similar subregional economic zones (SREZs) in Southeast Asia (SEA) as in China, but the expected benefits paled in comparison. This is clearly illustrated by the tricky triangular relationship where Johor and Riau benefited greatly from their relationship with Singapore. However, Malaysia and Indonesia are concerned that Johor and Riau would morph into a "corridor" subordinate to Singapore and attract key economic activities away from the traditional centres of Indonesia and Malaysia (Peng 2002). This is considered the prime reason for the failure of SIJORI, which limited the chain effect beyond the two locations. Johor and Riau had benefitted but their respective countries feared future developments could potentially compromise the authority of their central governments. The experience of the three countries holds a lesson for ASEAN as a whole.

Comparing the FTA and SREZ, the SREZ offers a better structure for advancing deeper economic integration that is more open than FTAs and not restricted to SREZ markets (Peng 2002). The three economies have the flexibility to withdraw from and/or not participate in SREZ.

Based on the discussion above on FTA and SREZ, it is apparent that Singapore strived to be a valuable partner to support the development and growth of its partners. Beyond growth, the city-state also made every effort to stay useful to the region when neighbouring ASEAN partners had attained a certain level of development.

The Region and Changing Investment Patterns in the Twenty-first Century

Besides finding new markets for existing businesses, another way to seek increased returns was to invest abroad. This would not increase GDP but would increase income. Distribution of that income would be another issue. As Fig. 6.12 shows, Singapore's direct investment abroad doubled in the final five years of the twentieth century and octupled since then. This is equivalent to roughly double the GDP of Singapore in 2016 as compared to a little more than one-third of GDP in 1994. The 1997 Asian

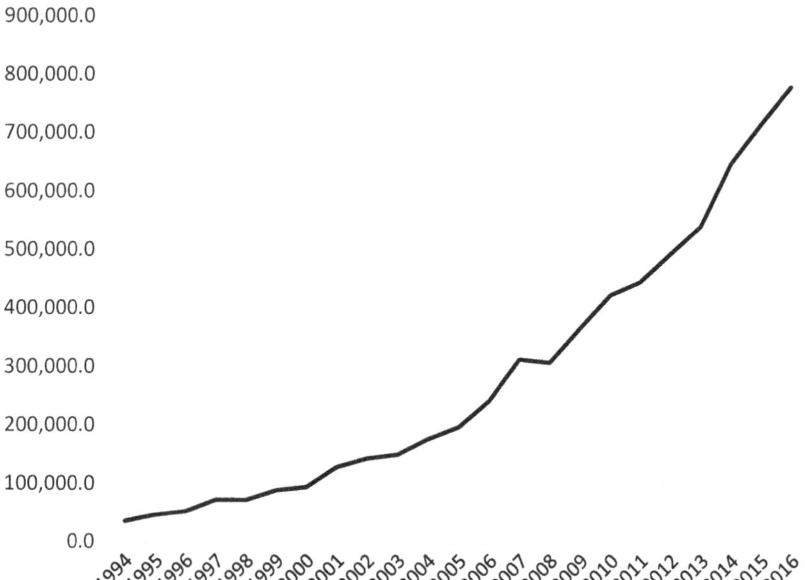

Fig. 6.12 Singapore direct investment abroad. Data source: SingStat

Table 6.3 Destinations of Singapore's outward FDI stock

Destination of outward FDI stock	*Amount of stock as of 2017 in billion US$*
China, P.R.: Mainland	105
Indonesia	62
India	35
China, P.R.: Hong Kong	35
Thailand	28
Malaysia	26
Mauritius	22
Russian Federation	15
Korea	12
Republic of Myanmar	9

Data source: Hers et al. 2018, p. 52, which in turn is based on derived instead of observed IMF CDIS data

financial crisis meant that there were many bargains available at the start of the new millennium. However, this change to increased investing abroad also derives from government encouragement.

Destinations were no doubt decided by investment opportunity, contacts and familiarity. A perusal of Table 6.3 suggests that proximity and size of economy were big factors. The case of Myanmar is notable since the 9 billion dollars invested there represents one-third of inward FDI to that country.

Eventually this should lead to a steeper increase in national income than in gross domestic product, but this has not proven to be the case so far, as Fig. 6.13 shows.

Conclusion

Unlike most of its neighbours, Singapore boasts a strong stable government that directs the economy towards greater prosperity rather than ceding to the interests of particular groups that exploit a protected status quo. It has repeatedly rebounded from external shocks to return to rapid long-term growth. This growth has been achieved by climbing a ladder of increasing sophistication in manufacture and in services for export—as a litmus test for competitiveness—as well as for internal consumption.

Recently, however, it has encountered challenges in slowing growth and possibly slowing returns to investment. After recovering from the global financial crisis, GDP growth has been dropping, varying between 2.5% and 3.5% for the last five years, with about 2% expected for 2019—

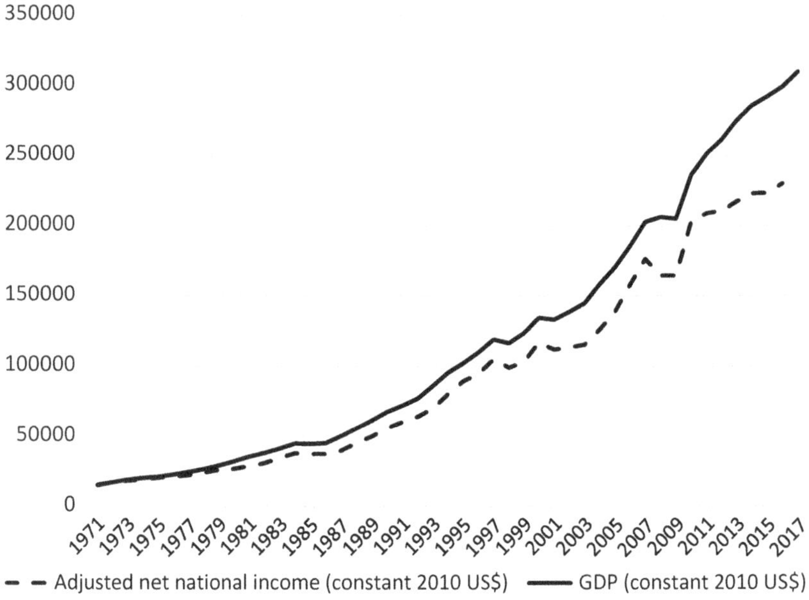

Fig. 6.13 GDP and adjusted national income. Data source: World Bank national accounts data, World Bank staff estimates and OECD National Accounts data files

much slower than in the past and similar to the established OECD economies rather than the more rapidly growing economies elsewhere in ASEAN. Although Singapore has been cultivating creative and innovative business and emphasized creativity over rote memorization in the schoolroom in pursuit of the "knowledge economy" popularized in the 1980s and 1990s, there is a limit to the extent of diverse knowledge that its population can possess. Can Singapore produce an Apple, an Amazon or Alibaba, a Google, Huawei or a Space X? It has two unicorns—start-up business valued over US$1 billion in Grab (which started in 2012 as MyTeksi in Malaysia) and Garena (SMU Social Media Team 2018), but there are at least 88 of these in China and 155 in the USA (CBInsights 2019). Conceivably, a Singaporean business could design a product as complex as a smartphone or a mid-sized aircraft and subcontract manufacture worldwide. But again, large wealthy countries can extravagantly explore the cutting edge of space and military development, leading to technological learning within their economies. To add to the speculative nature of planning for future growth now that Singapore has caught up to most of the wealthy nations, additive manufacturing (manufacturing objects by adding layers of material following computer-aided design) will probably reorganize advanced manufacturing over the next few decades, replacing the current patterns of global value-added networks that have been held in so many industries since the mid-1970s. Will this bring about an increased importance in the international trade of process and product design and a drop in the international trade of processed goods?

For someone seeking to do business in Southeast Asia, or even all of Eastern Asia, Singapore is an obvious option to prefer. Rents and wages are higher than elsewhere in the ASEAN region. However, the workforce is skilled and disciplined and usually speaks both English and Malay, Mandarin or Tamil (opening the doors to markets of a few hundred million or a billion and half people). Even more important is the business environment, with a streamlined bureaucracy and skilled bureaucrats seeking to facilitate your endeavours, not control them.

Appendix

The development of the economy of Singapore has been repeatedly described as a graduation up the ladder of value and technical know-how. The Economic Complexity Index (with scores labelled ECI and the more accurate ECI+) is an indicator of the degree of complexity of a nation's economy. One thus might expect ECI and ECI+ scores over the years to map out the evolution of Singapore's progress. However, ECI and ECI+ do not directly measure the complexity of processes producing goods and services. The fundamental calculation is based on the diversity of exports and their ubiquity (the number of countries able to produce them weighted by the complexity of each of those countries). Thus, complexity and sophistication are not synonymous. Complexity is measured by diversity and uniqueness of offerings. Sophistication is indicated by the technical refinement and complexity of a process as well as its educational requirements for operators.

Both the start and the end of the curve in Fig. 6.14 seem to contradict the narrative of Singapore steadily moving up the ladder of technical sophistication. One solution would be to argue that industrial policies took time to have an effect (although this would not explain the *decrease* in complexity from 1964 to 1967 and 1970) and that either those policies were abandoned with the Asian financial crisis (ECI+) or in 1993 (ECI) or

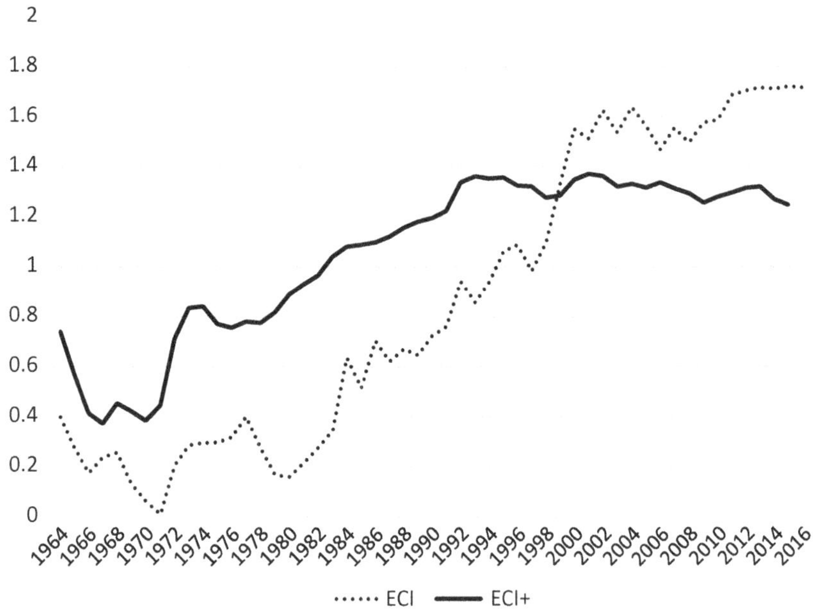

Fig. 6.14 Index of complexity for Singapore 1964–2016. ECI+ is a better indicator than ECI according to Albeaik et al. 2017. Data source: Observatory of Economic Complexity

there was no room for greater complexity at those points. Regarding the latter part of the curve, human ingenuity, current developments in technology and the higher rankings of other countries belie the last explanation. Nor has the government of Singapore abandoned the pursuit of greater sophistication among its businesses.

One problem is the data on which the index is based: services are excluded. This is not an oversight of the creators of the index, but simply a limitation of the data available across countries (Hausmann et al. 2018, p. 23). Because Singapore has a population under six million, it does not aspire to extremely complex manufacturing requiring a vast domestic network of tributary producers. Rather, it seeks sophistication in services. This is not captured by the Economic Complexity Index.

A second limitation of the index in its current form is revealed in Fig. 6.15.

Indonesia, Malaysia and Singapore have curves of a similar shape. They have different starting points, and the curve for Indonesia has the most

Fig. 6.15 Evolution of complexity compared. Data source: Atlas of Economic Complexity

dramatic slope of the three from 1976 to 1992, rising more sharply than that of Singapore. This corresponds to the better years under Suharto, during which economic policy was dictated by the "Berkeley Mafia" and foreign direct investment skyrocketed. This more pronounced slope might make sense. However, the general similarity of the curves for the three countries is a little surprising. Further, although the curves for Thailand and the Philippines are different, the general upward trend is there.

What is happening? There seem to be two factors at play. First, the world economy is more complex today than it was in 1964. A country could be losing ground with respect to the rest of the world but still increase in economic complexity. So there could well be a general upward trend in the curve of a country like the Philippines even though that economy was relatively stagnant from 1982 to 2004. Second, the data for economic complexity are taken from exports. Exports represented between 150% and 200% of GDP in Singapore until 2018 excepting the anomaly years to 1972 and the four years thereafter (see Fig. 6.16). As a result, the complexity of the economy adding value is diluted by the trade throughput.

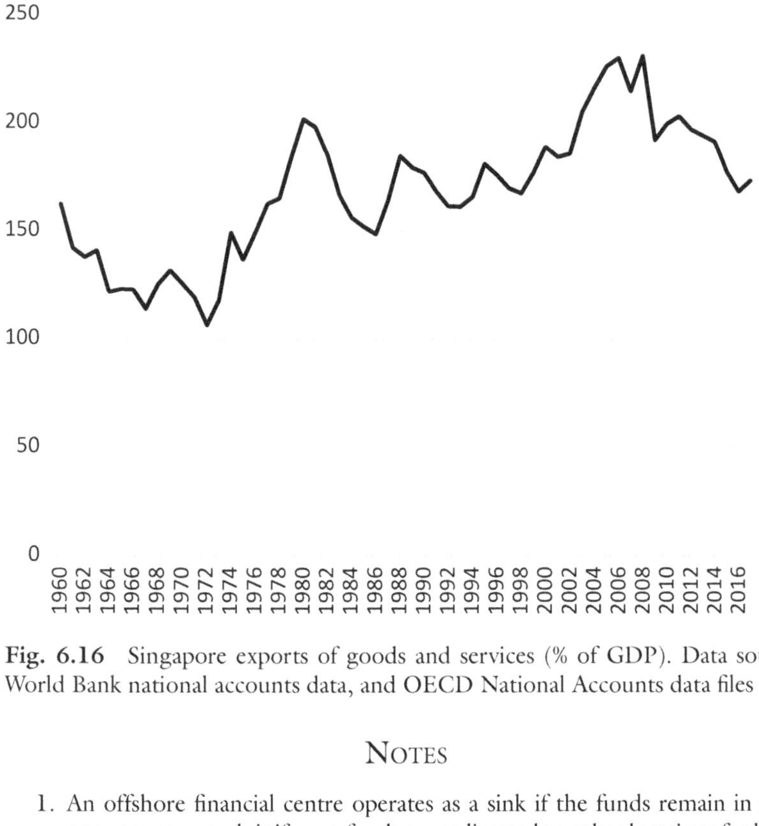

Fig. 6.16 Singapore exports of goods and services (% of GDP). Data source: World Bank national accounts data, and OECD National Accounts data files

Notes

1. An offshore financial centre operates as a sink if the funds remain in it. It operates as a conduit if most funds are redirected to other locations for long-term deposit. Expressed in terms of Garcia-Bernardo et al. (2017), "Sink-OFCs [offshore financial centres] attract and retain foreign capital while conduit-OFCs are attractive intermediate destinations in the routing of international investments and enable the transfer of capital without taxation."
2. One apparent exception to this is Singapore's prominent place on *The Economist's* "crony capitalism index." However, this has little to do with rent seeking within Singapore and much to do with expat billionaires exploiting protected industries in their home countries. See Anonymous 2016.
3. This is the estimate of Sim et al. (2014), based on Bloomberg data for 2008–2013. Stock market capitalization is the total value of all shares traded on the stock market. In 2008, 26 of the largest 100 business corporations

were government linked (Tan 2010). However, the principle state-owned holding company, Temasek, has been diversifying out of Singapore, halving from about 50% holdings within Singapore in 2004 to about 27% in 2018 (Temasek 2018).

King (2017) estimates revenues of the diverse holdings of Temasek are roughly equal to 20% of Singapore's GDP.

4. Popular wisdom conceives economic governance as a theatre in which business competes against private citizens for the allocation of wealth that is produced. The attraction of this lobbying model is the limitation of government power. Unfortunately, it omits a simple truth: because businesses organize private citizens for the production of wealth, social welfare is a key element in planning economic development. Singapore calculated expenditures on social welfare as part of development planning.
5. Mr Lim Kim San spearheaded Singapore's public housing in the 1960s to address the critical shortage of housing. He was the first chairman of Housing Development Board; one of the early projects was to build two blocks of flats in Tanjong Pagar (in Central Singapore) to house workers employed by the Tanjong Pagar Harbour Board (now the Port Authority of Singapore).
6. This had a curious effect upon the demand side make-up of GDP (C+I+G+(X−M)) or households and NPISHs' final consumption expenditure + gross capital formation + general government final consumption expenditure + external balance on goods and services. (NPISH stands for non-profit institutions serving households such as churches and political parties, and their expenditures are normally considerably less than those of households. Most data sources such as the World Bank combine their expenditures with those of households.) The average profile of OECD countries serves as a reference: private consumption at 60%, investment a little over 20%, government consumption expenditure around 20% and more or less balanced trade (0%). General government final consumption expenditure in Singapore has hovered around 10%, half the proportion of OECD countries. Gross capital formation has at times varied markedly, and will be discussed in the section "The Twenty-First Century: New Horizons" but otherwise hovered around 35%. External balance on goods and services and households and NPISHs' final consumption expenditure together have totalled about 55–60% as in the OECD countries, but the proportions of the two have varied dramatically GDP. This has led some critics to claim that households are being squeezed in Singapore with less and less disposable income to spend. Statistics of household expenditure show steady increase with the exception of the external shocks of the *Konfrontasi* campaign, the Asian financial crisis and the recession caused by the global financial crisis.

Household expenditure has not been squeezed but rather simply has been displaced by trade because of the basic algebra of the demand side of GDP.
The total of trade and household expenditure maintaining a level of about 60% except for a couple of troughs in the early 1970s and early 1980s. These troughs coincide more or less with peaks in gross capital formation in Singapore, otherwise around 35% for the last 30 years of the twentieth century.

7. There are several good descriptions of the "stages" in Singapore's development, for example, in Soon and Stoever (1996):

   - import substitution (1959–1965)
   - labour-intensive export-oriented manufacturing (1966–1973)
   - first attempts at upgrading the economy (1973–1978)
   - economic restructuring (1979–1984)
   - retrenchment and further diversification (1985 onwards)
   - Menon (2015) adds the rise of services

   Other descriptions of stages can be found in Lan 2001, Seetoh and Ong 2008, Auyong 2014 and 2016. For a capsule summary, see Economic Development Board n.d.

References

Ahmad, M. 1992. *Economic Cooperation in the Southern Growth Triangle: An Indonesian Perspective.* Conference on Regional Cooperation and Growth Triangles in ASEAN, organised by the National University of Singapore, Singapore, pp. 23–24.

Albeaik, Saleh, Mary Kaltenberg, Mansour Alsaleh, and Cesar A. Hidalgo. 2017. Improving the Economic Complexity Index. *arXiv:1707.05826v3.* https://arxiv.org/ftp/arxiv/papers/1707/1707.05826.pdf. Accessed February 5, 2019.

Anonymous. 2016. Our Crony-capitalism Index; The Party Winds Down. *The Economist* 419 (8988, May 7): 54.

Auyong, Hawyee. 2014. *Singapore's Productivity Challenge: Parts I, II and III.* Case Study Under the Guidance of Donald Low, Lee Kuan Yew School of Public Policy, National University of Singapore.

———. 2016. *Singapore's Productivity Challenge: A Historical Perspective.* Case Under the Guidance of Donald Low, Lee Kuan Yew School of Public Policy, National University of Singapore.

Baer, W., and L. Samuelson. 1977. Editor's Introduction. *World Development* 5 (1/2): 1–6.

Bruton, H. 1998. Reconsideration of Import Substitution. *Journal of Economic Literature.*, XXXVI: 903–936.

CBInsights. 2019. *The Global Unicorn Club*. https://www.cbinsights.com/research-unicorn-companies. Accessed February 21, 2019.

Chan, Heng Chee. 1986. Singapore in 1985: Managing Political Transition and Economic Recession. *Asian Survey* 26 (2): 158–167.

Chang, T.C. 2001. Configuring New Tourism Space: Exploring Singapore's Regional Tourism Forays. *Environment and Planning A* 33: 1597–1619.

Daquila, T.C., and H.H. Le. 2003. Singapore and ASEAN in the Global Economy: The Case of Free Trade Agreements. *Asian Survey* 43 (6): 908–928.

Debrah, Y.A., I. McGovern, and P. Budhwar. 2000. Complementarity or Competition: The Development of Human Resources in a South-East Asian Growth Triangle: Indonesia, Malaysia and Singapore. *International Journal of Human Resource Management* 11 (2): 314–335.

Economic Development Board. n.d. https://www.edb.gov.sg/content/dam/edbsite/news-and-resources/resources/singapore-business-environment/Singapore%20Business%20Environment%20-%20Singapore%20Today(June2017).pdf. Accessed February 21, 2019.

Freedom House. 2018. *Freedom of the World Report*. https://freedomhouse.org/report/freedom-world/2018/singapore. Accessed January 30, 2019.

Garcia-Bernardo, Javier, Jan Fichtner, Frank W. Takes, and Eelke M. Heemskerk. 2017. Uncovering Offshore Financial Centers: Conduits and Sinks in the Global Corporate Ownership Network. *Scientific Reports* 7: 6246.

Global Financial Centres Index. 2018. https://www.longfinance.net/media/documents/GFCI_24_final_Report.pdf. Accessed February 2, 2019.

Goh, C.B., and Gopinathan, S. 2006. *The Development of Education in Singapore Since 1965*. Background Paper Prepared for the Asia Education Study Tour for African Policy Makers, June 18–30, 2006, National Institute of Education, Nanyang Technological University.

Grice, Kevin, and David Drakakis-Smith. 1985. The Role of the State in Shaping Development: Two Decades of Growth in Singapore. *Transactions of the Institute of British Geographers* 10 (3): 347–359.

Grundy-Warr, C., K. Peachey, and M. Perry. 1999. Fragmented Integration in the Singapore-Indonesian Border Zone: Southeast Asia's 'Growth Triangle' Against the Global Economy. *International Journal of Urban and Regional Research* 23 (2): 304–328.

Guinness, P. 1992. *On the Margin of Capitalism: People and Development in Mukim Plentong, Johor, Malaysia*. Singapore: Oxford University Press.

Hausmann, Ricardo, César A. Hidalgo, Sebastián Bustos, Michele Coscia, Sarah Chung, Juan Jimenez, Aleander SImoes, and Muhammed A. Yildirim. 2018. *The Index of Economic Complexity. Mapping Paths to Prosperity*. Center for International Development, Harvard University; Macro Connections Media Lab, MIT Press.

Hers, Johannes, Joost Witteman, Ward Rougoor, and Koert van Buiren. 2018. *The Role of Investment Hubs in FDI, Economic Development and Trade*. Brussels: SEO Amsterdam Economics.

Hodjera, Zoran. 1978. The Asian Currency Market: Singapore as a Regional Financial Center. *Staff Papers (International Monetary Fund)* 25 (2): 221–253.

Huff, W.G. 1994. *The Economic Growth of Singapore: Trade and Development in the Twentieth Century*. Cambridge University Press.

Infopedia Singapore. 2011. *Marina Bay Sands*. http://eresources.nlb.gov.sg/infopedia/articles/SIP_1607_2011-11-01.html Accessed February 19, 2019.

King, Alistair. 2017. *Investigating the Scale of State-owned Business in Singapore*. Bureau Van Dijk. https://www.bvdinfo.com/en-gb/blog/compliance-and-financial-crime/investigating-the-scale-of-state-owned-business-in-singapore. Accessed January 30, 2019.

Kumar, Sree, and Sharon Siddique. 2010. *The Singapore Success Story: Public-private Alliance for Investment Attraction, Innovation and Export Development*. CEPAL – Serie Comercio Internacional No 99. United Nations Publications.

Lan, Chao-Wei. 2001. *Singapore's Export Promotion Strategy and Economic Growth (1965–84)*. University College London. Development Planning Unit Working Paper No. 116.

Lee, Lai To. 1987. Singapore in 1986: Consolidation and Reorientation in a Recession. *Asian Survey* 27 (2): 242–253.

Lee, Hsien Loong. 2005. *Ministerial Statement. Proposal to Develop Integrated Resorts*. http://www.nas.gov.sg/archivesonline/speeches/view-html?filename=2005041803.htm Accessed February 19, 2019.

Lim, Kim San. 1966. *Budget Statement by the Minister for Finance, Mr Lim Kim San, in Parliament on 5th December, 1966*. http://www.nas.gov.sg/archivesonline/data/pdfdoc/PressR19661205d.pdf Accessed February 2, 2019.

Lim, Yan Liang. 2015. Parliament: "No Plans" Currently to Offer Additional Casino Licences After 2017. *The Straits Times*. https://www.straitstimes.com/singapore/parliament-no-plans-currently-to-offer-additional-casino-licences-after-2017. Accessed February 19, 2019.

Low, James. 2016. *Milestone Programs for the Administrative Service in the Singapore Public Service*. Chapter 9 in Podger 2016.

Maynes, G.W. 2011. *Human Capital Accumulation: A Comparative Study of Singapore and Malaysia—1975 to 2006*. Masters of Business (Research) Thesis, Royal Melbourne Institute of Technology, Australia, pp. 79–126.

Meinhardt (Singapore). n.d. *Resorts World Sentosa*. https://www.meinhardt.com.sg/projects/resorts-world-sentosa/. Accessed February 19, 2019.

Menon, Ravi. 2015. *An Economic History of Singapore: 1965–2065**. Speech at the Singapore Economic Review Conference 2015. http://www.mas.gov.sg/News-and-Publications/Speeches-and-Monetary-Policy-Statements/Speeches/2015/An-Economic-History-of-Singapore.aspx. Accessed February 1, 2019.

Ministry of Finance. 1961. *State of Singapore Development Plan 1961–1964*. http://eservice.nlb.gov.sg/data2/BookSG/publish/2/28b66e5a-79a9-4304-9896-ffe676a2ed74/web/html5/index.html?opf=tablet/BOOKSG.xml&launchlogo=tablet/BOOKSG_BrandingLogo_.png&pn=51. Accessed February 2, 2019.

———. 2016. *Understanding Singapore Government's Borrowing and Its Purposes. An Overview*. https://www.mof.gov.sg/Portals/0/feature%20articles/PDR_2016.pdf. Accessed February 6, 2019.

Ministry of Trade and Industry. 2008. *Economic Survey of Singapore*. Third Quarter 2008.

Parsonage, J. 1992. Southeast Asia's 'Growth Triangle': A Sub-regional Response to a Global Transformation. *International Journal of Urban and Regional Research* 16: 42–63.

Peng, D. 2002. Subregional Economic Zones and Integration in East Asia. *Political Science Quarterly* 117 (4): 613–641.

Perry, M. 1992. The Singapore Growth Triangle: State, Capital and Labour at a New Frontier in the World Economy. *Singapore Journal of Tropical Geography* 12 (2): 138–151.

Podger, Andrew, and John Wanna. 2016. *Sharpening the Sword of State. Building Executive Capacities in the Public Services of the Asia-Pacific*. ANU Press, The Australian National University.

Reporters Without Borders. 2019. https://rsf.org/en/singapore. Accessed February 1, 2019.

Rigg, Jonathan. 1988. Singapore and the Recession of 1985. *Asian Survey* 28 (3): 340–352.

Seetoh, K.C., and A.H.F. Ong. 2008. Achieving Sustainable Industrial Development Through a System of Strategic Planning and Implementation: The Singapore Model. In *Spatial Planning for a Sustainable Singapore*, ed. T.C. Wong, B. Yuen, and C. Goldblum. Springer.

Siddiqui, K. 2010. The Political Economy of Development of Singapore. *Research in Applied Economics* 2 (2): 1.

Sim, Isabel, Steen Thomsen, and Gerard Yeong. 2014. *The State as Shareholder: The Case of Singapore*. Centre for Governance, Institutions and Organisations, National University of Singapore Business School.

SMU Social Media Team. 2018. *In Search of Singapore's Unicorns*. https://blog.smu.edu.sg/academic/institutes/iie/in-search-of-singapores-unicorns/. Accessed February 21, 2019.

Soon, Teck-Wong, and William A. Stoever. 1996. Foreign Investment and Economic Development in Singapore: A Policy-Oriented Approach. *The Journal of Developing Areas* 30 (3, April): 317–340.

Sparke, M., J.D. Sidaway, T. Bunnell, and C. Grundy-Warr. 2004. Triangulating the Borderless World: Geographies of Power in the Indonesia–Malaysia–Singapore Growth Triangle. *Transactions of the Institute of British Geographers* 29 (4): 485–498.

Stolarchuk, Jewel. 2019. Ho Ching Claims Investment Returns by GIC, MAS, and Temasek Are the "Single Largest Contributor to SG Budget" More Than Income Tax or GST. *The Independent*. http://theindependent.sg/ho-ching-claims-investment-returns-by-gic-mas-and-temasek-are-the-single-largest-contributor-to-sg-budget-more-than-income-tax-or-gst/. Accessed February 14, 2019.

Tan, Lay Hong. 2010. *Exploring the Question of the Separation of Ownership From Control: An Empirical Study of the Structure of Corporate Ownership in Singapore's Top 100 Listed Companies*. Working Paper. http://docs.business.auckland.ac.nz/Doc/exploring-the-question-of-ownership-from-control.pdf. Accessed February 1, 2019.

Tan, S.S. 2015. *Goh Keng Swee: A Portrait*. Singapore: Editions Dider Millet.

Tan, Seam. 2018. *Redesigning Jobs for Our Silver Age to Drive Our Thriving Economy*. Singapore Perspectives 2018. https://lkyspp.nus.edu.sg/docs/default-source/ips/presentation_sp2018_sean-tan.pdf. Accessed February 19, 2019.

Temasek. 2018. *Temasek Overview 2018*. https://www.temasekreview.com.sg/assets/media-centre/downloads/pdf/temasek-overview-2018.pdf?v=7614208cbaf6a0de3d9131662ef1d5a5. Accessed February 1, 2019.

UNDP Global Centre for Public Service Excellence. 2015. *UNDP and the Making of Singapore's Public Service – Lessons from Albert Winsemius*. Global Centre for Public Service Excellence.

Woo, Jun Jie. 2018. *Singapore's Approach to Managing Economic Crises*. Lee Kuan Yew School of Public Policy.

CHAPTER 7

Indonesia: Choosing Between the Privileged and Prosperity

Roderick Macdonald and Hotniar Siringoringo

Introduction

With a total population of 265 million, the Republic of Indonesia is the world's fourth largest country by population. A land area of 1,900,000 square kilometres gives it a population density of 144 persons per square kilometre. However, 60% of the population live on the island of Java, which has a population density of 940–1117 persons per square kilometre (depending on estimates) and seven cities with over a million people. This contrasts with the province of West Papua, the Indonesian portion of the island of New Guinea, with under ten persons per square kilometre. Overall, 55% of the population lives in cities. There are many active volcanoes across Indonesia, and floods, droughts, earthquakes and

R. Macdonald (✉)
Université du Québec à Montréal, Montréal, QC, Canada
e-mail: macdonald.roderick@uqam.ca

H. Siringoringo
Universitas Gunadarma, Depok, Indonesia
e-mail: hotniars@staff.gunadarma.ac.id

R. Macdonald (ed.), *Southeast Asia and the ASEAN Economic Community*, https://doi.org/10.1007/978-3-030-19722-3_7

tsunamis are always threats. Slash and burn agriculture by small farmers as well as large palm oil plantations also produce serious haze.

There are hundreds of ethnic groups and languages in Indonesia, united by one standard language (Indonesian, very nearly the same as Malaysian) and dominated by two ethnic groups, Javanese (a little over 40% of the population) and Sundanese (15% of the population), both coming from Java. Predominately Muslim, Indonesia is also home to Animists, Christians, Hindus (Bali), Buddhists and Taoists. The government recognizes six official religions: Islam, Catholicism, Confucianism, Hinduism, Buddhism and Protestantism. About 25% of ethnic Chinese self-identify as Christians.

This diversity has two sources. On the one hand, there is historical outside influence from Chinese, Indian and Arab traders as well as Dutch colonists. On the other is the multitude of distinct cultural traditions that co-existed under the Dutch colonial power and have been inherited by twentieth-century independent Indonesia.

This chapter describes the economy of Indonesia. This description would be misleading however, unless some insight is provided into the workings of government and politics. As with any country, economic governance can have a large impact. Indonesia is distinct in that the manner of governance has varied considerably since its independence, and there are forces in play that may affect that governance in the future. For this reason, four sections follow this introduction. The first is on the economy of Indonesia and provides basic economic statistics with some historical background. The next section delves behind the statistics to examine the underlying factors that have limited the economy's potential for growth in the past. Because these factors are to a large part a result of government economic policies and actions, the subsequent section provides a short history of the political regimes since independence and their economic policies. The final section is a short note on how the ideas Indonesian Muslims have of their religion impact on the political arena in Indonesia.

Economic Overview

While the economy of Indonesia has been growing rather quickly, much potential remains untapped.

Indonesia's economy surpassed the US$1 trillion mark in 2016 and has been growing steadily at a healthy rate since the global financial crisis, as seen in Fig. 7.1 (GDP (million constant 2010 US$) 2008–2017).

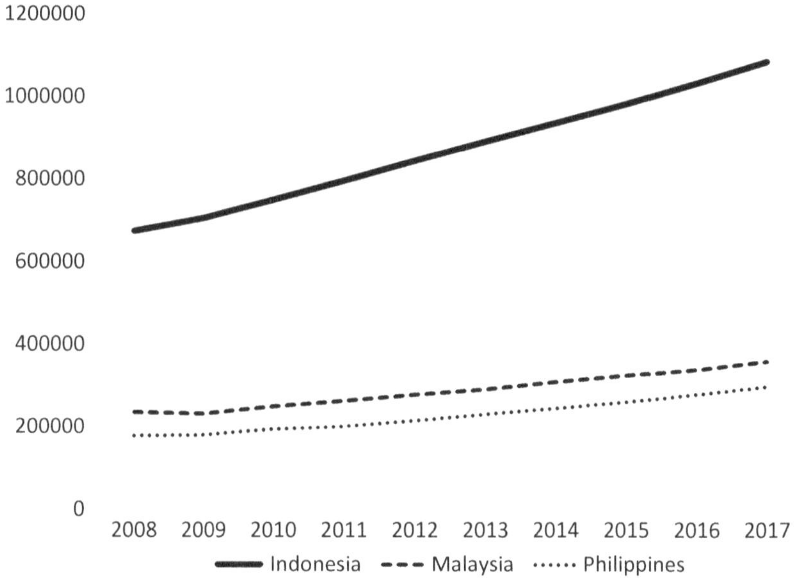

Fig. 7.1 GDP (million constant 2010 US$) in 2008–2017. Data source: World Bank national accounts data, and OECD National Accounts data files

Indonesia's statistical authority (BPS) reports 2.87% of GDP coming from mining of oil, gas and geothermal energy, 2.38% from coal and lignite mining and 2.27% from refining coal, oil and gas. Nearly 20% more oil is imported than exported. Indonesia would have 9.5 years of proven crude oil reserves at its current consumption rate without importing. Table 7.1 lists the principle categories of wealth creation in Indonesia. Mining and quarrying include 5.25% GDP for oil and coal; the remaining 2.32% include minerals such as bauxite, coal, nickel and tin. Indonesia was the world's seventh largest producer of gold in 2017. Rubber, palm oil and forestry products are classified among the principle agricultural products. Besides oil and gas, important manufacturing industries are tobacco (although sales have been in decline since 2016, over 340 billion cigarettes were produced that year), palm oil, the automotive industry (Thailand was the only ASEAN country besting Indonesia's production of 1,216,615 motor vehicles in 2017), electrical appliances and apparel and footwear. Travel and tourism contributed 1.8% of GDP in 2016, compared with

Table 7.1 Contribution to GDP by industries of origin for 2012

Contribution to GDP by industries of origin	*% contribution*
Agriculture, livestock, forestry and fishery	14.50
Mining and quarrying	11.81
Manufacturing industry	23.96
Electricity, gas and water supply	0.76
Construction	10.26
Trade, hotel and restaurants	13.96
Transport and communication	6.67
Finance, real estate and business services	7.27
Services	10.81
Total gross domestic product	100.00

Data source: BPS Indonesia

10% of global GDP and jobs worldwide (World Travel & Tourism Council 2017). The health industry is also quite small.

Palm oil (current US$13.9 billion), coal briquettes (US$13.6 billion), petroleum gas (US$7.35 billion), crude petroleum (US$5.04 billion) and rubber (US$3.74 billion) were the largest exports of Indonesia in 2016. Refined petroleum (US$9.6 billion), crude petroleum (US$5.76 billion), telephones (US$3.54 billion), vehicle parts (US$2.63 billion) and planes, helicopters and/or spacecraft (US$2.15 billion) were the top imports (Observatory of Economic Complexity 2018). Trade (imports plus exports) was only 40% of Indonesia's GDP, as compared to 93% for the entire ASEAN region in 2015. Although in part a consequence of Indonesia's large domestic market, this is also a result of the effort of local producers wishing to restrict foreign competition. The trade statistics also suggest that Indonesia is weak in processing capacity since products exported are less processed while products imported are more processed. Competitive advantage may lie in resources for a period of time. This period of time may be prolonged when a country's territory is large compared to its population, but this is not the case of Indonesia. The current account balance is slightly negative (see Fig. 7.2), and governments have striven to correct this by reducing imports rather than increasing exports. This suggests that protectionism, rather than fostering a domestic industry, has been at the expense of the Indonesian consumer (for the impact of non-tariff measures on retail prices since 2011, see Marks 2017). Figure 7.3 shows that this tendency has not abetted under the Joko Widodo administration.

Fig. 7.2 Current account balance as % GDP. Data source: International Monetary Fund, Balance of Payments Statistics Yearbook and data files and World Bank GDP estimates

Government finances are sound, with debt at 29% of GDP in 2017, of which nearly 60% was in rupiah, the Indonesian currency. Deficits have been under 3% for at least 25 years. The private sector presents financing that appears extremely conservative, with credit to the private sector at around 30% of GDP as compared to 129% for the world. Myanmar is the only ASEAN country with a lower ratio (ASEAN 2018). Foreign direct investment (FDI) is also low for Indonesia: while it generates 37% of ASEAN's GDP, it attracts only 28% of ASEAN FDI inflow (see Fig. 7.4).

Indonesia's trillion dollar economy is the sixteenth largest in the world and the largest in Southeast Asia. It is about half the size of India's economy and one-tenth the size of China's. This is not because it is a wealthy country, but because it is a large country. The GDP of Indonesia is three times those of Singapore and of Malaysia, but it has over 40 times the population of Singapore and nearly nine times the population of Malaysia. This translates into the GDP per capita shown in Fig. 7.5.

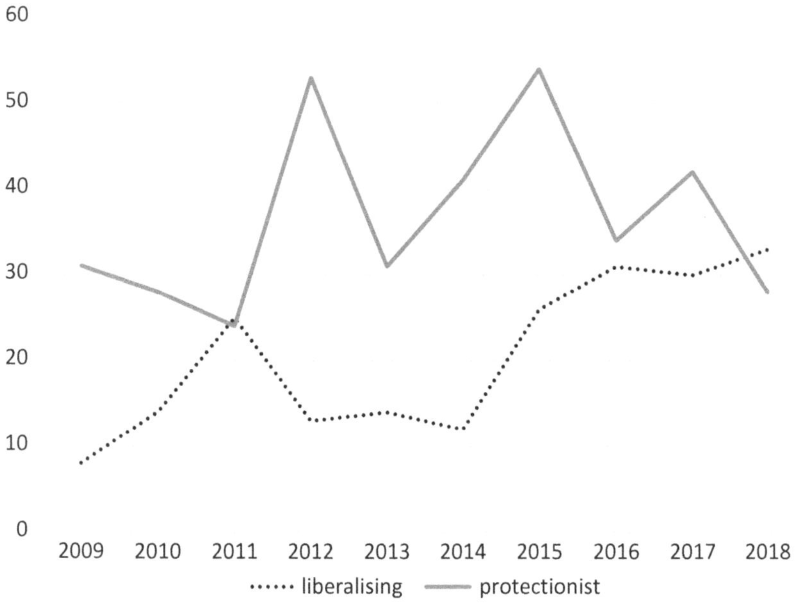

Fig. 7.3 Policies for and against free trade. Source of data: https://www.globaltradealert.org/country/96

The structure of the economy of Indonesia has evolved, although more slowly than in the case of its neighbours.[1] Agriculture is far less important today than 20 years ago. Comparing ratio of value added by agriculture to value added by industry is a proxy for comparing structures. The evolution of that ratio for Indonesia and for Malaysia follows more or less parallel curves since 1983 (see Fig. 7.6), and industry in both countries contributed similar portions of GDP in 2017 (see Fig. 7.7). However, Indonesia is a far more agricultural country than Malaysia or even the Philippines, both in terms of value added and in terms of people employed in each sector. Most notably, while the portion of Indonesia's GDP produced by agriculture, fisheries and forestry is 50% higher than that of Malaysia, the portion of total employment is three times as high. This means that there is potential for considerably more structural change. In this way, the remaining agricultural workers would produce more value per capita, and a greater portion of the working population could move on to higher

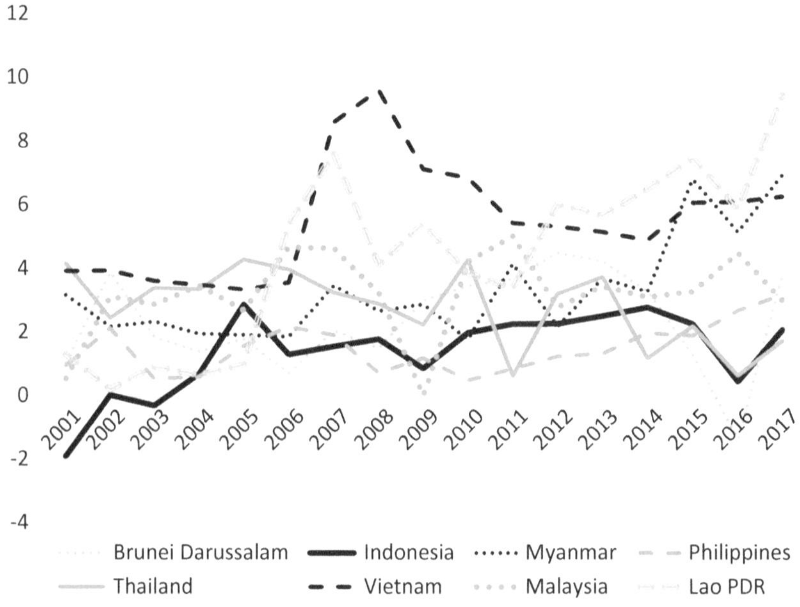

Fig. 7.4 FDI inflows as per cent of GDP for ASEAN countries. Singapore and Cambodia are excluded as outliers with FDI/GDP several times that of other ASEAN countries. Source of data: International Monetary Fund, Balance of Payments database, supplemented by data from the United Nations Conference on Trade and Development and official national sources

value producing jobs in industry and services—if adequate skills and opportunities are provided.

One of the ways opportunities are provided is through factories and machinery that multiply the productivity of workers. An indicator for the increase in such investment at the country level is the rate of capital formation. In Indonesia, the rate of capital formation[2] is high at about 33% of GDP, markedly higher than the 25% of Malaysia and the Philippines. This has been the case since 2004 with respect to Malaysia, and since 1984 with respect to the Philippines, excepting a few years following the Asian financial crisis. So why isn't Indonesia markedly richer than either Malaysia or the Philippines?

When comparing investment rates between different economies, the ratio of capital formation to GDP makes sense. However, the figure for

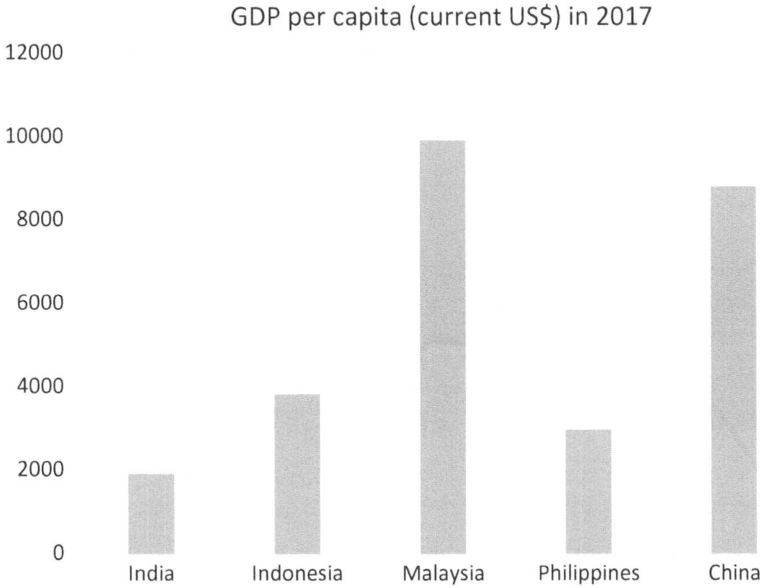

Fig. 7.5 GDP per capita of 2017 compared. Data source: World Bank national accounts data

capital formation also bears a relation to population, in the sense that this new capital multiplies the effectiveness of the work of a certain number of people.[3] One million dollars in machinery operated by one employee will probably boost his productivity considerably. If the million dollars' worth of machinery is operated by a thousand employees, the boost to each individual's productivity will probably be less. GDP per capita for Indonesia (in constant 2010 US$) was 40% that of Malaysia in 1968 and under 60% that of the Philippines. The capital formation *per capita* was lower (see Fig. 7.8) even if the ratio to GDP was higher in Indonesia. And it was not. The first year that Indonesia had a higher gross capital formation rate as per cent of GDP superior to that of Malaysia was 2004, with the exception of an episode from 1986 to 1989. Thus, one reason that Malaysia is wealthier than Indonesia is the latter's lower capital formation **per capita**.

Why is the fixed capital formation per capita lower in Indonesia? Indonesia simply disposed of more limited funds. We have seen in the previous section that Indonesia is underfinanced relative to other countries.

Fig. 7.6 Ratio of value added in agriculture to industry. Data source: World Bank national accounts data

An examination of the principle countries in Southeast Asia with Australasian roots gives further insight into this and raises a few questions.

Indonesia, Malaysia and the Philippines have very different GDP per capita. Malaysia is the richest country of the three with current US$9945 GDP per capita in 2017. Indonesia had US$3837 and the Philippines US$2989. While the Philippines is on the periphery and experienced a colonial history that led to a different religion and culture, Malaysia and Indonesia share a language and dominant religion and are in close proximity (although the easternmost extremes of Indonesia are closer to Australia due to the extent of Indonesia's territory). Why is it that Malaysia is more than twice as rich as Indonesia as measured by GDP per capita? There are four reasons.

First reason: The World Bank data on GDP per capita begins in 1960, 3 years before the foundation of Malaysia and 15 years after the independence of Indonesia. Although Malaysia has experienced a marginally

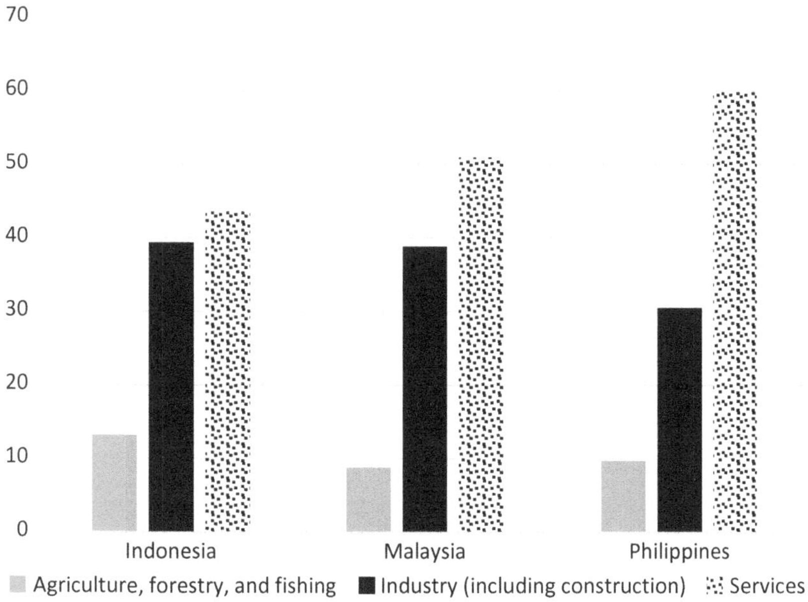

Fig. 7.7 Economic structure by value added. World Bank national accounts data

higher growth rate in GDP per capita than Indonesia, this is insufficient to explain today's wealth gap, even with the exponential effect. The logistics advantage of Malaysia (it covers predominantly two landmasses and is located between two rich neighbours, Singapore and Thailand) and the historical linkage with Singapore are probably sufficient to explain much of the slight difference in growth rates. The first year in the data series places the question further back in time. Malaysia's 1353.85 GDP per capita (constant 2010 US$) in 1960 was already twice as high as Indonesia's 690.04.

The Maddison historical statistics, although based on varied sources and estimates, permit an examination of GDP per capita back to 1950, using Geary Khamis dollars (unit with the same purchasing power parity that the US dollar had in the United States at the given dates). Malaysia had a lost decade before independence (negative growth), then far outstripped Indonesia from 1960 to 1970. Over the two decades 1950–1970, Indonesia's GDP per capita grew 50% more quickly than that of Malaysia. Neither country grew very quickly, however. While the West experienced

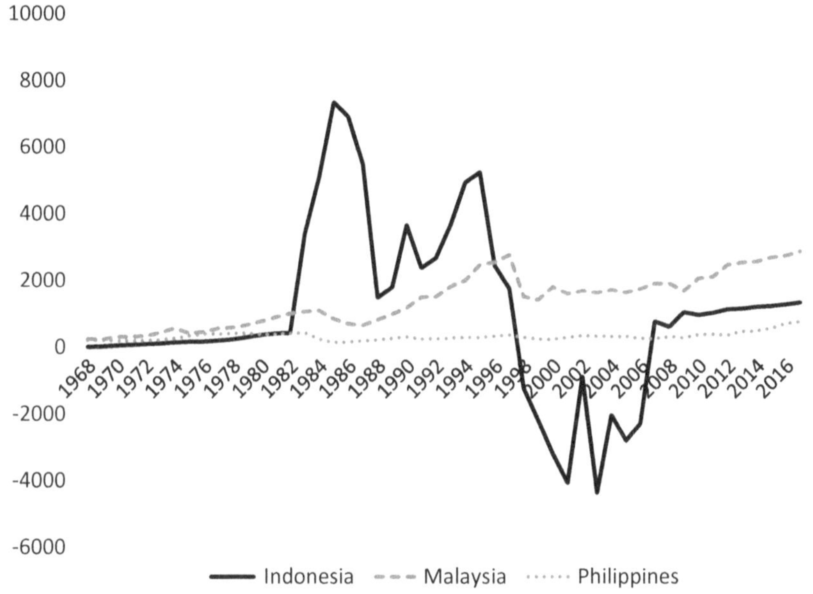

Fig. 7.8 Gross fixed capital formation per capita. Data source: World Bank national accounts data

a post-war boom, Indonesia grew at 2.4% and Malaysia at 1.8%. Malaysia grew at 3% during the 1960s.

Most important of all, Malaysia's GK$1559 GDP per capita was already nearly twice the US$817 of Indonesia in 1950. The original difference in GDP capita is probably explained by differing experiences either under Japanese occupation, European colonization or both.[4]

GDP grew at a 6.3% rate in 2007, fluttered during the global financial crisis and then stayed above 6% through to 2012, after which it dropped to "only" 5.6% and then around 5% for the next few years. Thus, the economy of Indonesia is growing quickly at over 5% but does not keep pace with China or India, and the rate of growth is lower than that of the Philippines. On the other hand, the growth rate of Malaysia is more volatile: it seems to be doing a little better than Indonesia based on the GDP growth figures, but growth in GDP per capita suggests that Indonesia has been doing somewhat better over the last few years. Both countries are growing more slowly than they had been before the Asian financial crisis.

Table 7.2 Logistics performance index for AEC countries, China and India

Country	*Overall LPI score*	*Customs*	*Infrastructure*
Singapore	4.00	3.89	4.06
China	3.61	3.55	3.66
Thailand	3.41	3.14	3.14
Vietnam	3.27	2.95	3.01
Malaysia	3.22	2.90	3.15
India	3.18	2.96	2.91
Indonesia	3.15	2.67	2.90
Philippines	2.90	2.53	2.73
Brunei Darussalam	2.71	2.62	2.46
Lao PDR	2.70	2.61	2.44
Cambodia	2.58	2.37	2.14
Myanmar	2.30	2.10	2.50

Data source: World Bank Group

Second reason: While the bulk of Malaysia covers two land masses, Indonesia is dispersed over an archipelago of over 17,000 islands. Sea transport is theoretically cheaper than air or land transport but requires investment in ships, ports and loading facilities, as well as transfer to land transport for local delivery. This complication further requires a control system both for the private firms involved and for the government. This system may be more or less effective and expeditious. Table 7.2 indicates that Indonesia scores more poorly than Malaysia in logistics, but this is only part of the picture. Even if Indonesia were to score as high as Malaysia or even Singapore, the challenges of connecting its population across land and sea would remain. One thing that does militate in Indonesia's favour is the density of population in most areas, particularly Java. In order for Indonesia to obtain a higher return on its investments, it would require superb infrastructure.

The **third reason** has to do with skills. Less than one-third of Indonesians complete secondary school and less than half complete lower secondary. The data for primary school is less complete but gives the same impression: 77% of Indonesians complete primary school (2015 data) compared to 91% in Malaysia (2010 data) and 84% in the Philippines (2013 data of the World Bank). The World Competitiveness Report (see below) confirms that Indonesia does poorly in primary education, so it also should be a priority to ensure that all of the new generation complete primary school. The math skills and basic general knowledge of primary school are prerequisite for effective participation in the economy; high school knowledge and the additional experience of learning are important for later acquiring somewhat more advanced new skills in the workplace. The World Bank does not have data for university education in Malaysia. What data there is suggests that Malaysia and the Philippines had only slightly better attainment rates for short-cycle tertiary education in 2000. Since then the Philippines has triple the rate, with 27% in 2013 as compared to 9% for Indonesia in 2015.

If we dig deeper into the skills of the workforce, we find that Indonesia is somewhat weaker in human capital than Malaysia and the Philippines. Indonesia does better in capacity and development and more poorly in deployment and particularly in know-how.[5] This suggests that the improvement that would bring the highest return would be skills training in the workplace and that, besides increasing the attainment levels for primary, secondary and tertiary education, Indonesia needs especially to take advantage of the current level of knowledge to allow the workforce to acquire new work-relevant skills.

The fourth and final reason for Indonesia's performance relative to Malaysia resides in the organization of the economy. Some indication is given by the residual that is total factor productivity (the portion of output not explained by inputs of labour and capital), although this is a "noisy" indicator—it includes more than the organization of the economy. Table 7.3 indicates that total factor productivity is much more important in the Philippines and somewhat more important in Malaysia. In the case of the Philippines, its importance rivals that in China's growth, explaining better than one-third of that growth (in other words, capital and labour explain less than two-thirds). This suggests that perhaps the organization of the economy (the rules and regulations, institutions and administrative processes, bureaucratic costs in time and money, etc.) may well be a factor in which growth has been limited and, more importantly, growth can eventually be unleashed if properly addressed.

Table 7.3 Sources of economic growth

Sources of economic growth 2000–2015	*Total GDP growth*	*Labour*	*Capital*	*TFP*
China	9.1	0.4	5.6	3.1
Indonesia	5.2	0.8	3.5	0.9
Malaysia	5.2	0.9	3.1	1.2
Philippines	5	0.8	2.4	1.8

Data source: For labour, capital and total factor productivity: APO Productivity Databook 2017, p. 72

Organization of the Economy of Indonesia

A number of indices and surveys[6] developed over the last quarter century shine some light on this total factor productivity. The following paragraphs use them in an attempt to discern the areas where Indonesia most needs improvement. Indonesia will be placed repeatedly in a bad light. These negative observations must be placed in the context of the opportunity Indonesia represents in terms of size, growth, dynamism and sound monetary management.

The economic freedom score (an attempt to measure the degree to which individuals control their own labour and property) of Indonesia is superior to that of Malaysia and is only marginally bested by the Philippines (see Table 7.4). The strength of Indonesia lies in its management of money with a "sound money" score of 9.68 which earned it the 13th rank worldwide.[7]

The weakness of Indonesia is in its legal system and property rights with a score of 4.88, placing 92nd out of 162 countries. Particularly serious is the 3.15 score for the legal enforcement of contracts. It also placed 92nd in the freedom to trade internationally although the score was higher at 7.0. It also did particularly badly in the "regulations" score of 6.43 which placed it 125th worldwide. Within regulations, labour market regulations scored surprisingly poorly at 4.63, placing 147th out of 162. However, the labour market score includes an unexplained zero for employee dismissal. Employee dismissal perhaps refers to World Bank survey data regarding the number of weeks' salary to be paid upon dismissal. Given the lack of a social safety net in Indonesia, it is hard to criticize a number of weeks required. Indonesia receives a score of 1.1 for "hiring regulations and minimum wage". Again, this score is not explained in the report and

Table 7.4 Economic freedom rank and score 2018

Country	*Economic freedom rank*	*Economic freedom score*	*Sound money score*	*Legal system*	*Regulations*
China	108	6.46	8.64	5.65	6.36
India	96	6.63	8.20	5.16	6.50
Indonesia	65	7.16	9.68	4.88	6.43
Malaysia	79	6.92	5.79	5.76	8.62
Philippines	49	7.34	9.42	4.28	7.37

Data source: The Fraser Institute 2018

Table 7.5 Scores in the Global Competitiveness Index

Pillar	*Indonesia*	*Malaysia*	*Philippines*
Overall	4.7	5.2	4.4
Institutions	4.3	5.0	3.5
Infrastructure	4.5	5.5	3.4
Macroeconomic environment	5.7	5.4	5.8
Health and primary education	5.4	6.3	5.6
Higher education and training	4.5	4.9	4.6
Goods market efficiency	4.6	5.1	4.0
Labour market efficiency	3.9	4.7	4.0
Financial market development	4.5	5.0	4.2
Technological readiness	3.9	4.9	3.8
Market size	5.7	5.1	5.0
Business sophistication	4.6	4.9	4.1
Innovation	4.0	4.7	3.3

Data source: Schwab 2018

the minimum wage in the formal economy does not seem to be creating unemployment, although perhaps the effect is hidden by movement into the informal sector.[8]

The principle conclusion from the economic freedom index scores is a need for reform of the juridical system in Indonesia.

Another index that can provide us insight is the Global Competitiveness Index, which is built upon 12 sets of measurements that the World Economic Forum calls pillars. Malaysia dominates Indonesia in all these measurements (see Table 7.5), but the largest gaps are to be found in infrastructure, technological readiness, health and primary education, labour market efficiency, institutions and innovation. We have already seen the importance of infrastructure. The following paragraphs examine the other pillars with the greatest gaps.

Technological readiness covers two concepts: the availability and absorption of new technologies (as opposed to creating them, which is covered in innovation) and the information and communication technology (ICT) infrastructure. The measures of the first are a compilation of responses to survey questions and thus of widespread opinion of business executives. Executives in Indonesia are less optimistic than those of Malaysia regarding the availability of new technology and its incorporation into business. The ICT measures are of the infrastructure available (fixed and mobile) and of users. Indonesia clearly has less bandwidth than

Malaysia. Both countries show a rise in Internet users, particularly mobile Internet: neither country is strong in fixed-line connections. Interestingly, this part of the world is seeing the birth of numerous online services such as Bukalapak (an e-commerce marketplace), Tokopedia (an online marketplace for customer-to-customer trade, financial technology and other offerings) and Gojek (ride-hailing and logistics) that will have a great impact on the retail distribution network. Rather than substituting that network as Amazon and Lazada have tended to do in the past, these services support retail businesses, facilitating supply and linking to consumers. "Appropriate technology" and "small is beautiful" were mantras of the 1970s, 1980s and 1990s for development economics. However, Internet bandwidth is proving itself to be very appropriate, acting as a catalyst for value chains in less sophisticated economies. It follows that improving the bandwidth will contribute to the efficiency of the economy. While Internet service providers may be lagging in implementing infrastructure, users are proving rapid in adopting to the services that are available. Indonesia has the fastest growing Internet economy in Southeast Asia (Google Temasek 2018).

Malaysia and especially Indonesia are weak in the area of "Health and primary education", especially regarding the business impact of tuberculosis and HIV. As alluded to above, Indonesia does poorly in primary education, placing 106th worldwide. Indonesia made remarkable progress in the construction of new schools over the 1970s and 1980s and nearly quadrupled the number of teachers since 1970. However, adjusted net primary school enrolment is only 92% of the appropriate age group (2016 data) as opposed to 96% for the Philippines (2015 data) and 98.9% for Malaysia (2016 data). The problem perhaps is not so much the expense of attending school as the opportunity cost of a child not working. Also, the quality of in-school time needs to improve according to the Programme for International Student Assessment (OECD 2016). Results are not available for Malaysia or the Philippines, but scholastic performance for science, math and reading in Indonesia is markedly below the world average and somewhat below Thailand. Indonesia is nonetheless on an upward trend for these three basic areas of performance. Unfortunately, the gap between students coming from a privileged background and disadvantaged students is increasing.

A fact not captured by the Global Competitiveness Report, and perhaps the best motivation for combining health with primary education, is that 37% of children under the age of five are stunted, a phenomenon that adversely affects brain development. Stunting is caused by chronic malnutrition during pregnancy and chronic malnutrition and repeated illness during childhood. This is a clear case where the poverty of a nation is self-perpetuating, since hunger and limited health care lead to a less capable workforce. Although focus on tuberculosis and HIV might bring a higher score in the competitiveness rating since the index calls attention to these, in reality, it is the food and health services issues that will have a dramatic effect in a generation. The food issue is not one of food production. The problem is one of a distribution of wealth that leaves many with limited disposable income for the purchase food. There are limited data for the GINI coefficient (an indicator of inequality) for Indonesia. The World Bank coefficient for 2013 is 39.5; statistics from Indonesia show a drop from 40.8 in 2015 to 38.9 in 2018. However, the 40.1 coefficient for the cities is much higher than the 32.4 for the countryside in 2018. Since cities are much wealthier than the countryside, this reinforces the notion that wealth distribution is a factor in the population's health. Access to health services is both a wealth distribution issue and health network issue. Health expenditure as a per cent of GDP shows Indonesia to be spending similar amounts to other countries in the region, including Singapore.[9] This means little: because Indonesia is a poorer country, this percentage of the GDP translates to far less per person, even under purchasing power parity. The market is not going to overcome this issue since rising inequality means families where stunting is more prevalent are precisely those with less purchasing power to acquire health services.

As with the economic freedom index, Indonesia scores poorly in the labour market pillar of the Global Competitiveness Report, particularly regarding redundancy pay (how many weeks of salary must be offered in terminating an employee) and in female participation in the workforce. As mentioned above, redundancy pay must be put into the context of the limited social security net available in Indonesia. Female participation in the workforce, while it does have an objective impact on the productivity of a given population, is also a social choice dictated by more than the mere economic imperative.

While there is a gap between Indonesia and Malaysia regarding the Innovation pillar, this is more a result of Malaysia's strong showing (22nd worldwide). Indonesia's ranking at 32nd is not far behind. However, the World Banks Enterprise Survey reveals private firms' shortcomings in basic innovativeness and exploitation of whatever technological readiness that Indonesia offers. The results are dramatically lower than both the world average and the average for East Asia and Pacific in several basic and accessible areas: per cent of firms that have their own Web site, that use e-mail to interact with clients/suppliers, that introduced a new product/service, that introduced at least a single process innovation and that spend anything on R&D. The survey is done with registered businesses, who frequently claimed that their biggest obstacle was competition from informal firms (firms that are part of the economy not regulated by the state). It would be interesting to learn if the informal firms hustle more to innovate.

The Institutions score is calculated from survey results on questions about the protection of property rights, the ethical standards of politicians and so on. The aspects of this pillar where Indonesia does particularly poorly are public trust in politicians, irregular payments and bribes, favouritism in decisions of government officials and the efficiency of the legal framework in challenging regulations. Clearly, this goes hand in hand with reform of the juridical system. The playing field is tilted in favour of the powerful and connected. Also, decisions are not made based on merit, thereby bettering the economy, but based on favours, with at best a random effect upon the economy. The change is all the more difficult because the current system is efficient in a perverse way: the Enterprise Survey results indicate less time required for regulatory compliance in Indonesia than other countries in the East Asia and Pacific region (Singapore is not part of the survey). As a collectivity, Indonesia has a choice. It can reinforce the privileges of the powerful and remain a relatively poor country, or it can level the playing field and work its way towards greater prosperity, including for the current rich. Levelling the playing field will not on its own automatically lead to greater prosperity, but it would allow other factors to contribute to the progress of the nation.

Among those other factors are quality education of the poor, sufficient nutrition and improved infrastructure. These are all expenditures which means that monies will have to be diverted from consumption (other than food and health) and done so in an efficient way. If the Institutions score remains low, then it will be very difficult for those expenditures to be done in an efficient way, which requires both competence and good faith.

Short view: Joko Widodo introduced a universal health-care plan and education reform in 2014, his first year in office as president of Indonesia. He has since maintained a strong record of infrastructure spending and a reputation for honesty. However, his administration has been criticized because growth has remained near 5%, in contrast to his elections promise of 7% growth.

A further critique made by some opponents is that the reason for this slow growth is an unacceptably high incremental capital-output ratio (ICOR), a measure of the efficiency of investment. The political innuendo is that this inefficiency is caused by corruption: with the corruption of the Soeharto regime, ICOR was approximately 3.0; under Widodo, ICOR is around 6.0. Ergo, more corruption under Widodo (see Ketum Indonesian Tax Watch 2018). In order to assert his authority over the government, Widodo was compelled "to embrace, rather than challenge, the usual patterns of politics in Indonesia's patronage-driven democracy" (Warburton 2016). Indonesian politics are for Indonesians to resolve, but the observations do raise interesting issues that underlie the recent evolution of Indonesia's economy.

The incremental capital-output ratio (ICOR) is an attempt to measure the efficiency of investment. It is a ratio with a quantity of investment in the numerator and a quantity of GDP growth in the denominator. The quantities are both an increment over time periods. The time periods are both of the same length, but the investment period probably should be earlier since the idea is that earlier investment "causes" later growth. In practice, however, the same time period is used for measuring investment and growth. Further, both theoretical (Boianovsky 2018) and practical insufficiencies have led to ICOR being somewhat disregarded.

Two financial crises provide the context. The Asian financial crisis of 1997 underlined the dangers of trusting too much in global markets and forced several ASEAN countries to gain deeper experience in the management of monetary policy. Ten years later, Indonesia weathered the global financial crisis and subsequent recession well. The United States managed the crisis in part with a loosened monetary policy, indirectly causing an increased flow of capital to emerging markets. The close of the period of quantitative easing (the large-scale purchases of government bonds or other financial assets by the central bank from private financial institutions, thereby increasing private bank lending and stimulating the economy) has led to rising interest rates not only in the United States but also in the worldwide market. As a result, countries such as Indonesia have had to raise their interest rates. This tightened monetary policy throttles growth. Indonesia has had to pursue stability over growth.

The impact for ICOR is that earlier investment under lower interest rates is compared with later investment under higher interest rates. This contributes to the higher ICOR.

Another factor is the nature of investment. The World Bank statistic "gross fixed capital formation" (formerly gross domestic fixed investment) includes land improvements (fences, ditches, drains, etc.); plant, machinery and equipment purchases and the construction of roads, railways and the like, including schools, offices, hospitals, private residential dwellings and commercial and industrial buildings and, since 1993, "net acquisitions of valuables". Land improvements have a different productive life span than do plants (factories), than does machinery. Depending upon the complexity of the factory, ramping up time (the delay between construction and being fully operational) can vary from a few days to two or more years. All of this is "averaged out" arbitrarily when calculating ICOR and comparing results across countries. The Widodo administration in Indonesia has been spending heavily on infrastructure, with a return spread out over several decades, resulting in an increase of ICOR.

Although these two factors (slowed growth under tighter monetary policy and nature of investment) would excuse a recent rise in ICOR, it is also true that Indonesia (as well as Malaysia) has historically suffered higher ICOR rates than normal, with the exception of the aftermath of the Asian financial crisis when there was low investment. The deficiencies in the organization of the economy listed above as part of the "long view" help explain this performance. They are also in large part due to the legacy of interested parties corrupting government economic policies over the past 70 years.

The Governments of Indonesia Since Independence

At present, the president, who is chief of state and head of government, appoints his cabinet. Two houses constitute the People's Consultative Assembly: the regional *Dewan Perwakilan Daerah* (DPD) and the central and more powerful *Dewan Perwakilan Rakyat* (DPR). These are both elected to five-year terms. The DPR legislates and produces the government budget together with the president. The DPR also approves the candidates for the Supreme Court,[10] who are then confirmed by the president. The DPD represents the regions but can only advise the DPR. The republic is divided into provinces that in turn are sub-divided into cities and regencies, again sub-divided at further levels. From 1945 to 2001, power was centralized with the central government in Jakarta. Regencies and municipalities began to take on responsibility for providing most services after 2001. This help to suppress authoritarianism but slowed reform.

The political history of Indonesia since independence in 1945 covers three periods: the old order of Soekarno, the new order of Suharto that began in 1966 and ended with the Asian financial crisis of 1997–1998 and the "reform era" (1998 to present).

Soekarno worked against two forces to establish Indonesia. First, the Netherlands did not easily relinquish control. It was via collaboration with the Japanese occupiers that he managed to declare independence with a constitution in 1945. The Dutch did not accept this until 1949 and even influenced the writing of a new constitution for the "Republic of the United States of Indonesia". This constitution was replaced in 1950. The second force resisting Soekarno was the diversity of political ideologies and interests. The first general elections in Indonesia's history (1955) saw 75% of the popular vote divided among four different parties: the two Islamic parties Masyumi (21% of the vote) and Nahdlatul Ulama (18.5% of the vote), the Partai Nasionalis Indonesia that emphasized the individual over the state (over 20% of the vote) and the communist Partai Komunis Indonesia (16.5% of the vote). To these four political parties must be added the influence of the armed forces.

In the face of this logjam of influences, Soekarno began to promote the concept of "guided democracy". Faced by regional military coups over December 1956 and January 1957, Soekarno declared martial law. He invited the regional military leaders to negotiate a solution to the crisis in September of that year, but this was not fruitful. The head of his military, General Nasution, managed to subvert two of the dissident regional military councils in that same month. The other dissident councils, aided by the CIA, began a political and military campaign to overthrow the central government in Jakarta in February 1958. Jakarta responded militarily in April and had suppressed effective opposition by December.

Meanwhile, in December Soekarno had nationalized several hundred Dutch businesses.

The 13 months from December 1957 to December 1958 left Soekarno in a strong position. Building on this, his decree in July 1959 reinstated the 1945 constitution, formalizing his power. Soekarno then dissolved parliament in March of 1960 and named half the members of the new parliament. Eight months later he added the *Madjelis Permusjawaratan Rakjat Sementara*, a legislative assembly of whom some were appointed by him and some came from the parliament.

This was followed by a crackdown on the press and the suppression of one Islamic and one socialist political parties (perhaps favouring the communists as well as alternative Islamic parties). His principles of "Nasakom: nationalism, religion and communism" attempted to corral the support of the army (with a cloud of ideas involving nationalism and the individual versus the state), Islamic movements (emphasizing religion in general rather than Islam in particular to avoid alienating other groups) and communist groups.

The two decades of Soekarno rule were marked by consolidation of power both domestically and through foreign policy. The economy was neglected. Inflation reached hundreds of per cent per annum in the last few years of Soekarno's presidency.

Most of the military's top leaders were kidnapped and assassinated in September 1965. This left Suharto as the senior commander. He blamed the communists for the assassinations and began to purge communists in October 1965, leaving 400,000 dead by December 1966 and destabilizing Soekarno's power base. Suharto began to extend his power and that of the military, and by March 1967 he stripped Soekarno of his title of president. The Old Order had ended. The New Order was beginning.

Suharto then reorganized political life to strengthen his control. He took over the *Golongan Karya* (*Golkar*), which had been an executive and consultative organ under Soekarno that brought together "functional groups" such as labour unions, villages, farmer groups, business association and so on. He transformed it into both an electoral machine with a vast grass-roots network and an electable movement that participated in national elections for the first time in 1971. He thus presented the populace with the option to vote for "development" rather than a given ideology or political party. Supposedly it was above politics. In 1971 there were nine political parties in the elections besides this "non-political" participant. *Golongan Karya* obtained 71% of the vote. Suharto then imposed a merger of the current nine "political" parties into two—one Islamic and one secular democratic—and restricted future campaigning. He was re-elected in the five subsequent elections up to and including 1998. The military was an important element of his control of Indonesia society, although Suharto worked to decrease his dependence on the military from 1988.

This "non-political" approach was not merely a ploy. It was a step towards engineering the development of Indonesia, including its economy. The economy was in dire need of capital. As had been the case of Spain under Franco, Indonesia had suffered from a combination of ideas of *autarkeia* typical of pre-World War II, and the isolation from potential partners caused by the rejection by those of the country's leader, in this case because of Soekarno's dependence on Communist support. Suharto brought in the "Berkeley Mafia", a cadre of US-educated economists tasked with reforming policy and developing the country, analogous to the technocrats that Franco finally let correct Spain's policies in the late 1950s.

Three things boosted the economy in the 1960s and early 1970s: an influx of foreign investment, the rise of entrepreneurs in light industries that were still protected and an increase of oil revenue as a consequence of OPEC's manipulation of the world oil market. Unfortunately for Indonesia, corruption became deeply embedded under Suharto, particularly in the later years. Many state-owned enterprises were run by friends of Suharto, such as Pertamina, bailed out by government after defaulting on loans in 1975. Businesses obtained government licences and aid by having recourse (i.e. paying money) to *yayasan* (foundations), run by Suharto supporters, particularly in the military. As a consequence, there was real economic progress under Suharto, but there was also widespread corruption and a growing perception that the economy was benefitting foreign interests and the friends of Suharto more than the general population.

The Asian economic crisis of 1997 was the spark that led to Suharto's downfall. Riots had already begun in 1996 and continued through to May 1998. Although chosen for another five-year term as president in March 1998, by May 21 he resigned[11] and his Vice President Bacharuddin Jusuf Habibie succeeded him, ending the period of the New Order and commencing the period of reform.

The reform era consists of five presidencies: three of short duration immediately following Suharto, the ten-year administration of Susilo Bambang Yudhoyono and that of the current President Joko Widodo.

Bacharuddin Jusuf Habibie was president from May 1998 to October 1999, the shortest presidency to date. A doctor in engineering and an airplane pilot, Habibie was more a competent administrator than a political animal. Although he was unable to retain power, his administration saw numerous substantial reforms: authoritarianism was countered by a limitation to two terms as president and decentralization of power to the regions, political freedom was enhanced by the release of political prisoners, permitting the creation of new political parties and reviving the freedom of the press. Thirty new laws were passed under his presidency.

Abdurrahman Wahid was president from October 1999 to July 2001. Whereas Habibie had spent his formative years studying engineering in Germany, Wahid leaned towards the humanities or at least pursued Islamic studies, first spending time at an institute for Islamic and Arabic Studies in Egypt before continuing to Iraq. During his tenure as president, he tried to improve the situation of ethnic Chinese in Indonesia and sought improved trade relations with Israel.[12] He travelled extensively as president, and this is perhaps one reason that his power base was weak. He had hoped to reduce the role of the military but failed. Eventually he was impeached and replaced by his Vice President Megawati Sukarnoputri.

As her patronymic indicates, Megawati Sukarnoputri was a daughter of Soekarno. She had been actively seeking the presidency since running against Wahid in 1999. She accomplished nothing of major consequence during her presidency from July 2001 to October 2004. She still retains influence in Indonesia politics and is chair of the Indonesian Democratic Party of Struggle.

The five-year term that had begun with Wahid ended in 2004 and Susilo Bambang Yudhoyono was elected. Son of a military man, Yudhoyono received a military formation in Indonesia and the United States as well as obtained a masters in business administration and ultimately a PhD in agricultural economics in 2004. He pursued a military career that ended in 1999 as lieutenant general when he was named minister of Mining and Energy by Wahid. When Megawati replaced Wahid, she also named him Minister of Mining and Energy. After the 2004 elections, it was Yudhoyono who replaced her as president.

Yudhoyono believed that the military should not be involved in politics. He had the ideas, will and competence for reform. Half of his cabinet ministers were technocrats rather than partisans or ideologues. However, he faced the obstacles of a "slow and inefficient bureaucracy, opposing forces throughout society and widespread corruption (especially on the regional level)" (Indonesian Investments n.d.). His decade in power provided stability to the young democracy that had experienced 50 years of autocratic rule since independence. What had become a civil war in Aceh (the northernmost province) ended in 2008 under his watch; civil violence and conflict declined with the exception of isolated spectacular catastrophes and terrorist attacks (the 2004 Tsunami and the 2002 and 2005 Bali bombings) and the economy grew 5% annually during his presidency, with improving macroeconomic fundamentals such as debt and foreign reserves. However, this stability came at the cost of political concessions that resulted in the continuation of severe problems. In particular, although he had campaigned on eradicating corruption and nepotism, he did not curtail them (see Mietzner 2015, p. 11). The technocrats were forced out around 2009–2010, however, and were generally replaced by opportunists from the political and business worlds (Stephen V. Marks, personal communication). Much of the economic growth stemmed from an exploitation of commodities (cultivated or mined resources usually used as inputs in the production of other goods) that did not lead to the creation of many jobs or the increase of wages, so that the increasing wealth was not widely distributed. Although poverty did decrease, the Gini index did not. It increased beginning with the Asian financial crisis: Gini was a little over 0.3 in 1999 and had passed 0.4 by the end of Yudhoyono's presidency (Wicaksono et al. 2017).

The next president was Joko Widodo. He was born to a family of modest means and graduated in forestry. He then worked in a forestry company before returning to his father's furniture business and eventually started a furniture business of his own. A client in France gave him the appellative "Jokowi". He began his transition into politics at 41 when he became Chairman of the furniture manufacturers association of his hometown Surakarta. He ran for mayor of that town and won in 2005, remaining in office seven years. He then ran for the governorship of Jakarta and won that in 2012. In 2014, 53.15% of the popular vote made him the first president of Indonesia not from a military or elite background, against runner-up Prabowo Subianto, a former general who had also been a son-in-law of Suharto. Prabowo controlled a majority in parliament, while Jokowi had the backing of 37% there.

Joko Widodo promised an improved economy with better social welfare for the poor. Fuel subsidies represented 17–19% of the government budget when he came into power. These led to a heavy strain upon infrastructure as the number of vehicles increased rapidly. The fuel subsidies were important for political support and made life easier for the middle class. He cut fuel subsidies in his first year in office[13] and introduced 16 economic policy packages by August 2017 (Investments Indonesia 2017). This pace is particularly remarkable because he spent the first two years in office battling opposition in parliament and even disunity in his cabinet (Warburton 2016). In January 2018, his administration announced a 17th economic policy packaged designed to simplify and accelerate import and export processing but it had yet to be enacted as of November 2018.

Current criticism of the Widodo administration regarding the economy revolves around the weakening of the rupiah currency and the slow growth rate of "only" 5%.

The Impact of Islam on Indonesian Politics

Two surveys published in December 2017 indicate the views of Indonesians regarding politics and the government of Indonesia (see Simandjuntak 2018).

A survey of high school and university students found:

- 29% would not support a democratically elected non-Muslim;
- 22% would support the establishment of Sharia-based bylaws;
- 20% support the establishment of an Islamic caliphate in the country.

A survey of professionals found:

- 30% of respondents say they would not support non-Muslim leaders;
- 28% say they support the establishment of Sharia-based bylaws.

While these figures may not seem high, they configure a context in which politicians, sometimes without moral quibbles about truth, can provoke human emotion and manipulate mobs. Humans are not above using Islam to further their own ends, be they political ambitions or simple revenge on neighbours.[14] An illustration of this is provided by BTP (Basuki Tjahaja Purnama), previously known as Ahok, a blunt-spoken reformer who was Governor of Jakarta 2014–2017 in replacement of Jokowi.

In a 2016 speech, BTP remarked that some persons misuse the Koran to proscribe voting for a non-Muslim: "you were lied to **using** Al-Maidah 51". Buni Yani, an academic, edited a video clip of the speech and uploaded it to YouTube with the title: "You are lied to **by** the Qur'an Al-Maidah 51".[15] This video clip soon went viral on Facebook and Twitter (Sasongko 2016).[16] The *Front Pembela Islam* (FPI)[17] campaigned hard to bring BTP to trial for blasphemy, organizing massive demonstrations. BTP lost the gubernatorial election to Anies Baswedan as of April 19, 2017. That same day, Prabowo Subianto (rival of Jokowi in the 2014 and 2019 elections) publicly thanked Rizieq Shihab,[18] leader of the FPI, for having "defended the interests of the Indonesian public, upheld justice and saved our democracy and our future" (Siregar 2017). Anies Baswedan, winner of the governorship election, would later be considered as a vice presidential running mate of Prabowo in the 2019 general elections (Laturiuw 2018), although ultimately Sandiaga Uno would be chosen. BTP was sentenced to two years' jail the next month. Three of the five judges were given promotions a couple of days after his trial. In November 2017, Rizieq Shihab's lawyer, Eggi Sudjana, complained that Anies Baswedan had simply used the protestors to win the election (Wahid 2017). The fog of war envelopes this complicated series of events, but it would seem that Sudjana was correct. The timeline is presented in Table 7.6.

Indonesia has the largest Muslim population in the world, with 224 million of its population embracing Islam. Spread as it is over thousands of islands, the country owes its unity to Islam as well as to the Dutch colonizers. Generally, Muslims in Indonesia have been very successful in exercising their religious beliefs convivially with Buddhists, Hindus and Christians.

Table 7.6 Timeline of the Ahok/BTP case

Date	*Actor*	*Action*
September 27, 2016	Ahok/BTP	Comment that some distort the Koran to influence voting
October 5, 2016	Buni Yani	Uploads edited video clip to YouTube with inaccurate wording
November 4, 2016, December 2, 2016, and February 11 and 21, 2017	Front Pembela Islam	Demonstrations as part of a campaign to bring Ahok/BTP to trial for blasphemy
November 23, 2016	Buni Yani	Formally charged for violation of ITE law
December 2, 2016	Front Pembela Islam	Organization of massive demonstrations
February 15 and April 19, 2017	Electorate	Anies Baswedan defeats Ahok/BTP election for governorship
April 19, 2017	Prabowo Subianto	Thanks FPI (Rizieq Shihab) for saving democracy
May 9, 2017	Ahok/BTP	Sentenced to two years' imprisonment
May 11, 2017	Three judges	Given promotions after Ahok/BTP trial
November 4, 2017	Eggi Sudjana	Complains that the protestors had been used to win the election
November 14, 2017	Buni Yani	Sentenced to 18 months in jail for violation of the ITE law
November 24, 2018	Buni Yani	Supreme Court denies his appeal

Data sources: Authors' compilation from various newspaper accounts

The official legal status of these religions and Confucianism in Indonesia reflects a sociological reality.

Islam is very old in Indonesia[19] and at least some communication with the Middle East has continued since the first contact, mostly through traders and sailors. Still, Indonesians are proud of their rich culture and many reject what they see as outside influence. This rejection is reinforced by news of the mistreatment of Indonesian maids by some employers in Saudi Arabia (and other Middle Eastern countries such as Kuwait). Nonetheless, there was an increase of outside influence in the twentieth century, coming from Japan and from the Middle East, invoking a single interpretation of Islam and rejecting the presence of other visions and other religions. The next few paragraphs explain the historic diversity and more recent rejection of difference.

Indonesians do not all understand Islam in an identical manner. Allah, the Prophet Mohammed and the Koran are the three things that unite Muslims in Indonesia. However, Allah is invisible, Mohammed is no longer on earth and the only authoritative version of the Koran is in classical Arabic. While theoretically all Muslims may strive for the same pure submission to God, the sociological reality is vast diversity. Since some people spend more time learning about religion than others, it is natural that some of these *ulama* acquire a status as teachers of others. Some of the diversity stems from differing opinions among teachers who strive for the truth, and some stems from teachers who are more interested in status—be it economic or power—and subvert Islam to other ambitions. Perhaps many have mixed intentions. In any case, there are many traditions among Muslims in Indonesia.

Another consideration is that, if God is pure and infinite, humans are not. This leads to Islam often being acculturated—understood from the perspective of the culture of the believer. The understanding of Islam varied from island to island in the past, with varying Hindu and animistic influences (van der Kroef 1958). Among Muslims preoccupied with orthodoxy and purity are some who contend that their particular strain of Islam is an exception to the tyranny of the imperfect human capacity to embrace Islam. Of these, some intend to bring others to their way of thinking. And among these, some will resort to violence in order to impose their point of view. The nineteenth-century prince Diponegoro combined a spirit of reform in some ways similar to al-Wahhab, with acceptance of Hindu and animistic traditions (ibidem).

As part of Japan's effort to inculcate the vision Greater East Asia Co-Prosperity Sphere during its World War II occupation of Indonesia (Ricklefs 1993), the occupiers co-opted all Muslim organizations within the one organization called Masyumi (van Bruinessen 2002b), originally with the intent of suppressing nationalism (as a rejection of the Japanese) but eventually with the intent of inculcating nationalism (as a rejection of the West, including the Dutch) (Madinier 2015).

The influence of the homelands of Islam increased from the mid-1970s and 1980s to the twentieth century. Saudi Arabia, Qatar and Kuwait, in particular, have been generous with both money and scholars, leading to a growing influence of Salafism and what Westerners would call Wahhabism (see van Bruinessen 2002a; Wahid 2014; von der Mehden 2014). Both reject pluralism. There is, however, a plurality of views within Salafis in Indonesia, particularly regarding politics. Some opt for political quietism and submission to government, while others opt for political activism and still others, violence.

Two examples of Saudi influence are *Dewan Dakwah Islamiyah Indonesia* (DDII) (literally Indonesian Islamic Proselytizing Council) and *Lembaga Ilmu Pengetahuan Islam dan Arab* (LIPIA, literally the Institute for the Islamic and Arabic Fields of Knowledge). The former was founded by Mohammad Natsir in 1967. Natsir had served as Prime Minister under Soekarno but became estranged from him and from Suharto because of his theocratic vision for Indonesia. He was both an administrator and a prolific scholar and the principle reason that the Saudis have generously funded DDII, which has promoted Islam by providing materials, scholars and scholarships as well as through social works. LIPIA was an educational institution for Islamic and Arabic studies directly founded by the Saudis in 1980. Graduates and those returning from scholarships abroad further propagate this influence. In general, these do not preach or teach a *jihad*. They do however transmit a concern for "purity" that some may use to justify recourse to violence either to impose or to exclude ways of living.

Many commentators write of the rise of "conservatism" among Indonesian Muslims. While this would seem to be true given the survey results mentioned above, it would not be accurate to conclude that the more devout Muslims will vote for a specific candidate. "Conservatism" and devotion are two different things. Nor would it be accurate to assume that a large number of "conservative" teachers of Islam tell their flocks to vote for a specific candidate. The reality is more complicated and involves various actors subordinating religion to political gain. The dynamic is one of some actors, politicians and religious leaders with at best mixed intentions, transacting favours with one another to acquire power.

Economic policy still remains an area of debate but becomes secondary in the mind of a large number of voters when politicians raise the spectre of "unIslamic" governance. Combining this with facile economic critiques is a winning formula for attracting less educated voters. As in many countries, the populace does not have the inclination, time or education necessary to appreciate the economic arguments of various candidates, so that most politicians are able to craft a passable discourse on why he (or, occasionally, she) alone can save the country from decline.

Conclusion

Indonesia is an extensive country with a large and diverse population and a huge economic potential that has yet to be realized. The island of Java, in particular, has incredible possibilities since its high population density can increase the return on rail and road infrastructure. This return will not be automatic, however, and cannot be achieved without allowing the population to be more productive by providing it with better health and skills.

As in much of Southeast Asia, much wealth and power repose upon exclusive rent-generating fiefs that do little to promote the economic progress of the country. Those who enjoy these positions rally to whomever is in power, as long as policies do not threaten their advantage. For a portion of the vote, the role of Islam is a more vital issue than any other consideration, and politicians do not shrink from manipulating voters through this channel. As with many things, a little knowledge can be very dangerous. A simplistic view of Islam combined with a superficial understanding of the economy could lead voters to an elect stagnation.

Notes

1. About 10% of Indonesians are below the poverty line and spend 50% of their income on food. Agriculture (and fisheries) is fundamental for survival and the basis of any economy. However, the demand for food is limited, so that the size of agriculture need not increase as much as other parts of the economy. First, industry overtakes agriculture as a source of growth, and then industry is passed by the rate of growth of services as an economy evolves. Typically, industry is more productive of value than agriculture. Services vary.

2. The rate of capital formation is an indicator of the effort made to maintain and increase wealth-producing capacity rather than consume wealth, measured by the outlays on additions to the fixed assets of the economy plus net changes in the level of inventories.
3. It is more complicated than this since not all capital formation is work related. The insight remains real.
4. Some may ask why Indonesia has not grown more quickly than Malaysia since it was in a more extreme "catch-up" position than Malaysia, but this only leads to the need for more detailed research into the causes of growth. The Maddison historical estimates anterior to 1950 are incomplete. The Malaysian entity had a lower GDP per capita than the colony of Indonesia in 1911 but grew more quickly until the onset of World War II.
5. The Global Human Capital Report 2017 (p. vii) explains that:

> The Capacity subindex quantifies the existing stock [sic] of education across generations; the Deployment subindex covers skills application and accumulation of skills through work; the Development subindex reflects current efforts to educate, skill and upskill the student body and the working age population; and the Know-how subindex captures the breadth and depth of specialized skills use at work.

6. Measures such as the Economic Freedom Index of the Fraser Institute or that of the Heritage Foundation, the Global Competitiveness Index of the World Economic Forum and the results of the Enterprise Surveys of the World Bank Group are a far cry from the measures of reality used in disciplines such as physics, even more so than other economic indicators. It is difficult to verify the primary data on which the different indices are based, and there is probably some redundancy from one index to another. Many of the data are responses to surveys, meaning that the results from time 1 probably influence the results at time 2 as recent index scores become conventional wisdom. In spite of these limitations, these various reports and indices still provide insight as to what can be changed in order to increase economic performance.
7. The inflation rate was over 6% when Joko Widodo took office and dropped to under 4% by 2016. At first glance it looked like a new era of money management, with greater cooperation with the central bank. However, the situation was more complicated. Short-term variations come from annual flooding in most areas in January, Ramadan and Idul Fitri (varied dates) and the annual vacation period followed by the start of school. These are more or less regular and do not have long-term effects. Two other sources of volatility have been less predictable. Food price volatility comes from the impact of harvest time and weather variations on food prices. Fuel (oil and gas) and electricity subsidies by the government in the

past have kept these prices down. For this reason, core inflation in Indonesia is tracked by consumer prices excluding food and fuel.

However, the rupiah began to depreciate from mid-2017 through most of 2018, posterior to the data on which the Economic Freedom Index was based. Indonesia's currency had proven strong in the wake of the global financial crisis but began to weaken in 2011–2012. It did worse than the currencies of Malaysia and the Philippines from 2008 to 2014. However, this changed from 2015 to 2017, arguably years that the Widodo administration influenced. The rupiah held its own and even improved very marginally, while the Malaysian ringgit and the Philippine peso both declined by 10% relative to the US dollar. This boasting point began to disappear on April 11, 2017. The exchange rate then was 14,100 rupiah to the dollar. By October 15, 2018, the exchange rate was 16,615 rupiah to the dollar. The ringgit and the peso also declined, but the depreciation of the rupiah was twice as severe. Some accounts explain this depreciation by trade. The current account balance had turned negative in 2011 (see Fig. 7.2). The consequent change in relative demand for the currency should exert downward pressure on the rupiah. However, it is difficult to explain the seven-year lapse between the onset of negative trade balance and the depreciation of the currency. Another potential explanation would be the effect of the end of quantitative easing in the United States and other Western countries. This should have the effect of repatriating capital from emerging markets, including Indonesia, as evidenced by the misfortunes of Turkey and Argentina. This explanation does not explain the different depreciation rates of the rupiah, the Malaysian ringgit and the Philippine peso. The most likely explanation is the fall in foreign direct investment not because of the end of quantitative easing, but because of uncertainty stemming from the coming elections in 2019.

8. Aleksynka 2016 provides critiques of labour market indicators.
9. There is a discrepancy between the amounts reported.
10. The Supreme Court manifested its openness to influence in November 2018 when it sentenced a woman to six months jail for spreading information violating decency. The information in question documented sexual harassment by her superior (see Beo Da Costa 2018).
11. In 2004, Transparency International accused the Suharto family of having embezzled US$35 billion over the 31 years in power. Indonesian gross capital formation was only US$26 billion in 1998. Although Suharto's three decades of administration was characterized by concentration of power and corruption, it was nonetheless a period of growth for the economy of Indonesia. GDP per capita grew at a 7% rate (in constant 2010 US$). Gross fixed capital formation had increased from under 10% of GDP to 30%, so that the increased funds generated were being devoted to gen-

erating future growth. Some of the new wealth did reach the general population. The data for education are incomplete, but are available for 1971 and 2006, and provide proxies for the impact of the Suharto administration. In 1971, 22.5% of the population over 25 had completed primary school and 5.5% had completed lower secondary school. By 2006, these figures had increased to 80% and 43%, respectively. In 1971, the figures were half as high for females as for males; by 2006, they were three-quarters as high. Life expectancy increased from 53.4 years in 1968 to 65.9 years in 1998. This was helped by a massive drop in the infant mortality rate per thousand births, from 119.7 in 1968 to 44.5 in 1998. It was also partly due to increasing wealth (and thus improved nutrition and shelter) and partly to the thousands of village clinics erected under the Suharto administration.

12. Both Habibie and Wahid had to confront weaknesses in the unity of the sprawling territory of Indonesia that was after all a Dutch artifice. Habibie permitted a referendum to decide between autonomy and independence for East Timor, near the east-most end of Indonesia. East Timor opted for independence. Wahid permitted a referendum in Aceh, at the other end of the country. However, having learnt from the East Timor experience, he formulated the referendum as a choice about the kind of autonomy within Indonesia. This did not end the separatist movement in Aceh.
13. Fuel and electrical subsidies were a big influence on elections, but the Yudhoyono administration had made efforts to eliminate or reduce these subsidies since 2005. Variations in the world price for oil combined with election dates to create a background rhythm to time subsidy cuts. The 2004–2014 administration of Susilo Bambang Yudhoyono was not fortunate in the timing of the fuel subsidies. Three times it cut subsidies while world oil prices were high, since subsidies were bringing deficit spending too high. A cut in 2005 led to double-digit inflation. A short-term hike in 2008 also led to transient 10% inflation. Another cut to subsidies came in 2013 and led to new inflation. World crude oil prices had a local peak at over US$90 a barrel in July 2014 and plunged to US$35 in January 2016. Joko Widodo was able to introduce subsidy cuts early enough to be forgotten by the next election and also at a time they would have minimal impact upon the price at the pump and thus little inflation. He did so in 2015, keeping government control of prices but in line with the market price.
14. In late November 2018, Indonesia's Prosecutor Office released an Android application which would allow private citizens to report unorthodox beliefs or behaviour regarding any of the officially recognized religions.
15. "The original version of Ahok's speech is taken from video which has duration 21 minutes 32 seconds on YouTube. The original text script is 'dibohongi pakai Surat Al Maidah 51.' However, the word 'pakai' is erased by

Buni Yani before uploading the video to Youtube" (Anjanillah and Al-Farabi 2017).

16. The Jakarta Metro Police charged Buni Yani in November 2016 for inciting religious hatred by misleadingly conveying Ahok's (BTP's) speech, omitting words. A year later, the academic was sentenced to 18 months in jail for violation of the law on information and electronic transactions. Another year later still, the Supreme Court rejected his appeal. There would seem to be a contradiction between the sentences of Buni Yani and Ahok/BTP.
17. The *Front Pembela Islam* (Islamic Defenders Front—FPI) was founded in 1998 and funded, according to Wikileaks (2009), by the National Police.
18. On May 29, police named Rizieq Shihabwas a suspect in a case involving pornography and adultery with Firza Husein (they dropped the case citing lack of evidence in June 2018).
19. Islam arrived in Indonesia from Arabia (from perhaps the mid-seventh century) and via India, China and Persia (see Hafid 2012). Stable Muslim communities were present from the thirteenth century (van der Kroef 1958).

References

Anjanillah, Farah, and M. Ramdhan Fathin Al-Farabi. 2017. A Critical Discourse Analysis: Blasphemy Portrayed in Ahok's Speech. The 9th International Graduate Students and Scholars' Conference in Indonesia (IGSSCI) Sustaining the Planet: A Call for Interdisciplinary Approaches and Engagement. http://igsci.pasca.ugm.ac.id/archive/v2.0/assets/files/igsc-09-046-Farah%20Anjanillah.pdf. Accessed November 2030, 2018.

ASEAN. 2018. *SME Policy Index ASEAN 2018 Boosting Competitiveness and Inclusive Growth*. https://asean.org/storage/2018/09/ASPI-2018-Brochure_FINAL.pdf. Accessed December 3, 2018.

Beo Da Costa, Agostinus. Indonesian President Urges Woman to Be Jailed to Seek Justice. *Reuters*, November 19. https://www.reuters.com/article/us-indonesia-rights/indonesia-president-urges-woman-to-be-jailed-in-harassment-case-to-seek-justice-idUSKCN1NO1CY?il=0. Accessed November 20, 2018.

Boianovsky, Mauro. 2018. Beyond Capital Fundamentalism: Harrod, Domar and the History of Development Economics. *Cambridge Journal of Economics* 42 (2): 477–504.

van Bruinessen, Martin. 2002a. Wahhabi Influences in Indonesia, Real and imagined. *Journée d'Etudes Wahhabisme*. www.archivesaudiovisuelles.fr/11/163/martin_van_bruinessen-7.pdf. Accessed November 21, 2018.

———. 2002b. Genealogies of Islamic Radicalism in Post-Suharto Indonesia. *South East Asia Research* 10 (2): 117–154.

Fraser Institute. 2018. *Economic Freedom of the World*. https://www.fraserinstitute.org/economic-freedom/map?year=2016&geozone=world&countries=MYS,PHL,IDN,CHN,IND&page=map. Accessed October 12, 2018.

Google Temasek. 2018. e-Conomy SEA 2018. https://www.thinkwithgoogle.com/_qs/documents/6730/Report_e-Conomy_SEA_2018_by_Google_Temasek_v.pdf. Accessed December 4, 2018.

Hafid, Erwin. 2012. The Early of Islam in Indonesia. *Journal of Islamic Civilization in Southeast Asia*. http://journal.uin-alauddin.ac.id/index.php/jicsa/article/view/727. Accessed November 29, 2018.

Indonesian Investments. n.d. *Susilo Bambang Yudhoyono Administration*. https://www.indonesia-investments.com/culture/politics/reformation/susilo-bambang-yudhoyono/item7596. Accessed November 14, 2018.

Investments Indonesia. 2017. *16th Economic Policy Package: Single Submission System*. https://www.indonesia-investments.com/news/news-columns/16th-economic-policy-package-single-submission-system/item8154? Accessed November 15, 2018.

Ketum Indonesian Tax Watch and Wakil Sekretaris Pemimpin Pusat Lembaga Penyuluhan Bantuan Hukum Nahdlatul Ulama. 2018. Tabayun. https://tabayun.co.id/2018/04/10/pak-jokowi-icor-darurat-yang-harus-anda-gebuk/. Accessed December 4, 2018.

Laturiuw, Theo Yonathan Simon. 2018. Anies Baswedan Tolak Jadi Calon Presiden Karena Emosional dengan Prabowo Subianto. *Wartakota Live Online*. http://wartakota.tribunnews.com/2018/08/16/anies-baswedan-tolak-dicalonkan-jadi-calon-presiden-karena-emosional-dengan-prabowo-subianto. Accessed March 19, 2019.

Madinier, Rémy. 2015. *Islam and Politics in Indonesia: The Masyumi Party between Democracy and Integralism*. Singapore: NUS Press.

Marks, Stephen V. 2017. Non-Tariff Trade Regulations in Indonesia: Nominal and Effective Rates of Protection. *Bulletin of Indonesian Economic Studies* 53 (3): 333–357.

Mietzner, Marcus. 2015. *Reinventing Asian Populism. Jokowi's Rise, Democracy, and Political Contestation in Indonesia*. Policy Studies an East-West Center Series, 72. Honoloulu.

Observatory of Economic Complexity. 2018. https://atlas.media.mit.edu/en/profile/country/idn/. Accessed November 19, 2018.

OECD. 2016. *PISA Country Note on Indonesia*. https://www.oecd.org/pisa/PISA-2015-Indonesia.pdf. Accessed December 4, 2018.

Ricklefs, M.C. 1993. *A History of Modern Indonesia since c. 1300*. London: Palgrave.

Sasongko, Agung. 2016. Video Ahok: Anda Dibohongi Alquran Surat Al-Maidah 51 Viral di Medsos. *Republika*, October 6. https://www.republika.co.id/berita/dunia-islam/islam-nusantara/16/10/06/oem6xe313-video-ahok-anda-dibohongi-alquran-surat-almaidah-51-viral-di-medsos. Accessed November 30, 2018.

Schwab, Klaus. 2018. *The Global Competitiveness Report 2018*. World Economic Forum.

Simandjuntak, Deasy. 2018. Identity Politics Looms Over Indonesia's Presidential Election. *East Asia Forum*. http://www.eastasiaforum.org/2018/11/10/identity-politics-looms-over-indonesias-presidential-election/. Accessed November 21, 2018.

Siregar, Hotman. 2017. Prabowo Expresses Gratitude to FPI Leader for 'Saving Indonesia's Democracy'. *Jakarta Globe*. https://jakartaglobe.id/news/prabowo-expresses-gratitude-fpi-leader-saving-indonesias-democracy/. Accessed November 29, 2018.

van der Kroef, Justus M. 1958. The Role of Islam in Indonesian Nationalism and Politics. *The Western Political Quarterly* 11 (1): 33.

von der Mehden, Fred R. 2014. Saudi Religious Influence in Indonesia. Middle East Institute. https://www.mei.edu/publications/saudi-religious-influence-indonesia. Accessed 25 June 2019.

Wahid, Din. 2014. Nurturing Salafi Manhaj. A Study of Salafi Pesantren in Contemporary Indonesia. PhD thesis. Summary available in. *Wacana* 15 (2): 367–376.

Wahid, Ahmad Bil. 2017. Kecewa Anies Absen Peringatan 411, Eggi: Jangan Kacang Lupa Kulit. *detikNews*. https://news.detik.com/berita/d-3713056/kecewa-anies-absen-peringatan-411-eggi-jangan-kacang-lupa-kulit. Accessed November 30, 2018.

Warburton, Eva. 2016. Jokowi and the New Developmentalism. *Bulletin of Indonesian Economic Studies* 52 (3): 297–320.

Wicaksono, Eko, Hidayat Amir, and Anda Nugroho. 2017. *The Sources of Income Inequality in Indonesia: A Regression-based Inequality Decomposition*. ADBI Working Paper, No. 667. Tokyo: Asian Development Bank Institute (ADBI).

Wikileaks. 2009. *Indonesian Biographical and Political Gossip, Q4 2005/Q1 2006*. https://wikileaks.org/plusd/cables/06JAKARTA5851_a.html. Accessed November 30, 2018.

World Travel and Tourism Council. 2017. *Travel & Tourism Economic Impact 2017 Indonesia*. London: WTTC.

PART II

Four Smaller Economies

CHAPTER 8

Brunei Darussalam, a Country Profile

Siti Fatimahwati Pehin Dato Musa

Introduction

This chapter first provides a brief socio-political and economic overview of Brunei Darussalam. Next, it focuses on the economic challenges that Brunei is facing due to its characteristics of a *rentier* economy. The chapter then discusses the policies that the government is currently undertaking to sustain the economy and finally highlights how regional integration through the ASEAN Economic Community (AEC) has benefited Brunei, especially in terms of improvements in the business environment.

Socio-political Overview of Brunei

Brunei is a unique economy in ASEAN because of its small size, monarchical rule and wealth. Brunei is a small oil and gas-exporting country located on the northwest coast of the island of Borneo with an area of 5765 square kilometres. The official religion is Islam and the type of government is a Constitutional Sultanate whereby the king has the full authority of the state. Brunei is divided into four districts: Brunei Muara, Tutong and

S. F. P. D. Musa (✉)
Universiti Brunei Darussalam School of Business and Economics, Gadong, Brunei Darussalam
e-mail: fatimahwati.musa@ubd.edu.bn

R. Macdonald (ed.), *Southeast Asia and the ASEAN Economic Community*, https://doi.org/10.1007/978-3-030-19722-3_8

Belait in the west and Temburong in the east. The coastline is covered by mangrove swamps and sandy beaches and extends about 160 kilometres along the South China Sea. About 70 per cent of the land remains covered by dense equatorial forests except for coastal areas that have been cleared for permanent cultivation. About 500 kilometres north of the equator, Brunei experiences a hot tropical climate throughout the year: the mean monthly temperature is 27°C, and annual rainfall is more than 2300 mm (APERC 2010).

Brunei's population was 432,900 in 2017 with an annual growth of 1.6 per cent (Brunei Government 2017). Brunei is a multi-racial state comprising 67 per cent Malays and 15 per cent Chinese, and others are Indians, indigenous ethnic groups and expatriates. Brunei has a young population: 45 per cent are aged 15–39 years, 24 per cent are below 15 years while only 7 per cent are 60 years and above (Brunei Government 2017).

Brunei achieved independence on 1 January 1984 after 96 years as a British Protectorate, leading to the sultan resuming power as the absolute monarch in addition to holding positions as prime minister, minister of defence and minister of finance. Four policy councils, namely, the Religious Council, the Privy Council, the Council of Cabinet Ministers and the Legislative Councils (LEGCOs), are responsible for advising the sultan (Brunei Press 2010). The sultan appoints all members of these councils, some of which are chaired by members of the royal family (Oxford Business Group 2014). The structure of Brunei's government is similar to the United Kingdom's Westminster system. The Council of Cabinet Ministers has 11 ministries responsible for foreign affairs and trade, education, defence, finance, energy and industry, culture, youth and sports, health, religious affairs and communications (Oxford Business Group 2014). The sultan is advised by ministers and councils but he has the final say. This is in contrast with the United Kingdom, where the role of the monarchy is limited by convention and parliamentary law.

The ideology of Malay Islamic monarchy was introduced after independence in 1984. This is the ideology whereby the Malay language and culture are embedded in the administration system, Islam as the main religion and way of life and the monarch is the head of state (Oxford Business Group 2013; Brunei Press 2010). These traditional values have formed a firm foundation that has developed a prosperous nation with strong family bonds and leadership committed to the welfare and well-being of the entire nation's citizens. The system is one in which the monarchy is the force of the country's well-being and so must be respected and protected by all citizens. His Majesty the sultan occupies a central place in the day-to-day lives of Bruneians, who receive subsidies covering many everyday items, low-cost healthcare, free education and a range of other benefits from the government.

Economic Overview of Brunei

In order for a country to qualify as a *rentier* state, Beblawi (1987) argues that oil should account for at least 40 per cent of the country's gross domestic product (GDP). Brunei is a *rentier* economy: it is among the world's economies most dependent on oil and gas, accounting for around half of GDP and 90 per cent of export revenues (Deutsche Bank Country Report 2012). It is also the fourth-largest oil producer in Southeast Asia and the ninth-largest exporter of gas in the world (BEDB 2011). In 2017, GDP in Brunei was US$11.40 billion (Brunei Government 2017).

The theory of *rentier* state thus can be used as the general framework to understand Brunei, since it generates most of its revenue from the production and export of oil. According to Benli (2014), there are three main characteristics of a *rentier* state: first, oil revenues are paid to governments in the form of rent; second, oil revenues are externally generated from exports; and third, oil revenues are directly accumulated by the state.

Revenues from oil and gas have made GDP per capita levels in Brunei one of the highest in Southeast Asia: US$28,290 in 2017. Figure 8.1 shows the GDP per capita of Brunei over the last five years (2013–2017) in current USD. GDP per capita was its peak in 2013 at US$44,597 and lowest in 2016 at US$26,939. However, economic growth has been the slowest in the Southeast Asian region at 0.6 per cent in 2017 and it is predicted to continue to contract with the government running a deficit.

The over-reliance on oil and gas has led to a large and overemployed public sector, discouraging the growth of the private sector. The private sector outside the oil and gas industry has contributed steadily, around 20 per cent of GDP, in recent years as shown in Table 8.1.

Figure 8.1 shows real GDP growth for 2005–2017. It peaked in 2006 and 2011 with growth rates of 4.4 per cent and 3.4 per cent that coincided with high oil prices. The economy contracted in 2008–2009 with a growth rate of around −1.8 per cent due to the global financial crisis. GDP grew by 0.8 per cent on average during the period 2010–2012. In 2014, GDP contracted by an estimated −2.3 per cent for a second consecutive year as

Table 8.1 GDP by sector at current prices (per cent share)

GDP by Sector	*2014*	*2015*	*2016*
Oil and gas sector	63.3	55.9	51.8
Non-oil and gas sector	36.7	44.1	48.2
Government sector	14.2	16.8	18.3
Private sector	22.5	27.3	29.8
Gross value added	100.0	100.0	100.0

Data source: Brunei Government (2017)

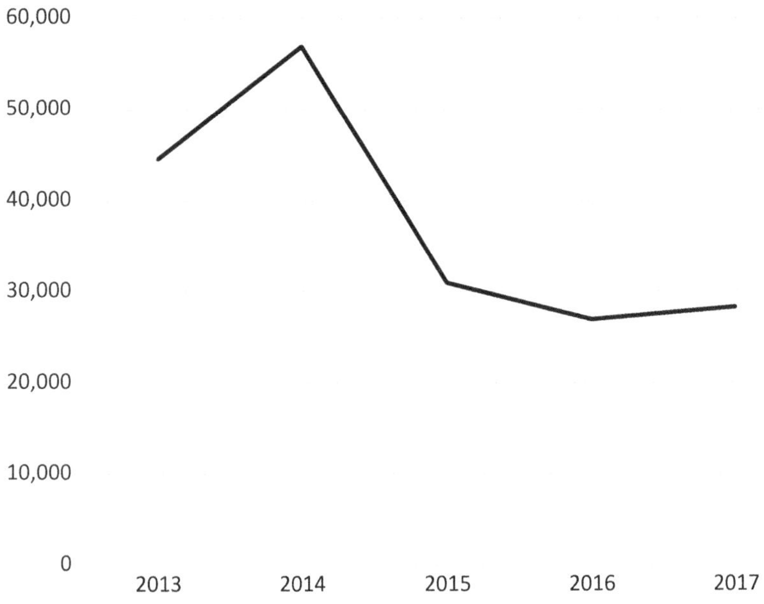

Fig. 8.1 GDP Per Capita of Brunei (Current USD) 2013–2017. Data source: The World Bank (2018)

the value of oil and gas production continued to fall (ADB 2015). Over the last ten years, real GDP has been growing at an average rate of 1.3 per cent *per annum*, whereas in the last five years it has grown by 0.2 per cent *per annum*. This economic performance is below the rest of Southeast Asia where the ASEAN economies grew by an average of 6 per cent from 2014 to 2017.

In 2009, hydrocarbon revenues declined by US$3300 million (37.4 per cent) compared to 2008 due both to a fall in crude oil prices and to the government's policy to cap production. At its peak, oil production reached 240,000 barrels per day (bpd) in 1979, but by 2009 production had fallen to 132,000 bpd. The policy of capping production was deemed necessary to extend the life cycle of the remaining reserves, currently estimated to expire within 25 years (Roberts 2011). Declining oil production and falling oil prices have reduced government revenue: in 2013, revenue fell by 17.3 per cent and further declined by 21.5 per cent in the first three quarters of 2014 (ADB 2015). The global price for a barrel of oil has plummeted 40 per cent since January 2015 and 78 per cent since its peak value in 2008. Due to the drop in the global oil price, the economy of Brunei contracted by 2.1 per cent in the year 2013 and continued to fall until it reached −1.7 per cent in 2016. Brunei's economy is slowly recovering following a 0.7 per cent growth in 2017 (Fig. 8.2).

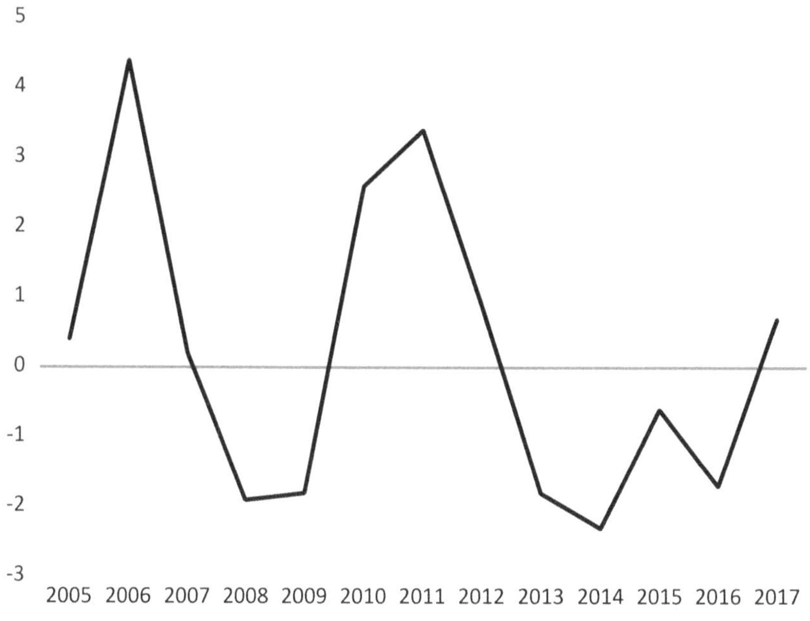

Fig. 8.2 Percentage growth rate of real GDP for Brunei, 2005–2017. Data source: Brunei Government (2017)

Mahdavy (1970) and Beblawi (1987) argue that overdependence on oil revenue can have negative political, economic and social impacts on a rentier state. On the economic side, it can cause enclaved development[1] which is termed "resource curse" or "Dutch Disease" whereby the booming oil sector distorts the growth of other sectors. The role of most rentier states is largely limited to the distribution of rent earnings among the population by providing public goods, welfare and by acting as the major employer. In addition, Brunei imports nearly all of its consumer and capital goods and 80 per cent of its food (Hashim 2010).

The redistribution of rent in terms of welfare is not favourable if it is not accompanied by an improvement in economic production. For example, the oil price drop from a peak of US$115/barrel in June 2014 to US$33 in February 2016 had a severe impact on Brunei's economy where government revenues fell by 70 per cent in 2014/2015 compared to 2012/2013 (Shahminan and Thien 2016). The combination of falling oil prices and falling government revenue meant that there was limited room for the government to create jobs. For 2016/2017, the government announced a freeze on public sector wages and hiring (Shahminan and Thien 2016). The public welfare budget during this difficult economic downturn was not sustainable and hence spending on health, national housing and aid for the needy was reduced.

In 2017, the working-age population (aged 15 years and over) was 310.4 thousand, of which 51.4 per cent were male. The labour force participation rate was 65.6 per cent and out of the total labour force of 203.6 thousand, temporary residents (non-local) accounted for one-quarter. Employment is heavily concentrated in the service sector, particularly in public administration at 27.3 per cent, followed by wholesale and retail trade at 11.8 per cent and education at 10.3 per cent. Agriculture, forestry and fishery accounted for less than 1.0 per cent of total employment (Brunei Government 2017). The government sector employs 40 per cent of the country's total labour force and the share of indigenous labour is 70 per cent (Siddiqui et al. 2012). Employment in the government sector attracts high incomes and is a major vehicle for redistributing the rents from oil revenue.

The overall unemployment rate was 6.9 per cent in 2016 (Brunei Government 2017) with the youth unemployment rate (aged 15–24 years old) being significantly higher at 25.3 per cent. It is the demographic characteristics and education attainments of the unemployed that are of primary concern to the government. In 2014, out of the 14,600 indigenous people unemployed, 72 per cent are youths and 90 per cent are primary or secondary school leavers. Some of the difficulties reported for securing jobs are low education levels, inexperience and job-hopping attitudes (Hong-Huat 2009).

The Brunei economy is still highly dependent on the oil exports with a ratio of more than 60 per cent of oil exports to GDP. The economy suffers from slow growth and high youth unemployment. In order to sustain the economy, diversification is important.

National Development Policies of Brunei

Brunei's economic policy since the beginning of independence and in particular its Fifth National Development Plan (1986–1990) has been to diversify the economy away from the oil and gas sector. Brunei went through nine five-year National Development Plans which attempted to promote economic diversification over the last few decades and yet the progress in achieving these goals had been much slower than expected.

The need to find a sustainable path for the non-oil economy led Brunei to create *Wawasan Brunei 2035* (The Brunei National Vision 2035). This current development plan for Brunei (2007–2035) consists of the National Vision, the Outline of Strategies and Policies for Development (OSPD, ten-year document) and the National Development Plan (NDP, five-year document). The Brunei National Vision 2035 aims to make Brunei, by 2035, a nation widely recognized for world-class education and skilled workforce, a high quality of life and a dynamic and sustainable economy.

In brief, the document described the situation of the economy of Brunei as unsustainable due to being over dependent on oil and gas and also due to the over-sized public sector. There is hence a need for more private sector participation to create more employment and generate more income for the economy (DEPD 2008).

His Majesty, in his recent speech in July 2017, acknowledged the two most important strategies to bring about sustained economic growth in Brunei. These are foreign direct investment (FDI) and encouraging the growth of small and medium enterprises (SMEs):

> Two core approaches have been focused on to ensure that growth really happens. The first approach is to step up foreign direct investment (FDI) and the second is to encourage small and medium-sized enterprises (SMEs) to penetrate the regional and international markets. (Othman 2017)

These two strategies are stated in the Brunei National Vision 2035 as follows:

- An economic strategy that will create new employment for our people and expand business opportunities within Brunei Darussalam through the promotion of investment, foreign and domestic, both in downstream industries as well as in economic clusters beyond the oil and gas industry.
- A local business development strategy that will enhance opportunities for local small- and medium-sized enterprises (SMEs) as well as enable Brunei Malays to achieve leadership in business and industry by developing greater competitive strength.

These two domestic strategies are congruent with AEC "pillars" (1) and (3).[2] The first AEC pillar seeks to create a single market and production base through free flow of goods, services, investment, skilled labour and freer flow of capital. This integration and market liberalization aim to provide more trade and business opportunities within the region. The third pillar of AEC, on the other hand, seeks to "achieve sustainable and balanced growth and development through equitable economic development" through initiatives that boost MSMEs' participation and integration in the regional and global value chains (The ASEAN Secretariat 2014).

The next section will focus on some of the benefits of regional economic integration that have indirectly contributed to the improvement of the business environment in Brunei. A conducive business environment is one of the contributing factors for greater MSMEs' participation in the economy and higher inflows of FDI.

Benefits of Regional Integration

This section will look at some of the potential benefits of regional integration to Brunei namely the harmonization of policies, standards and regulations, the reformation of domestic policies to improve the business environment and increased inflows of FDI.

Harmonization of Policies, Standards and Regulations

The AEC pillar of a single market is not only about liberalization of trade and investment, but in order to be a single market, there needs to be a harmonization of policies, standards and regulations across all the ASEAN economies. Hence, this pillar of the AEC indirectly acts as a catalyst for Brunei to improve its business environment.

Standardized business procedures across the ten ASEAN countries allow easier access for goods to be exported without much hassle. This will enable MSMEs to penetrate the larger regional market especially for products that require strict measures such as prepared-food products. In addition, as of mid-2016, 99.2 per cent of all intra-ASEAN tariffs in Brunei, Indonesia, Malaysia, the Philippines, Singapore and Thailand have been eliminated (Learning ASEAN Organization 2015). This allows Brunei to import raw materials at a cheaper price and improve the cost competitiveness of Brunei exports. Some of the successful MSMEs that have taken advantage of this are Sabli Foods, BMC, KTM, Tri-Sun and Hasmit Roofing. They have access to cheaper raw materials and subsequently export their goods more competitively to other ASEAN countries like Malaysia, Singapore and the Philippines.

Another benefit of regional integration would be a more efficient customs procedure for the transportation of goods among the ten ASEAN countries. This is made possible with the implementation of the ASEAN Customs Transit System (ACTS), an automated system that monitors the movement of goods in transit through ASEAN member states ensuring a smoother cross-border shipment procedure. Another standardized policy that the ASEAN countries have agreed upon is the ASEAN Comprehensive Investment Agreement (ACIA) in 2012. This agreement requires ASEAN countries to facilitate, liberalize, promote and protect cross-border investment in ASEAN and protects MSMEs against unlawful expropriation, thus lowering the risk of venturing into other ASEAN countries (Learning ASEAN Organization 2015).

It is thus important that MSMEs in Brunei take full advantage of the benefits offered by the AEC. MSMEs in Brunei need to be more exposed and upgraded to a more efficient and sustainable business in order to penetrate the regional market. Brunei MSMEs have been exposed to numerous training sessions and talks regarding AEC to ensure that these benefits are reaped. An example is the event organized by the US-ASEAN Business Council (US-ABC), through its joint initiative with the United States Agency for International Development (USAID): the US-ASEAN Business Alliance for Competitive SMEs. The event was held to help improve MSMEs competitiveness in preparation for the AEC. Alongside with that, the Ministry of Foreign Affairs and Trade (MoFAT) has also been actively conducting awareness campaigns to ensure greater understanding on the opportunities and benefits for Brunei as being part of the AEC (Brunei Press 2017).

Reformation of Domestic Policies to Improve the Business Environment

Dee and McNaughton (2011) argued that "domestic reform is better promoted by regional institutions, rather than unilaterally by market factors" (p. 4). They gave the example of the European Union (EU) success in promoting economic reforms. EU acts merely as the point of reference for any concerns regarding the policies. This eliminates the problem of loss of sovereignty of the member countries and allows the respective governments to take full authority over their domestic policies.

Regional integration encourages the implementation of effective domestic reforms and policies. These are called the "spillover effects" of integration (Dee and McNaughton 2011). For example, a number of reforms have been implemented to build a conducive business environment in Brunei to attract FDI and support the growth of MSMEs. According to the Energy and Industry Department of Brunei (2016), some of the recent reforms in this regard include the implementation of the Building Control Order to warrant building safety while streamlining the process for obtaining occupational permits; improvements to the Brunei Darussalam National Single Window (BDNSW), an online portal for documentary requirements related to import and export; the introduction of the Sutera Lane Merchant Scheme (SLMS) in September 2017 to assist importers and exporters; the streamlining of procedures in access to electricity by the Department of Electrical Services (DES) and enhanced monitoring of power supply.

Some of the latest legal reforms which aim to ease business start-ups include introducing an online business registration system whereby registering a company can now be done in a single step, within 24 hours, with the payment of a flat fee. Other reforms that increase the ease of doing business include:

1. the enforcement of the Secured Transaction Order (STO) and the launching of the Collateral Registry System in 2016 to facilitate lending;

2. improvements in the commercial court, such as the introduction of automatic discontinuance (Order 21) and use of the Judiciary Case Management System (JCMS) with improved features such as Electronic Filing System (EFS);
3. the Companies Act (Amendment) Order of 2016, which aims to protect investors and shareholders, and
4. the Companies (Corporate Governance) (Public Companies) Rules, 2016, introduce several mandatory rules for public companies to adhere to such as independence of the board from management and business relationships, and requirements to have independent directors, all of which aim to strengthen corporate governance which in turn will improve investor confidence.

In 2016, Brunei launched Darussalam Enterprise (DARe) which aims to nurture and support local enterprises across all stages of development. DARe provides capacity-building programmes and assistance regarding industrial land and complexes, marketing and promotion, financing and growth outside of Brunei (Brunei Press 2018). Another initiative is the establishment of Bank Usahawan or Enterprise Bank which offers financial products and advisory services that are compliant with the Islamic financing concept, helping businesses grow, expand and develop without the payment of interest. MSMEs that are registered, licensed and operating in Brunei for at least a year with a visible profitability trend are eligible to apply for a selection of financial plans (Brunei Press 2018).

The reforms mentioned above have improved the business environment in Brunei leading to an increase in the number of registered companies by 12 per cent in 2017 compared to 2016 (Brunei Government 2017). Brunei's global ranking has also improved to 72nd place in 2017, from 97th in 2016 in the Ease of Doing Business Index (Norjidi 2017). Due to this huge improvement in ranking, Brunei was named "Most Improved Economy in the World" for a second consecutive year by the World Bank. Brunei is now in the top five most competitive economies in ASEAN behind Singapore, Malaysia, Thailand and Indonesia (Norjidi 2017).

Despite the various initiatives already in place, there is still room to further strengthen the business environment to enable MSMEs to gain full advantage of AEC and penetrate the regional and international market.

Increased Inflows of FDI

Ismail et al. (2009) studied the relationship between regional economic integration and FDI inflows in ASEAN after the implementation of ASEAN Free Trade Agreement (AFTA) in 1993. FDI inflows into ASEAN were very low in the 1970s and 1980s. However, the trend of FDI inflows increased after AFTA until the financial crisis that affected most ASEAN countries in 1997/1998. Net FDI inflows into ASEAN in 1972 were only US$539 million. It increased in 1982 to US$343,095.85 million. In 1993, the amount of FDI inflows was US$14.737 billion and amounted to US$18.4 billion in 2003 which is a 22 per cent increase over a decade. Regional economic integration in this case acted as a medium to attract more FDI to the countries via the introduction of more attractive investment packages in the free trade agreements. These investment packages such as the ASEAN Industrial Scheme in 1996 and the ASEAN Investment Area in 1998 prompted countries to undergo domestic reforms to provide competitive and attractive investment environments.

Figure 8.3 shows the FDI net inflows, intra- and extra-ASEAN, in 2013, 2014 and 2015, respectively. It shows that there has been a rise in intra-ASEAN investment from US$19 billion in 2013 to US$22 billion in 2015. However, 2016 recorded the highest level of intra-ASEAN investment at US$24 billion (The ASEAN Secretariat and UNCTAD 2017). The rising interest of ASEAN firms in investing and expanding regionally is in line with the pillars of AEC. According to the World Bank, the AEC has the potential to increase GDP growth by 0.5–1 per cent and increase FDI stocks by 28–63 per cent (Oxford Business Group 2014). As of 2015, ASEAN attracted a total of US$121 billion of FDI within intra-ASEAN (The ASEAN Secretariat and UNCTAD 2017).

Table 8.2 shows FDI by economic activity in Brunei. There has been a huge drop in FDI over the years from [3]BND1080 million to BND238.2 million in 2012 and 2015, respectively. However, FDI in "other activities" other than oil and gas has risen from 2 per cent of the total in 2012, to 32 per cent in 2015 (Brunei Government 2017). The mining and quarrying sector continues to receive the largest share of FDI in Brunei. In 2015, intra-ASEAN FDI, particularly from Singapore, represents the largest share of total investment at BND69.2 million (29.0 per cent) followed by the United Kingdom, BND59.1 million (24.8 per cent), and Malaysia, BND52.8 million (22.2 per cent).

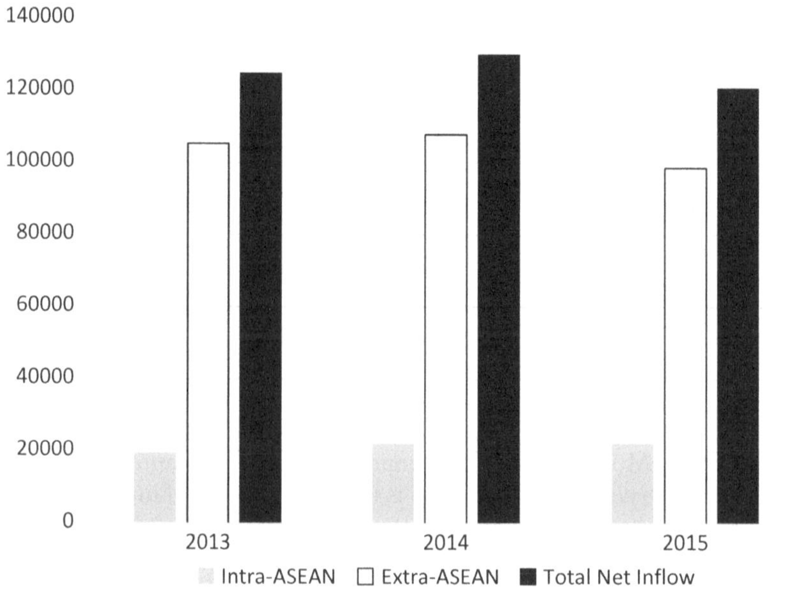

Fig. 8.3 FDI, Net Inflows, Intra- and Extra-ASEAN. Data source: The ASEAN Secretariat and UNCTAD (2017)

Table 8.2 FDI by economic activity

Economic Activity	*2012*	*2013*	*2014*	*2015*
Mining and quarrying	709.1	698.0	538.6	244.2
Manufacturing	96.8	142.0	77.3	66.6
Construction	47.8	52.5	28.5	12.3
Wholesale and retail trade	50.6	47.6	74.7	33.4
Financial and insurance activities	151.4	92.5	26.4	5.1
Other activities	25.1	42.9	26.9	76.7
Total	1080.8	970.5	719.5	238.2

Data source: Brunei Government (2017)

In 2017, 17 FDI projects estimated at about US$4 billion were in operation in Brunei, providing employment to 1321 local workers (Energy and Industry Department of Brunei 2016). In addition, there are nine more FDI projects in its initial implementation stages with a total investment value of over US$4.7 billion (Energy and Industry Department of

Brunei 2016). From 2017 to 2019, all the FDI projects will be operational and is projected to create 1600 direct job opportunities.

In its attempts to attract FDI inflows, Brunei Economic Development Board (BEDB) is promoting Brunei as an investment locale prioritizing four business segments namely life sciences, agri-business, ICT and services. The board eases the investment and business procedures and also provides information regarding the projects for potential investors. Other agencies such as Energy and Industry Department Prime Minister Office (EIDPMO) and Ministry of Foreign Affairs and Trade (MOFAT) International Trade Department play the role of coordinating investment development and regional negotiations, respectively.

However, the bulk of foreign direct investment originates outside the ASEAN region. One of the largest contributors of FDI in Brunei is Hengyi Industries Sdn Bhd from China. It has invested US$3 billion towards the Hengyi Pulau Muara Besar Petrochemical and Refinery plant. One of the spillover effects generated by Hengyi is the enhancement of human capital accumulation through its joint scholarship programme for chemical and process engineering majors. This scholarship sponsors students for further academic studies who receive industrial training at the Zhejiang University in China for 1.5 years. This human capital accumulation clearly supports the arguments brought about by numerous studies on the spillover effects of inward FDI. Utama (2012) in his paper listed down the many benefits of inward FDI. It includes “market expansion, employment creation, horizontal spillovers through productivity improvement, capital accumulation, innovation and technological advance, and vertical spillovers via backward and forward linkages to (intermediate) input markets” (p. 394). These spillovers of FDI will inevitably bring about increased economic growth and generate more employment.

The Way Forward for Brunei

The ASEAN Economic Community has created a sense of awareness within Brunei of the benefits of regional integration. As a small economy, regional integration is the way forward for Brunei to sustain and diversify its economy. Some of the benefits of regional integration for Brunei businesses are the harmonization of policies, standards and regulations, implementation of domestic reforms and the increased inflows of FDI. These benefits have subsequently contributed to an improvement of the business environment in Brunei attracting more FDI and allowing local MSMEs to access a wider market that will develop the private sector and provide more job opportunities to Bruneians. ASEAN can be seen as a building block for Brunei not only for regional integration but to participate more effectively in the global economy. In order to further capitalize on the benefits of AEC, preparation and proper implementation of policies are key factors for Brunei to consider.

Notes

1. Enclaved development is characterized by non-local capital extracting local resources.
2. The AEC Blueprint is built on four pillars: (1) a single market and production base, (2) a highly competitive economic region, (3) a region of equitable economic development and (4) a region fully integrated into the global economy (The ASEAN Secretariat 2014).
3. The current rate is 1BND = 0.92USD.

References

Asia Pacific Energy Research Centre (APERC). 2010. APEC Energy Demand and Supply Outlook. *Brunei Economy Review, 5th Edition.* www.ieej.or.jp/aperc/2010pdf/Outlook/Outlook_Volume_II_5E.pdf. Accessed March 14, 2018.

Asian Development Bank (ADB). 2015. *Asian Development Outlook 2015: Financing Asia's Future Growth.* http://www.adb.org/sites/default/files/publication/154508/ado-2015.pdf. Accessed March 30, 2018.

Beblawi, H. 1987. The Rentier State in the Arab World. In *The Rentier State: Nation, State and Integration in the Arab World, Vol. 2*, ed. G. Luciani. London: Routledge.

Benli, A.M. 2014. Rentier State Theory and the Arab Uprisings: An Appraisal. *International Relations* 11 (42): 75–91.

Brunei Economic Development Board (BEDB). 2011. *Economic Overview.* www.bedb.com.bn/why_ecoverview.html. Accessed April 14, 2018.

Brunei Government. 2017. *Brunei Darussalam Key Indicators 2017.* Brunei Darussalam: Department of Statistics, Department of Economic Planning and Development, Prime Minister's Office.

Brunei Press. 2010. *Borneo Bulletin Yearbook 2010: The Guide to Brunei Darussalam.* Bandar Seri Begawan: Brunei Press.

———. 2017. Dialogue to Discuss AEC Benefits. *Borneo Bulletin*, August 11. https://borneobulletin.com.bn/dialogue-discuss-aec-benefits/. Accessed March 20, 2018.

———. 2018. *Borneo Bulletin Yearbook 2018: The Guide to Brunei Darussalam.* Bandar Seri Begawan: Brunei Press.

Dee, P., and A. McNaughton. 2011. *Promoting Domestic Reforms Through Regionalism.* ADBI Working Paper No. 312. Tokyo: Asian Development Bank Institute. http://www.adbi.org/workingpaper/2011/10/13/4732.promoting.domestic.reforms.regionalism/ Accessed May 18, 2018.

Department of Economic Planning and Development (DEPD). 2008. *Wawasan Brunei 2035.* Brunei Darussalam: Department of Economic Planning and Development.

Deutsche Bank. 2012. *Brunei Darussalam Frontier Country Report 2012.* https://www.dbresearch.com/PROD/DBR_INTERNET_EN-PROD/PROD0000000000300330/Brunei_Darussalam.pdf. Accessed March 30, 2018.

Energy and Industry Department of Brunei. 2016. *US$4.7b Worth of FDI Projects in Implementation Stage.* http://www.ei.gov.bn/Lists/Industry%20News/NewDispForm.aspx?ID=263&ContentTypeId=0x0100585AA17FA637114E870034FE25016A22. Accessed April 20, 2018.

Hashim, A.A.H. 2010. Challenges in Achieving Wawasan 2035 Goals: Economic Diversification in Perspective. *CSPS Strategy and Policy Journal* 1: 29–54. Centre for Strategic and Policy Studies, Brunei Darussalam.

Hong-Huat, L. 2009. Economic Crisis, Unemployment and Training in Brunei Darussalam. *APEC Forum on Human Resource Development: Implementing Public TVET Programmes in the Midst of the Financial Crisis-HRD Policies in Collaboration with Employment Security*, Japan, 18–20 November 2009.

Ismail, N.W., P. Smith, and M. Kugler. 2009. The Effect of ASEAN Economic Integration on Foreign Direct Investment. *Journal of Economic Integration* 24 (3): 385–407.

Learning ASEAN Organization. 2015. *Brunei Will Benefit from AEC 2015.* http://learning.asean.org/news/brunei-will-benefit-from-aec-2015-36110.html. Accessed March 20, 2018.

Mahdavy, H. 1970. Patterns and Problems of Economic Development in Rentier States: The Case of Iran. In *Studies in Economic History of the Middle East*, ed. M.A. Cook, 295–315. Oxford: Oxford University Press.

Norjidi, D. 2017. Brunei Named Most Improved Economy in the World. *Borneo Bulletin*, November 1. https://borneobulletin.com.bn/brunei-named-most-improved-economy-in-the-world/. Accessed March 20, 2018.

Othman, A. 2017. *Boosting FDI, SMEs Key Growth Strategy: Sultan. Borneo Bulletin*, July 16. https://borneobulletin.com.bn/boosting-fdi-smes-key-growth-strategy-sultan/. Accessed March 20, 2018.

Oxford Business Group. 2013. *The Report: Brunei Darussalam 2012.* London: Oxford Business Group.

———. 2014. *The Report: Brunei Darussalam 2013.* London: Oxford Business Group.

Roberts, C. 2011. Brunei Darussalam: Consolidating the Foundations of Its Future? *Southeast Asian Affairs*, 33–50, Institute of Southeast Asian Studies.

Shahminan, F., and R. Thien. 2016. Brunei Deficit May Surpass $2.3b Amid Weak Oil Prices. *The Brunei Times*, January 20. http://www.bt.com.bn/frontpage-news-national/2016/01/20/brunei-deficit-may-surpass-2-3b-amid-weak-oil-prices. Accessed March 20, 2018.

Siddiqui, S.A., A.R. Athmay, and H. Mohammed. 2012. Development and Growth Through Economic Diversification: Are There Solutions for Continued Challenges Faced by Brunei Darussalam? *Journal of Economics and Behavioural Studies* 4 (7): 397–413.

The ASEAN Secretariat. 2014. *ASEAN Economic Community*. Indonesia: Association of Southeast Asian Nations.

The ASEAN Secretariat and UNCTAD. 2017. *ASEAN Investment Report 2017 Foreign Direct Investment and Economic Zones in ASEAN*. Indonesia. http://asean.org/storage/2017/11/ASEAN-Investment-Report-2017.pdf. Accessed July 1, 2018.

The World Bank. 2018. *The World Bank Data*. https://data.worldbank.org/indicator/NY.GDP.PCAP.CD?locations=BN. Accessed June 30, 2018.

Utama, N.P. 2012. A Survey on Socio-economic Development and FDI-led Strategy. *Procedia Economics and Finance* 1: 393–400. https://ac.els-cdn.com/S2212567112000457/1-s2.0-S2212567112000457-main.pdf?_tid=02dfd44d-683a-4b01-a7f9-dce03bb43635&acdnat=1526880134_f62c03bc4c042904bbcb6af33df39d02. Accessed May 20, 2018.

CHAPTER 9

Cambodia: Growth with a Red Flag

Sophal Ear and Sigfrido Burgos

Introduction

On April 17, 1975, the Khmer Rouge marched into Phnom Penh and declared an end to over 2000 years of Cambodian history. Thus began one of the most deadly and repressive social experiments, one marked by killing fields, malnutrition, and the total destruction of institutions, including the banning of money as a medium of exchange.

It is impossible to examine contemporary Cambodia without considering the incredible damage inflicted by the Khmer Rouge between 1975 and 1979. Led by Pol Pot, the Khmer Rouge emptied the urban centres of Cambodia, executed a genocidal policy and a campaign of terror that targeted the educated and urban elite. The regime instigated the evacuation of two million people from Phnom Penh over the course of three days, a

Funding for this chapter was provided by the John Parke Young Initiative on the Global Political Economy at Occidental College.

S. Ear (✉)
Occidental College, Los Angeles, CA, USA

S. Burgos
Independent Researcher (Foreign Affairs), Huntsville, AL, USA

R. Macdonald (ed.), *Southeast Asia and the ASEAN Economic Community*, https://doi.org/10.1007/978-3-030-19722-3_9

mass exodus that resulted in the death of 1.7 million Cambodians in a country with a population of only seven million over the next four years.

This is a period with which Cambodians continue to reconcile, obscured by corruption and political inference. Such conditions, coupled with the collective memory of trauma, continue to impede the peace-building process in Cambodia today.

The Khmer Rouge left their mark in the aftermath of mass atrocity crimes that have resulted in a lack of social coherence still felt in the country today, though the political landscape is no longer communist in terms of ideology. Through institutions like the Extraordinary Chambers in the Courts of Cambodia (ECCC), Cambodia's leadership has half-heartedly attempted to address the wrongdoings of Pol Pot's regime. At the national level, Cambodia's market economy has grown rapidly over the past decade, but it still lags behind in comparison to its neighbours and relies significantly on foreign aid or aid-like instruments from countries like China. In sum, Cambodia has made headway in recent years in terms of economic development, but challenges remain in spreading the wealth, and politically with a significant democratic backslide since the 2013 national elections and the 2017 commune elections. The 2018 national elections saw the main opposition party dissolved by Supreme Court order and all seats of the National Assembly going to the ruling Cambodian People's Party (CPP).

Located in Southeast Asia, Cambodia shares borders with Thailand, Laos, and Vietnam, with a relatively homogeneous population of 16 million, consisting of 90% ethnic Khmers, 5% Vietnamese, and 1% people of Chinese origin (World Services Group n.d.).

The official language of Cambodia is Khmer, with 96.3% of the population fluent in Khmer. The modern Khmer language spoken today is derived from Old Khmer, which was spoken under the Khmer Empire (802–1431). Southern Indian languages and religions had heavy influences, resulting in Old Khmer that borrowed much from Sanskrit and Pali. French was considered an important second language in Cambodia during French colonization of the early 1860s–1950s. However, since the mid-twentieth century, French influence diminished, leading to English becoming the second-most important language. Religion in Cambodia can also be traced back to the early influence of Indian culture on Cambodia: Theravada Buddhism is practised by 96.9% of the population, although other practices such as Hinduism and other forms of Buddhism are espoused by minute groups throughout the region.

Cambodia achieved its independence as a protectorate of France in 1953. However, the aforementioned decades of armed conflict, war, and genocide, including the period under the Khmer Rouge as well as violence from the Vietnam War, further destabilized the country. In 1981, Cambodia established a new constitution that was backed by the Socialist Republic of Vietnam. This was met with opposition by a coalition of three factions, which included the ousted Khmer Rouge. The coalition gained support from the United Nations and occupied Cambodia's UN seat, which brought Phnom Penh to the negotiating table. The Paris Peace Accords was signed in 1991, with the UN acting as a transitional oversight authority. By 1993, Prince Norodom Sihanouk led the coalition government and Cambodia became a multiparty liberal democracy under a constitutional monarchy, which still stands as the current form of government. King Norodom Sihamoni has been the head of state since October 2004 but does not govern; Prime Minister Hun Sen leads the cabinet and has been in power since 1985. The legislative branch follows a bicameral system with the National Assembly acting as a lower chamber and the Senate as the upper chamber. There are two main political parties in Cambodia: the CPP and the Cambodia National Rescue Party (CNRP), which was forcibly dissolved in 2018. The CPP traces its roots to 1951 with the formation of the Kampuchean People's Revolutionary Party. The CNRP was formed in 2012 as a merger between the Human Rights Party and the Sam Rainsy Party.

Cambodia consists of a three-tiered court system, with lower courts (municipal, provincial, or military courts), the Appeals Court, and the Supreme Court. This institutionalized system was established in 1982 (the Appeals Court was established later in 1992 as a result of the United Nations Transitional Authority in Cambodia). However, the judiciary is often accused of corruption due to its close association with the ruling party (Holligan and Abdulhak 2011). This is underscored by problems not just with everyday trials which are predetermined by bribes, but even at the level of the ECCC where corruption and political interference have been well documented. In a publication by the Open Society Justice Initiative from 2016, the authors observe that "The apparent ongoing government interference into the progress of Cases 003 and 004, particularly in the face of delayed and tepid responses from the UN and the international officials of the court, has an ongoing impact on the legacy and legitimacy of the entire court -well beyond Cases 003 and 004. It generates cynicism and basic distrust of the institution" (ECCC 2016).

The Economy in the Twentieth Century

In the early 1950s, as the world emerged from the ravages of the Second World War, Cambodia developed industries that produced cement, paper, plywood, processed foods, rubber tyres, and textiles. Subsequent conflicts and wars crippled many of these job-creating, growth industries, while fighting in Cambodia's rural and urban areas badly damaged primary and secondary infrastructure (i.e. bridges, roads, ports, dams, schools, and hospitals). As the economy started to recover from setbacks, the production of many of the abovementioned goods, especially garments, grew considerably beginning from the mid-1990s to today. However, despite its early successes in garment manufacturing, Cambodia still lacked big funding sources, development frameworks, and the political will to sustain the transition from agriculture to manufacturing and services. Much of the focus of Cambodia's elite remains in rent-seeking that has grown manifold with Chinese money.

Until the 1970s Cambodia's farm production was generally able to provide enough food for its own population in addition to exporting farm surpluses to neighbouring countries (such as Thailand and Vietnam). Many farms were destroyed during the Vietnam War (with France and then the US in 1957–1975) and later ravaged again by the Khmer Rouge. As a result of this destruction and the protracted rebuilding of lost capacity, the country did not regain the ability to produce enough rice for its own needs until the 1990s (in Southeast Asia, rice is a household staple). Today, Cambodia's main agricultural crops include cassava, coconuts, corn (maize), rice, rubber, sugar cane, and soybeans, in addition to value-added items, such as processed fish.

By the early 1990s, Cambodia had become "dollarized." This occurred as a result of massive dollar inflows stemming from a protracted post-conflict recovery. In 1992, following two decades of revolution and warfare, Cambodia began to normalize relations with the developed world (mainly Europe, Japan, and the US), and later with China. It started to accept large amounts of aid in the form of grants and loans from bilateral and multilateral sources such as the Asian Development Bank (ADB), the International Monetary Fund, and the World Bank, as well as from foreign government donors. It did so with the goal of becoming fully reintegrated into global trading blocs and realizing increased levels of steady economic growth, institutional modernization, and social development.

From the mid-1990s, a large percentage of Cambodia's income flows originated from manufacturing, services, exports (particularly of garments and footwear), and monetary transfers from abroad (principally remittances from migrant workers). Tourism also grew in importance owing to the country's natural resource endowments and ancient ruins, including the Great Lake (Tonlé Sap), unspoiled jungles, and the beautiful stone temples at Angkor—once the capital of the Khmer Empire. However, due to poverty, a historic dependence mindset, and underdevelopment, Cambodia still relies on external funding and technical assistance, creating dependency, especially from China (see below, Economic Priorities and International Funding). This will hopefully change as the economy grows and diversifies.

"With macroeconomic stability firmly entrenched by the time of Cambodia's accession to the [World Trade Organization] WTO in October 2004, the country embarked on the implementation of far-reaching reforms to achieve rapid and sustained socioeconomic development. International trade has been crucial to achieving this goal, as it has been the driving force behind much of Cambodia's economic growth and poverty reduction, linking its economy more firmly to regional and global markets" (WTO Secretariat 2011, p. vii). The European Union's "Everything But Arms" preferential trade scheme, which allows Cambodia to export most goods to EU member states without quotas and tariffs, has been a major contributor to the country's growth. In short, we can clearly see that Cambodia has grown in international and regional stature in the decade since 2006 (Figs. 9.1, 9.2, 9.3, and 9.4).

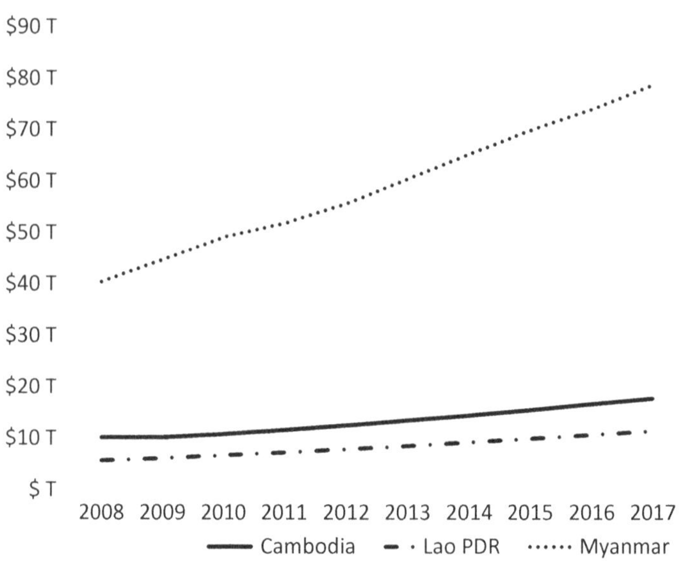

Fig. 9.1 GDP in constant US$2010. Data source: World Development Indicators, http://data.worldbank.org

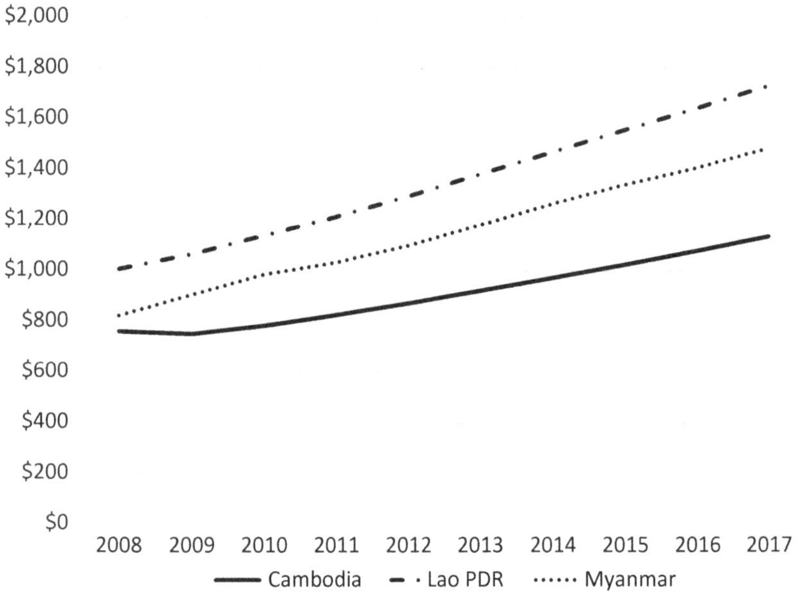

Fig. 9.2 GDP per capita. Data source: World Development Indicators, http://data.worldbank.org

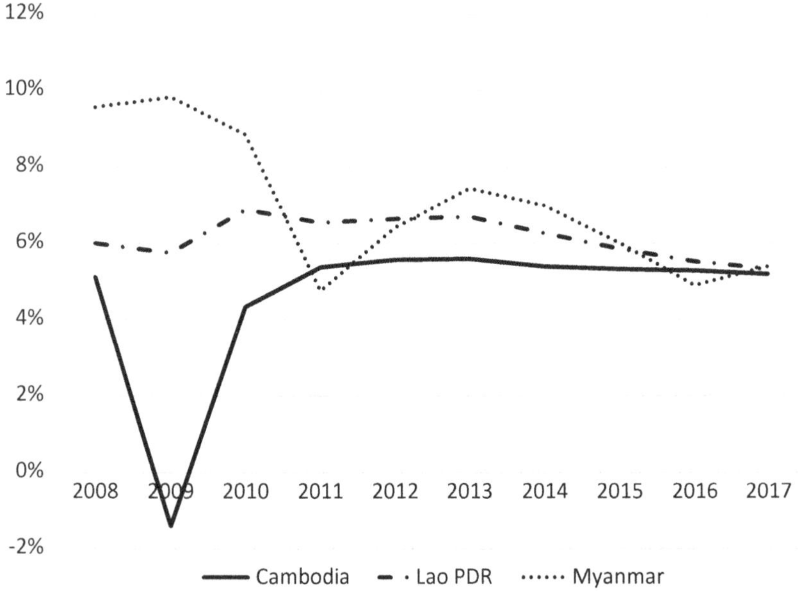

Fig. 9.3 GDP per capita growth. Data source: World Development Indicators, http://data.worldbank.org

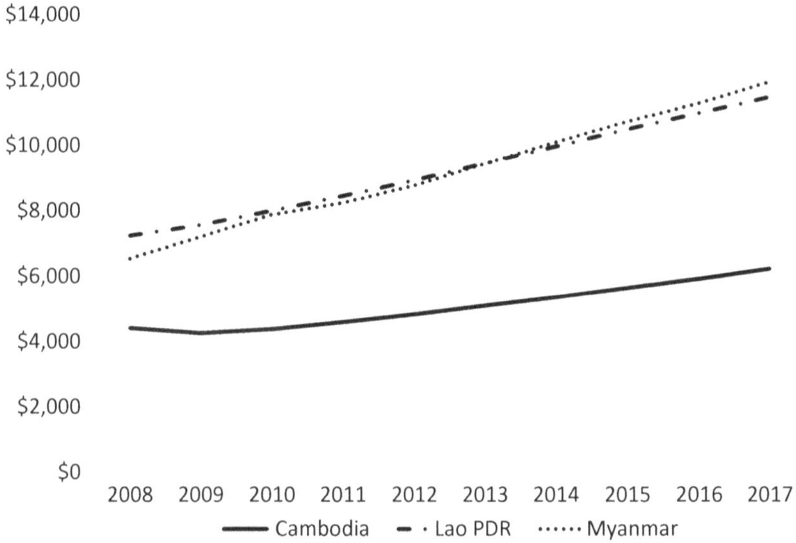

Fig. 9.4 GDP per person employed. Data source: World Development Indicators, http://data.worldbank.org

Economic Performance

"In recent years, Cambodia's economic growth has been one of the fastest among Southeast Asia's developing economies" (IMF 2015). As we see in Fig. 9.2, GDP at constant US$2010, GDP doubled between 2008 and 2017. From 1998 to 2007, the Cambodian economy grew at an average annual rate of almost 10% and, from 2010 to 2015, it averaged about 7.0% GDP growth. This robust growth has been driven by strong garments exports, real estate, and construction (IMF 2015). Analysts forecast that regional demand for goods and services as well as serious strengthening of living standards in China, Myanmar, Thailand, and Vietnam is expected to keep GDP growth steady.

"Inflation fell in 2015 and through 2016 owing to strong external disinflationary pressures from lower food and oil prices" (IMF 2015). Structures change, and the cost of locally produced goods has decreased; thus, prices have remained low and stable, whereas private sector profits have soared. For any given quarter, gross official reserves range from US$3 billion to US$6 billion, and this is believed to be enough to cover prospective imports for about four to five months. The fiscal deficit narrowed from over 8% in 2009 to less than 1% in 2017. According to the IMF, this gradual narrowing of budgetary deficits is supported by stronger revenues owing to improved enforcement in tax and customs administration as well as larger grants (IMF 2015).

Diversification of export industries and the expansion of the services sector drove economic advancement in the past decade. This advancement resulted in robust and sustained growth, which is expected of an economy transitioning away from agriculture. As agriculture falls behind, the economic transition into construction, manufacturing, heavy industry, and services signals socioeconomic progress as more jobs are available and higher incomes translate into higher living standards. Specifically, the largest source of growth is experienced within the services sector, including wholesale and retail trading, real estate services, and tourism-related services (Asian Development Bank 2014a).

However, Cambodia is primarily a farming nation. It is relatively flat and has plentiful water and fertile plains created by the flood waters of the Mekong River, the seventh largest river in Asia. Cambodia enjoys a year-round tropical climate, which makes it ideal for growing rice, fruits, and vegetables, as well as for raising livestock. The agriculture sector remains a major part of Cambodia's GDP, accounting for 44% of total employment and 25% of the GDP in 2016. Cambodia has undergone many structural economic changes transitioning the economy away from agriculture, and agriculture's contribution to GDP has decreased over the past two decades. The 2015–2025 Industrial Development Policy, which aimed to increase GDP share of the industrial sector, may be contributing to this change. Despite favourable weather conditions in 2017 as well as growth in subsectors such as livestock and fisheries, growth in agriculture is characterized by a stagnant performance as international prices for agricultural commodities remain low. It is important for Cambodia to successfully implement the 2016–2025 National Social Protection Policy Framework in order to avoid rural households based on agriculture falling back into poverty. Reduction in transportation and export costs while increasing farmer access to markets will also aid local farmers in becoming more competitive. Labour-intensive sectors, including agriculture, will continue to face challenges in jobs, income, and poverty reduction (World Bank 2017a).

By Western standards, farms are small in size. Farmers have few modern tools, use family labour (which partly explains why families are large in size), and lack contemporary inputs to increase productivity. Most farm output is consumed within the household, and any remainder is sold or traded. As a consequence, growth in the agricultural sector remains sluggish.

The principal exports are garments and footwear, which have remained steady although there is increasing competition from other low-cost producers such as Bangladesh, the Philippines, and emerging African nations. Nevertheless, the value of clothing and footwear exports may top US$8 billion in 2018, while the country claims near zero percent unemployment rate. In construction, including public and private projects, expansion and resilience remain evident—aided by the return of bullish confidence. These projects have been funded by inflows of foreign investments and with help from a rise in bank credit for the sector.

A dampening in the tourism sector as well as a visible weakening in the quantity and quality of industrial investments can be explained in part by the emergence of regional tensions (as China projects military power into the South China Sea, making neighbours nervous), the continued reports of corruption and nepotism cases, the appreciation of the US dollar, domestic political turmoil, and, in the garment industry, past labour unrest and the appearance in the market of other low-wage competitors in Southeast Asia. In terms of the country's external position, this remains stable as existing investments from high-income countries have remained operational due to significant upfront costs that have yet to be recovered.

The prolonged expansion of Cambodia's economy over the last decade has lifted gross national income per capita towards the US$1045 threshold for entry into lower-middle income status, as assessed by the World Bank (Asian Development Bank 2014a).

The incidence of individuals living in poverty has continued to decline, and this reduction can be explained by more and better jobs and rising urban incomes spilling over to rural areas. The national poverty line, at US$0.98 per person per day, is a low bar, but 13.5% of the population still lived in poverty in 2014. Recent statistics from the World Bank show three million poor people and eight million near-poor people, with 90% of these living in the countryside. Preliminary estimates also suggest that Cambodia achieved the goal of slashing poverty in half by 2010 (World Bank 2016). However, the vast majority who escaped poverty did so by a small margin, thus risking falling back if economic conditions worsen. The latest surveys and projections indicate that 0.5 million children under five years old are stunted, 12.2 million people don't have access to piped water, and 9.3 million don't have access to improved sanitation (World Bank 2016). While commendable, these figures are in line with assessments by the World Bank and the United Nations, suggesting that rural poverty remains more prevalent than urban poverty.

Talent, Human Capital, and Wages

An educated, healthy, and adequately fed labour force is essential to all economic sectors. Recent economic development is underpinned by four sectors: the garment and footwear sector, construction and real estate, tourism, and agriculture. The wage for workers in the garment and footwear industry is US$182 in 2019. Wages of unskilled workers in construction have risen to US$200 a month, a 9.2% year-on-year increase. Wages of skilled construction workers range from US$300 to 450 a month. The construction sector has played an increasingly significant source of income for workers migrating from rural to urban areas. Agricultural incomes have declined from 63% to 43% for total rural incomes, pointing towards a more diversified economy, which has driven poverty reduction. Non-agriculture income made up one-third of the total rural income, as opposed to the one-fifth in 2007 (World Bank 2017b). Overall, the minimum wage rose rapidly at an average of 17.6% per year during 2013–2017.

Increasing basic education remains a top priority as "Staying competitive by enhancing labour productivity will be key in compensating for rapidly rising real wages" (World Bank 2017b).

Cambodia is ranked 92nd out of 130 countries on World Economic Forum's "The Global Human Capital Report 2017." The importance of human capital is highlighted in the report, as "human capital is critical not only to the productivity of society but also the functioning of its political, social and civic institutions" (World Economic Forum 2017). Investment in human capital is key for Cambodia as it transitions towards a knowledge-based economy. This investment in human capital can be looked through the lens of not only employment rates in Cambodia, but also educational opportunities for Cambodian youth.

Currently, Cambodia has an unemployment rate of 0.2%. However, much of this labour is "characterized by low levels of education and skill" (Asian Development Bank 2018, p. 1). Primary education has improved in Cambodia as net enrolment in primary school in 2016 was 93.5%. Secondary school enrolment lags far behind as net enrolment in secondary schooling in 2016 was 37.1%, compared to 23.0% in 2007.

Cambodia's goal to transition from a lower middle-income country to an upper middle-income country by 2030 and eventually a developed country by 2050 has incentivized increased funding and the governmental role in improving the education sector. This is evident in the Education Strategic Plan (ESP) of 2014–2018. Implemented by the Ministry of Education, Youth and Sport (MoEYS), the project hopes to provide, "increasing focus on the expansion of Early Childhood Education, expanding access to quality secondary and post-secondary education and Non-Formal Education, Technical and Vocational Education. Specific measures will be taken to assure the education for marginalized children and youth" (MoEYS 2014). The World Bank has also supported education projects funded by the Global Partnership for Education, which granted scholarships and trained teachers, especially for early childhood education programmes.

Despite such initiatives from the Cambodian government, Cambodia faces many problems in providing basic education. The World Bank report highlights four main problems. First is the lack of access to pre-school education, which remains underfunded. Second is the large disparity in access and quality of education between regions, income groups, and gender groups. Despite the high enrolment rates, there are large performance disparities between urban and rural schools. In addition to that, the majority of the students moving into upper secondary education come from the richest income quintile that can afford education. Many families in poverty or based in the agricultural business either cannot afford to continue their children's education or children quit school in order to aid their family's business. There has been minor improvement in increased female enrolment in secondary school (female enrolment is 40.1% in 2016, as opposed to 22.2% in 2007), although there remains a large disparity between female and male literacy rate (86.5% literacy rate in males as opposed to 75.0% literacy rate in females). This disparity suggests a further gap in the classroom between male and female students. The third problem is a systemic problem in the lack of an institutionalized method of assessing student performance, which inhibits policymakers' and educational institutions' ability to make informed policy plans to improve education and hold accountability. Fourth is the lack of quality teaching in schools, particularly in rural, remote, and disadvantaged areas. (World Bank 2018). The lack of teacher training and teacher resources harms student retainment and performance rates.

Based on the age demographic of Cambodia, the present offers a wealth of potential for the labour market. A large proportion of Cambodia is of working age or getting ready to enter the labour market, yet only 37.1% are enrolled in secondary education, not to mention the single-digit enrolment in vocational training or university education. To solve these problems and take charge of the opportunity presented, the government approved the new Technical and Vocational Education and Training (TVET) Policy in 2017–2025.

Education should remain a top priority for Cambodia in order to maintain its strong economic growth. As it transitions and aims towards becoming a developed nation, it must transform its education and vocational training systems to provide a competitive labour force and increase its human capital.

Sources of Future Growth

As previously mentioned, the economy of Cambodia possesses four main sectors of growth: manufacturing (principally the garment and footwear industry), construction, tourism, and agriculture.

The manufacturing sector is mainly composed of the production of textiles and apparel articles for export. Over the first six months of 2017, it supported US$3.3 billion in exports as exports grew 5.4%. However, this was a fall from the 8.4% increase in 2016. Despite domestic rises in the minimum wage for garment workers, the price of exported garment products has been declining. Rising wages in tandem with increasing export competition led to pressure to cut costs within the textile sector while adding value to products. Initiatives have been taken, such as the Garment Training Institute in the Phnom Penh Special Economic Zone, which aim to upgrade the skills of workers while decreasing the cost of living of factory workers.

However, Cambodia must also diversify its export products and expand beyond textiles and footwear, the factories for which are predominantly owned by Greater China investors. Chinese officials have urged diversification of Cambodia's currently narrow export base (Khmer Times 2018). As Cambodia has grown more dependent on FDI, it should look towards investment in high-value manufacturing such as electrical appliances and components and auto parts. This can only happen with increased investment in electricity to the point of self-sufficiency and reexamination of electricity tariffs as well as the improvements to education mentioned above.

The construction sector is rising as the driving force behind growth and job creation. Urbanizing areas through modern high-rise commercial and residential projects propels the increased imports of fixtures, furnishing materials, and home equipment. This urbanization comes in support of the move towards increasing tourism within Cambodia. In an initiative to attract more tourists, Cambodia has attempted to urbanize areas and make them more tourist-friendly in the hope of diversifying tourist destinations. Despite these efforts, Angor Wat (the Angkor Temple) remains the most popular destination by far, consisting of 60% of the total international destination by air in 2016 (World Bank 2017a). Chinese tourism at Angkor drives much of this.

There is substantial growth potential in banking and financial intermediation, and plenty of demand remains in banking and financial services to Cambodians living on an average income in major urban centres. Such penetration may take time, as many rural migrants who have moved to cities still rely on cash and even livestock as their favoured means of saving. Nevertheless, financial penetration continues unabated, although the gap between credit and deposit growth rates has widened, thereby reducing bank liquidity. This reduction in bank liquidity has its roots in sociocultural factors, such as the banning of money under the Khmer Rouge, popular distrust of financial institutions run by corrupt politicians and their cronies, or of Chinese banks with close links to the Cambodian government. Other factors that may contribute to the increased loan to deposit ratios are, *inter alia*, those associated with firms losing revenues, inexperience in drafting business plans, poor execution of strategies, and bankruptcy.

Economic Priorities and International Funding

China's contribution to Cambodia's economic development over the past decade is indisputable. China actually invested more than did Cambodian sources in 2016. Indeed, Cambodia's Minister of Transport, Sun Chanthol, claimed that 70% of Cambodia's national roads and bridges were built under Chinese concessional loans. As quoted in Xinhua (2017), "In Cambodia, more than 2000 km of roads, seven river bridges, and a Phnom Penh Autonomous Port's new container terminal have been already built under the concessional loans from the People's Republic of China,"

Chanthol said, for a total of US$2 billion, while another four road and bridge projects were under construction with Chinese loans. The proportion of Cambodia's debt owed to China is unclear, by some estimates US$4 billion or 40% of Cambodia's public debt, exceeding the combined multilateral debt Cambodia owes to the World Bank and the Asian Development Bank. Meanwhile, "China is the biggest investor in Cambodia, accounting for up to 44% of the $19.2 billion in foreign direct investment between 1994 and 2014, according to the National Bank of Cambodia and the National Institute of Statistics" (Vannarin 2018).

The Cambodian government has lined up the support of banks, donors, and other economic partners to develop five areas that have been identified as priorities: transport (rural and provincial roads, including bridges, pavements, and access to farmlands); water supply, sanitation, and urban development (three factors that together ensure adult and infant health targets are achieved); agriculture and natural resources (the commercialization of agriculture, and irrigation support, including reforestation and sustainable management); education (primary, secondary, and tertiary education and vocational training); and finance (banking regulation, small and medium-sized enterprise finance, microfinance, and insurance) (IMF 2015). Clearly, these areas require long-term commitment and sustained government support, but in the development stage where Cambodia currently finds itself, it is possible to identify positive outcomes arising in the short term, especially in improving the economic and social environment.

As the aforementioned priorities move forward in time, the economic prospects for Cambodia will improve. Any growth strategy must be linked to a sober public sector management approach as a facilitating factor, covering public financial management, decentralization and de-concentration (i.e. legislating efforts to move away from monopolies and unproductive activities), anti-corruption measures, and capacity development (i.e. educating and training) (Bullen 2012). This is particularly important for the country, given that investors and the international community generally perceive Cambodia as corrupt and a place where the rule of law is flouted. A reinforcement of public sector management, combined with pragmatism and utilitarianism, can also be of support to Cambodia's critical challenges: both external and internal (e.g. aid usage, climate change, decentralization, rural-urban linkages, and regional co-operation). For any given country, an inclusive growth strategy should also incorporate five key interlinking themes: private sector development, good governance, gender equity, knowledge solutions, and true partnerships (IMF 2015).

Cambodia is continuing to expand and upgrade its physical infrastructure. The government is currently working on projects to improve road surfaces, manage fisheries, improve livelihoods from agriculture in targeted areas in rural communities, and increase access to health care (World Bank 2016). Not surprisingly, development partners' funding is still mostly focused on reducing poverty and improving the living conditions of poor and vulnerable Cambodians, both in rural and in urban settings (World Bank 2016). Evidently, efforts should stay in place to find creative ways to sustain productivity growth in the private sector, which is key to the manufacturing and industry and ultimately beneficial to the government as it tries to expand the revenue base for broad social programmes. For instance, as low-income farmers become more productive, they would use the increased earnings from the sale of surplus to buy a variety of goods and pay their children's school fees. These downstream effects, for the most part, are palpable improvements in many Cambodian households, and these feelings of doing better than the year before incentivize citizens to work harder and longer to achieve their aspirations.

Presently, the Cambodian government is working with the international community to help cover the costs of health services for the country's millions of poor people, reducing their out-of-pocket expenses and providing low-cost, long-term loans to build health facilities (World Bank 2016). Additionally, funds are being allocated to strengthen monitoring and evaluation of reliable health parameters, as well as pushing for sustained improvements to the quality of health services offered. The integrated water resource management of the Mekong River aims to improve sustainable management of water resources and fisheries and helps reduce chronic rural poverty along the basin in north-eastern Cambodia (World Bank 2016). As previous infrastructure development projects continue to be used and exploited, funds are being deployed to manage and maintain roads between major commerce centres. This maintenance work is intended to make the roads resilient to seasonal flooding, shortening vehicle travel times and providing better connectivity along national road corridors (World Bank 2016).

More generally, and in line with long-term development priorities, local banks and other financial institutions are working directly with donors to address the needs of urban and rural Cambodians, as well as to address the ever-increasing financing requirements of micro-, small and medium-sized enterprises (MSMEs) in the country. This direct financial assistance boosts economic prospects because it enhances the access of

MSMEs to longer-term finance, which in turn is critical to support poverty alleviation through income and employment generation in rural areas, where about 80% of Cambodia's poor live (Asian Development Bank 2014b). Under this inclusive approach, everybody wins: the government generates income through duties, fees, services, and taxes; the private sector satisfies its need for low-cost financing; and the people enjoy better financial services along with increased job opportunities and lower obstacles to succeed.

Hard and Soft Infrastructure for Business

The government implemented a project to decentralize rural sanitation service delivery to strengthen the capacity of districts to administer services in the provinces. Also, the improved management of roads has helped reduce travel from 2 hours to 1.5 hours per 100 kilometres (World Bank 2018). These gains run hand in hand with simplification of import and export procedures and border processes as part of an effort to improve its integration into regional and global markets. For example, between 2010 and 2015, customs clearance dropped from 6 to 1.5 days, which is a logistical accomplishment much appreciated by the private sector (World Bank 2018).

In cities throughout Cambodia, recent gains in peripheral public services are evident. For example, today, 40 provincial offices operate to provide construction permits, vehicle tags and plates, small business licenses, and motorcycle registration, among other services. Also, management of public finances now includes key achievements such as improved revenue generation capacity, debt sustainability, almost complete use of the banking system for government transactions, and modern information systems to facilitate payment and accuracy of financial reporting. These achievements are important to underscore given that they serve as stepping stones to further gains in other areas of the economy (World Bank 2018).

Cambodia's economic freedom score is 58.7 according to the Heritage Foundation's annual Economic Freedom Index, which ranks it at 101 for the year 2018. This marks a decrease from its 94th spot in 2017 with a 0.8 percentage point decrease in score. Among its Asia-Pacific neighbours, Cambodia is ranked 22nd out of 43 countries, with its overall score lying below both the regional and world averages. The score decrease comes from decline in property rights, labour freedom, and fiscal health. The social and political unrest from the Khmer Rouge led to lack of legal documentation of property ownerships, which were only complicated as government corruption led to farmers being taken advantage of or losing land all together. Labour freedom can be sourced to the lack of quality education. Despite wide primary school enrolment, secondary school enrolment took a sharp turn downwards. The Cambodian labour force is characterized by unskilled, uneducated, labour-intensive work as the garment and construction industries are becoming more important to Cambodia's economy. However, Cambodia has shown improvement in government integrity. The effects of the lack of property rights and systematized education are only amplified by pervasive corruption within the government and continue to constrain economic freedom. IMF 2015 enumerates several areas needing reform. Changes in property rights and education require long-term strategies and policy developments. The study highlights the need for a truly independent judiciary system in order to fully improve the judicial system. Despite this, Cambodia has been noted for improvement in government integrity. Over the past few years, Cambodia has increased in regulatory efficiency from which entrepreneurs have benefited. Still, Cambodia's economy is heavily dependent on trade and the financial system remains influenced by the ruling party (Heritage Foundation 2018, pp. 128–129).

Conclusions

The solid economic growth that Cambodia has experienced during the first 18 years of the twenty-first century has facilitated the creation of employment opportunities, which in turn has contributed to the decline in poverty—albeit narrowly defined as 98 cents per person per day. As a result of foreign, especially Chinese, investment in manufacturing, tourism, real estate, and new industries, the country has managed to make further progress in reducing poverty rates and increasing family incomes.

Cambodia has shown some growth and improvement for all, but based on an unstable foundation of corrupt government financed by China. There is great potential for return on investment hampered by the insecurity of that investment. The garment sector is a prime example—it has benefitted Cambodia tremendously, thanks to preferential trade agreements; however, much of the sector is now at risk as garment buyers cut back on purchases and investment shrinks.

Provided Everything But Arms from the EU is not suspended as has been warned, due to Cambodia's democratic backsliding, and the threat of Generalized System of Preferences suspension from the United States remains only a threat, the trajectory of Cambodia's economy remains strong. The warning signs, however, have been ignored for too long—Cambodia returned to the Financial Action Task Force's grey list of countries vulnerable to money laundering and terrorism financing. The number of casinos in Cambodia now exceeds Las Vegas and Macau combined.

Moving forward, focus will be directed to regional trade development, adaptation to climatic changes, educational and health improvements, and social protection schemes. To this end, the government aims to improve public financial management by strengthening the mobilization of public and human resources, the management of public institutions, implementing external audits; and to promote diversification in the manufacturing sector, Cambodia is expected to expand and sustain growth in construction, tourism, services, and agriculture.

References

Asian Development Bank. 2014a. *Asian Development Outlook 2014: Fiscal Policy for Inclusive Growth.* Mandaluyong City, Philippines: Asian Development Bank.

———. 2014b. Cambodia Needs Broader Economic Base to Sustain Growth. http://www.adb.org/az/node/150997&favtitle=Cambodia%20Needs%20Broader%20Economic%20Base%20to%20Sustain%20Growth%20%E2%80%93%20ADB%20Report. Accessed March 7, 2019.

———. 2018, February. *Toward Adopting a Skills Development Fund for Cambodia.* No. 90. https://think-asia.org/bitstream/handle/11540/8031/adb-brief-090-skills-development-fund-cambodia.pdf?sequence=1. Accessed March 7, 2019.

Bullen, Darryl. 2012. *Village Self-Reliance Review Cambodia.* Asia Refuge Projects. 37. http://leap201.org/wp-content/uploads/2014/09/Leap201-Cambodia-Village-Self-Reliance-Review-2012.pdf. Accessed March 7, 2019.

ECCC. 2016. *Extraordinary Chambers in the Courts of Cambodia.* May 12, https://www.eccc.gov.kh/sites/default/files/documents/court-doc/2016-05-17%2000:26/D198_EN.PDF. Accessed March 7, 2019.

Heritage Foundation. 2018. *2018 Index of Economic Freedom.* https://www.heritage.org/index/pdf/2018/countries/cambodia.pdf. Accessed March 7, 2019.

Holligan, Jennifer, and Tarik Abdulhak. 2011, April. *Overview of the Cambodian History, Governance, and Legal Sources.* Hauser Global Law Program. http://www.nyulawglobal.org/globalex/Cambodia.html#judicialbranch. Accessed March 7, 2019.

IMF. 2015. Cambodia: 2015 Article IV Consultation—Press Release; Staff Report; and Statement by the Executive Director for Cambodia IMF Country Report No. 15/307. International Monetary Fund. http://www.imf.org/external/pubs/ft/scr/2014/cr1433.pdf. Accessed March 7, 2019.

Khmer Times. 2018, November 7. *Cambodia Must Diversify Its Export Base, Says Chinese Official.* https://www.khmertimeskh.com/50547890/cambodia-must-diversify-its-export-base-says-chinese-official/. Accessed March 7, 2019.

MoEYS. 2014, March. *Ministry of Education, Youth, and Sport Education Strategic Plan 2014–2018.* http://www.moeys.gov.kh/images/moeys/policies-and-strategies/559-en.pdf. Accessed March 7, 2019.

Vannarin, Neou. 2018, July 20. *Friends with Benefits. Voice of America.* https://projects.voanews.com/cambodia-election-2018/english/feature/chinese-influence.html. Accessed March 7, 2019.

World Bank. 2016, June 9. *Cambodia and World Bank Expand Development Engagement to Reduce Poverty and Share Prosperity.* http://www.worldbank.org/en/news/press-release/2016/06/09/cambodia-and-world-bank-expand-development-engagement. Accessed March 7, 2019.

———. 2017a, October. *Cambodia Climbing Up the Manufacturing Value Chain.* http://documents.worldbank.org/curated/en/628341511277852360/pdf/121519-WP-PUBLIC-NOV21-7PM-October-2017-Cambodia-Economic-Update-Final.pdf. Accessed March 7, 2019.

———. 2017b, April. *Cambodia Economic Update.* http://documents.worldbank.org/curated/en/780641494510994888/pdf/114938-PUBLIC-may-16-8pm-Cambodia-Economic-report-v2-s.pdf. Accessed March 7, 2019.

———. 2018, September 27. *Country Overview: Cambodia.* http://www.worldbank.org/en/country/cambodia/overview. Accessed March 7, 2019.

World Economic Forum. 2017. The Global Human Capital Report 2017. http://www3.weforum.org/docs/WEF_Global_Human_Capital_Report_2017.pdf. Accessed March 7, 2019.

World Services Group. n.d. *Cambodia Business Guide.* https://www.worldservicesgroup.com/countries.asp?c=cb&country=Cambodia#people. Accessed March 7, 2019.

WTO Secretariat. 2011. *Trade Policy Review: Cambodia WT/TPR/S/253.* World Trade Organization. https://www.wto.org/english/tratop_e/tpr_e/s253_sum_e.pdf. Accessed March 7, 2019.

Xinhua. 2017, July 21. *70 pct of Roads, Bridges in Cambodia Built Under Chinese Support: Transport Minister.* http://www.xinhuanet.com/english/2017-07/21/c_136461623.htm. Accessed March 7, 2019.

CHAPTER 10

Laos in Need of Bolder Reforms for AEC Integration

Buavanh Vilavong

Introduction

Laos is the only landlocked nation in Southeast Asia. Because of this, the country faces development challenges due to high trade costs even though it is well endowed with natural resources. To overcome its landlocked status, Laos has embraced a process of opening up to the international economy. Economic liberalisation that started in the mid-1980s and the accompanying domestic reforms have paid off with a remarkable turnaround in its economic performance. As such, Laos has been among the fastest growing economies in the Association of Southeast Asia Nations (ASEAN).

However, recent growth is still driven by a narrow economic base dominated by natural resources and low-productivity agriculture. A major challenge for Laos is to continue to sustain development by opening up more of the economy to international competition while managing the process of structural change. Doing so will help sustain growth across a diversity of sectors and create jobs for a larger proportion of population.

B. Vilavong (✉)
Department of Industry and Handicraft,
Ministry of Industry and Commerce, Vientiane, Laos
e-mail: b.vilavong@moic.gov.la

R. Macdonald (ed.), *Southeast Asia and the ASEAN Economic Community*, https://doi.org/10.1007/978-3-030-19722-3_10

The ASEAN Economic Community (AEC), which commenced in January 2016, presents new opportunities for Laos, but it also underlines significant challenges. Laos has long been a country of promise given its resources and geographical location in Southeast Asia. Yet, despite relatively high growth in recent decades, the country remains among the world's poorest nations. Laos is a least developed country (LDC), and the goal to graduate from the LDC status presents a pressing need to explore how the country can sustain its current growth path and ensure sustainable and inclusive development.[1] Given this backdrop, this study seeks to assess how well Laos has performed following its economic integration and what the country needs to do to realise its potential in the face of the AEC.

The chapter proceeds as follows. The first section, recent developments in economic integration, provides a historical context for the recent economic integration that Laos has undertaken, while the next section tracks the country's economic performance. Economic reforms led not only to economic growth but also to structural change and a rising role of resources in the production and export base. Then follow discussions about some challenges and how Laos can move forward. The final section concludes.

Recent Developments in Economic Integration

Laos launched the 'New Economic Mechanism' (NEM) in 1986, aiming to transform the economy from one based on subsistence farming to a commercialised economy. The economic reforms fell into two phases. In the first period between 1986 and 1999, restrictions in domestic and foreign trade were eased and price controls were also liberalised (Douangboupha 2010). The reform and restructuring of state-owned enterprises commenced. The number of these enterprises fell from around 800 in the 1990s to 37 enterprises in 2002. Most state-owned enterprises that were privatised in the 1990s include those in service sectors such as telecoms, transport, insurance, real estate, and tourism (World Trade Organization 2012).

The tariff structure was simplified, and tariff rates were reduced following a major reform in 1995. Previously, there were 12 tariff bands, ranging from 5% to 100%. The top rate was lowered to 40% and the number of bands reduced to six: 5%, 10%, 15%, 20%, 30%, and 40%. Higher import tariffs were generally applied to agricultural products higher than to industrial products. Low tariffs (10% or less) were set on imported raw materials and agricultural inputs. The highest rate (40%) was applied to luxury goods, including alcohol and perfumes, as well as manufactured products (World Bank 2006).

Domestic reforms were temporarily stalled by the interrelated events that resulted in serious macroeconomic problems in Laos at the time of the 1997 Asian Financial Crisis. There was a short-term loss of macroeconomic control with a brief period of hyperinflation and a substantial depreciation in the nominal exchange rate. The exchange rate collapsed and economic contraction in other Asian economies put the reform momentum of Laos on hold.

The second phase of reforms resumed after Laos was able to restore macroeconomic stability in 2000. These reforms included further trade liberalisation, foreign exchange deregulation, and investment liberalisation. This has resulted in the gradual transformation of the Lao economy from a centrally planned system to a more open, market-driven one (Douangboupha 2010). The short period of central planning has mitigated the transition to a market economy. The smooth transition is attributed to geographical location, where the success of nearby Vietnam had a positive demonstration effect, and Laos was able to take advantage of the superior transport infrastructure of neighbouring countries (Bird and Hill 2010).

In the area of trade liberalisation, the priority was on integration into the regional and global economy. The economic liberalisation of Laos is, to a large extent, shaped by Laos' membership in ASEAN and its accession to the World Trade Organization (WTO).

From ASEAN to the ASEAN Economic Community

Laos joined ASEAN in July 1997. Under the ASEAN Free Trade Area (AFTA), the country committed to eliminate import duties on 96.3% of all products by 2018. Some products (such as fuels, automobiles, and alcoholic beverages), which had significant revenue effects, were phased in between 2015 and 2018. Laos maintains 87 tariff lines (such as arms, ammunition, and drugs) under the general exception list, which is not subject to any tariff reductions.

Apart from trade in goods, Laos is also a member of the ASEAN Framework Agreement on Services (AFAS). The AFAS sets out specific targets for lifting substantially all restrictions on trade in services: by 2010 for four priority sectors (air transport, computer and telecoms, healthcare, and tourism services), by 2013 for logistics services, and by 2015 for all other services sectors. By the end of 2015, nine AFAS packages were concluded. Laos liberalised 92 service subsectors out of the total of around 160 subsectors. By comparison, Cambodia made commitments in 94 sectors and Vietnam in 99 sectors (ASEAN Secretariat 2015b). Laos put forward the tenth package of AFAS in mid-2017, which raised sectoral coverage to 110 service subsectors.[2]

The AEC Blueprint sets a vision for the ASEAN region to become highly intra-regional integrated, competitive, and dynamic, with enhanced connectivity and integration with the global economy by 2025 (ASEAN Secretariat 2015a). Laos has been on track in implementing its AEC commitments, notably in cutting tariffs and creating the ASEAN trade repository through an online trade portal (Vilavong and Hess 2016). As of January 2017, 89.3% of Laos' products were zero, 7% were less than 5%, and the remainder were at 5%.[3] As the remaining tariff reductions are phased in, Laos is anticipated to lose considerable customs revenue. The government has therefore tried to shift its revenue base from import tariffs, in particular from vehicles and other luxury imports, to value-added and excise taxes. Lowering import duties is expected to help improve the efficiency of firms utilising imported inputs as well as benefit consumers through lower prices and allowing more choices.

Regional Connectivity to Overcome Landlocked Status

Laos has leveraged its geopolitical situation to transform the country's position from being 'landlocked' to 'land linked'. The construction of the Lao-Chinese railway began in December 2016. The cost of this mega-project is expected to reach US$6 billion (The Economist Intelligence Unit 2017b). This 427-kilometre railway link is expected to be finished by 2021 and will form part of the Kunming-Singapore rail route (Vilavong 2016). Laos is also working with Vietnam to prioritise the construction of a 600-kilometre rail link between its capital Vientiane and Vietnam's seaport Vung Ang. This project aims to improve Laos' access to the sea. Both countries also plan to construct a six-lane highway to connect their two capitals (The Economist Intelligence Unit 2017a).

These projects add to the regional connectedness efforts that Laos has already made with Thailand and Myanmar. The first Lao-Thai Friendship Bridge began operations in 1994. Four international bridges over the Mekong now connect Vientiane and other economically important cities of Laos to Thailand. Laos also opened its first friendship bridge with Myanmar in May 2015 (Vilavong 2018).

Better connectivity is expected to accelerate the integration of Laos into the region. This facilitates the country's access to the market of 600 million people in ASEAN and still larger markets when the regional trade agreements between ASEAN and dialogue partners are fully implemented.[4]

Accession to the World Trade Organization

Laos applied to join the WTO in 1997, the same year that it was admitted into ASEAN. The country took 15 years to complete the accession process and became a full member of the WTO in February 2013. Market access appears not to be a key concern for Laos in joining the WTO as it already has preferential access to a large number of markets. As a least developed country, Laos benefits from duty-free access to most developed country markets (such as Australia, Canada, the European Union, and Japan) along with some developing countries (such as China, India, and Russia).[5] Laos' expectations of WTO membership have therefore to do with access to the rules-based trading system of non-discrimination and predictability as well as locking-in the country's internal reforms (Pholsena and Vilavong 2015).

Thus, tangible benefits are expected to be derived from further and deeper integration into the regional economy given the intensity of trade and foreign investment that Laos has with its neighbouring countries. ASEAN countries are foreseeing to move closer together, economically following fuller integration under the AEC. Deeper regional integration, especially within ASEAN and with ASEAN dialogue partners, should provide more opportunities for Laos to further grow and diversify its economic base. Some sectors in which the country may gain stronger comparative advantage include agro-processing (particularly from tea and coffee), hydropower generation, mining, and assembly of machinery and electronics components (MPI and UNDP 2017).

Economic Performance

Laos has made tremendous efforts to integrate into the external economy while beginning to reap the benefits of economic growth and increased openness. Despite impressive economic progress, Laos remains dependent on a narrow range of export products and destinations. Key economic performance indicators are reviewed below.

Growth and Structural Change

The successes of market reforms were evident with an average growth rate of 7.5% since 2000 following the second phase of economic reforms. Laos is among the fastest growing economies in ASEAN (Asian Development Bank 2017). This has also been supported by two resource booms. The economic growth was initially powered by a mining boom in the early to mid-2000s. Since the late 2000s, strong expansion in hydropower development and associated construction activities has driven output growth (World Bank 2017a). The twin booms were estimated to contribute around three percentage points of economic growth and roughly 15% of total government revenue (Bird and Hill 2010).

Overall growth has been accompanied by structural change that has gradually shifted the economy away from agriculture. As shown in Fig. 10.1, agricultural value added in gross domestic product (GDP) declined from 45.2% in 2000 to 19.5% in 2016. Over the same period, an industrial value-added share increased from 16.6% to 32.5% of GDP, which was mainly driven by manufacturing output growth. Likewise, the share of services rose from 38.2% to almost 48% between 2000 and 2016, thanks to strong growth in tourism along with foreign investment inflows into the financial and distribution sectors.

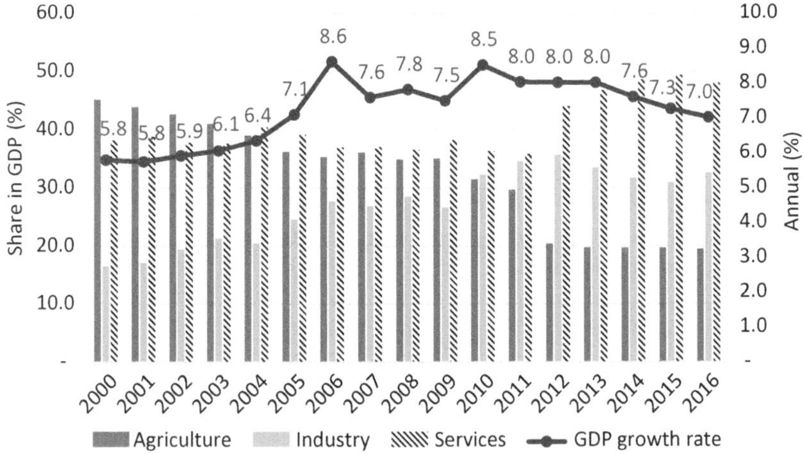

Fig. 10.1 GDP Growth and Composition, 2000–2016. Source: Author's calculations from the World Bank's Development Indicators

Despite its growing share, manufacturing still has weak backward linkages, especially with the service sector. Inadequate supply of financial and telecoms services (representing only 3% of total service inputs to manufacturing) may be an important constraint on the diversification and upgrading of manufacturing firms, inhibiting them from moving up the value chain (MPI and UNDP 2017). Region wise, domestic value added (49%) in manufacturing exports from Laos is below the levels in other countries such as Cambodia (76%), Thailand (80%), and Vietnam (64%).[6]

Between 2000 and 2011, gross national income (GNI) per capita rose substantially from US$280 to US$1120.[7] In 2011, Laos was upgraded from a lower-income economy to a lower middle-income economy under the World Bank's country classification. The GNI per capita further soared to US$2150 in 2016. A review by the United Nations in 2018 confirms that Laos has passed the thresholds for GNI per capita and for the human assets index (UNDP 2018). However, the economic vulnerability index is still to be fulfilled. If Laos meets the criteria again in the 2021 review, it will be officially removed from the list of least developed countries by 2024. Additionally, Laos has also cut the poverty headcount ratio from 39.1 in 1997 to 23.2 in 2012 (MOIC 2012).

In 2017, the Lao economy is expected to moderate to 6.7%, below historical averages (World Bank 2017b). Recent growth was underpinned by the strong increase in the contribution of hydropower development as well as from manufacturing. But it was partly offset by slight moderation in construction, flat output in the mining sector, and decreasing public spending.

Looking forward, economic prospects for Laos are projected to remain favourable over the years to come.[8] This is because of the vigorous pipeline of hydropower development projects and expanding opportunities for the non-resource sector likely to result from further integration into the AEC and the government's efforts to improve the investment climate. Around 20 hydropower dams are at different stages of construction with around 600 megawatts of electricity capacity estimated to be in operation by 2020. This is expected to both stimulate the Lao economy and raise electricity exports to neighbouring Thailand (World Bank 2017b).

Hydropower and mining are increasingly important aspects of the Lao economy. The country is among the most resource-rich economies in Asia, with significant mineral deposits (per capita), including gold, copper, zinc, and lead (PwC Laos 2012). The manufacturing sector remains primarily focused on garments and is expanding into simple assembling of electronics components, automotive wire harnesses, and other labour-intensive manufacturing. Laos' low population density and large markets for agricultural produces and livestock in neighbouring countries have brought new investors to explore investment opportunities in the agricultural sector (U.S. Commercial Service 2017). Laos also promotes tourism as a key area of future growth, with a 'Visit Laos Year 2018' campaign being launched.

The Growing Importance of Resource-Based Exports

Trade has acted as the primary driver of growth in the small landlocked economy of Laos. Merchandise trade has expanded 16.3% annually on average between 2000 and 2016. However, overall trade openness remains quite limited compared to other countries in East Asia and the Pacific. Laos' exports averaged 33% of GDP for the period 1999–2012 but this trade share in GDP remains relatively low compared with other countries in the region (Record et al. 2014).

Laos' trade is increasingly dominated by resource-based exports. Agricultural products used to be the country's main export items before being overtaken by minerals and electricity. The share of agricultural products fell from 39.2% of total exports in 2000 to 19.8% in 2016. Similarly, a manufactured export share declined from 57.1% to 22.3% over the same period. On the contrary, the export shares of ores and metals and fuels (electricity) rose rapidly, constituting, respectively, 21.6% and 24.7% of total exports in 2016 (see Fig. 10.2).

As for imports, manufactured products accounted for around two-thirds of the total, followed by agricultural products (18%) and fuels (12%) in 2016.[9] Within manufacturing, automobiles and electronics made up 16% and 12% of total imports, respectively. The recent growth in the importance of transport equipment, fuels, and machinery reflects the development of hydropower dams and transport infrastructure in Laos.

Concentration of Trade with Very Few Trading Partners

Thailand, China, and Vietnam account for 82.3% of Laos' total exports. As shown in Fig. 10.3, Thailand was the largest destination in 2016, with an export share of 40.1%, followed by China (28.5%) and Vietnam (13.7%). Other important export markets include India, Japan, Germany, Switzerland, and the United States. Vietnam used to be the largest market for Laos' exports in 2000, followed by Thailand and Germany.

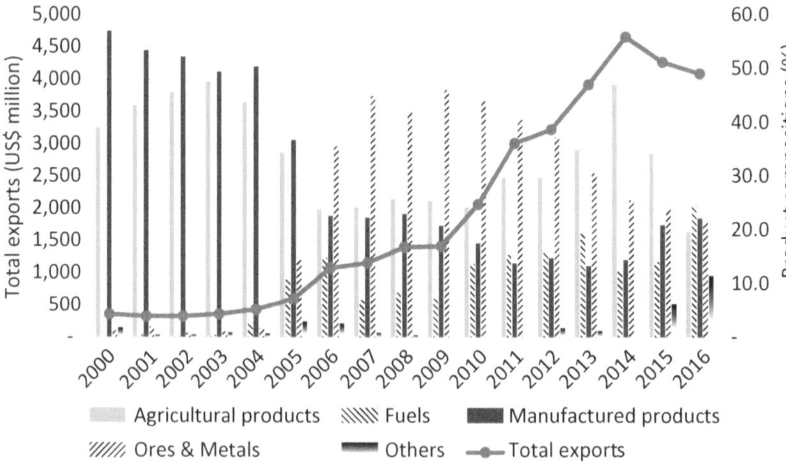

Fig. 10.2 Exports from Laos by Product Composition, 2000–2016. Note: Agricultural products (SITC 0+1+2–27–28+4), fuels (SITC 3), manufactured products (SITC 5+6–68+7+8+9), and ores and metals (SITC 27+28+68). Source: Author's calculations from UN Comtrade, using partner-reported data

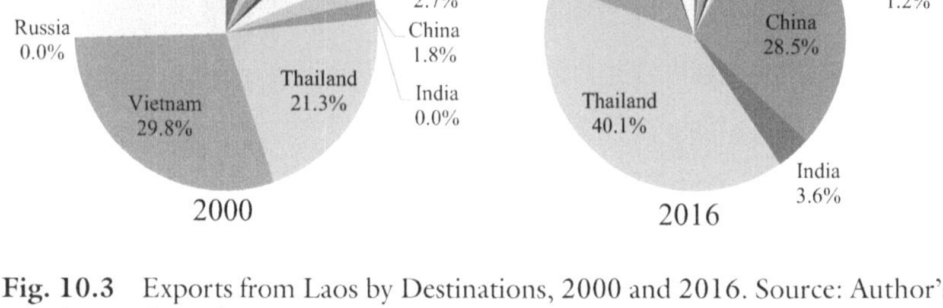

Fig. 10.3 Exports from Laos by Destinations, 2000 and 2016. Source: Author's calculations from the IMF's Direction of Trade

In terms of importation, almost 62% of imports were sourced from Thailand in 2000 while imports from Vietnam accounted for around 11% and China 6%. In 2016, Thailand was still the dominant source of imports, accounting for approximately 65% of Laos' total imports, followed by China and Vietnam with shares of around 16.5% and 9.4%, respectively. Other key import sources included South Korea, Japan, Singapore, Germany, and the United States (see Fig. 10.4).

Laos Participating in Labour-Intensive Production Sharing

The processes of manufacturing are geographically dispersed worldwide to take advantage of cost differentials across economies. This has resulted in the internationalisation of production sharing, in which countries participate in different stages of international production (Jones and Kierzkowski 1990). ASEAN members are among the economies that have emerged as dominant centres in global production sharing (Athukorala and Kohpaiboon 2013).

The participation of Laos in global production sharing had a humble start in garment manufacturing since the mid-1980s when Laos began to open up to the external economy. Over the years, this sector has contributed considerably to the Lao economy in terms of export earnings and

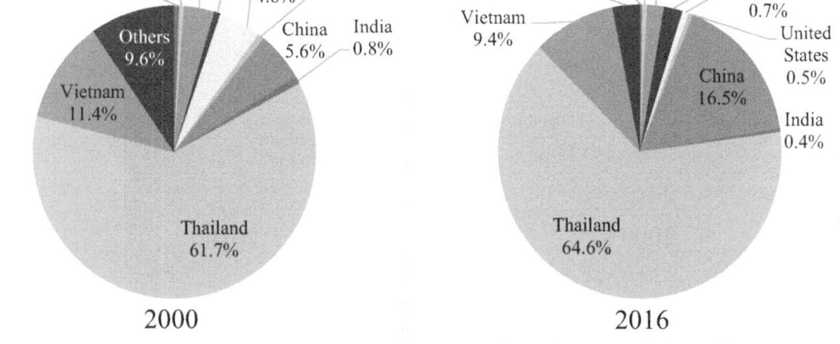

Fig. 10.4 Imports to Laos by Sources, 2000 and 2016. Source: Author's calculations from the IMF's Direction of Trade

manufacturing employment. Garments contributed 12.6% of manufacturing value added in Laos during the period 2005–2012 (Nolintha and Jajri 2015).

Later on, Laos started to attract foreign investment into non-garment manufacturing. This included companies assembling electronics components (such as Dai-ichi Denshi, Mitsubishi Materials, and Kitani), automotive wire harnesses (Daiwa and Toyota), camera parts (Nikon), and lens polishing (Essilor). Most of them started to invest in Laos after 2010 and concentrated investment in special economic zones in Vientiane, Savannakhet, and Champasack. This has resulted in rapid growth in parts and components assembly and exports in other labour-intensive manufacturing, overtaking the garment sector.

Some Challenges and the Way Forward

Laos has taken major steps towards outward-looking policy orientation since the mid-1980s. This has also been intended to enhance economic interaction with the international economy, which in turn helps support high levels of trade and economic growth. Despite impressive progress, Laos remains dependent on a narrow range of export products and destinations. Going forward, the AEC will lead to increased competition for Lao businesses combined with an uncertain global economic outlook at present.

Transforming Resource Wealth for Sustainable Development

One of the chief challenges for Laos is to transform natural resources into productive capital so that once such resource wealth is exhausted, there are other income-generating assets to take their place. More than half of Laos' wealth is in the form of natural resource assets (water, agricultural land, forests, and minerals). Overall, total wealth in Laos has been estimated to be around US$10,000 per capita. This is higher than in Mongolia or Vietnam, measured on a per capita basis. Nevertheless, physical capital accounts for only 9% of the country's wealth, which is markedly below the 17% average for low-income economies (World Bank 2010a). Therefore, transforming some of these natural resources into productive investments would benefit growth and long-term development prospects for Laos.

To achieve this objective, the revenues generated from resource exploitation need to be effectively managed. Development experience has shown that different sustainability strategies yield different outcomes in many countries. Vietnam, for instance, has been able to maintain a high savings rate while utilising a large amount of resources to maintain a high growth rate. In contrast, the savings rate of Zimbabwe became negative whereas the depletion of its resource wealth failed to generate growth (World Bank 2010a). For Laos, the government may consider diverting export revenues from natural resources into growth-enhancing investments. Such interventions should be in the form of delivery of public goods such as core infrastructure and skills training.

Supporting the Non-resource Sector for Broad-Based Growth

Economic growth in Laos in recent decades has been driven largely by natural resources. The contribution of mining and hydropower is expected to reach one-quarter of GDP by 2020, implying that the non-resource sector contributes the remaining 75% (Lord 2011). The fast-growing development of mining and hydropower projects employs only 1% of the total workforce. This suggests that the recent growth has not been broad based. Although the share of agriculture in national output has declined considerably, its importance in terms of employment remains significant as labour in the agricultural sector only lowered from 71.3% to 65.2% over the same period. The employment shares of the manufacturing and service sectors were 11.4% and 23.4% in 2015 (MPI 2016).

Therefore, the non-resource sector remains a vital contributor to employment and inclusive development. Expansion in agricultural production and exports is important given the significant share of this sector in employment. Manufacturing expansion is also expected to create job opportunities, especially for labour-intensive activities. Laos has already been engaged in regional production sharing in food processing and garments. It has also begun to tap into other elements of labour-intensive assembly such as electronics components, lens polishing, and automotive wire harnesses, as discussed above.

Boosting growth outside the resource sector will require a vibrant private sector. Despite ongoing domestic reforms, Laos is still ranked poorly in terms of doing business and economic freedom. It was ranked 139th out of 190 economies in the 2017 Doing Business Survey, reflecting weak and inconsistent law enforcement along with burdensome procedures.[10] In starting a business, for example, it takes entrepreneurs 67 days to complete enterprise registration in Laos, compared with 24 days on average in

East Asia and the Pacific. In the same vein, the time spent on complying with export requirements in Laos is as high as 216 hours whereas only 73 hours is needed on the regional average. Such delays may be partly attributed to Laos being a landlocked country, but policy barriers also play a substantial role. Laos scored 6.98 out of 10 on economic freedom in 2015, making it the 75th place compared to Cambodia and Myanmar that were rank 63rd and 151st, respectively.[11]

In addition, enterprise surveys conducted by the World Bank found that firms in Laos complained much more about tax rates in 2016 than in 2012. The Lao firms interviewed were more frequently visited by tax officials and the visits lasted longer compared to the East Asia and Pacific average (World Bank 2017a). This may be partly prompted by strengthened enforcement of tax collection against the backdrop of a shortfall in government revenue collection. Laos needs to continue domestic reform efforts with a greater focus on addressing these problems.

To grasp new opportunities and enjoy the benefits of the AEC integration, Laos needs to take bolder steps to create a more conducive business environment. These steps include continuing regulatory and policy reforms as well as ensuring effective implementation of commitments such as on trade facilitation in order to lower international trade costs (World Bank 2015). The full implementation of the AEC commitments also means instituting a national single window and eliminating other non-tariff barriers, which is considered quite a challenge for Laos (Vilavong and Hess 2016). Laos is not a special case though—complete AEC implementation will be challenging for other more developed ASEAN members as well.

Improving Hard and Soft Infrastructure

Exporting a standard container from Vientiane to Los Angeles adds as much as 45% to total shipping costs compared to exporting from Bangkok to the same final destination (World Bank 2010b). Putting landlocked status aside, the high shipping cost is also attributed to the unreliable national transport system. Road transport is the dominant mode of transport in Laos, which accounts for 70% of freight transport and 90% of passenger transport. Currently, Laos has no rail or water transport. In addition, transport is also hampered by mountainous terrain making up three-quarters of the country's area (MOIC 2012).

While there has been investment in numerous infrastructure projects with a bid to link Laos to the region as earlier discussed, Laos remains among the world's bottom ten in a recent survey on logistics performance. The country's overall logistics performance index (LPI) was 2.07 in 2016, which was down from 2.39 in 2014 (World Bank 2017c).[12] Laos was behind all other ASEAN members in almost all aspects including efficiency in border clearance, trade, and transport infrastructure and logistics competence. The only areas where Laos did not score last were timeliness and international shipments, in which Laos scored comparably to Myanmar.

This highlights the critical importance of improving not only hard infrastructure but also soft infrastructure in order to better connect Laos to the region. Hence, customs modernisation efforts are under way particularly in the organisation of clearance procedures. A prime example is the introduction of the United Nations Automated System for Customs Data (ASYCUDA) in order to reduce the time for customs clearance (Vilavong 2018). It is essential that the current efforts continue in order to boost customs enforcement and ensure effective regulation, as trade volumes are expected to increase when the AEC operates in full swing.

Conclusion

Laos has made impressive economic progress since adopting the NEM in the mid-1980s, shifting the economy from a centrally planned regime to the one that is more market driven. Laos is a full member of the WTO and increasingly integrated into the AEC. With economic growth of over 7% in recent decades, Laos is now a lower middle-income country, which shows positive momentum towards its target of LDC graduation. While Laos' economic progress has been impressive, the resource sector remains the main driver of the economy. Agriculture is still the main absorber of the labour force and the country's manufacturing base is narrow. Exports are also less diversified in terms of both product composition and markets. One of the key challenges for Laos is to manage its natural resource wealth in a manner that can ensure broad-based growth across a diversity of sectors and create jobs for the wider population. Going forward, the AEC will lead to increased competition for Lao businesses combined with an uncertain global economic outlook. Laos' future growth will depend upon how effectively the country can facilitate trade and improve connectivity. Sustaining long-term growth and development requires not only a strong political commitment to further reforms but also effective integration into the region. Apart from investments in upgrading transport infrastructure, particular focus should be on bolder reforms to improve the poor business environment and logistics performance. These efforts are expected to help Laos reap benefits from its integration into the regional and global economy and ensure a smooth transition after its graduation from least developed country status.

Notes

1. A country is eligible for LDC graduation if it meets the thresholds for two of three criteria: income per capita, human development assets (such as health and education), and economic vulnerability (MOIC 2012, p. 47).
2. Other areas include liberalising investment, harmonising a capital market regulatory framework, facilitating skilled labour mobility, promoting a regional framework in competition policy, consumer protection and intellectual property rights, promoting connectivity, and the narrowing development gap.
3. According to an interview with an official at the Foreign Trade Policy Department.
4. These include Australia, China, Japan, India, New Zealand, and South Korea. Negotiations have been ongoing to consolidate these agreements into the Regional Comprehensive Economic Partnership (RCEP) arrangement.
5. As an LDC, Laos has been granted preferential market access by over 44 countries. First, the Generalised System of Preferences is granted by Australia, New Zealand, Canada, the European Union, Norway, Switzerland, Japan, Turkey, and Russia, among others. The second scheme is known as the Special and Preferential Treatment Scheme, including those granted by China and South Korea (Douangboupha et al. 2007, p. 35).
6. See further discussions in Varela et al. (2016, p. 31).
7. According to the World Bank's World Development Indicators, based on the Atlas method at current prices.
8. While economic growth is expected to ease to 6.6% in 2018, it is projected to pick up slightly during 2019–2020 and get towards a more sustainable level (World Bank 2017b, p. 31).
9. According to the United Nations Commodity Trade Statistics (UN Comtrade) database, using data reported by partners.
10. By comparison, Cambodia and Myanmar were ranked at 131st and 170th, respectively.

11. Laos' score was combined from individual components: the size of government (8.51), legal system and property rights (5.98), sound money (7.35), freedom to trade internationally (6.74), and regulation (6.31). See Fraser Institute (2016).
12. The logistics performance index is on a scale from 1 (lowest) to 5 (highest). See https://lpi.worldbank.org/international/scorecard/radar/128/C/LAO/2016#chartarea.

References

ASEAN Secretariat. 2015a. *ASEAN Economic Community Blueprint 2025*. Jakarta: ASEAN Secretariat.

———. 2015b. *ASEAN Integration Report 2015*. Jakarta: ASEAN Secretariat.

Asian Development Bank. 2017. *Asian Development Outlook 2017*. Manila: Asian Development Bank.

Athukorala, Prema-chandra, and Archanun Kohpaiboon. 2013. *Global Production Sharing, Trade Patterns and Industrialization in Southeast Asia*. Working Papers in Trade and Development, no. 2013/18: 1–36.

Bird, Kelly, and Hal Hill. 2010. Tiny, Poor, Land-Locked, Indebted, but Growing: Lessons for Late Reforming Transition Economies from Laos. *Oxford Development Studies* 38 (2): 117–143.

Douangboupha, Latthana. 2010. Effects of Trade Policy Reforms on Economic Growth: The Case of the Lao PDR. *Lao Trade Research Digest* 1: 59–96.

Douangboupha, Latthana, Buavanh Vilavong, and Santisouk Phounesavath. 2007. *Addressing the Impact of the Phasing out of Textiles and Clothing Quotas in Lao PDR: Trade Negotiation Strategies*. Vol. 4. Addressing the Impact of the Phasing out of Textiles and Clothing Quotas in Lao PDR. Vientiane: National Statistics Centre.

Fraser Institute. 2016, December 22. *Economic Freedom of the World*. Fraser Institute. https://www.fraserinstitute.org/economic-freedom.

Jones, Ronald W., and Henryk Kierzkowski. 1990. The Role of Services in Production and International Trade: A Theoretical Framework. In *The Political Economy of International Trade*, ed. Ronald W. Jones and A. Krueger. Oxford: Basil Blackwell.

Lord, Montague. 2011. *The Lao PDR Diagnostic Trade Integration Study (DTIS): Resource Exports–Impacts and Linkages*. Vientiane: Ministry of Industry and Commerce.

MOIC. 2012. *Diagnostic Trade Integration Study: Trade and Private Sector Development Roadmap*. Vientiane: Ministry of Industry and Commerce.

MPI. 2016. *8th Five-Year National Socioeconomic Development Plan (2016–2020)*. Vientiane: Ministry of Planning and Investment.

MPI and UNDP. 2017. *National Human Development Report: Lao PDR Graduation from Least Developed Country Status*. 5th ed. New York: United Nations Development Programme.

Nolintha, Vanthana, and Idris Jajri. 2015. *The Garment Industry in Laos: Technological Capabilities, Global Production Chains and Competitiveness*. ERIA Discussion Paper Series, no. 2015–13: 1–21.

Pholsena, Khemmani, and Buavanh Vilavong. 2015. Accession of Lao PDR: Specific Commitments and LDCs' Integration into the Global Economy. In *WTO Accessions and Trade Multilateralism: Case Studies and Lessons from the WTO at Twenty*, ed. Uri Dadush and Chiedu Osakwe, 545–557. Cambridge: Cambridge University Press.

PwC Laos. 2012. *South East Asia: Investment Opportunities, Tax & Other Incentives*. PwC Laos. https://www.pwc.com/th/en/publications/download/south-east-asia-web.pdf.

Record, Richard, Konesawang Nghardsaysone, George Clarke, and Marlon Seror. 2014. *Lao PDR Investment Climate Assessment 2014: Policy Uncertainty in the Midst of a Natural Resources Boom*. Washington, DC: World Bank.

The Economist Intelligence Unit. 2017a. *Laos: Infrastructure Plans Will Help Regional Interconnectedness*. March 22. http://country.eiu.com/article.aspx?articleid=1985238582&Country=Laos&topic=Economy&subtopic=Forecast&subsubtopic=External+sector&u=1&pid=385906022&oid=385906022&uid=1.

———. 2017b. Laos: Railway Connection to China Is a Priority. *Laos Economy*, April 13. http://country.eiu.com/article.aspx?articleid=1285322512&Country=Laos&topic=Economy&subtopic=Forecast&subsubtopic=Policy+trends&u=1&pid=235906007&oid=235906007&uid=1.

UNDP. 2018. Lao PDR's Eligibility for Graduation from LDC Status Confirmed. UNDP, March 18. http://www.la.undp.org/content/lao_pdr/en/home/presscenter/pressreleases/2018/3/19/lao-pdr_s-eligibility-for-graduation-from-least-developed-countr.html.

U.S. Commercial Service. 2017. Doing Business in Laos. July 20. https://2016.export.gov/thailand/doingbusiness/laos/index.asp.

Varela, Gonzalo, Claire H. Hollweg, and Laura Gomez-Mera. 2016. *Services and Manufacturing Linkages: An Empirical Analysis for Lao PDR*. Vientiane: World Bank.

Vilavong, Buavanh. 2016. Can Laos Restore Growth While Global Economic Uncertainty Reigns? *East Asia Forum*, December 24. http://www.eastasiaforum.org/2016/12/24/can-laos-restore-growth-while-global-economic-uncertainty-reigns/.

———. 2018. Will Costs Continue to Cage Laos' Regional Connectivity? *East Asia Forum*, January 12. http://www.eastasiaforum.org/2018/01/13/will-costs-continue-to-cage-laos-regional-connectivity/.

Vilavong, Buavanh, and Simon Hess. 2016. What the AEC Means for Laos. *East Asia Forum*, January 1.
World Bank. 2006. *Diagnostic Trade Integration Study: Building Export Competitiveness in Laos.* Washington, DC: World Bank.
———. 2010a. *Lao PDR Development Report: Natural Resource Management for Sustainable Development.* Washington, DC: World Bank.
———. 2010b. Lao PDR Trade Facilitation Performance. *Trade Development Briefing Note* 2: 1–2.
———. 2015. "Lao Economic Monitor: Towards Restoring Macroeconomic Stability and Building Inclusive Growth".
———. 2017a. *Lao Economic Monitor: Challenges in Promoting More Inclusive and Shared Prosperity.* Vientiane: World Bank.
———. 2017b. *Lao PDR Economic Monitor: Lowering Risks and Reviving Growth.* Vientiane: World Bank.
———. 2017c. "Logistics Performance Index".
World Trade Organization. 2012. "Report of the Working Party on the Accession of Lao PDR to the World Trade Organization." World Trade Organization.

CHAPTER 11

Myanmar: On a Bumpy Road of Transition

Thomas Bernhardt and Aung Hein

Introduction

There are few countries on the globe that, in recent years, have attracted as much attention from the international media and community as Myanmar. After decades as a pariah state, the country received praise when it embarked on a transition toward democracy in 2010 which culminated in the first free elections in 25 years in 2015.

However, in view of allegations of ethnic cleansing and human rights abuses related to military interventions against the Rohingya minority in northwestern Rakhine State, repression against journalists, and slower than expected social and economic progress, international and local euphoria has lately given way to a more sober and at times skeptical perception of the

The views expressed here are those of the authors and do not necessarily reflect those of their affiliations.

T. Bernhardt (✉)
Department for International Financial Institutions,
Austrian Federal Ministry of Finance, Vienna, Austria

A. Hein
Woodrow Wilson School of Public and International Affairs,
Princeton University, Princeton, NJ, USA
e-mail: aungh@princeton.edu

R. Macdonald (ed.), *Southeast Asia and the ASEAN Economic Community*, https://doi.org/10.1007/978-3-030-19722-3_11

country's political and economic trajectory. This chapter will provide a snapshot on Myanmar's recent transformation with particular emphasis on its economic development and regional economic integration.

History, Society, and Culture

Myanmar is the largest country in mainland Southeast Asia. It has one of the ethnolinguistically most diverse populations in the world. The government recognizes 135 ethnic groups, of which the Bamar, at an estimated 68%, make up the majority. The official language is Burmese but various indigenous languages are also recognized. Since independence, this ethnic diversity has frequently led to ethnic strife, especially in border regions. Almost 90% of people practice Theravada Buddhism; other religious groups are the minority.

Arguably, the history of modern-day Myanmar began with British conquest and colonialization in three successive waves in 1824–1886. Britain administered Myanmar—then known as "British Burma"—as an Indian province until 1937. Under British rule, Myanmar's economy heavily depended on the export of rice, teak, petroleum, and mineral products. After a brief Japanese occupation during World War II, Myanmar gained independence in 1948. The civilian government that came to power lasted until 1962, when it was ousted by a military coup amidst an escalating civil war.

General Ne Win dominated politics in the period 1962–1988. He suspended the 1947 Constitution and ruled the country through the Revolutionary Council. Pursuing a "Burmese Way to Socialism", he implemented a command economy, nationalizing commerce and industry. The 1974 Constitution established a one-party rule by the *Burma Socialist Programme Party* (BSPP) with Ne Win as president. Toward the end of the 1980s, the economy suffered from mounting trade deficits and external debt payments. Ne Win's rule came to an end with the 1988 popular uprising and another coup by the military.

The *State Law and Order Restoration Council* (SLORC) that came to power suspended the 1974 Constitution and arrested several opposition leaders. It held general elections in 1990, which the opposition party *National League for Democracy* (NLD), headed by democracy icon and later Nobel-Laureate Aung San Suu Kyi, won in a landslide. The SLORC government refused to recognize the election results and began drafting a new constitution. It started dismantling the economic policies of the BSPP government in the early 1990s. However, it did not sustain economic reforms. A combination of economic mismanagement and external sanctions weighed down economic recovery (Charney 2009).

The 2008 Constitution is the culmination of the seven-step road map initiated by the military in 2003 (Kipgen 2017). The constitutional referendum that followed another popular protest in 2007 and amidst the humanitarian crisis from Cyclone Nargis was roundly criticized because it granted the military a de-facto veto on further constitutional change, 25% of parliamentary seats, and important ministerial posts (Home Affairs, Defense, and Border Affairs). The subsequent 2010 elections were boycotted by the NLD and saw a nominally civilian government headed by former General Thein Sein sworn into office.

The Thein Sein administration surprised many by embarking on a series of reforms. It released political prisoners, abolished censorship, and increased freedom of speech, assembly, and press. Upon release from house arrest, Aung San Suu Kyi participated in the 2012 bi-elections and was elected to Parliament. Internationally, Myanmar re-engaged with the outside world (Pulipaka 2017).

The administration also initiated sweeping economic reforms. In certain key areas, however, progress was limited. No serious attempt was made to amend the undemocratic features of the 2008 Constitution. Although the Nationwide Ceasefire Agreement (NCA) was signed with eight ethnic armed groups toward the end of Thein Sein's tenure in 2015, it was criticized for excluding other insurgent groups (Kipgen 2017).

After a landslide electoral victory, a new NLD-led government was sworn into office in March 2016, marking a historical return to civilian governance after a half-century of military rule. Since a provision in the 2008 constitution effectively barred NLD leader Suu Kyi from presidency, a new office of "State Counsellor" (with the functions and powers typically given to Prime Ministers) was created for her. Already during the election campaign, she had promised supporters to "be above the president" in case of victory (Pulipaka 2017).

The NLD government stated its objectives as (1) striving for a federal democracy, (2) improving socio-economic development, and (3) achieving peace and national reconciliation (Kipgen 2017). It revamped peace negotiations, initiating an all-inclusive twenty-first century Panglong Peace Conference, the namesake of the 1947 conference that created the Union of Burma. Progress so far has been limited. The fighting between

Myanmar military and several ethnic armed groups continued in different parts of the country. The sectarian violence between Buddhists and Muslims in northwestern Rakhine State has gripped both national and international attention (International Crisis Group 2017). Whereas critics have charged the NLD government with complacency, the reality is that key security apparatuses are not under civilian control. The civil-military contest and ethnic/sectarian conflict are, thus, key political challenges for the new government (Pulipaka 2017).

The social challenges to be addressed by the government are also enormous. Today, Myanmar's income per capita and life expectancy at birth are the lowest within the Association of Southeast Asian Nations (ASEAN).[1] The United Nations categorizes Myanmar among the "least developed countries" (LDCs) and ranks it 148th out of 189 countries in their Human Development Index. Poverty is widespread, affecting around a third of the population. The education and health systems are in poor shape. A quarter of adults are illiterate, every sixth inhabitant is undernourished, and only about half of the population has access to electricity.

The Myanmar Economy: A Snapshot

Myanmar's economy is undergoing a deep and swift transformation. Changes in the political regime have led to a gradual opening and liberalization of Myanmar's economic system. Central planning, inward orientation, and a state-dominated economy have given way to increased private sector activity, while international commercial and financial transactions have expanded.

Macroeconomic indicators paint a clear picture of recent achievements. First and foremost, Myanmar has seen impressive economic growth. In the 2000s, Myanmar's gross domestic product (GDP) grew at two-digit rates per year until the global financial crisis hit in 2008. After this shock, which led to a slowdown, GDP growth rates picked up again to about 6.5% a year—a pace much faster than in most other Asian countries (see Fig. 11.1). However, economic expansion has been slower than before and a return to double-digit growth rates seems unlikely. Still, with the International Monetary Fund (IMF) forecasting annual GDP growth to average 7% over the next five years, Myanmar is set to outpace all other ASEAN countries (see the shaded area of Fig. 11.1).

As a result of rapid economic growth, the size of Myanmar's economy has expanded from a GDP of US$10.3 billion in 2000 to US$66.5 billion

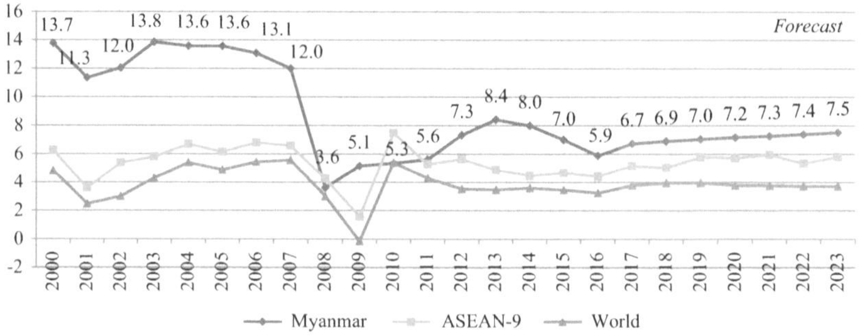

Fig. 11.1 Annual growth rates of real GDP, 2000–2023 (in %). Note: ASEAN-9 includes all ASEAN members except Myanmar. Source: IMF World Economic Outlook database

Table 11.1 Selected macroeconomic indicators for Myanmar, 2000–2017

	2000	*2010*	*2017*
Nominal GDP (billion US$)	10.3	49.5	66.5
GDP per capita (in current US$)	221	997	1264
Growth of real output (*in %*)			
Agriculture	11.0%	4.7%	−0.4%[a]
Industry	11.3%	18.6%	8.9%[a]
Services	13.4%	9.5%	8.0%[a]
Gross capital formation (*% of GDP*)	12.4%	23.2%	34.4%[a]
Inflation rate (*%*)	21.1%	7.7%	4.6%

Source: WDI database

[a]Figure for 2016

in 2017. Average incomes have risen as well. GDP per capita increased from a mere US$221 in 2000 to US$1264 in 2017 (see Table 11.1).

Underlying this fast economic growth is a process of structural change that Myanmar's economy is experiencing. Over the past couple of years, the services sector and, particularly, industry have significantly increased their contribution to economic output. Industry's share in GDP has risen from 9.7% in 2000 to 35.0% in 2016, while the services sector has expanded its contribution from 33.1% to 39.5% and today is the most important economic sector in terms of output. Meanwhile, the importance of agriculture for economic output is shrinking. Its share in GDP went down from 57.2% in 2000 to 25.5% in 2016 (see Fig. 11.2). Yet,

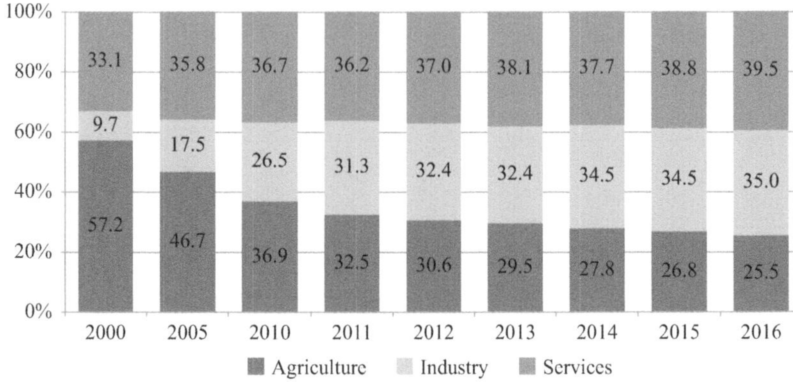

Fig. 11.2 Structure of output: share in GDP of different economic sectors, 2000–2016 (in %). Source: Myanmar Statistical Information Service

accounting for almost 50% of total employment (down from 76% in 2000), agriculture is still the most important provider of jobs. The services sector is catching up, today contributing 33.5% to total employment, up from 14.3% in 2000.

A key driver of economic expansion has been investment. Between 2000 and 2016, gross capital formation increased from 12.4% to 34.4% of GDP (see Table 11.1). Domestic investment was facilitated by the dynamic expansion of credit to the private sector which has grown by an annual 23% since 2010 (IMF 2018). At the same time, Myanmar has seen a tremendous rise in inflows of foreign direct investment (FDI). This rapid investment growth reflects the increased confidence in the prospects for Myanmar's economy, indicating that businesses are optimistic about the future returns on their investments.

Increasing foreign demand for Myanmar products has been another factor contributing to economic growth. Exports have expanded rapidly since 2010. However, imports have increased even faster, leading to a widening current account deficit. Another macroeconomic challenge relates to price stability. Myanmar's economic dynamism, together with expansionary macroeconomic policies, has resulted in inflationary pressures. The inflation rate has exceeded the 5% mark in almost all years since 2010 (see Table 11.1). Overall, however, Myanmar's macroeconomic environment is mostly favorable and the medium-term economic outlook predominantly positive (IMF 2018).

The Financial and Business Sectors

Decades of inward-oriented socialist and military junta economic governance have left a legacy (Bissinger 2014). Both Myanmar's business and financial sectors do not (yet) look much like those of a modern capitalist system.

Myanmar's financial sector is fairly underdeveloped and undersized. Notwithstanding notable progress, especially over the last years, it is lacking depth and breadth. It is strongly dominated by the banking sector, whereas capital markets and the insurance industry are just emerging: the insurance market, formerly a state monopoly, was liberalized in 2012 and the Yangon Stock Exchange opened only in 2015 (however, with currently just five listings and very little trading). Several financial services (including trade finance, venture capital, leasing, or factoring) that are common elsewhere are not or hardly available to Myanmar businesses (GIZ 2016; Turnell 2014).

Even the banking sector is comparatively underdeveloped—despite recent advances: total assets of Myanmar banks have grown more than tenfold since 2010 and their lending to the private sector has expanded rapidly. Yet, the density of the commercial bank branch network is still the second lowest in Southeast Asia after Laos. Myanmar banks tend to be very risk averse and their lending policies often do not conform to modern practices. In particular, re-financing lines are practically unavailable for enterprises. Most commercial banks only provide very simple financial services, and procedures can be lengthy and inefficient. Collateral requirements are stringent and loans of longer maturity extremely difficult to get (OECD 2013). State-owned banks currently account for about half of total assets, while foreign banks, allowed again since 2015, are basically limited to wholesale banking and foreign-owned companies as customers. Overall, while a sequence of reforms helped to modernize the legal framework and improved public trust, there is still a long way to go for Myanmar's financial sector to meet international standards (GIZ 2016).

Meanwhile, in the real economy, with the policy shift toward a market-oriented economic system, the number of private enterprises has multiplied. Private investment has been dynamic in the last couple of years, particularly into construction, manufacturing, and services. Approximately 127,000 businesses are registered in Myanmar, of which 99.4% are small and medium-sized enterprises (SMEs). For a country the size of Myanmar, this is still quite a low tally of enterprises. There are only about 2.6 registered SMEs per 1000 citizens—a ratio much lower than elsewhere in Asia.

Private business, hence, has not yet fully overcome a long history of oppression. It is estimated, however, that an additional 620,000 business entities operate in the informal sector, which thereby accounts for more than 83% of all Myanmar enterprises (OECD 2013). The bulk of firms are microenterprises. At the same time, large enterprises, while constituting less than 1% of the business population, account for a significant share of total employment (UNDP 2014). These figures point to the existence of a "missing middle", that is, the underrepresentation of medium-sized firms in Myanmar's enterprise population.

A number of these large companies are owned by or linked to the military. The two most prominent examples are the Union of Myanmar Economic Holdings Limited (UMEHL), the country's biggest conglomerate with presence in light industries and trading, and the Myanmar Economic Corporation (MEC), which concentrates on heavy industries. In many sectors, military-owned companies hold substantial market (sometimes even monopoly) power which they were able to build up during junta years, thanks to privileged access to licenses, permits, foreign exchange, and credit. However, the patronage system reaches further and additionally involves (often family-owned) businesses run by "cronies" whose ascent can be explained by their personal or family ties to leading military officers which helped them obtain licenses, concessions, and public contracts. Such crony businesses have benefitted from privatizations, accumulated wealth and power, and are important players in various sectors. The commercial interests of this military-economic complex have been among the driving forces for Myanmar's recent opening. Even under civilian rule, such military-owned and -linked companies are still powerful and retain huge stakes in the economy (Gabusi 2015).

On top of that, there are numerous state-owned enterprises (SOEs) that remain important, albeit less than in the past. Although their shares have been declining since the early 1990s, SOEs still dominate certain industries like agribusiness, forestry, mining, energy, construction, and telecommunications. Moreover, while a number of them are loss making, SOEs have been important investors in the economy (OECD 2013).

Labor Market

Myanmar is currently enjoying a demographic dividend. The size of its working-age population—about two-thirds of the total population—is the second largest in relative terms among CLMV—Cambodia, Laos,

Myanmar, and Vietnam. Its total dependency ratio is the second lowest. Yet, between 1960 and 2015, Myanmar's population growth has been the slowest among CLMV, posing the specter of future aging population.

Myanmar's labor force is sizeable with low female participation but widespread child labor. The labor force participation rate at 65% is among the lowest in ASEAN. Participation is high among elderly and children: about one in ten elderly persons (aged 80–84) and children (aged 10–14) are in the labor force. At 0.8%, the official unemployment rate is low.

The employment structure shows a traditional labor market with high dependency on the vulnerable primary and informal sectors. The primary sector—agriculture, forestry, and fishing—is the largest employer, accounting for just over half of all workers. The informal sector is large, employing 75.6% of workers.

Labor productivity is low, comparable only to Cambodia and Laos, while lagging behind all other ASEAN countries (Bernhardt 2017). Long working hours are common. More than half of the employed work at least 50 hours a week at their main job (MOLES and CSO 2015). Labor costs are among the lowest in the region (ADB 2014). Myanmar's minimum wage of around US$90 monthly is far below the levels in Vietnam and Cambodia and higher only than Bangladesh's.

Labor mobility is skewed toward urban areas where internal migrant workers can make up almost 50% of the workforce, as in Yangon. Moreover, many people seek work abroad. About 6% of households have at least one international migrant, with percentages being twice as high among rural compared to urban households (MOLES and CSO 2015). Myanmar's diaspora, estimated to be 4.25 million, is sizeable. About 70% of emigrants are based in Thailand, followed by Malaysia (15%), China (4.6%), and Singapore (3.9%).[2]

Since 2011, the legal framework has been modernized as the government has enacted five new labor laws and plans to amend 11 others. The new Labor Organization Law (2011) grants workers the right to join labor organizations, ending a decades-long ban of trade unions. The Social Security Law (2012) aims to increase coverage and expand benefits. The Minimum Wage Law (2013) enabled the setting of the first minimum wage in 2015. However, with a small labor inspectorate, enforcement of these laws is often incomplete (Bernhardt et al. 2017a).

Scarce human capital is a major challenge. Public expenditure on health and education is low but has risen recently. Secondary education is a major break point in the education system: the enrolment rate is only 56% and less than 10% of new entrants into Grade 1 will complete high school. Universities were closed down for years under military rule. Technical and vocational education is fragmented among various ministries and has been largely supply-driven. There is a substantial rural-urban disparity in access to education (ADB 2014).

Educational attainments are low: adults aged 25 years and older have, on average, spent only 4.7 years at school, less than in Cambodia and Laos. One-fifth of workers have no formal education, and 61.2% have only basic education. Merely 8.6% of them have secondary education—the lowest among CLMV along with Cambodia. Accordingly, large proportions of the labor force are low-skilled. Enterprises rank skills deficits among the most serious business constraints. Yet, only a minority of firms invests in staff training (World Bank 2017).

Turbulent industrial relations with incipient labor organizations pose a challenge. Overall, 88% of the employed are not a member of either an employers' or a workers' organization (MOLES and CSO 2015). Labor rights awareness is low. Industrial relations issues are often solved in confrontation, as testified by an increasing number of strikes. The absence of labor courts and weak arbitration mechanisms are obstacles to functioning industrial relations.

Going forward, challenges include reducing and eventually abolishing child labor, providing protection to workers in vulnerable and informal employment as well as expanding social security coverage. Occupational safety and health are emerging issues. Since the major boost to the labor market will come from increased female participation, the government needs to invest in broad-based education, while curtailing discrimination and enhancing opportunities for women.

Economic Policy

After taking office in 2011, the Thein Sein government surprised many with truly sweeping economic reforms. Driven by a desire to reduce Myanmar's overreliance on China, an ambition to spur economic development and, last but not least, the commercial interests of military-linked companies, it started to liberalize and open the economy. Myanmar's dependence on China had significantly intensified since the mid-1990s, when the West imposed sanctions. By around 2010, China had become Myanmar's largest trade and investment partner (Mizuno 2016). Western nations responded to this intended re-orientation away from China (and the steps taken toward democratization) and suspended or lifted most sanctions and began re-engagement in 2012. A substantial amount of Myanmar's external debt was either written off or rescheduled by the Paris Club. This allowed the International Financial Institutions to re-engage with Myanmar.

The Thein Sein government's *Framework for Economic & Social Reforms*, published in 2013, targeted sustained economic growth, macroeconomic stability, and a process of structural change into manufacturing and service sectors (Than 2014). Signature economic reforms included the new Foreign Exchange Management Law (2012), which corrected the distortionary exchange rate regime and strengthened the very thin financial sector. The parallel currency exchange markets were unified and a managed float exchange rate began. The revised Central Bank Law (2013) granted it operational autonomy away from the Ministry of Finance. The central bank cautiously opened the financial sector to foreign participation. In 2016, the Parliament enacted the Financial Institutions Law to bring banking supervision and corporate governance closer to international best practices (GIZ 2016).

The government also intervened in the real sector, opening the country for foreign investment while addressing weaknesses in the business environment. The new Foreign Investment Law (2012) replaced the 1988 law, clarifying ownership, land rights, and financial incentives. In 2013, Norway's Telenor and Qatar's Ooredoo were granted licenses to invest in the telecommunications sector, ending the State's monopoly. To circumnavigate the challenging business climate, the government passed the Myanmar Special Economic Zone (SEZ) Law (2014) and began the construction of Thilawa SEZ south of Yangon. It also liberalized state controls on international trade, reducing the export tax and easing licensing requirements for trade. The powerful and restrictive Trade Council was abolished and the private sector was allowed to engage in the hitherto prohibited trading of, inter alia, construction materials, motor vehicles, and rice exports (Than 2014).

The economy benefitted from the reforms and the general atmosphere of excitement. However, when the Thein Sein government stepped down in March 2016, the economy faced challenges: public objections to mega-projects, slow progress in SEZ implementation, rising economic nationalism, and inflating land prices (Than 2015). More difficult areas for reform also remained. In addition, the Thein Sein government's increased spending in its final months in office left the public exchequer virtually bankrupt. In this context, power was transferred to the first opposition-led government of Aung San Suu Kyi.

From the beginning, the NLD government had a clear focus on peace, national reconciliation, and cementing the democratic transition. By comparison, economic policy somewhat took a back seat, not least because the new decision-makers had much fewer stakes in business than their military-linked predecessors. The new government's 12-point economic policy, released in 2016, established broad targets such as improving public sector management, SOE reform, human capital investment, upgrading public infrastructure, job creation, private sector growth, financial stability, tax system reforms, and enhancing global economic integration. Yet, no detailed action plan was offered. The first acts by the NLD government were stabilizing public finances, relying less on the central bank to finance deficits, and downsizing ministries. As a major economic reform, in October 2016, the Parliament enacted the revamped Myanmar Investment Law which unifies previously separate laws for domestic and foreign investors, leveling the playing field between these two groups, and which aims to promote investments in underdeveloped regions.

Since then, economic reforms have stalled amidst the hangover from the humanitarian crisis in Rakhine State. The business community expressed disappointment with the perceived lack of reforms, policy uncertainty, and centralized decision-making (Nitta 2018). To be fair, the perception of a slowing reform momentum under the NLD administration also has to do with the fact that its predecessor tackled the easy part, addressing quick policy wins with rapid impacts (Gabusi 2015).

By mid-2018, the NLD government began addressing the criticisms. In March 2018, it announced the 238-point *Myanmar Sustainable Development Plan* to flesh out its economic policy and to provide coherence among existing and future strategies, policies, and investment plans (The Economist 2018). The much-anticipated Myanmar Companies Law followed in June 2018, allowing foreigners stakes of up to 35% in local companies without them losing their local status and setting up an online business registry for increased transparency and reduced paperwork.

The challenge for the government will now be to provide a clearer vision, consistency, and quicker decision-making and to initiate a second wave of reforms (IMF 2018). Translating all the reforms into practice will be equally important and will require efforts from Myanmar's civil service and improved coordination among implementing agencies. Going forward, the government's economic policy space will depend on how successful it is in raising tax revenues which, at 6.4% of GDP, are among the lowest around the globe.

Strengths and Weaknesses of the Myanmar Economy

In this time of transition, Myanmar's economic setup is changing quickly. Still, a number of current strengths and weaknesses can be identified.

Strengths

Large Pool of Labor
Myanmar has a large untapped pool of labor. Its population is relatively young. People below working age make up 29% of the country's total population, while the 15–29 age group accounts for around 40% of the working-age population. Moreover, labor is comparatively cheap (ADB 2014).

Rich Endowments
Myanmar's rich endowments provide its economy with various comparative advantages. Among its abundant natural resources are hydrocarbons, metals, and minerals, including precious stones. Myanmar has large areas of fertile and arable land. Moreover, it is well endowed with forests, including a variety of major commercially viable timber species. Its enormous water resources provide a rich basis for the fishery and aquaculture industry as well as for hydropower generation. Myanmar's natural beauty and its rich cultural heritage are also powerful tourist draws (OECD 2013).

Geostrategic Location
Myanmar is in a very advantageous geostrategic location. It is positioned between China and India, the world's two most populous countries with fast-growing markets. As a member of ASEAN, it also has easy access to the markets of this very dynamic grouping.

Trade Preferences
Exports from Myanmar enjoy preferential access to many markets. The European Union (EU) and the US re-admitted Myanmar into their *Generalized Systems of Preferences* (GSP) in 2013 and 2016, respectively. Myanmar also enjoys preferential treatment under the GSP regimes of other advanced economies.

Growing Availability of Official Development Assistance (ODA)
When Myanmar embarked on its path to democracy, international relations began to normalize and foreign-aid donors started to re-engage. Consequently, Official Development Assistance (ODA) flows to Myanmar grew rapidly. At US$1.5 billion, they were over three times higher in 2016 than in 2009 with increasing amounts going into upgrading Myanmar's economic infrastructure and production sectors.

Weaknesses

Political Stability and Governance
Ongoing ethnic conflicts, the yet-to-be-resolved humanitarian crisis in Rakhine State, and the power struggle between the armed forces and the civilian government undermine (confidence in) the country's political stability. Moreover, Myanmar appears to suffer from a "Burmese variant of the resource curse", whereby natural resources are the site of political contestation rather than important nodes of revenue generation (Pulipaka 2017).

Myanmar lacks robust governance and administrative frameworks, and the capacity of core economic policy-making institutions is limited. The rule of law, regulatory quality, government effectiveness, and inter-ministerial/inter-agency coordination are all deficient. Finally, despite recent improvements, corruption is still widespread—and perceived as an important obstacle by many businesses (World Bank 2017).

Macroeconomic Imbalances
With imports outpacing exports, the current account has moved into deep deficit territory. Foreign exchange reserves have gone down and can only pay for three months of imports (compared to eight months in 2011). The exchange rate has suffered as well, with the Myanmar Kyat depreciating by more than 60% vis-à-vis the US dollar over the last five years.

Lack of Diversification
As described above, Myanmar's economy is still a largely agrarian one. Extractive industries also play an important role, whereas the manufacturing sector is not very diversified. Exports are dominated by a few products, mainly raw materials and unprocessed goods. Neither export markets nor import markets are much diversified.

Infrastructure

For a long time, infrastructure in Myanmar suffered from underinvestment and lack of maintenance. First, deficiencies exist in the country's power system. Supply of electricity and its reliability are big challenges for enterprises (World Bank 2017). Second, shortcomings exist in the transportation infrastructure with Myanmar's roads, railroads, port, and air transport infrastructure often being of poor quality (ADB 2016). Third, despite the liberalization of telecommunication sector since 2013 and subsequent foreign investment, Myanmar's telecom infrastructure is still characterized by comparatively low coverage (biased toward large cities), reliability, and Internet speed.

Underdeveloped Financial System

Myanmar's financial sector is undersized and not up to modern standards. Access to finance is a key challenge for Myanmar's enterprises. This holds back long-term investments in machinery, equipment, and research and development (R&D) activities. Accessibility to banks, especially outside the large cities Yangon and Mandalay, is an underlying issue (Bernhardt 2017).

Low-Skilled Labor Force

A relatively large share of Myanmar's labor force is low-skilled. Under the military regime, public expenditure on education was among the lowest in the world and the quality of Myanmar's education system deteriorated. Accordingly, many enterprises view the labor force as inadequately educated and consider the shortage of skilled labor as a major constraint (World Bank 2017).

National Innovation System

Myanmar has only a rudimentary national innovation system. There are hardly any incubators or science and technology parks and very little collaboration between universities, research centers, and industry. The quality of scientific research institutions is very basic. Moreover, many of Myanmar's enterprises do not engage in innovation efforts. Firm-level spending on R&D is lower than in other ASEAN countries (Bernhardt et al. 2017b).

Low Firm-Level Productivity
After decades of seclusion, many Myanmar's enterprises operate on outdated business models and management practices. Quality management and the usage of cutting-edge technology are rare. In many firms, managerial skills and innovation efforts are deficient and investment in skills limited. As a result, productivity in most industries significantly lags behind that in more advanced Asian economies. In some cases, productivity in Myanmar is 50–75% lower than in China, India, Thailand, and Vietnam (Bernhardt 2017).

Fragmented Local Markets
With Myanmar's population being over 53 million, there is a potential mass market. However, local markets are largely fragmented due to lacking transport infrastructure, policy barriers, and ethnic conflicts.

Myanmar's Integration in the International Economy

For a long time, Myanmar has been a fairly closed economy. After decades of self-imposed isolationism under the military regime's "Burmese way to Socialism", the country was shut out of international markets in the late 1990s by Western economic sanctions. Only recently did it effectively re-enter the international commercial arena. Since 2010, its international trade has expanded rapidly. Exports have more than doubled, while imports quadrupled. This performance makes Myanmar ASEAN's import growth champion during that period; however, export growth was slower than in Cambodia, Laos, and Vietnam (see Fig. 11.3). An implication of this growth differential between exports and imports is that Myanmar's current account deficit has widened dramatically from 1.1% of GDP in 2010 to 5.3% of GDP in 2017. This imbalance represents an important macroeconomic challenge.

Moreover, despite the recent expansion of its international trading, Myanmar's economy is still relatively closed compared to other ASEAN countries. Exports and imports make up only 17% and 22% of GDP, respectively—the lowest and second lowest ratios in ASEAN. Also, at merely US$204, its exports per capita are only a quarter of those of Cambodia and Laos and a tenth of Vietnam's (see Fig. 11.4). Indeed, Ferrarini (2014) found Myanmar to be exploiting only 15% of its trading potential. There is, hence, still quite some leeway for catching up.

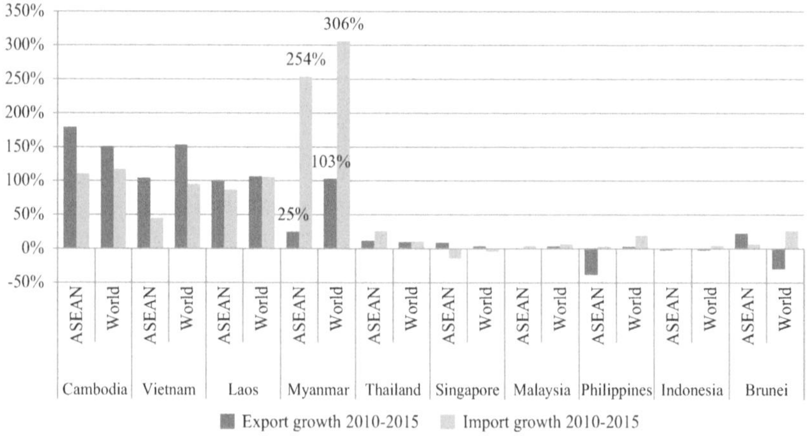

Fig. 11.3 Growth of exports to and imports from ASEAN and the world, 2010–2015. Source: UNCOMTRADE database

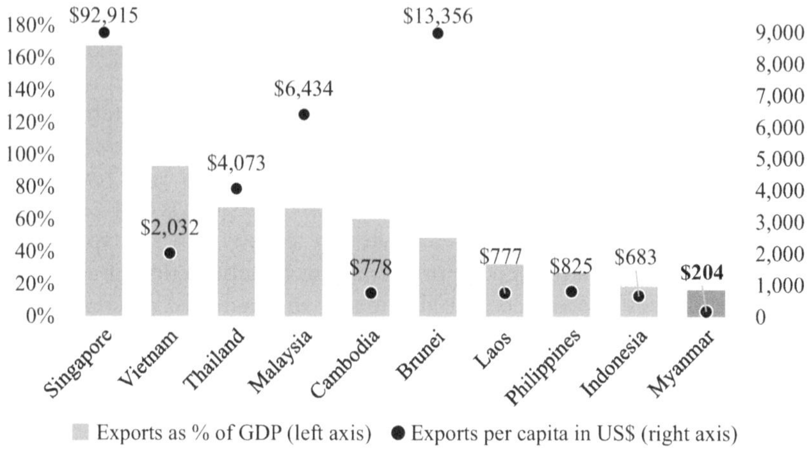

Fig. 11.4 Exports of goods and services as share of GDP and per capita, 2016. Note: The entries for Singapore and Brunei were re-scaled for better legibility. Source: WDI database

Most of Myanmar's trade is regional, that is, with Asian countries. This is partly a legacy from Western economic sanctions, partly the result of the region's recent economic dynamism. Its most important export markets are China, Thailand, the EU, India, and Japan. Together, they purchase 83% of Myanmar's exports. Regional partners are even more dominant as suppliers of imports. China is, by far, Myanmar's largest source of imports, followed by Singapore, Thailand, Japan, and India (see Fig. 11.5).

ASEAN is a vital market for Myanmar, accounting for 25% of its exports and 38% of its imports. These are the second and third highest shares among all ASEAN countries, respectively (see Fig. 11.6). Myanmar's ASEAN trade has also developed dynamically. Between 2010 and 2015, its ASEAN exports grew by 25% and its ASEAN imports even by 254% (see Fig. 11.3). Overall, however, over this period, ASEAN has lost in relative importance for Myanmar's external trade (see Fig. 11.6). This is mainly due to China, which has developed into Myanmar's most important trading partner by far, today accounting for more than a third of both Myanmar's exports and imports. Another reason is Myanmar's recent re-engagement with the US and particularly the EU, the latter now its third biggest export market.

Similar to the low degree of diversification in export markets and despite some improvement since 2010, Myanmar's export basket is highly concentrated in a few product groups (predominantly raw materials and resource-based products). This is even more true for its exports to ASEAN (where the top ten product groups account for 87% of export revenues) than for its exports to the world (where the top ten's share is 66%). Besides natural gas and crude oil (which make up almost 70% of exports to ASEAN), Myanmar's top ten export items also include agricultural, food, fishery, and forestry products as well as metals and minerals. Whereas manufactured goods are almost entirely absent from Myanmar's ASEAN export basket, various apparel products (mainly destined for the EU, Japan, Korea, and the US) have made it into the overall top ten list (see panels (a) and (c) of Fig. 11.7).

The composition of Myanmar's imports is quite different from its export structure. First, imports are much more diversified (with the top ten product groups accounting for only about half of both ASEAN and total imports). Second, they mostly consist of manufactured products, including motor vehicles, machinery, processed food products, construction materials, and pharmaceuticals. However, the ranking is topped by refined petroleum. Being imported mainly from Singapore, it constitutes

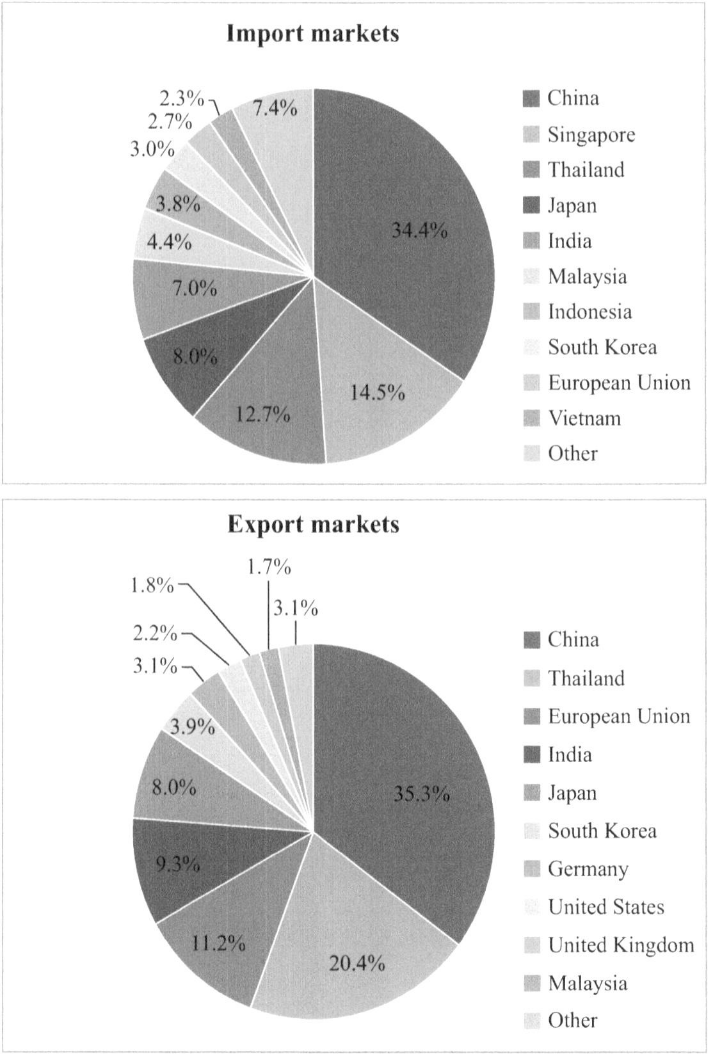

Fig. 11.5 Myanmar's top ten export and import partners, 2016. Source: UNCOMTRADE database

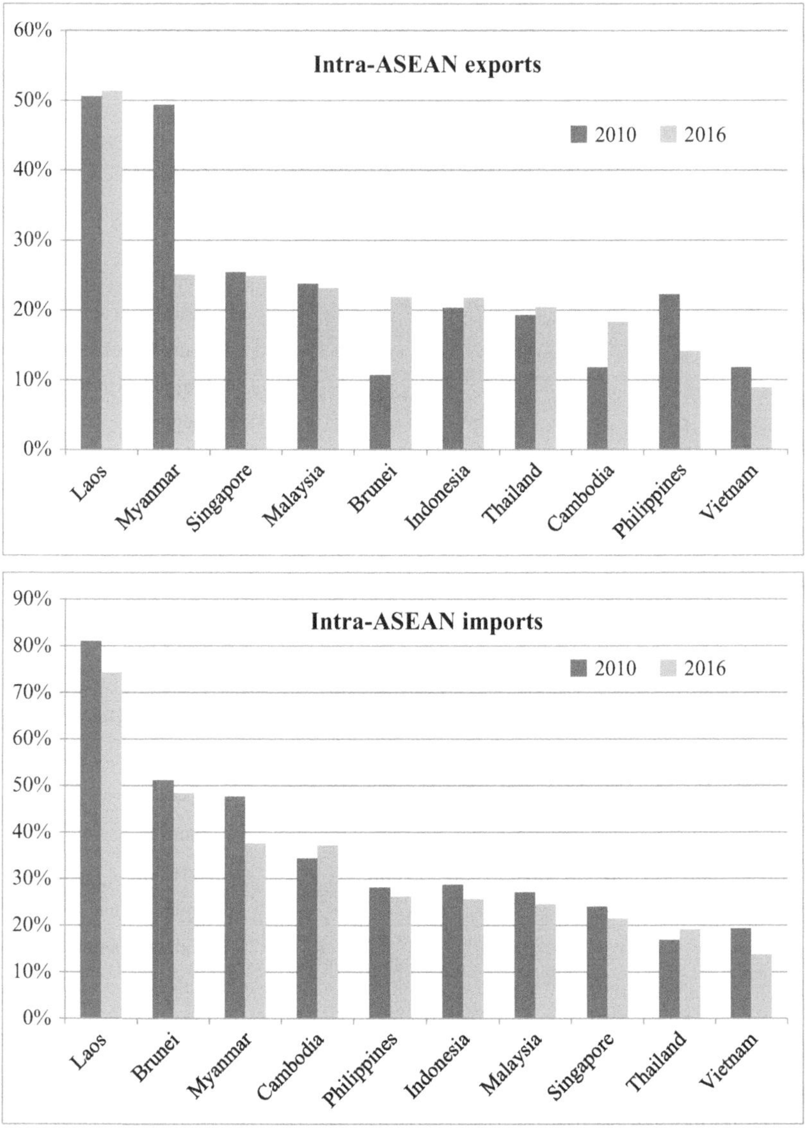

Fig. 11.6 Share of intra-ASEAN exports and imports (% of total). Source: UNCOMTRADE database

27% of Myanmar's imports from ASEAN (down from 45% in 2010; see panels (b) and (d) of Fig. 11.7).

Figure 11.7 reveals that Myanmar hardly engages in the trade of intermediate products, parts, and components. This exposes the fact that Myanmar's participation in cross-border production sharing and integration in global value chains (GVCs) is still very limited (Bernhardt 2017).

Along with a rapid expansion of international trade, Myanmar has also seen a rise in inflows of FDI. While there were some fluctuations over the years, approved incoming FDI in the financial year 2015–2016 (at US$9.5 billion) was twice as high as in 2011–2012 (when it stood at US$4.6 billion; see Fig. 11.8). As a share of GDP, FDI net inflows

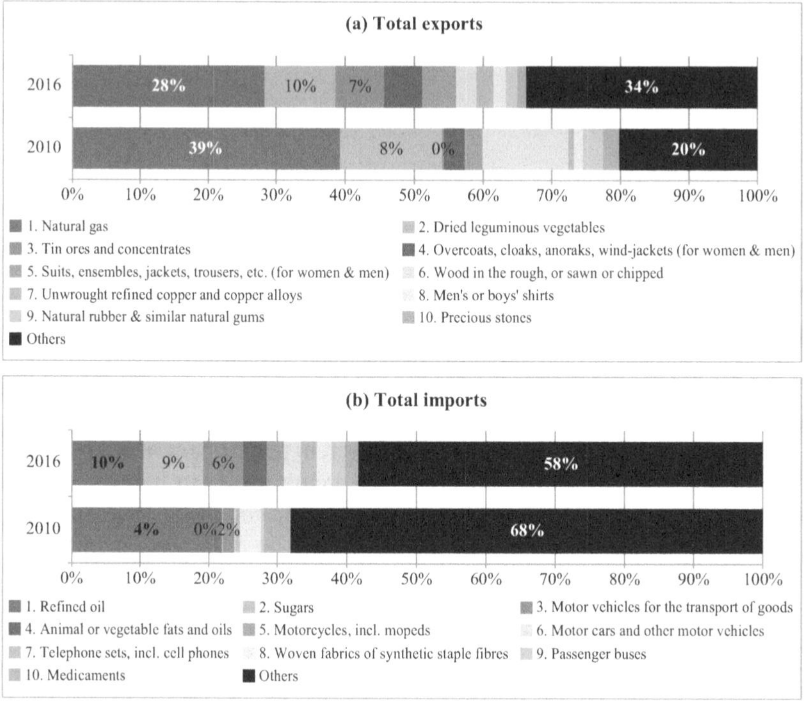

Fig. 11.7 Top 10 export and import product groups, 2010 and 2016. Source: UNCOMTRADE database

Fig. 11.7 (continued)

increased from 1.8% in 2010 to 5.2% in 2016, putting Myanmar in the midfield among ASEAN countries. However, in per capita terms, Myanmar still ranks last within ASEAN, its US$62 being less than half of the per capita FDI net inflows recorded in Laos, Cambodia, or Vietnam (see Fig. 11.9). Moreover, the last two years under the NLD government saw a slight downward trend in FDI (see Fig. 11.8).

A large majority of FDI inflows into Myanmar originates from countries such as Singapore, China, Thailand, South Korea, and Hong Kong. That is, regional investors are again at the forefront (Bernhardt et al. 2017b). Roughly half of all FDI comes from within ASEAN; this is one of the largest proportions among all ASEAN members.

A lot of incoming FDI is resource-seeking. The oil and gas and power sectors have traditionally been the recipients of the bulk of FDI inflows,

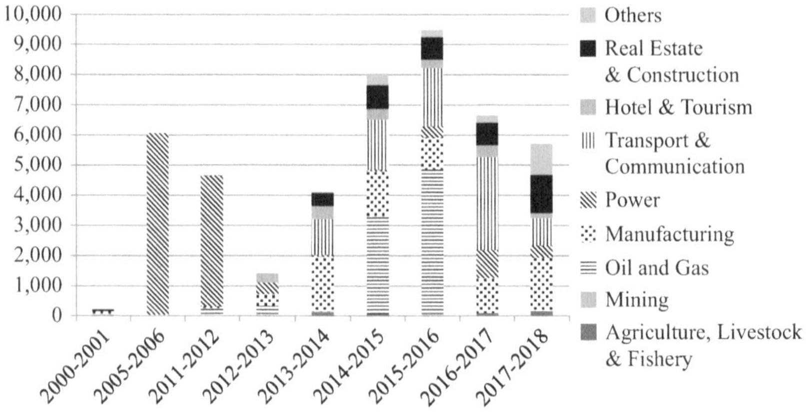

Fig. 11.8 Approved FDI flows to Myanmar, by sector (in million US$). Source: Directorate of Investment and Company Administration

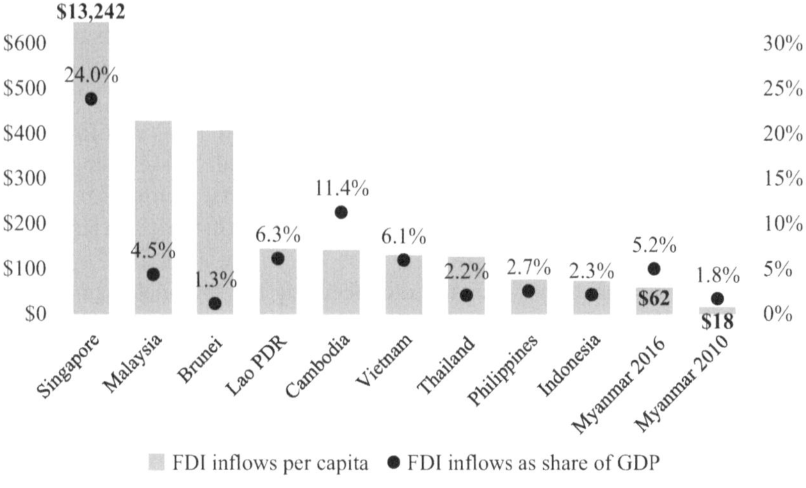

Fig. 11.9 FDI net inflows per capita and as share of GDP, 2016. Note: The entry for Singapore was re-scaled for better legibility. Source: WDI database

often originating from China. However, this has changed lately with FDI into manufacturing as well as into transport and communication strongly picking up. Together, these two sectors have accounted for about half of all FDI during the last five years (see Fig. 11.8).

Overall, the statistics reported in this section confirm that Myanmar's openness to international trade and cross-border capital flows has substantially increased over the last years.

Compliance with ASEAN Rules

Myanmar became a member of ASEAN in 1997. The ASEAN Economic Community (AEC) Blueprint 2025 enumerates several commitments that Myanmar needs to fulfill. Under the ASEAN Free Trade Area (AFTA), the AEC Blueprint 2025, and the ASEAN-plus-one FTAs with five other economies, Myanmar has been lowering tariff rates. Myanmar's Common Effective Preferential Tariff (CEPT) scheme under AFTA covers 99.3% of all tariff lines. Almost 93% of Myanmar's AFTA tariff lines are at 0% and none is higher than 10%. However, its tariff structure across all ASEAN-related FTAs is not always consistent (Nathan Associates 2016). Myanmar's negotiators need training to effectively participate in future rounds of trade negotiations, including the upcoming ASEAN Trade in Service Agreement. It lags behind other member states in implementing the National Single Window (NSW) and the National Trade Repository (NTR) to link up with their ASEAN-level counterparts. Among Myanmar enterprises, knowledge, understanding, and usage of trade preferences, including those under AFTA, are very low (Bernhardt et al. 2017b).

Myanmar still has a long way to go concerning the regional harmonization of (food safety, electrical equipment, etc.) standards. It also lacks national strategies to take advantage of the movement of skilled labor and investment within ASEAN. Regarding the freer flow of capital, with an investment liberalization rate of less than 80%, Myanmar lags behind most of its neighbors (Menon and Melendez 2017).

Progress is also necessary with respect to some behind-the-border issues. Myanmar needs to develop an effective enforcement mechanism for the national competition law. It still needs to enact a legal framework for consumer protection and intellectual property rights (Menon and Melendez 2017).

Outlook

The NLD's election victory created an enormous euphoria in Myanmar. However, since then the mood has become more sober as citizens realized that things will not change overnight and that the military still wields considerable power. The government will have to carefully manage expectations, both domestically and internationally, to avoid disappointments and preserve support for its project of transition. Even more important will be to achieve peace, reconciliation, and national unification. Success on this front will also help to stabilize the economy and the political system. One key question to be addressed in this context will be the extent to which the government is willing to decentralize power and follow a model of federalism in order to grant ethnic groups autonomy and participation in decision-making. An immediate priority is to address the humanitarian crisis arising from the conflict in Rakhine State—improving the living conditions of Rohingya in refugee camps in collaboration with Bangladesh, putting in place mechanisms for their eventual safe repatriation and reintegration, and devising a long-term plan for the peaceful coexistence of different communities. The future of the country will also depend significantly on how the civil government manages its relation with the military. Slowly cutting back the army's role and power will help render Myanmar's political system more democratic. It will also free public funds previously earmarked for military spending for social programs in areas like education and health. At the same time, the government needs to strengthen tax collection and public administration capacities. Further economic reforms, based on a long-term strategic vision and a clearly sequenced action plan, are needed to ensure macroeconomic stability, improve productive capacities, and deepen regional and global economic integration. To make economic growth inclusive, they have to be accompanied by well-designed social and labor market policies.

Notes

1. Unless otherwise noted, all statistics reported here are obtained from the World Bank's World Development Indicators (WDI) database (http://databank.worldbank.org/data/source/world-development-indicators).
2. See www.iom.int/countries/myanmar.

References

ADB. 2014. *Myanmar: Unlocking the Potential. Country Diagnostic Study.* Manila: ADB.

ADB (Asian Development Bank). 2016. *Myanmar Transport Sector Policy Note: How to Reduce Transport Costs.* Manila: ADB.

Bernhardt, Thomas. 2017. Myanmar, Say Hello to the World of Global Value Chains. In *Myanmar's Integration with the World: Challenges and Policy Options*, ed. Prabir De and Ajitava Raychaudhuri. Singapore: Palgrave Macmillan.

Bernhardt, Thomas, S. Kanay De, and Mi Win Thida. 2017a. *Myanmar labour issues from the perspective of enterprises: Findings from a survey of food processing and garment manufacturing enterprises.* Yangon: International Labour Organization.

Bernhardt, Thomas, Giles Dickenson-Jones, and S. Kanay De. 2017b. New Kids on the ASEAN Block: Myanmar SMEs and Regional Economic Integration. *Journal of Southeast Asian Economies* 34 (1): 4–38.

Bissinger, Jared. 2014. Myanmar's Economic Institutions in Transition. *Journal of Southeast Asian Economies* 31 (2): 241–255.

Charney, Michael. 2009. *A History of Modern Burma.* Cambridge: Cambridge University Press.

Ferrarini, Benno. 2014. Myanmar's Trade and Its Potential. *Journal of Southeast Asian Economies* 31 (2): 195–209.

Gabusi, Guiseppe. 2015. State, Market and Social Order: Myanmar's Political Economy Challenges. *European Journal of East Asian Studies* 14: 52–75.

GIZ. 2016. *Myanmar's Financial Sector. A Challenging Environment for Banks.* Yangon: GIZ.

IMF. 2018. *Myanmar: Staff Report for the 2017 Article IV Consultation.* Washington: IMF.

International Crisis Group. 2017. Myanmar's Rohingya Crisis Enters a Dangerous New Phase. www.crisisgroup.org/asia/south-east-asia/myanmar/292-myanmars-rohingya-crisis-enters-dangerous-new-phase. Accessed June 15, 2018.

Kipgen, Nehginpao. 2017. Militarization of Politics in Myanmar and Thailand. *International Studies* 53 (2): 53–172.

Menon, Jayant, and Anna Cassandra Melendez. 2017. Realizing an ASEAN Economic Community: Progress and Remaining Challenge. *Singapore Economic Review* 62 (3): 681–702.

Mizuno, Atsuko. 2016. Economic Relations Between Myanmar and China. In *The Myanmar Economy: Its Past, Present, and Prospects*, ed. Konosuke Odaka. Tokyo: Springer.

MOLES (Ministry of Labour, Employment and Social Security) and CSO (Central Statistical Organization). 2015. *Myanmar Labour Force, Child Labour and School-to-Work Transition Survey.* Nay Pyi Taw: MOLES.

Nathan Associates. 2016. *The Obligations of Membership: Myanmar in ASEAN*. Yangon: Nathan Associates.
Nitta, Yuichi. 2018. Two Years on, Myanmar's Lack of Reform Turns Investors Away. *Nikkei Asian Review*, March 30.
OECD. 2013. *Multi-Dimensional Review of Myanmar: Volume 1. Initial Assessment*. Paris: OECD.
Pulipaka, Sanjay. 2017. Myanmar's Political Transition, ed. De and Raychaudhuri.
Than, Tin Maung Maung. 2014. Introductory Overview: Myanmar's Economic Reforms. *Journal of Southeast Asian Economies* 31 (2): 165–172.
———. 2015. Myanmar's Economic Reforms: Hard Choices Ahead. *Social Research* 82 (2): 453–480.
The Economist. 2018. Myanmar's Government Unveils a 238-Point Economic Reform Plan, May 1.
Turnell, Sean. 2014. Banking and Financial Regulation and Reform in Myanmar. *Journal of Southeast Asian Economies* 31 (2): 225–240.
UNDP. 2014. *Myanmar One Pager Business Census 2013–2014*. Yangon: UNDP.
World Bank. 2017. *Enterprise Surveys – Country Profile Myanmar*. Washington: World Bank.

PART III

Some Context

CHAPTER 12

China and the ASEAN Economies: Interdependence and Rivalry

Stephen V. Marks and Cheryl Jia Min Yau

Introduction

Economic relations between Southeast Asia and China have been punctuated by a series of major policy developments over the past four decades. Following the death of Mao Zedong in 1976 and Deng Xiaoping's subsequent ascension to power in 1978, China began to turn outward and initiate market-oriented reforms internally. A visit by Deng to Southeast Asia in November 1978 left him impressed by the development of Singapore under Prime Minister Lee Kuan Yew, and he sent thousands of Chinese civil servants to learn from the experiences of Singapore and other countries.

During the Cold War era, diplomatic and trade relations between China and Southeast Asia were held back by concerns about the spread of communism in Southeast Asia. Since its accession to the World Trade

S. V. Marks (✉)
Pomona College, Claremont, CA, USA
e-mail: svm04747@pomona.edu

C. J. M. Yau
Pomona College, Claremont, CA, USA
e-mail: cyhg2015@MyMail.pomona.edu

R. Macdonald (ed.), *Southeast Asia and the ASEAN Economic Community*, https://doi.org/10.1007/978-3-030-19722-3_12

Organization in December 2001, however, with its double-digit growth and greatly increased integration into international commerce, China has become a major driver of economic conditions in Southeast Asia. It is a rival to Southeast Asian economies in export markets for apparel, electronics and other manufactures as well as an important market for raw materials and intermediate inputs from those countries. Association of Southeast Asian Nations (ASEAN)-China economic agreements have further propelled economic integration in the region. An Agreement on Trade in Goods entered into force in 2005 and will be fully implemented in all countries by 2020. An Agreement on Trade in Services followed in 2007 and an Agreement on Investment in 2010. By 2010, China had overtaken Japan as Southeast Asia's largest trading partner.

More Recent Developments

The maturation of the Chinese economy has driven an outward push from China to develop infrastructure and other activities in much of Eurasia. In speeches in Kazakhstan and Indonesia in 2013, President Xi Jinping announced a policy now known as the Belt and Road Initiative (BRI), through which China has arranged numerous infrastructure projects on a bilateral basis, mainly intended to enhance overland and maritime transportation routes that involve China. While the BRI is not specific to Southeast Asia, the region is an important venue for the initiative. In parallel with the launching of the BRI has been the founding under China's leadership of the multilateral Asian Infrastructure Investment Bank (AIIB), also announced by Xi in the visit to Indonesia.

A matter of considerable debate has been the extent to which China has undertaken these various initiatives with benign intentions for mutual economic benefit or to assert economic and political hegemony over developing countries in Asia and beyond. These concerns have been heightened by increased military activity by China related to various disputes in the South China Sea (SCS), a maritime region rich in natural resources and of geostrategic importance.

The perceived need to respond to a more assertive China in Asia had been a major motivation behind the "Pivot to Asia" under US President Barack Obama in 2012. The Obama Administration subsequently engaged with Asia and the Pacific, but not China, through negotiations on the Trans-Pacific Partnership (TPP) economic agreement, which included Singapore, Malaysia, Vietnam and Brunei among its Southeast Asian participants as well as Japan, Canada, Australia, New Zealand, Chile, Peru and Mexico.

The TPP was an ambitious agreement that in effect would have put a US imprimatur on regional commerce, with provisions on environmental standards, intellectual property, labour rights, investor-state dispute settlement and good governance, among others. It was signed by all 12 of the participating states in February 2016, but political resistance to the agreement within the United States culminated in withdrawal from the agreement by President Donald Trump on his fourth day in office in January 2017. Trump instead advocated for bilateral economic agreements with countries in the Indo-Pacific region, which he asserted would be more favourable to American workers and US economic interests in general.

The 11 other states that had participated in the TPP negotiations managed a pivot of their own and completed a revised agreement, the Comprehensive and Progressive Agreement for Trans-Pacific Partnership (CPTPP), which was signed by all in March 2018 and entered into force at the end of 2018, given that seven states had ratified it (Australia, Canada, Japan, Mexico, New Zealand, Singapore and Vietnam). Moreover, negotiations have been underway since 2012 on a Regional Comprehensive Economic Partnership (RCEP) agreement, to include the ten members of ASEAN and the six states with which ASEAN has trade agreements—China, Japan, South Korea, India, Australia and New Zealand. The agreement would be the largest free trade agreement (FTA) in the world in terms of population and GDP of the participating states, though it would be much more limited in scope than the TPP.

Trump Administration trade actions in early 2018 escalated into a trade war with China, based on US claims that China had given its producers unfair advantages in international competition, such as by coercing technology transfers from companies seeking to do business in China, but also on US concerns with the persistent bilateral trade deficits with China. The conflict was a source of economic disruption to Southeast Asia: it introduced the possibility of expanded manufactured exports to the United States and other countries, but also of reduced exports of raw materials and intermediate inputs to China. It also threatened to cause a regional or even global economic slowdown.

Plan of the Chapter

To appraise how dependent the various ASEAN states are on China, we first survey developments in trade in goods, in particular with reference to international supply chains, as well as recent issues related to trade agreements and policies, such as the spread of non-tariff barriers to trade. We then summarize the findings of an event study we have conducted to assess the impact of the US-China trade war on the corporate sectors of various economies, which casts light on matters of rivalry and interdependence between China and Southeast Asia through the lens of asset markets. We also consider demographic, education and research and development trends expected to influence trade between China and Southeast Asia in the future.

We next turn to issues related to foreign direct investment (FDI). We examine the nature and magnitude of FDI flows between Southeast Asia and China, and then discuss the implications of infrastructure investments under the BRI and the AIIB. Although arguably the ultimate goal of the BRI was to supplant the United States as a regional hegemon in Asia in particular, we contend that it will expose China to some of the economic and political liabilities of interdependence as well.

We lastly touch on other aspects of the relationship between China and the ASEAN countries—monetary cooperation, environmental concerns and territorial disputes—and then pull our various themes into a broader discussion of power relations between China and the ASEAN member states. We seek to offer insight into China's motivations in its relations with Southeast Asia and into how leaders in that region have navigated the complexities of their relationships with the United States and China.

Trade Relations Between China and Southeast Asia

Trade between Southeast Asia and China began to climb with the end of the Cold War and has grown explosively in the new millennium. In 2010 US dollars, total merchandise trade between China and Southeast Asia in 2016 was more than ten times its level in the year 2000. Figure 12.1 shows Southeast Asian exports to China, and Fig. 12.2 shows Southeast Asian imports from China, over 2000–2016, broken down into capital goods, primary industrial inputs, processed industrial inputs and consumption goods.[1]

It is notable that real exports from ASEAN to China have not increased since 2011, whereas ASEAN imports from China have continued to grow vigorously. Part of the explanation rests in Indonesia, which in 2014 imposed strict limits on exports of unprocessed minerals and metal ores, partly to encourage development of downstream processing sectors.

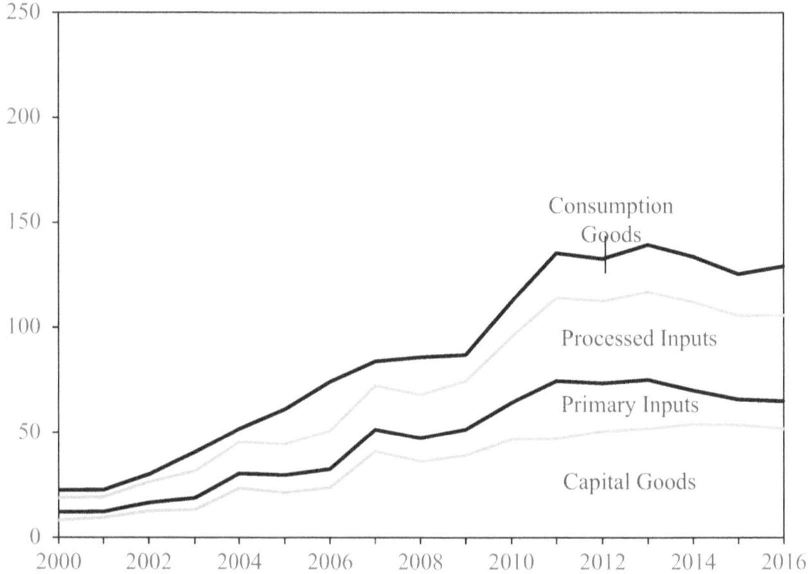

Fig. 12.1 Southeast Asian exports to China, 2000–2016 (billions of 2010 US dollars). Data source: UN Comtrade database, Broad Economic Categories; calculations by authors

However, Fig. 12.1, and the Indonesian data behind it, indicates considerable shrinkage of exports of primary products to China after 2013, without much of a concomitant rise in processed exports. Figures 12.1 and 12.2 also indicate that primary commodities play a much larger role in China's imports from than its exports to ASEAN countries. This is consistent with the scholarship that identifies Southeast Asia as a strategic natural resource hinterland for a rapidly growing China (Arase 2015).

Table 12.1 shows how dependent on China the various ASEAN economies were in 2016 relative to their global merchandise exports, imports and total trade. Myanmar and Laos were heavily dependent on China as an export market, while Cambodia, Myanmar, Vietnam and even Indonesia were quite dependent on China as a source of imports. Myanmar, Laos, Cambodia and Vietnam were the most dependent on China for trade overall.

Figures 12.1 and 12.2 together indicate that the ASEAN countries overall have slid towards increased merchandise trade deficits with China

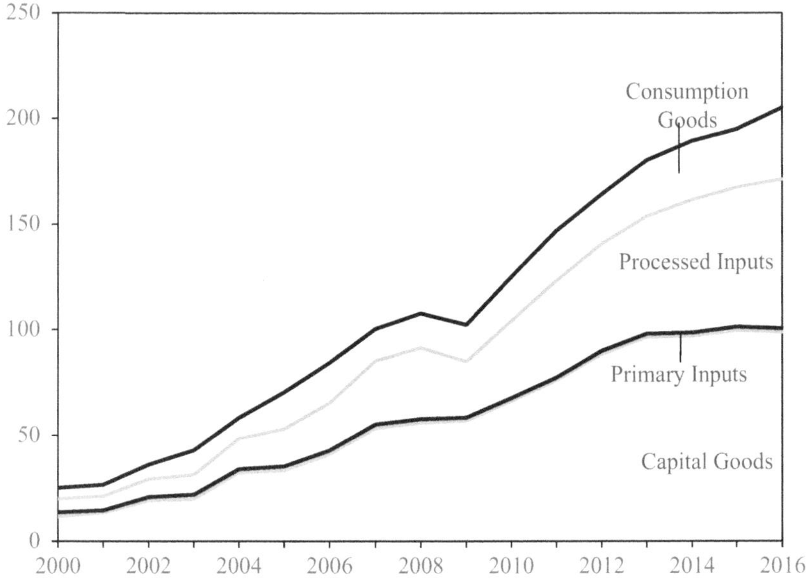

Fig. 12.2 Southeast Asian imports from China, 2000–2016 (billions of 2010 US. dollars). Data source: UN Comtrade database, Broad Economic Categories; calculations by authors

Table 12.1 Share of exports, imports and total trade with China, 2016 (per cent)

	Exports	*Imports*	*Total*
Brunei	4.7	13.0	7.6
Cambodia	6.1	36.8	23.0
Indonesia	11.6	22.7	17.0
Laos	36.1	18.2	26.0
Malaysia	12.5	20.4	16.2
Myanmar	40.8	34.4	37.2
Philippines	11.0	18.5	15.5
Singapore	13.1	13.9	13.5
Thailand	11.0	21.6	16.1
Vietnam	12.4	28.6	20.5
All ASEAN	12.5	20.7	16.5

Data source: UN Comtrade database, Broad Economic Categories; calculations by authors in recent years. Bilateral trade imbalances are of no particular consequence economically but may be problematic in terms of domestic politics or perceived dependency. Except for Singapore, the ASEAN countries experienced deterioration in their bilateral balances with China around 2010–2012, as the ASEAN-China FTA had been mostly phased in and these countries recovered from the global recession of 2008–2009. The only notable bilateral trade deficits with China by 2016, however, were 19.7 per cent of GDP in Cambodia and 13.7 per cent of GDP in Vietnam.[2]

The overall current account deficit is a better indicator of macroeconomic sustainability, and by that measure, the only major deficit countries have been Cambodia (8.9 per cent of GDP, 2016), Laos (7.8 per cent, 2016) and Myanmar (5.7 per cent, 2017), the least developed countries in ASEAN.

Production Networks in East Asia

While Southeast Asia has generally shared in the growth from the economic boom in China, the rise of China as an exporter of manufactured goods has prompted numerous studies examining whether this represents a threat to the exports of other developing countries, in East Asia in particular. A selective look at the literature is useful.

Holst and Weiss (2004) conclude from their econometric analysis that there is potential for both competition and complementarity between China and Southeast Asia: while the rise of Chinese exports has led to increasing competition for Southeast Asian exports in third markets like Japan and the United States in the short run, there is potential for export growth of all the economies of East Asia in the long run, if policymakers are able to facilitate an optimal regional division of production processes.

In a departure from prior gravity model studies of the impact of the rise of China on the export performance of other Asian countries,[3] Athukorala (2009) separates trade in parts and components from that in final goods. Based on analysis of annual data over 1992–2005, he finds that the bulk of Chinese manufactured exports, even of advanced-technology products, did not involve value added in advanced-technology activities in China. Instead, labour-intensive final assembly in China complemented the manufacture of parts and components in other East Asian countries. China's expansion into world markets for these goods had a positive effect on all East Asian exporters, but less so on South Korea and Japan, which have lost comparative advantage in labour-intensive activities. China drew significantly on parts and components as well as machinery from Indonesia, Malaysia, Thailand and the Philippines. Singapore was at an intermediate position between the two groups.

Kong and Kneller (2016) examine exports of eight Asian countries over 1994–2008, using a gravity model that reflects the latest theoretical developments but that can only be used to infer relative and not absolute effects on exports of other countries. For exports of parts and components, countries with greater endowments of human capital have benefited more from the growth of China's exports, given that parts and components tend to be more sophisticated technologically; Japan, South Korea and Malaysia ranked the highest in human capital, among the eight included countries. In contrast, for exports of final goods, countries with higher ratios of physical capital to labour benefited more from the growth in China's exports, though only in the period prior to China's entry into the World Trade Organization (WTO); Japan, Singapore and South Korea ranked highest among the included countries in these terms. Given that Indonesia, Thailand and the Philippines are all at the low end in terms of human and physical capital, and that South Korea and Japan are at the high end; these conclusions seem rather inconsistent with those of Athukorala, particularly for the earlier period, though the differences may be partly due to the difference in the years examined in the two studies.

Further analyses of the effects of China's exports on exports of other Asian countries no doubt will emerge. In any case, economists have a strong intuition that countries that have different relative endowments of factors of production than China should tend to do better, given the expansion of exports from China. It is also clear that patterns of competitive advantage have evolved rapidly in Asia in recent years, as capital accumulation and technological advance in China in particular have propelled it upward in product value chains.

Table 12.2 offers some simple perspectives on the linkages between the various ASEAN economies and international production networks in 2016: it shows the share of capital goods (including parts and accessories but excluding transportation equipment) and processed industrial inputs (excluding fuels and lubricants) in the exports and imports of each ASEAN country as well as China, South Korea and Japan. The share of capital goods exports is a rough indicator of the relative level of manufacturing development within the country: it is especially low for Cambodia, Brunei, Laos, Myanmar and Indonesia—though Brunei and Indonesia have large oil and gas sectors, particularly Brunei in relative terms, while Indonesia also exports large amounts of other primary industrial inputs. Among the

Table 12.2 Share of capital goods and processed industrial inputs in exports and imports (per cent), 2016

	Exports		*Imports*	
	Capital Goods	*Processed Inputs*	*Capital Goods*	*Processed Inputs*
Brunei	3.6	5.5	20.1	26.5
Cambodia	3.4	7.4	11.6	54.5
Indonesia	6.8	23.2	26.3	35.9
Laos	5.1	24.5	22.9	28.2
Malaysia	41.2	20.3	40.6	25.2
Myanmar	5.7	6.7	15.8	29.5
Philippines	56.3	15.1	36.9	24.2
Singapore	50.2	20.2	43.2	17.9
Thailand	26.6	24.7	31.1	32.8
Vietnam	34.9	14.6	37.8	37.3
China	40.3	23.1	38.5	24.5
South Korea	41.1	26.1	30.4	23.6
Japan	36.4	24.7	23.0	18.5

Data source: UN Comtrade database, Broad Economic Categories; calculations by authors

ASEAN economies, if capital goods and processed inputs are combined, the Philippines, Singapore, Malaysia and Thailand are the most linked on the export side with international production networks relative to their total exports, while Vietnam, Cambodia, Malaysia, Thailand and Indonesia are the most linked on the import side to such networks relative to their total imports.

To provide a more detailed perspective on dependence on trade with China among the ASEAN economies, the top combined import shares of capital goods and processed inputs from China in 2016 were 31.7 per cent of total imports for Cambodia, 22.6 per cent for Myanmar, 17.9 per cent for Vietnam, 15.1 per cent for Indonesia, 14.3 per cent for Thailand and 10.3 per cent for Malaysia. The top equivalent figures on the export side were only 5.5 per cent for Singapore and 4.8 per cent for Malaysia. The inference is that the ASEAN countries are far more dependent on China as a supplier than as a user of capital goods and processed inputs, consistent with the impressions given by comparison of Figs. 12.1 and 12.2. Contrary to the traditional perception that China is the assembly point for regional value chains in Asia, then, there is evidence that these value chains have evolved, with more of final assembly now being done in Southeast Asia. These trade developments go hand in hand with developments in foreign direct investment, as we discuss below.

Trade Agreements and Policies

An influential paper by Richard Baldwin (2008) observed that East Asia had been remarkably successful at integrating production processes across national boundaries. Nevertheless, Baldwin argued that "Factory Asia" was fragile, because it depended critically on the openness of the regional trading system. Baldwin noted that, unlike the most-favoured-nation tariff rates administered by the WTO, regional preferential tariffs negotiated under ASEAN rubrics are not bound within certain levels. However, the recent history of Indonesian trade policy does not bear out this particular concern: under pressure from various domestic interests in 2010 because of the increase in imports due to the ASEAN-China FTA, for example, Indonesia stood by its tariff commitments, in deference to the ASEAN alliance.

Baldwin identified another threat in the "Noodle Bowl Syndrome": under the ASEAN FTA as well as the ASEAN-China FTA, and all the rest that would come later, a complex tangle of bilateral agreements emerged. In the ASEAN-China agreement, for example, there are effectively ten bilateral agreements. In simplified terms, each country specifies a sensitive list of products for which it will not allow major tariff concessions. For each pair of countries, a country is not eligible to receive preferences for items on its own sensitive list, and is not granted preferences for items on the sensitive list of the other country. The multiplicity of tariff schedules and the rules of origin necessitated by the multiple schedules can impose transaction costs on all firms.

Kawai and Wignaraja (2011) have presented firm-level survey evidence that noodle-bowl effects do exist.[4] In addition, Cadot and Ing (2016) use a product-level gravity model to identify the effects of ASEAN's rules of origin on trade in the region, and estimate that the average tariff equivalent of these policies is 3.4 per cent over all rules and sectors. The trade-weighted average is 2.1 per cent.

Despite the success in regional tariff cutting, and partly because of it, the new millennium has witnessed a proliferation of non-tariff trade barriers throughout the ASEAN economies, particularly since 2010.[5] Indonesia has imposed an array of opaque barriers that in some cases are counter not only to its regional commitments but also to the rules of the WTO.[6] ASEAN countries also have more restrictive policies on services trade than almost any other part of the world.[7]

China similarly maintains many restrictions on trade and investment. Devadason and Chenayah (2014) find evidence that technical barriers to trade in China have had a depressive effect on ASEAN exports.[8] China's restraints on exports of various raw materials,[9] intended at least in part to protect downstream industries, may be partly responsible for the miniscule portion of primary products in China's exports to ASEAN countries shown in Fig. 12.2. Moreover, a number of the trade and investment barriers maintained by China have not proven readily resolvable through the WTO, much less through narrowly drawn regional pacts. For example, state enterprises, which are extensive in the Chinese economy, may favour domestic purchases over imports. Domestic subsidies favour local businesses, and the anti-monopoly law may protect state enterprises to some extent.

Recognition of the benefits of more complete economic integration has contributed to the push for the ASEAN Economic Community (AEC)—the cumulation of agreements and initiatives within ASEAN on trade in goods and services, investment, financial capital flows, immigration and other trade-related matters. It has also led to the broader regional push for the RCEP and the CPTPP. It remains uncertain how much political will exists to conclude negotiations on the RCEP, particularly given that China would be the most powerful party to the agreement, or to ward off the domestic interests that have so far undermined genuine realization of the goals of the AEC.

Southeast Asia and the Trade War Between the United States and China

The ongoing trade conflict between the United States and China offers a natural experiment on the extent to which the various Southeast Asian economies are in a rivalrous or dependent relationship with China. Marks and Yau (2019) examine how the conflict has affected the corporate sectors of these and other economies through an event study of the trade war, looking at the impact of news in the conflict on stock market valuations in various countries, as indicated by abnormal daily returns of country-specific exchange traded funds (ETFs) traded on US stock exchanges. These ETFs mimic broad indexes of share prices in the various countries.

The relationship between developments in the trade war and economic activity in Southeast Asia is complex. Intensification of the conflict could depress global market prospects in the short run, through macroeconomic uncertainties or financial contagion. Over the longer run, some sectors in Southeast Asian and other developing countries might be harmed, but others benefited, by increased US import tariffs on Chinese products or Chinese tariffs on US products. Exporters of raw materials or intermediate inputs to China could lose, for example, while exporters of finished manufactured consumer or capital goods to that country could gain.

Similarly, exporters in competition with Chinese exports to the United States could gain. However, even if China's exports to the United States are significantly affected, depreciation of the renminbi, ultimately under the control of the state in China, could offset the higher US tariffs to some extent and make Chinese exports even more competitive in other markets.

If resolution of the trade war does not curb coerced technology transfers by China, Beijing may continue to leverage its vast market to gain technological advantages over ASEAN countries, among others. Southeast Asia could benefit from a reshaping of supply chains, however, given that the threat of a prolonged war has accelerated the relocation of some manufacturing businesses to Southeast Asia from China.[10]

Our approach was to let financial markets summarize all these complex effects of the conflict on corporate sectors of various countries. We find that abnormal returns in much of Southeast Asia—notably Malaysia, the Philippines, Singapore and Thailand—have tended to be positively correlated with those in China.

Two countries are less in conformity with this pattern, however, and for different reasons. As China in particular has become a formidable rival, Indonesia has turned inward to a considerable extent, as reflected in the dramatic spread of non-tariff trade barriers in that country. In contrast, Vietnam is not nearly as far along in its development, but has embraced globalization through key reductions in trade barriers and regulatory reforms, and has offered investors lower labour costs and a geopolitical-risk hedge compared to China. Korean manufacturer Samsung now makes most of its smartphones in Vietnam, for example, and is the largest firm there.[11]

Over 2005–2015, Indonesia's manufactured exports rose by a respectable 71.0 per cent; the domestic value-added share in those exports rose from 75.4 to 82.4 per cent, while China's share rose from 2.2 to 3.9 per cent. In contrast, Vietnam's manufactured exports rose by a spectacular 461.3 per cent, but the domestic value-added share decreased from 58.2 to 51.8 per cent, while China's share rose from 6.1 to 15.9 per cent. In electronics and electrical exports from Vietnam, the domestic value-added share decreased from 52.8 to 38.8 per cent, while China's share rose from 5.7 to 20.9 per cent and South Korea's from 3.9 to 10.0 per cent. This is consistent with expectations: expansion of final assembly manufacturing in Vietnam can lead to rapid growth in exports, but also to increases in imports of intermediate inputs.

Each of these policy approaches has potential drawbacks. Applying opaque non-tariff trade barriers in Indonesia undermines good governance and risks further escalation of domestic costs, while Vietnam risks excessive dependency on external markets.

In terms of stock market outcomes, Indonesia exhibits some positive correlation with China, but less regularly than other ASEAN economies, and the market there appears to have been driven more by idiosyncratic factors. This is consistent with Indonesia being a large country that has turned inward and disengaged from regional supply chains to some extent, which could lessen its susceptibility to external economic shocks.

Vietnam also has been less affected by the trade war than many ASEAN economies. With its outward turn in recent years, Vietnam is integrated into regional supply chains. However, like Indonesia, Vietnam has a relatively small amount of value added at stake in China's exports. Moreover, as an emerging manufacturing hub, Vietnam is poised to benefit as firms consider relocating their factories from China. Le Dang Doanh, a former senior economic adviser to five prime ministers, argued that Vietnam could gain as the lowest-cost location for manufacturing in the CPTPP bloc. The company that manufactures AirPods wireless earphones for Apple announced in late 2018, for example, that it would move its production operation from China to Vietnam, because of the trade war.[12] Companies already present in Vietnam do not necessarily view further investment as an unalloyed benefit, however, since it could lead to higher labour costs or cause Vietnam to be targeted next by the United States.

Demographic Trends

To anticipate future developments in the economic relationship between China and Southeast Asia, it is important to examine demographic trends in the region. Wei, Xie, and Zhang (2017) observe that the one-child policy maintained by China between 1979 and 2015 contributed for a time to rapid economic growth in that country, by lowering the dependency ratio, as fewer children were being born, allowing entry into the labour force by working-age adults who might otherwise have had parental responsibilities. The growth dividends paid by the policy have now become liabilities, however. Wei, Xie and Zhang note that the working-age cohort in China has been shrinking in absolute terms since 2012. Further, the relaxation of the one-child policy will mean that, for a time, the dependency ratio will increase to the extent that there is an increase in the birth rate, although the latest data from the World Bank indicate that, with the ending of the policy, the birth rate in China has ticked upward only slightly, from 1.60 births per woman in 2012 to 1.62 in 2016. Moreover, the policy has contributed to the rapid ageing of the population. Recent projections are that 36.5 per cent of China's population will be aged 60 or older by 2050, versus 15.2 per cent in 2015.[13]

In terms of projected working-age population (15 to 64 years) growth rates between 2015 and 2050, China is at −21.1, South Korea at −26.4 and Japan at −28.4 per cent, while in Southeast Asia the Philippines is at 54.6, Malaysia at 28.0, Indonesia at 22.9, Vietnam at 6.1, Singapore at −9.8 and Thailand at −26.8 per cent.[14] For most of Southeast Asia, then, labour force growth trends will be opposite those in China over the next several decades.

Finally, the exceptional rates of growth in industrial production in China in recent years could not have been achieved without drawing down the labour force in agriculture. For a substantial loss of agricultural output to be avoided, labour productivity has had to increase in that sector, which has further raised the opportunity cost of labour time employed in industry.

These trends have contributed to the rise of labour costs in China relative to other developing countries in Asia, making its traditional labour-intensive role in "Factory Asia" increasingly untenable. One set of international labour cost comparisons indicates that US dollar labour cost per employee in manufacturing rose over 2010–2017 by 113.6 per cent in China, versus only 24.8 per cent in Singapore and 26.1 per cent in South Korea, while real value added per worker rose by 71.7 per cent in China versus 29.9 per cent in Singapore and 11.5 per cent in South Korea. Thus, labour costs adjusted for productivity changes increased substantially in China relative to these two countries.[15] There is also widespread anecdotal evidence that the escalation of labour cost in China is one factor pushing manufacturers to shift production to Southeast Asia in "China-plus-one" strategies, in which companies retain a presence in China but put much of their incremental investments into other countries.[16]

Trade and Made in China 2025

China is staking much of its economic future on its ability to boost productivity through technological innovation, and announced in 2015 its intention under the "Made in China 2025" strategic blueprint to make China the world leader in advanced manufacturing, in sectors such as robotics, biotechnology and aerospace.[17] Part of the transformation would involve supplying domestically far greater portions of components and parts for various advanced-technology products. The policy is driven by concern whether China can avoid the middle-income trap for developing countries whose labour and other costs have risen above those of other developing countries but whose technological capabilities and innovation have not risen to a level competitive with developed economies.[18] The concern is acute in China in light of the demographic trends noted above.

Not only is there evidence that the transformation envisioned in Made in China 2025 is underway, but that the economies of Southeast Asia will be affected as well. Table 12.3 indicates backward linkages in international value chains within East and Southeast Asia from 2005 to 2015, based on the Trade in Value-Added database of the Organisation for Economic Co-operation and Development (OECD). Note first that nominal gross exports of goods and services measured in US dollars more than doubled from ASEAN, and more than tripled from China, over this period. For ASEAN's exports, the share of value added that came from within ASEAN edged upward, from 68.6 to 71.1 per cent; for China's exports, the share from within China increased much more markedly, from 73.7 to 82.7 per cent. However, China's share of value added in ASEAN's gross exports more than doubled, from 2.9 to 6.2 per cent. Much of the increase has come at the expense of Japan, the United States and the European Union.[19] In contrast, ASEAN's value-added share in China's exports has shrunk, from 2.4 to 1.8 per cent.

The impression, then, is that growth in the absorption of foreign raw materials and intermediate inputs has slowed in Asia, particularly in China, but that China has emerged as a more prominent exporter of intermediate inputs to other Asian countries. Similar trends are evident on a more disaggregated basis. For example, in the coveted computer, electronics and electrical equipment sectors, OECD data shows that China's gross exports rose by 195.7 per cent between 2005 and 2015; its value-added share sourced domestically rose from 59.9 to 73.0 per cent, while its share sourced from ASEAN diminished from 4.5 to 3.5 per cent. ASEAN, in contrast, enjoyed an increase in gross exports of only 37.0 per cent; the value-added share sourced within ASEAN rose from 51.9 to 57.4 per cent, while the share sourced from China doubled, from 5.6 to 11.2 per

Table 12.3 Origin of value added in gross exports of all goods and services, ASEAN and China, 2005–2015

	2005	*2006*	*2007*	*2008*	*2009*	*2010*	*2011*	*2012*	*2013*	*2014*	*2015*
ASEAN's Exports in USD (2005 = 100)	100.0	116.7	135.1	154.2	135.3	171.5	205.2	209.4	213.1	219.3	203.3
Value-Added Share (%)											
ASEAN	68.6	69.2	69.9	69.5	71.9	71.6	71.1	70.9	71.0	70.8	71.1
China	2.9	3.1	3.4	3.4	3.6	3.5	3.8	4.3	4.7	5.3	6.2
Japan	5.2	4.6	4.4	4.3	4.0	4.2	3.7	3.6	3.1	3.2	3.3
South Korea	1.6	1.6	1.8	1.4	1.4	1.6	1.4	1.5	1.6	1.6	1.7
Taiwan	1.5	1.4	1.4	1.0	1.1	1.1	1.0	0.9	0.9	1.0	1.2
Other	20.3	20.0	19.2	20.4	18.0	18.1	18.9	18.8	18.8	18.1	16.5
China's Exports in USD (2005 = 100)	100.0	128.0	163.9	195.3	162.1	207.4	261.8	283.1	305.5	327.9	314.9
Value-Added Share (%)											
ASEAN	2.4	2.5	2.4	2.1	2.0	2.2	2.2	2.1	2.1	1.9	1.8
China	73.7	74.1	75.2	77.0	80.5	78.9	78.3	79.2	79.7	80.5	82.7
Japan	4.6	4.2	3.8	3.2	2.6	2.6	2.4	2.1	1.8	1.7	1.6
South Korea	3.1	2.9	2.7	2.0	1.9	2.0	1.8	1.9	2.0	1.9	2.0
Taiwan	2.8	2.7	2.4	1.8	1.7	1.7	1.5	1.5	1.6	1.5	1.6
Other	13.4	13.6	13.5	13.8	11.2	12.6	13.8	13.2	12.9	12.4	10.3

Data source: OECD Trade in Value Added (TiVA) database, 2018 update; calculations by authors cent. These trends align with the Made in China 2025 goal to technologically upgrade Chinese industry and exports.

Made in China 2025 placed major emphasis on indigenous technological development but also stated that transfer of advanced technologies from abroad should continue. Thus, the plan became a flash point in the trade negotiations between the United States and China. While media reports suggested that its targets could be postponed, or the plan discarded altogether,[20] it is doubtful that Beijing will abandon its long-run development goals.

Education and R&D Trends

The impact that China will have on Southeast Asian economies over the long run depends in part on trends in education and research and development (R&D), which clearly are closely tied to the realization of its Made in China 2025 goals.

There is evidence that China is pushing ahead of some Southeast Asian countries in education. The OECD reports on international educational assessments based on standardized testing in mathematics, reading and science through the PISA (Program for International Student Assessment) database.[21] Table 12.4 shows PISA assessments for OECD countries and OECD partner countries in Asia. In terms of mean assessments, China ranked ahead of Indonesia, Thailand and Malaysia in all three fields, ahead of Vietnam in mathematics and reading, and ahead of South Korea in mathematics and science. Scores in all three fields had higher standard deviations in China than in other countries, however, indicating unevenness in educational outcomes there.

To provide a sense of relative trends, Table 12.5 shows data from the United Nations Educational, Scientific and Cultural Organization (UNESCO) on gross enrolment ratios in various Asian countries at the primary, secondary and tertiary levels of education in 2012 and 2017.[22]

Most of the countries recorded increases in both secondary and tertiary enrolments over 2012–2017, but the surge in higher-education enrolments in China was truly impressive: China passed Indonesia, the Philippines, Malaysia and Thailand in the rankings and, by 2017, was behind only South Korea, Singapore and Japan. While China scholar David Shambaugh (2015) notes that higher education in China is subject to major deficiencies, including corruption and emphasis on rote memorization, these problems are shared by educational institutions in much of Southeast Asia.

Table 12.4 Mean PISA assessments, all 15-year old students, 2015, available Asian countries[a]

	Mathematics	*Reading*	*Science*
China	531.3	493.9	517.8
	(4.9)	(5.1)	(4.6)
Japan	532.4	516.0	538.4
	(3.0)	(3.2)	(3.0)
Indonesia	386.1	397.3	403.1
	(3.1)	(2.9)	(2.6)
Malaysia	446.1	430.6	442.9
	(3.3)	(3.5)	(3.0)
Singapore	564.2	535.1	555.6
	(1.5)	(1.6)	(1.2)
South Korea	524.1	517.4	515.8
	(3.7)	(3.5)	(3.1)
Taiwan	542.3	497.1	532.3
	(3.0)	(2.5)	(2.7)
Thailand	415.5	409.1	421.3
	(3.0)	(3.3)	(2.8)
Vietnam	494.5	486.8	524.6
	(4.5)	(3.7)	(3.9)

Data source: OECD Program for International Student Assessment

[a]Standard errors in parentheses

Expansion of higher education and R&D capabilities go hand in hand. Evidence from the recent past indicates a strong commitment in China to domestic R&D. Table 12.6 shows UNESCO data on R&D expenditures by global and regional technological leaders in 2016.[23]

Although the United States is the global leader in total R&D, China spends more on commercially applicable product and process development than any other country. Moreover, average annual real growth in total R&D expenditure by China, at 11 per cent, vastly exceeds the growth rates in the United States, Japan and Germany.[24]

In their granular look at developments in R&D in China, Wei, Xie and Zhang argue that the prospects for rapid advance by China in innovation and labour productivity growth depend in part on government policy reforms that allow a greater share of R&D to be conducted by private firms compared to state-owned enterprises, along with continued commitment to protection of intellectual property rights of Chinese firms and education of the population.

Table 12.5 Gross enrolment ratios by education level, 2012 and 2017

	Primary		*Upper Secondary*[a]		*Tertiary*	
	2012	*2017*	*2012*	*2017*	*2012*	*2017*
Brunei	105.9	104.8	104.5	86.8	22.4	32.9
Cambodia	121.8	107.8	58.1	69.3	13.1[b]	13.1
China	105.2	102.1	81.1	85.1	28.0	51.0
India	109.8	114.5[c]	57.7	65.5[c]	24.4	26.9[c]
Indonesia	109.3	103.5	69.5	80.1	28.7	36.3
Japan	101.3	98.2[c]	101.6	102.2[c]	61.4	63.6[c]
Laos	121.3	107.0	33.6	52.6	17.6	15.7
Malaysia	103.5	103.1	72.4	83.3	36.3	41.9
Myanmar	101.9[d]	113.0	35.2[d]	49.2	13.9	16.0
Philippines	113.9[d]	110.9[c]	75.1	77.8[c]	31.2	35.3
South Korea	99.7	97.0[c]	94.9	101.0[c]	96.6	93.8[c]
Singapore	–	100.8[c]	–	110.0[c]	–	83.9[c]
Thailand	96.9	99.6	72.9	112.3	50.7	49.3[c]
Vietnam	106.8	107.9	90.2	98.7[c]	25.0	28.3

Data source: UNESCO Institute for Statistics, http://data.uis.unesco.org/

[a]Lower secondary for Cambodia and Vietnam

[b]2015 data

[c]2016 data

[d]2014 data

Table 12.6 Research and development expenditure comparisons, 2016

	United States	*China*	*Japan*	*South Korea*
R&D in Billions of Current PPP[a] US Dollars				
Total R&D	511.1	451.9	165.7	77.7
Basic Research	86.3	23.7	20.8	12.4
Applied Research	100.3	46.4	31.2	17.5
Development	323.4	381.8	106.1	47.8
Not specified	1.1	0.0	7.5	0.0
Total R&D as % of GDP	2.7	2.1	3.1	4.2
Annual Growth in Total R&D in 2005 PPP US Dollars, 2011–2016	1.9	11.0	0.6	5.4

Data source: UNESCO Institute for Statistics, UIS.Stat database (http://data.uis.unesco.org/); calculations by authors

[a]Purchasing power parity

R&D expenditure data for Southeast Asia are incomplete, but for the region overall UNESCO estimates that total R&D was 0.9 per cent of GDP in 2015, versus the 2.1 per cent of GDP shown in Table 12.6 for China in 2016, and that the average annual real growth rate of R&D expenditure was 7.0 per cent over 2011–2015, versus the 11.0 per cent rate for China over 2011–2016. The region thus lags the Asian and global R&D leaders, China in particular.

The impression from the education and R&D data is that China seeks to compete more with industrialized countries than the middle-income countries of Southeast Asia, consistent with the goals of Made in China 2025. ASEAN countries with lower labour costs may enjoy further opportunities to export labour-intensive products, particularly as China continues to move production offshore, but will face tough competition from China in trying to upgrade their production capabilities in human-capital-intensive sectors that rely on advanced technologies. Moreover, the automation of production is eroding the cost advantages of dispersed supply chains, and further technological advance in China and other regional leaders will continue to do so over the long run.

Capital Flows Between China and Southeast Asia

Flows of foreign direct investment have also interconnected China and Southeast Asia, and have largely been complementary to trade. Under the "Go Out" policy initiated by China around the start of the new millennium, state and private actors invested upstream around the globe to secure natural resources, and to recycle China's current account surpluses. With the passage of time, more and more investments have been made downstream in international supply chains, and the government has coordinated outward capital flows to develop infrastructure in other developing countries, in particular under the rubric of the Belt and Road Initiative.

Historical and Recent Trends and Data

Figure 12.3 compares net inflows and outflows of foreign direct investment for China over 1990–2017. Particularly in the years prior to its accession to the World Trade Organization, China was aided by inward flows of FDI. Ye (2014) observes that, over 1978–1993, the earliest years of the reform era in China, investment by the ethnic Chinese diaspora (mostly in Hong Kong and Taiwan, but also in Southeast Asia) provided

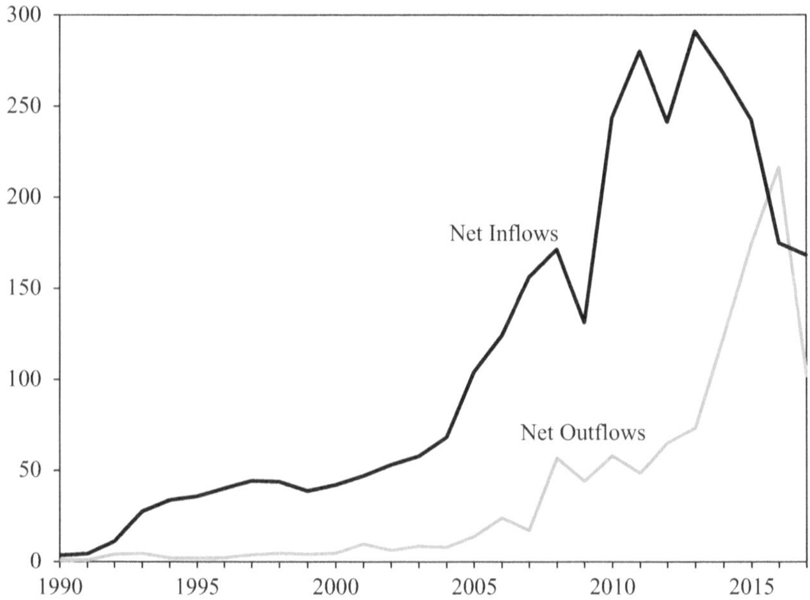

Fig. 12.3 China: net FDI inflows and outflows, 1990–2017, billions of current US dollars. Data source: World Bank

88.3 per cent of total external capital in China. In conjunction with local governments in China, diaspora investors had a hand in the relaxation of central government policies towards FDI, and played a critical role in rescuing and reforming struggling state-owned enterprises in the mid-1990s.

Yeung (1999) focuses on the internationalization of Chinese business firms from Southeast Asia, and argues that their competitive advantage is partly culturally determined. Given their familiarity with opaque business environments, ethnic Chinese businesses have leveraged their social networks and knowledge of China to form joint ventures there with local enterprises or state institutions, or to form joint ventures with Western companies that have supplied branded products or technology.

Finally, Rauch and Trindade (2002) find that the presence of Chinese diaspora around the world has facilitated trade with China, particularly in differentiated products, for which contractual relations are more complex than for bulk commodities. One reason may be that, in many countries, community sanctions may provide an effective contract enforcement alternative to inefficient judicial systems. In any case, the presence of an extensive ethnic Chinese diaspora in Southeast Asia boosts trade in differentiated products by at least 60 per cent, the authors estimate, and thus should facilitate complementary foreign direct investments as well. Indeed, Gao (2003) provides statistical evidence of the role of ethnic Chinese diaspora in countries around the world in FDI into China over 1984–1997.

In total, Southeast Asia provided 3.9 per cent of the utilized foreign direct investment in China in 2017 versus 6.0 per cent in 2010 and 5.5 per cent in 2003.[25] The vast majority has come through Singapore, which to some extent is a conduit for capital from the rest of the region.

Both inflows and outflows of foreign direct investment remain heavily regulated in China. Indeed, the lines blur between private and official investments, since some private companies have been nationalized, while most take direction from the state or Communist Party, and outward FDI has been undertaken by state enterprises as well. In any case, as China has prospered and labour and land have become costlier, and perhaps as political risks of exportation from China to countries like the United States have grown, its outward flows of FDI by private and state-owned entities have grown as well.

A jump in outflows in 2013 coincided with the announcement of the BRI under Xi Jinping, but a sharp contraction followed in 2017. About one-fourth of the decline that year can be attributed to a net decrease in the outflow of Chinese investments to the United States, due to greater regulatory scrutiny by both China and the United States, the former for fear of capital flight and the latter for national and economic security concerns. There was also a greater appreciation in Beijing of the risks of outward FDI, as China's Ministry of Commerce observed early in 2018 that "irrational outward investment was effectively restrained" in 2017, although "investment in the countries along the Belt and Road routes and the cooperation with them were promoted steadily."[26]

Table 12.7 shows the shares of FDI in each ASEAN country from China, Hong Kong and the top two other investor countries. Our goal in the table is to indicate dependency on China and Hong Kong for long-term external finance.

ASEAN publishes FDI inflow data for each member country by source country.[27] We have used the ASEAN data except for the Philippines, for which we use national data. The Philippines reports FDI flows via new equity, debt and reinvested earnings separately, but only breaks down the equity data by country of origin; ASEAN reports debt and reinvested

Table 12.7 Foreign direct investment shares in ASEAN Countries (per cent): China, Hong Kong and top two other countries, 2013–2017

	China	*Hong Kong*	*Other*	*Source*	*Other*	*Source*	*Total (US$ billions)*
Brunei	N/A	30.7	32.5	Malaysia	16.7	Netherlands	1.775
Cambodia	25.7	9.8	7.4	Vietnam	6.9	South Korea	9.714
Indonesia	5.0	4.7	58.8	Singapore	26.1	Japan	83.881
Laos[a]	63.6	1.2	9.2	Thailand	4.6	South Korea	5.190
Malaysia	6.9	15.2	16.9	Singapore	15.2	Japan	53.890
Myanmar	12.5	6.5	46.3	Singapore	12.9	Thailand	13.384
Philippines[b]	34.1	4.1	8.7	Japan	7.0	United States	33.453
Singapore	6.3	2.5	20.9	United States	17.3	Unspecified	333.145
Thailand	5.2	8.7	55.6	Japan	10.6	United States	40.695
Vietnam	5.9	6.4	27.3	South Korea	16.3	Japan	56.600

Data sources: ASEAN (https://data.aseanstats.org/fdi-by-hosts-and-sources); Bangko Sentral ng Pilipinas, BSP Online Statistical Database, Foreign Direct Investments, By Country, BPM6 Concept; calculations by authors

N/A not available
[a]Covers only 2012–2017
[b]See further discussion in text

earnings as being from an unspecified country. However, the debt flow data for the Philippines jumped in 2013 and subsequent years, and we attribute that jump to China, given the introduction of the BRI in 2013.[28]

The data indicate that Laos, the Philippines, Cambodia, Brunei and Myanmar are the ASEAN members most dependent on China and Hong Kong for FDI inflows. The relatively low level of Chinese investment in Vietnam may partly reflect historic tensions in the relationship between the two countries; a Pew Research Center poll shows that Vietnam is the only ASEAN country in which a majority of the public believes that growth in China's economy is not a good thing.[29]

The Belt and Road Initiative

Official thinking in China for some years has envisioned a major role for China in infrastructure investments in developing Asia. Indeed, in 2010, in the midst of pushback within Indonesia against the ASEAN-China Free

Trade Agreement as the trade balance deteriorated, a meeting between the Minister of Trade of Indonesia and the Minister of Commerce of China led to promises of Chinese infrastructure investments in Indonesia, among other measures.

The Asian Development Bank estimated in 2017 that developing Asia would need more than US$26 trillion for infrastructure development between 2016 and 2030, mostly in electrical power and transport, and including costs of climate mitigation and adaptation—so additional sources of finance for infrastructure clearly are needed.[30] The announcement of the Belt and Road Initiative by Xi Jinping in 2013 thus responded to a genuine need.

The BRI was conceived specifically as a conglomeration of China-financed infrastructure projects and trade and investment deals mostly in countries located along ancient land routes through Central Asia and beyond, as well as along a maritime route through Southeast Asia and all the way to Africa and Europe.[31] As many as 71 countries have agreed to participate. One estimate is that under BRI up to US$1.3 trillion could be spent on infrastructure by 2027.[32]

The official discourse within China on the BRI is idealized: "China will join hands with countries along the Belt and Road to build a community of common interests, common responsibilities and a shared future, featuring political mutual trust, economic integration and cultural inclusiveness," in the words of Vice-Premier Zhang Gaoli in February 2015.[33] At the other end of the spectrum of public opinion on the BRI was US Vice President Mike Pence, who stated in November 2018 that the United States does not "drown our partners in a sea of debt" or "offer a constricting belt or a one-way road."[34] Assuredly the reality is between these extremes.

Economist David Dollar (2015) offers a pragmatic view of BRI, pointing to economic reasons within China for the turn outward: slowing growth of total factor productivity and declining marginal product of capital—the latter reflected in vacant apartment buildings and excess capacity in some manufacturing sectors—motivated Beijing to seek alternative, external sources of growth. Other goals for China were to prompt development in non-coastal regions, especially provinces bordering mainland Southeast Asian countries, to secure strategic maritime routes, and to set forth a trademark foreign policy for Xi Jinping to mark his legacy.[35] The infrastructure projects have in many cases been accompanied by the construction of special commercial and industrial zones used primarily by Chinese businesses. Shaffer and Gao (2019) note that by January 2019

China had announced the building of 82 such zones in BRI countries, with a total investment of US$29 billion.

David Arase (2015) notes that the infrastructure intended as part of BRI is both hard and soft—the latter including various institutional and social foundations of international commerce. Shaffer and Gao similarly argue that the BRI should not be conceived only as an infrastructure undertaking, but as a package of deals and agreements that will fundamentally extend the footprint of the Chinese model of governance of trade, investment and innovation, and that will allow China to move up the value chain. Jennifer Lind (2018) puts it even more starkly: BRI is part of a broader effort by China to secure regional dominion in Asia, much like past regional hegemons around the world.

There are legitimate criticisms of BRI. Infrastructure projects have been mostly debt-financed, as in the Philippines, with risks borne primarily by host countries.[36] China's bilateral lending in general, including under the BRI, has not been transparent: there is some public information on the magnitude and timing of the loans, but not of the terms and conditions applied.[37] The vast majority of BRI construction projects have been done by Chinese companies employing a preponderance of Chinese workers. Host-country elites have been co-opted, but questions remain about whether projects funded bilaterally by China have been economically sustainable or in the national interest of the recipient countries.

Regardless of Beijing's intentions, connecting China with the rest of the world can facilitate future commerce. Recent research at the World Bank quantifies the effects of BRI infrastructure developments: de Soyres et al. (2018) estimate that BRI projects that reduce shipping times will cut transport costs for BRI economies by 1.5–2.8 per cent and for the world overall by 1.1–2.2 per cent.[38] Given Southeast Asia's central role in the BRI, this initiative could be a potential game-changer for a region with vast infrastructure needs. Among the ASEAN economies, and based on a conservative scenario, Cambodia, Brunei, Malaysia, Vietnam, Myanmar and Thailand are expected to enjoy the most substantial decreases in transport costs.

Nevertheless, there are signs of pushback in some BRI host countries. In Malaysia, Mahathir Mohamad returned as Prime Minister in May 2018 as head of a new political party. The electoral coalition he had previously led was brought down by a morass of corruption charges against his predecessor, Najib Razak, and his government. During the campaign, Mahathir had questioned Chinese investments in Malaysia, and in office, he tried to renegotiate and then cancelled a US$20 billion China-backed railway project and later three Chinese oil-gas pipeline projects valued at US$2.5 billion.[39]

It was similarly reported that in Myanmar a US$7.5 billion port project was being scaled back to US$1.3 billion, and that in Indonesia the 2019 presidential challenger had pledged, if elected, to review a number of BRI projects, including a US$4.5 billion Jakarta railway project.[40]

There is some evidence that China's leaders are responding to the criticisms of the BRI—by being willing to renegotiate terms, focus more on project quality, recognize economic and political risks and work with other partner countries such as Japan.[41] As debt problems have become unmanageable, as in Sri Lanka, China has done debt-for-equity swaps along with long-term lease arrangements to offload some of the risks from the host country.

The Asian Infrastructure Investment Bank

The Asian Infrastructure Investment Bank is a second Chinese initiative for infrastructure finance, but is multilateral and far more transparent than the BRI. It is aimed more at Southeast Asia than the BRI, though not focused on that region alone.[42]

The AIIB can be viewed as a rival to the traditional multilateral financial institutions, notably the World Bank and the Asian Development Bank (ADB). As of December 2018, it had 93 member countries worldwide; the United States and Japan, the founders of the ADB, are the only industrial countries not to have joined.

Establishment of the AIIB reflected in part China's frustration with governance structures of the traditional multilateral financial institutions, which have been slow to evolve even as the global balance of economic power has shifted. The United States appeared to many Chinese to have been diminished by the Great Recession of 2008–2009, but nevertheless retained voting shares sufficient to veto major board decisions in the International Monetary Fund and World Bank. With a voting share of more than 26 per cent in the AIIB, China has a greater share than Japan and the United States combined have in the ADB.

At the end of 2017, the ADB reported US$151.2 billion in member subscriptions, with US$7.6 billion paid in and the remainder callable, while the AIIB reported US$95.0 billion in subscribed capital, with US$19.0 billion paid in.[43] However, the AIIB had invested only a modest

US$4.1 billion and approved only 23 projects. The ADB had invested in a wide array of projects throughout Asia, with 60.9 per cent of 2017 operations in infrastructure in the form of energy, transport, telecommunications, water supply and sanitation.[44]

Other Dimensions of the Relationship

We now examine several other aspects of the relationship between ASEAN countries and China: monetary relations, environmental issues and territorial disputes.

Monetary Relations

China and Malaysia have maintained a currency swap arrangement since 2009, renewable every three years. The motivation is to use local currencies for international transactions. The arrangement fits with China's longer-term goal to establish the renminbi as a global vehicle currency to rival the US dollar in particular.[45] It is also consistent with the occasional anti-Western rhetoric of Malaysian Prime Minister Mahathir Mohamad and his protégé Najib Razak.[46]

Environmental Issues

Air and water pollution have become increasingly salient in Asia, and governments have at least paid lip service to environmentally sustainable development.

The AIIB states that its mode of operation is "Lean, Clean and Green"—a slogan that rings rather hollow, given that a 2017 report by the Global Environmental Institute noted that, by the end of 2016, China had been involved in 240 coal-fired power projects in 25 BRI countries; 52 of the projects were in the pipeline.[47] More abundant electricity in BRI countries will power Chinese industrial investments in special economic zones as well as the consumption of appliances and electronics manufactured by Chinese companies.

The unfortunate reality is that alternative sources of electricity are not necessarily environmentally sound either: construction within China of a series of hydropower dams on the Mekong River, ten so far, with several more planned, has impacted Myanmar, Laos, Cambodia, Thailand and Vietnam downstream.[48] These dams threaten vital fisheries, water resources for irrigation and human consumption, and even the flow of sediments that provides rich soil for agriculture and protects the Mekong delta in Vietnam from erosion. Other threats to the river include hydropower dams already built or planned for Mekong tributaries in Laos and Cambodia, some backed by Chinese capital, and one for the main channel of the river in Cambodia, along with planned blasting by China of stretches of the river outside its borders to allow larger vessels to navigate along it. The problem is expected to become more acute in the future with further climate change and as demands for water increase throughout the region.

Territorial Disputes

Territorial disputes over the South China Sea (SCS) have long been an irritant in relations between China and several ASEAN countries, and indeed among these countries themselves. The SCS is of considerable geostrategic significance. It encompasses major maritime passages, and has oil and gas reserves as well as fisheries resources. The SCS also provides a strategic buffer for southeastern China and can accommodate China's nuclear submarines.

China and Taiwan both claim on historic grounds a territory bounded by a "nine-dash line" that extends far to the south in the Sea. It includes several vital areas: the Paracel Islands, which are roughly equidistant from Vietnam and China; the Spratly Islands, parts of which are claimed by Malaysia, the Philippines, Brunei and Vietnam; and Scarborough Shoal, close to the Philippines.

The Philippines, under then-President Benigno Aquino III, brought a case against China over Scarborough Shoal and vicinity to the Permanent Court of Arbitration (PCA) in the Hague in 2013, and in 2016 the Court denied China's historic claims to the nine-dash line on the basis that these had been superseded by application of the territorial system of the UN Convention on the Law of the Sea, which both countries had previously ratified. China rejected the decision of the Court, but Rodrigo Duterte had by then assumed the presidency in the Philippines and did not press the claim.

Much earlier, in 2002, ASEAN members and China had negotiated a non-binding Declaration of Conduct on the South China Sea, but neither that nor the later PCA ruling stopped China from building artificial islands and enlarging its military presence in the disputed island groups.

Indeed, in disputes over the SCS, China has not hesitated to bring its power resources to bear. It established control over the Paracel Islands in 1974 following a naval battle with South Vietnam, which had attempted to expel the Chinese navy from the area. During a 2012 Scarborough Shoal standoff, Beijing put severe economic pressure on the Philippines—demanding payment for a US$500 million infrastructure loan, issuing an advisory against travel to that country and restricting imports of key Philippine exports. By pressuring the weaker and more dependent members of ASEAN, China has also been able to leverage the consensual decision-making structure within the organization to gain influence. In 2012, for example, with no SCS claims of its own, Cambodia infamously blocked a joint ASEAN communiqué on the South China Sea disputes, an action that was widely regarded as a sign of China's machinations.

Recent developments, such as the election of President Trump and the subsequent US withdrawal from the Trans-Pacific Partnership, have undercut confidence in the United States as a reliable presence in the region. Thus, in 2017, though it did not lessen its military grip on the SCS, China did ease its diplomatic stance, perhaps to exploit the new opening. In August 2018, the foreign ministers of the ASEAN member states and China announced agreement on a single draft negotiating text, which was to serve as the basis for the adoption of a final code of conduct in the SCS. In October 2018, China and ASEAN members conducted joint maritime exercises in disputed areas of the South China Sea.[49] We conjecture that Beijing was being particularly mindful of the importance of good relations with the ASEAN states, given the trade war with the United States. It remains unclear whether China was playing for time or seriously trying to negotiate a détente.[50]

There have also been low-grade territorial disputes in which popular resentment has arisen in Vietnam and Cambodia over long-term leases granted to Chinese investors for development of special economic zones and other valuable coastal areas, which have facilitated the creation of Chinese enclaves such as the resort area of Sihanoukville in Cambodia.

Power Relations in the Region

The various dimensions of the relationship between China and Southeast Asia need to be understood in the context of broader power dynamics. The narrative that has emerged since 2012 is that ASEAN and national political elites have been increasingly pressed to choose sides, given the intensification of US-China competition.

In an analysis of China's global ambitions, David Shambaugh (2013, p. 1) offered a 2012 quote from former US Secretary of State Henry Kissinger: "China does not see itself as a rising, but a returning power. It does not view the prospect of a strong China exercising influence in economic, cultural, political, and military affairs as an unnatural challenge to world order—but rather as a return to a normal state of affairs." Indeed, under Xi Jinping, since 2013, China's leadership has pursued expanded roles for the state and the Communist Party within China, and a much more influential role among its neighbours and on a global stage (Economy 2018).

China possesses formidable economic and military resources and is increasingly aggressive in using its influence, with a preference for bilateral negotiations in which power disparities can be leveraged most effectively. As we argued above, Southeast Asian nations are economically dependent on China, giving Beijing considerable scope to exert economic leverage. In Southeast Asia, China's influence is strongest within the Mekong subregion. Chinese gunboats regularly patrol the river downstream to remind its neighbours of its power.[51] The states in Cambodia and Laos, among the poorest of the ASEAN countries, have mostly acceded to the arrangements that China has pushed, and short-term regime interests have often prevailed over long-term national interests.

Shambaugh (2018) argues that economic relations are at the centre of China's engagement with Southeast Asia; its diplomatic, military and other ties with the region are increasing, but still not as extensive as those of the United States. Moreover, China's hold on soft power remains tenuous: years of efforts to improve its global image—such as through foreign aid and the establishment of the AIIB—have by no means met with unreserved success.

Goh (2016) underlines that, despite strong latent capabilities, China's power resources have not necessarily translated into influence over developing Asia. For example, Goh and Steinberg (2016) note that Myanmar was able to leverage the existence of local Chinese investments as well as popular protests to achieve a less unequal balance of power with China by 2011, since these investments depended on the Myanmar government for protection. Thus, President Thein Sein was able to suspend the controversial Myitsone Dam hydropower project, in which the imperatives of Chinese pressure, energy security, ethnic conflict and environmental concerns all figured prominently.[52]

Thus, while a common view is that the BRI will lead to debt traps that could bind BRI host countries to China for decades, we argue that China could find itself bound, particularly if debts are unable to be repaid and are instead swapped for equity positions. Not only could these become economic burdens for China, but also political hostages to host states.

More generally, China could find itself subject to the pottery store rule: "You break it, you own it." Playing a more assertive role in the internal political, security and economic affairs of its neighbours will create costly tensions and win few genuine allies.

Given memories of Western colonization, Japanese occupation during World War II and centuries of the Chinese imperial tribute system, which had run as far south as the Straits of Malacca (French 2017), ASEAN enshrined the principles of non-interference and respect for sovereignty at its founding. In 1971, the member states signed a declaration that the ASEAN region would be a Zone of Peace, Freedom and Neutrality free from interference by outside powers. This historical aversion towards great power domination has persisted to this day: ASEAN is careful not to commit itself to an alliance with a single power, instead engaging in a complex web of partnerships.

ASEAN member states have similarly strategically hedged between Washington and Beijing in order to maintain greater autonomy.[53] For example, this was a primary reason that Vietnam was an eager participant in the TPP, the demise of which represented a lost opportunity for the United States to strengthen its influence in the region.

Popular anger in Vietnam against Chinese actions has also allowed Hanoi to plausibly insist that its hands are tied by domestic politics, such as in recent street protests over exclusive economic zones created in Vietnam for Chinese businesses.[54] Baviera (2016) points out that too-obvious patronage relations between China and the Philippine elite have in the past given rise to nationalist protests that have limited China's ability to achieve its objectives in the South China Sea.

Shambaugh (2018) summarizes the ASEAN states in terms of their closeness to Beijing: Cambodia is a "capitulationist," Laos and Myanmar "chafers," Thailand and Malaysia "aligned accommodationists," Brunei and the Philippines "tilters," Singapore and Vietnam "balanced hedgers" and Indonesia an "outlier." It is of interest that the two states rated by Shambaugh as most distant from China—Vietnam and Indonesia—are the ones whose stock markets we found to be least closely associated with that of China in our event study.

Concluding Remarks

The economic and political fates of China and the ASEAN states are tied by geography into "a community of common destiny" in the words of Xi Jinping, driven not only by the imperatives of mutual interest but also by rivalry.[55] Intricate supply chains created through foreign direct investment and facilitated by Chinese diaspora communities have bound China to its neighbours in Southeast Asia, and have produced vast quantities of manufactured goods at low cost. Even so, China has undertaken an ambitious programme to upgrade its technological capabilities, which will make it harder for Southeast Asian nations to achieve their own goals in this respect.

ASEAN as an organization is at a critical juncture. It imposes an institutional discipline on members to some extent, as in the case of Indonesia following implementation of the ASEAN-China free trade agreement. ASEAN has also constituted a power resource for close neighbours of China like Vietnam, and to some extent has provided a forum for more unified negotiation with China over the South China Sea and other issues. Member states have had a history of allowing national interests to get in the way of regional unity, however, which has resulted in slow trade liberalization in the past and more recently in the protracted implementation of the ASEAN Economic Community. It remains to be seen whether Southeast Asian elites can muster sufficient political will to band together, create a more powerful political voice and navigate the complex straits of great power politics in the future.

Notes

1. We have compiled the trade data from the Broad Economic Categories data in the UN Comtrade database and have performed a crude deflation of the data using the US producer price index (from International Financial Statistics of the International Monetary Fund). All ASEAN countries are included except Brunei, Laos and Myanmar, for which some years of data were missing.
2. Vietnam also had a bilateral merchandise trade deficit with South Korea that year, of 6.8 per cent of GDP, much of which is explicable by the huge cellular telephone assembly presence that Korean manufacturer Samsung has established there. Trade data from the UN Comtrade database, and GDP data from the World Development Indicators database of the World Bank.

3. The gravity model posits that exports from one country to another are related positively to the gross domestic products of the two countries and negatively to the geographic distance between them. Other variables are added to the econometric specification as control variables or as policy variables to be investigated.
4. The survey included 841 firms in Japan, China, South Korea, Singapore, Thailand and the Philippines. Some 28 per cent of respondents indicated that they used FTA preferences. Only 20 per cent stated that multiple rules of origin added significantly to their costs, but this view was more prominent in the ASEAN countries (Singapore 38, the Philippines 28 and Thailand 26 per cent).
5. Malaysia, Brunei and Singapore have had the smallest increases. See Ing et al. (2016).
6. See Marks (2015) for further discussion of the political economy of the ASEAN-China trade agreement in Indonesia, and Marks (2017) for nominal and effective rates of protection associated with non-tariff trade barriers imposed in Indonesia, particularly between 2011 and 2015.
7. Jayant Menon and Anna Cassandra Melendez, "Will 2025 be the final deadline for the ASEAN Economic Community?" Asia Pathways blog, Asian Development Bank Institute, July 14, 2017.
8. See also the most recent *Trade Policy Review* for China from the World Trade Organization, July 2018.
9. See, for example, the China section of the *2018 National Trade Estimate Report on Foreign Trade Barriers*, Office of the United States Trade Representative.
10. See, for example, Karl Lester M Yap, "Southeast Asia Has an Investment Boom, Thanks to the Trade War," *Bloomberg*, October 22, 2018.
11. "Phone Home: Why Samsung of South Korea is the Biggest Firm in Vietnam," *The Economist*, April 12, 2018.
12. Bac Pham and Bennett Murray, "Here's Who Wins and Also Loses in US-China Trade War: Vietnam," *South China Morning Post*, November 18, 2018.
13. Japan, South Korea, Hong Kong and Taiwan have all been ageing even more rapidly. *World Population Ageing 2015*, New York: United Nations, Department of Economic and Social Affairs, Population Division, Tables A.III.4 and A.III.5.
14. Calculations by authors based on Jong Woo Kang and Grendell Vie Magoncia, "How to fill the working-age population gap in Asia: A population accounting approach," ADB Economics Working Paper Series No. 499, Asian Development Bank, November 2016.
15. Comparisons are not available for other ASEAN countries. Conference Board International Labor Comparisons Program, July 2018. International

wage comparisons are tricky for China for other reasons, as pointed out by Dmitriy Plekhanov, "Is China's Era of Cheap Labor Really Over?" *The Diplomat*, December 13, 2017.

16. See, for example, Jun Endo, "Southeast Asia's production gains speed as China slows," *Nikkei Asian Review*, September 20, 2018.
17. State Council of the People's Republic of China, "Made in China 2025," unofficial translation by IoT ONE, July 7, 2015, http://guide.iotone.com/made-in-china-2025.
18. Yu and Cui (2017) argue that we should expect to see China rely more on consumption and less on investment and exports, as well as more on services and less on industry, and that this will create opportunities for ASEAN countries for further growth through international commerce. The thrust of the Made in China 2025 report seems to indicate that China will go down that path only reluctantly.
19. The diminishment of Japan's share cannot be fully explained by trade diversion related to the ASEAN-China FTA, given that Japan has had its own free trade agreement with ASEAN.
20. See, for example, "China Airbrushes Out Industrial Plan That U.S. Loves to Hate," *Bloomberg*, March 4, 2019.
21. Assessments are conducted every three years, the most recent being 2015, which was the first year such an assessment was done for China. The China assessment included only Beijing, Jiangsu, Guangdong and Shanghai provinces, among the most developed in the country.
22. The gross enrolment ratio measures enrolments relative to the population in the age group expected to be in school at the various levels. It can exceed 100 per cent because of the presence of students who are younger or older than those in the official age group. Vietnam and the Philippines are notable in having high enrolment ratios for post-secondary, non-tertiary studies: 21.9 per cent in Vietnam in 2016 and 25.8 per cent in the Philippines in 2017.
23. The purchasing power parity numbers allow for more precise cross-national comparisons in terms of real resources being devoted to R&D.
24. A detailed breakdown for Germany was not available, but total R&D expenditure there in current PPP US dollars was 118.8 billion in 2016, and the growth rate over 2011–2016 was 2.9 per cent.
25. *China Statistical Yearbook*, National Bureau of Statistics of China, various issues. The most recent can be found at http://www.stats.gov.cn/tjsj/ndsj/2018/indexeh.htm.
26. "Comments on China's Outward Investment Cooperation in 2017," Ministry of Commerce, Department of Outward Investment and Economic Cooperation, January 18, 2018.

27. The official data mask the truth to some extent, given that unspecified countries—evidently tax havens like the Cayman Islands—were the second-largest investor in Singapore over 2013–2017, for example.
28. Publicly acknowledged FDI from China in the Philippines is miniscule. To determine a reasonable amount for the jump, we used official annual data on FDI financed by debt over 2005–2017, applied a structural shift dummy variable for 2013 and later years in a linear regression framework, and tested and corrected for non-stationarity of the debt data. We estimate an annual jump of US$2.3 billion in 2013 and afterward, versus an average of US$0.5 billion over 2005–2012. Total debt-financed FDI in the Philippines was officially nearly US$20 billion over 2013–2018. Recent news reports have estimated that the total debt owed by the Philippines to China could eventually be much higher—on the order of US$180 billion. "China Won't Allow Philippines to Fall into a 'Debt Trap': Envoy," *Reuters*, July 17, 2018. We assigned reinvested equity earnings to each investor country, in proportion to its share of cumulative net equity investment over 2005–2017.
29. Laura Silver, "How people in Asia-Pacific view China," Pew Research Center, Fact Tank blog, October 16, 2017.
30. *Meeting Asia's Infrastructure Needs*, Asian Development Bank, 2017.
31. Outside China the BRI is typically dated from the visits by President Xi Jinping to Kazakhstan and Indonesia in 2013, but inside China it was formally recognized at the March 2015 Boao Forum for Asia in Hainan, at which the National Development and Reform Commission, the Ministry of Foreign Affairs, and the Ministry of Commerce jointly issued the "Vision and Action to Promote the Construction of the Silk Road Economic Belt and the twenty-first Century Maritime Silk Road." An English translation is at https://www.fmprc.gov.cn/mfa_eng/zxxx_662805/t1249618.shtml.
32. Morgan Stanley, March 14, 2018 (https://www.morganstanley.com/ideas/china-belt-and-road). Much research on the BRI relies on official policy and media sources, which tend to report on intentions rather than actual progress, overstating the scale of the programme.
33. From a speech to a conference of senior officials in Beijing in February 2015. "China Sketches out Priorities of 'Belt and Road' Initiatives," *Xinhua News Service*, February 2, 2015.
34. Remarks at the Asia Pacific Economic Cooperation (APEC) Summit in Papua New Guinea, November 2018. Unstated was that infrastructure loans offered by the United States have been a small fraction of the amounts the BRI is expected to deliver.
35. William Callahan (2016) explores further the ideational origins of the BRI within China as part of a reformulation of its grand strategy of foreign

policy under Xi Jinping, who had China focus more on its periphery even as it enlarged its aspirations to reshape the global order.

36. In an analysis of the debt implications of the BRI, Hurley et al. (2018) include only one ASEAN country, Laos, the host for a costly China-Laos railway project and a hydropower project, among the eight most vulnerable BRI lending recipients.
37. Carmen M. Reinhart, "Exposing China's Overseas Lending," *Project Syndicate*, October 31, 2018.
38. Baniya et al. (2019) extend the analysis to its impact on trade flows.
39. Hannah Beech, "'We Cannot Afford This': Malaysia Pushes Back Against China's Vision," *New York Times*, August 20, 2018.
40. David Tweed, Iain Marlow, and Dandan Li, "Souring Deals Put China's Belt and Road Dreams Under Pressure," *Bloomberg*, January 29, 2019.
41. Iain Marlow and Dandan Li, "How Asia Fell Out of Love with China's Belt and Road Initiative," *Bloomberg*, December 10, 2018.
42. China also has led an initiative of the BRICS (Brazil, Russia, India, China, South Africa) countries since 2012 to form a bank that is now the New Development Bank, dedicated to infrastructure investment and sustainable development in emerging and developing economies.
43. *Asian Development Bank Financial Report December 31, 2017*, Asian Development Bank, 2018, and *2017 AIIB Annual Report and Financials*, Asian Infrastructure Investment Bank, 2018.
44. "Total ADB Operations 2017, by Sector and by Region," Operational Data accompanying *Asian Development Bank Annual Report 2017: Sustainable Infrastructure for Future Needs, Asian Development Bank, 2018.*
45. Eichengreen (2011) offers broader perspectives on the competition to be the top international vehicle currency.
46. Khalid (2011) discusses the origins and continuity of political and policy styles of these two Malaysian prime ministers.
47. Ren Peng, Liu Chang and Zhang Liwen, "China's Involvement in Coal-Fired Power Projects Along the Belt and Road," Global Environmental Institute, May 2017.
48. Michael Sullivan, "China Reshapes the Vital Mekong River to Power its Expansion," transcription of report heard on Weekend Edition Saturday, National Public Radio (United States), October 6, 2018.
49. Singapore, Brunei, Thailand, Vietnam and the Philippines deployed ships, while Cambodia, Indonesia, Malaysia and Myanmar sent observers. "China, ASEAN Start Inaugural Joint Maritime Drills," *Agence France-Presse*, October 22, 2018.
50. Tom Mitchell and John Reed, "China Softens Tone in Drive for Asia Influence: Diplomatic and Economic Charm Offensive Exploits Regional Doubts over US under Trump," *Financial Times*, January 3, 2018.

51. Sullivan supra note 48.
52. See also Yeophantong (2016).
53. See Goh (2016), Ang (2016) and Kang (2017).
54. See, for example, David Hutt, "Does China Really Dominate Southeast Asia?" *Asia Times*, August 23, 2018.
55. The phrase was also used by President Hu Jintao in 2007. Jin Kai, "Can China Build a Community of Common Destiny?" *The Diplomat*, November 28, 2013.

References

Ang, Cheng Guan. 2016. China's Influence Over Vietnam in War and Peace. In *Rising China's Influence in Developing Asia*, ed. Evelyn Goh. Oxford: Oxford University Press.

Arase, David. 2015. China's Two Silk Roads Initiative: What It Means for Southeast Asia. In *Southeast Asian Affairs 2015*, ed. Daljit Singh. Singapore: ISEAS, Yusof Ishak Institute.

Athukorala, Prema-chandra. 2009. The Rise of China and East Asian Export Performance: Is the Crowding-out Fear Warranted? *World Economy* 32 (2, February): 234–266.

Baldwin, Richard E. 2008. Managing the Noodle Bowl: The Fragility of East Asian Regionalism. *Singapore Economic Review* 53 (3, December): 449–478.

Baniya, Suprabha, Nadia Rocha, and Michele Ruta. 2019, January. *Trade Effects of the New Silk Road: A Gravity Analysis*. Policy Research Working Paper 8694. World Bank.

Baviera, Aileen S.P. 2016. The Domestic Mediations of China's Influence in the Philippines. In *Rising China's Influence in Developing Asia*, ed. Evelyn Goh. Oxford: Oxford University Press.

Cadot, Olivier, and Lili Yan Ing. 2016. How Restrictive Are ASEAN's Rules of Origin? *Asian Economic Papers* 15 (3, Fall): 115–134.

Callahan, William A. 2016. China's 'Asia Dream': The Belt Road Initiative and the New Regional Order. *Asian Journal of Comparative Politics* 1 (3, September): 226–243.

de Soyres, François, Alen Mulabdic, Siobhan Murray, Nadia Rocha, and Michele Ruta. 2018, October. *How Much Will the Belt and Road Initiative Reduce Trade Costs?* Policy Research Working Paper 8614. World Bank.

Devadason, Evelyn S., and Santha Chenayah. 2014. Proliferation of Non-tariff Measures in China: Their Relevance for ASEAN. *Singapore Economic Review* 59 (2): 1–28.

Dollar, David. 2015. China's Rise as a Regional and Global Power: The AIIB and the 'One Belt, One Road' *Horizons* (4, Summer): 162–172. Belgrade: Center for International Relations and Sustainable Development.

Economy, Elizabeth C. 2018. *The Third Revolution: Xi Jinping and the New Chinese State*. Oxford: Oxford University Press.

Eichengreen, Barry J. 2011. *Exorbitant Privilege: The Decline of the Dollar and the Future of the International Monetary System*. New York: Oxford University Press.

French, Howard W. 2017. *Everything Under the Heavens: How the Past Helps Shape China's Push for Global Power*. New York: Alfred A. Knopf.

Gao, Ting. 2003. Ethnic Chinese Networks and International Investment: Evidence from Inward FDI in China. *Journal of Asian Economics* 14 (4, August): 611–629.

Goh, Evelyn. 2016. Introduction. In *Rising China's Influence in Developing Asia*, ed. Evelyn Goh. Oxford: Oxford University Press.

Goh, Evelyn, and David I. Steinberg. 2016. Myanmar's Management of China's Influence: From Mutual Benefit to Mutual Dependence. In *Rising China's Influence in Developing Asia*, ed. Evelyn Goh. Oxford: Oxford University Press.

Holst, David Roland, and John Weiss. 2004. ASEAN and China: Export Rivals or Partners in Regional Growth? *World Economy* 27 (8, August): 1255–1274.

Hurley, John, Scott Morris, and Gailyn Portelance. 2018, March. *Examining the Debt Implications of the Belt and Road Initiative from a Policy Perspective*. CGD Policy Paper 121. Washington, DC: Center for Global Development.

Ing, Lili Yan, Santiago Fernández de Córdoba, and Olivier Cadot, eds. 2016. *Non-Tariff Measures in ASEAN*. Jakarta: Economic Research Institute for ASEAN and East Asia (ERIA) and United Nations Conference on Trade and Development (UNCTAD).

Kang, David. 2017. *American Grand Strategy and East Asian Security in the Twenty-First Century*. Cambridge: Cambridge University Press.

Kawai, Masahiro, and Ganeshan Wignaraja. 2011. Main Findings and Policy Implications. In *Asia's Free Trade Agreements: How Is Business Responding?* ed. Masahiro Kawai and Ganeshan Wignaraja. Cheltenham: Edward Elgar.

Khalid, Khadijah M. 2011. Malaysia's Foreign Policy Under Najib: A Comparison with Mahathir. *Asian Survey* 51 (3): 429–452.

Kong, Yoke Fong, and Richard Kneller. 2016. Measuring the Impact of China's Export Growth on Its Asian Neighbours. *World Economy* 39 (2, February): 195–220.

Lind, Jennifer. 2018. Life in China's Asia: What Regional Hegemony Would Look Like. *Foreign Affairs* 97 (2, March/April): 71–82.

Marks, Stephen V. 2015. The Asean-China Free Trade Agreement: Political Economy in Indonesia. *Bulletin of Indonesian Economic Studies* 51 (2, August): 287–306.

———. 2017. Non-Tariff Trade Regulations in Indonesia: Nominal and Effective Rates of Protection. *Bulletin of Indonesian Economic Studies* 53 (3, December): 333–357.

Marks, Stephen V., and Cheryl Jia Min Yau. 2019, February. *The U.S.-China Trade Conflict and Stock Price Indexes in Asia and Beyond*. Unpublished paper, Pomona College, Claremont, CA.

Rauch, James E., and Vitor Trindade. 2002. Ethnic Chinese Networks in International Trade. *Review of Economics and Statistics* 84 (1, February): 116–130.

Shaffer, Gregory, and Henry Gao. 2019, February 15. *China and the Changing Ecology of the Global Trade Regime: Developing a New Finance-Trade-Investment Model*. Presented at the Southern California International Law Scholars workshop, Los Angeles.

Shambaugh, David. 2013. *China Goes Global: The Partial Power*. Oxford: Oxford University Press.

———. 2015. China's Soft-Power Push. *Foreign Affairs* 94 (4, July/August): 99–107.

———. 2018. U.S.-China Rivalry in Southeast Asia: Power Shift or Competitive Coexistence? *International Security* 42 (4, Spring): 85–127.

Wei, Shang-Jin, Zhuan Xie, and Xiaobo Zhang. 2017. From 'Made in China' to 'Innovated in China': Necessity, Prospect, and Challenges. *Journal of Economic Perspectives* 31 (1, Winter): 49–70.

Ye, Min. 2014. *Diasporas and Foreign Direct Investment in China and India*. Cambridge: Cambridge University Press.

Yeophantong, Pichamon. 2016. China's Hydropower Expansion and Influence Over Environmental Governance in Mainland Southeast Asia. In *Rising China's Influence in Developing Asia*, ed. Evelyn Goh. Oxford: Oxford University Press.

Yeung, Henry Wai-Chung. 1999. The Internationalization of Ethnic Chinese Business Firms from Southeast Asia: Strategies, Processes and Competitive Advantage. *International Journal of Urban and Regional Research* 23 (1): 103–127.

Yu, Miaojie, and Xiaomin Cui. 2017. The Impact of China's Trade on ASEAN's Trade. In *Production Networks in Southeast Asia*, ed. Lili Yan Ing and Fukunari Kimura. Abingdon: Routledge and Economic Research Institute for ASEAN and East Asia (ERIA).

CHAPTER 13

ASEAN's Economic Community: ASEAN Way or Beijing's Way?

David Martin Jones and Sarah Choong Ee Mei

In 1997, the 30th anniversary of the Association of South East Asian Nations (ASEAN), the organization enunciated a vision of where it would be in 2020. An integral part of that ASEAN *Vision 2020* required the creation of an ASEAN Economic Community (AEC), a single market and production base affording a free flow of goods, services, investments, capital and skilled labour. Six years later, in Bali, the Declaration of ASEAN Concord II reaffirmed the commitment to the AEC and recognized it as one of the three pillars of an evolving economic, security and cultural community. In 2007, the Cebu Declaration brought the formation of the AEC forward to January 2015 and introduced the AEC Blueprint (2008), which developed into a roadmap in 2009, to drive the implementation of the AEC. In 2011, ASEAN also introduced regular 'scorecards' to assess implementation rates: in establishing a single market; achieving a competitive market; promoting equitable economic development and facilitating integration into the global economy. The first two scorecards ASEAN

D. M. Jones (✉) • S. C. E. Mei
War Studies Department, King's College, University of London, London, UK

International Organization for Migration (IOM), Grand-Saconnex, Switzerland
e-mail: d.jones2@uq.edu.au; sarah.choong@kcl.ac.uk

R. Macdonald (ed.), *Southeast Asia and the ASEAN Economic Community*, https://doi.org/10.1007/978-3-030-19722-3_13

published, moreover, indicated that ASEAN 'appeared to be on track' to achieve its 2015 goal (ASEAN 2012a, Ji 2014, p. 2). However, by December 2014, it was apparent that whilst ASEAN had achieved some success in reducing intra-ASEAN tariff barriers, non-tariff barriers had actually grown, whilst the economic disparity between the richest and poorest ASEAN states had increased (Balboa and Wingaraja 2014, Das 2015). Given that ASEAN has been established for five decades, what has it achieved and what challenges does it still face in its endeavour to realize an integrated ASEAN Economic Community?

ASEAN's Vision for Economic Integration

In August 2017, the Association of Southeast Asian Nations (ASEAN) celebrated its 50th anniversary as a regional security arrangement. Over this period it has enjoyed a somewhat checkered history. In its first decade, its founding members rarely met. In its second, it played a diplomatic role in the resolution of the Indochinese conflict. In its third, it widened its embrace to include the grouping's former protagonist, Vietnam, as well as Laos, Cambodia and Burma-Myanmar, and extended its diplomatic style into Northeast Asia via an ASEAN Regional Forum (ARF). Its fourth decade witnessed ASEAN extending its institutional reach. After 1997, ASEAN held regular summits with China, Japan and South Korea in an arrangement termed 'ASEAN Plus Three (APT)'. This mechanism incubated an embryonic East Asian Community which has been meeting annually from December 2005.

This incremental evolution earned plaudits both from the region's political leaders and from a wider scholarly community which had, through second-track fora, become increasingly involved in ASEAN's self-definition. More particularly, from a political economy perspective, the 1997 Asian Financial Crisis (AFC) spurred the arrangement into both deepening its economic integration into an AEC and projecting its socialization processes into Northeast Asia.

In its premonitory attempt to galvanize regional integration, the ASEAN Free Trade Area (AFTA) was established in 1992 with the aim of removing all tariffs on traded manufactured goods and processed agricultural products, as well as removing non-tariff barriers. Building on AFTA, the ASEAN Economic Community (AEC 2003) proposed via the Bali Concord II to mould the region into a single market and production base, in an effort to increase the overall competitiveness of ASEAN.

Yet, it was not entirely clear whether this greater ASEAN-inspired community would constitute an 'open region' that embraced a wide variety of states in its vicinity, including Australia, New Zealand and India, as well as, potentially, Canada, Russia and the United States or a more exclusively East Asian arrangement. This ambiguity concerning the geographical extent of the proposed community reflected a deeper, less advertised, ambivalence about the nature of ASEAN itself. *The Report of the Eminent Person's Group on the ASEAN Charter*, published in December 2006, emphasized the fact that ASEAN's traditional principles and objectives had to adapt to 'the new realities confronting ASEAN', if ASEAN wished to remain in the 'driving seat' of greater regional relations.

Indeed, given the generally positive evaluations of an expanded ASEAN 'to socialize the [East Asian] region with the same norms and values that have proved successful in Southeast Asia' (ASEAN Secretariat 2006), it comes as something of a disappointment to find that both official statements and the scholarship they generated after 1997 have exaggerated what the association actually has achieved both in the area of intra-ASEAN trade, development and connectivity and in terms of ASEAN's role in driving wider East Asian economic integration, the precursor to any future political integration. Having established ASEAN's guiding propositions and the cooperative practices they seek to instantiate, we shall, therefore, test their efficacy in facilitating both ASEAN and wider regional economic integration. The Asian Financial Crisis (1997) and ASEAN's economic response to it illustrates the strengths and weaknesses of its distinctive path-dependent processes. ASEAN's conduct, we shall argue, reveals that the absence of a supranational authority to implement agreed rules, together with its conflict avoidance formula, rather than facilitating a single economic market, in fact lends itself to more powerful actors in the Asia-Pacific, shaping ASEAN's economic destiny. With weak economic growth in Japan and the withdrawal of the United States from the Trans-Pacific Partnership in 2017, we will further argue that China's Belt and Road Initiative (BRI) plays an increasingly significant role in shaping the economic development and bilateral political posture of individual ASEAN member states.

Norms, Processes and the ASEAN Way

The defining ASEAN norm, identified in the Treaty of Amity and Cooperation (TAC) in Southeast Asia, requires non-interference in the affairs of member states. All who conform to the ASEAN process, therefore, accept the non-negotiable inviolability of national sovereignty.[1] Secondly, ASEAN eschews the use of force. The organization resolves disputes peacefully. In 1971, ASEAN declared itself a Zone of Peace Freedom and Neutrality (ZOPFAN) and subsequently a Nuclear Weapons Free Zone (NWFZ). These norms are by no means unique. The United Nations Charter (1949) and the Non-Aligned Movement at its Bandung meeting in 1955 had expounded them prior to ASEAN's formation. Non-intervention represented the core principle of the Chinese Communist Party's five principles of peaceful co-existence. The language of both the ASEAN Declaration and the TAC, thus, reflects the internationalist and post-colonial values of the post-war era.

What in fact distinguishes ASEAN's norms is not their content but their implementation in a framework of regional interaction. The ASEAN way, as Acharya tells it, is 'about the *process* through which such interactions are carried out' (Acharya 1997, p. 329). This process requires the cultivation of certain habits, notably discreetness, informality, expediency, consensus building and non-confrontational bargaining. Consequently, the ASEAN way contrasts vividly with the 'adversarial posturing' and 'legalistic decision-making procedures' found in multilateral negotiations conducted according to 'Western' diplomatic criteria. A preoccupation with expediency and discreteness, itself a reflection of member state weakness and insecurity, requires the practice of sensitivity to the 'comfort level' experienced by participants. The effort to raise the comfort level entails the avoidance of open disagreement between participants (ibid.).

The comfort process, therefore, and the distinctive pattern of socialization it entails means either evading the discussion of bilateral disputes between member states or addressing them obliquely in nonbinding 'workshops', second-track fora and dialogue sessions. For Michael Leifer, the cultivation of non-confrontation defined the ASEAN process, making it a 'conflict avoidance and management' tool rather than a conflict resolution mechanism (Leifer 1998, p. 4). As Rudolfo Severino, a former ASEAN Secretary General, explained: 'When ASEAN cannot solve a problem what does it do? First, it may put the problem under the carpet and not highlight it. What is a problem today may cease to be so in the future' (cited in Acharya 1998, p. 62). Rather than formal, legally binding rules, the ASEAN process promotes instead the practice of consultation and consensus. For ASEAN scholar diplomat Kishore Mahbubani, consensus building represents the key to ASEAN's 'unique corporate culture' (ibid., 55, Mahbubani 2008, p. 12).

Given the nonbinding character of ASEAN agreements, those who dissent are rarely discomforted. The ASEAN process 'is about agreeing to disagree rather than allowing disagreement to cloud and undermine the spirit of regionalism' (Acharya 1998, p. 62). This apparent informality further entails that close interpersonal ties between leaders and senior governmental figures trump official rules and bureaucratic mechanisms. As Acharya explains: 'whilst ASEAN is not lacking regularised ministerial and bureaucratic consultations, it has not embraced the idea of a centralised permanent bureaucracy with decision making authority' (ibid., 63). Indeed, ASEAN possesses no clear format for decision-making and meetings 'often lack a formal agenda' (ibid., 59). The cumulative effect of these processes is ASEANs weak or 'soft' institutionalism.

Nevertheless, a structure of a distinctively intergovernmental kind has evolved incrementally over time. Since the fourth ASEAN Summit held in Singapore in 1992, and given additional momentum by the APT, ASEAN has developed a complicated framework of meetings and formal and informal summits both to discuss and to agree on policy. As one analyst notes, 'since 1992 the ASEAN Heads of Government meetings have been regularised', meeting initially biennially with 'informal' summits occurring in between and since 2008 annually as part of wider discussions with a variety of dialogue partners culminating in the East Asian Summit (Chin 2003, p. 36). Below this level, the annual ASEAN ministers meeting of foreign ministers constitutes the intergovernmental 'receptacle' of the 'political sovereignties of the regional arrangement' (ibid.). Annual meetings of ASEAN economic and finance ministers evolved to complement this format, which dates from ASEAN's founding. Since 1977, the ASEAN Economic Ministers (AEM) and, in the aftermath of the AFC, the ASEAN finance ministers have also met annually. The ASEAN Standing Committee coordinates the work of the Association between these annual meetings, whilst the ASEAN chair and vice chair rotate on an annual basis between member states. The ASEAN Secretariat, headed by the secretary general of ASEAN, manages this increasingly complex arrangement of formal and informal summits, dialogues, meetings and standing committee (ASEAN Secretariat 2013a). From 2013 the secretary general holds office for a five-year non-renewable term and is chosen from candidates proposed by member states. In order to improve the organization's efficiency in the aftermath of the financial crisis and implement the post-crisis Hanoi Plan of Action (1998) Vientiane Action Programme (2003), and the roadmap for the AEC (2009), the ASEAN secretary general received 'an enlarged mandate to initiate, advise, coordinate and implement ASEAN activities' (ASEAN Secretariat 2009).

This enlarged mandate responded to the fact that ASEAN policymaking accelerated dramatically after the AFC. After 1997, ASEAN summits agreed on a plethora of protocols and plans designed both to increase Southeast Asian integration and to establish a regional leadership role for the organization. By 2012 the Table of ASEAN Treaties, Agreements and Ratification ran to 98 pages and 359 treaties or agreements.[2] They embraced a prospectus ranging from relatively technical sectorial protocols to declarations that refine and develop the character of the organization like the Declaration of ASEAN Concord 11 (2002) that established a framework to achieve an integrated ASEAN Economic Community (AEC), along with the two other pillars of the ASEAN community in the security and cultural realms, and the Kuala Lumpur Declaration on the Establishment of the ASEAN Charter (2005) that endowed the organization with a legal personality. They also cover framework agreements, like those establishing an ASEAN Investment Area (AIA) (1998) and an ASEAN Development Fund (2005), that sought to give substance to the organization's *Vision 2020* (1997), revealed at the informal Kuala Lumpur Summit 1997 (ASEAN Secretariat 1997). Both the Hanoi Plan of Action and Vientiane Action Programme sought to strengthen macroeconomic and financial cooperation, enhance greater economic integration and promote the development of science and technology. Subsequently, the decision to bring forward the completion of the AEC to 2015 and the various scorecards and roadmaps after 2009 to measure its implantation together with the Master Plan for ASEAN Connectivity to connect ASEAN's economies 'to each other and the world' reinforced the vision (ADB 2009).

To this end, ASEAN has had some success in facilitating greater connectivity across the region. Formulated in 2010, the Master Plan for ASEAN Connectivity 2025 focuses on both physical (transport, ICT and energy) and institutional (trade, investment and services) liberalization, as well as people-to-people connections (education, culture and tourism). In particular, ICT, through digital innovation, and mobility, through tourism, have seen distinct growth. With the rise of online retail and ride-hailing services such as *Grab* and *Go-Jek*, Southeast Asia's massive consumer market of over 600 million people fuels the rapid expansion of digital economies and digital innovation. If ASEAN adopted a coherent digital agenda, it could add US$1 trillion to ASEAN's GDP over the next decade (Menon

2016). Recognizing this potential, ASEAN policymakers support the adoption of technology by micro, small and medium enterprises (MSMEs), developing digital financial inclusion frameworks and promoting open data use (ASEAN 2016, p. 7).

Similarly, to boost the tourism industry, the ASEAN Framework Agreement on Visa Exemption (AFAVE) signed in 2006 'exempts citizens of any other Member Countries holding valid national passports from visa requirement for a period of stay of up to 14 days from the date of entry' (ASEAN 2012d). Following the Master Plan for Connectivity, 'ASEAN lanes' have been implemented at airports to encourage regional identity and allow ASEAN nationals to enjoy improved access throughout the region. In 2011, ASEAN received 79 million international tourists, of which 34 million were intra-ASEAN travellers, making up 43% of all tourists (Chheang 2013). Both the Cebu Plan for Cooperation, promoting ASEAN as a collective tourism destination, and the ASEAN Tourism Strategic Plan (2011–2015) saw visitors to ASEAN increase by 50% between 2003 and 2013 (ASEAN Secretariat 2013b). This evinces some success for ASEAN's connectivity strategy.

After 1997, the ASEAN process also established a structure governing ASEAN's external trade via framework agreements on economic partnership with Japan and India and a Strategic Partnership for Peace and Prosperity with China (2003). By 2012, ASEAN had concluded trade agreements, covering goods and services, with Japan, China, Australia and New Zealand (2008), the Republic of Korea (2009) and a comprehensive India-ASEAN FTA in 2014.

In this context of constructing a normative order via the process of dialogue and trust building, ASEAN scholars consider particularly influential the role that Track Two meetings and workshops—involving both diplomats and scholars—play in clarifying the evolving character of the organization and extending its processes into the ASEAN Regional Forum (ARF) and ASEAN Plus Three (APT) mechanisms. Acharya considers 'an important feature of regional security debates in ASEAN is the role of think tanks specializing in international relations and security studies in sponsoring what has (sic) been called second track dialogues and discussions on regional security issues' (Acharya 1998, p. 75).

Thus, ASEAN's *Vision 2020* foresaw Southeast Asia 'bound by a common regional identity' (ASEAN Secretariat 1997). Meanwhile, the Kuala Lumpur Declaration on the Establishment of the ASEAN Charter, December 2005, desired 'to realize an ASEAN Community, as envisaged in the Declaration of ASEAN Concord 11... and the ASEAN Vision 2020', which considers ASEAN "a concert of Southeast Asian nations; outward looking; living together in peace, stability and prosperity, bonded together in partnership in... a community of caring societies"' (ASEAN Secretariat 2005).

However, socialization through discursive construction notwithstanding, words are not deeds. Central to the case for ASEAN transforming both its member states and the wider region is the contention that the process of meeting and dialogue in an atmosphere of unstructured informality over time promotes trust, creates shared norms and induces a shared identity (see Wendt 1999 ch. 7). This should be observable both in the changing practice of the organization and in its manner of addressing a range of regional economic, political and security problems. In the economic arena in particular, the publication of scorecards after 2011 assessing the implementation of an ASEAN single market, common production base and the extent of the free flow in goods, services, investments, capital and skilled labour afforded a tool for measuring compliance and effecting the connectivity central to an integrated market (Balboa and Wingaraja 2014, Larkin 2015b, p. 5).

One difficulty with this transformation appears almost immediately when we examine the actual administrative practice of the organization, which, despite the ASEAN Charter's (2008) enhanced mandate for the ASEAN Secretariat, lacks adequate supranational capacity (Ji 2014, p. 3). In other words, despite the proliferation of meetings, declarations, protocols, blueprints, scorecards and master plans, the structure of ASEAN remains determinedly intergovernmental.

Thus, although Article 22 (2) of the 2007 ASEAN Charter (cf ASEAN Charter 2008) mandated that 'ASEAN shall maintain and establish dispute settlement mechanisms in all fields of ASEAN cooperation', member state preference for nonbinding decisions undermines this process. Member states still consider the enforcement of supranational decision-making a threat to national sovereignty—a sensitive issue for a region that experienced a history of colonialism. According to Sukma (2014), ASEAN is still characterized by the lack of a dispute-settlement mechanism to enforce compliance and the lack of adherence to regional policies reflects the absence of effective economic regime sanctions.

Ultimately, ASEAN's dispute resolution mechanism follows the GATT/WTO process which allows states to initiate non-compliance suits against other states. As outlined in Chap. 8 of the ASEAN Charter, disputes can be resolved through the nonbinding and non-adjudicatory processes of the Advisory Mechanism and Consultative Mechanism or the binding Enforcement Mechanism. However, both the Advisory Mechanism and the Consultative Mechanism are informal procedures set up for resolving trade and investment disputes. Thus although the binding Enforcement Mechanism of the ASEAN Protocol on Enhanced Dispute Settlement Mechanism (EDSM) of 2004[3] may be invoked and the Senior Economic Officials Meeting (SEOM) may convene a panel to resolve the dispute if consultations fail to be resolved, or the dispute even may be referred to the ASEAN Summit itself should it remain unresolved (ASEAN 2012b), these mechanisms are ineffectual and rarely used.

Significantly, decisions from the SEOM require the consensus of all ASEAN member states and, since both the aggrieved party and alleged transgressor are part of SEOM, a mutually acceptable resolution is unlikely (Inama and Sim 2015). Moreover, should the dispute remain unresolved it is referred to the ASEAN Summit, an event which convenes only twice a year and is unlikely to come to a decision within its short timeframe. While consensus is the default ASEAN practice, member states soon discover that achieving unanimity is not always feasible and poses an ongoing impediment to intra-regional trade and greater regional economic integration.

This pattern of state-driven interaction is particularly evident in the areas of economic cooperation. In fact, it is the staff of each member state's ASEAN National Secretariat (ANS), housed in their respective foreign ministries, that proposes and, once accepted at a heads of government meeting, disposes policy. As Zakaria Haji Ahmad explained, it is the ANS that 'coordinates' each country's position at ASEAN meetings (Zakaria 1986, pp. 192–212, Ji 2014). A total of 80% of ASEAN business conducted by the ANS machinery concerns fairly mundane technical and economic matters. The press and ASEAN scholarship, by contrast, glamorize ASEAN's political role. The ANS forms the actual bureaucracy of ASEAN. Moreover, at this level, what distinguishes the ASEAN process is not informality but a high degree of formality and hierarchy. In fact, the actual implementation of ASEAN policy across member states is 'structured in terms of collaboration not cooperation' (ibid.).

The dissonance between an official declaratory intent of deepening ASEAN integration and extending its nonbinding processes to the wider region, and the actual intra-ASEAN policy practice that remains intergovernmental and bureaucratic, has important implications not only for how

ASEAN functions, but also the extent to which its aspiration to build a common regional identity based on shared norms can be realized. In order to explore this dissonance, let us examine ASEAN's rhetorical and practical response to its first economic crisis.

Unravelling the 1997 Financial Crisis and Its Economic Implications

Prior to the financial crisis of 1997, those enamoured of the region at the expense of the state envisaged polymorphous economic and security arrangements, like ASEAN, together with the economic and security arrangements it spawned, like the ARF, ASEAN Free Trade Area (AFTA) and ASEAN Plus Three as the necessary mechanisms for building what many considered to be a new, multilateral, regional order. Yet ASEAN, as a regional economic grouping, was far from integrated. The structure of the more dynamic ASEAN economies was export oriented. They competed between themselves both for foreign direct investment (FDI) and as low-cost manufacturing bases for Northeast Asian, European or North American multinational corporations. Only in 1989 did some ASEAN states establish cross-border economic growth zones.[4] These growth triangles relied upon FDI from Northeast Asia and, with the onset of the financial crisis, fell into desuetude.

Unlike increasingly economically integrated regions such as the European Union (EU) where intra-European trade, amongst the core economies, accounted for over 60% of total EU trade by the mid-1990s, intra-ASEAN trade represented a mere 20% of total ASEAN trade at the time of AFTA's formation in 1992 (Herschede 1991, pp. 181–182). Indeed, continuing dependence on external markets made the notion of a 'customs union unacceptable to ASEAN members' (Bowles 1997, p. 222). As Andrew MacIntyre observed in 1997, despite the rhetoric of ASEAN economic cooperation, 'the bound tariff levels of the ASEAN countries are among the very highest in the world' (MacIntyre 1997, p. 239).

The financial meltdown of 1997 plunged the individual economies of a number of ASEAN states into a deep recession. Moving from the boundless optimism of the Asian miracle to financial crisis constituted a shock to the Asian model of economic development, undermining previous certainties and leaving both regional politicians and academics floundering for explanations and solutions. In this context, the ASEAN orthodoxy holds that even if attempts at economic integration had been largely rhetorical prior to the crisis, its consequence encouraged both a deepening of ASEAN integration and a widening of its processes to embrace Northeast Asia (Higgott 1998, p. 6). The 1997 financial crisis thus offers an excellent case for testing claims about the role of ASEAN and its capacity to build an integrated economic community, one of the pillars of the enhanced Declaration of ASEAN Concord (2003).

The crisis, which began in Thailand in June 1997, spawned two essentially contested understandings. The prevailing economic orthodoxy maintained that the structural features of the Asian economic model comprised the efficient cause of meltdown. By contrast, the market-unfriendly school, led by the then and current Malaysian Prime Minister Mahathir Mohammad, and abetted by a curious group of cheerleaders that ranged from Paul Krugman to Jeffrey Sachs, Joseph Stiglitz and President Suharto, maintained that the crisis was an effect of deregulated global capitalism.

Ultimately the crisis stimulated the desire to do something collectively to counter regional vulnerability. Here, Mahathir's diagnosis achieved increasing traction. As the meltdown spread from Southeast Asia to Northeast Asia, most notably South Korea, it induced a sense of regional humiliation. Shame induced resentment as Western institutions like the IMF and World Bank appeared to punish East Asia (Lewis 1999, p. 1).

Consequently, designing Asian solutions for Asian problems would both engender a greater sense of East Asian independence and strengthen regional economies against further externally induced shocks. The years following the crisis therefore witnessed an upsurge in the rhetoric of pan-Asian economic renewal (*The Financial Times* 13 May 2001). The Sixth ASEAN Summit in Hanoi, in December 1998, committed its members to 'a higher plane of regional cooperation in order to strengthen ASEAN's effectiveness in dealing with the challenges of growing interdependence within ASEAN and of its integration into the global economy' (ASEAN Secretariat Point 5 1998).

The years following the crisis witnessed an upsurge in the rhetoric of pan-Asian economic renewal. Thus, Singapore Ambassador-at-Large, Tommy Koh, argued that the economic crisis had 'stimulated a new sense of East Asian regionalism and brought the countries closer together' (Financial Times, 13 May 2001). A feeling of shared destiny and a commitment to renewal galvanized ASEAN. In the months following the outbreak of the economic crisis, ASEAN sought to institute a dialogue partnership with Northeast Asian states, China, South Korea and Japan, through an East Asian Summit (EAS), the first of which met in Kuala

Lumpur in December 1997. The Sixth ASEAN Summit in Hanoi committed its members to 'a higher plane of regional cooperation in order to strengthen ASEAN's effectiveness in dealing with the challenges of growing interdependence within ASEAN and of its integration into the global economy' (ASEAN Secretariat 1998).

The same summit further agreed to formalize these meetings into the arrangement known as ASEAN Plus Three, subsequently extended further into a nebulous East Asian Community, including Australia, New Zealand and India, in a subsidiary 'Asian' category after 2007 and by 2013 including both Russia and the United States. The push for greater East Asian institutionalization also produced a number of 'visions' to reinforce economic cooperation. South Korean President Kim Dae-jung proposed an 'East Asia Vision Group' that would report on proposals to deepen long-term cooperation among members of the APT grouping (East Asia Vision Group Report 2001, p. 1). Not to be outdone, the Japanese suggested creating an Asian Monetary Fund specifically to address regional needs in a more effective and sensitive manner than the IMF (Johnstone 1999, p. 125). Even more grandiose visions were floated including an Asian free trade area and a monetary union (Soesastro 2001, pp. 7–9), while Wanandi speculated that one day East Asia might develop into 'a community' on similar lines to the European Union (Wanandi 1999).

The crisis, therefore, inspired numerous official declarations of regional solidarity and identity. It was the AEC, the APT and subsequently the East Asian Summit (EAS) mechanism that constituted its lasting institutional fruit, constituting the 'embryo of an East Asian regional organization' (Soesastro 2001, p. 1). The arrangement was intended as a vehicle to regenerate ASEAN. Moves towards a more developed sense of East Asian regionalism seemingly entailed a new and enhanced role for the Association. As one of its proponents, ex-Indonesian Foreign Minister Ali Alatas averred the APT, like the practice informing the ARF, 'should, at least during the initial phase, continue to be ASEAN driven' (Alatas 2001, p. 4). Following the ASEAN way the process informing future summits would be gradual, consensual and nonbinding (Soesastro 2001, p. 2).

Perhaps the most distinctive feature of the APT/EAS arrangement was that it represented an exclusive understanding of regional cooperation. Unlike more open regional forums like APEC (Asia-Pacific Economic Cooperation), the APT implicitly set the boundaries of 'East Asia' in a way that excluded those countries on the Asian periphery that were, *ipso facto*, deemed 'external' to the region. Those most obviously designated outsiders were the United States, Australia and New Zealand. In this respect, the arrangement bore a resemblance to the East Asian Economic Caucus (EAEC), a putative group comprising the ASEAN states along with a number of Northeast Asian states like China, South Korea, Japan and Taiwan proposed by Prime Minister Mahathir in the early 1990s as a counterweight to US influence in APEC (Wanandi 2000, Alatas 2001, p. 2).[5] If EAEC was the avatar of East Asian collaboration, its later manifestation in the APT framework represented for both regional officials and analysts alike the primary mechanism for constructing an integrated East Asian region linked into the EAC through what the Asia Development Bank 2009 saw as the need for a massive (US$8 trillion) and coordinated investment in national and regional infrastructure (ADB 2009).

However, declarations of regional solidarity are frequently made for demonstrative effect. In fact, trans-Pacific economic and trade practice since ASEAN launched its deepening and widening initiatives reveals a rather different economic story than the official version of strengthening regional economic resilience conveys. This requires a brief account of the ambiguous, but transformative, role that China has come to play in the wider region's economic and financial and infrastructural integration. China's rapid growth since 1997 is the economic fount of the latest source of pan-Asian enthusiasm as well as the potential source of the next regional recession. This renewed sense of a profound and irreversible economic shift to the Asia-Pacific hemisphere has paradoxically been reinforced by the deep financial crisis that engulfed both Europe and North America after 2008.

By 2003, the OECD reported that of US$62 billion in global foreign direct investment, China accounted for US$52 billion (*Jakarta Post* 29 June 2004). China's heavy industries, power, steel and petrochemical voraciously consume resources especially from resource-rich Southeast Asia (*The Australian Financial Review* 27 April 2004).[6] Its demand for automobiles, industrial parks and apartments and its emergence as the globe's low-cost manufacturing base for everything from baseball caps and footwear to computers and televisions revived growth across Northeast Asia after 2002, the year that the PRC joined the WTO. This growth, however, has not been an unmixed blessing, especially for the ASEAN economies. Whilst China's growth has revived the high-technology economies of Japan, South Korea and Taiwan, it has simultaneously sucked investment out of Southeast Asian economies who rely on manufacturing. The rise of China after 1998, and its attraction for foreign investors, actually affected growth negatively in Southeast Asia particularly during the recession from 1997 to 2003. Here also low-tech manufacturing industries depend upon foreign direct investment. In zero sum terms, ASEAN's deteriorating investment attractiveness for low-cost manufacturing reflected the rapid growth of the Chinese 'titan'. After the AFC, ASEAN attracted only 16% of Asian FDI compared with China's 66%—the exact reverse of the position in 1990 (*Australian Financial Review*, 26 April 2004). By 2004, Chinese competition had devastated the Indonesian and Filipino garment and footwear industries. Global brands like Nike and Gap increasingly source China and Vietnam for new supplies where 'wages are lower and productivity higher' (Das 2013, p. 12, Napoli 2014, p. 245). As the IMF announced, somewhat euphemistically, 'countries whose factor endowments are similar to China and which... compete with it in world markets will need to undertake sizable adjustments and display flexibility in product and labour markets' (IMF 2003, p. 63).

In a bid to attract more FDI, the ASEAN Free Trade Area (AFTA) conceived in 1992 officially came into existence a decade later. In fact, AFTA reduced intra-ASEAN tariff rates under the Common Effective Preferential Tariff and the ASEAN Trade in Goods Agreement (ATIGA) that replaced it in 2010. The average tariff which stood at 12.76% in 1993 has been gradually reduced with the aim to meet the range of 0–5% tariff rates for all items in the Inclusion List for the ASEAN-6 by 2002 (ASEAN 2012c). By 2015, the ASEAN-6[7] had achieved an almost complete elimination of tariffs reducing them to 0.03%, whilst amongst ASEAN's more recent members, Cambodia, Laos, Myanmar and Vietnam, tariffs stood at 0.54% (ASEAN 2016). The reduction in tariffs has helped to promote trade flows within the region and boost intra-regional consumption. According to Hapsari and Mangunsong (2006), the reduction of tariff rates increased the bilateral exports of the ASEAN-5[8] and has made import and export profiles more complementary, thus increasing the potential for intra-ASEAN trade flows. Meanwhile, a study conducted by Calvo-Pardo et al. (2009) found that imports between the ASEAN-6 increased over a 13-year period from 1993 to 2006 and reported that AFTA has contributed to a limited trade creation, rather than a trade diversion, effect in the region.

Nevertheless, even with AFTA and the AEC, achieving full economic integration as a bloc remains difficult. The problem is that despite all its memoranda and action plans, scorecards and blueprints, ASEAN remains 'not a single country, but a group of countries with differing languages, legal systems and political risks. These differences erode the comparative advantage of the bloc', especially *vis a vis* China's growing regional hegemony (Napoli 2014, p. 246).

To the extent that the ASEAN economies have grown since 2002, it has been a result of both its role as a low-cost base for manufacturing goods assembled in Southeast Asia for export to the United States and Europe and its emerging role as a supplier of commodities to China. Thus, whilst ASEAN's exports to the EU were 'the same as China's in 2000…by 2012, China's exports to the EU were more than triple ASEAN's' (ibid., 348). Moreover, although trade with China rose by 18% in 2002, this reflected China's appetite for the region's raw materials. ASEAN, unlike Northeast Asia, has had little success in exporting higher value products to China.

As an indirect consequence of the China effect on trade flows, the slow adoption of economic and financial reforms meant that ASEAN had not achieved a single undivided market by 2015. Indeed, the ASEAN Secretariat observed in 2013 that ASEAN members had adopted less than 50% of single-market policy provisions (Napoli 358).

At the same time, the more market-oriented states in the region increasingly act autonomously of AFTA, evolving a pattern of overlapping, preferential trade deals both within and beyond the region (ASEAN-China Expert Group 2001, p. 91). As John Ravenhill argued, the Japan-Singapore Economic Partnership Agreement in January 2003 constituted a 'dramatic… turn in East Asia to preferential trade' (Ravenhill 2002, p. 182, ASEAN 2012a, Das 2015, pp. 8–9). The conclusion of bilateral trade deals between Singapore and New Zealand, and Singapore and Australia, as well as between Thailand and Australia and Australia and Malaysia (2012), followed. Such bilateralism since the AFC altered both the direction and pattern of trade in the region and illustrates that ASEAN's most developed economies, Thailand and Singapore, are concentrating on their own markets and depriving ASEAN of its best integrators in the process (*The Economist*, 31 July 2004).

In other words, despite the widely advertised aspiration amongst regional elites for an 'ASEAN-incorporated' model, the regional aspiration sits at variance with state-led development that the member states of ASEAN continue to practise. As Joe Studwell demonstrated, the ASEAN economy 'is a product' at the state level of 'a relationship between economic and political power' where political elites 'grant members of an economic elite monopoly concerns, mainly in domestic service industries that enable the latter to control vast amounts of wealth' (Studwell 2007,

p. xii). A relatively small group of tycoons form an economic aristocracy that works 'hand in glove' with local political elites at the state level. State and market are so intertwined that one commentator describes the relationship as 'nomenklatura capitalism' (Jayasuriya 2003, p. 34).

Whilst the political and economic structure at the state level remains an essentially crony capitalist one, meltdown and recession dramatically altered the economic landscape of Southeast Asia after 2003. Prior to the crisis, it was plausible to speak of shared developmental commonalities such as export-oriented growth, dependent on Japanese, Korean, Taiwanese or US and European foreign direct investment, technocratic planning, single-party rule and a governed labour and domestic market. Since 1997, the strategies adopted to deal with the meltdown and recovery, particularly in Southeast Asia, have created distinctive differences amongst the ASEAN political economies that presage not greater integration but growing economic disparity. With a number of its core components undermined by the crisis of 1997, and by the economic crisis in Europe and North America after 2008, the direction in which the wider Asian economic model moves can no longer be as smoothly interdependent or as export oriented as it was before the financial crisis era. Southeast Asia, in particular, is less dependent on traditional sources of Northeast Asian investment and increasingly reliant upon Chinese FDI. Since the ASEAN-China FTA came into effect in 2010, the ASEAN states have therefore become collectively more dependent on exports to and foreign investment from a rising China (Napoli 2014, pp. 358–359).

Any attempt to broaden East Asian economic and financial integration has to take into account that, since 2001, economic growth in Asia remained dependent on the WTO order that facilitated both US and European consumption together with Chinese growth and investment, after China entered the WTO in 2002. At the same time, East Asia's high savings rates and budget surpluses, after 1998, together with central bank interventions in the foreign exchange markets to keep currencies cheap, supported both the US current account deficit and the greenback.

For its export-led growth model, East Asia requires accommodating markets and willing inward investors. The United States is the most accommodating final market and, before the US banking crisis of 2008–2012, the most willing inward investor. In a Faustian bargain, the Asian economies financed the US twin deficits, as well as the European currency as a form of collateral against the direct investments they receive from multinational conglomerates (Dooley et al. 2006, p. 3).

At the same time, ASEAN's recovery from the Asian Financial Crisis (AFC) and continued growth during the Northern Financial Crisis relied upon its growing bilateral trade with China. Significantly, however, ASEAN runs a trade deficit with China which has created difficulty for small- and medium-sized enterprises (Lo, 5).

In other words, despite the post-financial crisis enthusiasm for deeper regional integration there is little to sustain a 'stable, prosperous and highly competitive ASEAN region in which there is a free flow of goods, services [and] investment' (ASEAN 2003). As Razeen Sally observed in May 2014, the 'AEC is well behind its targets to produce and abolish non-tariff and regulatory barriers in goods services and investment' (Sally 2014, p. 8, Balboa and Wingaraja 2014). Instead, the rise of China and to a lesser extent India, together with Japan's dominance in high technology and its aversion to technology transfer, leaves ASEAN increasingly dependent on Chinese investment and export markets open to a WTO-sponsored world trading order.

All Roads Lead to China or ASEAN and Unequal Treaties

After 1997, the response to the Asian economic crisis notably sharpened Sino-Japanese rivalry for Southeast Asian influence and distanced the region from the United States. This was for two reasons. Firstly, the conduct of Japanese financial institutions and *sogososha* during the crisis damaged Japan's standing in Southeast Asia. Japanese financial institutions took flight as the currency turmoil struck and returned only reluctantly. Meanwhile the United States seemed to a number of regional statesmen and think tanks to have unleashed the 'electronic herd' to speculate on regional currencies and impose what Thomas Freidman termed 'golden straitjacket' of accountability and transparency on Asian financial conduct (Friedman 1999, p. 101). These circumstances afforded China the opportunity to 'strengthen its influence over ASEAN members in order to challenge Japan's leadership in the region' (NIDS 2015, p. 209) and sideline a United States increasingly distracted by its global war on terror after 2001. The refusal to devalue the *renminbi*, which might have exacerbated Southeast Asia's financial crisis, indicated China's responsibility and regional leadership. It reassured the ASEAN states that China would not exploit the crisis for self-aggrandizing purposes. Over the same period (1998–2008) China acted with analogous self-restraint over the South China Sea dispute and promoted a good neighbourliness policy to reinforce its enhanced regional credentials.

Closer ties between ASEAN and China necessarily affected Japan. China's rise and its increasing assertiveness over a number of unresolved historical issues had already impacted negatively on Japan's regional image. Accordingly, the fact that China had increased its leverage over Southeast Asia in the aftermath of the crisis elicited a countervailing response. This assumed the form of the New Miyazawa Initiative of 1998 and subsequently the Obuchi-ASEAN plan to provide large-scale financial assistance to facilitate regional recovery (Ministry of Foreign Affairs 1998).

Mounting Sino-Japanese competition for regional influence explains their interest in the APT/EAS process. Both the APT and the East Asian Community Summit of 2005 constituted a stage upon which the major powers of Northeast Asia might play for the economic and political leadership of Southeast Asia. Indeed, Japan had few illusions that, without the United States, Indian and Australian participation in the regional process, China had 'an ideal framework within which it can exercise its influence, making it easier for China to play a leading role in forming a free-trade area in East Asia' (NIDS 2015, p. 210). Japan thus views China's participation in the APT, and its promotion of the Regional Comprehensive Economic Partnership (RCEP) as a regional free trade agreement, not as a prelude to deeper integration and community building, but as a strategy to diminish both Japanese and US influence in Southeast Asia. In order to pre-empt this outcome Japan sought to reignite its influence 'cooperating with ASEAN members' in terms of investment, technology, human resources and security because only 'through such measures, can Japan match the growing influence of China' (ibid., 215). In this context, former Japanese Prime Minister Koizumi's doctrine, promoting 'an expanded East Asian community', was not an idealist attempt to forge regional identity but a tactic to balance China's regional ascendancy by involving Australia, New Zealand, India and, ultimately, after the Obama pivot between 2012 and 2016, the United States in the process. Indeed, 'using ASEAN as their stage, it appears that Japan and China are jockeying for a leadership role in East Asia' (ibid., 215).

However, economic stagnation and deflation has adversely affected the extent of Japan's influence over Southeast Asia in recent years, while China-ASEAN trade grew substantially. Over the decade, since 2003, China-ASEAN trade has increased 24% year on year from US$78 billion to US$444 billion (Lo 2014, p. 5). By 2018, China was ASEAN's largest trading partner for the ninth consecutive year, with trade reaching US$514.8 billion in 2017 (Sun 2018). Moreover, the return of FDI to Southeast Asia after 2003 reflected Chinese rather than Western, Japanese and South Korean investment. 'Chinese FDI into ASEAN increased 11 times' between 2003 and 2008 (Napoli 358). Meanwhile, ASEAN exports to China offset their losses in Western market share.

Trade between ASEAN and China will continue to rise. Official state-run news agency *Xinhua* reports that China-ASEAN trade will reach US$1 trillion by 2020, as China continues to deepen capacity building and promote, in the PRC's estimation, 'win-win' development for all (Cao 2017). The ASEAN-China Free Trade Area (ACFTA) signed in 2002 and implemented in 2010 further facilitates this growth in trade. Since 2012, ASEAN and China have promoted an extension of their bilateral FTA to include Australia, India, Japan and South Korea as well. This is the basis for what China envisages as 'the maritime silk road' through the formation of an ostensibly ASEAN-led Regional Comprehensive Economic Partnership (RCEP). Reflecting and informing this partnership is China's Asian Infrastructure Investment Bank (AIIB) with 50, primarily Asian, members, but including the United Kingdom and Germany, and with assets of more than US$1 billion to invest in regional infrastructure. Even so, ASEAN countries will require infrastructure investments amounting to US$1.08 trillion between 2010 and 2020 (Larkin 2015a, p. 6). Significantly, the AIIB initiative complements China's bold Belt and Road Investment (BRI) initiative that seeks to build land transportation corridors that connect China to Europe and South Asia, as well as with Southeast Asia, whilst the Maritime Silk Road promotes port development, 'a string of pearls', to enhance trade from the Bay of Bengal to Hong Kong (Larkin 2015b, p. 4).

Yet, the 'Belt and Road' model not only complements ASEAN's Master Plan for ASEAN Connectivity (MPAC), it also enhances China's connectivity regionally and globally. In other words, it promotes China's strategic interests in the region. Ultimately the BRI integrates the smaller ASEAN economies more fully into 'China-centric regional production networks' (Das 2015, p. 7). In other words, although infrastructure development is crucial in realizing ASEAN's MPAC and AEC market, the AIIB and the BRI potentially facilitate intra-ASEAN competition for infrastructure funding rather than enhancing cooperation. In fact, China's increasingly proactive economic diplomacy in Southeast Asia is part of a broader strategy that seeks to bind its neighbours in 'a web of incentives that increase their reliance on China and raise the cost to them of adopting a confrontational policy towards China' on either territorial or economic disputes' (Glaser and Lal 2014, p. 2).

Southeast Asia's reliance on China and its political costs are becoming increasingly evident, especially in the wake of US President Trump's capricious withdrawal from former US President Obama-led Trans-Pacific Partnership that offered a potential economic balance to China's regional hegemony. As of 2018, Indonesia is the largest recipient in ASEAN of China's BRI funding, with investments amounting to US$87 billion in repayable loans. In April 2018, President Joko 'Jokowi' Widodo secured five contracts with Beijing. They included the construction of a US$17.8 billion hydropower plant on the Kayan River, a US$2 billion hydropower plant in Kayan in North Kalimantan, a US$700 million dimethyl ethercoal conversion plant, a power plant in Bali costing US$1.6 billion, and the development of steel smelters worth US$1.2 billion (Fuad 2018). Meanwhile, China Railway Corp (CRC) is constructing Indonesia's first high-speed railway, the first in Southeast Asia, by connecting Jakarta and Bandung. Indonesia urgently needs this investment to achieve nationwide access to electricity and service a rapidly increasing urban population.

Whilst a familiar refrain of China's diplomacy is its 'good neighbour' approach to its Southeast Asian brothers, its economic 'benevolence' comes at a price. Indonesia is notably reluctant to assert its territorial sovereignty over the resource-rich Natuna Islands which lie in an area of the South China Sea claimed by an increasingly assertive China. Despite holding legal sovereignty over the islands under the United Nations Convention on the Law of the Sea (UNCLOS) 1982, Indonesia has not asserted its territorial rights as strongly as other claimant states in the South China Sea dispute that has become increasingly contentious since 2012. According to the *Jakarta Post*, China's economic diplomacy poses unwritten obligations that recipients of its largesse reciprocate in the political sphere (Utama and Kim 2016). Thus while Indonesia—the largest Muslim country in the world—vociferously condemns the treatment of Muslim communities in Israel or the Rohingya in Myanmar, it is notably silent when it comes to the treatment of the Uighur minority in Xinjiang.

Economic reliance leads to a loss of sovereignty and erodes the already disproportionate bargaining power that China exercises over BRI recipients. Although developing countries freely consent to these infrastructure loans, the inability to repay the loans and their accumulated interest renders recipient states vulnerable to China's geopolitical demands. Thus Mustofa (2018) compares contemporary Chinese investment with nineteenth-century Dutch colonial policy and argues that the Indonesian government should beware of *penjajah kulit kuning* (yellow-skinned colonization) which he asserts has already reduced Angola and Zimbabwe to Chinese dependencies.[9] Fuad (2018) also sees history repeating itself via the BRI, which to Indonesian ears echoes *Vereenigde Oostindische Compagnie (VOC* Dutch East India Company) promises of trade and investment that led to 350 years of colonization. Nonetheless, in the absence of a Western economic counterweight, it seems inevitable that China will continue extending its geoeconomic influence not only in Indonesia but across the region.

The Philippine case further illustrates this phenomenon. Traditionally a US ally, under the presidency of Rodrigo Duterte (2016–), the Philippines has sought investment from China, supressing its justifiable claims in the South China Sea in return for infrastructure investment. Despite winning a historic legal victory at the Permanent Court of Arbitration (PCA) in the Hague in 2016 over China's right to disputed islands in the Paracel island chain, President Duterte ignored the Hague ruling opting instead for Beijing's financial largesse. In order to achieve a 'golden age of infrastructure', spur economic growth and reduce poverty from 21.6% in 2015 to 13–15% by 2022, Duterte needs China's FDI (Estrada 2018). President Duterte's pivot towards China, moreover, occurred after President Obama and Western human rights advocates criticized his aggressive prosecution of a war on drugs that featured a penchant for extrajudicial killing. The president informed foreign companies, worried over human right violations, to 'pack up and leave', observing that Chinese businesses would gladly take their place (Muggah 2017).

Duterte's economic and foreign policy has rendered Manila almost exclusively reliant on Chinese capital to achieve its ambitious 'Build Build Build' programme. Aligning with the Philippine Development Plan (2017–2022) and *Ambisyon Natin* 2040 ('our vision'), China pledged US$7.34 billion in soft loans to fund several infrastructure projects: the North–South Railway in Southern Luzon (US$2.91 billion); the 70 km Subic-Clark Railway (US$947.64 million); the Davao City Expressway (US$424.81 million) and the Kaliwa Dam project (US$234.92 million) (Rabena 2018). This investment will necessarily deepen Manila's dependence on China.

Beijing's strategy of fostering asymmetrical economic dependence among weaker states allows it to shape their foreign policies in ways congenial to China's interests. In this context, Malaysia offers an interesting case study of how this policy can have unanticipated consequences. In

2015, the *Sarawak Review* and *The Wall Street Journal* (WSJ) unearthed a paper trail that exposed a corruption scandal at the highest levels of Malaysian politics. In 2009, former Prime Minister Najib Razak had established 1 Malaysia Development Berhad (1MDB), a government investment arm to boost Malaysia's economic growth. However, the investment fund quickly amassed US$11 billion in debt. At the same time close to US$700 million found its way into Mr. Najib's personal bank account (Wright and Clark 2015). In a bid to rescue the state investment fund, and allay further suspicions over financial irregularities, Najib's government developed increasingly close links to China. In November 2015, the government sold 1MDB's power assets Edra Global Energy Berhad to China General Nuclear Power Corporation (CGN) for RM9.83 billion (US$2.3 billion). In return, CGN assumed the gross debt that Edra Global Energy Berhad and its operating companies had accumulated (Chin 2015).

This Chinese bailout guaranteed Malaysia's silence on China's increasingly assertive stance in areas like the South China Sea. In an increasingly fiscally challenged environment of corruption allegations and mounting debt from 1MDB, Malaysia's economic dependence on China translated into a shift from a non-partisan foreign policy to a pro-China stance. Following an official state visit to Beijing in 2016, Prime Minister Najib Razak wrote, in *China Daily*, 'we believe it is incumbent upon larger countries to treat smaller ones fairly. And this includes former colonial powers. It is not for them to lecture countries they once exploited on how to conduct their own internal affairs today' (Razak 2016). This statement was in response to lawsuits filed by the US Department of Justice implicating 'Malaysian Official 1' with money laundering, a charge the government considered as interfering in its internal affairs. Undoubtedly, China's tolerance of kleptocratic behaviour and human rights abuses leads weak or illiberal regimes to deal with Beijing, rather than face the scrutiny that the West or transnational organizations like the IMF might impose on their financial conduct.

After Najib's state visit in 2016, Malaysia enjoyed a substantial increase in investment to fund a variety of infrastructure projects. Najib agreed a total of 11 high-profile projects backed by US$134 billion worth of Chinese capital. These projects included the US$15 billion East Coat Rail Link (ECRL), a railway connecting Malaysia's underdeveloped east coast with Kuala Lumpur, as well as a controversial US$100 billion luxury real estate project in Johor. Failure to repay these BRI loans could leave

Malaysia exposed to the fate of countries like Sri Lanka, forced to cede Hambantota Port and 15,000 acres of land to China for 99 years to erase US$1 billion worth of China-denominated debt (Abi-Habib 2018). The port affords China a strategically critical foothold in the Indian Ocean. In this context, the construction of Forest City on four artificial islands off the coast of Johor has raised Malaysian concerns that it is being built for Chinese nationals and that former Prime Minister Najib Razak sold off Malaysian territory to a foreign government (Abu Bakar 2017).

It was only with the fall of Najib's government in the Malaysian general election of May 2018 that doubts about the nature of Chinese investment and the potential debt trap it created could be openly expressed. Whilst the new government has become more sceptical about BRI investment, its economic dependence may be difficult to reverse. Since assuming office in May 2018 following a surprise victory that toppled the *Barisan Nasional* after 61 years of uninterrupted rule, new Prime Minister Dr Mahathir Mohamad cancelled the China-backed East Coast Rail Link and two pipeline projects in Sabah and Melaka. Significantly, Mahathir described the BRI-sponsored projects as 'unequal treaties', a term the Chinese government had used—不平等条(*bu ping deng tiao yue*)—to refer to a series of treaties signed with Western powers that witnessed the erosion of its sovereignty in the nineteenth century. Nevertheless, despite the Mahathir-led *Pakatan Harapan* administration's attempt to reverse the Najib strategy, China remains Malaysia's second-largest export trading partner and largest source of imports (Lee and Huang 2018). Thus, reduced reliance on BRI does not equate to diminished dependency on China, and in the absence of a strong counterweight, Malaysia, like the other ASEAN economies, depends on the China trade and Beijing's financial largesse.

This dependence has become more evident since Donald Trump decided to abandon the Obama administration's Trans-Pacific Partnership (TPP) in 2017, impose restrictions upon Chinese imports and launch a trade war with China, for its apparent breach of WTO rules. Paradoxically, the TPP had briefly posited an alternative to the China-backed RCEP, as a US-led bid to determine the rules for Asian trade. A cornerstone of Obama's 'Pivot to Asia' policy, this partnership involved 12 countries, but (four from ASEAN) together with Japan, New Zealand, Australia, Canada and three South American states.[10] Whilst Australian Trade Minister Craig Emerson (2012) asserted that this meant two pathways to the same destination, this was somewhat disingenuous. China promotes the former, the United States the latter. China belongs to the former and not the latter, and the United States, until 2017, vice versa. The ASEAN-led RCEP brings under one umbrella the various bilateral and trilateral preferential trade deals concluded between ASEAN and a number of regional states. However, the 'free' in these RCEP trade agreements is notional. Key agricultural and manufacturing sectors remain protected. The now emasculated TPP, by contrast, envisaged a far more comprehensive and rule-binding trade agreement, which a number of ASEAN states, as well as China, resisted.

In this context, President Trump's 'America First' policy followed by the decision to withdraw from the TPP in 2017 has given China further opportunity to extend its economic influence and financial stake in Southeast Asia. Consequently, Southeast Asia has been drawn into the China-backed but ASEAN-led Regional Comprehensive Economic Partnership (RCEP), which comprises 16 participating countries: 10 ASEAN nations, China, India, Japan, South Korea, Australia and New Zealand. On 13 October 2018, the Sixth RCEP Inter-Sessional Ministerial Meeting held in Singapore witnessed all participating members reaffirming their resolve to conclude the region-wide trade pact. If successfully concluded, RCEP will be the largest trade deal in the world, accounting for 45% of the world's population (3.4 billion people) and one-third of the global GDP (US$20 trillion) and global total trade (US$10 trillion) (Shira 2018).

Although the RCEP is an ASEAN-led initiative, it is evident that this economic bloc is increasingly dependent upon the interests of the larger economic players in the region. Zhang (2016) notes that one of the prominent issues facing RCEP is ASEAN's incapacity to drive the regional negotiation processes. The need for all ten ASEAN member states to reach consensus prior to dealing with external partners delays trade negotiations and once again exhibits the structural constraints of the regional grouping. Moreover, the economic potential of the RCEP is further handicapped by political complications such as the South China Sea island dispute between China and ASEAN; territorial issues between China, Japan and South Korea; and historically competitive China-India and China-Japan relations. The inability to conclude the trade pact is also being hindered by India, who is at odds with other RCEP members over protectionist policies. Thus the National Institution for Transforming India, a government think tank, found that trade liberalization with ASEAN, Japan and South Korea has exacerbated India's trade deficit. It also argued that that a free trade agreement with China would put further pressure on the rupee and exacerbate India's trade deficit with Beijing which stood at US$59.4 billion in 2017 (Nakano 2018). Inevitably, ASEAN lacks the bargaining power necessary to persuade members to agree to a comprehensive multilateral free trade agreement and thus, the RCEP is ultimately contingent on whether it aligns with the political and economic will of more powerful states and not the other way around.

Moreover, as a result of Washington's withdrawal from the TPP, China is strategically positioned, as the dominant regional economic player, to rewrite the rules for international trade and establish a Sinocentric regional order via the Silk Road and the RCEP. The RCEP will not only potentially improve China's trade relations with neighbouring countries but propel China to a dominant position facilitating its geoeconomic interests and normative orientation. In fact, Mao and Ding (2016) state that the China-ASEAN free trade area and 'Belt and Road' countries could collectively form a 'One Belt, One Road' regional market reshaping the international economic order. Indeed, as ASEAN relies even more on China for both investment capital and as its primary export market, the liquidity of its decision-making and ability to counter China's geopolitical advances are likely to erode further.

Conclusion: Norms Are What Strong States Make of Them

Both regional scholars and diplomats have long maintained that ASEAN represents an evolving economic and security community. They further contended that the norms that the distinctive ASEAN process implemented over time transformed Southeast Asia and were, after 1997, in the process of building a shared East Asian regional identity. ASEAN's deeper integration into a cultural, economic, political and security community and its extension into the ASEAN-driven APT process after 1997 offers an interesting test case of the dominant assumptions in both ASEAN scholarship and liberal and idealist accounts of international relations and political economy. A process of discourse would transform, it was argued, state interests into shared norms creating the ideational basis of a shared identity. Nation speaking unto nation would see nations evolving progressively into post-national constellations like the frequently applauded, but increasingly discredited, European Union model. This idealist and historicist teleology that came to influence, if not dominate, the discipline of international relations after the Cold War found its quotidian exemplification in the evolution of ASEAN and its purported mutation into an East Asian Community. This collocation of weak states seemed in the course of its incremental evolution over 50 years to epitomize the transfiguration that norms could achieve, first in Southeast Asia's identity, then in the wider region.

However, actual intra- and extra-ASEAN economic practice reveals that its crucial norm of non-interference and its practice of nonbinding consensus inhibit deeper integration either within ASEAN or the wider East Asian region. Despite its slow progress towards a single market, an AEC was not achieved in 2015. Instead the ASEAN economies continue to 'compete rather than cooperate' to attract funding (Das 2013, p. 9). Ultimately, the norms and economic practices that ASEAN promotes can only sustain a pattern of limited intergovernmental and bureaucratically rigidified interactions. Norms, even ASEAN ones, cannot cultivate a regional sense of 'we-ness' if states continue to act, as all East Asian states do, within the paradigm of the nation-state.

Thus, whilst the official view of ASEAN emphasizes its political role and the informal, unstructured, cooperative and consensus-oriented character of the organization, at the quotidian level of policy formulation and implementation, the organization remains an essentially intergovernmental one, dealing primarily with trade and economic issues and dominated by member state bureaucracies, rather than one that possesses the institutional infrastructure to develop into a 'mature' security community or establish a common identity or an integrated single market and production base. The intergovernmental practice that the community norms paradoxically reinforce undermines the official rhetoric of community and regional identity building.

Following the essentially intergovernmental practice of the ASEAN regime, states pursue bilateral or trilateral arrangements rather than building a supranational practice. This is evident in the political economy of the ASEAN states, where the attempt to achieve an ASEAN economic community masks an actual practice of growing bilateralism and the fragmentation rather than integration of the ASEAN political economy together with the growing dependence of these smaller states on the wider region's illiberal economic powerhouse, China.

Meanwhile, extending ASEAN's conflict avoidance strategies to a wider East Asian Community has not altered the strategic reality of the economic fragility and economic diversity of the Southeast Asian states individually and collectively. In fact, what seems to be a Japanese and Chinese acculturation to ASEAN norms is far from it. Instead, these dominant powers manipulate ASEAN's shared norms and nonbinding processes for their own strategic advantage given that a more aggressive posture on either side would have countervailing effects—Japan would invoke memories of 1942, whilst China is still regarded with a degree of regional suspicion. Whatever strategic mutation ASEAN assumes in terms of its wider community building it can only mask the fact that weaker states cannot shape the economic or strategic fate of stronger ones.

Ironically, ASEAN was a Cold War creation supported by the United States to shore up regional resilience against the spread of Communism during and after the Vietnam war. ASEAN could sustain its distinctive approach to regional diplomacy largely because the United States tolerated its posturing and facilitated access to US markets. Although ASEAN, after 1997, resented Western financial and political intrusion in its internal affairs and sought to build an East Asian Community, it little appreciated the economic consequences of both China's rise and a US presidency more interested in economic nationalism than an increasingly open world trading order in the Asia-Pacific and beyond.

Notes

1. The Treaty was amended in 1987 and again in 1998 to provide 'that States outside Southeast Asia may accede to the Treaty with the consent of all the States in Southeast Asia'. *Protocol Amending the Treaty of Amity and Cooperation in Southeast Asia* Philippines, 15 December 1987.
2. The *Table of ASEAN Treaties Agreements and Ratifications* as of March 2012 reveals that of the 359 agreements, declarations, memorandums of understanding, protocols and treaties governing inter-ASEAN conduct or made between the organization and states external to it, over 250 have been codified, ratified or declared since 1997. http://www.asean.org/archive/document/Table%20of%20Agreement%20and%20Ratification%20as%20of%20March%202012.pdf.
3. Also referred to as the Vientiane Protocol.
4. Singapore, Johor in Malaysia and Batam in Indonesia formed a regional growth triangle in 1989. This was followed in 1991 by a northern growth triangle embracing Northern Sumatra, Southern Thailand and Northern Malaysia.
5. Proponents of ASEAN Plus Three denied that the framework had any correspondence to EAEC. Even so, in the sense that ASEAN Plus Three arose

from the perceived mistreatment of Asian states by Western countries and their financial institutions, there is no doubt that EAEC bears a family resemblance to ASEAN Plus Three.

6. China consumed 31% of the world's coal, 30% of its iron ore, 40% of its cement and 17% of its oil by 2003.
7. ASEAN-6 comprises Brunei, Indonesia, Malaysia, Philippines, Singapore and Thailand.
8. ASEAN-5 consists of the original five member states: Indonesia, Malaysia, Philippines, Singapore and Thailand.
9. For instance, due to the hyperinflation of its currency and debt incurred to China, Harare struck a deal in 2015 which witnessed the cancellation of US$40 million worth of Chinese debt in exchange for solidifying the *renminbi* as legal tender.
10. The four ASEAN states are Singapore, Brunei, Malaysia and Vietnam. The three South American states are Mexico, Peru and Chile.

References

Abi-Habib, M. 2018. How China Got Sri Lanka to Cough Up a Port. *New York Times*. https://www.nytimes.com/2018/06/25/world/asia/china-sri-lanka-port.html.

Abu Bakar, S.K. 2017. Mukhriz: Najib Satu-Satunya PM Jual Tanah Hak Milik Kekal Kepada Warga Asing [Mukhriz: Najib the Only PM to Sell Permanent Land to Foreigners]. *Free Malaysia Today*. https://www.freemalaysiatoday.com/category/bahasa/2017/10/19/mukhriz-najib-satu-satunya-pm-jual-tanah-hak-milik-kekal-kepada-warga-asing/. Accessed October 13, 2018.

Acharya, A. 1997. Ideas, Identity and Institution Building: From the ASEAN Way to the Asia Pacific Way. *Pacific Review* 10 (2).

———. 1998. Culture, Security, Multilateralism: The 'ASEAN way' and Regional Order. *Contemporary Security Policy* 19 (1).

Ahmad, Z. 1986. The World of ASEAN Decision Makers: A Study of Bureaucratic Elite Perceptions in Malaysia, the Philippines and Singapore. *Contemporary Southeast Asia* 8 (5).

Alatas, A. 2001. *"ASEAN Plus Three" Equals Peace Plus Prosperity*. Regional Outlook Forum, 2. Singapore: Institute of Southeast Asian Studies.

ASEAN Charter. 2008. *The ASEAN Secretariat*. Jakarta. https://asean.org/storage/images/archive/publications/ASEAN-Charter.pdf

ASEAN Secretariat. 1997. *A Community of Caring Societies, Vision 2020*. Jakarta: ASEAN Secretariat. http://www.asean.org/news/item/asean-vision-2020.

———. 1998. *Hanoi Declaration, 6th ASEAN Summit Southeast Asian Science Policy Advisory Network*. Jakarta: ASEAN Secretariat. http://www.icsea.or.id/sea-span/1198/RG1228LL.htm.

———. 2003. *ASEAN Declaration of Concord II*. Jakarta: ASEAN Secretariat. http://www.asean.org/news/item/declaration-of-asean-concord-ii-bali-concord-ii.

———. 2005. *Kuala Lumpur Declaration on the Establishment of the ASEAN Charter*. Jakarta: ASEAN Secretariat. http://www.aseansec.org/18030.htm.

———. 2006. *The Report of the Eminent Person's Group on the ASEAN Charter*. Jakarta: ASEAN Secretariat. aseansec.org/19247.pdf.

———. 2009. *Basic Mandate, Functions and Composition*. Jakarta: ASEAN Secretariat. http://www.aseansec.org/11856.htm.

———. 2012a. *ASEAN Economic Community Scorecard Charting Progress Toward Regional Economic Integration Phase I (2008–2009) and Phase II (2010–2011)*. Jakarta: ASEAN Secretariat. http://www.asean.org/resources/publications/asean-publications/item/asean-economic-community-scorecard-3.

———. 2012b. *ASEAN Protocol on Enhanced Dispute Settlement Mechanism*, pp. 1–6. http://asean.org/?static_post=asean-protocol-on-enhanced-dispute-settlement-mechanism. Accessed December 16, 2016.

———. 2012c. *ASEAN Free Trade Area: An Update*. https://asean.org/?static_post=asean-free-trade-area-afta-an-update. Accessed October 22, 2018.

———. 2012d. *ASEAN Framework Agreement on Visa Exemption Kuala Lumpur, 25 July 2006*. https://asean.org/?static_post=asean-framework-agreement-on-visa-exemption-kuala-lumpur-25-july-2006-2. Accessed October 22, 2018.

———. 2013a. *Illustrative ASEAN Organizational Structure*. Jakarta: ASEAN Secretariat. http://www.aseansec.org/13103.htm.

———. 2013b. *ASEAN Tourism Ministers Meeting*. Jakarta: ASEAN Secretariat. http://www.asean.org/communities/asean-economic-community/category/asean-tourism-ministers-meeting-m-atm.

———. 2016. *Master Plan on ASEAN Connectivity 2025*. Jakarta.

Asian Development Bank. 2009. Infrastructure for a Seamless South East Asia. http://www.adb.org/adbi/files/2009.08.31.book.infrastructure.seamless.asia.pdf.

Balboa, J, and G. Wingaraja. 2014. *ASEAN Economic Community: What Happens Next?* Asia Pathways: A Blog of the Asian Development Bank Institute. http://www.asiapathways-adbi.org/2014/12/asean-economic-community-2015-what-is-next/.

Bowles, P. 1997. ASEAN, AFTA and the New Regionalism. *Pacific Affairs* 70 (2).

Calvo-Pardo, H., C. Freund, and E. Ornelas. 2009. *The ASEAN Free Trade Agreement Impact on Trade Flows and External Trade Barriers*. The World Bank.

Cao, Y. 2017. 财经观察:中国东盟携手共谱繁荣新篇章 [Financial Observation: China and ASEAN Join Hands to Share A New Chapter of Prosperity]. Xinhua News Agency [新华社]. http://www.gov.cn/xinwen/2017-11/12/content_5239121.htm.

Chheang, V. 2013. *Tourism and Regional Integration in Southeast Asia. Institute of Developing Economies.* Japan External Trade Organization.
Chin, K.W. 2003. ASEAN Institution Building. In *The 2nd ASEAN Reader*, ed. S. Siddique and Sree Kumar. Singapore: Institute of Southeast Asian Studies.
Chin, J. 2015. 1MDB Sells Edra Power Assets to China Firm for Nearly RM10Billion Cash. The Star. Institute of Developing Economies, Japan External Trade Organization. https://www.thestar.com.my/business/business-news/2015/11/23/1mdb-sells-edra-power-assets-to-china-firm-for-nearly-rm10b-cash/. Accessed October 6, 2018.
Das, S. 2013. Conclusion. In *Enhancing ASEAN's Connectivity*, ed. S. Das. ISEAS: Singapore.
———. 2015. *Can the China Led AIIB Support the ASEAN Connectivity Master Plan?* ISEAS Perspective 30.
Dooley, M.P., D. Folkerts-Landau, and P. Garber. 2006. *Direct Investment, Rising Real Wages, and the Absorption of Excess Labor in the Periphery.* NBER Working Paper 10626. Cambridge, MA: National Bureau of Economic Research.
Emerson, C. 2012. Australia Joins Launch of Massive Asian Regional Trade Agreement. Department of Foreign Affairs and Trade. trademinister.gov.au/releases/2012/ce_mr_121120.html. Accessed October 14, 2018.
Estrada, D. 2018. China's Belt and Road Initiative: Implications for the Philippines. *Foreign Service Institute Insights* 5(3). http://www.fsi.gov.ph/wp-content/uploads/2018/03/Vol-5-No-3-China's-Belt-and-Road-Initiative-Implications-for-the-Philippines-Estrada1.pdf. Accessed October 13, 2018.
Friedman, T. 1999. *The Lexus and the Olive Tree.* New York: Viking.
Fuad, A. 2018. Apa Untungnya Indonesia Masuk Belt and Road Initiative? [What Is Indonesia's Gain in Joining the Belt and Road Initiative?]. Watyutink. https://watyuting.com/topik/ekonomika/Apa-Untungnya-Indonesia-Masuk-Belt-and-Road-Initiative. Accessed September 23, 2018.
Glaser, B, and Deep Lal cited in Schreer, B. 2014. Should Asia Be Afraid? *The National Interest*, August 20.
Hapsari, I.M., and C. Mangunsong. 2006. Determinants of AFTA Members' Trade Flows and Potential for Trade Diversion.
Herschede, F. 1991. Trade Between China and ASEAN: The Impact of the Pacific Rim Era. *Pacific Affairs* 64 (2).
Higgott, R. 1998, January 30. Shared Response to the Market Shocks? *The World Today.*
Inama, S., and E.W. Sim. 2015. *The Foundation of the ASEAN Economic Community.* Cambridge University Press.
International Monetary Fund. 2003. *The Global Implications of the U.S. Fiscal Deficit and of China's Growth.* Washington, DC: IMF.
Jayasuriya, K. 2003. Governing the Asia Pacific – Beyond the 'New Regionalism'. *Third World Quarterly* 24 (2).

Ji, X. 2014, September. Why the ASEAN Economic Community Will Struggle. *The Diplomat*. http://thediplomat.com/2014/09/why-the-asean-economic-community-will-struggle/.

Johnstone, C. 1999. Strained Alliance: US-Japan Diplomacy in the Asian Financial Crisis. *Survival* 41 (1).

Larkin, S. 2015a. The Conflicted Role of the AIIB in South East Asia. ISEAS Perspective, 23.

———. 2015b. China's Great leap Outward: The AIIB in context. ISEAS Perspective, 27.

Lee, H., and Y.Y. Huang. 2018. 对马来西亚投资:中国的机遇与风险 [Investment in Malaysia: China's Opportunities and Risks]. 新华丝路 [Xinhua Silk Road]. http://silkroad.news.cn/2018/0813/106248.shtml. Accessed October 13, 2018.

Leifer, M. 1998. *ASEAN Regional Forum: A Model for Cooperative Security in the Middle East*. Working Paper 1998/1. Canberra: Australian National University.

Jeffrey Lewis 1999. Asian vs. International: Structuring an Asian Monetary Fund. *Harvard Asian Quarterly* 3 (1). http://www.fas.harvard.edu/~asiactr/haq/199904/9904a005.htm.

Lo, J. 2014, December 12. Forging Ahead with Shared Vision. *China Daily*.

Macintyre, A. 1997. South-East Asia and the Political Economy of APEC. In *The Political Economy of South-East Asia*, ed. G. Rodan, K. Hewison, and R. Robison. Melbourne: Oxford University Press.

Mahbubani, K. 2008. *The New Asian Hemisphere The Incontestable Shift of Global Power to the East*. New York: Public Affairs.

Mao, X., and X. Ding. 2016. 一带一路"倡议与区域经贸融合发展 [The "Belt and Road" Initiative and the Development of Regional Economic and Trade Integration]. 当代世界与社会主义 [Contemporary World and Socialism] 3.

Menon, N. 2016. Asean's Digital Economy. *Asian Management Insights* 3 (2): 28–33.

Ministry of Foreign Affairs, Tokyo. 1998, October 3. A New Initiative to Overcome the Asian Currency Crisis: The New Miyazawa Initiative. http://www.mof.go.jp/english/if/e1e042.htm.

———. 1999. *Diplomatic Bluebook 1999: Japan's Diplomacy with Leadership Toward the New Century*. Tokyo: Ministry of Foreign Affairs. http://www.mof.go.jp/policy/other/bluebook/1999/I-c.html.

Muggah, R. 2017. Duterte's Drug War in the Philippines Is Out of Control, He Needs to Be Stopped. *The Guardian*. https://www.theguardian.com/global-development-professionals-network/2017/jan/05/rodrigo-dutertes-drug-war-in-the-philippines-is-out-of-control-he-needs-to-be-stopped. Accessed October 13, 2018.

Mustofa, A. 2018. Penjajahan Kuning Sedang Mengintai Indonesia [Yellow Colonisation Is Lurking in Indonesia]. *Law Justice*. https://law-justice.co/penjajah-kuning-sedang-mengintai-indonesia-.html. Accessed September 28, 2018.

Nakano, T. 2018. RCEP Accord Dims as India Frets Over Trade Liberalization. *Nikkei Asian Review*. https://asia.nikkei.com/Politics/International-Relations/RCEP-accord-dims-as-India-frets-over-trade-liberalization.

Napoli, C. 2014. China's Economic Rise Implications for ASEAN Trade Flows. *Journal of South East Asian Economies* 31 (3).

NIDS. 2015. *East Asia Strategic Review*. Tokyo: National Institute for Defense Studies. http://www.nids.mod.go.jp/english/publication/east-asian/e2015.html.

Rabena, A.J. 2018. The Complex Interdependence of China's Belt and Road Initiative in the Philippines. *Asia and the Pacific Policy Studies* 5: 683–697.

Ravenhill, J. 2002. A Three Bloc World? The New East Asian Regionalism. *International Relations of the Asia Pacific* 2 (2).

Razak, N. 2016. Fruits Harvested From Seeds of Trust. *China Daily*. http://www.chinadaily.com.cn/opinion/2016-11/02/content_27245852.htm. Accessed October 6, 2018.

Sally, R. 2014, May 8. Report Card on ASEAN Economic Integration. *The Straits Times*.

Shira, D. 2018. RCEP Negotiations Reach Critical Stage – Likely to Be Inked by Year-End. ASEAN Briefing. https://www.aseanbriefing.com/news/2018/09/07/rcep-negotiations-reach-critical-stage-likely-inked-year-end.html. Accessed October 14, 2018.

Soesastro, H. 2001. *Whither ASEAN Plus Three?* Bangkok: PECC.

Studwell, J. 2007. *Asian Godfathers Money and Power in Hong Kong and South East Asia*. London: Profile Books.

Sukma, R. 2014. ERIA Discussion Paper Series ASEAN Beyond 2015: The Imperatives for Further Institutional Changes.

Sun, J. 2018. 中国连续 9 年成东盟最大贸易伙伴 去年交易 5148 亿美元 [China is ASEAN's Largest Trading Partner for 9 Consecutive Years, Trading US$514.8 Billion Last Year]. 新浪网 [Sina]. http://finance.sina.com.cn/china/hgjj/2018-07-18/doc-ihfnsvyz7227839.shtml.

Utama, J., and M. Kim. 2016. More Than Just Economy: Maritime Implications of China's Investment. *The Jakarta Post*. http://www.thejakartapost.com/academia/2016/06/27/more-than-just-economy-maritime-implications-of-chinas-investment.html. Accessed September 23, 2018.

Wanandi, J. 1999. *Moving East Asia Forward Again*. Washington, DC: Annual Meeting of the Trilateral Commission. http://www.trilateral.org/annmtgs/trialtxts/t53/wan.htm.

———. 2000. East Asian Institution-Building, Tokyo: Annual Meeting of the Trilateral Commission Tokyo. http://www.trilateral.org/annmtgs/trialtxts/t54/wan.htm.

Wendt, A. 1999. *The Social Theory of International Politics*. Cambridge: Cambridge University Press.

Wright, T., and S. Clark. 2015. Investigators Believe Money Flowed to Malaysian Leader Najib's Accounts Amid 1MDB Probe. *The Wall Street Journal*. https://www.wsj.com/articles/SB10130211234592774869404581083700187014570.

Zhang, Y.H. 2016. 没有 TPP, 中国还有 RCEP [No TPP, China Still Has the RCEP]. 世界知识 [World Affairs] 8: 64–66.

CHAPTER 14

Conclusion: The ASEAN Economic Community

Roderick Macdonald

This book has provided an introduction to the Association of Southeast Asian Nations (ASEAN) Economic Community (AEC). The previous chapters described the economies of the member nations, as well as a brief overview of their geography and histories. The AEC organization itself was described and the rising influence of China discussed.

The region of Southeast Asia is divided between the maritime nations of the Philippines, Indonesia, Brunei, Singapore and Malaysia and the mainland nations of Myanmar, Thailand, Cambodia, Laos and Vietnam. With the obvious exceptions of Singapore and (somewhat) Brunei, the countries are further subdivided into lowlands and highlands, with logistic and cultural implications. The 650 million people of the region speak nine standard languages and dozens more local languages, using half a dozen forms of writing. Although each nationality draws from hundreds or thousands of years of history, Thailand is the only independent country predating the Second World War and has seen 20 constitutions since 1932. All of these countries were relatively poor at the end of the war and

R. Macdonald (✉)
Université du Québec à Montréal, Montréal, QC, Canada
e-mail: macdonald.roderick@uqam.ca

R. Macdonald (ed.), *Southeast Asia and the ASEAN Economic Community*, https://doi.org/10.1007/978-3-030-19722-3_14

have followed varying trajectories since that time, with Singapore becoming one of the wealthiest and orderly countries in the world, while the Philippines stagnated since the mid-1970s until very recently. Two factors led to a series of regional treaties after the Second World War: the need for economic improvement locally and the Cold War[1] at the worldwide geopolitical level. Thus, many treaties were neither the initiative of countries of Southeast Asia nor limited to their participation. The Association of South East Asian Nations was preceded by the establishment of the Association of Southeast Asia (ASA) on July 21, 1961. Five nations (Indonesia, Singapore, Malaysia, the Philippines and Thailand) eventually founded ASEAN on August 8, 1967, and other nations joined in subsequent years. While security was a dominant issue in the early years, economic advancement soon became the predominant preoccupation. Technocrats of the various nations saw that this advancement would require the acquisition of expertise in governance of economies and in the creation of a larger market through integration across national frontiers. This eventually led to the declaration of the ASEAN Economic Community on December 31, 2015. The realization of this community is a work in progress. The proliferation of additional bilateral treaties between member nations and other countries outside of ASEAN, as well as multilateral treaties between ASEAN or several members and other countries, does not contradict the purpose of the ASEAN economic Community but can reinforce the pursuit of the region's prosperity.

Two sections constitute this concluding chapter. First, a summary will be made of the country profiles in the previous chapters, with additional observations about individual nations. Second, the extent to which the region has integrated will be considered against the backdrop of Chap. 13 on the ASEAN Economic Community and Chap. 12 on the interdependence and rivalry between China and the ASEAN economies.

Member Nations of the AEC

The Philippines had been one of the wealthier countries of the region previous to the Second World War. Sicat (2003) has estimated that at the end of the war (1945), Philippine gross domestic product (GDP) in 1945 was close to 30% of the output of 1940. The American effort to recapture Manila from the Japanese left 300,000 civilians dead, severely damaging the economic and political capital of the country. The country was poorer than both British colonies of Singapore and Malaysia in 1947, but GDP per capita surpassed Malaysia and was about somewhat over half that of Singapore by 1960. Growth continued throughout the 1960s and 1970s, but manufacturing growth was in uncompetitive protected industries. GDP per capita shrunk from 1983 to 1985. It rose again thereafter, but what growth there was had become increasingly debt-based from about half way through the Marcos regime, and new wealth was poorly distributed.

Development after Marcos was marred by the continued influence of self-seeking business parties upon economic policy, leading to high prices for consumers and impeding economic growth.

At the turn of the millennium, cash remitted from abroad by Filipinos forced to seek employment outside their country amounted to more than 12.5% of GDP.

The economic fortunes of the Philippines began to improve in 1998. The country has enjoyed 6–7% growth annually since 2010, with the exception of 2011 (a little under 4%). This is the result both of current and recent administrations' efforts to free up economic actors and of the injection of foreign cash both from remittance by overseas workers and via the industry of business process outsourcing. In a sense, remittances have sped up the onset of middle-class spending, stimulating the economy. Foreign direct investment (FDI) has also grown but remains limited by the legacy protectionist policies. Absent those policies, the Philippines could become the Ireland of Southeast Asia and surpass the growth of the Celtic Tiger years, participating in manufacturing networks as well as providing regional marketing offices and research centres. Indeed, among the large economies of ASEAN and excepting the outlier Singapore, the Philippines currently enjoys the highest portion of value-added in medium-to-high-technology goods.[2]

Very similarly to the case of Ireland in Europe, the Philippines provides access to the region with a large English-speaking population, ever-improving education and great depth in the labour pool, thanks to the low median age of the population, as well as a reservoir of workers both abroad and in the overly numerous agricultural workforce. Fiscal and monetary policies have been responsible, with deficits under 3%, debt shrinking from 50% in 2010 to under 40% in 2017 and inflation averaging under 3% since 2013. Unfortunately, competition policy and other aspects of Ireland's blueprint are lacking, especially in contrast to Singapore (the other "Ireland"), although changes are forthcoming. As a result, trade is limited to about 70% of the economy with a slight trade deficit. Exports are weaker than they should be because domestic industry is not competitive. In fact, the Philippines is the least competitive of the larger economies in the ASEAN Economic Community. Institutional shortcomings are combined with the structure of the economy: too high a portion of the population works in relatively unproductive agriculture, fishery and like industries. The population born into these industries have little freedom to move into higher paying employment and overcome this impediment by working abroad. While there might be some hope for cash injection via incoming tourism, this industry is hobbled with respect to other countries in the region because of the structure of the real estate industry, which resembles Hong Kong more than Thailand. A mid-range hotel costs twice as much in the Philippines as in Thailand and other countries; an expenditure that will get you 40–50 square metres in a hotel on the mainland procures 20–25 square metres in any somewhat developed region of the Philippines.

Protectionism is not limited to trade and investment. It also involves capture of many government procedures for the governance of the economy and is the main obstacle not only for economic freedom, but also for full participation in the springboard that is the ASEAN Economic Community.

Rich in a multi-millennial history as well as legacy influences from China, but impoverished by decades of resistance and war, the current state of Vietnam came into being in 1975. It has a geography similar to Chile's in having a long South to North coast that rises up to mountains on the interior border, albeit with a latitude similar to that of Venezuela. Two five-year plans delivered poor results before *Đổi Mới* (see Chap. 3) began to introduce more feasible objectives within a "socialist-oriented market economy" in 1986. A consequence is that, today, state-owned enterprises continue to dominate the economy of Vietnam at the same time as private enterprise, both domestic and foreign, contributes a growing portion of GDP.

The USA had imposed a trade embargo on Vietnam until 1993, and most Western nations and non-communist Asian nations joined this embargo in 1979 after Vietnam invaded Cambodia to end the Khmer Rouge regime. Imports and exports have grown 60-fold since 1990, and today trade represents 185% of GDP.[3] GDP per capita has grown nearly 30-fold, from under US$100 in 1990 to US$2545 in 2018. However, much of this export is FDI related, and much of that FDI results in limited value-added exports, being in labour-intensive and assembly-based manufacturing or relatively unprocessed resources (Le 2018) such as electrical equipment, footwear, coffee and so on. Debt has become somewhat of an issue, with external debt at 45% of GDP and public debt at 63% of GDP; non-performing bank loans were at 9.5% in 2017, although falling. Interestingly, state-owned enterprises have a far lower return on capital (2.1%) than FDI-related firms (5.5%) although far more highly leveraged (Debt to equity of 3.2 compared to 1.7). Of course, higher returns are what attracts FDI, but it would seem the state is maintaining weak performers. Reflecting tightened monetary policy, gross fixed capital formation has dropped from about 30% in 2010 to about 23% in 2017. FDI is about 6% of GDP, about the same as in 2010, although less than the 9.6% of 2008. This reduced funding is not very productive either, with incremental capital output ratio (ICOR) varying between 6 and 7 since the global financial crisis. However, there has been much investment in infrastructure that typically gives rise to lower ICOR.

In summary, Vietnam has achieved amazing growth, but is in danger of being stuck with diminishing returns to diminishing capital. Governance needs to be more technocratic but less directive, focusing on facilitating and motivating growth, providing health and educational services rather than capture of returns. The underlying social trends are promising. The workforce, young and growing, is ever-better educated, with mastery of English a much sought-after skill. Should a Caucasian sit down at any park bench in Ho Chi Minh City, he or she will find herself approached by young people wishing to practise their English.

A tourist visiting Thailand might garner the impression that English is as widespread there as it is in the Philippines. The reason for this is the well-developed tourist industry that represents over 15% of employment and contributes, directly and indirectly, 20% of GDP. The impression would be inaccurate, however: wander from the tourist zones and English is left behind. Only the better-educated have a working knowledge of English. Thailand is a country divided between the less-educated agricultural hinterlands and a prospering urban sprawl that extends from Bangkok. In the past, the former voted for patronage, the latter for a modernization entrusted to an elite. In spite of this political tension, the result has been one of the most prosperous of the ASEAN nations. However, Thailand suffers from slowing productivity growth with rising wages in its established industries at least at present. The government has responded with efforts to restructure industry, first with targeted tax incentives and other means under Thaksin, and more recently (since 2014 under the Prayut government) with the Thailand 4.0 strategy (see Chap. 4).

Typically, children of agricultural families either remain in agriculture or move into labour-intensive work in tourism (as massage therapists, tuk-tuk drivers, etc.). Although the portion of the workforce in agriculture has steadily dropped from 70% in 1980 to 32% in 2018, much of it has moved into services that create limited value. The country needs to bring more of the domestic workforce into progressively sophisticated manufacturing. Past manufacturing was based on cost-based competition for export; costs were controlled in part by low salaries. This created a context in which Thais eschewed unskilled manufacturing jobs, and migrant labour filled the vacuum. As a result, a portion of the Thai population remains in agricultural and services employment that generates limited value. It is this portion of the population that is trapped by disincentives to move up the economic ladder. This impediment to increasing prosperity is reinforced by the ageing population of Thailand.

Malaysia is even richer than Thailand. Besides physical proximity to Singapore (a bridge spans the border), Malaysia enjoys historical ties to that country, which is dependent upon it for most resources. Trade averages near 150% of GDP. However, Malaysia has developed trade with other countries, so that Singapore's part of trade has declined from about 20% to about 12%. Further, Malaysia's economy is not resource-based. The contribution of agriculture to GDP was already down to 40% in 1960 and represented less than 10% in 2016. Industry now contributes four times more to GDP, and manufacturing is the source of 82.2% of total exports. However, industry could be bigger still, and only employs a little over a quarter of the workforce. Instead, its role is declining as commodities have begun to contribute to a larger portion of exports. Since Malaysia's manufactures participate in international production networks, (Chap. 5) imports are reworked and exported again. Unfortunately, value-added in the country is less than 50% of the final export; this low value-added is more pronounced in the electrical and electronics industries that are responsible for the largest portion of exports. Now that other countries in the region have begun to offer to sufficient infrastructure and qualified lower cost labour, inward FDI has shrunk from 5.9% to 3.3% of GDP since 1990. Malaysia needs to move into more complex products and services. To do so, it requires a combination of improved educational outcomes, incentives for on-the-job training and more visionary strategy on the part of multinational firms. These firms have to see Malaysia as more than a static source of low-cost labour. The government of Malaysia has to provide infrastructure, education and incentives to encourage these firms to move forward to more progressive strategy. For a discussion of the challenges of both Malaysia and Thailand, see Suehiro (2019).

Singapore is an outstanding economy in the region and worldwide. A lower income country when founded in 1963, it is now one of the world's wealthiest. While it is true that Singapore was richer (on a per capita basis) than any other nation of today's ASEAN Economic Community, the country has also grown far more quickly than these other nations, from 70% richer than the next wealthiest to nearly six times wealthier—excluding the special case of oil-rich Brunei. Singapore's economy is diversified: it is an important international port upon a key sea lane; it exports high-value services such as health, finance and high-end tourism and boasts advanced manufacturing. Its infrastructure (physical and digital) is among the best in the world. Of its four official languages, most citizens are fluent in both Mandarin and English, allowing them to operate directly in the largest markets in the world. The education system is performance and economy oriented (although there is growing awareness of the role of the liberal and fine arts), producing a very competent workforce. Aside from taxi drivers, most low-skilled jobs are filled by migrant workers who accumulate savings to later establish themselves in their home country. In the past, expatriates flocked to Singapore, attracted by opportunities and excellent remuneration, increasing the availability of talent and connections. Government facilitates business, and procedures are as streamlined as possible.

Two elements, citizens and government, contributed to this turnaround. In addition to supporting business as transparently as possible, the government has been directive, in the past going so far as to provide housing in exchange for sterilization, hoping to select for greater economic performance. Citizens have also pursued prosperity, although there has been an evolution in their values. The first generation sacrificed itself, working hard and educating many children. The second generation worked hard and had fewer progeny. The third generation resembles the West and the wealthy areas of China, pursuing high income and status, replacing children with unnecessary cars and extra maids from Indonesia. Like China and the West, Singapore faces a demographic time bomb. Striving for performance also comes with a cost: some children as young as 11 suffer from depression as they compete to enter various education streams.

One might be tempted to see business success irradiating from Singapore, with wealth decreasing stepwise through Malaysia, Thailand

and Vietnam. This would be an incomplete vision. Indonesia, also a near neighbour to Singapore and Malaysia, does have the largest economy in Southeast Asia with 40% of the total GDP in the region, but less than half the GDP per capita of Malaysia, and is poorer than Thailand, as is Myanmar. There are other factors at play. The portion of the workforce working in agriculture is three times greater in Indonesia than it is in Malaysia, and its work is less productive than that of Malaysian agricultural workers. Indonesia has been poorer than Malaysia since colonial times, making it difficult to invest and borrow its way to acquire the machinery and infrastructure that would allow its workers to produce on par with Malaysian workers. Infrastructure is also a challenge since Indonesia is a sprawling archipelago subject to volcanoes, earthquakes and tsunamis, although it does not have to deal with the numerous typhoons that harass the Philippines annually. A huge educational effort is also necessary to bring the vast populace up to a minimal standard for on-the-job training, leading to more advanced skills. Health services need also to be improved to enhance both learning performance and employability. All of this—investment, education and health—requires expenditure.

In the past, expenditure and governance by the Indonesian government have often been influenced by interested parties seeking to benefit from rules and regulations. For some, the appropriation of wealth and its distribution is part of the formula for power, and the ambition to monopolize power trumps the economic well-being of the nation. Usually, however, this acquisitiveness is not explicit or dominant in anyone's mind but rather is subject to the overriding belief that "Indonesia is different" or that Indonesia must not follow the footsteps of Western nations in economic governance. The economic wisdom of successive administrations seems to have increased, but the political context in no way guarantees this for the future. Continuity or not in wise economic governance in turn impacts the technical expertise of the administrative apparatus through which the administration executes its policies.

Like the Philippines, Indonesia is admirable in its management of monetary policy, but suffers from an ineffective and manipulated legal system. Its regulatory system performs even worse than that of the Philippines. Nonetheless, Indonesia is a land of opportunity both because of extensive resources and because of an abundant workforce ready to perform and to learn to perform if given adequate incentives. The rapid adoption of mobile Internet service both by small business and by consumers is an indicator of that readiness.

The Philippines, Vietnam, Thailand, Malaysia, Singapore and Indonesia are the large economies of the ASEAN Economic Community. Brunei Darussalam, Cambodia, Laos and Myanmar are the four smaller economies that complete the list of AEC member nations.

Brunei's economy is small, but its population is even smaller at 430,000. The GDP per capita is the second highest in the economic community: at US$33,000, it is about half that of Singapore. Although a great swath of that wealth is held by government and nobility, the population at large still benefits greatly from that wealth in the form of good salaries, as well as health and educational services up to the university level. The country is blessed with considerable oil reserves. However, oil reserves remain finite (estimated at about 20 years), and the country must rely on outside expertise and capital to exploit these reserves and search for new ones. The government has been seeking to diversify the economy, but it is not easy to do so because the cash flow from oil makes other endeavours appear less interesting. Calm and security of income take the edge off entrepreneurial instincts.

Myanmar is by contrast a large country. With the fourth largest population at 52 million, it also has the lowest GDP per capita at US$1340 in 2018. The only reported Gini measurement was 38.1 in 2015. Gini is lower in the countryside because everyone there is poor. Further, this poverty is greatest among excluded groups. Buddhism and political power in the land have been intertwined since the eleventh century. The Buddhist Bamar are the dominant ethnic group, at 68% of the population, but there are well over a hundred native ethnic groups in Myanmar, as well as the Indians and Chinese remaining after many fled racial discrimination and nationalization of business in the early 1960s. There are reports of discrimination and persecution of non-Buddhist groups, most conspicuously of the Rohingyas.

This country enjoys extensive natural resources, and industry has grown from under 10% of GDP in 2000 to 35% in 2016. Growth was in the double digits up to the global financial crisis, dropped to zero in 2009 and has been in the 6–8% range since then. Capital markets and insurance are undeveloped; the banking industry is evolving as foreign banks have been given freer rein to compete. Although Western tourists are abstaining somewhat in abhorrence of the fate of the Rohingyas, tourists from East Asia increased 50% in 2018. Petroleum and natural gas are poised to boom as the government has scheduled an international tender for 2019.

The economy of Cambodia virtually began in the 1990s, after violent conflict in the 1970s, and the West had resisted a Vietnam-sponsored government in the 1980s and replaced it by the current constitutional monarchy in 1993. The economy began to change at the turn of the century. Agriculture employed 80% of the workforce in 1980, 70% from 2001 to 2008, then dropped to under 27% by 2017. Industry varied around 5% from 1993 to 1999, then around 8.5% from 2000 to 2008 and finally growing to over 27% of GDP by 2017. From the US$2533 million in 1993, GDP inched upward to US$3120 million in 1998 and then ballooned to US$22,158 million in 2017. Exports followed a similar pattern, from US$347 million in 1993 to US$13,267 million in 2016. The economy is relatively undiversified, with knitted garments contributing to over 50% of exports. Nonetheless, domestic value-added of exports is 76%.

Geopolitical play lies behind the dramatic economic change. After Vietnam freed Cambodia from the Khmer Rouge regime, the West and the United Nations (UN) pushed aside Vietnam's influence, and then withheld funds when Prime Minister Hue Sen appeared less than democratic. China sent $US6 million within a month of the coup by which Hue Sen consolidated his power; investment from China tripled from US$36 million in 1997 to US$113 million in 1998. Since then, both aid and investment from China have soared and the economy of Cambodia with it. Annual aid from China reached nearly US$350 million by 2012, and Chinese government and companies invested US$4.89 billion in greenfield projects[4] between 2008 and 2017 (Davis 2018). It appears that Chinese investment may now begin to diversify into the financial sector with an emphasis on lending to small- to medium-size businesses (Amarthalingam 2018).

A quarter of a million square kilometre buffer between Vietnam and Thailand, Laos stretches from China on the North to Cambodia on the South. Its 7 million people give it a population density of about 30 persons per square kilometre. It is slightly richer than Vietnam and poorer than the Philippines on a per capita basis. The economy of Laos—market oriented with heavy oversight by the communist state—has manifested strong growth since 2002 (from a GDP of $US1758 million to US$16,853 million in 2017). Electricity (19% of total exports in value) and copper (ore at 11%; refined at 7.7%) are the biggest exports, and resources are important to the economy. However, industry has doubled its contribution to GDP, passing 32% in 2016, thanks principally to growth of manufacturing output. Manufacturing is dominated by clothing, assemblage of electronics components, automotive wire harnesses (cabling and connectors for cars) and other labour-intensive manufacturing. Unfortunately, domestic manufacturing adds to only 49% of the value of gross exports (contrasting with Cambodia at 72% and the Philippines at 79%). Thailand, China and Vietnam account for 82.3% of Laos' total exports.

Various sources report between 135 and 183 state-owned enterprises with total assets above US$5 billion.

The country needs to divert part of the earnings of resource-based business into infrastructure and more complex manufacturing, as well as the usual development of human capital by education and health services. It also needs to streamline the governance of business.

More capital will speed development, although debt in the form of poorly structured or overly massive leverage would bring future problems. China surpassed Thailand as the largest investor in Laos towards the end of 2013. In a 2018 conference, Minister of Energy and Mines Dr. Khammany Inthirath reported that Chinese investment in energy and mines reached US$10 billion, of which US$5 billion went directly to the government of Laos and US$5 billion to Chinese businesses investing in Laos. Smaller Chinese entrepreneurs have also contributed to GDP growth, for example, by renting out land from farmers who are thus freed to pursue other work. Many of these smaller businesses export back to China. The government of Laos introduced a plan to privatize state-owned real estate in 2013, and this led to Chinese and Chinese firms owning much of the best land in the capital, Vientiane. Much of the recent growth in the economy can be explained by funding from China.

Integration of the ASEAN Economic Community

ASEAN, originally created for security purposes, gradually took on an economic vocation, leading to the erection of the ASEAN Economic Community. The logic was that a larger market and a larger production base would facilitate the creation and circulation of wealth.

However, a number of factors have frustrated that logic. The region has experienced impressive growth, but less than could legitimately be expected. While technocrats in each country and within the organization of ASEAN and the AEC have pursued the goal of economic "boundarylessness" while respecting national sovereignties, other forces have resisted. While every nation stands to gain from economic integration, at least in theory, established rent-seekers believe they will suffer if they lose their protection. Based on this belief, it is only rational for them to resist.

Local interests in Indonesia, the Philippines and other ASEAN members would be disadvantaged by full market integration because they would no longer be able sell goods and services at high prices to the local market.

In a series of well-researched books, Dr. Joe Studwell (2008, 2014) has described the policies by which some East Asian economies have flourished and some have languished. He includes Vietnam in the northeastern group, excludes the city states of Singapore and Hong Kong, the almost city state of Brunei with its oil-centric economy, and ignores the more extremely underdeveloped countries in Southeast Asia that are Cambodia, Laos and Myanmar.

He argues that development from lower income and breaking the middle-income trap was achieved by the successful nations because of strong governments taking action in three ways listed below (see "Dr. Studwell proposed three common groups of policies…"). He observed that this was not the case in most of Southeast Asia where economic elites hijack economic governance to pursue their own business ends. The economies of the region are the result of political elites granting "members of an economic elite monopoly concerns, mainly in domestic service industries [i.e. local service industries] that enable the latter to control vast amounts of wealth" (Studwell 2008, p. xii). This influence of interested parties is tolerated across the AEC countries by an electorate that is unsophisticated in economic matters and seeks short-term benefits from patronizing local politicians.

The temptation is to condemn this behaviour and confront the perpetrators. However, these "perpetrators" have not set out to impoverish their countrymen. They simply act pragmatically within the current configuration of the economy as they experience it. Attempting change where established economic powers are adversaries would be futile for these businesses. The reality is that no one person or organization can radically alter the configuration of the economy (short of violence); the collaboration of all or many would be best. Professor Fabella (2018) has proposed that it is precisely though the large domestic "conglomerates" that economies under weak institutions must develop: "Rather than threaten to shackle the conglomerates in our midst, we should re-channel them to the Tradeable [sic] goods sector …"

Another theme common to many countries is the poverty of farmers and fishermen. For some reason or another, they are trapped in "things as they are." They continue to farm (or to fish) as did their ancestors, with little change beyond the purchase of imported fertilizer to get the most out of a parcel of land before slashing and burning their way onto another. And often, they have weak or no legal title to the land they farm. Many work as labourers on large semi-industrialized farms that are a less productive use of land than the more highly labour-intensive small-scale farming—when these small-scale farmers are provided sufficient training and have access to efficient procurement and sales markets. This mismanagement of agriculture has a double negative effect upon the economy. Countries may be less than self-sufficient in spite of their fertile soil, and the price of foods can be higher. More importantly, it deprives the nation of what Dr. Studwell calls a "capitalism laboratory" where large numbers of households could enjoy a small disposable income, thanks to their hard work.

This state of affairs is not very encouraging. It contrasts strongly with the upbeat reports of McKinsey and Company, PwC, Google (in tandem with Temasek) and others in recent years. These businesses dispose of armies of bright hard-working people working with amazing resources (data, contacts, money, etc.) to speed their research. The presentation of the results is somewhat compromised by the companies' purpose and can be expected to please the collaborators (such as the ASEAN Secretariat and the ADB Bank) and encourage companies and governments to have recourse to their services to prioritize building out backbone infrastructure for the mobile Internet, big data, the Internet of Things, the automation of knowledge work and cloud technology in order to improve productivity, to use the words of "three global megatrends" in a 2014 McKinsey report. Nonetheless, the research is valuable and should not be ignored.

Demographic dividend (a large portion of the population in the workforce), growing urbanization and a recent history of considerable stable growth recommend the region to McKinsey. According to PwC, "people power" (people that produce and consume), increasing FDI and fiscal strength indicate a bright future for the AEC nations, with reservations in various countries. Challenges include recent reduction in growth, low productivity, dependence on external trade, deficient infrastructure, deficient economic institutions (pervasiveness of corruption, obscure or complicated bureaucracy, etc.), weak monetary leverage and Industry 4.0 and digital disruptors.[5] This last observation might seem to contrast with the McKinsey perspective, but the same argument is made: the AEC must prepare for technological change to benefit more from global value chains,[6] or else be doomed to participate less.

Basically, these blue-ribbon consultants are arguing that the AEC nations have arrived at a "can-do" moment for prosperity. Does this contradict the somewhat pessimistic diagnosis of Dr. Studwell? In part, but not completely. Dr. Studwell proposed three common groups of policies that permitted economic prosperity among East Asian nations: land reform leading to a generation of agricultural capitalists, an emphasis on ever more sophisticated manufacture for export (via temporary protection for domestic rivals among whom the weakest are gradually weeded out) and a financial regime that channels funds into a more advanced productive capacity rather than cash flow (thus leading to a temporarily underperforming stock market).

Regarding land reform, the lot of farmers is not much better in many poor countries; however, foreign remittances and outsourced business services, especially in the Philippines, have partially filled the role of providing extra cash to the poor. Part of the foreign work is low value-added services—Myanmar citizens braving scams (by their compatriots) to work in Singapore, Malaysia and Thailand; Filipina maids braving abuse and prejudiced courts to work in Saudi Arabia and Kuwait; Indonesian maids often working long hours in Singapore or facing abuse in Saudi Arabia. Part of the foreign work is by engineers and managers who can earn more money abroad. So, land reform is lacking, but part of the benefit that land reform would have provided has been obtained by people leaving husbands, wives and children behind to receive their remittances. And food pricing is not that high, although vegetables are expensive in the Philippines, and Vietnamese poor at times buy spoiled fruit and vegetables in the market when world food prices take a jump. A further observation is that GDP per person employed has been increasing, more or less doubling in real terms since 1991 (see Fig. 14.1), so that individual work has been creating more value, at least a portion of which comes back to employees.

Regarding the emphasis on manufacturing for export, the consultants' reports repeat the recommendation of Dr. Studwell in more specific terms for the current economic context.[7]

Regarding a financial regime that channels funds into evermore advanced productive capacity, this is omitted by the consultants in their reports, although perhaps if hired by governments they will recommend

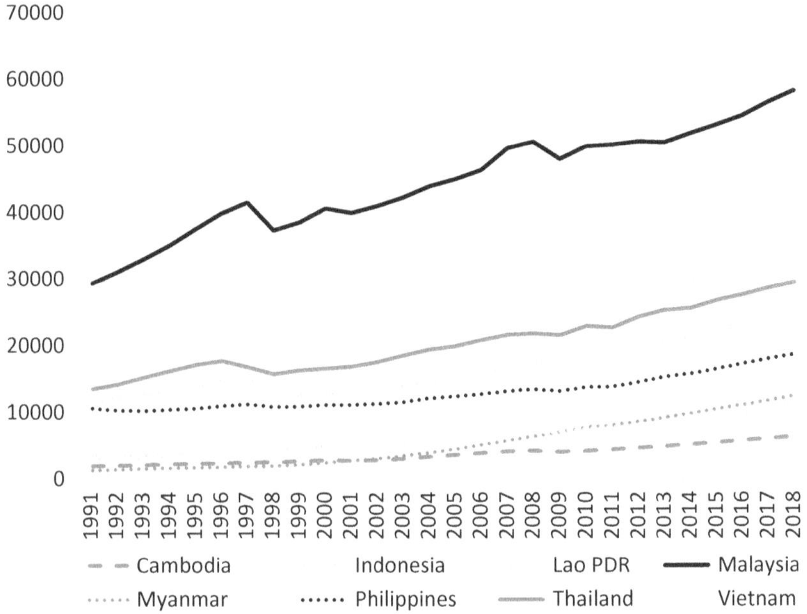

Fig. 14.1 GDP per person employed (Constant 2011 PPP $) for eight ASEAN nations. Singapore and Brunei Darussalam are excluded since both have had high outlier figures for the period covered. Data source: International Labour Organization, ILOSTAT database, via the World Bank

it. If hired by firms, their recommendations still will direct funds into more advanced capacity.

It would seem that Dr. Studwell's observations still stand, but that a larger swath of the population disposes of funds to influence the economy through purchase, saving and direct investing choices. Greater disposable income distributed across large numbers of people increases the impact of the market forces as opposed to government dictates. However, the local economic elite remain in place in most ASEAN economies. What about their resistance to integration? Has the AEC had an impact?

The principle goal of the AEC is to create a large market zone on both the demand and the supply sides for goods, services, capital and people. Daria Taglioni has observed that Southeast Asia has embraced global value chains with increasing participation in knowledge-intensive industries.[8] Some commentators are very upbeat about integration, perhaps confusing

AEC policies and blueprints with realities on the ground. Other commentators are extremely negative, arguing that the consensus-driven AEC, without power to impose policy upon participating nations, has done little to integrate markets. Who is right? This question cannot be fairly answered as yet since the community is still less than five years old—too short a time for its modus operandi to have had an impact. However, we can get a quick appreciation of the impact of the ASEAN as an organization regarding integration of markets.

Integration of markets might seem to be a clear-cut concept of free trade versus the classic barriers of tariffs and non-tariff barriers (impeding trade through bureaucratic delays, quotas, arbitrary standards, etc.). A standard narrative about ASEAN is that tariff barriers have been all but eliminated, but that non-tariff barriers of some members are frustrating integration. This is true but incomplete. The purpose of integration is to cultivate ASEAN businesses so that they can trade competitively on the world market. Increasing trade within ASEAN should not reduce trade with the outside world. One of the ways to get a better valuation for products and services and to sell higher volumes is to trade with partners with greater disposable income. So, trade outside the region is also important, with the European Union (EU), the USA, Japan, Oceania and, more recently, China, contributing to the growth of ASEAN economies. Further, trade within ASEAN is frustrated not only by tariff and "non-tariff" barriers but also by the complexities of exporting across nine different bureaucratic frontiers, and also by the very basic issue of having goods that are worthwhile trading, such as goods that are made in one country but are desired in another. The first difficulty will be addressed by ASEAN Single Window initiative. In operation in Indonesia, Malaysia, Singapore and Vietnam (OECD 2018), and possibly fully implemented by the end of 2019, it will unify customs procedures of all ten nations and allow them to be cleared through a unique platform. The second difficulty is deeper and will only be resolved if the different ASEAN national economies develop more sophisticated manufacturing that is complementary to that in other ASEAN countries.

Some notion of the progress of integration can be garnered first by examining recent legislation in the various countries and, second, by examining trade between the countries.

Some of the data available on legislation favouring free trade within the ASEAN region and that which is harmful to free trade within the ASEAN region are presented in Table 14.1. More detailed data is available at

Table 14.1 Interventions favouring and harmful to free trade with other ASEAN countries 2009

Year	*Total interventions favouring free trade with ASEAN 2009–2018*	*Total interventions harmful to free trade with ASEAN 2009–2018*
Vietnam	19	33
Thailand	14	28
Singapore	3	5
Philippines	10	16
Myanmar	2	2
Malaysia	124	161
Laos	0	0
Indonesia	94	211
Cambodia	5	4
Brunei	1	0
Total	272	460

Data source: Globaltradealert.org and author's calculations

globaltradealert.org regarding specific products and countries targeted. The data in the table should be interpreted with care. It does not take into account the state of protection versus free trade previous to 2009 and so indicates only change over time. Again, an intervention harmful to world trade also counts as an intervention harmful to ASEAN trade. The methodology simply counts interventions, treating them all as equal units without discriminating between an omnibus act freeing or protecting all industry and another act freeing or protecting a single product. Nor does it distinguish between levels of tariffs, although tariffs are less relevant as almost now absent in intra-ASEAN trade. Non-tariff measures are the principle issue.

Mindful of the limits and caveats of the previous paragraph, Table 14.1 indicates that Malaysia and Indonesia have been the most active in manipulating trade, followed at a distance by Vietnam, Thailand and the Philippines. More research would be necessary to surpass the limits mentioned above and, more importantly, to understand the motivation of the interventions in each country: whether to protect a stagnant economic elite or to actively nurture technological upgrading within domestic industries. Certainly, the content of previous chapters suggests little propensity for climbing the technological ladder in Indonesia and the Philippines, with some ambition in Malaysia and Thailand. An exception is Vietnam, although anecdotal evidence indicates it is meeting with some difficulties.[9]

Does trade data reinforce this impression of several countries resisting integration? Surprisingly not, although the results are mixed and complex.

The two countries most active in manipulating trade, Indonesia and Malaysia, are among the six ASEAN nations that trade more with ASEAN nations than any external partner. Laos, Myanmar, Singapore and Thailand are the other four. Myanmar is a borderline case, however: that earliest data is from 2010, and 2015 saw China and Hong Kong combined overtake the share of ASEAN in Myanmar's exports. See Fig. 14.2 for the evolving shares of these countries' export destinations.

Brunei, Cambodia, the Philippines and Vietnam deal with other partners more than with ASEAN. Each country presents a special case. Oil is almost the sole export of Brunei, and is shipped to Japan and Korea, although Malaysia and Thailand also take about 10% each. Cambodia used to send half its exports to the USA, but those days seem to have passed. Since 2009, the share of Europe and Central Asia has skyrocketed, thanks to the preferential treatment Europe has afforded Cambodia. However, on February 11, 2019, Europe started a process leading to the suspension of Cambodia's preferential access to the EU market under the Everything But Arms (EBA) trade scheme, due to deficient human rights and labour rights. The China + Hong Kong share of exports might rise in consequence, although some light manufacturing, such as bicycles, is relocating to Cambodia from China because of the US-China trade war, and these items might sell within ASEAN. Vietnam's principle trading partners are the USA (21%) and China + Hong Kong (16%). The former can be ascribed to post-war reconciliation relations; the latter to geographic proximity. China and Hong Kong combine for nearly 23% of exports by the Philippines and their share has been increasing, Japan's share has been varying around 21%, while ASEAN has received about 15% for many years. See Fig. 14.3 for the evolution of the principle export destinations of these countries.

What this somewhat bewildering array of exports data suggests is that proximity is a big factor for trade. ASEAN and AEC's efforts to integrate the ASEAN markets depend not only upon dragging the local economic elites kicking and screaming into the twenty-first century but especially upon infrastructure—particularly hard infrastructure such as rail, seaports, airports and roads as well as telecommunications. Infrastructure quality impacts heavily upon participation in global value chains (Ignatenko et al. 2019).

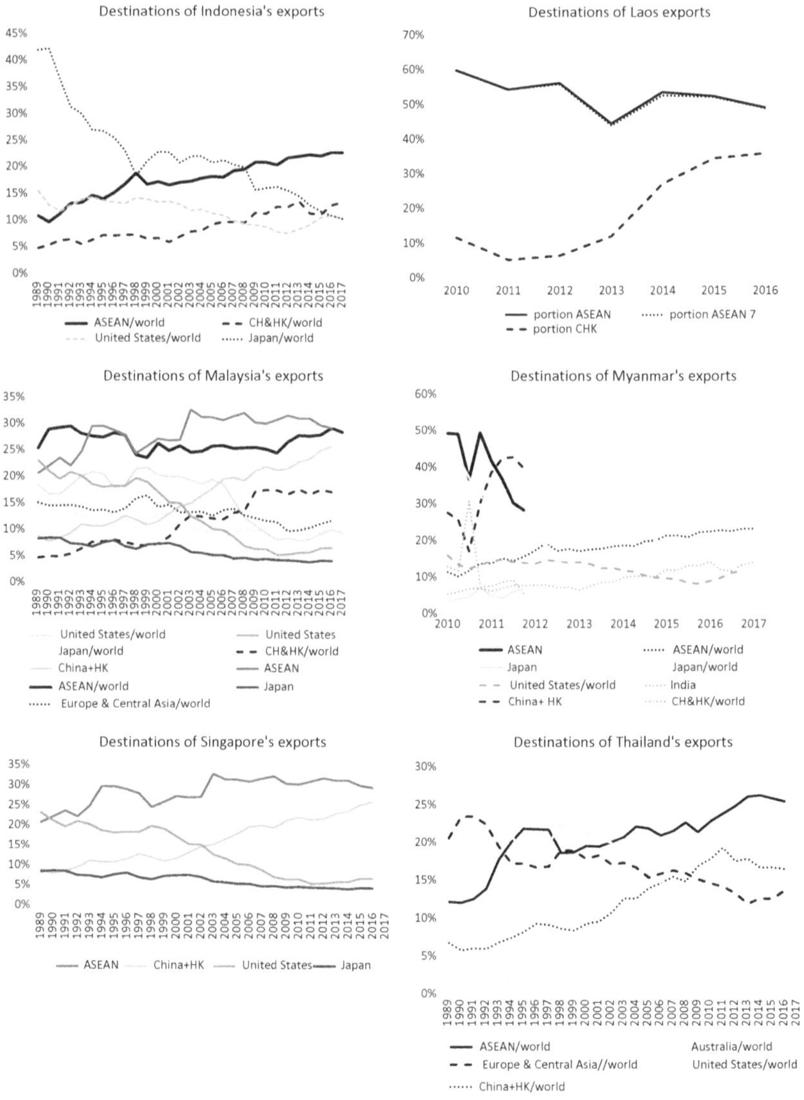

Fig. 14.2 Principle export destinations of six ASEAN nations. Data source: World Integrated Trade Solution (WITS) and author's calculations

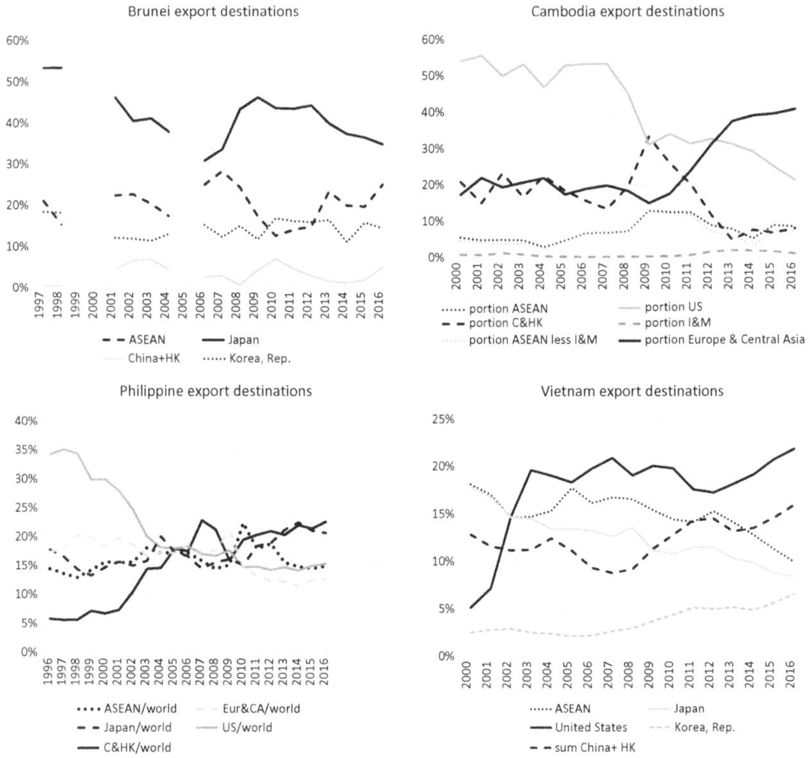

Fig. 14.3 Principle export destinations of four ASEAN nations. Data source: World Integrated Trade Solution (WITS) and author's calculations

Southeast Asia is deficient in this area, with some exceptions such as Singapore's world leading seaport and airport. Not only are the major cities home to some of the worst traffic in the world in spite of a modest count of vehicles per capita, the countryside and inter-country spaces are bereft of efficient routes. Non-residents doing visa runs on mainland ASEAN typically fly because it is so much simpler, safer and often cheaper, even when borders are less than 200 kilometres away. Sea travel is necessarily somewhat developed in Indonesia and the Philippines, but there are annual disasters, and the ports leave much to be desired from the commercial viewpoint. The reality is that the infrastructure is good enough for many of the local economic elites who are happy enough trucking sugar and palm oil from the countryside to major cities and can afford an extra day or few hours. Exportation, on the other hand, needs efficient throughput across borders. The World Bank and the ADB have been discussing the need for larger infrastructure expenditure for some years, bandying about the figure of US$1.7 trillion per year needed versus US$880 billion spent for the East Asia-Pacific region. For example, the World Bank and the Financial Times have organized eight annual infrastructure finance summits in Singapore. ADB has hoped to provoke an increase in investment in infrastructure by offering about US$14 billion in financing for infrastructure annually, about 1% of the expenditure. The World Bank and ADB expect their clients to spend about 12% of infrastructure budgets to deal with climate change.

China has also dealt with the need through two programmes: the Belt and Road Initiative and the Asian Infrastructure Investment Bank (AIIB), as explained in Chap. 12. The latter is overshadowed by the former, far more direct and aggressive.

As of June 2018, the AIIB had lent about US$5 billion for 28 projects, fewer than a quarter of which were in ASEAN countries. As of March 2019, 7 of 34 projects were in ASEAN countries—5 in Indonesia, 1 in Myanmar and 1 in the Philippines. This represents the first three years of operation of the bank, so its activity appears to be about an order of magnitude smaller than ADB.

Not so the Belt and Road Initiative. Huge projects are underway across East, South, Central Asia and Africa. Even Italy has returned to its history in the silk trade and shown support for the Initiative. A number of these projects are in Southeast Asia, both for the land and sea routes. These should help with ASEAN needs for ports, rail, roads and bridges, and thus with market integration. Two considerations should be borne in mind, however: scale and difficulties in implementation.

The Center for Global Development provides the highest estimate for the size of the initiative: about US$8 trillion over ten years. This is about equal to the shortfall in Asia-Pacific infrastructure spending, but spread over 36 countries in three continents, with the centre of gravity outside the ASEAN zone. Most other estimates of the size of the initiative are far more modest. The Belt and Road Initiative may help, but it does not fill the gap.

The second consideration is that several projects in the ASEAN zone have bogged down. Management of the projects (particularly who gets the jobs that are created), financing conditions and suitability of projects are among the factors that have slowed implementation. Local politics, Chinese companies and directives from the government of China itself have probably all contributed to woes of the already considerable burden of managing large and complex projects. In part, this is a learning experience and a difficult situation, where local politicians have mixed motives varying from patriotism to betrayal of their country's best interests for personal gain. China has been criticized extensively in the Western media for the Initiative but, in fairness, perhaps it has been learning from experience.

Telecommunications and other digital infrastructure are also crucial to the future development of the countries of the AEC. New digital-based businesses are providing new jobs outside of the protected and uncompetitive fiefdoms in many ASEAN countries.[10] Besides the obvious ICT (information and communication technology) industries, digitalization can impact manufacturing, fisheries and agriculture (with both education and information on weather, markets, etc.), transport, and has led to the Internet economy.

Four specific areas of the Internet economy (online transactions) are e-commerce, financial service, travel and ride hailing, and digital entertainment. E-commerce might have been expected to replace the developed retail network of ASEAN countries. Digital financial services were supposed to be impeded by the populations' limited participation in the banking system. Travel would be a modest business due to limited tourism by locals and ride-hailing was expected simply to supplement inadequate taxi service. The creativity of entrepreneurs has defied these assumptions. Online services are supporting the pervasive network of neighbourhood sundry stores, digital payment is facilitated for those without bank accounts or credit cards, and the ride-hailing services are resolving many of the logistic difficulties posed by the traffic of most ASEAN cities. And the unicorns and smaller start-ups happily move from one specialty to another, building on their customer base, data and expertise.

The Internet economy alone is expected to reach US$240 billion by 2025, adding about 7% to the region's total GDP. Given that the growth of the region is already in that range, this may not seem a major contribution. But there are additional effects of digitalization through new businesses, greater participation in global value networks and increasing productivity in existing business. Government plans in Brunei, Cambodia, Malaysia, the Philippines, Singapore and Vietnam aim for a 20–30% contribution of the digital economy (Internet transactions included) to total GDP. The digital economy has been projected to contribute between US$0.8 and 1.1 trillion increase to total ASEAN GDP by 2025 (Hoppe et al. 2018; A.T. Kearney 2016). As a point of reference, the International Monetary Fund (IMF) projects a regional GDP of US$4.1 trillion for the region in 2023 (IMF n.d.), which one could extend to US$4.5 trillion in 2025 at a 5% growth rate. Although projections about the future are educated guesses, the digital economy seems to be important for AEC development.

Growth of the digital economy requires funding. The telecommunications systems require massive investment, as do data centres. And the various businesses require investment. Venture capital, greenfield FDI projects as well as cross-border mergers and acquisitions in ICT (information and communication technology) are all important sources of financing. The top 10 foreign investors in ICT greenfield projects during 2013–2017 were Korea (US$14 billion), the USA (over US$14 billion), China (over $US4 billion), Japan and Germany, in decreasing order of importance. However, this may well change radically with the coming implementation of 5G. Cross-border investors in ICT mergers and acquisitions hailed from China (US$4.5 billion), Indonesia (over US$2 billion), Japan (a little under US$2 billion), Singapore, Austria and the USA. Both foreign and domestic venture capitals are active. Foreign sources include Alibaba, Didi Chuxing, JD.com, Meituan-Dianping and Tencent (China), Softbank (Japan), Venture International Corporation (Republic of Korea), and Temasek Holdings (Singapore).[11] China and the USA have been vying for the number one and number two top spots in venture capital funding for fintech, virtual reality, autonomous driving, wearables, education technology, robotics and drones, 3D printing (Woetzel et al. 2017). The government of China announced (July 8, 2017) its desire to be a world leader in artificial intelligence by 2030, and major Chinese firms are rapidly ramping up the use of artificial intelligence to deal with big data. The biometric IDs and centralized personal information that are distasteful to the West but embraced in China resolve many issues for transacting with hundreds of millions of persons without credit or banking history. It also suits a few of the governments in the region. Given this shared interest as well as the proximity and the sheer size of China, it seems likely that much funding and much of the orientation of the digital orientation of ASEAN will come from that country.

Notes

1. The Cold War was a standoff between the USA and her allies against the Union of Soviet Socialist Republics (and to some extent China) consisting in a large build-up of nuclear arsenals and geopolitical positioning. This lasted from the end of the Second World War until the fall of the communism in the USSR in 1989. The so-called domino theory that nations in Asia and Europe could sequentially fall under Marxist influence inspired much of the diplomatic and military acts of the USA during this time, bringing them to military involvement in Korea and then Vietnam, and stationing considerable assets in Germany.
2. Many manufacturing processes are carried out by stages in different countries, so that country A adds so much value, country B additional value, and so on. Adding more value within this chain of production contributes more to the gross domestic product of the country and is advantageous.
3. GDP is calculated by summing the value-added within the country. Trade (imports plus exports) is calculated by summing the total value of merchandise and services crossing the border, including the value-added in other countries. Trade is greater than GDP for many countries in Southeast Asia.
4. A greenfield project establishes a new economic activity in the host country, as opposed to a brownfield project that incorporates existing elements by acquisition or leasing.
5. Industry 4.0 refers to automation and data integration in manufacturing, such as the Internet of Things. A digital disruptor is a business, technology or event that changes the basic rules of business through computers or telecommunications.
6. A global value chain is the worldwide sequence of activities required to conceive, develop, produce and market a good or service. For example, various Philippines businesses participate in the global aerospace value chain via the manufacture and assembly of a small number of components and sub-assemblies in the interiors and fight controls systems, as well as some post-sales services such as MRO (maintenance, repair and overhaul).
7. Economic prosperity is linked to the notion of value, which ultimately depends upon the desires of the solvent buyer. The following focuses on the supply side of value to simplify the argument. Value is produced by humans working. Organization, discipline, time and effort all contribute to the amount of value a human can produce, but one other factor is predominant: knowledge. Knowledge takes the form both of the skill of the worker and of the design of the tools which he or she uses to produce value. This is what nineteenth-century Germany and the USA, late nineteenth century and again post-Second World War Japan, then Taiwan, Korea and Singapore did so well, and China is now doing. To do so, they

may have strayed over ethical limits in acquiring knowledge from other countries, manipulating property rights to favour local firms, hiring knowledge away from competitors and engaging in industrial espionage.

Once they have climbed the technological ladder, they become masters in foiling the attempts of other nations to acquire knowledge from them. Although this is rational for the firms involved in the short term, it is most unfortunate for the world economy operating on a chain reaction: the more wealth is dispersed, the faster economies can grow.

8. "Southeast Asia is an example of a region that has integrated with several GVCs. Following the investments of many major multinational corporations attracted by the low costs of production, it has become known as a trusted hub for producing not only electronics parts and automobile components, but increasingly knowledge-intensive goods and services." Quoted at http://www.worldbank.org/en/topic/trade/publication/book-making-global-value-chains-work-for-development. Accessed March 28, 2019.
9. One personal communication to the author was that a Korean semiconductor plant was careful to exclude Vietnamese from any proprietary knowledge.
10. Although even this can be complicated: Indonesia's Go-Jek is currently in a battle to enter the Philippines where Grab has the ride-hailing market almost to itself. The Land Transportation Franchising and Regulatory Board blocked Go-Jek's entry bid based on rules requiring 60% Filipino ownership, so Go-Jek has begun to negotiate with Ayala Corp to explore shared ownership in the Philippine venture. Founded in 1834, the Ayala Group is among the largest conglomerates in the Philippines, operating in real estate, financial services, water and telecommunications among other fields.
11. UNCTAD ASEAN 2018, pp. 163–261, provides an extensive overview of investment in the ASEAN digital economy, and Hoppe et al. 2018 investigate future transformation of small- to mid-sized businesses in the region.

References

A.T. Kearney. 2016. *The ASEAN Digital Revolution*. A.T. Kearney. https://www.atkearney.com/digital-transformation/article?/a/the-asean-digital-revoluti-1. Accessed March 23, 2019.

Amarthalingam, Sangeetha. 2018. Chinese Investment in Cambodia to Diversify into SME Finance. *Khmer Times*, December 4.

UNCTAD ASEAN. 2018. *ASEAN Investment Report 2018 – Foreign Direct Investment and the Digital Economy in ASEAN*. ASEAN Secretariat and United Nations Conference on Trade and Development (UNCTAD).

Davis, Emerson. 2018. China Investment Signals Support for Cambodia. *fDi Magazine.* https://www.fdiintelligence.com/News/China-lends-Cambodia-FDI-support. Accessed January 8, 2019.

Fabella, Raul. 2018. *Capitalism and Inclusion Under Weak Institutions.* Center for Integrative and Development Studies, University of the Philippines.

Hoppe, Florian, Tony May, and Jessie Lin. 2018. *Advancing Toward ASEAN Digital Integration. Empowering SMEs to Build ASEAN's Digital Future.* Bain & Company.

Ignatenko, Anna, Faezeh Raei, and Borislava Mircheva. 2019. *Global Value Chains: What Are the Benefits and Why Do Countries Participate?* IMF Working Paper.

IMF. n.d. https://data.imf.org/?sk=ABFF6C02-73A8-475C-89CC-AD515033E662&sId=1390030341854. Accessed March 23, 2019.

Le, Quoc Phuong. 2018. *Vietnam's Low National Competitiveness: Causes, Implications and Suggestions for Improvement.* Korea Institute for International Economic Policy (KIEP).

OECD. 2018. *Economic Outlook for Southeast Asia, China and India 2018: Fostering Growth Through Digitalisation.* Paris: OECD Publishing. http://dx.doi.org/9789264286184-en.

Sicat, Gerardo P. 2003. *The Philippine Economy During the Japanese Occupation, 1941–1945.* UP School of Economics Discussion Papers 200307, University of the Philippines School of Economics.

Studwell, Joe. 2008. *Asian Godfathers: Money and Power in Hong Kong and South East Asia.* Grove Press.

———. 2014. *How Asia Works.* Grove Press.

Suehiro, A. 2019. Responses to the Middle-Income Trap in China, Malaysia, and Thailand. In *Emerging States at Crossroads. Emerging-Economy State and International Policy Studies*, ed. K. Tsunekawa and Y. Todo. Singapore: Springer.

Woetzel, Jonathan, Jeongmin Seong, Kevin Wei Wang, James Manyika, Michael Chui, and Wendy Wong. 2017. *China's Digital Economy. A Leading Global Force.* McKinsey Global Institute Discussion Paper.

Index[1]

A

B

[1] Note: Page numbers followed by 'n' refer to notes.

R. Macdonald (ed.), *Southeast Asia and the ASEAN Economic Community*, https://doi.org/10.1007/978-3-030-19722-3

H

I

The manufacturer's authorised representative in the EU is Springer
Nature Customer Service Centre GmbH, Europaplatz 3, 69115 Heidelberg,
Germany. If you have any concerns regarding our products, please
contact ProductSafety@springernature.com

Printed and bound by CPI Group (UK) Ltd, Croydon, CR0 4YY
30/09/2026
02225661-0014